E–Entrepreneurship and ICT Ventures:
Strategy, Organization and Technology

Tobias Kollmann
University of Duisburg–Essen, Germany

Andreas Kuckertz
University of Duisburg–Essen, Germany

Christoph Stöckmann
University of Duisburg–Essen, Germany

BUSINESS SCIENCE REFERENCE

Hershey · New York

Director of Editorial Content:	Kristin Klinger
Director of Book Publications:	Julia Mosemann
Acquisitions Editor:	Mike Killian
Development Editor:	Beth Ardner
Publishing Assistant:	Kurt Smith
Typesetter:	Devvin Earnest
Quality control:	Jamie Snavely
Cover Design:	Lisa Tosheff
Printed at:	Yurchak Printing Inc.

Published in the United States of America by
Business Science Reference (an imprint of IGI Global)
701 E. Chocolate Avenue
Hershey PA 17033
Tel: 717-533-8845
Fax: 717-533-8661
E-mail: cust@igi-global.com
Web site: http://www.igi-global.com/reference

Library of Congress Cataloging-in-Publication Data

E-entrepreneurship and ICT ventures : strategy, organization, and technology / Tobias Kollmann, Andreas Kuckertz, and Christoph Stöckmann, editors.   p. cm.
  Includes bibliographical references and index.   Summary: "This book provides a unique overview of the current state of conceptual and empirical research at the interface of e-business and entrepreneurship"--Provided by publisher. ISBN 978-1-61520-597-4 (hardcover) -- ISBN 978-1-61520-598-1 (ebook) 1. Electronic commerce. 2. Entrepreneurship. 3. Technological innovations-- Economic aspects. I. Kollmann, Tobias. II. Kuckertz, Andreas, 1972- III. Stöckmann, Christoph, 1980- IV. Title.

  HF5548.32.E5855 2010
  658.8'72--dc22

                    2009047130

British Cataloguing in Publication Data
A Cataloguing in Publication record for this book is available from the British Library.

Table of Contents

Section 1
Strategy

Section 2
Organization

Section 3
Technology

Detailed Table of Contents

Section 1
Strategy

On the basis of Schumpeterian innovation, this chapter will pioneer in describing business model innovation as addendum to Abernathy's and Utterback's dynamic model of process and product innovation. Thereby, an integrated business model innovation approach will be initiated, overcoming the drawbacks of unilateral innovation. The integrated business model innovation approach proposes a framework for long-term differentiation and competitive advantages. Different examples, in particular regarding ICT-ventures, will clarify the effect of integrated business model innovation.

Recent literature highlights the fact that research in the fields of internationalization and entrepreneurship appears to overlook the internal and external context in which the international strategies are conceived. This chapter contributes to filling that gap by answering two basic questions: What is it about e-ventures that allows them to compete globally? And what is it about e-ventures that makes it a specific mix of strategy shaping processes necessary to formulate a born global strategy?

Chapter 3

While studies on the effect of market orientation in established and young companies have indicated a positive influence on firm performance, the questions whether and in what form this effect can also be found empirically in emerging firms is still a largely unexplored issue. Applying rigorous procedures in the development of the measurement instrument and using a unique sample of 141 young companies, this chapter confirms that market orientation does also have a significant and positive effect on the performance of emerging firms. However, results indicate significant differences to established firms, which are discussed. In conclusion, founders of emerging firms should pursue an individual way of market-oriented behavior that seems most appropriate when considering the company-specific liabilities.

Chapter 4

This article explores how some non-urban counties that are contiguous but located in different US states have worked with their state governments, developing institutional mechanisms to overcome the artificial barrier to technology-based economic development that state borders create. The chapter argues that political boundaries that transect otherwise integrated economic regions often impede economic development coordination and cooperation in general, and for technology access, workforce training, and business innovation in particular. Case study evidence from several successful cross-border efforts in the United States and internationally demonstrates the critical success factors required to overcome political boundaries and initiate technology-based development. These success factors include the creation of diverse funding sources, effective leadership by a coordinated team, and the development of formal legal entities to confront legal and infrastructure challenges.

Organizational legitimacy is a key resource that is necessary for every venture to acquire other crucial resources, which will subsequently stimulate growth. This chapter illustrates this legitimacy-growth relationship by analyzing the case of Europe's first online pharmacy DocMorris. Given that this ICT venture started as extremely illegitimate, this case provides a rich background to identify various strategies that are potentially helpful to enhance a venture's level of legitimacy. Building on interview data collected from the firm's key actors, the chapter shows how the perception of a firm's legitimacy from the viewpoint of various internal and external stakeholders can be managed strategically.

Chapter 6

This chapter investigates the ownership structure, operating characteristics and sustainability of six rural internet portals located in Scotland. The study based on in-depth interviews discovered that two distinct forms of ownership structure existed. The first form of ownership structure involved dedicated private individuals, who self-funded their internet portal activities, while the second form was managed by not-for-profit organizations, such as charitable trusts. Differences between these forms are discussed. Despite the differences, both forms of ownership structure struggled to achieve commercial viability.

Chapter 7

This chapter describes organizational features of a particular kind of social enterprises that have emerged since the development of Web 2.0: peer to peer charities and e-social banking. The chapter will explain how the philosophy of Web 2.0 offers new opportunities for the development and growth of social enterprises. Furthermore, the chapter details their main features obtained from the study of twelve initiatives. The chapter finally offers some reflections on main dilemmas and challenges that could be faced in a short term future.

Section 2
Organization

Chapter 8

Information dissemination, which can enhance the success of on-line and off-line products, is increasingly outside the realm of influence of companies because in many markets, on-line communicators can play a central role in influencing others' purchase decisions. E-Mavens are recognized as a consumer type that engages in on-line communication. Using a sample of more than 2,500 consumers, the chapter profiles e-Mavens using demographic and psychographic characteristics as well as explore their motives for visiting music web sites. In addition, changes in e-Mavens' music-related consumption behavior are investigated. Next, using cluster analysis, the chapter develops a typology of e-Mavens.

Chapter 9

Debbie Richards, Macquarie University, Australia
Peter Busch, Macquarie University, Australia
Ayse Bilgin, Macquarie University, Australia

As the importance of creativity and in turn innovation for individuals, organizations, nations and thus the global community as a whole becomes recognized, so too does the value of identifying those individuals with the potential to become entrepreneurs. With opportunities for innovation afforded by the internet, the identification and development of a new breed of individuals known as e-entrepreneurs seems particularly worthwhile. This chapter focuses on scenarios within the field of information and communication technology. Results indicate innovators may present multiple personality styles, which offer strengths to entrepreneurial activities. Finally through identification of creative personnel, our approach offers a way for organizations to cultivate promising entrepreneurs.

Chapter 10

Cecilia Hegarty, University of Ulster, Northern Ireland

This chapter explores entrepreneurship education through the lens of ICT-enabled learning within university education. In the case study presented, learners extol the benefits of ICT-enabled learning on their entrepreneurship module. There are a number of implications for employers and educationalists. In this chapter, the value of entrepreneurship education via ICT-enabled learning is discussed. For the entrepreneurial firm, recommendations are made about providing training in entrepreneurship for employees.

Chapter 11

Harald von Kortzfleisch, University of Koblenz-Landau, Germany
Mario Schaarschmidt, University of Koblenz-Landau, Germany
Philipp Magin, University of Koblenz-Landau, Germany

The objective of this chapter is to conceptually transfer the concept of open source software (OSS) development to scientific entrepreneurship and to hypothetically discuss the support potentials of this rather new development philosophy for what the authors than call open scientific entrepreneurship. The main thrust of the chapter presents open scientific entrepreneurship from two points of origin: OSS development as a specific form of scientific e-entrepreneurship and further on potential benefits of opening 'traditional' scientific entrepreneurship up by looking at specific action fields. The general benefits as well as downsides of the concept of openness are discussed on a generic level.

This chapter reviews the current status of Open Source (OS) and provides new insights into the prerequisites of the OS process as well as the profile of OS contributors. Moreover, it extends the scope of possible business models such to augment those that exist or were already discussed in the past. While the term OS was coined in the context of software development and redistribution, this chapter presents and discusses the concept of OS to include any Open Collaborative Innovation in both software and hardware.

This chapter addresses the Enterprise Resource Planning (ERP) entrepreneurial venture challenge for developing an ERP database using standard generic database software within existing resources and available data at lowest cost in minimum time for the Australian Department of Defence. The anticipation of the developers of the ERP database was that this entrepreneurial venture could not only help the Australian Department of Defence to become an inclusive knowledge based learning society, but to subsequently provide an inexpensive database model for other organizations, large or small.

In the Net Economy, delivery often has to leave the Net and be provided through traditional means. The firm's delivery mechanism influences the design of the firm's Net presence. This chapter examines the pursuit of e-entrepreneurial ventures by existing businesses with specific attention to the architecture of Web portals and to the delivery mechanisms of products. Additionally, outlined are features and facets of Web portals necessary to sell and deliver mark-up based and production based products and services in the B2C sector of the Net Economy.

Section 3
Technology

Both Web 1.0 and Web 2.0 were linked directly to new stages in the development of e-business. Whereas the distinction between Web 1.0 and Web 2.0 became widely accepted in both literature and practice, we are merely at the beginning of the possibilities arising from current trends culminating in our information society. Information emerges increasingly as a major factor of production, allowing for the activation of innovative business opportunities. Against the background of an increasing information overload, the question to be asked is how technological and market-oriented future developments will cope with these challenges. This paper aims at clarifying this overall development with the objective of giving impulses for the 3rd generation of e-business. For this purpose, the characteristics of each generation (Web 1.0, Web 2.0, and Web 3.0) are clearly highlighted.

Chapter 16

The OpenSocial standard enables Internet-based businesses to create new kinds of value-creating partnerships without extending themselves beyond their own means or competencies. This chapter argues that by entering structured partnerships, e-ventures and social networks can gain a sustainable competitive advantage by integrating their highly complementary resources and capabilities. Building on the Resource-based View (RBV) of the firm and the concept of core competencies, it is shown that both partners can significantly benefit from the technology-induced possibilities that arise from the OpenSocial standard.

Chapter 17

This chapter introduces the concept of Ambient Intelligence (AmI) with regard to the enabling technologies and how they are combined to assist e-entrepreneurs. AmI is a new paradigm in the area of Information and Communication Technology (ICT). The aim of the chapter is to provide a better understanding of the AmI process and knowledge of the AmI system and tools. To this end, three of the enabling technologies are discussed, semantic web, multi-modal services, and radio frequency identification tags. These technologies are then examined within the AmI reference model.

Chapter 18

The chapter provides a case study analyzing the creation and development process of ARTIFICIAL INTELLIGENT AGENTS, S.L. (AIA), a company spin-off from the University of Girona (Spain). It describes all phases, from concept to implementation, as well as the problems and challenges faced by the entrepreneurial team composed of academics and professionals. Furthermore, it lays out the path from developing a technology in the field of human automation attempting to sell a user-friendly technology that would help customer intelligence and management.

Preface

The formation of new ventures plays a decisive role in the social and economic development of the world and is often based on technological innovations. This is by and large due to the fact that with each new venture created, a market participant comes into existence, which potentially stimulates the competition and drives the economic vitality further. Over the last decades, information and communication technologies (ICT) in particular were associated with numerous entrepreneurial opportunities. Many of the world's most reputed companies such as *Microsoft*, *IBM*, or *SAP* have benefited from this development and significantly shaped how business is done today. In recent times, those particular information and communication technologies that are related to digital networks such as the Internet have enabled numerous start-ups to exploit innovative entrepreneurial opportunities. Business models making use of information and communication technologies allowing for the execution of interactive, inter-business processes are usually labeled as electronic business or e-business. Until now, two significant waves of such ICT ventures could be witnessed: Well-known winners of the dot-com boom that ended around the year 2000 were companies like *Amazon*, *eBay*, or *Google*; the subsequent Web 2.0 excitement gave rise to, for instance, start-ups such as *YouTube*, *Facebook*, or *Flickr*, all of them established after the year 2003. Even if the long-term success of some of these ICT ventures is still uncertain, there is without a doubt one lesson to be learned from these events: The ongoing rapid technological development within the electronic business environment still makes even more innovative business models possible and will continue to do so in the future. Since young companies are especially likely to implement such business models based on digital networks, electronic entrepreneurship (or e-entrepreneurship) has emerged as a central theme within the academic discourse. E-entrepreneurship addresses the theoretical interface of electronic business and entrepreneurship research and is defined as (based on Kollmann 2006: 333)

"[...] establishing new companies with innovative business ideas within the e-business environment, which, using an electronic platform in data networks, offer their products and/or services based upon a primarily electronic creation of value. This value proposition becomes only possible through the intelligent utilization of information technology."

The present edited volume, *E-Entrepreneurship and ICT ventures: Strategy, Organization and Technology*, provides a unique and much needed overview of the current state of conceptual and empirical research at the interface of e-business and entrepreneurship research. Because of its exclusive focus on this interface, two largely separate streams in the academic literature are merged, which closes an important gap in current research. The papers collected in this volume are therefore essential reading material for students, academics, practitioners (managers and entrepreneurs), and political decision makers interested in applying and fostering e-business concepts in an entrepreneurial environment. Over the years, at the *E-Business and E-Entrepreneurship Research Group* at the *University of Duisburg-Essen*, Germany, we came to the conclusion that especially three aspects are essential to understand and manage young e-businesses or ICT ventures, namely their strategy, their organization, and their technology. Consequently, this edited volume is divided into three corresponding sections collecting the experiences, ideas, and results of the work of many international experts on this topic. Section 1, *Strategy*, discusses various issues related to general strategic questions such as an ICT venture's positioning, its internationalization strategy, its innovation approach, or the effects of market orientation. Section 2, *Organization*, focuses primarily on human relations, methods of collaboration, and communication. Last, Section 3, *Technology*, presents the state-of-the-art of selected technologies that enable e-business activities and provides an outlook on future developments such as the long awaited semantic web or Web 3.0. In the following paragraphs, we briefly introduce the main contribution of each chapter of *E-Entrepreneurship and ICT ventures: Strategy, Organization and Technology*.

Section 1, *Strategy*, consists of seven chapters. Chapter 1, "*An Integrated Business Model Innovation Approach: It is Not all about Product and Process Innovation*," by Roman Boutellier, Markus Eurich and Patricia Hurschler, Swiss Federal Institute of Technology (ETH) Zurich (Switzerland), addresses business model innovation as an addendum to Abernathy's and Utterback's dynamic model of process and product innovation. Their integrated business model innovation approach proposes a framework for long-term differentiation and competitive advantages. They use different examples, in particular ICT-ventures, to clarify the effect of integrated business model innovation. Chapter 2, "*Internationalization Strategy in New E-Ventures: Towards a General Model and New Research Agenda*," by María Gracia García-Soto and Antonia Mercedes García-Cabrera, University of Las Palmas de Gran Canaria, (Spain), highlights the fact that research in the fields of internationalization and entrepreneurship appears to overlook the internal and external context in which the international strategies are conceived and aims at filling that gap by answering two questions. First, the authors ask what it is about e-ventures allowing them to compete globally? The second questions focuses on what it is about e-venturing making it a specific mix of strategy shaping processes necessary to formulate a born global strategy? Chapter 3, "*Market Orientation in Emerging Firms: Towards a More Rigorous Understanding of Entrepreneurial Marketing*," by Malte Brettel, Andreas Engelen, Florian Heinemann, RWTH University of Aachen (Germany) and Andreas Kessell, GFIU mbH / Antikoerper-online.de (Germany), focuses on entrepreneurial marketing. Applying rigorous procedures in the development of the measurement instrument and using a unique sample of 141 young companies, the authors confirm that market orientation does have a significant and positive effect on the performance of emerging firms. However, results indicate significant differences to established firms. They conclude that founders of emerging firms should pursue an individual way of market-oriented behavior that seems most appropriate when considering the company-specific liabilities. Chapter 4, "*Crossing Borders: Overcoming Political Barriers to Technology-Led Economic Development*," by Nicholas Maynard, RAND Corporation (USA), Aaron McKethan, Brookings Institute (USA), Michael I. Luger, University of Manchester (UK) and Alekhya Uppalapati, The University of North Carolina at Chapel Hill (USA), argues that political boundaries that transect otherwise integrated economic regions often impede economic development coordination and cooperation in general, and for technology access, workforce training, and business innovation in particular. Case study evidence from several successful cross-border efforts in the United States and internationally demonstrates the critical success factors required to overcome political boundaries and initiate technology-based development. Chapter 5, "*Legitimizing Innovative Ventures Strategically: The Case of Europe's First Online Pharmacy*" by Andreas Kuckertz and Karsten Jörn Schröder, University of Duisburg-Essen (Germany), focuses on the central question how radically innovative ICT ventures can build organizational legitimacy, which is essential to acquire other key resources. Based on an in depth case analysis of an extreme case, they illustrate how ICT ventures can manage their various stakeholder groups strategically. Moreover, they develop a number of novel strategies that entrepreneurs can employ to legitimate their innovative business model. Chapter 6, "*Internet Portals in Rural Areas: An Investigation of their Provision in Rural Scotland*," by Laura Galloway, Heriot-Watt University (Scotland), David Deakins, Massey University (New Zealand) and John Sanders, Heriot-Watt University (Scotland), investigates the ownership structure, operating characteristics and sustainability of six rural internet portals located in Scotland. Based on in-depth interviews, the authors discover that two distinct forms of ownership structure exist. Despite differences, both forms of ownership structure struggled to achieve commercial viability. Chapter 7, "*E-Social Entrepreneurship and Social Innovation: The Case of On-Line Giving Markets*," by Alfonso Carlos Morales Gutiérrez and J. Antonio Ariza Montes, Universidad de Córdoba (Spain), describes organizational features of a particular kind of social enterprises that have emerged since the development of Web 2.0: peer to peer charities and e-social banking. Moreover, the authors explain how the philosophy of Web 2.0 offers new opportunities for the development and growth of social enterprises and detail their main features. They finally offer some reflections on main dilemmas and challenges that could be faced in a short term future.

Section 2, *Organization*, consists of seven chapters. Chapter 8, "*Enlisting Online Communicators in Web 2.0*," by Gianfranco Walsh, Simon Brach, University of Koblenz-Landau (Germany) and Vincent-Wayne Mitchell, City University (UK), focuses on e-Mavens, which are recognized as a consumer type engaging in on-line communication. Using a sample of more than 2,500 consumers, the authors profile e-Mavens using demographic and psychographic characteristics as well as explore their motives for visiting music web sites. In addition, changes in e-Mavens' music-related consumption behavior are investigated. Moreover, using cluster analysis, they develop a typology of e-Mavens. Chapter 9, "*The role of Creativity (and Creative Behaviour) in Identifying Entrepreneurs*," by Debbie Richards, Peter Busch and Ayse Bilgin, Macquarie University (Australia), aims at identifying those individuals with the potential to become entrepreneurs. The authors focus on scenarios within the field of information and communication technology. Their results indicate that innovators may present multiple personality styles, which offer strengths to entrepreneurial activities. Chapter 10, "*Education and Training for the Entrepreneurial Employee: Value of ICT-Enabled Learning*," by Cecilia Hegarty, University of Ulster (Northern Ireland), explores entrepreneurship education through the lens of ICT-enabled learning within university education. In this case study presented, learners extol the benefits of ICT-enabled learning on their entrepreneurship module. There are a number of implications for employers and educationalists. Moreover, the value of entrepreneurship education via ICT-enabled learning is discussed. For the entrepreneurial firm, recommendations are given about providing training in entrepreneurship for employees. Chapter 11, "*Open Scientific Entrepreneurship: How the Open Source Paradigm can Foster Entrepreneurial Activities in Scientific Institutions*," by Harald von Kortzfleisch, Mario Schaarschmidt and Philipp Magin, University of Koblenz-Landau (Germany), conceptually transfers the concept of open source software (OSS) development to scientific entrepreneurship and hypothetically discusses the support potentials of this rather new development philosophy for what the authors call open scientific entrepreneurship. The main thrust of the chapter presents open scientific entrepreneurship from two points of origin: OSS development as a specific form of scientific e-entrepreneurship and further on potential benefits of opening 'traditional' scientific entrepreneurship up by looking at specific action fields. The general benefits as well as downsides of the concept of openness are discussed on a generic level. Chapter 12, *"Open Source: Collaborative Innovation,"* by Avi Messica, The College of Management (Israel), reviews the current status of Open Source (OS) and provides new insights into the prerequisites of the OS process as well as the profile of OS contributors. Moreover, the author extends the scope of possible business models such to augment those that exist or were already discussed in the past. While the term OS was coined in the context of software development and redistribution, the author presents and discusses the concept of OS to include any Open Collaborative Innovation in both software and hardware. Chapter 13, *"Enterprise Resource Planning: An E-Entrepreneurial Challenge,"* by J. Doug Thomson, RMIT University, Melbourne (Australia), addresses the Enterprise Resource Planning (ERP) entrepreneurial venture challenge for developing an ERP database using standard generic database software within existing resources and available data at lowest cost in minimum time for the Australian Department of Defence. He shows that the anticipation of the developers of the ERP database was that this entrepreneurial venture could not only help the Australian Department of Defence to become an inclusive knowledge based learning society, but to subsequently provide an inexpensive database model for other organizations, large or small. Chapter 14, *"Delivery in the Net Economy,"* by Anthony Scime, Purdue University (USA) and Anthony C. Scime, State University of New York (USA), examines the pursuit of e-entrepreneurial ventures by existing businesses with specific attention to the architecture of Web portals and to the delivery mechanisms of products. Additionally, outlined are features and facets of Web portals necessary to sell and deliver mark-up based and production based products and services in the B2C sector of the Net Economy.

Finally, Section 3, *Technology*, consists of four chapters. Chapter 15, *"Web 1.0, Web 2.0 and Web 3.0: Revealing New Vistas for E-Business Founders,"* by Tobias Kollmann, University of Duisburg-Essen (Germany) and Carina Lomberg, Ecole Polytechnique Fédérale de Lausanne (Switzerland), addresses the distinction between different generations of the web. The authors argue that whereas the distinction between Web 1.0 and Web 2.0 became widely accepted in both literature and practice, we are merely at the beginning of the possibilities arising from current trends culminating in our information society. The authors aim at clarifying this overall development with the objective of giving impulses for the 3rd generation of e-business. For this purpose, the characteristics of each generation (Web 1.0, Web 2.0, and Web 3.0) are highlighted. Chapter 16 *"OpenSocial: Structured Partnerships in the Context of Social Networking Platforms,"* by Matthias Häsel, XING (Germany), argues that by entering structured partnerships, e-ventures and social networks can gain a sustainable competitive advantage by integrating their highly complementary resources and capabilities. Building on the Resource-based View (RBV) of the firm and the concept of core competencies, the author shows that both partners can significantly benefit from the technology-induced possibilities that arise from the OpenSocial standard. Chapter 17, *"Enabling Technologies in an Ambient Intelligence (AmI) System,"* by Simrn Kaur Gill and Kathryn Cormican, National University of Ireland (Ireland), introduces the concept of Ambient Intelligence (AmI) with regard to the enabling technologies and how they are combined to assist e-entrepreneurs. The aim of the authors is to provide a better understanding of the AmI process and knowledge of the AmI system and tools. To this end, three of the enabling technologies are discussed, semantic web, multi-modal services, and radio frequency identification tags. These technologies are then examined within the AmI reference model. Chapter 18, "*Creating Value through Entrepreneurship: The Case of Artificial Intelligent Agents,*" by Andrea Bikfalvi, Universitat de Girona (Spain), Christian Serarols Tarrés, Universitat Autònoma de Barcelona (Spain) and Josep Lluís de la Rosa Esteva, Universitat de Girona (Spain), provides a case study analyzing the creation and development process of ARTIFICIAL INTELLIGENT AGENTS, S.L. (AIA), a company spin-off from the University of Girona (Spain). It describes all phases, from concept to implementation, as well as the problems and challenges, faced by the entrepreneurial team composed of academics and professionals. Furthermore, it lays out the path from developing a technology in the field of human automation attempting to sell a user-friendly technology that would help customer intelligence and management.

Taken together, the chapters of *E-Entrepreneurship and ICT ventures: Strategy, Organization and Technology* contribute to an enhanced understanding of the important interface of e-business and entrepreneurship by bringing together leading academics and practitioners worldwide.

Tobias Kollmann
Andreas Kuckertz
Christoph Stöckmann
University of Duisburg-Essen, Germany

REFERENCES

Kollmann, T. (2006). What is e-entrepreneurship? Fundamentals of company founding in the net economy. *International Journal of Technology Management, 33*(4), 322-340.

Section 1
Strategy

Chapter 1

An Integrated Business Model Innovation Approach:
It is Not All about Product and Process Innovation

Roman Boutellier
Swiss Federal Institute of Technology (ETH) Zurich, Switzerland

Markus Eurich
Swiss Federal Institute of Technology (ETH) Zurich, Switzerland

Patricia Hurschler
Swiss Federal Institute of Technology (ETH) Zurich, Switzerland

ABSTRACT

This chapter will foster the understanding of business model innovation with a focus on the Information and Communication Technology (ICT) industry and e-entrepreneurship. A general overview of business models and their elements as well as an introduction to innovation alternatives will provide the necessary background for business model innovation. On the basis of Schumpeterian innovation, this chapter will pioneer in describing business model innovation as addendum to Abernathy's and Utterback's dynamic model of process and product innovation. Thereby an integrated business model innovation approach will be initiated overcoming the drawbacks of unilateral innovation. The integrated business model innovation approach proposes a framework for long-term differentiation and competitive advantages. Different examples, in particular ICT-ventures, will clarify the effect of integrated business model innovation.

INTRODUCTION

Not long ago Information and Communication Technology (ICT) was reserved to a few specialists. In the last decades, however, ICTs became ever easier to use and are nowadays open to the majority of western society. Modern ICTs have become part of our daily lives and have even changed our way of life. We are getting used to checking our e-mail inboxes on a daily basis, connecting with our friends via social networking websites such as Facebook (http://www.facebook.com), being reachable 24/7, writing documents on personal computer applications, finding the fastest train connections via an

DOI: 10.4018/978-1-61520-597-4.ch001

Internet application, and browsing the Internet to find products that offer the best value for the money. In the course of this development information is no more limited to being an auxiliary factor that supported the production of physical products as in the "Real Economy". Information became a product of its own in the so-called "Net Economy". Net Economy refers to the economically used part of electronic data networks. Net Economy is thereby a network economics that benefits from the network effect through electronic platforms that enable the processing of information, communications and transactions (Kollmann, 2006a). The economic opportunities within the Net Economy are termed e-business (Kollmann, 2006a). ICTs are playing a decisive role in business model innovation as the advent of modern ICTs facilitated the development of new services and the realization of innovative e-business ideas. We call a start-up in e-business an ICT-venture. ICT-ventures, such as Skype Technologies S.A. (http://www.skype.com), Joost N.V. (http://www.joost.com), MySpace (http://www.myspace.com), or Adobe Systems Inc. (http://www.adobe.com), have shown to be scoring particularly well in developing and deploying the latest ICTs. The business logic of an ICT-venture is influenced by ICT as either its products can only be developed by the means of ICTs or the ICT-venture develops new or more sophisticated ICTs itself. This chapter explains the effects of the net on business models: the Internet enables electronic products, electronic processes, new ways of reaching customers, and new value networks. The business scope of a company, which traditionally did business in the Real Economy, can be redefined on the basis of ICT-enabled business transformation (Venkatraman, 1994) and ventures can accomplish innovations in industries, in which innovation has no longer been considered as being possible anymore. An ICT-venture is typically doing business in the Net Economy. Moreover, ICT-enabled ventures can break the mold of doing business through the introduction of ICT in the Real Economy. Enter-

prises developing and deploying sophisticated ICTs offer their products or services on the basis of either direct electronic creation of value (e.g. Adobe Systems Inc.) or ICT-enabled creation of value (e.g. Blacksocks S.A.). The global market has tremendously increased competition and the appearance of ICT-ventures entering the global market has the potential to tighten this competition yet more. The act of establishing a venture in the Net Economy is termed "e-entrepreneurship" (Kollmann, 2006b).

Against this background, effective research and development become ever more important for companies in order to protect or increase their market shares and to sell their products on the market for as long as possible. However, many companies still rely either on pure product or on process innovation, which is not an adequate approach to remain in mature markets. Toyota successfully showed that there is no contradiction between product leadership (based on product innovation) and cost leadership (based on process innovation). For a long time, these two approaches were considered to be contrasting each other. Porter (1985) described the combination of both as "stuck-in-the-middle" (p. 72). However, a successful combination of product and process innovation might need to be complemented or enhanced with further innovation approaches: it is the time for integrated business model innovation! Interviews with 765 CEOs from the Americans, Europe and Asia Pacific showed that most companies still trust in product and process innovations, while not even a third of them emphasized the business model as innovation type of choice. However, the study also revealed that business model innovation is prioritized by about 30% of outperformers compared to only 15% of underperformers, which could be interpreted as a hint that business model innovation pays off (Pohle, & Chapman, 2006).

This chapter aims at fostering the understanding of business model innovation. Therefore, it starts with an introductory description of business models, different innovation possibilities, and business model innovation. Several examples help to understand specific innovation possibilities and indicate how competitive advantages can stem from innovation. Based on this theoretical background, a simplified framework for integrated business model innovation is proposed for long-term differentiation. Case studies exemplify the successful realization of integrated business model innovation.

BACKGROUND

It is nearly impossible to find a generally accepted definition of the term business model. In practice, the usage of the term business model varies strongly and even managers often fail to spontaneously explain the business model of their company as they do not precisely know what is actually meant by business model. In theory, a literature review revealed that many authors define the term differently, and some authors even use the term without definition (Frischmuth, 2001). Rolf Caspers discovered that the term business model has not been defined clearly in literature (Bieger, Bickhoff, Caspers, zu Knyphausen-Aufseß, & Reding, 2002). In electronic commerce, Paul Timmers (1998) found that the term is not used consistently. This section will therefore present some popular definitions of the term business model especially in the context of ICT.

Timmers (1998) defined business model as the "architecture for the product, service and information flows, including a description of the various business actors and their roles; and description of the potential benefits for the various business actors; and description of the sources of revenues" (p. 2). In accordance to this definition, Timmers (1998) determined eleven types of business models in the Net Economy, including e-shop, e-procurement, e-auction, e-mall, third-party marketplace, virtual communities, value-chain service providers, value-chain integrators, collaboration

platforms, information brokers, and trust services. In the e-business domain, Amit and Zott (2001) refer to a different definition. They declare that a "business model depicts the content, structure, and governance of transactions designed so as to create value through the exploitation of business opportunities" (p. 511). In their approach to clarify the role of the business model in capturing value from innovation, Chesbrough and Rosenbloom (2002) perceive a business model as mediator between technical potential and the realization of economic value. Technology development is taken as input. The business model converts this input through different elements and functions into economic value. According to Chesbrough and Rosenbloom (2002), it is absolutely essential that technology and business model fit as the inherent value of a technology might remain hidden until it is somehow commercialized. Thus the business model has the potential to release latent value from technology (Chesbrough, & Rosenbloom, 2002).

A more general definition of the term business model comes from Gary Hamel (2000). His business model definition contains four main components, three relations between them and four basic requirements. The four main components are: customer interface, core strategy, strategic resources, and value chain network. The customer interface describes how a company reaches its customers and which channels are used. The customer interface is established through relations, information, and support and price structure. The core strategy defines the business mission, the product and market scope, and the differentiation basis. The strategic resources contain core competences and processes as well as strategic assets. The value chain network completes the own resources with suppliers and partners. The relation "customer's benefit" connects the customer interface and core strategy. Core strategy and strategic resources are linked by the relation "configuration". The third relation "boundaries of a company" relates strategic resources with the value chain network. The four basic requirements are: efficiency, inimitability, fitting accuracy, and profit multiplier (Hamel, 2000).

A similar explanation has been proclaimed by Osterwalder and Pigneur (2002), who refer the term business model to a "conceptual tool that contains a set of elements and their relationships and allows to express the business logic of a specific firm" (p. 1). They included four major elements into their business model framework: product innovation, customer management, infrastructure management, and financial aspects (Osterwalder, & Pigneur, 2002). However, the literature review raised some confusion about which elements and functions belong to a business model and which do not. Depending on the author, a business model comprises different elements and functions. Amongst many others, the list includes: value proposition, market segment, structure of the value chain, cost structure, profit potential, position within the value network, revenue generation mechanism, identification of potential complementors and competitors, and reaching customers distributing a product or delivering a service (Chesbrough, 2007; Chesbrough, & Rosenbloom, 2002; Magretta, 2002). The discussion about which elements and functions are part of the business model and which are not is out of scope of this chapter, but there are two points to be stressed: first, a business model is much more than just a revenue generation mechanism, and, second, a business model should not be mixed up with the strategy (Magretta, 2002).

As there are just too many different definitions, this chapter uses a simple and yet general definition: breaking down the term into its two words - "business" and "model" - can facilitate the formulation of a useful definition of the term. A business is a company that aims at making profit. A model is a simplified picture of the reality, which consists of elements and their relations to each other. Consequently, a business model can be understood as simplified picture of a company that aims at generating revenue, and that comprises

essential elements of the company plus the relations between those elements (Hoppe, & Kollmer, 2001). This definition is close to Peter F. Drucker's thoughts in his disquisition on the theory of the business (Drucker, & Stone, 1998, chap. 1).

The ultimate goal of a business model for an ICT innovation is that the new technology provides value to the consumer (Chesbrough, & Rosenbloom, 2002). The sole development of a promising technology is worthless without an appropriate business model. The identification, modification and execution of a business model can be considered as an "entrepreneurial act" (Chesbrough, & Rosenbloom, 2002, p. 550). The modification and innovation of an extant business model, however, is crucial to sustain the success of the company. Chesbrough (2007) claims that "no great business model lasts forever" (p. 15). Companies might lose market shares if the growth of their business is restricted to the constraints of their extant business model. In this chapter, business model innovation refers to the modification of an extant business model.

Business model innovation is of importance for both, new ventures and established companies. Ventures must identify an appropriate business model on a basis of their innovations and modify the business model in accordance to their needs. If established companies incorporate new ICTs in their business they must recognize what kinds of changes are required to innovate their business models. ICTs can enable business transformation and even lead to a business scope redefinition. ICTs provide the opportunity to enlarge or shift the original business mission and scope through substitution of traditional capabilities with ICT-enabled skills (Chesbrough, 2007; Venkatraman, 1994).

Before describing an integrated business model innovation approach, an introduction is provided to Schumpeterian innovation. Amit and Zott (2001) identified four sources of value creation in e-business: efficiency, complementarities, lock-in, and novelty. In the context of ICT-ventures and e-entrepreneurship, this chapter focuses only on the value creation source "novelty". In accordance with Amit and Zott (2001), the main theoretical anchor of the source "novelty" lies within the framework of Schumpeterian innovation, novel ICTs and new combinations of resources are the basis of innovation. Therefore, Schumpeterian innovation is taken as the main theoretical foundation of the integrated business model innovation approach.

Joseph Schumpeter (1931) initiated the theory of business development and new ways of value creation on the basis of technological change and innovation. Schumpeter (1931) describes five distinctive areas of innovation in a company:

- Creation of new products or modification of product quality: product innovation
- Implementation of new production methods: today's process innovation
- Development of new markets: addressing new customers
- Development of new sources: finding new suppliers
- Development of new organizational structures

Joseph Schumpeter actually never speaks about innovations, but about implementation of new combinations. In 1943, Schumpeter elaborated the conception of creative destruction, which states that long-term economic growth is based on the entrance of innovative entrepreneurs, even if it destroys the value and power of established companies. At the time the innovation becomes an established practice, the entrepreneur's advantages diminish: economy is never in an equilibrium state, it is dynamic. Creative destruction can also take place within an established company (Amit, & Zott, 2001; Schumpeter, 1943). The five areas of innovation in a company may be consulted for the definition of business model innovations. This allows broader understanding of the meaning of business model innovations than the definitions

by a lot of innovation researchers and managers. The presented business model definitions try to reduce reality to a few components. Models abstract and simplify the reality. A simplified framework will be described in the following section, which includes only the most important innovation possibilities and represents a generic basis for business model management.

BUSINESS MODEL INNOVATION

Towards Integrated Business Model Innovations

The dynamic model of James M. Utterback and William J. Abernathy (1975) addresses only two of Schumpeter's five areas of innovation: product and process innovation. The authors distinguish between two subsequent waves of innovation: the first wave describes product innovation, the second process innovation. Product and process innovations are usually at the beginning of product life cycles. Afterwards business model innovation can be an addendum (see Figure 1).

The number of different product innovations is high at the beginning until a dominant design emerges. After this stabilization, product innovations go on routinely. The products become more and more similar and radical innovation gives way to incremental improvement (Boutellier, & Rohner, 2006), for example there have been no radical innovations in the cement industry for more than 40 years.

Adobe Systems' success, for instance, is based on product innovation. Their first product innovation was PostScript, a page description language. Adobe Systems innovated further products like Adobe Photoshop, which became the flagship product of Adobe Systems. With its innovative and sophisticated features, Adobe Photoshop made Adobe Systems market leader for commercial image manipulation (cf. http://www.adobe.com).

Figure 1. Business model innovation enables differentiation after product and process innovations slow down.

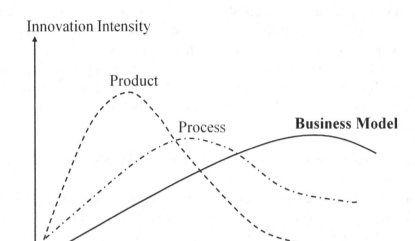

Process innovation becomes high priority after the dominant design has emerged and cost pressure increases. New production methods aim at producing the product cheaper, faster or at a better quality. All processes along the value chain are considered. As an option, companies can start to introduce e-procurement, i.e. purchasing standardized products via the Internet. Delivery and accounting can be managed in the enterprise resource system. ICT enables the company to introduce efficient processes with standardized product catalogues.

In mature markets products change slowly, e.g. the design and features of cars do not change quickly. Product and process innovations are still important, but business model innovation adds a new dimension of novelty. Business model innovation, however, asks for a different management approach than do product and process innovation, which is a significant barrier hindering a lot of companies to do business model innovations.

Product and process innovations represent the basis for business model innovation. After product and process innovation, business model innovation takes place: either by finding new sources and suppliers or by reaching new markets and new customers. Organizational structure innovations often follow these two innovation areas. Schumpeter denominated the five areas of innovation nearly 75 years ago. In modern wording, Hamel's school of thought is linked to Schumpeter's ideas and the terms "value chain network", "customer interface", and "organizational structure" are used. The simplified model provides starting points for innovations (see Figure 2).

In the simplified framework Schumpeter's development of new sources and suppliers is termed as "value chain network". In a globalized world supply chain management and the value chain network become important for innovative companies. By concentrating on core competences and outsourcing the rest, suppliers become important business partners. The transportation from the supplier's manufacturing plant to the company and finally to the customers is challenging, especially when speed is crucial. Radio Frequency Identification (RFID) technology, for example, can enable innovative solutions for supply chain

Figure 2. A simplified framework for business model innovations integrating the most important types of innovation.

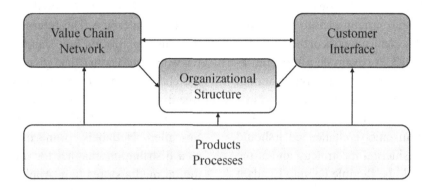

problems such as real-time tracking and tracing. New technologies, such as RFID, help to refine existing applications for Vendor Managed Inventory (VMI). The Internet is about to extend its reach to the physical world through the integration of technologies such as RFID, (wireless) Sensor and Actuator Networks, and Networked Embedded Devices. The integration of those technologies enables an electronic network between physical objects that is commonly termed the Internet of Things (Floerkemeier, Langheinrich, Fleisch, Mattern, & Sarma, 2008). The Internet of Things aims at bridging the physical with the digital world. Therefore the scope of business is between the Real Economy and the Net Economy. The Internet of Things could, for example, contribute to a more precise inventory accuracy and improve VMI and Continuous Replenishment Programs (on basis of European Supply Chain Institute, 2007; Pramatari, Doukidis, & Kourouthanassis, 2004). The selection of suppliers may dependent on the capability of suppliers to cooperate in a global track and trace infrastructure, like the EPCglobal network (Schuster, Allen, & Brock, 2007).

Hamel's component customer interface comes close to Schumpeter's development of new markets. Development of new markets may consist of geographical new regions or new customer segments. New markets need a new interface between the company and the targeted customers. To reach new customers, the customer interface might be changed, for example by using the Internet to contact the customers. Consider for instance the vast number of e-shops existing solely on the Internet without stores – their customer interface and distribution channel is the Internet. Amazon. com (http://www.amazon.com), for example, makes use of the Internet as exclusive sales and distribution channel, which means a change of the interface to the customer. By comparison, Barnes & Noble Inc., founded in 1917, became the United States' largest book retailer with about 800 stores. Barnes & Noble is the only bookseller with a fully operational multi-channel strategy – with retail locations and an online subsidiary (cf. http://www.book.com). The website was launched in 1997. Today, Barnes & Noble's web pages serve as the company's largest shop, enabling customers to order any book at any time from everywhere. With the Internet retailing Barnes & Noble is able to reach new customers. Another example comes from the fashion and sports industry in which some companies even integrate their customers in the design and development of their products: http://www.niketalk.com is an example of such a web platform by Nike.

Organizational structure is the fifth element of business model innovation. "Structure follows strategy", states Chandler (Foss, 1997; Hall, & Saias, 1980), which means that the organizational structure aligns itself with the strategy, and not vice versa. Organizational structure has to be adapted whenever the value chain network or the customer interface are changed. For example, after optimizing the value chain network, the organizational structure of procurement can be centralized in a way to enable the bundling of all subsidiaries' demands. The organization is challenged: it should constantly be considering its strategy and at the same time it should be flexible enough to adapt to new suppliers and new customers.

Innovations are only worthwhile if they can be protected. Patents guarantee a limited protection for products and processes. However, imitators often succeed to copy products, because they are directly available. To copy process innovations, access, experience, and technological know-how are needed. However, by outsourcing processes to suppliers, even process innovations are no longer protected. Business model innovations are different: though they cannot be patented, they are difficult to imitate as it is a combination of many innovations, to all intents and purposes an integrated approach. These business model innovations can be incremental or radical. In mature markets there are often incremental business model innovations from existing companies, because big changes in the organizational structure, such as complete reorganizations, are difficult to manage. For existing companies it is difficult to completely change their organization, therefore, ventures fill this gap and enter the market with radical new concepts. The music industry is an example, in which ventures popped up to provide music via the Internet.

The five major record companies used to divide up more or less the complete market, only some independent labels had minor shares. The major record labels dominated the music industry by contracting artists, producing records, and selling them on the market. Labeling and retail market accounted for over 50 percent of the

value creation. During the past few years new technologies, most notable digital audio encoding formats such as MP3, enabled the Internet as new customer interface. The Internet paved the way for music platforms (e.g. Jamendo S.A.: http://www.jamendo.com) that give unknown artists the chance to build up their reputation through free distribution of some of their songs over the Internet and make their money later in concerts. So-called "Netlabels" primarily use the Internet as a distribution channel for music, and online digital media stores (e.g. Apple's iTunes Music Store: http://www.apple.com/itunes) entered the value chain network of established record companies. The software-based media stores allow the customer to download her favorite songs one by one. She only pays for the songs she likes and does not have to purchase the whole album. During the first half of 2007 417 million songs have been downloaded in the United States while only 24 million records were bought (Nielsen Sound-Scan, 2009). As the major labels failed to set up their own online digital media stores, e.g. Apple signed deals with the major records labels to sell their songs. Online digital media stores take their share of the profit margins and thereby reduce the profit margins of the major record labels.

Cases of the Integrated Business Model Innovation Approach

Companies have improved customer relationship management and reorganized their global supply chain. Only few companies are as yet aware of the opportunities provided by an integrated business model innovation approach. In this section, it will be explained how innovation potentials can result in competitive advantage. Three cases will clarify the effect of an integrated approach.

The first case describes the ICT-venture Skype and its integrated business model innovation approach in a mature ICT market. The second case deals with the Village Phone program that shows how Grameen Telecom developed an untapped market. Grameen Telecom innovated a business model through adaptation of its value chain network, its customer interface and its organizational structure. In this case there have been no product and process innovations at all. The final case, Blacksocks, an ICT-enabled venture in the mature textile industry, highlights innovations at the customer interface that are integrated in an adapted value chain network and organizational structure, in a market, in which product innovation itself is not possible anymore.

Skype: Business Model Innovation in a Mature ICT Market

The ICT-venture Skype Technologies S.A. is the first major peer-to-peer (P2P) Internet telephony operator. Skype succeeded to provide software of the same name (Skype) that enables free and easy use of Internet telephony at an acceptable voice quality. Telecommunication operators and Internet telephony service providers have existed before Skype entered the market, but Skype innovated in terms of both technological development and business modeling.

Skype bases its Voice over Internet Protocol (VoIP) services on P2P technology, which leads to a lean organization with minimal network infrastructure. The company uses protocols that can bypass firewalls and manage to hide its technical complexity from the user. It requires no expert knowledge to install and configure the software. Above all Skype offers software that converges voice communication, instant messaging, chatting, and video-conferencing to one single application. Therefore users can benefit from an all-in-one solution and do not have to switch applications anymore. The combination of several free of charge communication services at a good quality into one application is the foundation of Skype's large base of hundreds of millions users. While Internet telephony services are offered for free, Skype generates revenue through value-added services. The company proposes their large user base premium services such as voicemail or gateway connectivity to the Public Switched Telephone Network (PSTN). The premium service SkypeOut, for example, is liable to pay for the expenses and enables phone calls from the Skype application to normal PSTN phones. The service SkypeIn allows phone calls from normal PSTN phones to Skype. The Skype user has to pay for the provision of the number.

Skype's success bases on its consequent business model innovation of the extant business models of telecommunication companies. Skype changed the product 'telephony' and enriched it with formerly separated communication methods such as chatting and video-conferencing. The process was changed as the underlying PSTN technology was substituted for VoIP P2P technology. These changes entailed changes to the value chain network. New actors appear in the value network of Skype, for example, hardware manufacturers for the login servers. Moreover, the costumer interface changed as well, which is now a graphical user interface on a computer screen. As a consequence, the organizational structure is different to those of established telecommunication companies. The services provided by Skype require different employee profiles and different knowledge, for example, knowledge in session initiation protocols or P2P technology (Alby, 2008; Bulk, 2004; Tapio, 2005).

Village Phone: ICT as Key to Business Model Innovation in an Untapped Market

Bangladesh is one of the world's poorest and most densely populated countries. Most homes and almost all rural villages lack a telephone connection. The lack of connectivity sustained underdevelopment and poverty and made Bangladesh's rural area an untapped market. To improve the situation Grameen Bank, a micro-finance institution, founded two subsidiaries: Grameen Telecom and Grameen Phone. Grameen Telecom provides phone services in Bangladeshi rural areas (the so-called Village Phone program), while Grameen Phone provides phone services to the urban areas.

ICT is the key to the disruptive Village Phone business model that provides modern telecommunication services to the poor people of Bangladesh and thereby fosters their development. The basic idea of Grameen Telecom's business model is to enable cell phone services by creating micro enterprises that can generate revenue and provide connectivity to the people in their villages. The micro enterprises are entrepreneurs, whose development has been supported by Grameen Telecom and Grameen Bank. Grameen Telecom supports the entrepreneurs in the start-up phase by buying a cell phone subscription, providing the connection, and training them. The entrepreneurs purchase a cell phone with a credit granted from Grameen Bank and sell phone services to customers by the call. With about 70 customers a month using each cell phone, the shared-access business model creates reasonable cash flows. This enables the entrepreneurs to amortize their investment. Repayment rates to Grameen Bank are over 90%. With its high revenues Grameen Telecom's shared-access business model has proven to be successful: sustainability and success stem from the Village Phone program that ensure benefits for all stakeholders. Each phone generates revenue of about $90 each month and gives the entrepreneurs and the Bangladeshi villagers social and economic benefits.

Grameen Telecom did not innovate on the product. Indeed, the cell phones are simple, just good enough and could hardly attract wealthy customers. From a process innovation point of view, Grameen Telecom was faced with the lack of infrastructure and was therefore forced to an alternative connectivity option namely via cell phones. Neither the product nor the processes can be considered as an innovation, but Grameen Telecom succeeded with its business model innovation. The introduction of an intermediate entity,

namely the entrepreneurs, and the interdependency with Grameen Phone and Grameen Bank means a significant change to the common value chain network of existing telecommunication providers. The customer interface is designed human centered. Bangladeshi poor people with low literacy do not get directly in touch with Grameen Telecom but interact with entrepreneurs they know. The business interdependency between Grameen Telecom and its holding company Grameen Bank and its sister company Grameen Phone implies an organizational structure that is essential for the business model. Grameen Phone subsidizes Grameen Telecom and therefore makes Grameen Telecom superior to rural-only competitors (Cohen, 2001; Lawson, & Meyenn, 2000; Richardson, Ramirez, & Haq, 2000).

Blacksocks: ICT-Enabled Business Model Innovation in a Mature Market

The ICT-enabled venture Blacksocks S.A. sells subscriptions for black socks. It has solved the old problem of sorting socks in an innovative way. Once every few months a pair of socks is delivered to the customer by post. All these socks are black and identical. Meanwhile, white T-shirts and drawers are also available.

In a short time Blacksocks succeeded to establish a sizeable market share in the Swiss socks market – a market which is characterized by cut throat competition and crowding out, where nobody would have expected to succeed with an innovation. The company's market channel is the Internet (cf. http://www.blacksocks.com) which offers a cheap way to reach millions of potential customers. Since Blacksocks went online in 1999 it has sold several hundred thousand sock subscriptions in the small Swiss market. Blacksocks sells a product which seems to be difficult to differentiate: black socks are indeed just black socks. The Swiss company outsources almost all processes and concentrates exclusively on marketing and direct customer contacts. Outsourcing and standardization of business processes contributed to cost reductions. According to the CEO's opinion only the customer service cannot be outsourced, even though this process is mainly handled by email. To guarantee the functioning of such a business solution, cooperation with partners is paramount. The prospective dynamic safety stock per period is calculated electronically by balancing inventories, sales and purchases. The CEO budgets future sales, buffer capacity and lot size electronically. Small stocks are desirable to avoid capital lockup. At the beginning of the year the sock producer in Italy gets the total number of orders to better balance seasonality. One of the supplier selection criteria was geographical proximity: if there is a problem in the production, the CEO of Blacksocks travels to Italy and back within a day. Another criterion was size: the supplier should be big enough to guarantee quality and deadlines, but not too big for Blacksocks to still represent an important customer. Blacksocks also cultivates the relationship with its distribution partner and therefore the CEO of Blacksocks visits his logistic partner once a month. Daily business operations run via e-mail and twice a day the packer receives a delivery bill. A barcode on the receipt is matched with the database and the sock deliveries.

Blacksocks has neither performed a product nor a process innovation but rather a radical business model innovation. By using the Internet as new customer interface it quickly reaches new customers. By outsourcing all processes, except for marketing and customer services, Blacksocks differs from the traditional textile value chain network: with only one supplier the sock procurement process is kept as lean as possible. The long-term business relationship guarantees for a highly efficient value chain and distribution and data management require other business partners than usual sock sellers. Moreover, the organization is as small as possible and the organizational structure fits its overall market approach. Only four people, who are specialized in customer communication and web design, form Blacksocks' team.

Traditional sales persons' skills are not necessary in this organizational structure. Competitors tried to copy the business model, but without having an integrated approach they remained without success. Blacksocks was then able to take over databases from failed imitators and enlarged its own customer base. Blacksocks' integrated approach enables protection from imitators (S. Liechti, CEO Blacksocks, personal communication, February 7, 2006).

FUTURE RESEARCH DIRECTIONS

The findings of this chapter smooth the way for developments in business model innovation. It could be interesting to better understand which forces, e.g. top management awareness, can facilitate or hinder the change of an extant business model.

Novel ICTs as well as changes of the manufacturers' and service providers' business models might entail necessary changes to the business models of the other stages in the value network, like suppliers or distribution centers. Further research could invest in understanding how business model innovations at one stage in the value network may trigger business model innovations at other stages and which impact mutual reactions and reciprocation has on the overall value creation of the value network.

As described in the background section there is still no unique definition of the term business model. A generally accepted business model framework could remove some of the great confusion that goes along with the term business model. An evaluation of the generic elements that belong to a business model might be a starting point.

The business model innovation framework proposed in this chapter focuses on changes to extant business models, i.e. changes to an extant business model within one specific firm or changes of an adopted business model by a venture. Novel ICTs can, however, even pave the way to establish new business models from the scratch. ICTs could enable completely new services and applications that have never been available before, such as online ordering. The Internet of Things (Floerkemeier et al., 2008), sophisticated wireless sensor and actuator networks, or novel collaboration platforms, for instance, could enable new applications in e.g. supply chain management or healthcare, or provide mass customized services. As totally new products and services may evolve, it is not possible to rely on changes of extant business models. Insights into markets as well as technological developments are significant to arrange products, processes, distribution channels, exchange mechanisms and transaction architectures. On the one hand, novel ICTs are a great opportunity for ICT-ventures to enter the market but, on the other hand, it is a great challenge for them to construct new business model innovations for totally new products.

CONCLUSION

This chapter described Schumpeterian innovations as sources of business model innovation and thereby introduced business model innovation as an addendum to Abernathy's and Utterback's product and process innovation cycles. For ICT-ventures as well as for established companies it is important to understand innovation approaches that go beyond product and process innovation. The model of Abernathy and Utterback has proven its value in many industries, but is limited to product and process innovations.

In order to innovate it is not necessary to have a precise definition of the term business model. It could be helpful, however, to know potentials and examples of business model innovations and to follow an integrated approach. Many companies succeed because their business model innovations integrate different innovations going on in their companies simultaneously. If a company innovates in one of the five Schumpeterian innovation areas,

it should adapt the others. For instance, a change to the customer interface may implicate changes to the suppliers' or the organizational structure. An integrated approach of the five innovation possibilities offers long-term differentiation and a much higher protection against copying.

It is well understood that companies require specialists for product and process innovations. For organizational adaptations consultants are temporarily mandated. In contrast to product innovation, companies may have no second thoughts to reveal parts of business model innovations to their competitors. The strategic relevance is underestimated, the resource management is minimal and the results are generated during many years in an uncoordinated patchwork of small adaptations. Similar to core competences business modeling relies on a long learning process which is partly based on implicit know-how: it is difficult to coordinate many different innovation streams in a company. Business models are driven by visions and corporate culture, not only strategy. An integrated approach of business model innovations becomes manageable with concentration on five basic elements: products, processes, value chain network, customer interfaces, and organizational structures. Therefore an innovative business model is the best protection against imitators when product and process innovations slow down. Business models are not only intellectual constructs, as described by Hamel (2000), but rather emerge from concrete changes in the five innovation types of Schumpeter (1931).

A framework derived from Schumpeter's innovation areas provides the basis for business model innovations, in which value network and the customer interface play a major role. The described case studies in the ICT domain show different approaches and clarify the effect of an integrated business model innovation approach. Companies customize the customer interface, change the value chain network and organize the structure according to the interface and the network. Innovations on the customer side suffice just as little as innovations on the supplier side: if changes are managed according to the five Schumpeterian innovation types, business model innovation could make the difference!

REFERENCES

Alby, T. (2008). *Web 2.0 Konzepte, Anwendungen, Technologien* (3rd Ed.). München, Germany: Hanser.

Amit, R., & Zott, C. (2001). Value Creation in E-Business. *Strategic Management Journal, 22*(6/7), 493–520. doi:10.1002/smj.187

Bieger, T., Bickhoff, N., Caspers, R., zu Knyphausen-Aufseß, D., & Reding, K. (Eds.). (2002). *Zukünftige Geschäftsmodelle: Konzept und Anwendung in der Netzökonomie*. Berlin, Germany: Springer.

Boutellier, R., & Rohner, N. (2006). Technologiegeschwindigkeit und Technologieplanung. In J. Gausemeier (Ed.), *Vorausschau und Technologieplanung* (pp. 291-316). Paderborn, Germany: W.V. Westfalia Druck GmbH.

Bulk, F. (2004). *Final Project: Skype* [Electronic Version]. Retrieved February 11, 2009 from http://www1.cs.columbia.edu/~salman/skype/frank.pdf

Chesbrough, H. (2007). Business Model Innovation: It's Not Just About Technology Anymore. *Strategy and Leadership, 35*(6), 12–17. doi:10.1108/10878570710833714

Chesbrough, H., & Rosenbloom, R. S. (2002). The Role of the Business Model in Capturing Value from Innovation: Evidence from Xerox Corporation's Technology Spin-Off Companies. *Industrial and Corporate Change, 11*(3), 529–555. doi:10.1093/icc/11.3.529

Cohen, N. (2001). What Works: Grameen Telecom's Village Phones [Electronic Version]. *World Resources Institute Digital Dividend*, 1-15. Retrieved February 11, 2009 from http://pdf.wri.org/dd_grameen.pdf

Drucker, P. F., & Stone, N. (1998). *Peter Drucker on the Profession of Management*. Boston, MA: Harvard Business School Publishing.

European Supply Chain Institute. (2007). *Euro RFID: Your Guide to RFID & GDS Solutions* [Electronic Version]. Retrieved February 11, 2009 from http://www.escinst.org/pdf/euroRFID2007.pdf

Floerkemeier, C., Langheinrich, M., Fleisch, E., Mattern, F., & Sarma, S. E. (2008). *The Internet of Things: First International Conference, IOT 2008, Zurich, Switzerland, March 26-28, 2008, Proceedings*. Berlin, Germany: Springer.

Foss, N. J. (1997). *Resources, Firms, and Strategies: A Reader in the Resource-Based Perspective*. Oxford, UK: Oxford University Press.

Frischmuth, J. (2001). *Strategien und Prozesse für neue Geschäftsmodelle Praxisleitfaden für E- und mobile Business*. Berlin, Germany: Springer.

Hall, D. J., & Saias, M. A. (1980). Strategy Follows Structure! *Strategic Management Journal, 1*(2), 149–163. doi:10.1002/smj.4250010205

Hamel, G. (2000). *Leading the Revolution*. Boston: Harvard Business School Press.

Hoppe, K., & Kollmer, H. (2001). *Strategie und Geschäftsmodell*. Unpublished.

Kollmann, T. (2006a). *E-Entrepreneurship Grundlagen der Unternehmensgründung in der Net Economy* (2nd Ed.). Wiesbaden, Germany: Gabler.

Kollmann, T. (2006b). What is e-entrepreneurship? Fundamentals of company founding in the net economy. *International Journal of Technology Management, 33*(4), 322–340. doi:10.1504/IJTM.2006.009247

Lawson, C., & Meyenn, N. (2000). Bringing Cellular Phone Service to Rural Areas [Electronic Version]. *Public Policy for the Private Sector*, 1-4. Retrieved February 11, 2009 from http://rru.worldbank.org/documents/publicpolicyjournal/205lawson.pdf

Magretta, J. (2002). Why Business Models Matter. *Harvard Business Review, 80*(5), 86–92.

Osterwalder, A., & Pigneur, Y. (2002). *Business Models and their Elements* [Electronic Version]. Retrieved February 11, 2009 from http://inforge.unil.ch/aosterwa/Documents/workshop/Osterwalder_Pigneur.pdf

Pohle, G., & Chapman, M. (2006). IBM's global CEO report 2006: business model innovation matters. *Strategy and Leadership, 34*(5), 34–40. doi:10.1108/10878570610701531

Porter, M. E. (1985). *Competitive Advantage: Creating and Sustaining Superior Performance.* New York: The Free Press.

Pramatari, K., Doukidis, G. I., & Kourouthanassis, P. (2004). Towards Smarter Supply and Demand Chain Collaboration Practices Enabled by RFID Technology. In P. H. Vervest, E. Van Heck, K. Preiss & L.-F. Pau (Eds.), *Smart Business Networks* (pp. 187-210). Berlin, Germany: Springer.

Richardson, D., Ramirez, R., & Haq, M. (2000). *Grameen Telecom's Village Phone Programme in Rural Bangladesh: a Multi-Media Case Study; Final Report* [Electronic Version]. Retrieved February 11, 2009 from http://www.telecommons.com/villagephone/finalreport.pdf

Schumpeter, J. A. (1931). Theorie der wirtschaftlichen Entwicklung (3rd Ed.). München, Germany: Duncker & Humblot.

Schumpeter, J. A. (1943). *Capitalism, Socialism and Democracy.* London: Allen and Unwin.

Schuster, E. W., Allen, S. J., & Brock, D. L. (2007). *Global RFID: The Value of the EPCglobal Network for Supply Chain Management.* Berlin, Germany: Springer.

Tapio, A. (2005). *Future of Telecommunication - Internet Telephony Operator Skype* [Electronic Version]. Retrieved February 11, 2009 from http://www.tml.tkk.fi/Publications/C/18/tapio.pdf

Timmers, P. (1998). Business Models for Electronic Markets. *Electronic Markets, 8*(2), 3–8. doi:10.1080/10196789800000016

Utterback, J. M., & Abernathy, W. J. (1975). A Dynamic Model of Process and Product Innovation. *Omega, 3*(6), 639–656. doi:10.1016/0305-0483(75)90068-7

Venkatraman, N. (1994). IT-Enabled Business Transformation: From Automation to Business Scope Redefinition. *Sloan Management Review, 35*(2), 73–87.

ADDITIONAL READING

Barabba, V., Huber, C., Cooke, F., Pudar, N., Smith, J., & Paich, M. (2002). A Multimethod Approach for Creating New Business Models: The General Motors OnStar Project. *Interfaces, 32*(1), 20–34. doi:10.1287/inte.32.1.20.18

Berkhout, G., Van Der Duin, P., Hartmann, D., & Ortt, R. (2007). *The Cyclic Nature of Innovation: Connecting Hard Sciences with Soft Values.* Amsterdam, The Netherlands: Elsevier Jai.

Brenner, W., & Hamm, V. (1996). Information Technology for Purchasing in a Process Environment. *European Journal of Purchasing & Supply Management, 2*(4), 211–219. doi:10.1016/S0969-7012(96)00017-2

Brenner, W., & Wenger, R. (Eds.). (2007). *Elektronische Beschaffung: Stand und Entwicklungstendenzen*. Berlin, Germany: Springer.

Christensen, C. M. (2006). *The Innovator's Dilemma: The Revolutionary Book that Will Change the Way you Do Business*. New York: HarperCollins.

Drucker, P. F. (1993). *Post-Capitalist Society* (3. ed.). New York: HarperBusiness.

Fleisch, E. (2005). *Das Internet der Dinge: Ubiquitous Computing und RFID in der Praxis Visionen, Technologien, Anwendungen, Handlungsanleitungen*. Berlin, Germany: Springer.

Floerkemeier, C., & Fleisch, E. (2008). RFID Applications: Interfacing with Readers. *IEEE Software, 25*(3), 67–70. doi:10.1109/MS.2008.71

Foray, D. (2004). *Economics of Knowledge*. Cambridge, MA: MIT Press.

Kay, J. (1996). *The Business of Economics*. Oxford, UK: Oxford University Press.

Kay, J. (2004). *The Truth About Markets - Why Some Nations Are Rich but Most Remain Poor*. London, UK: Penguin Books.

Looney, C. A., Jessup, L. M., & Valacich, J. S. (2004). Emerging Business Models for Mobile Brokerage Services. *Communications of the ACM, 47*(6), 71–77. doi:10.1145/990680.990683

Omae, K. (1983). *The Mind of the Strategist* (Reprinted Ed.). Harmondsworth, UK: Penguin Books.

Penrose, E. T. (1959). *The Theory of the Growth of the Firm*. Oxford, UK: Blackwell.

Prahalad, C. K., & Hamel, G. (1990). The Core Competence of the Corporation. *Harvard Business Review, 68*(3), 79–91.

Prahalad, C. K., & Hammond, A. (2002). Serving the World's Poor, Profitably. *Harvard Business Review, 80*(9), 48–57.

Prahalad, C. K., & Krishnan, M. S. (2008). *The New Age of Innovation: Driving Cocreated Value Through Global Networks*. New York: McGraw-Hill Professional.

Pynnonen, M. (2008, 27-31 July). *Customer Lock-In in ICT Services Business: Designing and Managing Customer Driven Business Model*. Paper presented at the PICMET '08 - 2008 Portland International Conference on Management of Engineering & Technology, Cape Town, South Africa.

Rogers, E. M. (2003). *Diffusion of Innovations* (5th Ed.). New York: Free Press.

Salomann, H., Dous, M., Kolbe, L., & Brenner, W. (2007). Self-service Revisited: How to Balance High-tech and High-touch in Customer Relationships. *European Management Journal, 25*(4), 310–319. doi:10.1016/j.emj.2007.06.005

Sanchez, A. M. (1995). Innovation Cycles and Flexible Automation in Manufacturing-Industries. *Technovation, 15*(6), 351–362. doi:10.1016/0166-4972(95)96596-L

Shafer, S. M., Smith, H. J., & Linder, J. C. (2005). The Power of Business Models. *Business Horizons, 48*(3), 199–207. doi:10.1016/j.bushor.2004.10.014

Son, M., Hahn, M., & Kang, H. (2006). Why Firms do Co-Promotions in Mature Markets? *Journal of Business Research, 59*(9), 1035–1042. doi:10.1016/j.jbusres.2006.04.002

Teece, D. J. (1993). Profiting from Technological Innovation: Implications for Integration, Collaboration, Licensing and Public Policy. *Research Policy*, 22(2), 112–113. doi:10.1016/0048-7333(93)90063-N

Timmers, P. (2000). *Electronic Commerce: Strategies and Models for Business-to-Business Trading*. Chichester, UK: Wiley.

Utterback, J. M. (1994). *Mastering the Dynamics of Innovation: How Companies Can Seize Opportunities in the Face of Technological Change*. Boston: Harvard Business School Press.

Vickers, M. (2000). Models from Mars. *Business Week*, 106–107.

Voelpel, S., Leibold, M., Tekie, E., & von Krogh, G. (2005). Escaping the Red Queen Effect in Competitive Strategy: Sense-testing Business Models. *European Management Journal*, 23(1), 37–49. doi:10.1016/j.emj.2004.12.008

Voelpel, S. C., Leibold, M., & Tekie, E. B. (2004). The Wheel of Business Model Reinvention: How to Reshape your Business Model to Leapfrog Competitors. *Journal of Change Management*, 4(3), 259–276. doi:10.1080/1469701042000212669

Chapter 2

Internationalization Strategy in New E–Ventures:
Towards A General Model and New Research Agenda

María Gracia García Soto
University of Las Palmas de Gran Canaria, Spain

Antonia Mercedes García Cabrera
University of Las Palmas de Gran Canaria, Spain

ABSTRACT

Recent literature highlights the fact that research in the fields of internationalization and entrepreneurship appears to overlook the internal and external context in which the international strategies are conceived. That oversight occurs even though the international activity of new ventures needs to be understood within the context and requirements of the respective industry. That gap is accentuated when we focus our interest on the electronic business industry since the literature contains no models conceived to explain the advantage and the process of the internationalization of new e-ventures. This work contributes to filling that gap by answering two basic questions: (1) what is it about e-ventures that allows them to compete globally? and (2) what is it about e-ventures that makes it a specific mix of strategy shaping processes necessary to formulate a born global strategy?

INTRODUCTION

E-ventures represent a group of firms that carry out innovative business. To that end they use knowledge and advanced technological capability to offer services based on a predominantly electronic creation of value (Kollman, 2006). In fact, e-ventures are so called because, unlike traditional businesses, they perform their economic transactions on line via the Internet (Matlay, 2003), which is why their business activity is called e-business (Fillis, & Wagner, 2005). Within that framework, e-entrepreneurship refers to the start up of a new e-venture, which we label e-born global when it operates in international markets from its inception.

Although the study of new ventures in the field of e-business is relatively new, its development

DOI: 10.4018/978-1-61520-597-4.ch002

has been notable, with interesting studies and manuals being published in recent years. Those articles have basically tried to verify and put in context the conclusions reached in the field of entrepreneurship to date about the peculiarities of businesses operating in the e-industry (Fillis, & Wagner, 2005; Kollman, 2006; Lal, 2004; Matlay, & Westhead, 2005). A study of the literature reveals two clear stages in the venture creation process: opportunity recognition and opportunity exploitation, the latter occurring when the new venture is started up (Morse & Mitchell, 2006). In both stages, certain decisions, such as those related to strategies and the organizational resources that make their implementation possible, assume great importance since they condition the success of the new venture in general (Kakati, 2003), and technological business in particular (Chorev & Anderson, 2006). Thus, it can be said that strategy shaping is a critical factor in the process of creating a new venture.

In the particular case of electronic start-ups, the entrepreneur must consider the specifics of e-businesses that affect strategic decisions –e.g., the impact of new information and communications technologies makes international operations less costly than before (Knight & Cavusgil, 1996). These special features can particularly influence the definition of the target market, giving rise to a growing number of new ventures that are born with an international vocation, and whose competitive advantages and rate of growth, in the short term, are surprising by their exponential character. To refer to this type of company, the term born global has been coined, as well as global start-up, instant exporter, micro-multinational, international venture and international new venture (Fernhaber, McDougall, & Oviatt, 2007; Karra, Phillips, & Tracey, 2008; Kuivalainen, Sundqvist, & Servais, 2007; Weerawardena, Mort, Liesch, & Knight, 2007).

A number of partial studies –e.g., Fernhaber et al. (2007), Kuivalainen et al. (2007), Zahra, Korri, & Yu (2005)–, have aimed to explain the born global phenomenon. These partial studies do not satisfy the expectations of the researchers who emphasize the importance of finding a new integrated theoretical framework that would permit the explanation of this complex phenomenon (Crick, & Spence, 2005; Jantunen, Nummela, Puumalainen, & Saarenketo, 2008; A. Rialp, J. Rialp, & Knight, 2007; Weerawardena et al., 2007; Zahra et al., 2005; Zhou, 2007). Moreover, Boter and Homquist (1996) warn that the internationalization of new businesses needs to be understood within the context and requirements of the respective industry. However, if we focus our attention on the e-business industry, the literature contains no models conceived to explain the advantage and the process of the internationalization of new e-ventures. On the basis of those arguments, the primary objective of this work is to analyze the internationalization strategy and the process through which it is formed in firms operating in electronic sectors. More specifically, we aim to answer two fundamental questions related to that objective: (1) what is it about e-ventures that allows them to compete globally? and (2) what is it about e-ventures that makes a specific mix of strategy shaping processes necessary to form a born global strategy? To that end, we apply various concepts from strategic management to the context of e-entrepreneurship so that this chapter contributes to filling a gap in the literature that is of particular relevance to academics and professionals interested in the e-business sector.

In pursuit of the proposed objective, this chapter is structured as follows: (1) background, which includes the study of the born global strategy, as well as its antecedents and processes for shaping the international strategy for venture creation; (2) proposal of an integral model for the shaping of the born global international strategy in the new e-venture; (3) new research agenda, which includes research issues requiring new contributions in order to advance research in this field; and (4) conclusions.

BACKGROUND

New Venture and Born Global Strategy

There is a broad consensus on the sequence of the process of venture creation. That process begins with opportunity recognition, in other words, with the perception of, and search for unsatisfied market needs or under-employed resources, the screening of the idea, and the formulation of a business plan. According to Kirzner (1979), most entrepreneurs, both recent and experienced, are likely to consider the recognition of the opportunity and its evaluation as an important step toward the launch of new products and services. However, Shane, and Venkataraman (2000) affirm that appropriate opportunity recognition is a necessary but insufficient condition for new venture success. This is because entrepreneurs do not always recognize the path to capitalize on the identified ideas and convert them into profitable businesses (Thukral et al., 2008). Once the opportunity has been recognized, the process continues with the exploitation of that opportunity, which occurs when the business plan is implemented and the new venture started up (Morse, & Mitchell, 2006). Therefore, the opportunity exploitation requires attention to be paid to variables such as strategies and other organizational resources which make possible their implementation, thus conditioning the success of the new venture.

There are different strategies that a firm must formulate to guide its actions in the market (e.g., product and market development, competitive strategy, etc.) and we are interested in the internationalization strategy since firms that operate in the e-business sector tend to enter new foreign markets much earlier and have an internationalization pattern that differs from the one which is usual in low-tech industries (Crick, & Spence, 2005). After reviewing the literature, Crick and Spence (2005), Gabrielsson, Kirpalani, Dimitratos, Solberg, and Zucchella (2008) and Jantunen et al. (2008) agree

to distinguish, in terms of strategy, two choices related to internationalization: traditional firms and born globals.

Traditional firms follow the model based on the offer of a narrow range of services aimed at, and adapted to, a local market in order to achieve business consolidation and undertake international expansion later –i.e., incremental internationalization process. This slower route that avoids excessive risks only provides low opportunities to obtain a high level of performance. This is the classic view of internationalization that emphasizes the importance of domestic experience as a precursor to internationalization, but this path is increasingly less relevant for many new firms (Karra et al., 2008).

Born globals are entrepreneurial firms that internationalize shortly after start-up (McDougall, & Oviatt, 2000). As opposed to traditional firms, the venture should be conceived from inception as a project with the capacity to offer products targeting a global market (Karra et al., 2008), which will maximize growth and performance in a shorter period of time (Crick, & Spence, 2005). For this sub-set of international new ventures, size and age are no longer prerequisites for doing international business (Gabrielsson et al., 2008). Nevertheless, there is no widespread definition of born global firms. When referring to this kind of firm, many authors emphasize three dimensions of a born global: scope, scale and speed of internationalization (Oviatt & McDougall, 1994). Scope of internationalization is related to the narrow or broad range of targeted geographic markets because born globals operate in multiple countries from their very outset (Oviatt, & McDougall, 1994). According to Kuivalainen et al. (2007) the ambiguity associated with the term "multiple countries", which ignores the location and possible institutional distances between them –e.g., language, consumer behavior, cultural standards, legal framework, etc. (Stöttinger, & Schlegelmich, 1998)–, makes it difficult to conceptualize the born global firm precisely.

Scale of internationalization relates to the extent of a firm's international operations and is measured by the proportion of international sales –e.g., the original definition of born global by Knight and Cavusgil (1996) requires an export volume greater than 25% of total sales. More recently, many authors have criticized definitions based on the level of exports. That group of researchers includes Gabrielsson et al. (2008), who state that the levels established in these definitions are not adapted to the socio-economic circumstances of all countries and are not valid to identify born globals. Karra et al. (2008) also consider that the definitions based on international sales hamper the analysis of the key differences between domestic and international entrepreneurship. Those authors consider that international entrepreneurship requires the configuration of a firm's resources across international boundaries.

Finally, speed of internationalization is the period of time between the inception and the moment when a firm initiates international operations and has been a factor included in the traditional definitions of born globals –e.g., the original definition by Knight and Cavusgil (1996) required that exports should start within 3 years of inception. More recently, new definitions have appeared in the literature without reference to the period of starting international operations. De Clercq, Hessels, and van Stel (2008), for example, refer to born globals as "[...] ventures that view their operating domain as international at or near their inception" (p. 283). Gabrielsson et al. (2008) are more demanding when they state that born globals have a global market vision at inception. For the purposes of this study, we follow the approach of that last author to analyze the early internationalization of a new e-venture. That decision was taken because we understand that the approach is broad enough to cover born globals of different size –i.e., it ignores the number of countries and the percentage of international sales– while sufficiently restrictive to distinguish this type

of firm from those that take other paths to enter international markets.

Antecedents of Born Global Strategy

On reviewing the literature concerning early entry of new firms into foreign markets, we have found that researchers have used multiple variables to explain antecedents of born global strategy; some authors have linked those variables to the processes of shaping that strategy (Crick, & Spence, 2005; Gabrielsson et al., 2008; Spence, & Crick, 2006). Basically, such research has analyzed individual-level factors, team-level factors, firm-level factors, industry-level factors and macro-level factors. This section analyzes those factors as antecedents of the formulation of a born global strategy while their role in the process of shaping that strategy is analyzed in the following section.

As far as the individual is concerned and making use of a cognitive perspective, some research works explain how the entrepreneur recognizes and exploits the international opportunities based on his motivations and mental models, as Zahra et al. (2005) describe. For those authors, the cognition approach as an antecedent of the new venture's international strategy highlights the importance of both the economic and non-economic motivations in the choice of born global strategy. Additionally, both subjective characteristics –e.g., attitudes, perceptions, personality, etc.–, and objective attributes –e.g., knowledge, experience, etc.–, influence decision-makers' views about the risks involved in entering new export markets (Loane, Bell, & McNaughton, 2007). Few authors have used this approach to address the founding team's influence on the rapid internationalization process in new ventures (Oviatt & McDougall, 2005). Such teams can create and enhance the core internal capabilities, skills and knowledge. The founding team composition refers to the collective characteristics of team members whose diversity and complementary traits, experience and business backgrounds (Inkpen & Tsang, 2007) have a relevant effect, particularly, in achieving a better performance (Loane et al., 2007).

From a firm's point of view, the knowledge-based theory explains the traditional internationalization process, which is based on the accumulated business experience. However, some authors, like Autio, Sapienza, and Almeida (2000) or, more recently, Zhou (2007), have used it to explain born global internationalization. According to Zhou (2007), the accumulation of knowledge that explains the appearance of the born global is different from the traditional internationalization models. Specifically, for the former, which is born global, knowledge is gained by exploring opportunities, while for the latter, it is obtained by resolving problems in the international market (Zhou, 2007).

On the other hand, entrepreneurial orientation represents the rules and norms by which a firm makes decisions, that is, its organizing principles (Sapienza, De Clercq, & Sandberg, 2005) which define the firm's fundamental philosophy (Lumpkin, & Dess, 1996); this has been conceptualized along various dimensions. On the international level, it applies to its international operations (Kuivalainen et al., 2007). This philosophy or identity of the firm can be described, for example, in terms of its proactiveness, capacity for risk taking and competitive aggressiveness (Lumpkin, & Dess, 1996). This orientation is related to the willingness of the company to export to distant markets (Madsen, 1989), to a strong involvement in the process of internationalization in very early phases, or to following the true born global path (Kuivalainen et al., 2007). More specifically, entrepreneurial orientation promotes a greater level of information-scanning activities, fosters an increased knowledge base and greater responsiveness to foreign markets (Zhou, 2007). The knowledge-based approaches and the entrepreneurial orientation have also been combined to give place to the strategic orientation as an antecedent of the new venture's international strategy.

Regarding the firm level, the role of networking in the rapid internalization process has been widely discussed. Mort and Weerawardena (2006) reviewed the literature on this topic and found eleven relevant works that explain how networks make possible the smooth running and the higher performance of born global firms. Born globals tend to be vulnerable because they are frequently small and depend on a few products which they sell in multiple markets and sometimes the geographical location of those markets is not important (Mort, & Weerawardena, 2006). Due to this, these firms often seek partners that complement their own competencies in those foreign markets (Madsen. & Servais, 1997) by developing effective networks (Mort, & Weerawardena, 2006).

On the industry level, research on international new ventures suggests the relevance of the industry structure. Industry structure is defined as the basic underlying characteristics that shape the competitive strategy for a group of firms producing goods or services that are close substitutes for one another (Porter, 1980). Many research works have analyzed a single industry and, more particularly, they tend to focus on high-technology industries (Fernhaber et al., 2007). This is probably due to the use of modern technology, technological process innovation and level of product complexity in these sectors (Crick, & Spence, 2005). If we look at the industry structure from an overall view –i.e., concentration, global integration, local industry internationalization, venture capital, etc. (Fernhaber et al., 2007)–, we can indicate that this offers opportunities related to internationalization by a new venture (Bloodgood, Sapienza, & Almeida, 1996).

Finally, at the country level, research has provided different factors to explain why some countries have more export-oriented new ventures than others (De Clercq et al., 2008). From that perspective, the existence of export spillovers –as a result of the export activities of established businesses, inward FDI (Foreign Direct Investment), and outward FDI–, can have a significant

Table 1. Antecedents and strategy formation processes for venture creation

Strategy formation process	Description	Theoretical bases	Key antecedents
Formal	Based on carrying out an evaluation of the initial idea and the formulation of a business plan.	Planning	Stability of the sector
Emergent	Based on daily, fragmented, and flexible decisions, which allow the entrepreneur to combine the information with the available resources to start up the new venture.	Learning	Business size
Visionary	Based on the entrepreneur's intuitive capacity, experience and long term vision.	Cognitive	Entrepreneur
Collective	Based on the cultural values shared by the entrepreneurial team, which provide common mental models to recognize business opportunities, evaluate them and start up the new venture.	Cultural	Entrepreneurial team
Negotiation	Based on the debate and agreement process between founders and other social actors who play a relevant role in the start-up process. Both parties have different preferences, business concepts and goals.	Power	Network
Reactive	Based on the frequent structural inertia in the environment produced by well established norms and procedures which are accepted by social and economic actors.	Environmental	Industry and country
Transformation	Based on the co-existence of the above processes in a certain moment of time and/or different specific contexts.	Configuration	All the above

influence on the adoption of an international strategy by new ventures.

International Strategy Formation in Venture Creation Process

As shown in the previous section, there is a broad range of literature that analyzes and explains the antecedents of an international strategy from different partial perspectives and levels of analyses. None of the antecedents could individually explain the strategy formation process followed by the new venture. These partial approaches do not satisfy the expectations of most researchers, who emphasize the importance of finding new integrated frameworks to explain this complex phenomenon (Crick, & Spence, 2005; Jantunen et al., 2008; A. Rialp et al., 2005; Weerawardena et al., 2007; Zahra et al., 2005; Zhou, 2007).

In order to analyze the role of each antecedent in the process of shaping the born global strategy from a new holistic perspective, we turn to the approaches of Mintzberg (1990) and Mintzberg,

Alhstrand, and Lampel (1998). According to that literature, the entrepreneur can use different processes to formulate the strategy with which the new venture will compete; those processes can be used in both the recognition and the exploitation of opportunity, since the strategy is modeled in both stages of the creation of a new firm. While Mintzberg (1990) and Mintzberg et al. (1998) originally addressed ten different processes for strategy shaping, Bailey and Johnson (2000) summarized them in six in order to analyze them in a more robust way. On the basis of the approaches of those authors, we adapt the main characteristics of the processes of strategy shaping to the initial stages of new venture creation (see Table 1). The process or combination of processes that the entrepreneur uses to formulate a strategy for a new venture will be determined by the relevance of certain antecedents—i.e., participation in networks, entrepreneurial team, etc.

We now describe the processes of international strategy shaping in the opportunity recognition and exploitation stages of a new venture.

Formal Process, Based on the Planning Approach

The international strategy formulated for the new venture would stem from the carrying out of an evaluation of the initial idea and the formulation of a business plan, following the usual process to create a venture (Morse, & Mitchell, 2006). This evaluation should be present throughout the opportunity recognition stage. As the entrepreneurs analyze the business idea and their expectations about the potential viability of the idea improve, a more formal process to evaluate its feasibility begins. This technical evaluation includes, for example, market research or a financial viability study (Lumpkin, 2005). Finally, if the business plan indicates that the opportunity is feasible in economic terms, the entrepreneur would initiate the exploitation stage. The formal process will be particularly valid when the entrepreneur analyzes the viability of possible new businesses in stable sectors of activity. In such sectors, it is possible to gather valuable information on which to base strategic decisions and the preparation of a business plan (Newbert, 2005).

Emergent Process, Based on the Learning Approach

The strategy formation is based on daily, fragmented, and flexible decisions, which allow the entrepreneur to combine the information with the available resources to start up the new venture. Fillis and Wagner (2005) emphasize that new firms tend to emerge as an unplanned decision facing specific opportunities rather than as part of a formalized strategy (Jennings, & Beaver, 1997). Most specifically, the importance of the emergent process for the formation of the international strategy of the new venture is justified on the basis of its youth and its normally small size. It is then unlikely that the new venture has the available resources to be able to follow a formal process (O'Donnell, Gilmore, Carson, & Cummins, 2002).

Visionary Process, Based on the Knowledge Approach

The strategy formation in the new venture is supported by the entrepreneur's intuitive capacity, experience and long term vision. From this point of view, strategies are in the entrepreneur's mind and are based on his cognitive traits which constrain his/her ideas and decisions on where to position a new venture. Later, by exploiting the identified opportunity, the entrepreneur will attempt to transform his/her vision into a real venture that achieves the expected performance. Under that approach, born-global opportunity recognition and exploitation depend on the existence of individuals with certain personality traits - such as creativity, optimism, the concept of self-efficacy, the propensity to assume risks, the need for achievement, and locus of control (Park, 2005)-, which, along with their own personal circumstances, give rise to the creation of a new firm (Zahra et al., 2005). It must be taken into account that international entrepreneurs have to transfer business concepts between national contexts and make them relevant to people in different countries (Zhou, 2007), which entails greater risk that can only be assumed by individuals with the previously mentioned characteristics. Regarding the educational and professional profiles, the entrepreneur who faces the development of a born global should have had higher education (Bloodgood et al., 1996) and previous international experience in foreign markets (Crick, & Spence, 2005). Karra et al. (2008) provide an interesting list of specific competences to operate in cross-national environments—e.g., abiliy to identify international opportunities, to span the institutional distance between national contexts, to build international ties with partners, etc.

Collective Process, Based on the Culture Approach

The international strategy formulated for the new venture is based on the cultural values shared by the members of the entrepreneurial team. This implies that team members use their common mental models to identify a business opportunity, evaluate it and choose the most appropriate way to apply the international strategy. Although every member of the team will have individual perspectives and different cognitions about the opportunity and the possible new venture, as suggested by West (2007), what the collective process brings to strategy formation is the set of decisions adopted on the basis of the similarities among the team members and their shared criteria. The collective process is specifically based on the rules and norms that guide the decision-making by the entrepreneurial team, that is, their work philosophy (Lumpkin, & Dess, 1996). This philosophy includes, in the field of international entrepreneurship (Kuivalainen et al., 2007; Madsen, 1989), proactiveness, risk-taking abilities, competitive aggressiveness (Lumpkin, & Dess, 1996), learning orientation, willingness to participate in networks, orientation to growth and success, etc.

Negotiation Process, Based on the Power Approach

The international strategy stems from a negotiation process between new venture's founders and other social actors who play a relevant role in the start-up process. Both founders and social actors have different preferences, business concepts and objectives, which could eventually influence the debate among them and the final agreement on the international strategy. The starting point to understand the negotiation process is the entrepreneur's lack of resources. In fact, it is difficult for the entrepreneur to recognize a born global opportunity and exploit it on his/her own. It is important to consider that we study the born

global as a new independent business project, that is, it has no relationship with spin-off processes or other corporate strategies from pre-existing firms. Therefore, access to technology, financial resources, customers and suppliers in international markets, local institutions' knowledge, etc., must be provided by networks in which the entrepreneur is embedded (Batjargal, 2007; Crick, & Spence, 2005; Mort, & Weerawardena, 2006). In line with those ideas, Neergaard (2005) emphasize the relevance of networks because they can solve the entrepreneurs' initial restrictions to operating in a multinational context.

Reactive Process, Based on the Environmental Approach

International strategy shaping in a new venture responds to the common structural inertia that is produced in the environment. This inertia is the result of well established norms and procedures that are accepted by social and economic actors within that environment (Zahra et al., 2005). Two basic issues cover this environmental influence: the cultural values and the recurrent decisions made by other ventures previously started up. First, cultural values have a significant effect on entrepreneurial behavior in general (Gupta, MacMillan, & Surie, 2004) since some values generate more entrepreneurial behavior than others. For example, when low uncertainty avoidance values prevail, individuals are interested in exploring new ways of doing things, make decisions even in situations where information is limited and are more ready to assume risks and exploit any opportunity that they can identify in their environment (Busenitz & Lau, 1996). All this creates an atmosphere where individuals display greater disposition to formulate offensive strategies and international growth strategies. Second, within a geographic area or a specific industry, the decisions related to the scope, scale and speed of internationalization made by established entrepreneurs may significantly affect the decisions that will be made by new entrepreneurs in the future (Fernhaber et al., 2007). That imitation supports decision making under uncertain conditions –e.g., when the company and/or the entrepreneur have no experience in foreign countries (DiMaggio, & Powell, 1983). As international new ventures are not yet consolidated firms and also operate in a very risky environment –e.g., international scope, etc.– imitation could be highly relevant (Fernhaber et al., 2007), and that provides an interesting approach to understand the creation of an international new venture. As a result of that imitative behavior, uniformity in company decisions emerges (DiMaggio, & Powell, 1983), and the structural inertia is reinforced. This structural inertia justifies the fact that the greater the local industry internationalization is, the more likely it is that new ventures within that industry will internationalize (Fernhaber et al., 2007).

Transformation Process, Based on the Configuration Approach

According to this approach, the formation of the strategy on which the new venture will compete is based on the co-existence or combined action of the aforementioned processes. The configuration and importance of these processes vary according to the new venture's peculiarities in terms of its organization and processes, entrepreneur profile, and the structural characteristics of the environment in which it competes.

An Integral Model for the Formation of the Born Global International Strategy in the New E-Venture

Most prior analyses appear to overlook the internal and external contexts in which the international strategies are conceived (Zahra et al., 2005). On that line, Boter and Homquist (1996) warn that the internationalization activity of new businesses needs to be understood within the context and requirements of the respective industry. However,

when we focus our attention on the e-business industry, we find that the literature contains no models conceived to explain the suitability and the process of the internationalization of new e-ventures. On the basis of those arguments, we propose two basic questions for those enterprises: (1) what is it about e-ventures that allows them to compete globally? and (2) what is it about e-ventures that makes a specific mix of strategy shaping processes necessary to form a born global strategy? To answer those questions, the following sections first describe the distinctive characteristics of e-ventures and then analyze how those characteristics are particularly valid for e-ventures to carry out a born global international strategy.

E-Ventures: New Business Projects in the Electronic Economy

In the transition from the 20th to the 21st century, we witnessed an unprecedented development in ICT in general, and the Internet in particular. The spread of that phenomenon covers not only technology but also its use by firms and individuals, giving rise to a new virtual space for the establishment of interactions between them. As a result, business competitiveness has spread from the traditional channels of commerce to electronic commercial transactions. Thus, we saw the appearance of the e-Economy (Magretta, 1999), also known as the electronic economy, digital economy, new economy or Internet economy (Matlay, & Westhead, 2005). This new economy is supported by digital technology and communication networks, which provide a global platform where people and companies can send and receive information, collaborate, and buy and sell different products and services (King, Warkentin, & Chung, 2002). Although the economic impact of the Internet and ICT on the entrepreneurship field has still not been empirically demonstrated (Matlay, 2003), there can be no doubt that these new technological trends are the seeds of e-entrepreneurs (Matlay, 2003) and e-ventures. In fact, e-ventures are so called because, unlike traditional businesses, they perform their economic transactions on line, via Internet (Matlay, 2003). Based on that conceptualization, e-entrepreneurship, which is where the e-start-up is embedded, refers to the establishment of new e-ventures.

More specifically, online economic transactions provide a new set of business opportunities, which we refer to as e-opportunities. In order to identify them, some firms analyze the functions or activities carried out by a great many traditional enterprises and then develop informatic applications and services that are either standardized or adapted to each possible customer. Later, they distribute those products/services from their remote data center via Internet or by means of a private network. The many possibilities offered by e-opportunities seem to be inexhaustible since we are witnessing a continuous process of the development of new business initiatives that are Net-related or Web-based. These new opportunities support the development of innovative and heterogeneous business concepts, many examples of which can be found in business practice. Beyond the mere virtual shops that market and manage the buying and selling of products and services, and distribution via the Net –e.g., self-tests to evaluate the needs for, and purchase of, occupational hazard prevention products, real estate website, etc.–, other electronic businesses can be developed, such as: virtual universities, virtual publishers and libraries, virtual means of communication and diffusion, software services (e.g., development of intranets, and extranet that connect the firm with customers and suppliers, corporate webs, digital signature, electronic invoicing, telematic communications with the administrations, web-conferencing, electronic transactions with third parties, etc.), infoware services (e.g., control of the use of computer-based resources by employees, generation of internal statistics, data bases, etc.), humanware services (e.g., remote control of job absenteeism, human resource training,

implementation of virtual training platforms in the firm, etc.), and others.

Although various research works have identified some specific characteristics of these firms, there is still no integral description of e-ventures. In the following lines, we classify three groups of factors that capture their distinctive character: factors related to the organization and its processes; characteristics of the individuals that undertake and participate in such initiatives, and the structural characteristics of the sector in which such companies compete (see Table 2).

With regard to its organization and internal processes, the e-venture is characterized by developing innovative business concepts which, using advanced technological knowledge and capabilities, enables it to offer services based on a predominantly electronic creation of value –i.e., e-business, e-commerce– (Kollman, 2006). Fillis and Wagner (2005) define the term e-business as any business activity carried out over an electronic network (exchanging data files, having a website, using other companies' websites or buying/selling goods and services online). Therefore, when we talk about e-ventures, we are referring to those companies that take advantage of electronic technology (IT) to meet their information needs at every organizational level –i.e., storage, processing and communication–, and make use of formal electronic processes (IS) to compile, recover, process, store and spread information in order to facilitate planning, control, coordination and decision making processes (Fathian, Akhavan, & Hoorali, 2008).

The intangible services offered by these firms generate lower costs of communication and transportation (Lal, 2004) and so have high export potential (Fernández Sánchez, 2005). Therefore, the e-venture enjoys greater opportunity to carry out international activities that lead to rapid growth. Additionally, e-ventures develop uncontaminated business activities, thus being very attractive for sustained development of the territories in which

Table 2. Characteristics of e-ventures

Categories of factors	Characteristics
Organization and internal processes	Innovative business ideas. Services in advanced technology. Electronic platform in data networks. Services based on electronic processes. Constant updating in new technologies. Ability to adapt quickly. Intangible character of the activity. Short products and services life cycle. Low degree of environmental contamination. Services with a high added value. High economic risk. Services with high level of exportation potential. Perspective of better international coordination. Reduction of the importance of intermediaries. Financial barriers. A high investment in R&D. Low operations, communication and transportation costs. Low impact of the geographical distance from the market of origin. Need for good relationship with firms for business purposes.
Individual profiles	High level of education. High entrepreneurial personality. High capacity to establish good relationships with other firms. Previous experience in high technology sectors. High learning and continuous education capacities. High economic rewards.
Structural characteristics of the sector	Highly dynamic. Complexity. Innovative. Constant change. Inability for financial institutions to hire qualified personnel to evaluate ICTs. High presence of venture capital funds. Support from public administrations.

they act. They can also render services with a high added value and can contribute to the development of information and communication infrastructures in the areas in which they are established. In consequence, public administrations are very interested in this kind of company.

As far as human resources are concerned, e-ventures have highly qualified personnel (Crick, & Spence, 2005) and a great capacity for learning. In fact, these companies generate quality employment by hiring highly qualified personnel and offering good remuneration (Fernández Sánchez, 2005; Lal, 2004). On the same line, these firms need a strong entrepreneurial vision and attract highly entrepreneurial individuals (Park, 2005). Their founders have high capabilities and edu-

cational levels as well as previous professional experience in high-technology sectors. Moreover, they possess the skills to develop and maintain agreements with other companies in order to get valuable tangible and intangible resources –such as complementary technology, access to distribution channels, etc. (Colombo, & Grilli, 2007).

These technological organizations compete in highly dynamic, complex and innovative industries (Blomqvist, Hurmelinna, Nummela, & Saarenketo, 2008) –the technological sector could be defined as a truly entrepreneurial environment. For that reason, e-start-ups must be constantly updated in new technology and have the ability to adapt quickly to rapidly changing environments. To that end, these companies must make significant investments in R&D (Lal, 2004), thus assuming high level risk. Financial institutions also play a key role as they sometimes cannot recognize successful ICT projects; this is caused by asymmetric information between the two parties (Colombo, & Grilli, 2007). This conditions the decision making of the financial institutions that are more disposed to finance business projects that are, a priori, less risky. As a result, e-firms usually face barriers to obtaining financial resources to start and consolidate the new venture with finance from such institutions; thus, venture capital funds constitute the alternative source of finance for these innovative, high technology projects that correspond to the target sought by such investors.

Having described the specific characteristics of the e-venture, we now answer the two key questions proposed in this work.

What Is It About E-Ventures That Allows Them To Compete Globally?

A combined analysis of the peculiarities of e-ventures and the characteristics of a born global reveals how electronic companies meet important conditions that make them especially suitable to compete with the born global strategy (see Table 3).

With regard to organization and internal processes, we emphasize how the use of Internet, the support of ICT, and the intangible character of the activity of e-ventures, provide important advantages for the new venture to face rapid internationalization and compete abroad with large multinationals. In effect, Matlay and Westhead (2005) emphasize that in recent years traditional markets have changed and new markets have appeared, especially worldwide e-markets (Chaston, 2001). Although national markets continue to be important, new spaces have been created for the firm to expand its competitive scope (Gregorio, Kassicieh, & De Gouvean, 2005). According to Kakati (2003), a relevant constraint for this decision is the availability of resources, which

represents an additional challenge for start-ups (Chorev, & Anderson, 2006; Kakati, 2003). However, the peculiarities of e-ventures mean that the barriers linked to the initial lack of resources can be overcome, since they make international expansion more feasible. This is because electronic companies need infrastructures and economic resources to a lesser extent for them to be able to enter or operate in foreign markets.

Moreover, ICT and the Internet support the company's commercial transactions abroad (Wood, 2004) by offering opportunities to reduce the cost of operating in those markets (Lal, 2004). More specifically, ICT reduces transaction costs by improving coordination in business activities between geographically distant locations (Lal, 2004), reducing the time required to carry out international business operations (Damaskopoulos, & Evgeniou, 2003; Fathian et al., 2008) and decreasing imperfect information between suppliers and buyers (Matlay, & Addis, 2003). At the same time, e-commerce, as opposed to other distribution channels, is characterized by lower operational costs –e.g., advertising costs (Quelch, & Klein, 1996)– and by the fact that electronic information is likely to be more accurate, timely and more easily available (Damaskopoulos, & Evgeniou, 2003).

In addition, born globals tend to be vulnerable because they are frequently small and depend on a few products that they sell in multiple markets. Therefore, such firms often seek partners that complement their own competencies in those foreign markets (Madsen, & Servais, 1997) by developing effective networks that make possible the smooth running and the higher performance of born global firms (Mort, & Weerawardena, 2006). In that context, and in the case of e-ventures, Internet provides easier access to international partners and offers ways to coordinate relations with them more efficiently. In that respect, it should be taken into consideration that the geographical distance to the foreign markets and potential partners has little effect on the operations of e-ventures

Table 3. E-ventures and born global strategy in the e-Economy

Characteristics of the E-venture		Characteristics of the born global	Connection
Organization and internal processes	Use of the Internet and other forms of communication aided by the development of ICT	Company's resources	The Internet offers new ventures an important opportunity to internationalize and compete with the large multinationals since it is not essential to have infrastructures and other costly investments to operate abroad –e.g., ease of communications, ease of identifying and developing new markets, lower transaction costs.
		World wide markets	The e-firm expands its competitive scope by using Internet to access electronic world markets.
		Knowledge of the specificities of the local markets	Internet makes it possible to access relevant information about local markets –e.g., regulations, distribution companies, sociocultural characteristics of the local population, etc.–, to undertake on-line surveys and to identify new markets by means of the profiles and patterns of access of Internet users in different countries.
		International partners	A reduction of the negative impact of the geographical distance between partners on business coordination and negotiation.
			Removes many barriers for international commerce, such as imperfect information between suppliers, as well as between the company and other partners.
		Coordination between the company and its subsidiaries, and between subsidiaries	The Internet reduces the time required exchange information and improves the efficiency of the mechanisms of coordination in business activities in geographically distant locations.
		Operating costs	Because it is possible to manage and coordinate international business via the Internet, it is not necessary to install physical logistics for production and sales; consequently, the operating costs decrease and international expansion becomes more rapid.
		International advertising costs	The Internet constitutes a means with extensive, low cost coverage to promote the company's products and services and also makes it possible to implement promotion campaigns adapted to the different customer profiles in terms of both content and the virtual spaces through which the promotion is undertaken –i.e., personalized e-mails, company website, forums and chats aimed at the target market, on-line news, electronic bulletins, advertising on search engines, etc.
		Control of overseas operations	The Internet enables companies to directly manage the relationship with the customer, thus reducing the need for intermediaries. By means of Internet, the firm can give the customer the required information about the product, the prices and order management in an accurate, timely and easily available fashion.
	Intangible character of the activity	Cost of transport, customs tariffs	The geographical distance to the foreign markets does not hinder the international distribution of the products/services offered by e-ventures, as opposed to the high impact that geographical distance can have in other sectors.
	High R&D costs	International scope and scale of target market	Importance of attaining a minimum efficient size that permits the amortization of the high costs of R&D undertaken by these companies.

compared to the high impact it can have in other sectors. The Internet also makes it possible to reduce dependence on intermediary distributors for the delivery of the products and services to the target markets (Quelch, & Klein, 1996). In fact, the new forms of communication provided by ICT have removed many of the barriers to international commerce.

With regard to the person, we should highlight the correspondence between the educational and highly entrepreneurial profiles of the individuals who act in the e-business sector, and the profiles of those motivated to initiate international businesses. To be more specific, certain attributes in these individuals, such as a proactive character, the capacity to assume risks, the concept of self-efficacy and the need for achievement, are combined with university studies, broad and varied professional careers and a high capacity for learning. That set of attributes and resources, sometimes possessed by the individual entrepreneur and sometimes by an entrepreneurial team, explains the greater predisposition of e-entrepreneurs to adopt international strategies.

Finally, and as regards the structural characteristics of the sector, the uncertainty associated with technological development, where groundbreaking changes are frequent and the life cycle of products and services becomes shorter, can affect the company's strategy. Thus, the company that decides to compete only in its domestic market takes the risk of being unable to renew its offer of products and services at the speed required by the sector and compete with other internationalized companies. In turn, the high investment in R&D that continuous innovation entails could also be difficult to recover. As a result, internationalization has become an important strategy for the survival and growth of the new e-venture (Chorev, & Anderson, 2006). Furthermore, the amount of venture capital invested in firms in an e-industry affects the level of international new ventures in that industry, according to the approach of Fernhaber et al. (2007). That could be true since venture capital firms provide financial resources to mainly technology based, growth-oriented new ventures. Thus, new e-ventures wishing to access those funds should formulate an international strategy in order to achieve the high growth required by the venture capital firm.

What is it About E-Ventures that make it Necessary a Specific Mix of Strategy Shaping Processes to form a Born Global Strategy?

The strategy with which the new venture will compete can be formulated by means of a combination of processes–i.e., transformation. The importance of these processes varies according to the company's internal and external contexts. In the specific case of e-ventures, their peculiarities justify the adoption of a specific mix of strategy shaping processes. From that approach, we can

propose a new global model which, based on the characteristics of the e-venture, integrates the processes of shaping the born global strategy with the antecedents of that strategy and the sequence of the process of venture creation (see Figure 1).

The works of Crick and Spence (2005) and Gabrielsson et al. (2008) are of great relevance to the integrative perspective, which we study, since those authors distinguish different phases in the process of venture creation in order to analyze the adoption of a born global strategy. Moreover, the work of Crick and Spence (2005) is undertaken in the context of new, technology-based companies and so provides a vision that approaches the e-born global –i.e., an e-venture with a global international vision from its inception. In that respect, this present work discusses the processes of strategy shaping in the stages of e-opportunity recognition and exploitation. If we focus the analysis on the first of those phases, the shaping of the born global strategy will fundamentally depend on the characteristics and motivations of the founder of the e-venture (Gabrielsson et al., 2008), his/her capacity to act in the face of unforeseen events (Crick, & Spence, 2005) and the availability and use of contacts with networks (Crick, & Spence, 2005; Gabrielsson et al., 2008). Consequently, those last authors refer to the antecedents of the visionary, emergent and negotiation processes as cornerstones of the recognition of the born global opportunity. Although we agree with the general reflections of those authors, from our point of view, the importance of the business environment to the shaping of the international strategy supports the significant role that the reactive process plays in the e-opportunity recognition stage.

Many authors have emphasized the problems of competing in dynamic and complex environments such as the e-industry. This makes it difficult to identify the critical variables on which to base decision making (Aldrich & Martinez, 2001). Furthermore, unpredictable, rapid and nonlinear changes hinder the systematic analysis and understanding of the environments because,

Figure 1. Integral model for the formation of the born global international strategy in the new e-venture: processes and antecedents

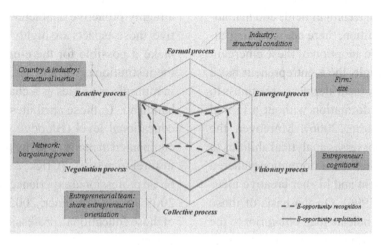

in the short term, the speed of changes means that the already gathered data quickly becomes out of date. Thus, the formal process for strategy planning is somewhat unuseful (Newbert, 2005). Moreover, due to that highly dynamic character and the flexibility required in decision making, entrepreneurs do not always have the time needed to carry out formal evaluations in the e-opportunity recognition stage.

Those obstacles are greater in the case of start-ups, in that such ventures do not have the necessary resources to deal with the formal process. Therefore, the preparation of a formal plan is usually omitted by the e-entrepreneur. Thus, the international strategy seems to stem from unplanned opportunity recognition (Crick, & Spence, 2005). However, Newbert (2005) considers that, if the entrepreneur requires external funding to start up the venture, he/she will make the effort to prepare a business plan that justifies the viability of his/her project to the financial investors. Due to the lack of reliable information, that plan will mainly be based on the business's expectations of success, the justification for the necessary funding, predicted repayment period and other aspects (Newbert, 2005). In our opinion, that plan

will not be formulated during the e-opportunity recognition stage so that decisions can be made; instead, once the decision has been adopted, the business plan will be drawn up to guarantee the capture of the funds necessary to develop the e-opportunity exploitation stage.

As a result of the aforementioned notions, Spence and Crick (2006) state that, while formal planning may be important, the relevance of emergent strategies must be taken into consideration when studying the internationalization of new ventures in technological sectors. This is due, firstly, to the up-to-date information available in the opportunity screening stage and, secondly, to the learning obtained through informal process to evaluate the e-opportunity. This learning in the opportunity recognition stage is due to factors that include access to useful information on possible markets and clients (West, 2007), on key agents in the international markets (Karra et al., 2008) and on new technological trends (Colombo, & Grilli, 2007). The existence of ideas and diverse knowledge in the entrepreneurial team is also very important, especially the different profiles and professional backgrounds of its members (Weerawardena et al., 2007) –e.g., experience as managers, experience in international markets, experience in commercial and financial positions, university degrees in technical fields and in management, etc. In addition, there are several arguments that justify the adoption of these emergent strategies: for example, the e-entrepreneur has a capacity for technological alertness –readiness to perceive relevant information without a formal search process (Baron, 2006). Moreover, the entrepreneur also possesses analytical abilities to establish valid links between information gathered from the environment and his/her creative ideas (Fine, & Deegan, 1996). On the basis of those arguments, we can indicate that, only prior to the opportunity exploitation stage can the entrepreneurs decide about the suitability of the born global strategy; however, it will be difficult for them to formulate a full international strategy that includes decisions about scale, scope and speed –i.e., in the opportunity recognition stage, the emergent process has an influence, albeit only moderate, on the shaping of a born global strategy.

However, in the e-opportunity recognition stage, the e-entrepreneur's intuitive capacity and long-term vision are often the only criteria that can be applied in the evaluation of the business idea and the shaping of a particular strategy. In those cases, the strategy responds to a visionary process. The high relevance of this process in the formulation of the strategy lies in the actual profile of the individuals starting up e-ventures. That profile is characterized by being highly entrepreneurial (Park, 2005) and, consequently, the motivations and expectations of business growth are high (Sadler-Smith, Hampson, Chaston, & Badger, 2003). In fact, Zahra et al. (2005) state that the decision to create a born global and, in particular the choice of scale, scope, speed, and the allocation of tangible and intangible resources basically depends on the entrepreneur's motivation and ego. According to those authors, there is a close link between the entrepreneurs' personal objectives and the goals and needs of their ventures. Furthermore, the entrepreneur's personality traits define

him/her as an individual with high self-esteem, a need to achieve, a capacity to assume risks and a highly proactive character. From our perspective, those aspects are highly relevant, since they make it possible for the e-entrepreneur to view the institutional barriers associated to operating in multiple countries as a challenge rather than a handicap. To those attributes, we can add a high educational level (Bloodgood et al., 1996), accompanied in many cases by previous experience in foreign markets (Crick, & Spence, 2005) and broad professional experience (Colombo, & Grilli, 2005; Fillis, & Wagner, 2005). The combination of those educational, professional and personality attributes form the model of an individual with a high capacity to make risky decisions on the basis of his/her intuition and criteria.

On occasions, that visionary process is the result of the action of a group of entrepreneurs since new technological ventures rely increasingly on entrepreneurial teams –according to Cooper (1986), on average, 70% of the high technology start-ups are created by a team of founders. Thus, the synergy derived from the continuous interaction between entrepreneurs with complementary backgrounds adds value to the visionary process. This is because the knowledge resources and entrepreneurial character in the new e-venture multiply as a result of the complementary backgrounds of the team members –e.g., experience in venture creation in general (Colombo & Grilli, 2005; Sarasvathy, 2001) and in the ICT industry in particular, complementary educational specialty (Colombo & Grilli, 2005; Sarasvathy, 2001), etc. However, the short time that these entrepreneurs spend working together in the initial stage of the process that gives rise to a new venture justifies the absence of a solid, consolidated group of shared cognitions –i.e., cultural values forged during the joint work and common experiences of the members of the entrepreneurial team. Therefore, the collective process hardly affects the decision taken in the opportunity recognition stage regarding the adoption of a born global strategy.

Moreover, embeddedness in networks is critical to the recognition of e-opportunities (Batjargal, 2007) since it provides the entrepreneurs with some of the information resources that they need in this first stage for the creation of a new venture. The support of these networks is of great importance and, in that regard, Neergaard (2005) stresses that a greater number of founder partners results in a greater number of contacts and, therefore, provides a wider range of resources. However, since the actors in the networks have different preferences, business concepts and goals, the formulated strategy is a result of the process of negotiation with them. In the opportunity recognition stage, the networks that support the entrepreneur are fundamentally close to him/her –i.e., groups of friends, family, etc.–, with the entrepreneur maintaining weak links with them in the shape of conversations and casual access to new information (Baron, 2006). Therefore, the entrepreneurs can access valuable support without which the strategic decisions would be influenced by discussion with the actors participating in the networks. Thus, while we agree with Crick and Spence (2005) and Gabrielsson et al. (2008) about the importance of the availability and use of contacts with networks, we should highlight the low impact that the process of negotiation with those networks has on the adoption of the strategic decision.

Finally, regarding the reactive process, we emphasize the structural characteristics of the technological industry, its special need for telecommunications infrastructures and the structural inertia usual in any territory and industry. More specifically, the structural conditions both of the country in which the new venture is going to start up and of the e-business industry determine the suitable strategic decision. If we focus first on the economic and technological conditions in a country, a new e-venture would internationalize only if the foreign country possesses advanced ICTs. For example, access to broadband cannot be established or modified by the company,

since it is part of the country's infrastructure (Lal, 2004). Similarly, the existence of human capital with technical higher education and/or foreign language skills are local resources that influence the starting up of an e-born global. In relation to the sector level, the structural conditions in e-business sectors require the adoption of international strategies. Specifically, the high investment in R&D dictates the need for a minimum efficient size to be achieved in order to return the investment. However, that is almost impossible if the new e-venture operates in a narrow local market. The globalization of e-markets is also a relevant structural condition since small ventures and multinational firms compete head-to-head. The relevance of those structural conditions justifies the e-venture's adoption of the reactive process as an alternative for shaping a born global strategy.

Once the e-born global strategy formation process has been analyzed in the opportunity recognition stage, we focus on the exploitation stage. In that respect, Crick and Spence (2005) and Gabrielsson et al. (2008) coincide in highlighting the importance of learning and the capacity to act when faced with unforeseen events while Crick and Spence (2005) also stress the development of current networks and entry into new networks. Therefore, emergent and negotiation processes turn out to be more relevant since they attain the importance of the visionary process as the entrepreneur goes through the opportunity exploitation stage. We add the reactive and collective processes, because they also play key roles in the e-born global strategy formation in that second phase. As previously mentioned, the formal process maintains its low relevance to the shaping of the e-born global strategy due to the dynamic character of the electronic sector (see Table 4).

The relevance of the emergent, visionary, negotiation and reactive processes is explained by similar arguments to those used for the opportunity recognition stage, although the critical antecedents differ for the first three. Concerning

Table 4. Born global strategy formation processes in e-ventures

Strategy formation process	E-opportunity development stage			
	E-opportunity recognition		E-opportunity exploitation	
	Key antecedents	Impact	Key antecedents	Impact
Formal	Need for external funding	Very low	Need for external funding	Very low
Emergent	Available up-to-date information Speed of response Learning by exploring	Medium	Available up-to-date information Firm alertness Learning by solving problems	High
Visionary	Motivations, personality, experience and education of entrepreneurs Complementary background of entrepreneurial team Entrepreneurial nose for a business idea	High	Motivations, personality, experience and education of entrepreneurs Complementary background of entrepreneurial team Entrepreneurial flair for fulfilling the idea	High
Collective	Shared cognitions	Very low	Shared cognitions International entrepreneurial orientation	High
Negotiation	Initial access to social networks Access to business ideas	Low	Business network building Resources to exploit ideas	High
Reactive	Cultural values International knowledge spillovers Structural conditions in the country and industry	High	Cultural values International knowledge spillovers Structural conditions in the country and industry	High

the emergent process, the learning that takes place in the opportunity exploitation stage follows a different pattern from that in the recognition stage (Zhou, 2007). While knowledge and experience are gained by exploring opportunities in the opportunity recognition stage, in the exploitation stage it occurs while the entrepreneurs face problems and solve them. Once the opportunity exploitation process has begun, the new e-venture needs up-to-date information to guide decision making. In that context, the new venture often tries to develop a technological alertness system that detects the technological trends and changes in the market and makes it possible to develop a flexible organization in its capacity to respond to the information provided by the alertness system (García-Cabrera & García-Soto, 2008). This system, continuous in nature, includes both active and passive search, which is fundamental for technology-based firms. Given the volatility of the environment, it will be the emergent process, based on the up-to-date information obtained and the capacity to respond to it, that allows the

entrepreneur to shape the entire born global strategy –i.e., to decide the scale, scope and speed of internationalization. Thus, the emergent process for strategy shaping assumes greater importance in the opportunity exploitation stage than in the previous recognition stage.

With regard to the visionary process, the highly entrepreneurial profile of the founders conditions the new decisions about the born global strategy that are adopted in the opportunity exploitation phase. This is because the vision of the leaders and their notion of the desired e-venture constitute a clear guide throughout the decision process. That vision, which in the recognition stage provides the criteria for the evaluation of the initial idea, plays a part in the second stage by bringing about chance events that help the shaping and exploitation of the born global strategy. In that respect, Crick and Spence (2005) indicate that the entrepreneurs do not always act in ways that increase the likelihood of events presenting themselves or even recognize and use these international opportunities. Therefore, the relevance of the emergent process in contributing to the shaping of the born global strategy will depend on the entrepreneurial profile of the founder. In the case of e-ventures, the characteristics of the individuals who initiate electronic ventures guarantee the highly entrepreneurial vision necessary for the visionary and emergent processes to contribute to the shaping of the born global strategy.

As far as the negotiation process is concerned, the relevance of accessing close networks –e.g., family, friends, etc.– leads to patently strong interest in forming part of new business networks (Loane & Bell, 2006; Mort & Weerawardena, 2006; O'Donnell, Gilmore, Cummins, & Carson, 2001). This justifies the growing importance of the negotiation process, due to the debate and search for agreements between the founders of the new venture and the partners and other economic actors participating in those networks. As a result of each party's bargaining power, their respective preferences, business concepts and goals will be more or less prevalent in the specification of the aspects that define the e-born global strategy in the opportunity exploitation stage. It is interesting to see how the volatile, dynamic and complex context, and the e-venture's need for resources simultaneously affect the decision to proactively promote the development of new entrepreneurial networks –i.e., business networks building (Loane & Bell, 2006; Mort & Weerawardena, 2006; O'Donnell et al., 2001). From a broad perspective, the development of alliances must consider intra- and inter-sectorial partners. In that respect, the existence of an entrepreneurial team represents greater value for the venture since it facilitates access to a greater number of networks (Neergaard, 2005): this is an aspect that has been confirmed in the case of firms operating on the Internet (Batjargal, 2007).

These networks not only support product marketing, they also provide ongoing feedback on technological trends that support the development of new products or services. However, although networks speed up internationalization by pro-

viding synergistic relationships with other firms (Crick & Spence, 2005; Mort & Weerawardena, 2006) and access to the market, the growth of the e-born global in the international market will be faster if it decides to cooperate with an MNE rather than participate in networks of smaller companies (Gabrielsson et al., 2008). That decision will have significant repercussions on the new e-venture's bargaining power within those alliances and, consequently, on the importance of the negotiation process to the shaping of the born global strategy. In fact, although participation in networks is positive for the success of the born global (Neergaard, 2005), the born global's position in the networks could be either an important facilitator or inhibitor (Chetty & Campbell-Hunt, 2003). In that respect, when the entrepreneur joins networks by developing strong ties –e.g., agreements for physical delivery of the products on the market– and, at the same time, the entrepreneur is in a weak position –e.g., he/she manages a new venture without sufficient reputation and resources to guarantee long-term survival–, the new venture's strategy could mainly depend on the interests and objectives of actors with greater bargaining power. However, as the e-born globals advance in the exploitation stage and successfully consolidate in the market, their bargaining power will increase.

As previously mentioned, in the opportunity recognition stage, entrepreneurial team members lack a common history that brings shared criteria and guides to support the decisions in line with a collective process. However, in the opportunity exploitation stage, that process becomes increasingly important. As the entrepreneurs work together, a shared work philosophy is developed and reinforced (Lumpkin & Dess, 1996). That work philosophy defines the way in which the entrepreneurial team as a whole understands the industry, the business and the combination of resources to create a profitable business. The consolidation of those shared cognitions strengthens the role of the collective process in the strategic decision although it may prejudice the shaping of a born global strategy. In effect, the existence of an integrated entrepreneurial team with converging thoughts could have a negative impact when the new venture operates in technological sectors (West, 2007) and if those cognitions do not lead to flexibility, innovation or creativity. This is due to the fact that competitiveness in technological sectors is based on innovation and so the born global strategy requires the continuous development of new products and services. Thus, the collective process is relevant to the shaping of the born global strategy when shared cognitions support the international entrepreneurial orientation of the e-venture –i.e., proactiveness, innovativeness, risk taking, competitive aggressiveness (Kuivalainen et al., 2007; Zhou, 2007).

Based on the previous assumptions, we can assert that the e-opportunity recognition and exploitation stages cannot be approached from a single perspective, since no individual process is able to explain the decision to start up an e-born global. Moreover, the relevance of those processes and the antecedents that define them differs in the recognition and exploitation stages. This confirms the basic hypothesis of the configuration approach for the shaping of the international strategy in e-ventures.

FUTURE RESEARCH DIRECTIONS

Future research lines include the study of additional antecedents of the new e-venture's international strategy, based on the different formation processes, as well as different methodologies to approach its analysis. Specifically, we believe that, due to the entrepreneur's role as a project initiator and seed of the new venture (visionary process), a deeper understanding of the factors that affect this actor's behavior is necessary. In that respect, emotional intelligence represents a research line that could contribute new evidence about the entrepreneur's ability to cooperate with

other founding partner, and also to build the necessary links to networks that allow him/her to enter industries related to e-economy and act with a global market vision. Based on both the psychological distance –as opposed to institutional and cultural distance constructs– between domestic and foreign markets perceived by entrepreneurs, and the factors influencing that distance, new research could shed light on the scale, scope and speed of the internationalization strategy of the new e-venture. Moreover, the study of affective, normative and calculated commitment levels –focused toward the founder team, the business idea, or the business networks– could also provide new evidence of the founders' will to stay in the firm and in the network and, consequently, of the strategic decisions formulated in a collective and in a negotiation way. With regard to the negotiation process, new research should also explore various issues, such as the new venture's position in the network, the types of links developed in the network, the relevance of links via intermediaries, the information asymmetries stemming from the actors' different technological levels, etc., and so analyze the cases in which the network represents a facilitator rather than an inhibitor of the development of a born global strategy.

Secondly, longitudinal empirical studies could clarify the actual influence that imitation –as a behavior that aims to legitimize decisions made and reduce the risks taken– and other institutional pressures –i.e., coercive, normative, etc – has on the thriving of e-born globals in a particular territory or industry, thus giving information about the impact that reactive processes have on strategy formation in the new e-venture. Emergent processes in strategy formation could also be better understood in the e-venture context if future studies used a longitudinal perspective to analyze the learning process that takes place in the e-opportunity recognition stage versus the opportunity exploitation stage. This new venue could explain, according to Zhou (2007), the born global phenomenon. Similarly, this longitudinal approach could clarify the entrepreneurial network building process from a dynamic and evolutionary perspective.

Finally, and given that the interdisciplinary use of theories and approaches to explain international strategy formation in the new e-venture remains unexplored, we suggest that such research should be carried out. It would allow the empirical comparison of the relevance of some processes –and antecedents– with others in both the opportunity recognition and exploitation stages of an e-born global business –i.e., transformation process. In addition, from this integrative approach, we believe it is necessary to develop comparative research studies that help explain the relevance of strategy formation processes in different contexts. For instance, comparative studies for sub-sectors in the e-business context, successful new e-ventures versus failed initiatives, e-born global versus traditional path for e-venture internationalization, comparative cross-cultural studies concerning regional cultural differences that affect e-ventures, etc. Lastly, in order to advance in this integrative line, qualitative researches based on case studies and those quantitative in nature would be well received.

CONCLUSION

Mintzberg et al. (1998), in their book Strategy Safari, made use of a fable in which six blind men tried to describe an elephant; each contributed his partial and certain point of view, although all of them were wrong in the holistic idea. In our chapter, and paraphrasing those authors, we can affirm that the complex born global strategies formed for new e-ventures –i.e., a true elephant– make it impossible to identify the antecedents and process to formulate this strategy from a single theoretical perspective. Actually, the work we carried out has enabled us to identify the most relevant partial approaches to formulate the strategy. We also drew upon a solid framework,

based on Mintzberg (1990) and Mintzberg et al. (1998), to propose an integration of past research and pending research issues.

From our perspective, an integrated and solid theory building for the study of the e-born global does not go against the development of new partial researches. It would be accompanied by new evidence to progress in the knowledge of our particular elephant. However, the complexity of the topic means that it is not feasible to develop empirical works that bring together all the relevant variables associated with each strategy formation approach. Following Mintzberg et al. (1998), to be able to capture the whole we have to understand each and every constituent element.

Practitioners, administrators and public policy makers should be aware of those antecedents that, in every process stage and in every geographic area, help develop e-born globals. In this sense, there should be an exhaustive analysis of every socio-economic macro-environment (e.g., development level of telecommunications infrastructures, cultural values, spillovers of international knowledge, technological and entrepreneurial spillovers, etc.), instead of adopting recipes from other countries or other regions of their country. Based on the present situation, public and private agents could support and foster those factors that give rise to the creation of e-born globals in their territory.

REFERENCES

Aldrich, H. E., & Martinez, M. A. (2001). Many are called, but few are chosen, an evolutionary perspective for the study of entrepreneurship. *Entrepreneurship . Theory into Practice, 25*(4), 41–56.

Autio, E., Sapienza, H. J., & Almeida, J. G. (2000). Effects of age at entry, knowledge intensity, and imitability on international growth. *Academy of Management Journal, 43*(5), 909–924. doi:10.2307/1556419

Bailey, A., Johnson, G., & Daniels, K. (2000). Validation of a Multi-Dimensional Measure of Strategy Development Processes. *British Journal of Management, 11*, 151–162. doi:10.1111/1467-8551.t01-1-00157

Baron, R. A. (2006). Opportunity recognition as pattern recognition. How entrepreneurs 'connect the dots' to identify new business opportunities. *The Academy of Management Perspectives, 20*(1), 104–119.

Batjargal, B. (2007). Internet entrepreneurship: social capital, human capital and performance of Internet venture in China. *Research Policy, 36*, 605–618. doi:10.1016/j.respol.2006.09.029

Blomqvist, K., Hurmelinna, P., Nummela, N., & Saarenketo, S. (2008). The role of trust and contracts in the internationalization of technology-intensive Born Globals. *Journal of Engineering and Technology Management, 25*(1-2), 123–135. doi:10.1016/j.jengtecman.2008.01.006

Bloodgood, J. M., Sapienza, H. J., & Almeida, J. G. (1996). The internationalization of new high-potential US ventures: antecedents and outcomes. *Entrepreneurship Theory & Practice, 20*(4), 61–76.

Boter, H., & Homquist, C. (1996). Industry characteristics and internationalization processes in small firms. *Journal of Business Venturing, 11*(6), 471–487. doi:10.1016/S0883-9026(96)89166-X

Busenitz, L. W., & Lau, C. M. (1996). A cross-cultural cognitive model of new venture creation. *Entrepreneurship Theory and Practice, 20*(4), 25–39.

Chaston, I. (2001). *E-Marketing Strategy*. Maidenhead, UK: McGraw-Hill.

Chetty, S., & Campbell-Hunt, C. (2003). Explosive international growth and problems of success amongst small to medium-sized firms. *International Small Business Journal, 21*(5), 5–27. doi:10.1177/0266242603021001719

Chorev, S., & Anderson, A. R. (2006). Success in Israeli high-tech start-ups: critical factors and process. *Technovation, 26*, 162–174. doi:10.1016/j.technovation.2005.06.014

Colombo, M. G., & Grilli, L. (2005). Founders' human capital and the growth of new technology-based firms: a competence-based view. *Research Policy, 34*, 795–816. doi:10.1016/j.respol.2005.03.010

Colombo, M. G., & Grilli, L. (2007). Technology policy for the knowledge economy: public support to young ICT service firms. *Policy, 31*, 573–591.

Cooper, A. C. (1986). Entrepreneurship and high technology. In D. L. Sexton & R. W. Smilor (Eds.), *The Art and Science of Entrepreneurship* (pp. 153-68). Cambridge, UK: Ballinger.

Crick, D., & Spence, M. (2005). The internationalisation of high performing UK high-tech SMEs: a study of planned and unplanned strategies. *International Business Review, 14*, 167–185. doi:10.1016/j.ibusrev.2004.04.007

Damaskopoulos, P., & Evgeniou, T. (2003). Adoption of new economy practices by SMEs in Eastern Europe. *European Management Journal, 21*(2), 133–145. doi:10.1016/S0263-2373(03)00009-4

De Clercq, D., Hessels, J., & van Stel, A. (2008). Knowledge spillovers and new ventures' export orientation. *Small Business Economics, 31*, 283–303. doi:10.1007/s11187-008-9132-z

DiMaggio, P. J., & Powell, W. W. (1983). The iron cage revisited: institutional isomorphism and collective rationality in organizational fields. *American Sociological Review, 48*, 147–160. doi:10.2307/2095101

Fathian, M., Akhavan, P., & Hoorali, M. (2008). E-readiness assessment of non-profit ICT SMEs in a developing country: the case of Iran. *Technovation, 28*, 578–590. doi:10.1016/j.technovation.2008.02.002

Fernández Sánchez, E. (2005). *Estrategia de innovación*. Madrid: Thomson.

Fernhaber, S. S., McDougall, P. P., & Oviatt, B. M. (2007). Exploring the role of industry structure in new venture internationalization. *Entrepreneurship Theory and Practice, 31*, 517–542. doi:10.1111/j.1540-6520.2007.00186.x

Fillis, I., & Wagner, B. (2005). E-business development – An exploratory investigation of the small firm. *International Small Business Journal, 23*(6), 604–634. doi:10.1177/0266242605057655

Fine, G., & Deegan, J. (1996). Three principles of serendip: insight, chance and discovery in qualitative research. *Qualitative Studies in Education, 9*(4), 434–447. doi:10.1080/0951839960090405

Gabrielsson, M., Kirpalani, V. H. M., Dimitratos, P., Solberg, C. A., & Zucchella, A. (2008). Born globals: propositions to help advance the theory. *International Business Review, 17*(4), 385–401. doi:10.1016/j.ibusrev.2008.02.015

García-Cabrera, A. M., & García-Soto, M. G. (2008). Reconocimiento de la oportunidad y emprendeduría de base tecnológica: un modelo dinámico. *Investigaciones Europeas de Dirección y Economía de la Empresa, 14*(2), 109–125.

Gregorio, D. D., Kassicieh, S. K., & De Gouvean, R. (2005). Drivers of e-business activity in developed and emerging markets. *IEEE Transactions on Engineering Management, 52*(2), 155–166. doi:10.1109/TEM.2005.844464

Gupta, V., MacMillan, I. C., & Surie, G. (2004). Entrepreneurial leadership: developing and measuring a cross-cultural construct. *Journal of Business Venturing, 19*, 241–260. doi:10.1016/S0883-9026(03)00040-5

Inkpen, A. C., & Tsang, E. W. K. (2005). Social capital, networks, and knowledge transfer. *Academy of Management Review, 30*(1), 146–165.

Jantunen, A., Nummela, N., Puumalainen, K., & Saarenketo, S. (2008). Strategic orientation of born globals - Do they really matter? *Journal of World Business, 43*, 158–170. doi:10.1016/j.jwb.2007.11.015

Jennings, P., & Beaver, G. (1997). The performance and competitive advantage of small firms: a management perspective. *International Small Business Journal, 15*(2), 63–75. doi:10.1177/0266242697152004

Kakati, M. (2003). Success criteria in high-tech new venture. *Technovation, 23*, 447–457. doi:10.1016/S0166-4972(02)00014-7

Karra, N., Phillips, N., & Tracey, P. (2008). Building the born global firm. Developing entrepreneurial capabilities for international new venture success. *Long Range Planning, 41*, 440–458. doi:10.1016/j.lrp.2008.05.002

King, D., Lee, J., Warkentin, M., & Chung, H. (2002). *Electronic commerce: a managerial perspective*. Upper Saddle River, NJ: Pearson Education International.

Kirzner, I. (1979). *Perception, opportunity and profit*. Chicago, IL: University of Chicago Press.

Knight, G. A., & Cavusgil, S. T. (1996). The born global firm: a challenge to traditional internalization theory. In S.T. Cavusgil, & T. Madsen (Eds.), *Advances in International Marketing* (pp.11-26). Greenwich, CT: JAL Press.

Kollman, T. (2006). What is e-entrepreneurship? – Fundamentals of company founding in the net economy. *International Journal of Technology Management, 33*(4), 322–340. doi:10.1504/IJTM.2006.009247

Kuivalainen, O., Sundqvist, S., & Servais, P. (2007). Firm's degree of born-globalness, international entrepreneurial orientation and export performance. *Journal of World Business, 42*, 523–267. doi:10.1016/j.jwb.2007.04.010

Lal, K. (2004). E-business and export behavior. Evidence from Indian firms. *World Development, 32*(3), 505–517. doi:10.1016/j.worlddev.2003.10.004

Loane, S., & Bell, J. (2006). Rapid internationalization among entrepreneurial firms in Australia, Canada, Ireland and New Zealand. *International Marketing Review, 23*(5), 467–485. doi:10.1108/02651330610703409

Loane, S., Bell, J., & McNaughton, R. (2007). A cross-national study on the impact of management teams on the rapid internationalization of small firms. *Journal of World Business, 42*, 489–504. doi:10.1016/j.jwb.2007.06.009

Lumpkin, G. T. (2005). The role of organizational learning in the opportunity-recognition process. *Entrepreneurship Theory and Practice, 29*(4), 451–472. doi:10.1111/j.1540-6520.2005.00093.x

Lumpkin, G. T., & Dess, G. G. (1996). Clarifying the entrepreneurial orientation construct and linking it to performance. *Academy of Management Review, 21*(1), 135–172. doi:10.2307/258632

Madsen, T. K. (1989). Successful export marketing management: some empirical evidence. *International Marketing Review, 6*(4), 41–57. doi:10.1108/EUM0000000001518

Madsen, T. K., & Servais, P. (1997). The internationalization of born globals: an evolutionary process? *International Business Review, 6*(6), 561–583. doi:10.1016/S0969-5931(97)00032-2

Magretta, J. (1999). *Managing in the new economy.* Boston, MA: Harvard Business School.

Matlay, H. (2003). Small tourism firms in e-Europe: definitional, conceptual and contextual considerations. In R. Thomas (Ed.), *Small Firms in Tourism: International Perspectives* (pp. 297-312). Oxford, UK: Pergamon.

Matlay, H., & Addis, M. (2003). Adoption of ICT and e-commerce in small businesses: an HEI-based consultancy perspective. *Journal of Small Business and Enterprise Development, 10*(3), 321–335. doi:10.1108/14626000310489790

Matlay, H., & Westhead, P. (2005). Virtual teams and the rise of e-entrepreneurship in Europe. *International Small Business Journal, 23*(3), 279–302. doi:10.1177/0266242605052074

McDougall, P. P., & Oviatt, B. M. (2000). International entrepreneurship: the intersection of two research paths. *Academy of Management Journal, 43*(5), 902–906. doi:10.2307/1556418

Mintzberg, H. (1990). Strategy formation: schools of thought. In J. W. Fredrickson (Ed.), *Perspectives on Strategic Management* (pp. 105-235). New York: Harper Business.

Mintzberg, H., Ahlstrand, B., & Lampel, J. (1998). *Strategy safari.* London: Prentice Hall Europe.

Morse, E. A., & Mitchell, R. K. (2006). *Case in Entrepreneurship.* London: Sage Publications, Inc.

Mort, G. S., & Weerawardena, J. (2006). Networking capability and international entrepreneurship. How networks function in Australian born global firms. *International Marketing Review, 23*(5), 549–572. doi:10.1108/02651330610703445

Neergaard, H. (2005). Networking activities in technology-based entrepreneurial teams. *International Small Business Journal, 23*(3), 257–278. doi:10.1177/0266242605052073

Newbert, S. L. (2005). New firm formation: a dynamic capability perspective. *Journal of Small Business Management, 43*(1), 55–77. doi:10.1111/j.1540-627X.2004.00125.x

O'Donnell, A., Gilmore, A., Carson, D., & Cummins, D. (2002). Competitive advantage in small to medium-sized enterprises. *Journal of Strategic Marketing, 10*(3), 205–223. doi:10.1080/09652540210151388

O'Donnell, A., Gilmore, A., Cummins, D., & Carson, D. (2001). The network construct in entrepreneurship research: A review and critique. *Management Decision, 39*(9), 749–760. doi:10.1108/EUM0000000006220

Oviatt, B. M., & McDougall, P. P. (1994). Toward a theory of international new ventures. *Journal of International Business Studies, 25*(1), 45–64. doi:10.1057/palgrave.jibs.8490193

Oviatt, B. M., & McDougall, P. P. (2005). Defining international entrepreneurship and modeling the speed of internationalization. *Entrepreneurship Theory & Practice, 29*(5), 537–553. doi:10.1111/j.1540-6520.2005.00097.x

Park, J. S. (2005). Opportunity recognition and product innovation in entrepreneurial hi-tech start-ups: a new perspective and supporting case study. *Technovation, 25*, 739–752. doi:10.1016/j.technovation.2004.01.006

Porter, M. E. (1980). *Competitive Strategy: techniques for analyzing industries and competitors*. New York: The Free Press.

Quelch, J. A., & Klein, L. R. (1996). The internet and international marketing. *Sloan Management Review, 37*(3), 60–75.

Rialp, A., Rialp, J., & Knight, G. A. (2005). The phenomenon of early internationalizing firms: what do we know after a decade (1993-2003) of scientific inquiry? *International Business Review, 14*, 147–166. doi:10.1016/j.ibusrev.2004.04.006

Sadler-Smith, E., Hampson, Y., Chaston, I., & Badger, B. (2003). Managerial behavior, entrepreneurial style, and small firm performance. *Journal of Small Business Management, 41*(1), 47–67. doi:10.1111/1540-627X.00066

Sapienza, H. J., De Clercq, D., & Sandberg, W. R. (2005). Antecedents of international and domestic learning effort. *Journal of Business Venturing, 20*, 437–457. doi:10.1016/j.jbusvent.2004.03.001

Sarasvathy, S. D. (2001). Causation and effectuation: toward a theoretical shift from economic inevitability to entrepreneurial contingency. *Academy of Management Review, 26*(2), 243–264. doi:10.2307/259121

Shane, S., & Venkataraman, S. (2000). The promise of entrepreneurship as a field of research. *Academy of Management Review, 25*(1), 218–228. doi:10.2307/259271

Spence, M., & Crick, D. (2006). A comparative investigation into the internationalisation of Canadian and UK high-tech SMEs. *International Marketing Review, 23*(5), 524–548. doi:10.1108/02651330610703436

Stöttinger, B., & Schlegelmich, B. B. (1998). Explaining export development through psychic distance: enlightening or elusive? *International Business Review, 15*(5), 357–372.

Thukral, I. S., Von Ehr, J., Walsh, S., Groen, A., Van der Sijde, P., & Adham, K. A. (2008). Entrepreneurship, emerging technologies, emerging markets. *International Small Business Journal, 26*(1), 101–116. doi:10.1177/0266242607084656

Weerawardena, J., Mort, G. S., Liesch, P. W., & Knight, G. (2007). Conceptualizing accelerated internationalization in the born global firm: a dynamic capabilities perspective. *Journal of World Business, 42*, 294–306. doi:10.1016/j.jwb.2007.04.004

West, G. P. III. (2007). Collective cognition: when entrepreneurial teams, not individuals, make decisions. *Entrepreneurship Theory and Pratice, 31*(1), 77–102. doi:10.1111/j.1540-6520.2007.00164.x

Wood, C. M. (2004). Marketing and e-commerce as tools of development in the Asia-Pacific region: a dual path. *International Marketing Review, 21*(3), 301–320. doi:10.1108/02651330410539639

Zahra, S. A., Korri, J. S., & Yu, J. (2005). Cognition and international entrepreneurship: implications for research on international opportunity recognition and exploitation. *International Business Review, 14*(2), 129–146. doi:10.1016/j. ibusrev.2004.04.005

Zhou, L. (2007). The effects of entrepreneurial proclivity and foreign market knowledge on early internationalization. *Journal of World Business, 42*, 281–293. doi:10.1016/j.jwb.2007.04.009

ADDITIONAL READING

Ardichvili, A., Cardozo, R., & Ray, S. (2003). A theory of entrepreneurial opportunity identification and development. *Journal of Business Venturing, 18*, 105–123. doi:10.1016/S0883-9026(01)00068-4

Audretsch, D. B., & Keilbach, M. (2007). The theory of knowledge spillover entrepreneurship. *Journal of Management Studies, 24*(1), 29–46.

Bell, J., McNaughton, R., & Young, S. (2001). Born-again global firms: an extension to the born global phenomena. *Journal of International Management, 7*(3), 173–189. doi:10.1016/S1075-4253(01)00043-6

Brynjolfsson, E., & Kahin, B. (2002). *Understanding the digital economy: data, tools and research.* Cambridge, MA: The MIT Press.

Cavusgil, S. T. (1984). Organizational characteristics associated with export activities. *Journal of Management Studies, 21*(1), 3–22. doi:10.1111/j.1467-6486.1984.tb00222.x

Chandler, G. N., & Hanks, S. H. (1994). Founder competence, the environment, and venture performance. *Entrepreneurship Theory & Practice, 18*(3), 77–89.

Chetty, S., & Blankenburg Holm, D. (2000). Internationalization of small to medium-sized manufacturing firms: a network approach. *International Business Review, 9*(1), 77–93. doi:10.1016/ S0969-5931(99)00030-X

Chulikavit, K., & Rose, J. (2003). E-commerce and the internationalisation of SMEs. In H. Etemad, & R. Wright (Eds.), *Globalisation and Entrepreneurship: Policy and Strategy Perspectives* (pp. 205-222). Montreal, Canada: Edward Elgar Publishing Limited.

European Commission's DG Enterprise and Industry. (2009). *E-business in Europe - 2008. Industry perspectives on e-business development and ICT impact.* Retrieved July, 2009, from http://www. ebusiness-watch.org/key_reports/documents/ BRO08.pdf

Evans, P. B., & Wurster, B. S. (1997). Strategy and the new economics of information. *Harvard Business Review, 75*(5), 70–83.

García-Cabrera, A. M., & García-Soto, M. G. (2008). NTC Co.: Seeking and screening technological venture opportunities in entrepreneurial start-ups. In J. A. Medina-Garrido, S. Martínez-Fierro, & J. Ruiz-Navarro (Eds.), *Cases on Information Technology Entrepreneurship* (pp. 122-147). New York: IGI Global.

Grant, R. M. (2002). *Contemporary strategy analysis. Concepts, techniques, applications.* Oxford, UK: Blackwell Publishers Ltd. Fourth edition.

Jack, S. L., & Anderson, A. R. (2002). The effects of embeddedness on the entrepreneurial process. *Journal of Business Venturing, 17*, 467–487. doi:10.1016/S0883-9026(01)00076-3

Johanson, J., & Vahlne, J. E. (1977). The internationalisation process of the firm. *Journal of International Business Studies, 8*(1), 23–32. doi:10.1057/palgrave.jibs.8490676

Knight, G. A., & Cavusgil, S. T. (2004). Innovation, organizational capabilities, and the born-global firm. *Journal of International Business Studies, 35*, 124–141. doi:10.1057/palgrave.jibs.8400071

Korhonen, H., Luostarinen, R., & Welch, L. (1996). Internationalization of SMEs: inward-outward patterns and government policy. *Management International Review, 36*(4), 315–329.

Martin, L., & Matlay, H. (2003). Innovative use of the internet in established small firms: the impact of knowledge management and organisational learning in accessing new opportunities. *Qualitative Market Research, 6*(1), 18–26. doi:10.1108/13522750310457348

McDougall, P. P., & Oviatt, B. M. (1996). New venture internationalization, strategic change, and performance: a follow-up study. *Journal of Business Venturing, 11*(1), 23–40. doi:10.1016/0883-9026(95)00081-X

McPherson, A., Jones, O., & Zhang, M. (2004). Evolution or revolution? Dynamic capabilites in a knowledge-dependent firm. *R & D Management, 34*(2), 161–176. doi:10.1111/j.1467-9310.2004.00331.x

Milliken, F. J., & Martins, Ll. (1996). Searching for common threads: understanding the multiple effects of diversity in organizational groups. *Academy of Management Review, 21*, 402–433. doi:10.2307/258667

Mueller, S. L., & Thomas, A. S. (2000). Culture and entrepreneurial potential: a nine country study of locus of control and innovativeness. *Journal of Business Venturing, 16*, 51–75. doi:10.1016/S0883-9026(99)00039-7

Porter, M. E. (1985). *Competitive Advantage: creating and sustaining superior performance.* New York: The Free Press.

Scherer, F. (1999). *New perspectives on economic growth and technological innovation.* Washington DC: Brookings Institution Press.

Schrader, R., & Siegel, D. S. (2007). Assessing the relationship between human capital and firm performance: evidence from technology-based new venture. *Entrepreneurship Theory and Practice, 31*(6), 893–908. doi:10.1111/j.1540-6520.2007.00206.x

Steensma, H. K., Marino, L., & Weaver, K. M. (2000). Attitudes toward cooperative strategies: a cross cultural analysis of entrepreneurs. *Journal of International Business Studies, 31*(4), 591–609. doi:10.1057/palgrave.jibs.8490924

Zahra, S. A., & George, G. (2002). International entrepreneurship: the current status of the field and future research agenda. In M. A. Hitt, R. D. Irelands, S. M. Camp, & D. L. Sexton (Eds.), *Strategic entrepreneurship: creating a new mindset* (pp. 255-288). Oxford, UK: Blackwell Publisher.

Chapter 3
Market Orientation in Emerging Firms:
Towards a More Rigorous Understanding of Entrepreneurial Marketing

Malte Brettel
RWTH Aachen, Germany

Andreas Engelen
RWTH Aachen, Germany

Florian Heinemann
RWTH Aachen, Germany

Andreas Kessell
RWTH Aachen, Germany

ABSTRACT

Most studies on the effect of market orientation in established and young companies have indicated a positive influence on firm performance. Whether and in what form this effect can also be found empirically in emerging firms – despite their numerous particularities – is still a largely unexplored issue. Applying rigorous procedures in the development of the measurement instrument and using a unique sample of 141 young companies, the authors confirm that market orientation does also have a significant and positive effect on the performance of emerging firms. However, results indicate significant differences to established firms regarding two aspects: (1) the items included in the measurement instrument diverge considerably from the established scales in this area, adding behavioral aspects characteristic for emerging firms and leaving aside items specific to larger organizations; (2) firms do not show a single consistent pattern of market-oriented behavior contributing to company success. Therefore, founders of emerging firms should pursue an individual way of market-oriented behavior that seems most appropriate when considering the company-specific liabilities.

DOI: 10.4018/978-1-61520-597-4.ch003

INTRODUCTION

Discussion about market orientation in established companies started as early as the 1950s with Peter Drucker and other researchers claiming that marketing involves the entire organization being seen from the customers' perspective (Drucker, 1954). Systematic conceptualization of market orientation in established companies was first provided by Kohli and Jaworski (1990), Narver and Slater (1990), Shapiro (1988), and Webster (1988). Subsequent empirical studies mostly used measurement scales that are based on the MARKOR and MKTOR scales introduced by Jaworski and Kohli (1993), Kohli, Jaworski, and Kumar (1993), and Narver and Slater (1990). The majority of these studies clearly indicate that market-orientated behavior has a positive effect on performance in established firms (Grether, 2003, who provides a comprehensive review of more than 70 empirical studies in this area).

In general, it seems admissible to assume that this positive influence of market orientation on company success can also be in found young and/or small companies (Fischer, & Reuber, 1995; George, & Zahra, 2002; Pelham & Wilson, 1996). However, as young firms differ significantly from established companies (Hills, & LaForge, 1992; Muzyka, & Hills, 1993; Storey, 1994), it is very likely that the market-oriented behavior in these firms, and its relationship with performance, displays particularities that are worth examining in more detail.

Results of such a study promise to be highly relevant from a practical perspective: in order for entrepreneurs to benefit systematically from market orientation as a potential success factor they need to understand which activities lead to higher levels of market orientation and how these can contribute to the success of their company. Therefore, from a research perspective a measurement instrument of market-oriented behavior is needed that incorporates the particularities of young companies. Thus far, to our knowledge none of the attempts to examine the effects of market orientation for small and medium enterprises (SMEs) has lead to a generally accepted, valid, and reliable measurement instrument.

As a consequence, following the multi-stage process of construct development recommended by Churchill (1979), we

1. develop a measurement instrument for market-oriented behavior building on the specific characteristics of emerging firms as a subset of SMEs that we define as young, growth-oriented enterprises (Muzyka, & Hills, 1993) and
2. test this measurement instrument in terms of the effect shown on performance. This will then be used as a basis for deriving practical implications for founders of young firms.

We begin our discussion with the specification of the domain. Here, we a) describe the dimensions of market-oriented behavior as introduced by Kohli and Jaworski (1990) for established companies, b) characterize the specific nature of emerging firms, and c) conclude this section by analyzing the adequacy of Kohli & Jaworski's (1990) conceptualization for emerging firms. Based on both literature searches and also interviews with experts we generate additional measurement items within this conceptualization in order to adequately capture the particularities of market-oriented behavior in emerging firms. Using data from a sample of 141 emerging firms (data collection), we then purify the measurement instrument. The empirical results applying this instrument are presented in the subsequent section. We conduct our analysis using the partial least square (PLS) structural equation approach (cf. Chin, 1998a; Wold, 1985). Finally, we discuss the implications of our findings together with potential avenues for further research.

DOMAIN SPECIFICATION – DIMENSIONS OF MARKET-ORIENTED BEHAVIOR IN EMERGING FIRMS

Dimensions of Market-Oriented Behavior in Established Companies

Following Kohli and Jaworski (1990) and Shapiro (1988), we take a behavioral perspective on market orientation. Accordingly, Deng and Dart (1994) define market-oriented behavior as a process: "Market orientation is the generation of appropriate market intelligence pertaining to current and future customer needs, and the relative abilities of competitive entities to satisfy these needs; the integration and dissemination of such intelligence across departments; and the coordinated design and execution of the organization's strategic response to market opportunities" (Deng, & Dart, 1994; Jaworski, & Kohli, 1993 and 1996; Kohli, &1996 Jaworski, 1990). So, while maintaining the three dimensions of market-oriented behavior that were originally identified by Kohli and Jaworski (1990), i.e. a) information generation, b) information dissemination, and c) responsiveness to information, Deng and Dart (1994) moreover differentiate customer and competitor orientation, both of which they see as essential components of market orientation (Kohli, & Jaworski, 1996; Narver, & Slater, 1990). Whereas customer orientation focuses on fulfilling customer expectations, competitor orientation aims at establishing a competitive advantage based on superior knowledge of the competitive landscape (Oxenfeldt, & Moore, 1978).

Characteristics of Emerging Firms

As outlined, the focus of the present article is on emerging firms as a subset of SMEs. In a behavioral context, they are generally characterized by some of the following liabilities which we will build on in subsequent paragraphs:

Liability of age/newness: Stinchcombe (1965) attributed the significantly higher "mortality risk" of young companies to the need to define new, unfamiliar roles, tasks, and processes. Moreover, young companies have to establish new, often trust-based relationships with formerly unknown exchange partners (Stinchcombe, 1965; Aldrich, & Auster, 1986).

Liability of size/smallness: Complementing Stinchcombe's (1965) findings Aldrich & Auster (1986) also observed that the smallness of a company has a negative impact on survival rates – mainly due to a lack of financial and human resources (Bruederl, & Schuessler, 1990).

Liability of adolescence/growth: In addition to operating the "daily business", emerging firms face the challenge that they have to implement structures and processes as the organization grows. This will require a substantial share of the founders' attention (Kazanjian, 1988; Drazin, & Kazanjian, 1990; Churchill, & Lewis, 1983).

Liability of uncertainty: Emerging firms are experimental in character as to whether a particular new combination of resources will actually serve the market better than existing solutions (Starr & MacMillan, 1990). Therefore, such companies by definition are exposed to a high level of uncertainty resulting from a lack of market experience (Kirzner, 1973) and unsettled market conditions (Tushman, & Anderson, 1986; Bhide, 2000).

Owner dominance and dependence: Although not explicitly labeled a liability in entrepreneurship literature, in most cases small firms are largely dependent on and limited by the know-how and capabilities of their founders (Shane, & Stuart, 2002).

Dimensions of Market-Oriented Behavior in Emerging Firms

Studies that have analyzed market orientation in SMEs agree on the importance of the first and the third dimension of market-oriented behavior, i.e. information generation and responsiveness, in this specific context (Pelham, 1997; Wickham, 2001). With regard to the second dimension, information dissemination, however, there is disagreement: Fischer and Reuber (1995), for example, have argued that due to the small number of actors involved in young firms (liability of size/smallness), activities aiming for information dissemination within the organization are only of minor importance. On the other hand, Sinkula (1994) has described information dissemination as an essential activity for market information processing, particularly in young organizations. He claims such activities – though informal in nature – to be a prerequisite for the initiation of a learning process within an entrepreneurial team (Sinkula, 1994). It is important to note, however, that activities for information dissemination in established organizations as well do not necessarily refer to formal coordination or communication mechanisms. As Kohli and Jaworski (1990) have already pointed out "[…] informal 'hall talk' is an extremely powerful tool for keeping employees tuned to customers and their needs" (Kohli, & Jaworski, 1990, p. 5). The above mentioned learning process appears particularly important considering the liability of uncertainty that emerging firms are facing. Sinkula's view is also supported by Fischer and Reuber's (1995) empirical findings that – despite their argumentation stated above – have shown items measuring internal communication activities to be significantly correlated with success measures. Therefore, in the present study we maintain the original conceptualization of market-oriented behavior proposed by Kohli and Jaworski (1990). More formally:

H₁: The three dimensions of market-oriented behavior identified by Kohli & Jaworski (1990) as well as their inherent causality can also be found in emerging firms.

This hypothesis receives additional support from the fact that for developing the original conceptualization of market oriented behavior

Kohli and Jaworski (1990) also included smaller companies. When developing the MARKOR scale, however, Jaworski and Kohli (1993) and Kohli, Jaworski, and Kumar (1993) had a clear focus on business units of larger corporations.

Retaining the dimensions of Kohli and Jaworski (1990) we will account for the specific nature of emerging firms on the item level.

MEASURING MARKET-ORIENTED BEHAVIOR IN EMERGING FIRMS

Additional Items Capturing the Particularities of Emerging Firms

The starting point for developing our measurement instrument was the MARKOR 32-scale of Jaworski and Kohli (1993). As the sample data used for generating the MARKOR 32 scale also included information from smaller companies, we used the complete set of 32 items originally proposed by Jaworski and Kohli (1993) because some of the items eliminated for MARKOR 20 (Kohli, Jaworski, & Kumar, 1993) might be relevant for emerging firms. However, we modified the tense of these items to capture market-oriented behavior during the market entry phase. On the basis of extensive literature searches we then developed additional items in order to capture the particularities in the behavior of emerging firms. As the next step, for the purpose of discussing clarity and the practical relevance of these items in order to ensure face validity (Churchill, 1979), we conducted 20 personal interviews with experts in this area. Each of the interviews had a minimum length of 45 minutes. Following Churchill's (1979) recommendation we chose a heterogeneous group of experts to include as many perspectives on market-oriented behavior in emerging firms as possible. Experts included founders of emerging firms, marketing executives in emerging firms, venture capitalists, business angels, and academics with a background in entrepreneurship and/

or marketing research. The interviews led to the adoption and removal of some of the additional items as well as to the inclusion of aspects not previously taken into consideration. The overall process of adding and removing items can be summarized as follows:

Information generation: Liabilities of smallness and newness often result in limited availability of resources in emerging firms. This lack of resources causes these firms to rely on informal methods for gathering market-related information rather than on formal market research (Gilmore, & Carson, 2000; Muzyka, & Hills, 1993; Roberts, 1991). Moreover, the high level of uncertainty favors a trial and error approach to testing possible product-market combinations (Geursen, 2000; Geursen, & Conduit, 2002; Stokes, 2000). This is also one of the reasons why emerging firms tend to target those potential customers with the highest level of technological competence and innovativeness (Moore, 1995). Moreover, smallness and owner dependence imply a central role of founders in information generation activities, especially with regard to customer contact (Roberts, 1991; Shane, & Stuart, 2002; Stokes, 2000). To reflect these particularities in emerging firm behavior, 9 indicators were added to the original MARKOR-scale in this dimension (cf. Appendix A).

Information dissemination: Within this dimension it seems important to cover the communication activities of those people within the emerging firm that are in closest contact with actual or potential customers (Fischer, & Reuber, 1995). As outlined above, due to the high level of owner dependence this role is usually played by one of the founders. Furthermore, with regard to smallness and newness the degree of institutionalization of the marketing function should be included in the measurement as it seems essential to ensure adequate information dissemination (cf. Roberts, 1991). In total, 7 indicators were added to account for these aspects (cf. Appendix B).

Responsiveness: Compensating for the lack of formalized market-research and continuing to pursue the above-mentioned trial and error approach, product development is often done incrementally as firms receive market feedback (Bhide, 2000; Moore, 1995; Roberts, 1991). Moreover, based on expert feedback we added two further characteristics of emerging firm behavior to this dimension: First, due to newness of companies studied, the implementation of a formally existing marketing plan was considered an essential differentiator between successful and unsuccessful firms. Second, as a result of smallness experts found reactive behavior towards competitor activities to be another aspect characteristic for young firms. However, interviews with experts also led to the elimination of one indicator measuring whether as a result of their smallness emerging firms tend to enter partnerships with other companies along the value chain (Gilmore, & Carson, 2000; Moore, 1995). Overall, 8 items were added to this dimension (cf. Appendix C).

In total, a set of 56 indicators was developed as input for the purification of the measurement instrument. This set consisted of the original 32 MARKOR items plus an additional 24 items to account for the specific behavior of emerging firms. Summarizing these findings leads to our second hypothesis:

H_2: *Including additional items in the measurement instrument that capture the specific nature of market-oriented behavior in emerging firms leads to an improved measurement quality in this particular context.*

Formative vs. Reflective Constructs

Generally, one differentiates between a) formative indicator constructs or composite latent variable models and b) reflective indicator constructs or principal factor models (Bollen, & Lennox, 1991;

Jarvis, MacKenzie, & Podsakoff, 2003). Whereas formative indicators are defined as observed variables that cause a latent variable (Bollen, 1989), reflective indicators are assumed to be influenced by a latent variable, i.e. the "direction of causality is from the construct to the indicators" (Jarvis, MacKenzie, & Podsakoff, 2003, p. 200).

Analyzing the marketing activities of emerging firms one encounters a high degree of individuality and variability (Gibson, 2002). In other words, there does not appear to be one consistent pattern of market-oriented behavior supporting company success. Rather, there exists a large variety of company-specific approaches which can be attributed to several reasons: First, as small firms are owner-dominated and their founders tend to vary substantially in terms of personalities and competencies, their behavioral patterns are likely to differ as well. Then, the lack of resources commonly found in emerging firms comes in varying forms, thus inducing different types of responses (Gilmore, & Carson, 2000). Moreover, the exposure to internal and external uncertainty demands for high flexibility in terms of processes and structures (Muzyka, & Hills, 1993) facilitating the development of firm-specific behavioral patterns. Therefore, we assume that the individual items used to capture different aspects of market-oriented behavior do not necessarily have a common origin and as a consequence cannot be expected to correlate, which would be a precondition for reflective constructs (Jarvis, MacKenzie, & Podsakoff, 2003). Summarizing these aspects:

H_3: For emerging firms it is more appropriate to measure market-oriented behavior as a formative rather than as a reflective measurement model.

Timing of Measurement

Since processes and structures in emerging firms tend to be highly dynamic (Kazanjian & Drazin, 1990), it is very likely that the market-oriented behavior observed varies significantly across the different phases of company development. Comparing the importance of these different stages, it is particularly during the market entry phase when initial technology-market-segments are determined and the foundation for potential growth is laid (Moore, 1995; Stokes, 2000). Therefore, at the latest beginning in this stage the market orientation of the young organization should begin to exert influence on company success. However, Noble, Sinha & Kumar (2002) pointed out the existence of a time lag between market-oriented behavior and its effect on performance. As a consequence, the measurement of market-oriented behavior and of company success relate to two different points in time: market-oriented behavior is measured during the market entry phase and causally linked to subsequent performance at a later stage of company development.

MEASURING PERFORMANCE IN EMERGING FIRMS

Instruments Measuring Performance in Emerging Firms

"Traditional" indicators of company success such as profit, cash-flow or market share seem inappropriate to comprehensively cover the performance of emerging firms which are often losing money during their early years of existence (Timmons, 1999). For emerging firms the mere fact of survival over a substantial period of time can already be seen as a success (Stinchcombe, 1965). Moreover, as size correlates positively with the probability of survival (Aldrich, & Auster, 1986), growth is an important indicator for the performance of emerging firms.

In order to assess comprehensively the success of a company Jaworski and Kohli (1996) recommend using a combination of objective and subjective performance measures. Accordingly, we developed the objective measures based on Roberts (1991), focusing particularly on growth in terms of turnover and the number of employees (7 items). For subjective measures (6 items) we built on Desphandé, Farley, and Webster (1992) as well as Pelham (1999).

Hypotheses on the Performance Effect of Market-Oriented Behavior in Emerging Firms

A strong market orientation supports a company in constantly delivering customer value that is superior to that of potential competitors (Narver, & Slater, 1990). The generally positive effect of market orientation on company success resulting from this has been shown empirically as well as argued for on the basis of theoretical concepts (Narver & Slater, 1990 using the market-based view). As outlined earlier, the positive impact of market orientation is also likely to be found in emerging firms (Fischer, & Reuber, 1995; George, & Zahra, 2002; Geursen, 2000). This view receives further support from authors who claim that emerging firms tend to be too technology- rather market-driven (Roberts, 1991). Thus, differentiating by dimension:

H_4: *Exhibiting dedicated activities for the generation of market-related information in the market entry phase has a positive effect on the performance of emerging firms at a later stage.*

H_5: *Exhibiting dedicated activities for the dissemination of market-related information in the market entry phase has a positive effect on the performance of emerging firms at a later stage.*

H_6: *Exhibiting dedicated activities for responding to market-related information in the market entry phase has a positive effect on the performance of emerging firms at a later stage.*

DATA COLLECTION

Continuing to follow the process suggested by Churchill (1979), a questionnaire with 56 behavioral and 13 performance items using a 7-point Likert scale was sent to a national sample of emerging firms in Germany (N = 1,000). The sample was drawn randomly from membership data of the German Chamber for Industry and Commerce using the following criteria: Included were firms that a) had been founded at the most five years ago, and b) were active in innovation intensive sectors. Our definition of innovation intensive sectors was drawn from Grupp and Legler (2000). The survey was addressed to one of the founders. Three contact attempts were made with the firms.

Of the 1,000 companies, 158 responded (16% response rate) which appears acceptable for a survey among SMEs (Dennis, 2003). 17 responses did not meet our sample criteria or were incomplete, leaving 141 usable answers. Of these, 118 firms (84%) were active in a B2B setting, whereas 23 (16%) served B2C markets. t-tests and F-tests were used to compare the answers of the two groups on all 69 variables in the survey (56 behavioral and 13 performance items). t-tests showed 32 out of 138 means were not within the 95% confidence interval. 11 out of 69 F-tests were significant (10% significance level). Thus, we conclude that there is no significant difference between the two groups. 70% of respondents were owners/managers, the remaining 30% were members of the second hierarchy level. Testing for informant bias, however, did not lead to significant differences. 50 out of 138 means were not within the 95% confidence interval, but only 7 out of 69 F-tests were significant (10% significance level). Moreover, in order to test for non-response bias we compared the answers of early with late respondents (Armstrong, & Overton, 1977) which did not reveal any significant differences either. 31 out of 138 means were not within the 95% confidence interval. 10 out of 69 F-tests were significant (10% significance level).

Figure 1. Results of construct measurement for objective performance

Variable	Indicator (Text)	Loading
Y11	Number of employees this year	0.52**
Y12	Sales this year (in Mio EUR)	0.49**
Y13	Growth rate of the sales to previous year in percent	0.7566
Y14	Average growth rate of sales in percent since foundation of the company	0.7651
Y15	Growth rate of the number of employees to previous year in percent	0.8017
Y16	Average growth rate of the number of employees since foundation of the company in percent	0.7531
Y17	EBIT this year as a percentage of sales	0.25**

**: item did not meet threshold criterion

Construct Reliliabiliy Measures:
Composite Reliability	0.916
Average Variance Extracted (AVE)	0.731
Cronbach's Alpha	0.877

PURIFICATION OF MEASUREMENT INSTRUMENT – ASSESSMENT OF CONSTRUCT RELIABILITY AND VALIDITY

Assessment of Performance Measures

As we use the performance measures for assessing the validity of our behavioral constructs, contrary to our structure thus far, we start with analyzing reliability and validity of the performance constructs. In order to adequately conduct this analysis, we first have to establish whether the respective construct is either formative or reflective (Bollen, 1989; Diamantopoulos, & Winklhofer, 2001). A quantitative assessment by means of a Tetrad-test (Bollen, & Ting, 1993) cannot be conducted, as software available to date, e.g. SAS, is only able to calculate Tetrads for constructs with 4 or 5 indicators. Instead, we have to rely on the qualitative criteria suggested by Jarvis, MacKenzie, and Podsakoff (2003). Applying these criteria to our performance measures we conclude: a) direction of causality is from construct to indicators, b) interchangeability of indicators/items is given, c) correlation/covariation among indicators is given,

and d) indicators have the same antecedents and consequences. This clearly leads us to the conclusion that the constructs are reflective.

As the next step, following the established procedures for reflective constructs indicator loadings are estimated as a measure for indicator reliability. Due to an indicator loading of less than the threshold criterion of 0.7 we eliminated 3 items to purify the objective performance construct (Carmines & Zeller, 1979). Construct reliability measures for the objective performance then showed sufficient accuracy as presented in Figure 1. The threshold criteria used in this case are: a) composite reliability – 0.7 (Nunnally, 1978), b) AVE – 0.5 (Fornell, & Larcker, 1981), and c) Cronbach's Alpha – 0.7 (Cronbach, 1951).

With regard to the construct measuring *subjective performance* all 6 indicators meet the threshold criterion of 0.7. Determining the measures for construct reliability again (using the same threshold criteria as in Figure 1) leads to satisfactory results as displayed in Figure 2. Both performance measures demonstrate construct and indicator discriminant validity (Fornell, & Larcker, 1981). Moreover, they show a significant correlation (significance level of 0.01) with a correlation coefficient of r=0.31.

Figure 2. Results of construct measurement for subjective performance

Variable	Indicator (Text)	Loading
Y21	Concerning the development of the company in comparison to other companies of the same industry sector, we are…	0.8962
Y22	Concerning the company growth in comparison to the most important competitor, we are...	0.8875
Y23	Concerning the outlook on company profits over the next years, we are...	0.8358
Y24	Concerning new product success compared to our competition, we are...	0.8887
Y25	Concerning the number of new customers we are able to win compared to the most important competitor, we are…	0.8018
Y26	Concerning the degree of customer retention to the company compared to other companies in our industry sector, we are…	0.7774

**: item did not meet threshold criterion

Construct Reliliabiliy Measures:

Composite Reliability	0.938
Average Variance Extracted (AVE)	0.715
Cronbach's Alpha	0.920

Assessment of Measurement Items for Market-Oriented Behavior

As outlined, a total of 56 items was used to measure market-oriented behavior during the market entry phase: a) 19 items for information generation, b) 15 for information dissemination, and c) 22 for responsiveness to information. Again, in such circumstances Tetrads cannot be calculated to establish the formative or reflective nature of the constructs. However, in order to substantiate the qualitative reasoning leading to our third hypothesis, that market-oriented behavior in this context should be specified as a formative measurement model, we analyzed the correlations among all 56 items (Jarvis, MacKenzie, & Podsakoff, 2003): Of the 1,540 possible correlations only 114 (7.4%) display a correlation coefficient of r > 0.4. Hence, we continue treating market-oriented behavior in emerging firms as a formative composition model of three latent variables. As a consequence, adequate measurement implies creating an index, not a scale as would be done for reflective constructs (Bollen, & Lennox, 1991).

Following the process of index construction recommended by Diamantopoulos and Winklhofer (2001), the first step is to ensure measurement reliability of the formative constructs by testing for multicollinearity. In this case, no variance inflation factor (VIF) as indication for multicollinearity is higher than 2.9 and thus well below the accepted threshold criterion of 10.0 (Diamantopoulos, & Winklhofer, 2001). Therefore, we do not have to eliminate any indicator due to multicollinearity problems.

The very nature of formative constructs renders the assessment of single indicator validity by testing internal consistency impossible (Diamantopoulos, & Winklhofer, 2001). However, as it is the one of the main goals of this study to develop an adequate measurement instrument, we still have to identify the most adequate items for this context. For this purpose, the external validity of the measurement has to be determined using a variable or construct that is theoretically connected but not explicitly part of the measurement model (Bollen, & Lennox, 1991; Jarvis, MacKenzie, & Podsakoff, 2003). In this study, we tested the correlation of all 56 indicators with the constructs measuring a) objective and b) subjective performance of emerging firms as these two constructs meet the criteria just mentioned. Using the power analysis algorithm resulted in an alpha of 16% as a threshold for the elimination of indicators

Table 1. Results of reliability and validity analysis

Information Generation			
	Path coeff.	**t-value**	**During the market entry phase...**
X213	0.5422	4.6330	... we did a lot of in-house market research.
X214	0.3343	2.9868	... we were slow to detect changes in our customers' product preferences. *(inverted item)*
X312	0.2138	2.6040	... we often talked with or surveyed those who can influence our end users' purchases (e.g., retailers, distributors).
X313	0.3034	2.5156	... we collected industry information by informal means (e.g. lunch with industry friends, talks with trade partners).
X114	0.3209	2.4193	... we gathered information on what is our competitive advantage.
X211	0.1676	2.0319	... we met with customers at least once a year to find out what products or services they would need in the future.
Information Dissemination			
	Path coeff.	**t-value**	**During the market entry phase...**
X122	0.2736	2.5341	... nobody in our firm felt responsible for gathering market- and customer-related information. (inverted item)
X322	0.2834	2.4075	... our firm periodically circulated documents (e.g. reports, newsletters) that provided information on our customers.
X126	0.3194	2.3859	... we developed a marketing plan for our firm.
X221	0.2908	2.1678	... we had "interdepartmental" meetings at least once a quarter to discuss market trends and developments.
X225	0.2321	2.0402	...: When one "department" found out something important about competitors, it was slow to alert other "departments". *(inverted item)*
X323	0.1624	1.7699	... a lot of informal "hall talk" in our firm concerned our competitors' tactics or strategies.
X232	0.2062	1.6695	... the activities of the different "departments" in our firm were well coordinated.
Responsiveness to Information			
	Path coeff.	**t-value**	**During the market entry phase...**
X137	0.4401	4.1353	... analysis and understanding of different market segments has led to new product development activities in our firm.
X235	0.3582	3.5391	...: Even if we had come up with a great marketing plan, we probably would not have been able to implement it in a timely fashion. *(inverted item)*
X113	0.3229	3.2483	... we quickly tested which markets and which customers were most appropriate for our product.
X331	0.2929	3.0735	...: When we found out that customers were unhappy with the quality of our service, we took corrective action immediately.
X332	0.2684	2.7532	... our business plans were driven more by technological advances than by market research. *(inverted item)*
X239	0.1793	1.7670	... it took us forever to decide how to respond to our competitors' price changes. *(inverted item)*
X333	0.1765	1.6822	... principles of market segmentation drove new product development efforts in our firm.
X335	0.1743	1.6758	... we were quick to respond to significant changes in our competitors' pricing structures.
alpha=16%, critical t-value of 1.397, df=139			

(Cohen, 1992). The underlying assumptions were n = 141 and an equal weighting of type I and type II error. In total, we eliminated 15 indicators that did not show a significant correlation with at least one of the performance constructs. However, in alignment with Diamantopoulos and Winklhofer's (2001) recommendation, we retained one item for conceptual reasons although it did not meet this criterion. This item captures whether business plans are technology- rather than market-driven, which we consider an essential facet of market orientation in emerging firms.

For further improvement the remaining 41 items were exposed to yet another validation approach, focusing on nomological aspects. Due to conceptual reasons a valid indicator should not only show a significantly positive correlation with at least one of the performance constructs, but one would also expect a significantly positive path coefficient with its corresponding behavioral construct (Diamantopoulos, & Winklhofer, 2001). In the first step, we tested whether any of the 41 items displayed a negative path coefficient, resulting in the removal of 8 items. As a second and final step, we tested the path coefficients for the remaining 33 items for significance. Here, we removed those 12 indicators with a non-significant path coefficient leaving us with a total of 21 items. Due to space limitations the detailed results for these analyses are not provided in this paper. They are available from the authors upon request. Figure 1 represents the 21 indicators – of the original 56 – which display at least one significantly positive correlation with a performance construct as well as a positive and significant path coefficient with one dimension of market-oriented behavior. 8 of these 21 items originate from MARKOR 20 (Kohli, Jaworski, & Kumar, 1993). Another 8 are part of the 12 additional items of the MARKOR 32-scale (Jaworski, & Kohli, 1993). The remaining 5 indicators come from the items that we developed as an integral part of this study in order to capture the particularities of market-oriented behavior in emerging firms.

EMPIRICAL RESULTS

Covariance- vs. Variance-based Techniques

As our behavioral constructs appear to be formative in nature the use of covariance-based techniques, such as LISREL or AMOS, is not recommended (Chin, 1998b). Issues such as "identification problems, the occurrence of implied covariances of zero among some measured variables, and the existence of equivalent models" (MacCallum, & Browne, 1993, p. 540) are likely to arise. Although these issues can be managed "[…] their resolution may involve altering the original model in terms of its substantive meaning or parsimony, or both" (MacCallum, & Browne, 1993, p. 540). Therefore, in the following we use PLS as a variance-based technique of structural equation modeling (Chin, 1998a; Wold, 1985).

Performance Effect Hypotheses

On the basis of the 21 reliable and valid items identified, we estimated path coefficients between constructs using PLS. All but 2 out of 8 path coefficients are significant as diagramed in Figure 3 (with alpha=16%, only significant paths shown, t-values provided in parentheses):

In the following, we interpret the results for each dimension:

Information generation: Path coefficients β_3 and β_4 indicate a positive and significant influence of information generation during the market entry phase on objective as well as subjective firm performance. Therefore, our hypothesis H_4 can be confirmed.

Information dissemination: For this dimension path coefficients β_5 (–0.177, t=1.3917) and β_6 (–0.096, t=.8268) are non-significant. Thus, direct influence of information dissemination on firm performance cannot be assumed. Accordingly, H_5 is not directly supported by our sample data which strengthens the critical views on the

Figure 3. Estimation of path coefficients

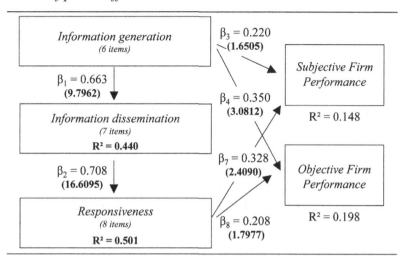

importance of dedicated activities to ensure information dissemination mentioned earlier. However, considering the role of this dimension within the inherent causality of market-oriented behavior that is shown by β_1 and β_2, it at least appears to have an indirect influence on firm performance.

Responsiveness: Here, path coefficients β_7 and β_8 indicate a positive and significant influence of responsiveness during the market entry phase on firm performance. Therefore, H_6 can be confirmed.

As mentioned, based on path coefficients β_1 and β_2, we can also confirm our first hypothesis H_1 claiming that Kohli and Jaworski's (1990) three dimensions of market-oriented behavior as well as their inherent causality also play an essential role in emerging firms.

Overall, the explanatory power of our model is comparatively strong showing an $R^2=0.148$ for subjective performance and an $R^2=0.198$ for objective performance. Thus, market-oriented behavior during the market entry phase is able to explain up to 20% in the variance of later firm performance. The R^2 values within the three behavioral constructs – which are 0.44 for information dissemination and 0.501 for responsiveness – moreover support the high level of appropriateness of our model for the sample studied.

Measurement Hypotheses

In order to evaluate our hypotheses regarding the measurement of market-oriented behavior – H_2: additional, emerging firm-specific items should be included, and H_3: market-oriented behavior in emerging firms should be measured using formative constructs – we compared our results to five alternative models applying different sets of items and measurement approaches to our sample data. The results are summarized in Figure 4:

In comparison, the newly developed index clearly demonstrates the highest level of nomological validity (cf. Bagozzi, 1979). Using only the MARKOR items and/or a reflective specification of the measurement model produces consistently lower values for construct reliability and validity. Moreover, the number of significant path coefficients turns out to be lower. Summarizing these findings, we conclude that adding additional items for capturing the specific nature of emerging firms as well as using a formative measurement model is more appropriate for measuring market-oriented behavior in this context. As a consequence, our hypotheses H_2 and H_3 can be confirmed

Figure 4. Comparison of alternative measurement approaches

	MARKOR 20	MARKOR 32	Index of 21 Items
Formative	R^2 *obj.* = **0.11** R^2 *subj.* = **0.11** # *sg. PC* = **5**	R^2 *obj.* = **0.17** R^2 *subj.* = **0.13** # *sg. PC* = **5**	R^2 *obj.* = **0.20** R^2 *subj.* = **0.15** # *sg. PC* = **6**
Reflective	R^2 *obj.* = **0.08** R^2 *subj.* = **0.06** # *sg. PC* = **3**	R^2 *obj.* = **0,11** R^2 *subj.* = **0,06** # *sg. PC* = **4**	R^2 *obj.* = **0.09** R^2 *subj.* = **0.05** # *sg. PC* = **5**

DISCUSSION

Considering the primarily qualitative nature of existing research on market orientation in young companies, the contribution of this study from a research perspective can be summarized as follows: Building on Kohli and Jaworski's (1990) original conceptualization as well as the MARKOR 20- and MARKOR 32-scales, we developed a formative index of market-oriented behavior that in the context of emerging firms demonstrates considerably stronger reliability and validity than existing measurement instruments. Apart from using a formative specification, this was achieved mainly by changing the focus of the measurement instrument. First of all, 5 additional items to account for behavior specific to emerging firms were included. These will be discussed in more detail below. Moreover, we eliminated 12 of the MARKOR 20-items capturing types of behavior that mainly require the existence of formalized structures and processes and thus can typically be found in established organizations. In contrast, only 4 of the 12 additional items originating from MARKOR 32 were removed. This supports our assumption stated earlier that considering the data

used for the development of MARKOR 32, the scale is more appropriate in the context of young firms than MARKOR 20.

The strong influence of market-oriented behavior in the market-entry phase on firm performance shown in this study clearly indicates also the practical relevance of our results. Two main implications for emerging firms can be derived: First, the formative nature of behavioral constructs suggests that there is no single consistent pattern of market-oriented behavior contributing to company success. Rather, founders of emerging firms should pursue an individual way of market-oriented behavior that seems most appropriate considering the company-specific liabilities. This also provides an important insight into the nature of entrepreneurial marketing in general and on how it differs from traditional marketing in established firms. Second, the 5 non-MARKOR items that are part of the index emphasize the particular importance of the following activities in order to differentiate successful from non-successful emerging firms:

Actively gathering information on competitive advantage: In terms of information generation actively gathering information on the competitive advantage of the product or service offered appears to be critical as a response to the liability of newness. This supports the assumption often stated in the literature that emerging firms tend to focus primarily on their product or its underlying technology while neglecting market aspects.

Institutionalizing the marketing function: For ensuring sufficient dissemination of market-related information, an emerging firm should designate a specific person to be responsible for the marketing activities. This early institutionalization of the marketing function proves to be an essential basis for future expansion, thus being an appropriate response to the liability of growth.

Developing and implementing an explicit marketing plan: Another central element of information dissemination activities seems to be the development of an explicit marketing plan. This emphasizes the importance also of an early implementation of formalized market-related processes in emerging firms. Similar to the institutionalization of the marketing function, a marketing plan potentially contributes to reducing owner dominance and owner dependence.

Starting market-driven new product development initiatives: In terms of responsiveness to information, systematically using one's knowledge about market segments – rather than about technology – to start new product development initiatives also shows strong influence on performance. This appears to be an adequate approach to reduce the uncertainty faced by the emerging firm.

Applying trial and error methods for testing product-market-combinations: As another response to the liability of uncertainty, early testing of which markets and which customers are most appropriate for the product or service offered is likely to enhance chances for company success. Herewith, another important differentiator between established firms in a stable environment on the one hand and emerging firms on the other that is often mentioned in the literature can be confirmed on the basis of our results.

FUTURE RESEARCH DIRECTIONS

From a methodological perspective, it has to be pointed out that neither the treatment of formative constructs nor the process of index development have been studied with the same intensity and rigor as the corresponding procedures for reflective constructs (Diamantopoulos & Winklhofer, 2001). Moreover, the measurement instrument has only been applied to one sample of emerging firms all based in one country. However, our findings prove to be stable also for two alternative datasets – one generated in Germany and another one in Thailand. The results are available from the authors upon request. Also, the study focuses on market-oriented behavior during a specific stage in company development, thus further limiting the possibility of generalizing our findings.

These limitations suggest the following avenues for further research: Thus far, research on market orientation in young firms has been predominantly qualitative in nature. More research on the development of appropriate measurement instruments applying rigorous procedures is needed, as it will likely lead to a better understanding of market-oriented behavior in young companies. A first step would certainly be to broaden the basis for empirical evidence of the constructs and items derived in this study – also in an international context. Moreover, future research should incorporate possible advances in the treatment of formative constructs. Once widely accepted behavioral constructs have been established, this will enable research on the antecedents of market orientation in emerging firms, e.g. the role of organizational culture or values (Homburg, & Pflesser, 2000 for established companies). This would be yet another important step in the research on market-oriented behavior in emerging firms and in young companies in general.

REFERENCES

Aldrich, H. E., & Auster, E. R. (1986). Even Dwarfs Started Small - Liabilities of Age and Size and Their Strategic Implications. In L.L. Cummings & B.M. Staw (Eds.), *Research in Organizational Behavior* (pp. 165-189). San Francisco, CA.

Armstrong, J. S., & Overton, T. S. (1977). Estimating Non-Response Bias in Mail Surveys. *JMR, Journal of Marketing Research, 14*(3), 396–402. doi:10.2307/3150783

Bagozzi, R. P. (1979). The Role of Measurement in Theory Construction and Hypothesis Testing - Toward a Holistic Model. In O.C. Ferrell, S.W. Brown & C.W. Lamb (Eds.), *Conceptual and Theoretical Developments in Marketing* (pp. 15-32). Chicago.

Bhide, A. (2000). *The Origin and Evolution of New Business*. New York: Oxford University Press.

Bollen, K. A. (1989). *Structural Equations with Latent Variables*. New York: Wiley & Sons.

Bollen, K. A., & Lennox, R. (1991). Conventional Wisdom on Measurement - A Structural Equation Perspective. *Psychological Bulletin, 110*(2), 305–314. doi:10.1037/0033-2909.110.2.305

Bollen, K. A., & Ting, K.-F. (1993). Confirmatory Tetrad Analysis. In P. Marsden (Eds.), *Sociological Methodology* (pp. 147-175). Washington, DC: Wiley-Blackwell.

Brüderl, J., & Schüssler, R. (1990). Organizational Mortality - The Liabilities of Newness and Adolescence. *Administrative Science Quarterly, 35*(3), 530–547. doi:10.2307/2393316

Carmines, E. G., & Zeller, R. A. (1979). *Reliability and Validity Assessment*. Beverly Hills, CA: Sage.

Chin, W. W. (1998a). Commentary - Issues and Opinion on Structural Equation Modeling. *MIS Quarterly, 22*(1), 7–16.

Chin, W. W. (1998b). The Partial Least Squares Approach to Structural Equation Modeling. In G.A. Marcoulides (Eds.), *Modern Methods for Business Research* (pp. 295-336). Mahwah, NJ: Lawrence Erlbaum Associates.

Churchill, G. A. (1979). A Paradigm for Developing Better Measures of Marketing Constructs. *JMR, Journal of Marketing Research, 16*(1), 64–73. doi:10.2307/3150876

Churchill, N. C., & Lewis, V. L. (1983). The Five Stages of Small Business Growth. *Harvard Business Review, 61*(3), 30–50.

Cohen, J. (1992). A Power Primer. *Psychological Bulletin, 112*(1), 155–160. doi:10.1037/0033-2909.112.1.155

Cronbach, L. J. (1951). Coefficient Alpha and the Internal Structure of Tests. *Psychometrika, 16*, 297–334. doi:10.1007/BF02310555

Deng, S., & Dart, J. (1994). Measuring Market Orientation - A Multi-Factor, Multi-Item Approach. *Journal of Marketing Management, 10*(8), 725–742.

Dennis, W. J. (2003). Raising Response Rates in Mail Surveys of Small Business Owners: Results of an Experiment. *Journal of Small Business Management, 41*(3), 278–295. doi:10.1111/1540-627X.00082

Deshpandé, R., Farley, J. U., & Webster, F. E. (1992). Corporate Culture, Customer Orientation and Innovativeness in Japanese Firms. In *MSI Report, Nr. 92- 100*. Cambridge, MA: Marketing Science Institute.

Diamantopoulos, A., & Winklhofer, H. M. (2001). Index Construction with Formative Indicators - An Alternative to Scale Development. *JMR, Journal of Marketing Research, 38*(2), 269–277. doi:10.1509/jmkr.38.2.269.18845

Drucker, P. F. (1954). *The Practice of Management*. New York: Harper & Row.

Fischer, E., & Reuber, A. R. (1995). The Importance of Market Orientation for Emergent Firms. In W.D. Bygrave et al. (Eds.), *Frontiers of Entrepreneurship Research - Proceedings of the Fifteenth Annual Entrepreneurship Research Conference* (pp. 90-104).

Fornell, C., & Larcker, D. F. (1981). Evaluating Structural Equation Models With Unobservable Variables and Measurement Error. *JMR, Journal of Marketing Research, 18*(1), 39–50. doi:10.2307/3151312

George, G., & Zahra, S. A. (2002). Being Entrepreneurial and Being Market-Driven - Exploring the Interaction Effects of Entrepreneurial and Market Orientation on Firm Performance. *Frontiers of Entrepreneurship Research*, 255-266.

Geursen, G. M. (2000). The Market And Entrepreneur Led Firms: A Model For Achieving Customer Relevance. In G.E. Hills, W. Siu, & D. Malewicki (Eds.), *Research at the Marketing/ Entrepreneurship Interface - Proceedings of the UIC Symposium on Marketing and Entrepreneurship* (pp. 33-56).

Geursen, G. M., & Conduit, J. L. (2002). Entrepreneurial, Market Relevant Strategies of Small and Large Firms. In G.E. Hills, D.J. Hansen, & B. Merrilees (Eds.), *Research at the Marketing/ Entrepreneurship Interface - Proceedings of the UIC Symposium on Marketing and Entrepreneurship* (pp. 15-41).

Gibson, B. (2002). Methodological Individualism as the Economic Core of the Small Firm Marketing Interface. In G.E. Hills, D.J. Hansen, & B. Merrilees (Eds.), *Research at the Marketing/ Entrepreneurship Interface - Proceedings of the UIC Symposium on Marketing and Entrepreneurship* (pp. 2-14).

Gilmore, A., & Carson, D. (2000). SME Marketing By Networking. In G.E. Hills, W. Siu, & D. Malewicki (Eds.), *Research at the Marketing/ Entrepreneurship Interface - Proceedings of the UIC Symposium on Marketing and Entrepreneurship* (pp. 192-200).

Grether, M. (2003). *Marktorientierung durch das Internet - Ein Wissenorientierter Ansatz für Unternehmen.* Mannheim, Germany: DUV.

Grupp, H., & Legler, H. (2000). *Hochtechnologie 2000 - Neudefinition der Hochtechnologie für die Berichterstattung zur technologischen Leistungsfähigkeit Deutschlands.* Karlsruhe/Hannover: Frauenhofer-Institut für Systemtechnik und Innovationsforschung, Niedersächsiches Institut für Wirtschaftsforschung.

Hills, G. E., & LaForge, R. W. (1992). Research at the Marketing Interface to Advance Entrepreneurship Theory. *Entrepreneurship Theory and Practice, 16*(3), 33–59.

Homburg, C., & Pflesser, C. (2000). A Multiple-Layer Model of Market-Oriented Organizational Culture: Measurement Issues and Performance Outcomes. *JMR, Journal of Marketing Research, 37*(4), 449–462. doi:10.1509/ jmkr.37.4.449.18786

Jarvis, C. B., MacKenzie, S. C., & Podsakoff, P. M. (2003). A Critical Review of Construct Indicators and Measurement Model Misspecification in Marketing and Consumer Research. *The Journal of Consumer Research, 30*(2), 199–218. doi:10.1086/376806

Jaworski, B. J., & Kohli, A. K. (1993). Market Orientation - Antecedents and Consequences. *Journal of Marketing, 57*(3), 53–70. doi:10.2307/1251854

Jaworski, B. J., & Kohli, A. K. (1996). Market Orientation - Review, Refinement, and Roadmap. *Journal of Market-Focused Management, 1*(2), 119–135. doi:10.1007/BF00128686

Kazanjian, R. K. (1988). Relation of Dominant Problems to Stages of Growth in Technology-Based New Ventures. *Academy of Management Journal, 31*(2), 257–279. doi:10.2307/256548

Kazanjian, R. K., & Drazin, R. (1990). A Stage-Contingent Model of Design and Growth for Technology-Based New Ventures. *Journal of Business Venturing, 5*(3), 137–150. doi:10.1016/0883-9026(90)90028-R

Kirzner, I. M. (1973). *Competition and Entrepreneurship*. Chicago: University of Chicago Press.

Kohli, A. K., & Jaworski, B. J. (1990). Market Orientation - The Construct, Research Propositions, and Managerial Implications. *Journal of Marketing, 54*(2), 1–18. doi:10.2307/1251866

Kohli, A. K., Jaworski, B. J., & Kumar, A. (1993). Markor - A Measure of Market Orientation. *JMR, Journal of Marketing Research, 30*(4), 467–477. doi:10.2307/3172691

MacCallum, R. C., & Browne, M. W. (1993). The Use of Causal Indicators in Covariance Structure Models - Some Practical Issues. *Psychological Bulletin, 114*(3), 533–541. doi:10.1037/0033-2909.114.3.533

Moore, G. A. (1995). *Inside the Tornado: Marketing Strategies from Silicon Valley's Cutting Edge*. New York: Harper Business.

Muzyka, D. F., & Hills, G. E. (1993). Introduction. In G.E. Hills, R.W. LaForge, & D.F. Muzyka (Eds.), *Research at the Marketing/Entrepreneurship Interface - Proceedings of the UIC Symposium on Marketing and Entrepreneurship* (pp. VII-XV).

Narver, J. C., & Slater, S. F. (1990). The Effect of Market Orientation on Business Profitability. *Journal of Marketing, 54*(4), 20–35. doi:10.2307/1251757

Noble, C. H., Rajiv, K. S., & Kumar, A. (2002). Market Orientation and Alternative Strategic Orientations: A Longitudinal Assessment of Performance Implications. *Journal of Marketing, 66*(4), 25–39. doi:10.1509/jmkg.66.4.25.18513

Nunnally, J. C. (1978). *Psychometric Theory*. New York: McGraw-Hill.

Oxenfeldt, A. R., & Moore, W. L. (1978). Customer or Competitor - Which Guideline for Marketing? *Management Review, 67*(8), 43–48.

Pelham, A. M. (1997). Mediating Influences on the Relationship Between Market Orientation and Profitability in Small Industrial Firms. *Journal of Marketing Theory and Practice, 5*(3), 55–76.

Pelham, A. M. (1999). Influence of Environment, Strategy, and Market Orientation on Performance in Small Manufacturing Firms. *Journal of Business Research, 45*(1), 33–46. doi:10.1016/S0148-2963(98)00026-5

Pelham, A. M., & Wilson, D. T. (1996). A Longitudinal Study of the Impact of Market Structure, Firm Structure, Strategy and Market Orientation Culture on Dimensions of Small-Firm Performance. *Journal of the Academy of Marketing Science, 24*(1), 27–43. doi:10.1007/BF02893935

Roberts, E. B. (1991). *Entrepreneurs in High-Technology - Lessons from MIT and Beyond*. New York: Oxford University Press.

Shane, S., & Stuart, T. (2002). Organizational Endowments and the Performance of University Start-ups. *Management Science, 48*(1), 154–170. doi:10.1287/mnsc.48.1.154.14280

Shapiro, B. P. (1988). What the Hell is "Market Oriented"? *Harvard Business Review, 66*(6), 119–125.

Sinkula, J. M. (1994). Market Information Processing and Organizational Learning. *Journal of Marketing, 58*(1), 35–45. doi:10.2307/1252249

Starr, J. A., & MacMillan, I. C. (1990). Resource Cooptation and Social Contracting - Resource Acquisition Strategies for New Ventures. *Strategic Management Journal, 11*(4), 79–92.

Stinchcombe, A. L. (1965). Social Structure and Organizations. In J.G. March (Ed.), *Handbook of Organizations* (pp. 153-193).

Stokes, D. (2000). Putting Entrepreneurship into Marketing: The Processes of Entrepreneurial Marketing. *Journal of Research in Marketing & Entrepreneurship, 2*(1), 1–16.

Storey, D. J. (1994). *Understanding the Small Business Sector*. London: Routledge.

Timmons, J. A. (1994). *New Venture Creation - Entrepreneurship for the 21st Century*. Burr Ridge, IL: McGraw-Hill.

Tushman, M. L., & Anderson, P. A. (1986). Technological Discontinuities and Organizational Environment. *Administrative Science Quarterly, 31*(3), 439–465. doi:10.2307/2392832

Webster, F. E. (1988). Rediscovering the Marketing Concept. In *MSI Report, Nr. 88-100*. Cambridge, MA: Marketing Science Institute.

Wickham, P. (2001). *Strategic Entrepreneurship - A Decision Making Approach to New Venture Creation & Management*. Englewood Cliffs, NJ: Prentice Hall.

Wold, H. O. (1985). Partial Least Squares. In S. Kotz & N.L. Johnson (Eds.), *Encyclopedia of Statistical Sciences* (pp. 581-591). New York: Wiley&Sons.

ADDITIONAL READING

Brettel, M., Claas, S., & Heinemann, F. (2006). Management, Market Orientation, and Performance in Entrepreneurial Firms. K. Weaver (Ed.), *Academy of Management - Best Paper Conference Paper*, Atlanta 2006.

Brettel, M., Engelen, A., & Heinemann, F. (2009). Der Einfluss nationaler Kultur auf Stellhebel und Wirkung der Marktorientierung in deutschen und thailändischen jungen Unternehmen. *Zeitschrift für Betriebswirtschaft, 79*(1), 59–92. doi:10.1007/s11573-009-0011-0

Brettel, M., Engelen, A., Heinemann, F., & Kessell, A. (2008a). Marktorientierte Unternehmenskultur als Erfolgsfaktor in jungen Wachstumsunternehmen. *Zeitschrift für Betriebswirtschaft, 78*(11), 1197–1220. doi:10.1007/s11573-008-0100-5

Brettel, M., Engelen, A., Heinemann, F., & Vadhanasindhu, P. (2008b). Antecedents of Market Orientation: A Cross-Cultural Comparison. *Journal of International Marketing, 16*(2), 84–119. doi:10.1509/jimk.16.2.84

Engelen, A. (2007). *Marktorientierung junger Unternehmen: Einflussgrößen und Wirkung im interkulturellen Vergleich zwischen Deutschland, Thailand und Indonesien*. Paper presented at Wiesbaden 2007.

Engelen, A., Heinemann, F., & Brettel, M. (2009). Cross-cultural entrepreneurship research: Current status and framework for future studies. *Journal of International Entrepreneurship, 7*(3). doi:10.1007/s10843-008-0035-5

Felix, R., & Hinck, W. (2005). Executive Insights: Market Orientation of Mexican Companies. *Journal of International Marketing, 13*(1), 111–127. doi:10.1509/jimk.13.1.111.58537

Grinstein, A. (2008). The effect of market orientation and its components on innovation consequences: a meta-analysis. *Journal of the Academy of Marketing Science, 36*(2), 166–173. doi:10.1007/s11747-007-0053-1

Hills, H., Hultman, C., & Miles, M. (2008). The Evolution and Development of Entrepreneurial Marketing. *Journal of Small Business Management, 46*(1), 99–112. doi:10.1111/j.1540-627X.2007.00234.x

Homburg, C. (2007). Betriebswirtschaftslehre als empirische Wissenschaft - Bestandsaufnahme und Empfehlungen. Zeitschrift für betriebswirtschaftliche . *Forschung, 56,* 27–60.

Homburg, C., & Hildebrandt, L. (1998). Die Kausalanalyse: Bestandsaufnahme, Entwicklungsrichtungen, Problemfelder. Hildebrandt, L., Homburg, C. (Eds.). Die Kausalanalyse: Instrument der empirischen betriebswirtschaftlichen Forschung, Stuttgart 1998, 15-48.

Homburg, C., Workman, J., & Krohmer, H. (1999). Marketing's Influence Within the Firm. *Journal of Marketing, 63*(2), 1–17. doi:10.2307/1251942

Kara, A., Spillan, J., & DeShields, O. (2005). The Effect of a Market Orientation on Business Performance: A Study of Small-Sized Service Retailers Using MARKOR Scale. *Journal of Small Business Management, 43*(2), 105–118.

Kessell, A. (2007). Marktorientierte Unternehmenskultur als Erfolgsfaktor junger Unternehmen: Kontextspezifische Konzeption und Empirische Untersuchung, Wiesbaden 2007.

Ketchen, D. J. Jr, Hult, G. T. M., & Slater, S. F. (2007). Toward greater understanding of market orientation and the resource-based view. *Strategic Management Journal, 28*(9), 961–964. doi:10.1002/smj.620

Kirca, A., Jayachandran, S., & Bearden, W. (2005). Market Orientation: A Meta-Analytic Review and Assessment of Its Antecedents and Impact on Performance. *Journal of Marketing, 69*(2), 24–41. doi:10.1509/jmkg.69.2.24.60761

Laforet, S. (2008). Size, strategic, and market orientation affects on innovation. *Journal of Business Research, 61*(7), 753–764. doi:10.1016/j.jbusres.2007.08.002

Li, Y., Yong Feng, S., & Liu, Y. (2006). An empirical study of SOEs' market orientation in transitional China. *Asia Pacific Journal of Management, 23,* 93–113. doi:10.1007/s10490-006-6117-9

Menguc, B., & Auh, S. (2008). Conflict, leadership, and market orientation. *International Journal of Research in Marketing, 25*(1), 34–45. doi:10.1016/j.ijresmar.2007.08.001

Narver, J., Slater, S., & MacLachlan, D. (2004). Responsive and Proactive Market Orientation and New-Product Success. *Journal of Product Innovation Management, 21*(5), 334–347. doi:10.1111/j.0737-6782.2004.00086.x

Narver, J., Slater, S., & Tietje, B. (1998). Creating a Market Orientation. *Journal of Market-Focused Management, 2*(3), 241–255. doi:10.1023/A:1009703717144

Powpaka, S. (2006). How Market Orientation Affects Female Service Employees in Thailand. *Journal of Business Research, 59*(1), 54–61. doi:10.1016/j.jbusres.2005.03.004

Roskos, S. (2005). *The Influence of Entrepreneurial and Market Orientation on the Degree of Innovation and Success of New Venture in Technology-Oriented Industries.* Paper presented at Lohmar 2005.

Siguaw, J. A., Simpson, P. M., & Enz, C. A. (2006). Conceptualizing Innovation Orientation: A Framework for Study and Integration of Innovation Research. *Journal of Product Innovation Management, 23*(6), 556–574. doi:10.1111/j.1540-5885.2006.00224.x

Simpson, P. M., Siguaw, J. A., & Enz, C. A. (2006). Innovation orientation outcomes: The good and the bad. *Journal of Business Research, 59*(10-11), 1133–1141. doi:10.1016/j.jbusres.2006.08.001

Siu, W., & Kirby, D. (1998). Approaches to Small Firm Marketing - A Critique. *European Journal of Marketing, 32*(1-2), 40–60. doi:10.1108/03090569810197417

Slater, S., & Narver, J. (1994). Market Orientation, Customer Value, and Superior Performance. *Business Horizons, 37*(2), 22–28. doi:10.1016/0007-6813(94)90029-9

Slater, S., & Narver, J. (1998). Customer-Led and Market-Oriented: Let's not Confuse the Two. *Strategic Management Journal*, *19*(10), 1001–1006. doi:10.1002/(SICI)1097-0266(199810)19:10<1001::AID-SMJ996>3.0.CO;2-4

Slater, S., & Narver, J. (1999). Market-Oriented Is More than Being Customer-Led. *Strategic Management Journal*, *20*, 1165–1168. doi:10.1002/(SICI)1097-0266(199912)20:12<1165::AID-SMJ73>3.0.CO;2-#

Smith, J. (1998). Strategies for Start-Ups. *Long Range Planning*, *31*(6), 857–872. doi:10.1016/S0024-6301(98)80022-8

Song, M., Di Benedetto, C. A., & Mason, R. W. (2007). Capabilities and financial performance: the moderating effect of strategic type. *Journal of the Academy of Marketing Science*, *35*(1), 18–34. doi:10.1007/s11747-006-0005-1

Verhoef, P. C., & Leeflang, P. S. H. (2009). Understanding the Marketing Department's Influence Within the Firm. *Journal of Marketing*, *73*(2), 14–37. doi:10.1509/jmkg.73.2.14

APPENDIX A – ITEMS MEASURING INFORMATION GENERATION

Table 2.

	Indicator	Source	Perf. correlation		Significance level		
	(Text)		Objective	Subjective	Objective	Subjective	
X111	... we gathered information on how potential customers used comparable products.	additional item	0.11	−0.01	0.21	0.89	n.s.
X112	... we spent a lot of time in direct contact with our customers to listen to their suggestions for our product.	additional item	0.12	−0.05	0.19	0.58	n.s.
X113	... we quickly tested which markets and which customers were most appropriate for our product.	additional item	0.27	0.12	0.00	0.15	
X114	... we gathered information on what is our competitive advantage.	additional item	0.30	0.12	0.00	0.16	
X115	... we used our personal contacts (other entrepreneurs, investors/business angels, consultants, commercial banks etc.) to gather market-related information.	additional item	0.23	0.00	0.01	0.96	
X116	.... we developed our product to the final stage before we first asked a potential customer for his opinion. *(inverted item)*	additional item	0.05	0.01	0.62	0.87	n.s.
X117	... we asked our most innovative customers to test our product intensively.	additional item	0.18	0.05	0.05	0.60	
X118	... we used our personal contacts with business partners to find out more about our competitors.	additional item	0.13	0.19	0.16	0.02	
X119	... we monitored our competitors to develop a better understanding of their behavior.	additional item	0.09	0.14	0.33	0.11	
X211	... we met with customers at least once a year to find out what products or services they would need in the future.	Markor 20	0.17	0.17	0.06	0.05	
X212	... we polled end users at least once a year to asses the quality of our products and services.	Markor 20	0.11	0.05	0.23	0.54	n.s.
X213	... we did a lot of in-house market research.	Markor 20	0.31	0.20	0.00	0.02	
X214	... we were slow to detect changes in our customers' product preferences. *(inverted item)*	Markor 20	0.00	0.18	0.98	0.04	
X215	... we were slow to detect fundamental shifts in our industry (e.g. competition, technology, regulation). *(inverted item)*	Markor 20	0.00	0.20	0.97	0.02	
X216	... we periodically reviewed the likely effect of changes in our business environment (e.g. regulation) on customers.	Markor 20	0.10	0.00	0.25	0.98	n.s.
X311	... individuals from our "manufacturing department" interacted directly with customers to learn how to serve them better.	Markor 32	0.12	0.15	0.20	0.08	
X312	... we often talked with or surveyed those who can influence our end users' purchases (e.g., retailers, distributors).	Markor 32	0.24	0.09	0.01	0.30	
X313	... we collected industry information by informal means (e.g. lunch with industry friends, talks with trade partners).	Markor 32	0.29	0.25	0.00	0.00	
X314	... intelligence on our competitors was generated independently by several departments.	Markor 32	0.12	0.04	0.19	0.67	n.s.

n.s.: item which is non-significant with alpha = 16% was eliminated

APPENDIX B – ITEMS MEASURING INFORMATION DISSEMINATION

Table 3.

	Indicator (Text)	Source	Perf. correlation		Significance Level		
			Objective	Subjective	Objective	Subjective	
X121	… information about our customers was passed on to our most important employees.	additional item	0.18	0.08	0.04	0.35	
X122	… nobody in our firm felt responsible for gathering market- and customer-related information. *(inverted item)*	additional item	0.09	0.19	0.34	0.02	
X123	… product ideas from customers were rarely passed on to our most important employees. *(inverted item)*	additional item	0.03	0.14	0.76	0.10	
X124	… the marketing of our product was a regular topic in meetings with our most important employees.	additional item	0.23	−0.01	0.01	0.90	
X125	… we had spontaneous meetings in order to discuss market trends and developments.	additional item	0.22	0.02	0.02	0.82	
X126	… we developed a marketing plan for our firm.	additional item	0.25	0.07	0.00	0.39	
X127	… we had regular and spontaneous meetings to discuss customer satisfaction issues.	additional item	0.12	0.07	0.19	0.44	n.s.
X221	… we had interdepartmental meetings at least once a quarter to discuss market trends and developments.	Markor 20	0.20	0.15	0.03	0.09	
X222	… marketing personnel in our firm spent time discussing customers' future needs with other functional departments.	Markor 20	0.27	0.09	0.00	0.32	
X223	…: When something important happened to a major customer of market, the whole business unit knew about it within a short period.	Markor 20	0.05	0.08	0.57	0.39	n.s.
X224	… data on customer satisfaction were disseminated at all levels in this business unit on a regular basis.	Markor 20	0.13	0.10	0.16	0.25	
X225	…: When one department found out something important about competitors, it was slow to alert other departments. *(inverted item)*	Markor 20	0.03	0.20	0.71	0.02	
X321	… there was minimal communication between marketing and manufacturing departments concerning market developments. *(inverted item)*	Markor 32	0.05	0.17	0.56	0.05	
X322	… our firm periodically circulated documents (e.g. reports, newsletters) that provided information on our customers.	Markor 32	0.28	0.00	0.00	0.96	
X323	… a lot of informal "hall talk" in our firm concerned our competitors' tactics or strategies.	Markor 32	0.15	0.03	0.11	0.70	
n.s.: item which is non-significant with alpha = 16% was eliminated							

APPENDIX C – ITEMS MEASURING RESPONSIVENESS
Table 4.

| | Indicator | Source | Perf. Correlation | | Significance level | | |
	(Text)		Objective	Subjective	Objective	Subjective	
X131	… we actively supported referrals of our product to new customers by word of mouth.	additional item	–0.01	0.10	0.94	0.26	n.s.
X132	… we paid a lot of attention to the satisfaction of our customers so that they referred us to others.	additional item	–0.05	0.17	0.61	0.05	
X133	… we focused on those customers where we could offer a relevant product advantage over our competitors	additional item	0.03	–0.06	0.73	0.46	n.s.
X134	… based on customer feedback we developed and improved our product on a continuous basis.	additional item	0.26	0.12	0.00	0.19	
X135	… we were not always able to react quickly and pragmatically on customer complaints. *(inverted item)*	additional item	0.03	0.08	0.75	0.36	n.s.
X136	… we were not able to implement our marketing plan as outlined. *(inverted item)*	additional item	–0.05	0.29	0.57	0.00	
X137	… analysis and understanding of different market segments has led to new product development activities in our firm.	additional item	0.18	0.21	0.05	0.02	
X138	… we reacted quickly on new information about products of our competitors.	additional item	0.13	0.20	0.14	0.02	
X231	… several "departments" of our firm got together periodically to plan a response to changes taking place in our business environment.	Markor 20	0.17	0.08	0.07	0.36	
X232	… the activities of the different "departments" in our firm were well coordinated.	Markor 20	0.09	0.19	0.35	0.03	
X233	… customer complaints fell on deaf ears in our firm. *(inverted item)*	Markor 20	0.02	–0.05	0.78	0.55	n.s.
X234	…: When we found that customers would have liked us to modify a product or service, the "departments" involved made concerted efforts to do so.	Markor 20	0.12	–0.10	0.17	0.27	n.s.
X235	…: Even if we had come up with a great marketing plan, we probably would not have been able to implement it in a timely fashion. *(inverted item)*	Markor 20	0.18	0.27	0.05	0.00	
X236	…: If a major competitor had launched an intensive campaign targeted at our customers, we would have implemented a response immediately.	Markor 20	0.09	0.07	0.32	0.43	n.s.
X237	… we periodically reviewed our product development efforts to ensure that they are in line with what customers want.	Markor 20	0.22	0.21	0.02	0.02	
X238	… for one reason or another we tended to ignore changes in our customer's product or service needs. *(inverted item)*	Markor 20	0.04	0.03	0.66	0.69	n.s.
X239	… it took us forever to decide how to respond to our competitors' price changes. *(inverted item)*	Markor 20	0.14	0.21	0.13	0.01	
X331	…: When we found out that customers were unhappy with the quality of our service, we took corrective action immediately.	Markor 32	0.18	0.09	0.05	0.29	
X332	… our business plans were driven more by technological advances than by market research. *(inverted item)*	Markor 32	0.03	0.12	0.71	0.18	n.s. **

continued on following page

Table 4. continued

	Indicator	Source	Perf. Correlation		Significance level		
	(Text)		Objective	Subjective	Objective	Subjective	
X333	... principles of market segmentation drove new product development efforts in our firm.	Markor 32	0.27	0.03	0.00	0.78	
X334	... the product line we sold depended more on internal politics than real market needs. *(inverted item)*	Markor 32	0.07	0.17	0.42	0.05	
X335	... we were quick to respond to significant changes in our competitors' pricing structures.	Markor 32	0.11	0.20	0.25	0.02	
n.s.: item which is non-significant with alpha = 16% was eliminated							
** despite non-significance item was retained for conceptual reasons							

Chapter 4

Crossing Borders:
Overcoming Political Barriers to Technology–Led Economic Development

Nicholas Maynard
RAND Corporation, Arlington, USA

Aaron McKethan
Brookings Institute, Washington, DC, USA

Michael I. Luger
Manchester Business School, University of Manchester, Manchaster, UK

Alekhya Uppalapati
Kenan-Flagler Business School, The University of North Carolina at Chapel Hill, Chapel Hill, USA

ABSTRACT

In the United States, many chronically depressed counties are adjacent to their state's border. This article explores how some non-urban counties that are contiguous but located in different states have worked with their state governments to develop institutional mechanisms to overcome the artificial barrier to technology-based economic development that state borders create. The story the authors tell can apply both to other countries that are also divided into states and to smaller countries within a federated region (such as the member states of the EU). The authors argue that political boundaries that transect otherwise integrated economic regions often impede economic development coordination and cooperation, in general, and for technology access, workforce training, and business innovation in particular. The authors use case study evidence from several successful cross-border efforts in the United States and internationally to demonstrate the critical success factors required to overcome political boundaries and initiate technology-based development. These success factors include the creation of diverse funding sources, effective leadership by a coordinated team, and the development of formal legal entities to confront legal and infrastructure challenges.

DOI: 10.4018/978-1-61520-597-4.ch004

INTRODUCTION

"Core-periphery" disparities have long been used to characterize spatial development in many regions of the world. Central place theory (Christaller, 1933) posited that centralization is a natural process that characterizes human settlements. The very geography of a circle makes distances between points at the outer boundary farther apart than points toward the center. That makes agglomeration (critical mass) harder to achieve at the periphery, and reinforces the center as the hub for transportation and other networks.

Many political jurisdictions have made the center more important by placing capitols, universities, and other public facilities in the center. While there is often economic, political, and social activity across state lines, economic development at the border has been inhibited to some extent by specific laws, policies, and/or customs. The historical practice of inter-jurisdictional competition for business locations, research and development facilities, federal funding, and other benefits has reduced the impetus for jurisdictions at the border (and elsewhere) to work together. Another key barrier to cross-border cooperation is the tendency for infrastructure and public service delivery areas to be defined functionally within state borders, rather than across them (Wood, 1961; Hawkins, 1976).

Because of these forces, many non-urban border regions (including suburban, rural, and remote areas) around the world still struggle today to keep pace with more developed central places. Border regions tend to lack the skilled workforce, infrastructure, and advanced technology required to compete in an economy where cheap land and proximity to resources once may have been sufficient to sustain a viable economic base (Cooke, 1997). Some sub-national governments in peripheral regions have addressed the problem of scale ineconomies and scant resources by developing means to cross borders, creating greater critical mass, and lessening destructive competition be-

tween neighboring jurisdictions. However, for the most part, such cooperation is the exception, not the rule (McDowell, 1995).

Of course, not all border or peripheral regions suffer economically. Seaports, by definition, are on the borders of their political jurisdictions, so cities like San Diego, Los Angeles, Seattle, Miami, Houston, and New York have thrived. Similarly, rivers and lakes often are used as political boundaries, so such cities as Chicago, St. Louis, and Philadelphia have achieved critical mass.

But, as figure 1 illustrates, many states in the U.S. appear to have border-periphery disparities. Many (but not all) border regions in New York, Pennsylvania, Virginia, North and South Carolina, Georgia, Arkansas, Mississippi, Texas, the four corners states, and elsewhere, are among the poorest in terms of per capita income. Similar patterns characterize the distribution of unemployment and poverty rates, educational attainment, and health conditions.

This article highlights the development challenges faced by non-urban border regions and identifies strategies developed by local leaders that have mitigated the economic consequences associated with being a border region. Specifically, we address the following research questions:

- What unmet needs in case study regions are now being satisfied by a cross-border economic development program or strategy?
- What are the common hurdles to executing a successful cross-border initiative in the case study regions?
- What are the critical success factors of existing programs of cross-border economic and technological development?

The particular challenges facing non-urban border jurisdictions raise questions about the nature of cross-border economic activity and the appropriate public policies that can meet the unique needs and challenges of those border places. Since the challenges facing border counties are common

Figure 1. US per capita income by county. (Source: Bureau of Economic Analysis, 2003)

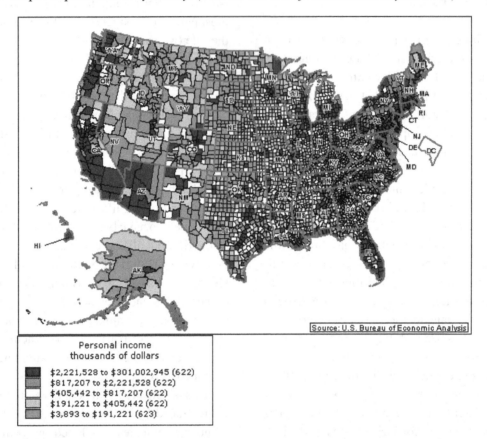

Personal income
thousands of dollars

$2,221,528 to $301,002,945 (622)
$817,207 to $2,221,528 (622)
$405,442 to $817,207 (622)
$191,221 to $405,442 (622)
$3,893 to $191,221 (623)

to many states and regions, the ability to identify critical success factors for cross-border collaboration and engagement could serve as a template for successful strategies and policies.

As we address these questions, we will assess three particular factors that we think are likely to influence the degree of success in cross border technology development programs: presence and maintenance of formalized organizational structure, funding mechanisms, and leadership. The latter two factors – funding issues and leadership - are intrinsically important to the success of economic development and other related initiatives. However, we expect to find that the first of the three factors – organizational structure and development – play a particular key role in the formalization and maintenance of efforts to facilitate and expand cross-border collaboration and technology development.

The next section (section two) provides a brief review of the academic and policy literature on the drivers for existing cross-border initiatives (CBIs), including technology programs, and a conceptual framework for technology-focused CBIs. In section three, we outline the research methodology used for this article. Section four includes an overview of our primary research findings. Section five follows to describe the critical success factors of these cross-border initiatives. The final section summarizes our findings and provides policy recommendations.

BACKGROUND

There is not abundant literature on this specific topic. The pertinent literature focuses on the existence and definition of border (periphery) problems, the logic of attempts to overcome scale ineconomies and other problems faced by border regions, including the impetus for cross-border initiatives as well as other forms of interjurisdictional cooperation, and accounts of innovative programs to cross borders and create economies that are more integrated.

The Border-Periphery Problem

The challenges of the core-periphery problem are apparent when surveying rural, border areas of states. Evidence indicates that rural counties "have lower performance indicators and higher percentages of stagnant or declining economies" than metropolitan regions (Stabler 1999).

One key challenge for peripheral counties is achieving a critical mass of knowledge workers and resources. Due this limited knowledge base, rural economies may offer lower return on investment than urban areas, thus discouraging innovation investment. In addition, there has been a recent "outflow of knowledge capital… from peripheral regions." (Bennewort, & Charles 2005; Virkkala 2006) In general, peripheral areas lack the resources to encourage innovation, such as networks, training programs, and technology transfer (Virkkala 2006).

A major challenge for peripheral regions is improving efficiency as these regions often lack an educated workforce and the advantage of economies of scale. The persistent income gap between rural and urban workers with similar skill levels can be traced to the low productivity levels of rural areas (Porter 2004, Glaeser, & Mare 2001). Literature suggests that rural employees have lower skill levels than their urban counterparts including an older population and lower college completion rates (Porter 2004, Quigley 1998 and 20022002). In addition, rural employees often lack the skills necessary to exploit modern services and advanced technologies. (Porter, 2004; Gale, & McGranahan 2001). Moreover, because rural areas lack scale economies, infrastructure

improvements are usually more expensive per job generated in rural areas (ERS 2006).

Sectoral clusters are also slow to develop in peripheral regions. It is difficult to pool resources and create a cluster in border areas, which lack the critical mass of firm-level resources and expertise necessary for developing a cluster. Rural economies also often lack the characteristics necessary to attract cluster development. Cluster development requires human resource development opportunities, close proximity to primary and secondary suppliers, and access to capital to create the firm-level and knowledge worker critical mass (Rosenfield 1995, & 2000). In addition to lacking in these traits, many rural areas also tend to have low education levels, limited patenting, and limited access to venture capital (Munnich, Schrock, & Cook 2002).

Overcoming the Border Problem

For many non-urban border regions, there are limited resources available to fund and support technology access and innovation programs (Malecki, 2003). Other limitations include having few regional personnel with technological expertise, a limited number of high-tech local firms, and a lack of science and engineering programs in the local universities. Without these initial resources, regional programs to bolster technology access and innovation may face overwhelming hurdles to their success. To overcome these limitations, border regions can reach across state lines to pool their resources and jumpstart their technology development efforts.

Technology access and innovation have become essential ingredients to regional economic development efforts (Malecki, 1997). Many regions and countries have been able to harness their human capital to create knowledge economies that boost productivity and economic growth while replacing their declining sectors (Kejak, 2002). These regions are able to compete nationally and internationally for jobs and investment and support this inflow of workers and capital with the requisite education facilities and infrastructure (Shefer, 2005). These inflows help create a critical mass of businesses within the high-skilled sectors where the region has a competitive advantage (Porter, 1998). This critical mass, or cluster, of businesses gives the region the ability to compete more effectively in the global marketplace. Such private sector success is in turn supported by the local and state governments who facilitate and coordinate resources for innovation and development (Muniagurria, 1995). With substantial public and private resources, these governments have sustained training programs, infrastructure, and entrepreneurship while developing extensive innovation capacity (Wonglimpiyarat, 2005).

To achieve this critical mass, non-urban border regions must overcome their peripheral locations by exploiting potential economic, social, and organizational linkages with neighboring jurisdictions across the border. The level of trade is one indicator the strength of the economic linkages among neighboring states. As cross-border economic integration intensifies, Economic incentives for implementing cross-border organizations include both an increase in trade and exports, many of which are from knowledge-based activities. Convergence of culture and values also contributes to the formation of cross-border region as shared culture and values are vital in creating organizations and making economic decisions (Williamson, 2000; North, 1990). Moreover, a similar cultures, ideological communities, and even identities encourage a favorable attitude toward cross-border relationships. (Policy Research Initiative, 2005).

The Emergence of Innovative Cross-Border Initiatives

Some border regions have begun to collaborate to connect complementary industries and to strengthen and market different competitive advantages among high-tech businesses that may exist in different locations in the broader region (Beyers, 1996). The latter activity is perceived to be better than the alternative practice of competing against each other in select technology fields. Collaboration can include training programs across industries, sharing of technological expertise, and coordination of inputs to lower costs. This collaboration can lead to expansion of the industrial base in both regions while offering productivity improvements within existing firms.

Cross-border regional organizations aspire to assist in reducing or mitigating economic transaction costs, which include the cost of collecting information when creating a contract or formal relationship, making decisions at the conclusion of a contract, and enforcing contracts across the border. By reducing these costs and facilitating contracts, cross-border relationships diminish the border effect caused by limited social and cultural similarities. (Helliwell 2002). Moreover, cross-border organizations may be useful in addressing local and regional issues often ignored by larger national organizations; they are also less scattered and have better identifiable costs and benefits than larger national organizations. (Policy Research Initiative, 2005).

By collaborating with regions across state lines, cross-border initiatives can achieve the critical mass of participants needed for a sustainable program. Rural counties may not have the critical mass of participants necessary to make their technology programs a long-term success as many border regions are both sparsely populated and losing their most talented students to urban areas (Gibbs, 1995). This drain on human capital prevents rural cross-border areas from sustaining the number of users required to make their technology programs successful.

There are three types of cross-border initiatives focused on technology access and innovation: information and communication technology (ICT) access for cross-border regions, technology training and education, and innovation development. There are typically two types of ICT access programs, including last-mile access and fiber network deployments. Many residents in border areas do not have access to ICT services or they are simply unaffordable from current suppliers. The second category consists of technology training and education programs. These include a wide array of efforts from short-term on-the-job training to bolstering higher education in science and engineering. The third category of initiatives focuses on regional innovation capacity and research and development (R&D) programs, which include supporting public and private regional research facilities through funding, incentives and infrastructure investment.

Stewart (1997), Feser (1998), and others have identified four types of critical factors that characterized successful cross-border efforts:

- *Tailored program structure:* Successful programs are tailored to fit the needs of the region while avoiding unnecessary overlap with current efforts. These programs also tend to be implemented in phases, to avoid program overreach and funding difficulties.
- *Sustained leadership engagement:* To achieve success, a program must have sustained involvement by key leaders in both states. Fostering personal connection between regional leaders can be vital to launching and sustaining a program.
- *Diverse program funding:* Programs that succeed in developing a diverse set of funding sources can help ensure financial sustainability long after the initial grant phase has concluded.
- Coordinated regulatory support: Programs may not pass the planning phase without close cooperation between state and local regulators and legislators. This is particularly important for cross-border technology parks, which require a high level of legal and regulatory coordination for deployment of the facilities.

RESEARCH METHODOLOGY

While there are many potential areas of study related to the economic development challenges faced by cross-border regions, this research focuses particularly on technology access and innovation and the impacts these factors can have on economic development. Many regions already face challenges related to technology access, developing a skilled workforce, and creating a critical mass of innovation. A close proximity to political borders only exacerbates these challenges for border counties and regions. However, very few of these counties have implemented a cross-border initiative specifically designed to utilize technology innovation and ICTs to bolster economic development. With this small number of existing programs, our research effort was able to include a large share of these technology-based CBIs.

Through a series of structured interviews and facilitated meetings, we summarized and analyzed the responses and perspectives of dozens of leaders in business, government, economic development, and higher education. These interviews provided a window through which to examine a long history of natural cross-border activity in a variety of forms as well as specific policy and business efforts underway to improve cross-border collaboration, information exchange, and ultimately, economic activity. Moreover, the interviews helped us to better understand the barriers to collaboration as well as the tangible opportunities and challenges necessary to realize successful cross-border economic development activity in a variety of forms.

Primary Research

To answer our research questions, this study's primary research included a series of interviews targeting border region leaders in business, economic development, higher education, and government. These border regions were limited to only those regions with an existing cross-border initiative that used technology deployment and innovation to accelerate economic development. We identified these programs through secondary materials and contacts with existing CBIs to ensure that only those with a technology-focus were included in the interview process. By eliminating those programs that were did not cross-border or focus on technology-based development, we were able to include a large sampling of existing programs in our interviews.

We sent a survey protocol to prospective interview participants in cross-border programs. The purpose of the protocol was to provide a standard set of questions and themes for interview respondents of different backgrounds, thus facilitating a comparison of these regions of study with each other and with different cross-border programs. We conducted in-depth interviews with approximately 40 leaders in the case study regions and leaders who represented other cross-border programs. These discussions were designed to gauge the opinions and perspectives of participants about potential opportunities and barriers to cross-border economic and technological development.

Secondary Research

Secondary research consisted of collecting and analyzing data, reports and other materials on a wide range of issues that touch on cross-border economic development, particularly those dealing with technology in rural and/or lower-wealth areas. The secondary research provided a helpful road map in identifying and navigating the important issues we explored in our interviews.

Case Studies

We conducted an in-depth literature review to identify cross-border economic development efforts in the United States, and to some extent efforts spanning international borders. Key criteria in our search included the centrality or importance

of technology-based economic development to each of the efforts. This search produced a very long list of nascent or ongoing efforts. We reduced this list to the extent possible through secondary research, and then contacted key representatives of each initiative to understand clearly the current goals and operational status of each program. We further reduced our list by focusing on efforts that have recently been operational in the last 3-4 years to ensure that we could identify key contacts for interviews. Finally, we reduced overlapping initiatives and focused on arriving at a final list of programs offering both geographic and programmatic diversity as well as cohesion, with an explicit focus on technology-based economic development opportunities across borders.

Based on an extensive number of interviews with cross-border technology and development programs already in operation, there are a number of key lessons that should be learned for future cross-border efforts. The following programs are a sub-set of those cross-border initiatives investigated as part of the research completed for this article. These ten offer the broadest set of best practices concerning program design, structure, funding, and regulation. The table below offers a brief synopsis of these programs, their focus, and critical success factors present.

Case Study Descriptions

For the cross-border programs studied, three linked attributes determine the structure and scope of the initiative. These three levels of program scope include geographic reach, extent of infrastructure development, and degree of formalized structure. This section outlines the key issues for each of these three program attributes.

Framework for Assessing Cross-Border Initiatives

Cross-border initiatives range in geographic scope from two counties collaborating across state lines

Table 1. CBI overviews

Program Name	Location	Programmatic Focus	Critical Success Factors
Cross-Border Business Innovation Center (CBBIC)	Northern Ireland; Republic of Ireland	Cluster development; training	• Tailored program structure • Sustained leadership engagement
Bi-National Sustainability Laboratory	New Mexico, Texas, Mexico	Technology park; training; R&D	• Diverse program funding • Coordinated regulatory support
Information and Telecommunication Technology Training Initiative	Massachusetts; Connecticut	Training	• Tailored program structure • Sustained leadership engagement
Buffalo Niagara Enterprise (BNE)	New York; Ontario	Cluster development; training	• Sustained leadership engagement • Diverse program funding
Heartland Foundation	Missouri; Nebraska; Kansas; and Iowa	Cluster development; training; leadership development	• Tailored program structure • Sustained leadership engagement • Diverse program funding
Clay-Towns Industrial Park	Georgia; North Carolina	Technology park; cluster development; training	• Tailored program structure • Diverse program funding • Coordinated regulatory support
Native American Access to Technology Program (NAATP)	New Mexico; Arizona; Utah; and Colorado	Technology access; training	• Sustained leadership engagement
The Advanced Materials Cluster	North Carolina; Virginia	Technology park; cluster development; training	• Tailored program structure • Diverse program funding • Sustained leadership engagement
International Center for Automotive Research (ICAR)	North Carolina; South Carolina	Technology park; cluster development; training	• Tailored program structure • Diverse program funding • Sustained leadership engagement
e-Polk and PANGEA	North Carolina; South Carolina	Technology access; training	• Tailored program structure • Diverse program funding

to more robust programs encompassing multiple states along national borders. From the interviews conducted with cross-border technology programs already in operation, personal ties of organizational and political leaders are a key determinant of the size and scope of cross-border initiatives. These ties are crucial in forging the organizational relationships and maintaining momentum for these programs. The geographic scope of a given program, particularly in its beginning phases, is typically shaped by these personal cross-border connections. This reflects, among other things, the personal trust and historical ties between stakeholders across the border region in designing cross-border collaborative interactions that can foster mutual gains.

Increases in geographic scope can also raise the complexity of organizing cross-border programs, which in turn can lead to additional challenges in maintaining these initiatives. These problems can include increased coordination problems due to a larger number of stakeholders, additional local or state regulatory requirements, the addition of a federal layer of requirements, and an increased likelihood of competition over location of program assets.

Infrastructure development for CBIs ranges from using existing infrastructure to developing a new industrial or research park on the border. Most cross-border technology training programs simply use existing facilities at local firms or universities to minimize expenses. ICT access programs usually include the deployment of network infrastructure while innovation capacity programs can involve the construction of a technology park on a state border. These parks can require transportation, communication, electricity, and water infrastructure in addition to the development of the park property itself.

Program formality is defined as the level of legal and regulatory structures enacted to support the creation of a cross-border program. For those programs with relative informality, there are few, if any, legal or regulatory requirements for creating or sustaining programs that can arise on an ad-hoc basis and be managed with loose agreements of short or indefinite duration. In contrast, an industrial or research park development with its requisite infrastructure has numerous legal and regulatory requirements necessitating a more formal partnership structure.

Cross-Border Business Innovation Center (CBBIC)

The Cross-Border Business Innovation Center (CBBIC) is a joint venture between Northern Ireland and the Republic of Ireland to offer business development assistance to create a regional high-tech cluster. In coordination with the private sector, the CBBIC offers skills development opportunities for local workers and supports high-tech entrepreneurship in a sparsely populated border region. The region served by the CBBICs is comprised of small cities and struggles with employment and investment as there is no central location attracting business investment and jobs.

For more than a decade before their formal partnership, the two CBBICs had been informally collaborating and sharing services. The directors were already acquainted with one another and the CBBICs were too small to independently establish cluster development programs: training programs and infrastructure deployment were too costly for an individual CBBIC to accomplish. This pre-existing relationship between the two directors was crucial in starting the formal program coordination. Under this partnership, the CBBICs are able to increase efficiency in serving a low-density population while addressing the common need for economic development across the region.

The program targets specific knowledge-based industries with local high employment, including manufacturing, construction, engineering, digital media, and IT. The program budget is supported by a combination of service fees and funding sources, namely the European Union (EU) as well as the central and local governments. Legal amendments to the European Company Statute were required to allow the CBBIC to incorporate in multiple countries. The biggest challenges for the CBBIC include underlying trust issues between the two CBBICs, which were accustomed to competing with one another for EU funds, making it harder to work together.

Bi-National Sustainability Laboratory Inc.

This is a US-Mexican program devoted to R&D and economic development. Started by Sandia National Labs, the program currently encompasses New Mexico and Texas and will expand to include ten US and Mexican states over the next several years.

The initial concept for the cross-border partnership was from the Sandia National Laboratories in New Mexico to create a bi-national entity promoting economic development, the use of developing techniques, and border security. The program's immediate goal was to use technology more effectively to increase border security coordination. In the long run, the program hopes to use economic development to help Mexican border areas increase opportunities thereby lowering economic pressures to immigrate to the US. Other priorities include business support services, secure commerce, health care collaboration, infrastructure needs, environment, and communication.

To provide initial funding for the program, a small New Mexico non-profit, Bi-National Laboratory, Inc., was established to apply for and receive state and federal grants. Organizations and entities contributing to the initiative include the Sandia National Laboratories, the State of New Mexico, New Mexico State University, the University of Texas El Paso, the US Economic Development Agency, and Mexican agencies for innovation and industrial development. While funding has been a challenge for the initiative, current financing is provided by the U.S. and Mexican governments with expected funding from the State of New Mexico and the University of Texas El Paso.

With regards to regulatory and legal restrictions, the main concerns deal with how funding will be channeled from both countries to one entity, taxation, multinational employee status, where infrastructure will be constructed, and what laws govern the infrastructure. For the project to be successful, both national governments and participating state governments must be supportive. Thus, one of the main concerns has been coordinating the various entities involved while considering the unique context of the border region.

Information and Telecommunication Technology Training Initiative (IT²)

The IT² was a Massachusetts-Connecticut IT training program funded through two Department of Labor grants from 2000 to 2005. The program offered services such as technology training, business support services, and education indirectly promoting economic development in the regions. IT²'s focus included raising skill sets to advance careers, improving wage levels, retaining trained workers, and improving the competitive advantage of the participating companies in the ICT sector. To accomplish these goals, the program coordinated with regional community colleges, workforce boards, and IT firms. The initiative directly supported company training and issuing vouchers to unemployed workers for IT training. However, the program ended when the Department of Labor shifted the focus of the grants from workforce IT

training to tertiary education efforts.

The program's success was supported by starting with a small grant and then growing and diversifying through a second grant. To keep the scope of the first grant manageable, all of the supported firms were within the IT sector, including JDS Uniphase, which was the largest partner. With the second grant, the initiative was able to expand its focus to other industries making it more resilient to economic fluctuations. During this second phase of the project, companies in the insurance, healthcare, and retail sectors were also among the program's participants.

Among the challenges faced by the initiative were organizational issues with coordinating across community colleges and business partners. Another key hurdle included customizing the process for employers by reducing paperwork required and still ensuring enough data would be tracked for the US Department of Labor.

Buffalo Niagara Enterprise

The Buffalo Niagara Enterprise (BNE) initiative is a multi-county program in New York that coordinates with its adjacent Canadian counterpart. BNE delivered a multi-year, multi-million dollar regional marketing campaign to entice workers and businesses to relocate to the area. The program's focus is to promote the expansion of US firms into Canada as well as bring Canadian firms into the US. Formed to be a one-stop shop, BNE walks firms through the bureaucracy associated with securing tax incentives, relocation and training employees, supports business development, and fosters public-private partnerships.

Primary services of BNE include seminars on human resources, business services, and training on entering a new national market. BNE has targeted several sectors, including life sciences, professional support centers, logistics and distribution, technology-intensive manufacturing, and information technology.

When BNE was started in 1999, a budget of $5 million per year was expected for the first five years. Currently, the budget is approximately $3 million. The organization is mostly funded by private sources, including membership fees from local organizations and firms. Before BNE, the economic development efforts were coordinated at the county level, resulting in heavy competition among the counties. Now, BNE ensures coordination and communication across regions allowing firms to find a location easily and avoiding a race to bottom by the counties when offering incentives to firms. Moreover, the region has become more economically diverse including industries from the steel and auto industries to financial services and life sciences.

Heartland Foundation

The Heartland Foundation funds and manages a cross-border community development program in Missouri and three neighboring states. Originally a non-profit foundation started to raise funds for hospital equipment, the Heartland Foundation began to focus on larger issues of community health in the early 1990s. Recently, it has transformed itself into a regional community development program. The program, based in St. Joseph, MO, covers 30 counties across Missouri, Nebraska, Kansas, and Iowa.

Among the priorities of the foundation are economic and infrastructure development, leadership, and youth empowerment. The foundation brings together three universities in the region, as well as economic development institutions, small business development centers, career centers, legislators, and chambers of commerce to support regional community development. Services offered by the foundation include healthcare collaboration, training, infrastructure development, healthy community programs, reading programs, public achievement programs, and leadership programs. The foundation is funded by endowment funds and fundraising events as well as state and federal grants for specific programs. To maintain this grant support, the Foundation continuously

evaluates their programs by developing a scorecard to measure program outcomes.

Challenges faced by the foundation include raising adequate funding to support all of their programs and creating connections across organizations. Since the foundation brings a wide range of organizations and people together to collaborate on region-wide efforts, the foundation also coordinates leadership development programs to help people form bonds across regions and organizations.

Clay-Towns Industrial Park

This dual-state program was initiated in February 2001 when Towns County, Georgia approached Clay County, North Carolina to partner on an industrial park across their border. Operated by a joint venture between two counties across state lines, this industrial park seeks to attract light industry to the region. The park coordinates transportation, communication, and power infrastructure while offering facilities to expanding local enterprises and relocating businesses.

The target sectors include small-scale manufacturing, wholesale trade, high-tech, and warehouse distribution. Since the region did not have affordable internet services, the program also deployed a $15 million fiber loop in Western North Carolina, Tennessee, and Georgia to bring low-cost connectivity to the park. Long-term connections across organizations were vital in coordinating a successful program.

The main challenges for this program were legal and political hurdles, which required amending laws in both states. While previous North Carolina law allowed counties to enter into agreements among one another, counties were not permitted to convey ownership to a partnership that included counties in another state. In contrast, previous law in Georgia did not recognize the legal authority of another state's counties, but counties were permitted to own property and covey it to another political or governmental entity.

Legislation was passed in both states to allow the creation of this joint partnership. The Clay-Towns Development Authority was also given the legal authority to sell property and use the revenue to fund its programs.

Native American Access to Technology Program (NAATP)

The NAATP works with Native American tribes in the Four Corners Region of the US (New Mexico, Arizona, Utah, and Colorado) to provide better access to technology and training for their communities. The initiate was prompted by the large gap in access to technology between the Navaho Nation and the US average as well as the apparent disparity within the Nation. Organizations involved in the partnership included NGOs, the University of Arizona, state libraries, Tribal Health Connections, and the Tribal College.

The project received its funding through the Gates foundation, with support from local state libraries and NGOs, for a total of $8 million budgeted across four years. While not currently funded from these outside sources, the effort continues in many of the communities through tribal support for the staff, training, and connectivity expenses. The key factors behind the program's success included the prior experience with IT, the commitment of the local Tribal Council, individual tribes' relationships with state agencies, and leadership within the tribal community.

The Advanced Materials Cluster

Advanced materials and composites are emerging into a technology-based cluster of interest in the NC/VA border region. The nascent Northwest North Carolina (NWNC) Advanced Materials Cluster is a public-private partnership designed to foster this industry's cluster development. Among the initiative's goals are to strengthen the region's ability to support advanced materials manufacturers and suppliers, stimulate regional

economic development, develop educational programs to strengthen the local workforce, and encourage strategic partnerships at the state and local level.

The initiative is centered on Martin Marietta, the second largest construction aggregates producer in the United States, and is facilitated by the Wilkes Community College (WCCC). The Wilkes Community College's main campus in North Wilkesboro offered a new certificate program for advanced materials in the fall of 2005. This certificate program was designed by the national composites industry to educate potential workers in the region. Other key supporters of the initiative include local firms, cluster councils, and business service agencies.

Community leaders aim to attract Martin Marietta's extensive supply chain, as well as its purchasers, to the region. The cluster geographically includes Alleghany, Wilkes and Ashe Counties, but its director does not object to expansion, even into Virginia. WCCC's counterpart in Virginia, Wytheville Community College, does not offer a similar certificate, even though one-third of the 45 Martin Marietta employees in the region are from Virginia.

International Center for Automotive Research (ICAR)

In the early 1990s, German automaker BMW announced a major plant location in Greenville, South Carolina. Before announcing its new regional location in South Carolina, several states (including North Carolina) had offered economic development incentive packages in an effort to lure the automotive giant and its thousands of jobs to their respective states. Economic development officials and local policy makers have suggested the presence of BMW in Greenville has literally transformed the regional economy. BMW has created hundreds of jobs and encouraged other firms in the automotive industry, such as Michelin, to locate additional facilities and jobs in the region.

Thus, the upstate South Carolina region has been branded as a major center for automotive manufacturing.

In an effort to make upstate South Carolina even more influential in the automotive industry, Clemson University and the State of South Carolina broke ground in 2003 on Clemson University's International Center for Automotive Research (ICAR). BMW Manufacturing and Michelin North America are ICAR's principal industrial partners and the research center is strategically located in close proximity to both Atlanta and Charlotte. According to Bob Geolas, ICAR's director, ICAR will be the premier global automotive engineering and motorsports research and educational center. The project has already generated over $90 million in public and private funding. Its primary objective is to foster innovation and develop technologies for the benefit of automotive manufacturers, suppliers and consumers. Technology and educational support will focus on automotive systems integration and related services. In addition, the program will create a stronger local workforce of technical leaders.

e-Polk and PANGEA

e-Polk, Inc., a community-based nonprofit organization, was formed in 2001 as a result of North Carolina's e-communities initiative and was formally established as a non-profit organization in 2003. e-Polk's mission is to promote internet initiatives in southwestern North Carolina and upstate South Carolina as a means to promote economic development, community-building and enhanced quality of life. e-Polk is an important economic development asset in Polk County and the surrounding region.

One important aspect of North Carolina's support of e-Polk was a $375,000 e-communities grant to lay a fiber-optic network in North and South Carolina. This advanced fiber-optic network, called PANGEA, is available to businesses, Internet Service Providers (ISPs) and governments at competitive prices. The telecommunications network covers the region with a combination of wireless and fiber networks. PANGEA is the biggest technology project linked to economic development in Polk County and aspires to foster local economic growth by making available telecommunications technology and benefits commonly found only in major metropolitan areas. e-Polk is currently working with the Polk County government as well as the Tryon Downtown Development Association and Advantage West North Carolina to attract businesses to their technologically advanced community.

INTERPRETATION: CRITICAL SUCCESS FACTORS

Our approach to analysis of these cases is to distill the common themes across these CBIs to determine their critical success factors. An important and recurrent theme that emerged from interviewing leaders in higher education, economic development, government, and business in border regions is the ongoing need to foster a new and stronger culture of regional entrepreneurial development and collaboration. Many interviewees see this culture as a pathway to greater economic vitality that can generate new employment, a growing tax base, and new and advanced innovation. Moreover, interviewees believe a more entrepreneurial climate would be a strong magnet to attract relocating firms to the area, bringing facilities and jobs.

At the outset of this study, we posited that three critical success factors in particular were likely to influence the success and maintenance of cross border technology initiatives: presence and maintenance of formalized organizational structures, funding mechanisms, and leadership. As noted previously, the latter two factors – funding issues and leadership - are no doubt important to most economic development initiatives regardless of scale or scope. However, we expected to observe that the presence of formalized structures – as opposed to ad hoc and informal mechanisms for collaboration – were valuable in terms of developing and maintaining critical involvement from stakeholders and facilitate trust in cross-border interactions and resource sharing.

Based on our study, below are some of the critical success factors that we identified as common across the case study regions.

Program Design and Structure

Most leaders of programs we studied reported they began their design process by examining current national, regional, and local policies and programs to understand the best practices as well as the gaps in technology support and training. Program managers sought to solve an unfilled niche of business support rather than replicate ongoing efforts. A majority of case study programs also focused their efforts on particular industrial sectors, such as IT or light manufacturing, for their training and technology access programs.

All of these programs were multi-year efforts with long time horizons for delivering results. The US-Mexican program has a time frame of over seven years, with three devoted to the planning and pilot phases alone. A long-term time horizon for measurable results can be a major hurdle for developing and maintaining support for cross-border initiatives. Long-term commitment increases the importance of having a pilot phase to secure an initial round of support and funding and gives the programs time to garner political support while refining the program's activities and goals. For ERC Broadband, profits made on broadband services were used to create economic development programs. For this program, connectivity was just the starting point to expand operating revenues to develop R&D, commercialization, and education efforts.

Another organizational structural issue these programs considered was the cost of including an additional organization within the initiative. In many instances, additional organizations simply brought financial, political and managerial support to the effort. However, costs of adding another organization include coordination issues and budget conflicts. One program, which allowed the community colleges to be the primary coordinators of a technology training effort, found the community colleges became territorial once they gained control of the project. This reduced coordination among the several colleges involved as well as with the program manager. Cross-border program managers should carefully consider the potential positive and negative impacts of including an additional organization—considering if those costs of adding the organization can be mitigated.

Leadership and Stakeholder Engagement

A key issue for the design of cross-border programs is the inclusion of various stakeholders. Effective outreach requires that program leaders build on and leverage their personal relationships among local leaders to ensure that the desired spectrum of interests is represented on the initiative's board. A majority of programs interviewed felt that leadership had been the decisive factor in advancing their organization to reach across state lines, expanding on its current mission, and securing funding for a multi-year effort.

One of the biggest hurdles repeatedly reported by programs has been coordinating across all the various stakeholders. For many of these organizations, which are accustomed to competing with each other for funds and assets, this is a new way of working together. As the program in Northern Ireland reported, there were significant trust issues between the innovation centers and these fights would grow in intensity as the cross-border activities expanded.

To overcome trust issues, the cross-border leadership needs to build connections among the participating organizations. The Heartland Foundation reported an innovative set of programs used to bring a wide range of individuals, not only CEOs and managers, from across the region to work on program steering committees and region-wide activities. By helping these individuals understand their common problems, the participants of the program were able to collaborative to design best practices for solving regional development issues. The Foundation also put these individuals through an annual leadership program, where they have formed lasting bonds across organizations. Moreover, the Foundation continues to work with previous leadership students, drawing on them as a collective pool to support the cross-border initiatives.

Program Funding

Directors of nearly all of the programs reported that funding was a significant hurdle for launching and sustaining the initiative. This includes securing the sufficient funds needed at the early phases of the initiative as well as managing the transition from grants to a blend of external support and service fee revenues. This transition to a mix of funding sources is not always necessary, according to respondents, but is particularly important in making the program financially sustainable. In turn, this sustainability works to ensure a program's long-term viability.

During the launch phase of the program, it may be necessary to secure funding from a variety of sources to ensure that the program can be sustained during its start-up. A mix of funding sources from state, local, and federal governments, foundations, private sector, and universities protects the program from funding shifts and economic impacts that may affect one or more of its supporting organizations. Such a strategy may insulate the program from emerging political hurdles that can arise if funding priorities change over time, creating competition between the use of funds for traditional constituencies and needs versus those devoted to cross-border activities that can generate indirect political and other benefits. Programs in later stages can also

benefit from a mix of sources; however, if there are service fees providing revenue as well, this should be less of an issue.

An example of the impact a single funding source can have on a cross-border program is the training program in Massachusetts and Connecticut. The program was funded through two consecutive federal grants that were secured from the Department of Labor. After 2001, there was a steep decline in funding and the Department's program was not renewed. Remaining funding was shifted to an initiative that focuses on building capacity within the community college. This has required the organization to shift its focus in response while reducing its cross-border activities.

Sources of support are likely to change as the initiatives progress through phases. Funding may need to change for each stage of planning, pilot phase, full-program launch, and program maintenance. For the US and Mexican cross-border program, current financing for the planning and pilot phases are from the US and Mexican governments, with upcoming funding from the State of New Mexico and the University of Texas at El Paso. As the program expands to encompass ten states, funding is expected to come from the member states and private industry.

Another important lesson gleaned from interviews with these programs is the importance of careful planning for the budget that covers a long period. This is particularly true for staffing issues, which can be a significant portion of the budget. One way to overcome this issue, as reported by the Heartland Foundation, was to spin off several of its more successful cross-border efforts. This can allow these programs to grow on their own while allowing a smaller cross-border initiative staff to focus on a tighter set of activities.

Legal and Regulatory Hurdles

The above factors were anticipated as likely critical success factors in developing and maintaining successful cross border technology initiatives. However, to the authors' surprise, legal and regulatory issues did not emerge in interviews and structured conversations as a major problem for most of the cross-border programs contacted for this study. However, three for which legal or regulatory problems were an issue were either cross-national border or had extensive infrastructure requirements.

The US-Mexican border program is currently assessing the regulatory and legal structure that will be in place to support the initiative. The major concerns include the funding mechanism used to channel support from both countries to one entity, taxation regulations, multinational employee status and the location of the headquarters. The program was considering placing the headquarters building directly on the border; however, this would have required a special treaty to allow a structure within 100 feet of border.

For the Clay-Towns industrial park, the project managers passed laws in Georgia and North Carolina to create a cross-state legal entity, the Clay-Towns Development Authority, with the novel authorization to hold title to real property. To lower political hurdles, the act that allowed the Clay-Towns Development Authority (CTDA) to hold property title was applicable only to Clay County rather than statewide. The CTDA does not have an agreement in place for sharing tax revenue across state lines. Currently, any tax revenue gained by one county stays within that county. To work around this tax-sharing hurdle, CTDA may retain the revenue it receives from selling property in the park. This avoids the issue of tax revenue sharing altogether while still raising funds for the industrial park.

FUTURE RESEARCH DIRECTIONS

Cross-border regional organizations aspire to assist in reducing or mitigating economic transaction costs, which include the cost of collecting information when creating a contract or formal relationship, making decisions at the conclusion of a contract, and enforcing contracts across the border. By reducing these costs and facilitating contracts, cross-border relationships diminish the border effect caused by limited social and cultural similarities. Moreover, cross-border organizations may be useful to address local and regional issues often ignored by larger national organizations; they are also less scattered and have better identifiable costs and benefits than larger national organizations. One direction for future research would include tracking and quantifying the potential impact of these cross-border organizations on transaction costs within their target regions. This would assist local policymakers and businesses in accurately assessing the value of participating in these cross-border arrangements, potentially making them more attractive to prospective stakeholders.

CONCLUSION

Technology-based new venture development has been touted in the academic policy literature as an ideal type of entrepreneurial economic development (Venkataraman 2004). Not only are high tech jobs becoming more plentiful nationwide, but their wages are also generally higher than average private sector wages (Platzer 2001). Technology research and development is a major driver of productivity gains and economic growth (Audretsch et al 2002). However, creating and sustaining an entrepreneurial economic region based on technology is decidedly more complex than merely trying to emulate some of the successful entrepreneurial sectors found in such places as Research Triangle Park, Route 128 in Boston, and Silicon Valley. The academic literature on fostering entrepreneurship, dating back to Penrose (1959), suggests that regions must acquire and nurture bundles of investments and resources. This requires taking stock of regions' existing entrepreneurial and technological assets and adapting and harnessing them to fit the unique needs and opportunities of the respective region.

Leaders in economic development and government clearly cited a historically embedded culture of competition across county and state lines, making cross-border collaboration the exception rather than the rule. The benefits to cross-border competition have historically been seen to flow to specific places rather that the broader cross-border region as a whole. This perception has been institutionalized over time as economic development, political, business, and other leaders have developed core constituencies with strong interests in competing with neighboring counties and states.

However, the goal of a cross-border regional strategy would not necessarily be to eliminate or suspend the historical competitiveness among counties and states. According to interview participants, previous regional efforts attempting to induce counties or states to act in a manner inconsistent with their own self-interest have failed. Instead, a formal mechanism is required to provide joint gains, which will foster cross-border collaboration and preserve natural competitiveness while also engendering new collaboration when working together can yield benefits for both states.

A regional approach to cross-border economic development must take into account this historical culture of competition. Rather than attempting to completely alter the nature of this competition in the short-term, a regional approach should instead offer a strong "business case" to each participating county or municipality for the advantages of cross-border collaborations. While a historical legacy of cross-border competition continues in many respects, there are explicit benefits to collaborating, especially sharing costs and revenues when new regional assets have the potential to spill over across political boundaries.

Through the series of structured interviews in across 10 regions, we identified several key findings that help to better understand the state of cross-border activity and the potential for additional collaboration across state lines that can lead to sustained economic development and growth. Accordingly, these key findings motivate the specific recommendations found below.

Overcoming (or Transcending) the Legacy of Competition and Territoriality

The legacy of cross-border competition and territoriality shapes the development of regional leaders and their roles. While we found many examples of cross-border initiatives in operation or under development, deep collaboration among leaders and their respective institutions across state lines has generally been rare. Reaching out to current leaders and developing the next generation of new leaders to think regionally may help cultivate a new culture of collaboration and partnership in the cross-border region. Regional leadership must be institutionalized, perhaps via greater collaboration among chambers of commerce or colleges and universities.

Importantly, we found strong interviewee consensus that beyond efforts to "reach out" to the right mix of leadership and ensure ample funding, one practically important way to overcome (or transcend) the legacy of competition and territoriality is to formalize non-profit or other legal structures that can bind participants together, establish consensus on key goals and resources, and outcomes. Absent formalized structures facilitating cross border exchanges and interactions, long-term and collaboration is unlikely to be established or to flourish for any meaningful length of time necessary for up-front investments of time and other resources to yield measurable positive benefits for all stakeholders.

It is not our belief that formalized structures, which themselves can be resource-intensive to establish and cumbersome administratively and legally to govern. are necessarily important for promoting collaboration within a region or promoting more modest goals (such as one-time efforts or opportunities). This study's contribution to the literature is primarily about the need for formalization to overcome the historically embedded inertia against cross border collaboration involving technology-based economic development.

Fostering Regional Leadership

In many ways, regional universities and community colleges are collaborating in a variety of ways across state lines and many of these initiatives are bearing fruit. However, many higher education and business leaders interviewed also cited the need for educational institutions to work together more directly and regularly in an ongoing, sustained manner. Regional universities and colleges can develop a joint regional mission statement outlining how the various colleges and universities can collaborate to provide the kinds of cross training, services, and support that can benefit a region. Despite years of progress, more work on reciprocal tuition agreements is also needed in harmonizing in-state tuition rules and procedures for colleges and universities serving students across the state line. Furthermore, universities can also act as potential catalysts for developing new regional leadership in the public and private sectors by playing the role of regularly convening and harnessing leadership in business, higher education, and government across a region.

Pursuing "Low-Hanging Fruit" and Longer-Term Collaboration Simultaneously

Interview participants suggested strengthening regional ties in the long-term would sometimes require changing laws and regulations that would create new opportunities for long-term and deeply embedded collaboration. However, these efforts need to be balanced with short-term projects, which can provide some momentum for longer-term efforts by building trust and strengthening

relationships among regional leaders on both sides of a state line. One interview participant called such short-term projects "easy victories" in a longer-term effort to build and sustain cross-border cooperation and collaboration. Examples of such projects include joint marketing and development of existing business parks along state lines, joint chambers of commerce meetings designed to form and strengthen relationships among leaders across state lines, and efforts by regional universities to jointly host a series of summits for business and technology leaders to learn new ways to expand activities across state lines.

REFERENCES

Benneworth, P., & Charles, D. (2005). University Spin-offs Policies and Economic Development in less Successful Regions: Learning from Two Decades of Policy Practice. *European Planning Studies*, *13*(4), 537–557. doi:10.1080/09654310500107175

Beyers, W. B., & Lindahl, D. P. (1996). Lone eagles and high fliers in rural producer services. *Rural Development Perspectives*, *11*(3), 2–10.

Christaller, W. (1933). *Die zentralen Orte in Süddeutschland*. Jena, Germany: Gustav Fischer.

Clemson University International Center for Automotive Research. (n.d.). Retrieved from http://www.clemson.edu/autoresearch/

Cooke, P., Uranga, M. G., & Goio, E. (1997). Regional innovation systems: Institutional and organisational dimensions. *Research Policy*, *26*(4), 475–491. doi:10.1016/S0048-7333(97)00025-5

Economic Research Service. (2006). *Rural development Strategies: Infrastructure*. United States Department of Agriculture. Employment Security Commission of North Carolina. (n.d.). *25 Largest Employers by County*. Retrieved November 11, 2005, from http://jobs.esc.state.nc.us/lmi/largest/largest.pdf

Feser, E., Goldstein, H., Renski, H., & Renault, C. (2002). *Regional technology assets and opportunities: The geographic clustering of high-tech industry, science and innovation in Appalachia.* Prepared for the Appalachian Regional Commission. Office of Economic Development, University of North Carolina at Chapel Hill.

Feser, Edward J., Harvey A. Goldstein, & Luger, M. (1998). *At the Crossroads: North Carolina's Place in the Knowledge Economy of the Twenty-First Century.* Report for the North Carolina Alliance for Competitive Technologies and North Carolina Board of Science and Technology. Chapel Hill, NC: Univ. North Carolina at Chapel Hill.

Fritsch, A., & Johannsen, K. (2004). *Ecotourism in Appalachia: Marketing the mountains.* Lexington, KY: University of Kentucky Press.

Gale, F., & McGranahan, D. (2001). Nonmetro Areas Fall Behind in the 'New Economy'. *Rural America, 16*(1), 44–52.

Gibbs, R. M. (1995). Going away to college and wider urban job opportunities take highly educated youth away from rural areas. *Rural Development Perspectives, 10*(3), 35–44.

Glaeser, E. L., & Maré, D. (2001). Cities and Skills. *Journal of Labor Economics, 19*(2). doi:10.1086/319563

Hawkins, R. B. (1976). Special Districts and Urban Services. In E. Ostrom (Ed.), *The Delivery of Urban Services* (pp. 171-188). Beverly Hills, CA: Sag.

Helliwell, J. (2002). *Globalization and Well-Being.* Vancouver, Canada: UBC Press.

Income, S. A., & Estimates, P. (n.d.). U.S. Census Bureau. Retrieved from http://www.census.gov/hhes/www/saipe/county.html

Kejak, M. (2003). Stages of growth in economic development. *Journal of Economic Dynamics & Control, 27*(5), 771–800. doi:10.1016/S0165-1889(01)00071-9

Local Area Bearfacts. (n.d.). Bureau of Economic Analysis. U.S. Department of Commerce. Retrieved from http://www.bea.doc.gov/bea/regional/bearfacts/countybf.cfm

Malecki, E. J. (1997). *Technology and Economic Development: The Dynamics of Local, Regional and National Competitiveness.* Essex, UK: Addison Wesley Longman Limited.

Malecki, E. J. (2003). Digital development in rural areas: potentials and pitfalls. *Journal of Rural Studies, 19*(2), 201–214. doi:10.1016/S0743-0167(02)00068-2

McDowell, G. R. (1995). Some communities are successful, others are not: toward an institutional framework for understanding the reasons why. In D.W. Sears & J.N. Reid (Eds.), *Rural Development Strategies* (pp.269-281). Chicago: Nelson-Hall.

Muniagurria, M. E. (1995). Growth and research and development. *Journal of Economic Dynamics & Control, 19*(1), 207–235. doi:10.1016/0165-1889(93)00779-4

Munnich, L. W., Jr., Schrock, G., & Cook, K. (2002). Rural Knowledge Clusters: The Challenge of Rural Economic Prosperity. *Reviews of Economic Development Literature and Practice, 12.* U.S. Economic Development Administration. Retrieved from http://www.eda.gov/ImageCache/EDAPublic/documents/pdfdocs/u_2eminn_2elit_2erev3_2epdf/v1/u.minn.lit.rev3.pdf

North, D. C. (1990). *Institutions, Institutional Change and Economic Performance.* Cambridge, UK: Cambridge University Press.

Northwest North Carolina Advanced Materials Cluster. (n.d.). Retrieved October 26, 2006, from http://www.advancedmaterials.org/

PANGEA. (n.d.). *e-Polk – Polk County Internet Access*. Retrieved October 26, 2006, http://www.pangaea.us/

Penrose, E. T. (1959). *The Theory of the Growth of the Firm*. New York: John Wiley & Sons.

Platzer, M. (2001). *Cyberstates 2001: A State by State Overview of the High Technology Industry*. Paper presented at American Economic Association, Washington DC. Policy Research Initiative. (n.d.). *The Emergence of Cross-Border Regions*. Retrieved October 26, 2006, from https://recherchepolitique.gc.ca/doclib/PRI_XBorder_e.pdf

Porter, M. E. (1998). *Clusters and the New Economics of Competition*. Cambridge, MA: Harvard Business Review.

Porter, M. E. (2004). *Competitiveness in Rural U.S. Regions: Learning and Research Agenda*. Institute for Strategy and Competitiveness. Cambridge, MA: Harvard Business School.

Quigley, J. (1998). Urban Diversity and Economic Growth. *The Journal of Economic Perspectives*, *12*(2), 127–138.

Quigley, J. (2002). Rural Policy and the New Regional Economics: Implications for Rural America. UCal Berkeley.

Rosenfeld, S. (1995). *Overachievers: Business Clusters that Work: Prospects for Regional Development*. Regional Technology Strategies, Inc.

Rosenfeld, S. (2002). *Just Clusters: Economic development strategies that reach more people and places*. Regional Technology Strategies, Inc.

Rosenfeld, S. (2003). *Clusters of Creativity: Innovation and growth in Montana*. Prepared for the Montana Governor's Office of Economic Opportunity. Regional Technology Strategies, Inc.

Rosenfeld, S. A., & Kingslow, M. (2000). *Clusters in Rural Areas: Auto Supply Chains in Tennessee and Houseboat Manufacturers in Kentucky*. Regional Technology Strategies, Inc. Retrieved from http://www.rural.org/publications/Rosenfeld00-11.pdf

Shefer, D., & Frenkel, A. (2005). R&D, firm size and innovation: an empirical analysis. *Technovation*, *25*(1), 25–32. doi:10.1016/S0166-4972(03)00152-4

South Carolina Employment Security Commission. (n.d.). Top Employers by County. Retrieved November 11, 2005, from http://www.sces.org

Stabler, J. (1999). Rural America: A challenge to regional scientists. *The Annals of Regional Science*, *33*, 1–14. doi:10.1007/s001680050088

State & County QuickFacts. (n.d.). U.S. Census Bureau. Retrieved from http://quickfacts.census.gov/qfd/

State and County Employment and Wages from the Quarterly Census of Employment and Wages. (n.d.). Bureau of Labor Statistics. U.S. Department of Labor. Retrieved from http://www.bls.gov/data/home.htm.

Stewart, L., et al. (1997, May). *Connectivity Plan for North Carolina's Region A: Cherokee, Clay, Graham, Haywood, Jackson, Macon, and Swain Counties, and the Qualla Boundary*. Connect NC Project.

Venkataraman, S. (2004). Regional Transformation through Technological Entrepreneurship. *Journal of Business Venturing*, *19*(1), 153–167. doi:10.1016/j.jbusvent.2003.04.001

Virginia Employment Commission. (n.d.). *Virginia's Top 50 Employers*. Retrieved November 11, 2005, from http://velma.virtuallmi.com/

Virkkala, S. (2006). *What is the role of peripheral areas in a knowledge economy? - A study of the innovation processes and networks of rural firms.* Conference Innovation Pressure, March 2006. Retrieved from http://www.proact2006.fi/chapter_images/302_Ref_B111_Seija_Virkkala.pdf

Wessner, C. (2002). The Economics of Science and Technology. *The Journal of Technology Transfer, 27,* 155–203. doi:10.1023/A:1014382532639

Williamson, O. E. (2000). The New Institutional Economics: Taking Stock, Looking Ahead. *Journal of Economic Literature, 38*(3), 595–613.

Wonglimpiyarat, J. (2005). The dynamic economic engine at Silicon Valley and U.S. Government programmes in financing innovations. *Technovation.*

Wood, R. (1961). *1400 Governments: The Political Economy of the New York Metropolitan Region.* Cambridge, MA: Harvard University Press.

Chapter 5

Legitimizing Innovative Ventures Strategically:
The Case of Europe's First Online Pharmacy

Andreas Kuckertz
University of Duisburg-Essen, Germany

Karsten Jörn Schröder
University of Duisburg-Essen, Germany

ABSTRACT

Organizational legitimacy is a key resource that is necessary for every venture to acquire other crucial resources, which will subsequently stimulate growth. The authors illustrate this legitimacy-growth relationship by analyzing the case of Europe's first online pharmacy DocMorris. Given that this ICT venture started as extremely illegitimate, this case provides a rich background to identify various strategies that are potentially helpful to enhance a venture's level of legitimacy. Building on interview data collected from the firm's key actors, the authors are able to show how the perception of a firm's legitimacy from the viewpoint of various internal and external stakeholders can be managed strategically.

INTRODUCTION

A venture's success does not only result from how smart its internal processes are designed, its environment plays a key role as well. Consequently, over the last few decades management research has placed an emphasis on analyzing environmental factors as well and showed that not only technological or material factors exert significant influence on a single firm, but that values, rules, or norms that are present in the relevant environment have to be taken into account as well (Meyer and Rowan, 1977). Thus, a firm's legitimacy (which could be roughly described as its integrity and trustworthiness form the perspective of its various stakeholder groups) becomes of utmost importance.

Usually, firms that are entering a market as so-called "first movers" (Kerin et al., 1992) are said to have competitive advantages over their followers. However, while such firms can certainly reap the benefits of this strategic move, they face additional

DOI: 10.4018/978-1-61520-597-4.ch005

challenges as well. Ventures that are radically innovative suffer from a lack of legitimacy since they are largely unknown to their relevant stakeholders and other market participants. An innovative business model might impede success as well, as such business models are most likely to be inconsistent with prevailing values and norms of the environment. Seeing that it is the main problem of any new venture to overcome the liabilities of newness (Stinchcombe, 1965), it becomes immediately evident that organizational legitimacy can serve as remedy to this problem. The literature considers legitimacy to be a resource that is essential to acquire other crucial resources (Dowling and Pfeffer, 1990; Zimmerman and Zeitz, 2002); the concept has therefore been applied to entrepreneurial phenomena by various researchers (e.g., Starr and Macmillan, 1990; Aldrich and Fiol, 1994; Zimmerman and Zeitz, 2002; Delmar and Shane, 2004).

This research suggests that legitimacy is not just "existent" as opposed to "not existent". In other words, there is a certain threshold of legitimacy that is necessary to operate and grow a business successfully. The challenge for radically innovative ventures is that they are usually farther away from this threshold than, for instance, ventures imitating established business models. However, firms can strive actively to achieve legitimacy through managing the process of legitimation strategically and do not necessarily have to accept the environmental factors they are exposed to. Rather, they may consciously decide to alter these factors in order to legitimate themselves. This is especially important in the context of ICT ventures, i.e., ventures utilizing electronic platforms in data networks and offering products or services based on a purely electronic creation of customer value (Kollmann, 2006), given that such ventures are usually more innovative than the average start-up. Unfortunately, until now the literature has been quite brief and abstract with respect to strategies that could be utilized to build legitimacy. With this paper we address

this apparent gap and aim to shed light on the following research question:

What strategies can innovative ventures employ to gain legitimacy from the perspective of their most important stakeholders?

To answer this research question, we will analyze the case of Europe's first online pharmacy *DocMorris* and extend the analysis of this firm previously presented by Fallgatter and Brink (2008). *DocMorris* started from an extremely low level of legitimacy, but nonetheless became a tremendous success. Therefore, *DocMorris* seems to be an appropriate candidate to learn more about how legitimacy can be build. The following paragraphs will introduce the concept of organizational legitimacy and its importance for entrepreneurial ventures. After reviewing the literature on strategies that can be utilized to build legitimacy, we will introduce our case study and discuss how *DocMorris* managed its various stakeholder groups strategically. The paper closes with some suggestions regarding how other ventures can benefit from the example of *DocMorris*.

THEORETICAL BACKGROUND

Legitimacy and Entrepreneurial Ventures

Admittedly, establishing a new venture successfully, especially in ICT industries, is one of the hardest management challenges. The reasons for this challenge are at least twofold: On the on hand, ICT ventures are quite often based on the development and exploitation of a new technology, on the other hand, just like any other venture in more traditional industries, such ventures usually start from a very restricted resource base. Thus, rapidly arriving at a legitimate standing seems to be of utmost importance. Legitimacy is usually understood as the status of being legitimate, whereas legitimation refers to the process of actually achieving legitimacy (Suchman, 1995). Scholars have suggested numerous definitions of organizational legitimacy over the last few decades (for a comprehensive catalogue of such definitions cf. Fallgatter and Brink, 2008: 305). From this rich literature we will introduce two definitions in this paper to emphasize the most important aspects of this theoretical concept. First, Ashforth and Gibbons define legitimacy in the following way (1990: 177):

"An organization is said to be legitimate to the extent that its means and ends appear to conform with social norms, values and expectations."

Legitimacy is thus a concept that goes way beyond the boundaries of an organization and which acknowledges the fact that every organization is to a large degree a product of its environment. However, contrary to classic strategic environmental factors such as the level of competition or the degree of market and technology turbulence, which have been taken into account by various strategic management concepts for quite some time, the focus is now on 'softer' external factors, such as norms and rules that are prevalent in an environment (e.g., external assumptions of how business should be conducted and for what purpose). Suchman extends this argument with his definition by underlining another major aspect of legitimacy (1995: 574):

"Legitimacy is a generalized perception or assumption that the actions of an entity are desirable, proper, or appropriate within some socially constructed system of norms, values, beliefs, and definitions."

While the first definition highlights what needs to be achieved by an organization in order to be legitimate, Suchman's definition underscores the fact that legitimacy can never be achieved solely by an organization itself. Actors external to a firm are essential, since they *perceive* the firm's action and behavior in a particular way and thereby sometimes ascribe legitimacy to an organization or venture and sometimes not. Thus, it is not only necessary to adhere to certain norms; doing so needs to be recognized by the environment as well – otherwise, legitimacy cannot be achieved. This is particularly challenging for ventures because of one common characteristic most of them share: They operate from a restricted resource base. In the legitimacy literature, a wide consensus can be found that legitimacy is a resource in itself, which can be build by employing other types of resources. However, especially ICT ventures usually do not only lack the legitimacy resource due to being largely unknown or innovative at their inception; they lack other crucial resources as well that are necessary to build legitimacy. For instance, resources that are quite often not available are experience in a certain industry, financial resources, or human capital (Aldrich and Fiol, 1994). While the decision to commit these resources to a venture (for instance by a venture capitalist (Kollmann and Kuckertz, 2006; Kollmann and Kuckertz, in press)) might be primarily *motivated* by the return on investment (ROI) that becomes possible through sustainable operations or even growth, such a decision can only be *justified* by organizational legitimacy serving as a signal that the venture is indeed capable to achieve the goal of generating the desired ROI (Zimmerman and Zeitz, 2002). Against this background, it becomes quite clear that a less than average resource base puts every venture at a competitive disadvantage in comparison to its more established (and therefore better equipped) competitors. Moreover, what potentially intensifies this issue is a venture's innovativeness, i.e., the more innovative the service, product or business concept is, the more likely conflicts will arise, because the venture stands in contradiction to established norms and rules.

Merely adhering to environmental norms and rules to legitimate oneself would, however, be a far too simple recommendation, given that legitimacy is a multidimensional concept. Suchman (1995) distinguishes between three types of legitimacy, i.e. pragmatic, moral, and cognitive legitimacy (for an alternative conceptualizations see, for instance, Aldrich and Fiol, 1994). An organization has achieved pragmatic legitimacy, if its stakeholders are willing to establish (long-term) relationships with it, because they perceive entering such a relationship as being associated with certain benefits. Therefore, the reason why an organization is granted a legitimate status is based on purely rational grounds. Not necessarily opposed to this, but based on a completely different rationale, would be the concept of moral legitimacy, which is based on an evaluation whether an organization complies with norms that are prevalent in the organization's environment. Last, cognitive legitimacy rests not upon perceived utility or morality as the previous types of legitimacy, but rather on the question, whether an organization's behavior is generally comprehensible and understandable by external parties. This last type of legitimacy is especially important in the context of venturing, given that many innovative ventures start with an unclear value proposition, which potentially prevents attaining the legitimate status from an external viewpoint.

Strategic Legitimation

The previous paragraphs highlighted the importance of being legitimate for every organization and for ventures in particular. Early works on legitimacy consider this desirable and necessary resource simply as 'given' and only achievable by conforming to external norms and rules. More recently, however, authors suggested that legitimacy can be actively influenced (Zimmerman and Zeitz, 2002) – even to such a degree that a firm creates an environment that naturally accepts the firms procedures and behavior. Thus, legitimacy is gained by pursuing appropriate strategies to build the perception of appropriateness, acceptance

and desirability of a venture's operations; once it has been established, the acquisition of additional resources becomes possible, the venture's likelihood of survival increases and growth (or at least sustainable operations) becomes possible (Zimmerman and Zeitz, 2002). There is clearly a legitimacy-resource-growth relationship for which empirical support was reported, for instance, by Singh et al. (1986).

Given that legitimacy is necessary to acquire resources, in most cases ventures will have to build legitimacy with little or no money (Zimmerman and Zeitz, 2002) due to their resource-restricted situation. The legitimation process thus needs to be complemented with bootstrapping instruments (Bhidé, 2000). As a consequence, the venture that legitimates itself successfully will have tremendous additional effects on the environment. This is due to the fact that legitimacy applies not only to individual organizations, but to industries as a whole as well (Aldrich and Fiol, 1994). Therefore, if a venture starts legitimating itself, it will – in the successful case – necessarily contribute to the legitimacy of the industry and its competitors, as any entrepreneurial activity reshapes the larger environment (Aldrich and Fiol, 1994).

Aldrich and Fiol (1994) suggest two very broad strategies on the organizational level to achieve legitimacy. These two strategies are based on the respective type of legitimacy that a firm wishes to achieve. First, founders should utilize encompassing symbolic language and behaviors in order to gain more cognitive legitimacy (i.e., "the spread of knowledge about a new venture" (Aldrich and Fiol, 1994: 648)). Second, they urge founders to communicate internally consistent stories with respect to their entrepreneurial activity, as this is likely to result in so-called sociopolitical legitimacy (i.e., the principal category of the subcategories pragmatic and moral legitimacy, in other words "the process by which key stakeholders […] accept a venture as appropriate and right, given existing norms and laws" (Aldrich and Fiol, 1994: 648)). Contrary to this, Zimmerman and Zeitz (2002) suggest four general strategies that can be roughly differentiated by the degree of confrontation an organization accepts in order to gain legitimacy. The first strategy comprises all activities aiming at achieving congruence between the organization and its environment, that is to say, the environment is strictly accepted as a given set of rules and norms to which the organization adapts. Second, organizations can choose an environment that is in line with the organization's values, which naturally requires less adoption (for instance, if an ICT venture consciously chooses to relocate to a technology cluster such as the Silicon Valley). Third, an organization can attempt to manipulate the environment in such a way that established external norms are changed and the organization thus achieves the status of being legitimate. The last and most challenging option would be the creation of a previously not existent environment.

However, up to now the literature on legitimation is quite vague about how such strategies can be adjusted to various different parties in the larger environment. There is consensus that legitimacy is ascribed to an organization from outside by certain stakeholder groups (Suchman, 1995). Such stakeholders are defined as follows (Freeman, 1984: 46):

"A stakeholder in an organization is (by definition) any group or individual who can affect or is affected by the achievement of the organization's objectives."

Given that different stakeholder groups form different expectations towards the venture, they are equally inclined to perceive different degrees of legitimacy. The challenge for entrepreneurs resulting from this fact is that different stakeholders pursue different objectives, and that their respective interests need not be congruent. A particular behavior that might help to build legitimacy with one group of stakeholders, might be detrimental with a second group and ineffective with a third.

Some scholars (e.g., Mitchell et al., 1997) have suggested methods and instruments to identify key stakeholders and to actively manage the relationship with them (for instance depending on a stakeholder's specific power, legitimacy, and urgency). However, these instruments were not developed with respect to an organization wishing to build legitimacy in the eyes of its stakeholders. This apparent research gap will be closed in the subsequent paragraphs.

METHOD AND DATA

The theory with respect to the different forms of organizational legitimacy is certainly well enough developed and sufficiently substantiated, and thus potentially allows to employ a quantitative, hypotheses-driven research design in the general entrepreneurial setting. However, against the background of our research questions, we felt that we needed to investigate an extreme case, which is inevitably a rare phenomenon. We found one such case with Europe's first online pharmacy *DocMorris*, which was founded in the year 2000. At this time, *DocMorris* was an extremely innovative venture merging for the first time an e-commerce business model with the more traditional business model of a pharmacy. *DocMorris* can therefore be considered a first mover in a new industry (Kerin et al., 1992); it has not only helped to establish a new segment within the e-commerce sector, but has significantly influenced adjacent industries as well. What is more, the venture experienced substantial resistance by established players (indicating its illegitimacy at the time of establishment), which considerably exceeded the challenges other more conventional ventures usually have to deal with. Given that the firm was sold successfully in April 2007 to a pharmaceutical wholesaler, we can assume with some certainty, that the legitimation process was successful, and – as the subsequent analysis will show – this legitimation process was managed strategically by the main actors.

DocMorris is thus an appropriate candidate for a qualitative single-case design investigating the strategies that radically innovative ventures can pursue in order to gain legitimacy (Fallgatter and Brink, 2008). Admittedly, such a design is extremely limited in terms of its potential generalizability (Lee and Baskerville, 2003), however, focusing on a single case and analyzing this single case in-depth can help to facilitate theoretical progress and potential modification of existing theoretical propositions and concepts (Eisenhardt, 1989; Eisenhardt and Graebner, 2007). Moreover, most published research on legitimation and the legitimacy concept has been quite theoretical so far, and applications to real-life-scenarios are still scarce. A single case study can help closing this apparent gap in the literature. We analyze this case along the lines of the theoretical discussion of organizational legitimacy, i.e., we utilize an established paradigm as the guiding line of our research (Yin, 2003), rather than pursuing a presuppositionless approach (Glaser and Strauss, 2008)

Data were collected through interviews with key actors and industry experts, i.e., the venture's founder and chief executive officer (CEO), one venture capital investor, whose firm had invested substantial amounts into the venture (VC), and a representative of a business association (REP). Interviews were conducted by phone, lasted for approximately one to two hours, and in two of three interviews two interviewers were present. Interviews were taped and subsequently transcribed. This interview data was triangulated with information that resulted from screening the general business press, the firm's press releases, information provided on the firm's website and other publically available information. To analyze the data we resorted to a content analysis software that allowed to code the data and to develop a system of categories (MAX Qualitative Data Analysis – MAXQDA 2.0).

CASE ANALYSIS

The Business Model

"There were main theatres of war and sidelines, there were allies and alliances, there were main opponents – the pharmacists – who have forged these alliances. We have smashed these alliances and isolated the pharmacists." (CEO)

As the introductory quote to this paragraph indicates, we selected a firm for our analysis which in the very beginning of its operations was characterized by an extraordinary level of illegitimacy. This illegitimacy caused tremendous resistance by certain stakeholder groups, which *DocMorris* needed to overcome. *DocMorris* started as Europe's first online pharmacy at the end of the dot-com-hype; the firm was established in October 1999 and started serving its customers in June 2000. The idea for the business was simple: As the CEO of the firm wanted to profit from the obvious benefits of starting an ICT venture at the end of the 20th century, he concentrated his search on goods that potentially could be delivered to customers through an e-commerce platform, but were at the time of start-up distributed traditionally. He found one such good with pharmaceuticals; the main idea thus was to cross two established business models, namely e-commerce and pharmacy. Given that under German law a pharmacist is only allowed to operate three branches, serving the complete German market through distance selling could place an online pharmacy at a significant competitive advantage due to for instance economies of scale in procurement. *DocMorris* achieved indeed substantially lower procurement costs in comparison to traditional pharmacies and is able to pass a considerable slice of these savings on to its customers. Pharmaceuticals offered by *DocMorris* are on average 10 to 15% cheaper when compared to the firm's stationary competitors. These lower prices are particularly interesting for chronically ill people.

While the economic rational for this business model is easy to comprehend, the venture nonetheless suffered from extreme illegitimacy in the very beginning. Not only was the venture itself illegitimate, but also its key communication channel (i.e. the Internet) was facing serious issues regarding its legitimacy (Kollmann and Kuckertz, 2004). Moreover, *DocMorris* did poorly on all three dimensions of legitimacy that were suggested by Suchman (1995). First, just like every other start-up, *DocMorris* had almost no cognitive legitimacy, as the firm was largely unknown to its potential customers. Second, the firm had to struggle with its moral legitimacy, as traditional pharmacies tried to put online pharmacies into the same league as dubious online retailers distributing anabolic steroids or impotence drugs. Even worse, distance selling of pharmaceuticals was illegal at the time of start-up in Germany, as the German legislation was based on the assumption that pharmaceuticals should not be sold without the personal advise of a qualified pharmacist. Overall, the venture could thus be characterized as having low pragmatic legitimacy as well, given that in the typical consumer's perception *DocMorris* potentially offered more problems than solutions to consumers' needs. Given these particular circumstances, especially the German law, *DocMorris* was consciously founded in a Dutch border town close to Germany, namely Heerlen. Distributing pharmaceuticals to German customers from Dutch headquarters was lawful under European Union legislation, but of course still illegal under German legislation. For the first three and a half years, *DocMorris* thus operated under extreme legal uncertainty, which was not resolved until the European Court of Justice dismissed a claim filed by the Federal Union of German Associations of Pharmacists (ABDA) in 2003.

Still, *DocMorris* has been a tremendous success. For instance, in its early years it was recognized as a 'Rising Star' in Deloitte's 'Technology Fast 500'-Ranking due to its sales growth of approximately 500% in the first three years. Over the years, the customer base has grown to more than one million and the firm's sales exceed more than € 200 million (Figure 1). These figures, together with a growing number of competitors entering the market for online pharmacies, indicate that the firm has successfully managed to build legitimacy for itself and for a whole new part of the e-commerce sector as well. In 2007, the firm was sold to Europe's largest pharmaceutical wholesaler *Celesio*, lending further support to the notion that *DocMorris* today is a legitimate business. In order to illustrate how this legitimacy was build, the following paragraphs will discuss the various strategies that were employed to manage the firm's various stakeholders. Our analysis focuses on two major stakeholder groups: internal and external stakeholders.

Legitimacy and Internal Stakeholders

Given the significant amount of external pressure caused by the firm's obvious illegitimacy, it was of utmost importance for *DocMorris* to be perceived as legitimate by three internal groups of stakeholders: management, investors, and employees. By focusing on stabilizing these internal stakeholders, the firm's founders achieved the required internal stability that was necessary to meet the external challenges.

With respect to the firms *management team*, legitimacy was achieved in two ways. First, the firm started with relatively low levels of hierarchy, thus being able to offer the management team the possibility to directly execute power and influence results. Each management team member had a huge amount of responsibility due to the fact that the venture had no middle management during the difficult launching process. Of course, it was the CEO's challenge to bring out the best of the management team and to continuously demonstrate that the company was on the right track. To do so,

Figure 1. DocMorris – Growth of sales and customers (2001 to 2007)

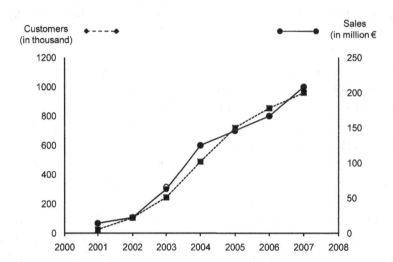

each team member was informed about all aspects of the business model at all times, which resulted in a high level of motivation and consequently in (pragmatic) legitimacy. Second, researchers have already highlighted the importance of charismatic leadership in order to strengthen the base of moral legitimacy (Aldrich and Fiol, 1994). This was exactly the case with *DocMorris*, the firm's CEO was indeed "the figurehead of the company with excellent communication skills" (VC). Through individual conversations he ensured that legitimacy was consolidated amongst his management team. Apart from that, he aimed to create an atmosphere of transparency and took care that misunderstandings were avoided.

Gaining legitimacy from *investors* is crucial as well. Due to the fact that new businesses quite often experience critical phases of turbulences during their start-up process, a reliable investor, who supports the new venture in periods of adversity, is essential. To create the needed atmosphere of trust, *DocMorris* utilized a number of specific strategies that ultimately resulted in legitimacy from the perspective of its investors. The firm's CEO puts it this way:

"We reap what we sow. I always tried to keep our investors informed how specific operations were running at DocMorris. That means that we briefed them about bad news as well. Thereby we were able to build a great base of trust amongst our investors and this was the reason that they relied on us in critical situations as well". (CEO)

In the case of *DocMorris*, the company established a continuous communication and information policy targeted at its stakeholders. This implied transmitting details about how the company was running and thereby occasionally briefing investors even about negative operations. By closely cooperating with the company's shareholders the investors could be persuaded to remain invested.

The last important group of internal stakeholders comprises the firm's *employees*. As with other stakeholders, a proper communication policy and the creation of a transparent internal environment seems to be an important factor to achieve pragmatic, moral, and cognitive legitimacy. *DocMorris* was permanently confronted with interim injunctions brought up by the *Federal Union of German Associations of Pharmacists*. These injunctions were intended to shut down the venture and to drive undesired competition out of the market. Understandably, these legal issues caused enormous tensions and doubts amidst the staff. Therefore it turned out to be necessary to explicitly take care of the employees' concerns:

"I had to maintain an intensive communication manner with my employees, to avoid great concerns about a failure of our company and to keep our staff at it." (CEO)

Due to the public hostility brought up by the market opponents of *DocMorris*, communication maintained through individual talks and its transparency were playing an important role to squash rumors and encourage employees. Fortunately for *DocMorris*, the firm was a quick success in terms of sales and the number of customers, which helped to strengthen the base of legitimacy from the perspective of the employees.

Legitimacy and External Stakeholders

Without a doubt, internal stakeholder are necessary to build the basis for organizational legitimacy. However, without being perceived as legitimate by key external stakeholders, no venture will be able to succeed in the long run. Given that external stakeholders can differ significantly in their respective goals and motivations, it is close to impossible to satisfy each and every need that may be articulated by a specific stakeholder group. In the subsequent paragraphs, we will analyze how *DocMorris* managed its various stakeholder groups strategically to exceed the threshold value of organizational legitimacy so that the firm would be perceived as legitimate from the perspective of most, but not all, stakeholder groups. As it seems to be – at least for the short term – an unachievable goal to satisfy all stakeholder groups simultaneously, *DocMorris* decided to pursue a form of 'contra-strategy' towards some stakeholders, i.e., the firm consciously provoked conflict with some

stakeholders (which reduced its legitimacy from the perspective of this particular group) in order to gain legitimacy from the perspective of another, more important stakeholder group. In the following paragraphs we will illustrate how *DocMorris* managed various stakeholder groups to achieve the goal of being perceived as legitimate in general, namely its customers, the traditional pharmacies, its suppliers, the general public, policy makers, and health insurance companies.

A firm's *customers* are certainly one of the most important groups that needs to be convinced that the business is legitimate. In the case of *DocMorris*, it was easy for customers to ascribe pragmatic legitimacy to the venture, as customers can save substantial amounts of money buying pharmaceutical products online. These inexpensive products can be bought largely anonymously online together with professional, high-quality advice. To compensate for the lack of physical, real-life advice that traditional pharmacies provide to their customers, a service telephone was installed. Moreover, customers find a plethora of information about products on the firm's website. However, in order to gain further legitimacy, the company inevitably had to adapt to certain business standards such as delivering products on time and offering the same quality products as traditional pharmacies. For every type of pharmacy, customer and after sales service as well as quality management in general are vital in order to satisfy customers' demands. Equally important seems to be a well defined complaint management:

"Everyone makes mistakes sometimes. If the online pharmacies make mistakes, it is essential to monitor the complaint management meticulously. At the moment I am responsible for the complaint management for the Online Pharmacists Association. When there are complaints, regardless of which triviality, there has to be an immediate reaction. One example: Someone transfers money, but the consignment is not complete and the refund is delayed. In this case the pharmacist has one

chance to react quick and accommodating. If he misses to do so, there will be an immense irritation and the customers are gone." (REP)

To highlight the fact that operations met the level of quality desired by its customers, *DocMorris* applied for external certification which was successful and allowed to emphasize that the firm bears a certain seal of approval.

Somewhat ironically, one of *DocMorris's* main opponents, the *traditional pharmacies*, significantly helped the firm to gain publicity extremely fast which resulted in enhanced cognitive legitimacy. As the traditional pharmacies felt that their business model was exposed to extreme danger by the advent of online pharmacies, they tried to rally their customers to support the traditional pharmaceutical distribution concept. However, as "one can assess cognitive legitimation by measuring the level of public knowledge about a new activity" (Aldrich and Fiol, 1994: 648), doing so can be consider a fatal flaw in the battle for the market:

"The traditional pharmacies accomplished to collect 7.7 million signatures against us. From now on 7.7 million potential customers were aware that the business model of the online pharmacy did exist and we invested nothing for that." (CEO)

Still, the traditional pharmacists and the *Federal Union of German Associations of Pharmacists* were important and powerful market participants. As the management of *DocMorris* realized the importance of this association quite early, they tried to isolate this group from other lobbies as soon as possible. The main goal of this effort was to avoid the formation of alliances. To achieve this goal, management entered intensive discussion with several other stakeholder groups. Beyond that, the company sought private talks with representatives of the pharmaceutical industry, the *Resident Doctors' Association* and

the pharmaceutical suppliers. While it could be ensured that *DocMorris* would not be a harm to the first two groups, it was difficult to convince the suppliers at first. They were deeply concerned to potentially annoy their main customers, the traditional pharmacies, by establishing business relationships with *DocMorris*.

Given these circumstance, the stakeholder group comprising the firm's *suppliers*, perceived the legitimacy of *DocMorris* as quite problematic in the beginning. In fact, when launching its venture, *DocMorris* was faced with a total boycott by potential suppliers, who did not want to put their established business relationships with traditional pharmacies at any risk. Therefore, *DocMorris* entered into a 'gentlemen's agreement' with them and agreed to remain silent about every delivery's origin. The CEO was personally acquainted with the most important pharmaceutical suppliers and had explained the business model to them in person. This was an important step forward to resolve doubts regarding the consequences of supplying *DocMorris* and therefore helped to gain legitimacy with the suppliers. After *DocMorris* had overcome these initial procurement problems, the company accomplished to build up a good reputation and the procurement process was simplified. Persuading the pharmaceutical wholesalers turned out to be tedious as well. However, after crossing a certain threshold, *DocMorris* benefitted from its growing market power, which had led to increased economies of scale. Suddenly, the whole situation had changed and the company was able to order necessary pharmaceuticals directly from the pharmaceutical companies.

The battle with the traditional pharmacies affected the level of legitimacy perceived by the *general public* as well. In an attempt to enhance its moral legitimacy, *DocMorris* actively created an image as a venture fighting the traditional pharmacies to the advantage of its customers:

"We were perceived as something like 'Robin Hood', who takes something from the well-established wealthy traditional pharmacies, to give it to the poor." (VC)

This image was cultivated by setting up an appropriate public relations strategy; the firm's success and growth was communicated continuously via all types of mass media channels. Positioning the CEO as 'Robin Hood' contributed to achieving the goal of positioning *DocMorris* as an industry leader, which is generally believed to create pragmatic and moral legitimacy (Aldrich and Fiol, 1994). From the perspective of the general public, it was equally helpful that the traditional pharmacies brought *DocMorris* to court whenever possible, which ensured that a great deal of attention was attracted to *DocMorris*. The CEO expresses the effects of the lawsuit somewhat tongue-in-cheek:

"It was part of the PR strategy that the pharmacist association would sue us. We founded DocMorris in June 2000 and were pretty nervous after there was no sign of bringing us to trial until the autumn of the same year. In the meantime, we considered if we should sue ourselves. In the end the lawsuit was filed against us in November 2000." (CEO)

Lobbyism to convince the stakeholder group of *policy makers* can be considered an important factor as well. During the legitimization process of *DocMorris*, communicating with key policy makers was a fundamental driver of the firm's later success. The CEO got in touch with a professional lobbyist, who was instructed to influence decision makers in the interest of *DocMorris*:

"I contacted a professional lobbyist who made contacts for me with decision makers. Next, I visited every member of the Bundestag [German parliament] who was a member of the health committee to explain to them our business model.

After that all rumors and prejudices which were propagated were scotched and the dialogue partners soon understood." (CEO)

This was the first step to change the regulatory framework. In the beginning, *DocMorris* had to establish its headquarters in the Netherlands to avoid the monopoly of the traditional pharmacies and the entirely regulated market in Germany as well as to operate legally under EU jurisdiction. After several lawsuits were filed against *DocMorris*, the company had to operate in a legal grey area. Hence, the firm's management exerted influence on German legislation with the explicit goal to legalize the business model of online pharmacies not only in the EU, but in Germany as well:

"Great parts of the legal text, which permits the mail order of pharmaceuticals, were drafted by us. We transmitted the text via the appropriate channels to the decision makers and managed to convince them. Afterwards we took care that the exact text appeared in the law which passed [the Germany parliament]." (CEO)

As a consequence, the business model of online pharmacies became legal in Germany, and the venture gained considerable (moral) legitimacy.

Policy makers most certainly felt quite easy about changing the law given that the venture managed to gather support from another key stakeholder group that is vitally important in the German health system: the *health insurance companies*. It was in the own interest of these companies that the heavily regulated German pharmacy market would be liberalized so that costs for pharmaceuticals could be reduced. The insurance companies naturally favor that their insurants order comparatively cheap medication to take the pressure off their budgets. For instance, the chairman of one particular health insurance company emerged as the champion of the new business model. After arguing publicly in favor of online pharmacies, he attracted high interest from the public to *DocMorris*. Given that the entire industry was still at a juvenile stage, having a prominent person being sympathetic for the new business model signaled to the public that the whole business was trustworthy and legitimate.

CONCLUSION

Analyzing the case of DocMorris *through the lenses of stakeholder and legitimacy theory has turned out to be quite fruitful. While the venture started indeed as quite illegitimate and – depending on what perspective is chosen – illegal, the growth of customers and sales is a clear indication of the tremendous legitimacy the firm has earned over the years. Equally, the rising number of competitors (Aldrich and Fiol, 1994) indicates as well that the industry and the online pharmacy business model is generally perceived as being legitimate. Nowadays, online pharmacies are represented by the* European Association of Mail Service Pharmacies (EAMSP).

Taken together, the findings from this case study of Europe's first online pharmacy suggest that ventures can take a number of measures to raise their legitimacy that go well beyond what has been suggested in prior studies. In particular, to build legitimacy with the various stakeholder groups every venture naturally encounters, we urge founders to consider one or more of the following strategies:

- Identify and analyze opponents, direct competitors, allies, and undecided parties,
- protect the day-to-day business and stabilize the firm's internal basis,
- gain customer trust and provide an optimal complaint management,
- isolate opponents wherever possible, manipulate them, systematically provoke resistance, and aim at winning the public opinion,
- ally with direct competitors,
- cooperate with allies, inform undecided parties, communicate, create transparency, persuade, and build networks,
- split opposing parties, and
- lobby policy makers through transparent communication.

While these strategies seem to be quite promising to build organizational legitimacy in the long run, it may in some cases be necessary to build legitimacy fast. This may be due to an extremely low level of actual legitimacy or a restricted resource base, which limits long-term efforts. To build legitimacy quickly, we suggest the following (low-cost) measures:

- Interpret resistance as a critical success factor and provoke such resistance,
- build omnipresence in mass media,
- create transparency for stakeholders by direct and open communication,
- lead charismatically,
- build networks with direct competitors and institutions outside of the respective industry,
- build a management team that is capable of perceiving opportunities and reacts fast.

Declaredly, these measures were derived from a single and extreme case, which at the moment obviously limits their generalizability. We therefore caution founders and managers of venture firms to carefully assess the applicability of these measures against the specific situation of their organization. Nonetheless, we are convinced that the example of DocMorris *has been quite informative and will stimulate more rational and strategic approaches to the entrepreneurial process – both in theory and in practice.*

REFERENCES

Aldrich, H. E., & Fiol, C. M. (1994). Fools rush in? The institutional context of industry creation. *Academy of Management Review, 19*(4), 645–670. doi:10.2307/258740

Ashforth, B. E., & Gibbs, B. W. (1990). The double-edge of organizational legitimation. *Organization Science, 1*(2), 177–194. doi:10.1287/orsc.1.2.177

Bhidé, A. V. (2000). *The origin and evolution of new business*. Oxford, UK: Oxford University Press.

Delmar, F., & Shane, S. (2004). Legitimating first: Organizing activities and the survival of new ventures. *Journal of Business Venturing, 19*(3), 385–410. doi:10.1016/S0883-9026(03)00037-5

Dowling, J., & Pfeffer, J. (1975). Organizational legitimacy: Social values and organizational behavior. *Pacific Sociological Review, 18*(1), 122–136.

Eisenhardt, K. M. (1989). Building Theories from Case Study Research. *Academy of Management Review, 14*(4), 532–550. doi:10.2307/258557

Eisenhardt, K. M., & Graebner, M. E. (2007). Theory building from cases: opportunities and challenges. *Academy of Management Journal, 50*(1), 25–32.

Fallgatter, M. J., & Brink, S. (2008). Zum Einfluss der Legitimation auf die Entwicklung junger Unternehmen: Eine State of the Art-Betrachtung am Beispiel von DocMorris. *Zeitschrift für Management, 3*(4), 303–319. doi:10.1007/s12354-008-0046-0

Glaser, B. G., & Strauss, A. (2008). *The discovery of grounded theory. Strategies for qualitative research* (3rd ed.). New Brunswick, NJ: Aldine.

Kerin, R. A., Varadarajan, P. R., & Peterson, R. A. (1992). First-Mover Advantage: A Synthesis, Conceptual Framework, and Research Propositions. *JMR, Journal of Marketing Research, 56*(4), 33–53.

Kollmann, T. (2006). What is e-entrepreneurship? Fundamentals of company founding in the net economy. *International Journal of Technology Management, 33*(4), 322–340. doi:10.1504/IJTM.2006.009247

Kollmann, T., & Kuckertz, A. (2004). Venture Capital Decision Making After the High-Tech Downturn: Considerations Based on German E-Business Investment Cases. *Journal of Private Equity, 7*(4), 48–59. doi:10.3905/jpe.2004.434766

Kollmann, T., & Kuckertz, A. (2006). Investor relations for start-ups: an analysis of venture capital investors' communicative needs. *International Journal of Technology Management, 34*(1/2), 47–62. doi:10.1504/IJTM.2006.009447

Kollmann, T., & Kuckertz, A. (in press). Evaluation uncertainty of venture capitalists' investment criteria. *Journal of Business Research*.

Lee, A. S., & Baskerville, R. L. (2003). Generalizing Generalizability in Information Systems Research. *Information Systems Research, 14*(3), 221–243. doi:10.1287/isre.14.3.221.16560

Meyer, J. W., & Rowan, B. (1977). Institutionalized organizations: Formal structure as myth and ceremony. *American Journal of Sociology, 83*(2), 340–363. doi:10.1086/226550

Mitchell, R. K., Agle, B. R., & Wood, D. J. (1997). Toward a Theory of Stakeholder Identification and Salience: Defining the Principle of Who and What Really Counts. *Academy of Management Review, 22*(4), 853–896. doi:10.2307/259247

Singh, J. V., Tucker, D. J., & House, R. J. (1986). Organizational legitimacy and the liability of newness. *Administrative Science Quarterly, 31*(2), 171–193. doi:10.2307/2392787

Starr, J. A., & Macmillan, I. A. (1990). Resource cooptation via social contracting: Resource acquisition strategies for new ventures. *Strategic Management Journal, 11*, 79–92. doi:10.1002/smj.4250110107

Stinchcombe, A. L. (1965). Social structure and organizations. In J. G. March (Ed.), *Handbook of organizations* (pp. 142-193). Chicago, IL: Rand McNally.

Suchman, M. C. (1995). Managing Legitimacy: Strategic and Institutional Approaches. *Academy of Management Review, 20*(3), 571–610. doi:10.2307/258788

Yin, R. K. (2003). *Case study research. Design and methods* (3rd ed.). Thousand Oaks, CA: Sage.

Zimmerman, M. A., & Zeitz, G. J. (2002). Beyond Survival: Achieving New Venture Growth by Building Legitimacy. *Academy of Management Review, 27*(3), 414–431. doi:10.2307/4134387

ADDITIONAL READING

Amit, R., & Zott, C. (2001). Value Creation in E-Business. *Strategic Management Journal, 22*(3), 493–520. doi:10.1002/smj.187

Bhave, M. P. (1997). A Process Model of Entrepreneurial Venture Creation. *Journal of Business Venturing, 9*(3), 223–242. doi:10.1016/0883-9026(94)90031-0

Brazeal, D. V., & Herbert, T. T. (1999). The Genesis of Entrepreneurship. *Entrepreneurship Theory and Practice, 23*(3), 29–45.

Bygrave, W. D., & Hofer, C. W. (1991). Theorizing about Entrepreneurship. *Entrepreneurship Theory and Practice, 16*(2), 13–22.

Covin, J. G., & Slevin, D. P. (1989). Strategic Management of Small Firms in Hostile and Benign Environments. *Strategic Management Journal, 10*(1), 75–87. doi:10.1002/smj.4250100107

Gartner, W. B. (1985). A Conceptual Framework for Describing the Phenomenon of New Venture Creation. *Academy of Management Review, 10*(4), 696–706. doi:10.2307/258039

Gruber, M., MacMillan, I. C., & Thompson, J. D. (2008). Look before you leap: market opportunity identification in emerging technology firms. *Management Science, 54*(9), 1652–1665. doi:10.1287/mnsc.1080.0877

Harms, R., Kraus, S., & Schwarz, E. (2009). The suitability of the configuration approach in entrepreneurship research. *Entrepreneurship & Regional Development, 21*(1), 25–49. doi:10.1080/08985620701876416

Harms, R., Reschke, H., Kraus, S., & Fink, M. (in press). Antecedents of Innovation and Growth: Analyzing the Impact of Entrepreneurial Orientation and Goal-oriented Management. *International Journal of Technology Management.*

Jaworski, B. J., & Kohli, A. K. (1993). Market Orientation: Antecedents and Consequences. *Journal of Marketing, 57*(3), 53–70. doi:10.2307/1251854

Kautonen, T. (2006). Trust as a governance mechanism in inter-firm relations: Conceptual considerations. *Evolutionary and Institutional Economics Review, 3*(1), 89–108.

Kazanjian, R. K. (1988). Relation of Dominant Problems to Stages of Growth in Technology-Based New Ventures. *Academy of Management Journal, 31*(2), 257–279. doi:10.2307/256548

Kennedy, M. M. (1979). Generalizing from single case studies. *Evaluation Quarterly, 3*, 661–678. doi:10.1177/0193841X7900300409

Kohtamäki, M., & Kuckertz, A. (Eds.). (in press). Value Creation (Focus Issue). *International Journal of Entrepreneurial Venturing*.

Kohtamäki, M., Varamäki, E., & Tornikoski, E. (2009). Strategic Management Competence of Small and Medium Sized Growth Firms. *International Journal of Entrepreneurship and Small Business*, *7*(1), 139–150. doi:10.1504/IJESB.2009.021614

Kollmann, T., Häsel, M., & Breugst, N. (2009). Competence of IT Professionals in E-Business Venture Teams: The Effect of Experience and Expertise on Preference Structure. *Journal of Management Information Systems*, *25*(4), 51–80. doi:10.2753/MIS0742-1222250402

Kollmann, T., & Kuckertz, A. (2006). Venture Archetypes and the Entrepreneurial Event: Cross-Cultural Empirical Evidence. *Journal of Enterprising Culture*, *14*(1), 27–48. doi:10.1142/S0218495806000039

Kollmann, T., Kuckertz, A., & Breugst, N. (in press). Organizational Readiness and the Adoption of Electronic Business - The Moderating Role of National Culture in 29 European Countries. *The Data Base for Advances in Information Systems*.

Kollmann, T., & Stöckmann, C. (in press). Antecedents of Strategic Ambidexterity: Effects of Entrepreneurial Orientation on Exploratory and Exploitative Innovation in Adolescent Organizations. *International Journal of Technology Management*.

Kollmann, T., Stöckmann, C., & Schröer, C. (2009). Diffusion and Oscillation of Telecommunications Services: The Case of Web 2.0 Platforms. In I. Lee, I. (Ed.), *Handbook of Research on Telecommunications Planning and Management for Business* (557-570). Hershey, PA: Information Science Reference.

Kuckertz, A., & Kohtamäki, M. (Eds.). (in press). The Interface of Strategy, Innovation, and Growth [Special Issue]. *International Journal of Technology Management*.

Kuckertz, A., & Kohtamäki, M., & Droege gen. Körber, C. (in press). The fast eat the slow - The impact of strategy and innovation timing on the success of technology-oriented ventures. *International Journal of Technology Management*.

Lee, A. S., & Baskerville, R. L. (2003). Generalizing Generalizability in Information Systems Research. *Information Systems Research*, *14*(3), 221–243. doi:10.1287/isre.14.3.221.16560

Politis, D. (2005). The process of entrepreneurial learning: A conceptual framework. *Entrepreneurship Theory and Practice*, *29*(4), 399–324. doi:10.1111/j.1540-6520.2005.00091.x

Porter, M. E. (2001). Strategy and the Internet. *Harvard Business Review*, *79*(3), 63–78.

Shane, S., & Venkataraman, S. (2000). The Promise of Entrepreneurship as a Field of Research. *Academy of Management Review*, *25*(1), 217–226. doi:10.2307/259271

Vuorinen, T., Varamäki, E., Kohtamäki, M., & Pihkala, T. (2006). Operationalising the Value of SME Network Resources. *Journal of Enterprising Culture*, *14*(3), 199–218. doi:10.1142/S0218495806000131

Chapter 6
Internet Portals in Rural Areas:
An Investigation of Their Provision in Rural Scotland

Laura Galloway
Heriot-Watt University, UK

David Deakins
Massey University, New Zealand

John Sanders
Heriot-Watt University, UK

ABSTRACT

This paper investigates the ownership structure, operating characteristics and sustainability of six rural internet portals located in Scotland. It builds upon a previous study conducted by Deakins et al. (2003), which examined the characteristics of internet portals. In-depth interviews were conducted with six owners or the operators responsible for maintaining and developing the internet portal. The study discovered that two distinct forms of ownership structure existed. The first form of ownership structure involved dedicated private individuals who self-funded their internet portal activities, while the second form were managed by not-for-profit organisations, such as charitable trusts, that either hired part-time staff or employed volunteer staff to operate their internet portal. The privately owned portals were most effective because they demonstrated a higher degree of commitment via content richness, fullness of the services offered, and the extent of community and local business usage. In contrast, the not-for profit owned internet portals suffered from limited content, a narrow selection of services, some political in-fighting, low employee commitment, and modest community and business usage. Despite the differences both forms of ownership structure struggled to achieve commercial viability.

DOI: 10.4018/978-1-61520-597-4.ch006

INTRODUCTION

In today's fast changing economy it is increasingly important for firms to participate in internet-based activity. Rodgers, et al. (2002) state that "for all intents and purposes, you cannot compete nowadays without some kind of e-business strategy" (p.184). The internet is a medium for achieving growth and global markets, but also opening up new niche market areas, which can facilitate entrepreneurial growth. Even for low growth rural businesses, some form of internet presence is increasingly important. For successful exploitation of opportunities presented, careful planning, strategy and management are said to be essential (Porter, 2001) (though conversely, in the Web 2.0 environment particularly, there is some evidence that progressive, most often pure-Web, firm owners are employing strategies more akin to prospecting and involving reactionary (to markets) activities to identify and exploit opportunities (Chen, 2005)).

Strategy is most often developed at firm level, but strategy can also be developed collectively. There is evidence that the internet has provided a means for collective action amongst rural business owners, for example, through local area marketing of rural locations, for example in Scotland (Galloway, et al., 2004); industry-focused marketing such as tourism (Pease, et al., 2005); and combinations of these, notably agri-food, for example in Greece (Baourakis, et al., 2002; Vakoufaris, et al., 2007) and Wales (Thomas, et al. 2002). Such strategies can benefit member firms that may not have a direct internet presence: as Pease and Rowe (2005) note, in many cases, particularly in rural locations, "the premise…is the realisation that on its own an SME is not able to cope with the increasingly complex [internet] environment… nor does it possess the skills and expertise needed to compete in that environment". This is, in part, as a result of a paucity of dissemination of useful information on how (rather than why) those in peripheral locations, with their itinerant issues, particularly relating to knowledge, skills and experience, can use evolving internet technologies to advantage (Thompson, 2005).

The current paper reports findings from a study supported by the Carnegie Trust for the Universities of Scotland that seeks to investigate the role of internet portals with rural entrepreneurs in selected rural business communities in Scotland. Internet portals are defined as collective activity using the internet to present businesses via a collective brand, most often industry or location-specific. It will build upon previous research supported by the Scottish Economist's Network (Deakins, et al. 2003) to examine the nature of changes (if any) in the role of internet portals and their impact over this five year period on the rural business communities that they serve. In the previous research internet portals were referred to as 'internet forums'. Since completion some five years ago, the term 'forum' has been adopted generally as referring to communications amongst online communities on specific topics or amongst particular interest groups. For this reason the more appropriate term to be used for the subjects of study in the present research was considered to be 'portal', as identified by writers such as Turban, et al. (2004) and Pease, et al. (2005), the latter of whom describe a portal as "an information gateway using internet technologies [that] can be used by the customer to view products and services and to place orders…and as a point of collaboration between businesses…They…serve as a single point of content management".

RURAL ENTREPRENEURSHIP

In the developing literature on rural business owners and entrepreneurs, it is claimed that there are a number of characteristics of rural entrepreneurship, compared to entrepreneurship in urban areas that determine its distinctiveness. It is now well established that rural areas have relatively more self-employment and business ownership than urban areas, and that in many areas the rural economy is increasingly supported by the small firms and self-employment sectors, as agriculture and traditional industry decline (Roberts, 2002). Despite greater proportions of independent economic activity, however, businesses in rural areas tend to be smaller in size, and are less likely to be classifiable as growth firms, resulting in part in the rural business environment being characterised as less volatile and exhibiting less 'business churn' relative to urban areas (Smallbone, et al. 2002). Other characteristics of the rural business environment include that there can be shortages of skilled labour, providing difficulties in recruitment (Patterson & Henderson, 2003) due in part to net outward migration of younger ages of the population (Courtney & Brydon, 2001). Other issues include reliance on local markets to a greater extent than in urban areas (Galloway & Mochrie, 2006), caused in part by remoteness from extended markets (Huggins & Izushi, 2002), and limited numbers and density of business networks (ibid). Further, Galloway and Mochrie (2006) found also that there is a high proportion of family-owned businesses in the rural economy and a business advice and support premium, due to the more spatially dispersed pattern and lack of business networks. More recently, the Small Business Service confirm that these issues and characteristics of the rural small businesses economy prevail in England (Telford, 2006), and it is likely that this can be generalised to the British and European contexts at least.

Rural Business and the Internet

The benefits, real and potential, associated with internet adoption for businesses are many, and they have been extensively reported elsewhere in the literature. It is not the intention here to reiterate these in detail, however, a summary of now established principles includes access to extended markets (Lawson, et al, 2003); increased trading hours (Buhalis & Main, 1998); product/service refinement and more efficient market targeting as a result of communications with and information from customers (Baourakis, et al., 2002); improved business to business dealings including supply chains (Bharadwaj & Soni, 2007); more efficient transaction arrangements as a result of online payment facilities (Leatherman, 2000); and supplementary networking channels (Swan, et al., 1999).

Despite these well-documented benefits, several studies have identified that rural firms have been relatively slow to take-up innovation and technology, including internet use, and rural SMEs have been presented as being slow to understand the benefits of internet adoption (Smallbone, et al., 2002). These types of findings have been identified as surprising by those who have theorised that since rural firms have more to gain from the benefits of the internet, especially access to extended markets (due to the issues associated with rurality and peripherality, already outlined), they would be more, and not less, likely to engage in internet-based business activities than urban firms (Vaessen & Keeble, 1995). It may be the case that where there was lag, this was characteristic of early use of the internet for business, as the study from which the current research builds found that in fact far from being laggards in the take-up of internet activity, levels of adoption can be high, but the full utilisation of the benefits of it may be more limited (Deakins, et al, 2003). This has been supported by other more recent research such as Dwelly, et al. (2005) and recent analysis of the Small Business Service's annual small business survey, in which was found, for example, that "for almost all purposes, businesses in rural areas with dispersed dwellings are significantly more likely than those in other types of area to use ICT" (Telford, 2006). Forman et al. (2005) go some way to explain this more recent reportage of high levels of internet activity amongst rural firms. Based on empirical testing of US data they found that current variation in internet technology up-take and use between urban and rural businesses comprises a concentration of innovative and enhanced technology use in urban firms in order to provide internal advantage, while common internet technologies are introduced more often and to greater advantage in rural firms in their pursuit of the benefits associated with participating in the external business environment.

The reported reticence of rural firms to adopt internet technologies in the late 1990's and early 2000's was undoubtedly associated with erratic roll-out of internet technologies appropriate for business use, such as broadband (Galloway, 2007). Additionally, information failures among potential users were implicated. Recent UK government commitment to technology solutions for rural and remote locations, most often in the form of subsidised ADSL provision is likely to have dispatched with the first of these issues (DTI, 2004). The issue of demand failure as a symptom of information deficit amongst potential users, however, has inherent the implication that gaps in knowledge can be filled though the provision of fuller information, training support and dissemination of good practice. It may be that policy promotion has encouraged the take-up of internet activity amongst rural entrepreneurs, or there may now be more generally an increased awareness of the benefits of it in rural areas.

Internet Portals

Research on the value of internet portals in rural localities is limited. In theory an internet portal is an additional resource that can add to the entrepreneurial capital of rural business owners. During the previous research project in 2003, six rural internet portals (referred to as forums at that time) were investigated. This qualitative part of the original study was intended to supplement the large survey of ICT use by rural firms by providing information about an additional service that had developed in some areas specifically for the purposes of exploiting the internet for additional business. It was found in that study that firms used these portals for getting started on the internet (most portal operators provides a website building service also), reaching extended markets, raising their profile and there was some evidence that networking and access to support and advice were being facilitated also (Deakins, et al., 2003). With the development of Web 2.0 and the semantic web and the extended communications inherent (Finin, et al., 2005) it may be the case that rural firms are more able now than before to participate in wider business and customer networks.

Interviews with those who had created and developed portals using the rural location as the common brand revealed that those individuals involved in their operation anticipated a significant contribution to economic activity in the area. The earliest of these portals were found to be privately created and operated, the rationale being that profit for the firm on the basis of effectiveness of the portal for businesses would reap profit for the portal operator. Indeed, the anticipation of the contribution such ICT could make to the rural economy was such that as Thompson (2005) points out in relation to Australia, "a raft of government policies and programs has been launched and reports published and disseminated, based around the theme of ICT and online capabilities" (p.219). The emergence of portals for rural areas, often with community and social, as well as business, agenda is one of these phenomena that has occurred in response to research and commentary about the potential advantages of internet technologies to rural areas: the why (rather than how) rationale for facilitating ICT participation. As such, portals developed by public agents or charities were represented in the original study also. Since that time, many more portals, rural and industry specific, have emerged, with Scotland being no exception. The specific nature and content varies by industry (if there is an industry focus), location, and the aims and objectives of the people or organisations responsible for their development. The previous research concluded that where the remit of the founding organisation was too broad, lack of focus was likely to result in the portal being less effective. Specifically, for the rural portals studied, those publicly funded with remits that included, for example, economic development through business provision, community engagement in the internet, provision of local internet services, provision of community information, and other community aims such as contributing to employability skills amongst the population by using the portal as a trainer and employer of those without jobs, would result in least effective achievement of the aims of the portal. Conversely, those that were highly focused on business objectives would be most successful.

The aim of the current study is to investigate five years on, the extent to which portals are sustainable, the effect they have on business and economic development in the rural locations they cater for, and identify the characteristics of successful portal operation.

Methodology

The current study replicated the part of the original research that investigated the structure, operations and strategy of internet portals in rural areas in Scotland. Rural area was defined as comprising a UK mainland settlement of fewer than 10,000 residents (PIU, 2000), however, Scotland's rural areas are very diverse, with some areas very isolated and others relatively well-served by an infrastructure that affords a proximity to urban services. As a result, remoteness was included in the description of firms, and this was based on the time it would take to travel (by normal methods, such as road on the mainland and boat on the islands) to an urban area (i.e., mainland settlement of more than 10,000). The size of the portal in terms of numbers of businesses in the locality that were hosted or advertised in it was included also. As Scotland has a strong tourist industry, the number of firms is given, and includes the number of these that are tourist accommodation providers. The 'size' of the portal in these

terms, from a business perspective, is very closely related to the 'size' of the community they represent, and this correlates closely with remoteness also[1]. Eight portal operators were contacted and invited to participate in the research. These eight included the five included in the original study and two 'new' ones for comparison. Four of the original portal operators and two of the operators included for the current study only agreed and an interview was conducted with them. Of these six portals, one was publicly funded, two were operated as a registered charity, and three were privately owner-managed. Table 1 below provides some details about the sample.

The owner or person assigned responsibility for the portal was contacted and in-depth interviews were conducted. Interviewees were asked about how the portal was started and issues thereof, and the aims, use and effectiveness (in the respondent's opinion) of the portal. Depending on location of the interviewee, some of these interviews were face-to-face and some were by telephone using a speaker. All interviews were tape-recorded and transcribed, and analysis was conducted by the authors separately in the first instance to check for consistency of interpretation of data. Collaboration on and comparison of interpretations of themes emerging was conducted thereafter and consensus was achieved ensuring reliability.

Results

Provision of services varies significantly amongst those included in the research. Portals A, D, E and F all provide a website building service to businesses and community groups, whereas B and C do not, instead providing links to websites. All portals facilitate or provide internet hosting of websites, and all contain a business directory. Portals D, E and F also host forums whereupon business and/or community groups can communicate and network. In fact, in the case of these three portals, the owners claimed that this is the most popular and commonly used part of their site.

Table 1. Description of sample

Portal	Age	Time from urban area	Funding status	Change in funding status?	Size: Total no. of firms (no of these accommodation)	Operation	In 2003 study?
A	12	3 hours (island)	Charitable status (training organisation)	Yes Originally privately operated	45 (14)	One person responsible as part of overall duties of employment with training organisation	No
B	10	30 minutes (mainland)	Public (LEC and tourist organisation)	No	202 (53)	Two part-time staff who operate it as part of duties for the LEC.	Yes
C	6	1 hour (mainland)	Charitable status (part of greater charitably funded regeneration activity)	Yes Previously funded through consultancy firm by public sector grants	40 (30)	One person as part of overall regeneration duties	Yes
D	7	20 minutes (mainland)	Private	No	123 (39)	One person	No
E	9	3 hours (mainland)	Private	No	1570 (204)	One person	Yes
F	12	5 hours (island)	Private	No	120 (45)	One person	Yes

Content

Portals A, D, E and F are all extensive sites in themselves, providing much content through links to their own pages and external websites, and including some interactivity facilitated by Web 2.0, such as availability of blogging areas, site feedback facilities, etc.. While portals B and C also provide links, these are most often to external websites and content of the portal itself is relatively limited to front page information and pictures.

Updating, developing and adding content was claimed by the operators of Portals D, E and F to be one of the most important activities in terms of maintaining interest in and relevance of their sites. That is not to say that continual change is advocated: on the contrary, these portal operators were consistent in advocating that the site be consistent over time in terms of structure, so that navigation becomes familiar to users. As the operator of Portal E puts it:

The structure of the site, the layout of it is basically the same and I know I've added lots of new sections but the actual layout with indexing is basically the same…I've not changed the structure for about seven or eight years. People are now very familiar with the layout.

In the same vein, Portal F operator notes that in terms of what is technologically possible, there is a sense that just because you can do it doesn't mean you should:

I've seen a lot of fads, a lot of crazes, a lot of flash in the pan developments come and go, and although my sites may initially look a little plain, I think there's a depth there and there's a sort of focus on not just the content and the readability but the simplicity and speed. In designing people's sites they ask "Can we have this and can we do this?" and I have to say "Well I don't know whether that's a good idea and that might make it a little harder to read". Portal F informant.

This may well be a point particularly pertinent to rural portals and websites; all respondents claimed that while broadband had been made available in their area, it was inconsistent in terms of speed and reliability, and the slower the download speed one experiences, the more difficult it is to engage with new or large software applications. This has specific implications for much of the utility of Web 2.0 applications that require real-time up- and down-load-ability. Moreover, while internet innovation is continual, the pace of change may not be optimal for many businesses and consumers, and again, this has implications for use of Web 2.0 applications. The owner of Portal F explains the importance of simplicity and predictability:

I'm not trying to show off or display my knowledge in different areas, its always from the ordinary man on the street. How would they like to find their way around a website? With mine, its not going to be the fanciest, its just going to be a nice website, a good website... A lot of alternative sites come and go, they burn bright, they are a shooting star. Then they just fall to the ground and they're gone. This one is consistent and reliable and it moves in an evolutionary manner.

Several of the portal operators claimed that the overall aim of the facility is to attract external markets to local businesses. All mentioned that they did some form of overseas marketing of the portal. Several respondents claimed that a focus on the external was, however, counterproductive. The owner of Portal E claims that revenues are often locally-based and as a result he is keen to keep the local population engaged. He includes linking on his site that directs local people to farming pages, police pages, what's on pages, etc.:

the way Visit Scotland or the Highland Tourist Board promoted the area was in a way that was only of interest to visitors. I always acted on the assumption that visitors were interested in what

was actually happening. So if you approached it from that perspective then you're supplying that for the local people then visitors will also be interested, as long as you give them what they're looking for.

Indeed, this respondent is keenly aware that what attracts external visitors is photographs of the area and information about goods, services and holiday accommodation, and he claims it is about balancing the attractions for the local and the global that is the key to recurrent and increasing interest in the site. This strategy has been demonstrably successful:

we get vast coverage from overseas that's a significant amount of audience from abroad.

Similarly the operator of Portal A claims that while the focus of the site is local and community events, the greatest beneficiary of the portal are the holiday accommodation establishments with enquiries from external markets.

The owner of Portal F claims:

If you know your neighbours and the things you come into contact with on a daily basis but you look out from that, then that's the best compromise of all because if you make it for the local population with a view to how they perceive that internationally, then you do get a nice combination, a nice mixture. I think if you just look globally it looks a bit naff. When you just think locally it's a bit too parochial. Its finding that balance – inward and outward. As long as you attract people from all over the world but its also very useful for locals.

In some cases the role of the portal was used for accessing resources, although this varied between the different portals. One of the operators indicated that in response to local demand, he had set up a section called *find tradesmen*, while another operator (D) commented that there was active Web 2.0-type use of the portal for seeking solutions to trading issues, with the portal acting as an information exchange. For example, he commented that:

If you know somebody has a technical problem, they go and describe the problem—they ask for an answer and they usually get it within half-an-hour—we have this kind of community in the forum –there is always someone who knows the answer.

Structure

The private status of Portals D, E and F means they are developed and managed by one individual. These respondents claimed that the key to their sustainability is the lack of interference from different groups of stakeholders with varying agendas. The current study does provide evidence that compromise and eclectic input can have a negative impact on sustainability and effectiveness. For example, Portal C as a part of a regeneration project that was funded by grants through a consultant firm, had failed to engage the local community (business and otherwise). The operator of this portal claimed that

There were lots of typical small village suspicions that we were all creaming off thousands for our own benefit and this sort of nonsense.

As a result, and to engage with the community better, charitable status was applied for and achieved in an attempt to become more transparent, and through this inclusive. Additionally, there is now less reliance operationally on volunteer staff, and a focus on professionalising activity. With the portal being only a small part of an overall regeneration remit, the effects of change of funding status remains to be seen however. Currently this portal is little more than an advert for the location, with little business or community

engagement. What may be its greatest hindrance may not be its transparency (or lack of it) in terms of spending, but the fact that as an entity the portal is not a focus in its own right, and critically, it is managed and operated by committee. As private owner of Portal F states:

In funding agencies and a lot of quango-type organisations, they continually have to have meetings about meetings and always have to be seen to be doing something new and fresh…Its all these meetings about websites and they all finish when the website goes live. Whats the use in starting it.

This criticism of committee and accountability and its lack of appropriateness for portals is important, as what is being claimed is that the focus in the public sector is often about creating the portal, whereas, owners of Portals D, E and F are consistent in their claims that the most important thing in terms of effectiveness and therefore feasibility is ongoing maintenance, management and development of content.

You know, when they first launch, its like a panacea to change…and the trouble is they're not developed and maintained. Its easier to get another swathe of Euro money and add a flash new site with a different domain than it is to nurture and develop the existing website. Owner of Portal F.

There was a site for the town which they had got European funding for. It was absolutely hopeless. There was nothing in it, it was never updated. If you look on Google its still there… its been like that for four years so its actually an embarrassment to the town. They pay a lot of money, they get a site up and then there's nobody to maintain it after that. Or they've got a few enthusiastic people and someone leaves the group and then there's nobody to do it. Owner of Portal D.

These kinds of statement illustrate what can be the case for portals run by committee and funded by public money. These comments come from owners of private portals, however, and they might be expected to be critical. There does seem to be some logic to the argument that too many interested parties results in no-one having ownership, though. It is likely that the inherent features and qualities of a being the owner of a private venture with antecedent levels of investment, personal and financial, are the drivers of success in the three private cases in this study, and this is what they perceive to be awry in publicly operated portals. However, none of the owners of privately-run portals claimed that the income generated was sufficient to yield a proper salary – all three owners had alternative means of income, such as pensions and interests in other businesses. Sustainability and success referred to was always measured in terms of amount of use of the portal by business, the community and by customers, rather than profit. All three of these owners regularly checked the statistics regarding visits to the portal - which pages were most popular, which links were used most often, etc - but none had achieved commercial sustainability, despite having long sought it, though revenues from advertising do provide some income. Case A corroborates this: it had originally been a privately-run portal, but had been offered to the local training agent because it was commercially unfeasible. On first sight this was considered to be because the area in which Portal A is located is very remote and lacks critical mass of community and businesses from which to derive revenue. However, Portals D and E in particular, are less isolated and have neighbouring towns and villages in the same greater area from which to cascade interest and revenue, and commercial feasibility remains elusive for them also. Despite this, success in terms of having a service that is used by many people is a strong indicator of effectiveness, and the privately-run portals had all experienced consistent growth in terms of interest in and use of the portal. Conversely, the two charity-based and one LEC-operated portal had not experienced use and growth to the same degree, and the portals themselves are limited in terms of content and facility for the local and external communities.

Characteristics of Successful Portals

The privately-run portals along with Portal A that had been privately-run previously all have much in the way of content, and this content is updated and new content created regularly, as noted above. Moreover, the private owners all had previous and ongoing experience of business (all had been or were currently active in the local business community). Perhaps most importantly, all three had a unique passion for the area in which they were located and a keen interest in contributing to the local economy. In this way, they were able to create and operate their portals (often by outsourcing the more technology-intensive parts to supplement their more basic web skills), and critically, to champion it. This blend of business and passion seems, for these cases at least, to be critical. The day-to-day operations of the portal were consistently referred to as things you could either learn, practice or outsource – all claimed to have applied the trail and error technique to provision and all obtained specialist technology services from a third party at one time or another. More important, according to the private owners was the application of good business practice to portal management and operation. Examples of this, common to the three private owners included consistency and reliability of experience. Approachability and communication was also identified:

Over the years I've built up a huge range of local contacts and if an individual is doing something they can contact me. Portal Owner E.

I've always stayed in the same place and I've always had the same email address. People will often contact me personally. There are just a handful of people that have the right blend of personality and technical skills. Portal Owner F.

Linked to these principles of personal representation, quality of service, reliability and consistency, is also the power of word of mouth. As Portal Owner D describes:

They look at my own website [the portal] ...and I'm getting a lot more people coming to me now because a lot of people that I've done websites for have been doing well and getting a lot of business from them.

These general business principles have sustained the owners of Portals D, E and F particularly, as has the belief that the portal is a worthwhile economic contribution to the area. The extent to which this is actually the case is difficult to gauge, however.

The Economic Contribution

The existence of portals, rural and otherwise, in itself demonstrates that economic contribution or development is anticipated, whether direct (as a result of affording access to markets) or indirect (in terms of including and encouraging firms to exist online at a time where the internet is becoming established as an essential for all firms). There is, however, no systematic research available to determine whether this comprises anything more than subjective, well-meaning conjecture. Certainly, operators of portals in the current study are convinced that they are a worthwhile endeavour:

Portal A:

We get good feedback from the people that do use it for accommodation. Its definitely worthwhile

for the holiday people. Its really good for them. Its made things more accessible.

Portal B:

The use of the place name brand has been very successful.

Portal D:

The accommodation business in particular, they do really very well...I couldn't give you any figures, I just go by feedback and people have been advertising for a number of years.

Portal E:

I think we've been very successful. I could never quantify that and without doing a great deal of research it would be quite difficult to quantify that. I get asked these kinds of questions by the local enterprise agency. I know its successful but I couldn't prove it to you.

Portal F:

Its consistent...It does bring in new business and it brings in goodwill.

These results broadly corroborate those of Thompson (2005) who arrives at similar conclusions in their study of two portals in Australia: i.e., that "well developed and well implemented online services can make a positive contribution to the future of regional and rural communities" (p.232), and along with business-related impacts, they include in their analysis non-economic impacts, such as charitable and social outcomes. The obvious and fundamental problem here is that these are entirely unscientific subjective evaluations about the impact of the portals. Herein lie obvious implications for further research, not only in terms of attempting to quantify economic gain as a result of portal provision, but also to investigate the extent to which portal use locally and from external trade comprises displacement activity. For example, several portals provided free adverting of goods and services, and a business directory. These functions had traditionally been the domain of local newspapers and telephone directories. It would be interesting to investigate if perceived economic gain was real or displaced, particularly in light of the findings that much of the orientation of the longest surviving portals is local, despite the rationale for this being a means of attracting global markets.

FUTURE RESEARCH DIRECTIONS

Opportunities for further research in this area include investigating from the demand-side, i.e, the point of view of the small firms, the effectivness of rural internet portals for business. The current paper reports that portal providers subjectively perceive their portals to be advantageous to the rural economy; it would be useful to know if this belief is shared by users. The current authors intend to pursue this line of enquiry, and within it build a more objective measure of effectiveness with which to guage the impact of internet portals for rural firms.

CONCLUSION

The current research is limited in that it has investigated only six portals. It would be interesting to compare these results with similar studies of rural business use of portals elsewhere in the world, and studies of other portals in Scotland and the UK, to test the generalisability and robustness of the results. With that in mind, the current study provides some evidence that internet portals in rural areas vary considerably in structure, function and operation, but their aims are basically the same.

They are all intended to provide a common link, in this case using the rural location as the common feature, to enhance economic activity and development in the area. They do not seem to be commercially sustainable enterprises, however there is robust data detailing their potential for extensive use locally and internationally, and much anecdotal evidence that they are effective economic contributors. In order to justify properly the value of a well-organised, professionally-managed and effective portal, systematic research to gauge the impact of those that can be demonstrated to be most successful in terms of extent and variety of use in needed. If this can be reliably quantified there would be a strong rationale for encouraging and supporting portals in rural areas. The current research identifies that assuming effectiveness of rural internet portals in terms of economic development is not a strong enough incentive to have people invest themselves in them as public projects. It is not appropriate either to use the portal agenda as a panacea for an eclectic mixture of rural social and economic issues. It is therefore insufficient in terms of effectiveness of a portal to provide funding for creation, particularly where that funding is intended to meet various and different socio-economic needs. The key to success of a rural internet portal seems to be personal, emotional investment in its success, affording (not necessarily real) personal ownership and entrepreneurship in those engaged in portal development. For areas that happen to have located in them local philanthropists who will pioneer and champion a portal using their own time and financial investment, the public sector may have a duty to ensure that it supports this person. For areas that do not have such an individual, the public sector may have role in terms of finding and encouraging this from within the local population. The identification and engagement of those with a genuine interest in the economic development of their locality and the drive to make a portal successful is a challenge undoubtedly. Comments from those who perceived their portals to be highly effective in terms of economic development suggest that this might be a challenge worth pursuing.

REFERENCES

Baourakis, G., Kourgiantakis, M., & Migdalas, A. (2002). The impact of e-commerce on agro-food marketing: The case of agricultural co-operatives, firms and consumers in Crete. *British Food Journal, 104*(8), 580–590. doi:10.1108/00070700210425976

Bharadwaj, P. N., & Soni, R. G. (2007). E-commerce usage and perception of e-commerce issues among small firms: Results and implications from an empirical study. *Journal of Small Business Management, 45*(4), 501521. doi:10.1111/j.1540-627X.2007.00225.x

Buhalis, D., & Main, H. (1998). Information technology in peripheral small and medium hospitality enterprises: Strategic analysis and critical factors. *International Journal of Contemporary Hospitality Management, 10*(5), 198–202. doi:10.1108/09596119810227811

Chen, S. (2005). *Strategic Management of e-Business* (2nd ed.). Chichester, UK: John Wiley & Sons.

Courtney, P., & Brydon, J. (2001). *Differential economic performance: Experience from two Scottish regions*. Paper presented at RICS Research Foundation Rural Research Conference, London.

Deakins, D., Galloway, L., & Mochrie, R. (2003). *The Use and Effect of ICT on Scotland's Rural Business Community*. Scotecon Report.

DTI. (2004). *UK National Broadband Strategy*. Retrieved July 23, 2009, from http://www.berr.gov.uk/

Dwelly, T., Maguire, K., & Truscott, F. (2005). *Under the Radar: Tracking and supporting rural home based businesses*. Live Network Report to the Commission for Rural Communities.

Finin, T., Ding, L., Zhou, L., & Joshi, A. (2005). Social networking on the semantic web. *The Learning Organization, 12*(5), 418–435. doi:10.1108/09696470510611384

Forman, C., Goldfarb, A., & Greenstein, S. (2005). How did location affect adoption of the commercial internet? Global village vs. urban leadership. *Journal of Urban Economics, 58*, 389–420. doi:10.1016/j.jue.2005.05.004

Galloway, L. (2007). Can broadband access rescue the rural economy? *Journal of Small Business and Enterprise Development, 14*(4), 641–653. doi:10.1108/14626000710832749

Galloway, L., & Mochrie, R. (2006). Entrepreneurial Motivation, Orientation and Realisation in Rural Economies: a study of rural Scotland. *International Journal of Entrepreneurship and Innovation, 7*(3), 173–184.

Galloway, L., Mochrie, R., & Deakins, D. (2004). ICT-enabled collectivity as a positive rural business strategy. *International Journal of Entrepreneurial Behaviour and Research, 10*(4), 247–259. doi:10.1108/13552550410544213

Huggins, R., & Izushi, H. (2002). The digital divide and ICT learning in rural communities: Examples of good practice service delivery. *Local Economy, 17*(2), 111–122. doi:10.1080/02690940210129870

Lawson, R., Alcock, C., Cooper, J., & Burgess, L. (2003). Factors affecting adoption of electronic commerce technologies by SMEs: An Australian study. *Journal of Small Business and Enterprise Development, 10*(3), 265–276. doi:10.1108/14626000310489727

Leatherman, J. C. (2000). Internet-based commerce: Implications for rural communities. *Reviews of Economic Development Literature and Practice*, 5. Washington, DC: US Economic Development Administration.

Patterson, H., & Henderson, D. (2003). What is really different about rural and urban firms? Some evidence from Northern Ireland. *Journal of Rural Studies*, *19*(4), 477–490. doi:10.1016/S0743-0167(03)00027-5

Pease, W., & Rowe, M. (2005). Use of information technology to facilitate collaboration and co-opetition between tourist operators in tourist destinations. In *Technology Enterprise Strategies: Thriving and Surviving in an Online Era Conference*, Melbourne.

Pease, W., Rowe, M., & Cooper, M. (2005). Regional tourist destinations – the role of information and communications technology in collaboration amongst tourism providers. Paper presented at *ITS Africa-Asia-Australasia Regional Conference*, Perth.

PIU – Postal Information Unit. (2000). *Counter Revolution: Modernising the Post Office Network*. London: PIU.

Porter, M. E. (2001). Strategy and the internet. *Harvard Business Review*, *79*(3), 63–78.

Roberts, S. (2002). *Key Drivers of Economic Development and Inclusion in Rural Areas*. Initial scoping study for the socio-economic evidence base for DEFRA.

Rodgers, J. A., Yen, D. C., & Chou, D. C. (2002). Developing e-business: A strategic approach. *Information Management & Computer Security*, *10*(4), 184–192. doi:10.1108/09685220210436985

Smallbone, D., North, D., Baldock, R., & Ekanem, I. (2002). *Encouraging and Supporting Enterprises in Rural Areas*. Report to the Small Business Service.

Swan, J., Newell, S., Scarbrough, H., & Hislop, D. (1999). Knowledge management and innovation: networks and networking. *Journal of Knowledge Management*, *3*(4), 262–275. doi:10.1108/13673279910304014

Telford, R. (2006). *Small businesses in rural areas – how are they different?* Paper presented at the 26th ISBE Conference, Cardiff.

Thomas, B., Sparkes, A., Brooksbank, D., & Williams, R. (2002). Social aspects of the impact of information and communication technologies on agri-food SMEs in Wales. *Outlook on Agriculture*, *31*(1), 35–41.

Thompson, H. (2005). Online services and regional web portals: Exploring the social and economic impacts. In H.K. Kehal & V.P. Singh (Eds.), *Digital Economy: Impacts, Influences and Challenges*. Hershey, PA: Idea Group Publishing.

Turban, E., & King, D. Lee, J., & Viehland, D. (2004). *Electronic Commerce 2004: A Managerial Perspective*. Upper Saddle River, NJ: Pearson Education Inc.

Vaessen, P., & Keeble, D. (1995). Growth-oriented SMEs in Unfavourable Regional Environment. *Regional Studies*, *29*, 489–505. doi:10.1080/00343409512331349133

Vakoufaris, H., Spilanis, I., & Kizos, T. (2007). Collective action in the Greek agrifood sector: evidence from the North Aegean region. *British Food Journal*, *109*(10), 777–791. doi:10.1108/00070700710821322

ADDITIONAL READING

Deakins, D., Mochrie, R., & Galloway, L. (2004). Rural business use of ICT: A study of the relative impact of collective activity in rural Scotland. *Strategic Change*, *13*, 139–150. doi:10.1002/jsc.683

Tatnall, A. (2007). *Encyclopedia of Portal Technologies and Applications, Vol.1.* Hershey, PA: Information Science Publishing.

Tatnall, A. (2007). *Encyclopedia of Portal Technologies and Applications, Vol. 2.* Hershey, PA: Information Science Publishing.

ENDNOTE

[1]   Interestingly, as one would expect, the further an island is from an urban centre, the fewer the number of businesses, but the opposite is the case for remote areas on the mainland, with the number of firms included in the portal increasing with distance from an unban centre. The cause, upon inspection, is that while an island is geographically isolated, a settlement on the mainland is part of a greater rural area or county, and as such, portal operators increase the geographic scope and reach of the portal to include other rural communities close by.

Chapter 7
E–Social Entrepreneurship and Social Innovation:
The Case of On–Line Giving Markets

Alfonso Carlos Morales Gutierrez
Universidad de Córdoba, Spain

J. Antonio Ariza Montes
Universidad de Córdoba, Spain

ABSTRACT

In this paper the authors mainly aim at describing some organizational features of a particular kind of social enterprises that have emerged since the development of web 2.0: peer to peer charities and e-social banking. They will define first the traditional social enterprise and how this phenomenon has evolved in recent years. Then they will explain how the philosophy of Web 2.0 offers new opportunities for the development and growth of these social initiatives. Thirdly, they will detail their main features obtained from the study of twelve inititatives – the most relevant at present – which they have called 2.0 social enterprises (peer to peer charities and e-social banking). The authors will finally offer some reflection on main dilemmas and challenges that could be faced in a short term future.

INTRODUCTION

Entrepreneurship, business social orientation and web 2.0 are three areas of growing interest in last years, which converges in this work into a kind of entities that emerged in the first decade of the twenty-first century: peer to peer Charities and social e-banking. This paper aims at identifying common features and patterns across this social entrepreneurial organizations adopting enterprise 2.0 and technology scope (Markfleet, 2008).

First of all, we would like to set this kind of entities at the intersection of two phenomena: social entrepreneurship and Web 2.0 development. Social enterprises were set up mainly in the last quarter of the twentieth century. Indeed, the demand of high levels of competitiveness in economic activities caused, in that period, a "natural selection" of sectors, territories and social groups that resulted in job losses in traditional sectors (agricultural and industrial) and consequently, in high rates of unemployment. This economic scenario made the defferent social agents adopt some strategies in order to include the excluded. Therefore, in most

DOI: 10.4018/978-1-61520-597-4.ch007

Western countries arise the social enterprises as a mechanism to alleviate this situation.

Later on, in the early twenty-first century, Internet opens to a new phase of development -Web 2.0-, emerging multitude of initiatives inspired by social networking and even other kinds of social organizations where main actors -rather than excluded people of developed countries as in the case of the traditional social enterprise-, are agents, projects and social entities that perform their work in developing countries, either directly or through local or international non-governmental organizations (NGOs). It is in this context where we can be locate peer to peer Charities, entities undoubtedly characterized by a social sense -their main targets are people with scarce resources, but very different from social enterprises of the end of the century- which are sources of funding for entrepreneurship, among other aspects.

In third place we will mention the main characteristics of peer to peer Charities and social banking, using data obtained from various sources: primary and secondary. We will attempt to describe its founders are, their organizational design, processes and growth strategies, among others.

Finally, as a result of obtained data and exposed features, we will propose a series of questions or dilemmas that can influence the development of such organizations in a short-term future because of their special characteristics.

THE TRADITIONAL SOCIAL COMPANY AS A STARTING POINT

Main Features of the "Traditional" Social Entrepreneurship

The term social entrepreneurship began to appear routinely both in the general-interest and specialist press in the early 1990s. First descriptions of social entrepreneurs ranged from "anyone who starts a not-forprofit" or "not-for-profit organizations starting for-profit or earned-income ventures" (Wolk, 2007) to "business owners who integrate social responsibility into their operations" (Dees, 2001).

Famous are those social entreprises specialized in recycling such as Green Works in England (Clifford, & Dixon, 2005) or in biodynamic agriculture as Sekem (Seeclos, & Mahir, 2003).

Although there is no universally agreed definition of a social enterprise, there appears to be a general consensus that it is a business with primarily social and/or environmental objectives, whose surpluses are principally reinvested for that purpose either in the business and/or a community rather than being driven by the need to maximize profits for shareholders and owners (DTI, 2002). In this definition, the following features are highlighted: double bottom line, commercial and autonomy orientation.

Double and Triple Bottom Line

Social enterprises can be distinguished from other nonprofits organizations by their strategies, structure and values (Dart, 2004). Social enterprises have two basic objetives, social and economic, which are integrated into their business strategy. Therefore, some authors suggested that the definition of entrepreneurship should be modified to include the creation of 'social and economic value' and thus applied to both private, entrepreneurial ventures as well as to social enterprises (Chell, 2007).

This way, it is acknowledged that contributions in the creation of companies are not only economic but also social, which in the case of social enterprises will be obviously larger.

Nowadays, the concept of the bottom line has expanded to include environmental (triple bottom line) outcomes. This trend has called the attention of policy makers and practitioners who are interested in the potential contribution of social enterprises to economic, social and/or environmental regeneration and renewal.

Figure 1. Structure and capital in social enterprise. (Fuente: Chertok et al, 2008)

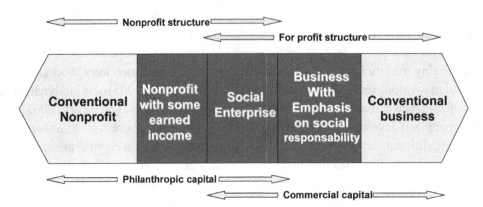

Business and Autonomy Orientation

The specific objetives of social enterprises need different sources of income: businesses and non-profit organizations (Hansmann, 1980). Donative nonprofits obtain their funds from donations and philanthropy, whereas social enterprise and non-profits enterprises generate at least some of their revenue from trading (Figure 1). If they are in competition with other nonprofit and/or for-profit organizations for resources and customers (Hansmann, 1980; Steinberg, 1993), then their tax and fiscal benefits (Glaeser, & Shleifer, 2001) and close stakeholder relationships have the potential to be exploited to generate competitive advantage.

Some examples of earned income strategies include fees for service, sale of goods, service delivery contracts, course and tuition fees, consulting, rental income, lease payments (Skloot, 1987; Frumkin, 2002; Zeitlow, 2001) and cause related marketing (Varadarajan, & Menon 1988; Weisbrod, 2004).[1] Social enterprises are engaged in revenue generation from trading (Zeitlow, 2001) with a benchmark of 50% and above (Department for Trade and Industry, 2002).

The commercial transformation of social enterprise has served to professionalize management (Alexander, 2000), focus their performance on the "bottom line" (Frumkin, 2002, p. 152), and

encourage them to adopt measures to evaluate their social and economic gains (OECD, 2003).

Social Enterprise and Social Innovation

A definition of social entrepreneurship is set out as "entailing innovation designed to explicitly improve societal wellbeing, housed within entrepreneurial organizations that initiate this level of change in society (Perrini, 2006). Many scholars take this focus on innovation even further. Social entrepreneurs are "change agents," (Ashoka, 2007) creating "large-scale change through patternbreaking ideas" (Light, 2007), "addressing the root causes" of social problems (Dees & Anderson, 2007), possessing "the ambition to create systemic change by introducing a new idea and persuading others to adopt it," (Kramer, 2005) and changing "the social systems that create and maintain" problems (Alvord et al, 2004).

These types of transformative changes can be national or global. They can also often be highly localized—but no less powerful—in their impact. Most often, social entrepreneurs who create transformative changes combine innovative practices, deep and targeted knowledge of their social issue area, applied and cutting-edge research, and political savvy to reach their goals. For all entrepreneurs, whether in the business or social realm, innovation is not a one-time event—but continues over time.

Evolution and Development of Social Enterprise in Some Countries

We place the interest in social enterprise in the nineties: Harvard University presented the Social Enterprise Initiative in 1993. From then, universities and private foundations created numerous initiatives to support training and strategic consulting to managers, including those of non-profit organizations.

In the European continent, the social enterprise soom emerged, particularly in countries characterized by one of these features: those with some gaps in the provision of certain social services and/or those with a significant development of the "social economy". We will discuss now the case of three countries with different models of social enterprise: Italy, UK and Spain.

The absence of the state as provider of basic social services, the political influence of large Italian cooperative federations and attention from academics in this country toward social enterprises explain to a large extent the relevance of a particular type of social enterprise: the social cooperatives in Italy.[2]

In the UK, the evolution of social enterprise followed a different pattern. Patricia Hewitt, Minister of Commerce and Industry in UK, published in 2002 the "*Social Enterprise: A Strategy for Success*" which undoubtedly hastened its spread and provided the British government with a set of tools to promote the implementation of this institutional form (Social Enterprise Unit, Training Programs, Social Enterprise Coalition, etc.[3]

In Spain, social enterprises have developed since the mid-nineties as insertion enterprises.[4] These entities have actually been transition businesses[5] that allocated a significant percentage of their jobs to individuals in the process of integration, who completed their apprenticeship and obtained a level of employability high enough

to enter the labour market.[6] Therefore, they are training centers for workers with low labour productivity.

Challenges and Issues in the Traditional Social Enterprise

In recent years, the concepts of social enterprise and social entrepreneurship have suffered a substantial increase in terms of real development and political attention (including media). However there are still some issues that focus the interest of diverse stakeholders in developing this type of organizations: institutional recognition, the integration into the market and its articulation as a partner in dialogue with different social actors.

The Problem of Institutional Recognition

In Europe two situations about this issue can at least be distinguished. On the one hand, countries where there is already a more or less formalized sector different from the public or private capitalist (social economy), and those that attempt to minimize potential conflicts between the cominant concepts (reluctant to recognize social enterprises) and conceptual schemes and existing practices. Moreover, in countries where there is no awareness of an alternative area where entrepreneurship and social welfare mix, these ideas should not be imposed on indigenous practices, whether formal or informal, as this would hinder the recognition of social enterprise by the same actors and consequently its legitimacy would be called into question, difficulting the privileged access to certain resources.

The Problem of Development in the Market

The convergence between traditional and social entrepreneurship is a source of new opportunities. However, this convergence entails serious risks and challenges for social enterprises in terms of sustainability and organizational culture. The access of social enterprises to various funding sources, the increasing level of professionalism, the opportunity to benefit from innovative ways of collaboration and technological advances require an investment that is not always possible for the agents themselves. New ways of transferring resources emerge alongside traditional forms of public and private support in order to make viable the survival of these enterprises in the long term.

However, the financial viability of social enterprises is still a big difficulty of the sector. When these organizations are said to mobilize hybrid resources, one should not just think of grants, donations or sales. In fact, to the amount of financial instruments that are now available for social enterprises, should be added the reduction of public aid and the difficulty of reconciling work and family life by citizens (with the consequent impact on the possibility of donating time or money). These circumstances are hints of a landscape in which innovation, value added, knowledge and experience will be essential values.

Vertebration as a Socially Significant Agent

The development of a European market where social enterprises are integrated demands the involvement of different stakeholders in each member state in debates and discussions at European level. At this level, the issue of financial support from public sector through tenders that have been awarded in terms of social services, general interest, are some of the debates where social enterprises can play a main role. The articulation of social enterprises interests is essential in order to influence decisions that affect them directly and thus exercise lobbying against public entities and private sector. The creation of these second-level players would allow the accumulation of know-how and the exchange of

experiences, unquestionably interesting for those involved agents.

WEB 2.0 AND THE NEW KINDS OF SOCIAL ENTERPRISE

Impact of Web 2.0 at Social And Business Level

New information and communication technologies have been a catalyst in accelerating these changes and especially the development of Web 2.0 philosophy. Thanks to the facilities, evolution and free development of technologies that were previously inaccessible to most users, Web 2.0 has allowed, among other things, elements that affect both the social and business dimension of new initiatives.

At the social level, this new stage in the digital age permits to develop new forms of social articulation through social networks and generation of communities and interest groups. Moreover, it permits the involvement of users (providing content, decision making...) developing a global collective intelligence. Thus, the power of citizens is currently more important than ever because they can express, directly and instantly, their views or their votes.

From the business point of view, Web 2.0 has important implications for marketing and advertising models, thus emerging numerous business opportunities. Web 2.0 social initiatives not only use the typical 2.0 tools (RSS, podscats, blogs...) as a complementary strategy. These new social enterprises are designed like networks and places where social needs and donnors can meet. In the future, the trend will be an intelligent virtual world, where avatars move and act accordcing to the facts and habits of each individual. Web 2.0 will be responsible for delivering users the type of news and advertising that could be of their interest, for educating in those fields that result more useful and for encouraging relationships among individuals with the same affinities and interests.

Web 2.0 is not only a good opportunity to create new businesses, but has also numerous applications for the traditional firm. Among the main reasons which will induce the traditional company to use Web 2.0 stands out the possibility of improving interaction with customers. At present, according to McKinsey, over 75% of managers affirm that their companies invest in Web 2.0 and plan to maintain or increase their investments in technology trends that encourage user collaboration.

Social Enterprises in the Social Web

Theoretically, entrepreneurship in Web 2.0 requires low investment, a short-term period to create a small business and small organizational structure. These features would permit new enterprises to compete quickly with traditional businesses already settled in the market. This can be applied to any kind of initiative. But to what extent does this new technological and business context contribute to the promotion of social enterprise? To answer this question we will provide at least two reasons: Web 2.0 permits a smooth operation of the allocation via markets (even social markets) and the potential for sustainability of social enterprises increase due to the global network effect.

Generation of Efficient Social Markets

Web 2.0 permits the generation of efficient markets with low transaction costs (perfect competition, transparency, penalization of opportunistic behaviors...). Furthermore, social needs can be addressed through the creation of markets where is possible to find a shared social need (which would be a market niche for a traditional company) and provide a good service that satisfies the existing demand. Are there people who can give small amounts of money without being affiliated to an organization? Are there small projects that can

cope with small investments and receive assistance with minimal intermediation? The answer to both questions explains in part the peer to peer Charities phenomenon that we will develop further on.

For the solidarity world, the advantages of the new scenario posed by Web 2.0 are obvious. On the one hand, in the case of donors, Web 2.0 increases significantly their chances of donation in amount (especially in the case of microgiving) as well as in the types of beneficiaries (health, education, business...) and even in the possibility of different participation types in social initiatives. Furthermore, potential beneficiaries include the possibility of increasing the visibility of their need on a massive scale.

Network and Sustainability Effect of Social Initiatives

The social enterprise must have a social impact and cover stably its structure costs. Business strategies in Web 2.0 derive their revenues from advertising, subscriptions, sales or transaction fees, which require a critical mass of users. If a business is created and nobody buys the product, the company disappears. If there are not justified needs (with sufficient and accurate information to be found), or people willing to donate (with the necessary security mechanisms), the encounter will not be possible.

Under the principle of "What is not shared is lost", the more the service is accessed, the higher the value for other users, and greater will be the chance of generating a permanent meeting place where the cost structure can be financed with a small amount, which depends on the number of transactions. New social enterprises (web 2.0 social companies) are oriented towards autonomy, financing their activities mainly with commissions per transaction (a percentage of the donation from the donor), although they also allow permanent and sporadic donations.

Table 1. Person to person social enterprises

	Organization	Founders	Impact
Micro-lending	**MyC4** (www.myC4.com)	2006 Mads Kjaer (1961) y Tim Vang (1972)	6374 inverstors in 68 countries, over €3,8 million in donations in 2300 business in Africa
	51Give (www.51give.com)	2007 Daniel Foa y Hiu Ng	No data
	Kiva (www.kiva.org)	Matt y Jessica Flanery	Facilitated loans to 60,000 entrepreneurs with a more than 95 percent repayment rate in its first three years
	RangDe (www.rande.org)	2008 Smita Ramakrishna y Ramakrisna	281 projects 123 social investors
Giving	**Globalgiving** (www.globalgiving.org)	2000 Mari Kuraishi and Dennis Whittle	- Over $14 million in donations since 2002 - Over 1,300 projects have received funding to date - More than 41,500 unique donors
	Donorchoose (www.donorchoose.org)	2000 Charles Best, a teacher at a public high school in the Bronx	In 2009, donors have funded $1,590,983 worth of resources for students in need. The projects have supplied 1,357,560 hours of instruction and homework. Resources provided were: 27% books; 20% technology; 42% classroom supplies; 2% field trips; 0% class visitors; 8% other resources.
	Microgiving (www.microgiving.com)	2007 John Ferber	No data
	Firstgiving (www.firstgiving.com)	2003 Hermanos Lingard y otros	1,526,245 people have helped raise $83,103,015 for 20,672 nonprofits using Firstgiving
	Change. Org (www.change.org)	2006 Ben Ratray (1982)	31000 members in 91 countries
	Apadrina un proyecto (www.apadrinaunproyecto.com)	Mundo Unido Cooperación	No data
	Nuru (www.nuruinternational.org)	2006 Jake Harriman and John Hancox	in Kenya directly impacting the lives of over 2,500 people
	Zazengo (www.zazengo.com)	Vicki Saunders	No data

PERSON TO PERSON AND SOCIAL ENTERPRISE: CHARITIES AND E-SOCIAL BANKING

An Exploratory Research

Given the limited extent of knowledge on social entrepreneurship with web 2.0 technologies, we deliberately opted for an exploratory research approach. The selection of cases (Table 1) was based on the following criteria. First, the chosen organizations had to be widely recognized as successful with global scope. Second, priority was given to organizations which had already been described and documented. We gathered data from several sources: existing case studies, published and unpublished reports and articles, internet sources and we have even participated in its operation as users and donors.

Figure 2. Capital market 2.0 and non-profit sector

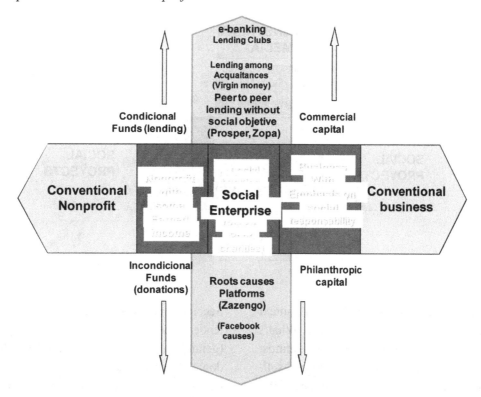

These data helped us identify and compare patterns across cases. Although we are aware of the limitations of our sampling and data analysis approach, we consider this study as a first important step that provides tentative propositions for a more inclusive empirical research agenda in the future. Following Miles and Hubermann (1994), we apply a comparative case analysis design to capture the complexity and richness of the underlying phenomenon and detect patterns and regularities across cases.

We have found two types of social enterprise 2.0 especialized in the design and development of on line giving markets with different strategy models (Figure 2):

- "peer to peer charities", social enterprises especialised mainly in micro-giving) and
- "e-social banking" entities, social enterprises 2.0 specialised in micro-lending.

As conventional businesses enter the market and obtain financial resources from banks, these kind of social enterprises of web 2.0 have a particular access to obtain those resources: the on line giving markets. With this mechanism, they can receive sporadic donations for a specific cause (inconditional funds) until they channel the generosity of small social investors who, with no profit motiv in mind, provide microcredits for small business in developing countries.

Organizational Design: Social Network Orchestrator

eBay is the archetype of company that has grown in the context of the new philosophy of Web 2.0 (also Charles Swab, CNET Networks and others). The eBay product is the collective activity of all its users (such as the Web itself). EBay grows organically in response to user activity, and the

Figure 3. Network social orchestrator

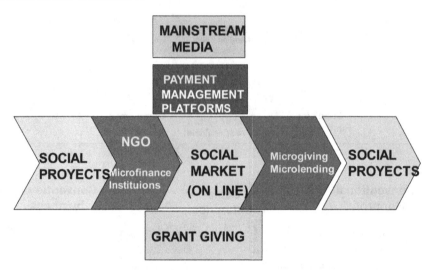

role of the company is the enabler of a context where the activity of the user takes place. What's more, eBay's competitive advantage comes almost entirely from the critical mass of buyers and sellers, which makes any new entrant offering similar services significantly less attractive. Häcki and Lighton (2001) call this peculiar organizational design network orchestrator, a specific type of virtual organization model. In the same way, social enterprises 2.0 to which we refer (known as giving on-line market places in the context of philanthropy) are a kind of replica –organizational isomorphism- of the online market that implies the development of eBay. In this case, instead of goods demand and offer, there is demand of nees and offer of donors as appropriate to the solidarity world. E-social entrepreneurs 2.0 (the orchestrators) stablish a common platform in the web for a number of participants (donors, lenders, local entrepreneurs, etc) that come into play at the right time with the necessary information and relevant channels of communication (Figure 3).

Firstly, we have the demand of economic resources. Micro-financing institutions and NGOs, which work in the field, on the one hand, filter and support fund petitions, and, on the other hand, guarantee the correct use of the obtained resources.

Secondly, we have the offer of donors or microlenders who choose, according to their preferences (gender, country, business or others) the use of donated funds. Finally, we find the internal mechanisms of the network that make platforms operative in the internet: platforms for safe payment, large donors that use them as responsibility image and even social media that spread the network beyond the internet.

The agents that make up this social network achieve functions similar to the major stakeholders of a traditional company (technical core, suppliers, customers, creditors, etc ...). Following the scheme proposed by Charles Handy (2000) about clover organization, three areas can be distinguished: the core business where the most strategic functions of the company are assigned, the outsourcing area (tactical functions that are performed in collaboration with other specialised agents that receive a remuneration for their services) and an operational area, which involves the stakeholders interested in the development of the activity.

The emergence of such initiatives in the network provides a number of advantages with respect to traditional models of solidarity (Table 2): more flexibility in the donation process, more transparency and lower costs of organization, among others.

Table 2. Different types of philanthropy

	Tratitional approach	**Person to Person approach** (Internet user uses a network to mobilize a social cause)	**Peer to Peer Charities**
Transaction	Donor to organization	Donor to recipient model with low control	Donor to recipient model
Donor participation	Fixed participation as a member	Puntual and variable participation	Puntual and variable participation and even returnable (microlending)
Information to donor	Global of all organization	Limited to personal skills	Focused on the use of resources
Possibilities of choise	Restricted to the organization's mission	Restricted to mobilized cases and membership in certain social networks	Wide in countries, projects and even organizations

Core Social E-Entrepreneurship: Human Resources

Social entrepreneurs may mean starting new organizations, or offering new products or services (Mahir & Martí, 2006). Innovative ideas can be completely new inventions or creative adaptations of existing ones (Peredo & Murdith, 2006). Like other entrepreneurs, social entrepreneurs are creative thinkers, continuously striving for innovation, which can involve new technologies –like web 2.0-, supply sources, distribution outlets, or methods of production (Dees, 2001). Under these conditions the organizational core is generally made up of an organizational team that combines technological trade and solidarity capabilities. In addition, this implies that exist individual entrepreneurs and teams which together combine the capabilities necessary for business development.

For example, Nuru was the vision of Jake Harriman (CEO) and John Hancox (Board Chairman), and shaped by the innovation engine of the Stanford Graduate School of Business (GSB). Since 2006, teams of Stanford GSB students have joined together with top academics, social sector experts and humanitarian practitioners to conduct exhaustive studies of dozens of top humanitarian NGOs. They identified best practices, key learnings, and cutting edge theories in a range of areas. When this research was analyzed they concluded that certain best practices work much better than others, and that by flexibly applying those practices in partnership with an empowered community, the poor can actually lift themselves out of extreme poverty. What started with those Stanford GSB students soon spread to the faculty, the Stanford Public Management Program and the Center for Social Innovation. Philanthropic foundations, venture capitalists and successful Silicon Valley entrepreneurs invested seed money to get Nuru off the ground, and in the past 6 months over 3100 friends have joined this cause on Facebook.

In other cases, social entrepreneurs are young professionals, who have experienced some activities in the network (not necessarily in the social sector, for example John Ferber from Microgiving previously founded an advertising company on the network that was acquired in 2004 by Time-Warner) or with extensive experience in organizations in the network (such as Jessyca and Matt Flannery of Kiva, with a long experience in eBay or TiVo). Therefore, the development of altruistic concern and caring can be very varied.[7]

The Offer of P2P Charities: Beneficiaries and Third Sector

The area that we have called operative is composed primarily by solidarity supplier agents (direct beneficiaries of the platform through personal or collective projects) and the intermediary organizations (indirect beneficiaries) and for solidarity client agents (donors or lenders without a motiv of profit).

Indeed, a peer to peer Charity has a common mission: to deliver resources to the neediest. So, the organization should have an offer that attracts potential donors. Kiva facilitates microloans to over 60,000 entrepreneurs in 45 developing countries. Potential creditors may examine the available profiles of the candidates to obtain a loan and grant loans to people that catches their attention. Potential borrowers are chosen according to their nationality, sex, type of business or level of need, among other factors. African widows tend to arouse much interest, while the male population in Central America (as well as butchers) has less support.

Normally, such platforms are fed of projects by NGOs and microfinance institutions. In fact, many of them allow the search given by NGO's reputation as these organizations have been operating in the traditional way. In the case of social e-banking platforms -the moment that a creditor gives a loan- the company sends the money to a microfinance institution in the country of origin of the borrower. This institution (for example Kiva does business with more than a hundred of these institutions) disburses the funds and works with the borrower to ensure that liquidation of the loan occurs on the correct term. Controlling this type of institutions is a key element for this type of solidarity platforms.[8]

The Various Forms of Demand for the Exercise of "Solidarity"

The network allows that anyone from anywhere in the world where Internet is available, can make a contribution. We have encountered the following profiles of altruistic donors who are somehow different alternatives of seed capital for local entrepreneurs: microdonors grant giving, lenders, social investors and volunteers.

Microdonors

Microdonors make small contributions non-recurrent and non-binding. The donor looks for a moral and even private gratification. In other markets on line (not social) buyers require a reputation system, for example, voting the seller. In these cases, there is of some discrimination regarding the commitment to feed back about the social action supported. Thus, platforms require minimum amounts for certain rights for accessing customized information on the monitoring of projects. Obviously, the most local approach to the strategy of the peer to peer Charities determines the local nature of the altruistic donors or lenders.

Grant Giving

Grant giving contributes significantly to the maintenance of the platform fixed costs. They usually appear as such on the main page of these institutions.

Non-Profit Lenders and Social Investors

The impact of Yunnus social innovation has been instrumentalised through the philosophy of Web 2.0. In this case the contributions made by donors are loans and it is possible to re-lend that amount once it has been returned, thus creating a virtuous cycle. Likewise in the case of Kiva, interest is not charged to the intermediary micro-credit institutions, but to borrowers in the developing world. This agreement creates a low cost funding source and also allows to generate funds for financing its operation costs.

There are also platforms that support the possibility of people who are willing to provide resources at an interest rate lower than market. In this case they demand a minimum investment for this type of figure.

The Volunteer as a Strategic Participant

Business models such as Ikea´s have a customer-centred approach. Customers are not just the recipient of a product, in this case a piece of furniture, but a collaborator of the company when assembling the product, motivated by lower costs or even a leisure opportunity. In social platforms could be implemented some mechanisms to engage potential volunteers not as mere time donors but as work donors:

a. In strategic tasks: efficient control of money raised and/or the planning and developing of the enterprise information.[9]
b. In tactical or operational tasks (translation of the site into other languages, advertising in blogs...). Articulated social networks (blogosphere, Facebook ...) provide a channel for the dissemination and consolidation of these initiatives as long as these alternatives are known by prospective donors. The creation of groups in social networks already in place (51give develops a group on Facebook about microfinance in China) or the use of the blogosphere (Daily Kos in the case of Kiva) are some of the most used strategies.

This does not imply that diffusion is restricted to the internet. In fact many organizations acknowledge the role played by traditional communication media in the dissemination of their experiences (interviews, newspapers, broadcast television programs ...).[10]

Outsourcing of Support Services

Social platforms can be supported by existing social institutions in a number of activities that can be considered for specialist support in relation to its core: information search for the development of supply, or the processing and management of donated funds. In the first case we find a search engine of non-profit organizations: Guidestar. Every day, nearly 22,000 people come to GuideStar to learn more about nonprofits; in 2008, their visits added up to more than 8 million visitors. Many are donors seeking information on organizations to support. Second profile within the normal partner of such platforms is Pay Pal. Organizations tend to use often this type of payment with your credit card.

QUESTIONS FOR DISCUSSION

Studying the different experiences of peer to peer Charities and e-social banking, we have identified some issues and dilemmas that we consider critical for their future development and for the possible evolution of e-business initiatives at society level: supplier control, donor´s loyalty, strategy and advertising.

Supplier Control

On-line markets generally allow stores to sell their products directly and/or indirectly. Reputation is important and is acquired progressively through participation in the market. In the case of social enterprise 2.0, its reputation is backed by NGOs or microcredit institutions that present the project and guarantee in some way that the need is real, that the funds will be used in the order given on the platform and will provide information on the impact of this initiative.

The risk of opportunism in this area increases once these platforms reach a certain volume of transactions. Thus, the possibility of losing reputation is higher because the information distributed by beneficieries can be incorrect, false or deliberately manipulated, not employing, therefore, the resources for their social ends.

For this reason it is necessary the development of control mechanisms to verify and monitor these aspects in the field. So cyber-volunteerism

Table 3. Person to person social enterprises

	Organization	Strategy
Micro-lending	MyC4	Micro-lending with low rates (but with benefits for lender) Local Specialization (Africa)
	51Give	Local (China) and types of beneficiaries (students and rural entrepreneurs)
	Kiva	Global (45 developing countries) and general (all types of entrepreneurs)
	RangDe (www.rande.org)	Local and general Two types of products (microlending and social investors)
Giving	Globalgiving	Global and general
	Donorchoose	Local (United States) and specialised (education)
	Microgiving	Local and general
	Firstgiving	Global and general
	Change. Org	Local (United States) but general (many causes)
	Apadrina un proyecto	Local and general
	Nuru	Local and specialised
	Zazengo	Local (United States) but general (many causes)

management and the increase in technological possibilities, like google-earth- geopositioning, can open up a range of options to exercise the necessary control over this type of platforms.

Loyalty Toward The Cause

A great advantage for donors in on-line giving markets is the flexibility of platforms as compared to more traditional models of donation. However, the ideal way to support these institutions is not the occasional donation, but a periodical quota. Likewise, in the case of e-social banking, it is socially desirable for the paid loans to be reinvested to support another new project.

From this perspective, the essential task for medium and long term objectives of this type of institutions is to achieve the donor´s loyalty with information, knowledge and recognition. It is very important to create feedback mechanisms where individuals and beneficiaries of nonprofit programs can immediately inform the program staff whether a service is having the desired effect. Information systems and Web 2.0 tools can

be equally necessary for the development of appropriate policies in this field.

Segmentation Strategy and Growth of the Platform

The sector of the retail market has at least two strategies for positioning at the point of sale: the generic superstores and hypermarkets, which offer a wide range of products, or the large specialized surface area (also known as category killers), specialized in one type of product. This emerging sector is also characterized by two types of platforms (Table 3): a multicause one (with an overall strategy for the use of proceeds) or the person-to-person specialized type (e.g. entrepreneurs, education, Africa). While this industry is in a very nascent stage, and the most popular peer to peers are more generalised, we notice a tendency towards more specialized and differentiated approaches that require further idiosyncratic knowledge. It should be pointed out that this type of business strategy requires balanced growth. It is not enough to have a lot of resources; the availability of attractive projects is also important.

Solidarity and Advertising

Solidarity can be an end in itself or can be transformed by certain firms in the network into an advertising medium: a way to attract a particular type of customer. We believe that an element of differentiation of these platforms is provided, as the advocacy of social enterprises is committed to social change and, why not, with a critical sense and capacity for social denounce.

REFERENCES

Alexander, J. (2000). Adaptive Strategies of Non-Profit Human Service Organizations in an Era of Devolution and New Public Management. *Nonprofit Management & Leadership, 10*, 287–303. doi:10.1002/nml.10305

Alvord, S. H., Brown, D. L., & Letts, C. W. (2004). Social Entrepreneurship and Societal Transformation: An Exploratory Study. *The Journal of Applied Behavioral Science, 40*(3), 260–282. doi:10.1177/0021886304266847

Ashoka. (2007). *Ashoka home page*. Retrieved August 29, 2007, from http://www.ashoka.org/ Ashoka. (n.d.). *What is a Social Entrepreneur?* Retrieved from http://ashoka.org/social_entrepreneur

Chell, E. (2007). Social Enterprise and Entrepreneurship: Towards a Convergent Theory of the Entrepreneurial Process. *International Small Business Journal, 25*(1), 5–26. doi:10.1177/0266242607071779

Chertok, M., Hamaoui, J., & Jamison, E. (2008, Spring). The funding gap. *Stanford Social Innovation Review*, 44–47.

Clifford, A. M., & Dixon, S.A. (2005). Greenworks: un modelo de negocio que combina la iniciativa emprendedora social con la mejora del medio ambiente. *Iniciativa emprendedora, 48*, 69–79.

Dart, R. (2004). The Legitimacy of Social Enterprise. *Nonprofit Management & Leadership, 14*(4), 411–425. doi:10.1002/nml.43

Dees, J. G. (2001). *The Meaning of Social Entrepreneurship*. Durham, NC: Duke University. Retrieved January 2009, from http://www.fuqua.duke.edu/centers/case/documents/dees_ sedef.pdf

Dees, J. G., & Anderson, B. B. (2007). Framing a Theory of Social Entrepreneurship: Building on Two Schools of Practice and Thought. *Association for Research on Nonprofit Organizations and Voluntary Action (ARNOVA) Occasional Paper Series—Research on Social Entrepreneurship: Understanding and Contributing to an Emerging Field, 1*(3), 39–66.

Dees, J. G., Emerson, J., & Economy, P. (2001). *Enterprising nonprofits: A toolkit for social entrepreneurs*. New York: John Wiley & Sons.

DTI. (2002). *Social Enterprise? A Strategy for Success*. The Department of Trade and Industry. Retrieved from http://www.dti.gov.uk

Frumkin, P. (2002). *On Being a Non-Profit, A Conceptual and Policy Primer*. 432 H. Haugh. Cambridge, MA: Harvard University Press.

Glaeser, E. L., & Shleifer, A. (2001). Not-For-Profit Entrepreneurs. *Journal of Public Economics, 81*, 99–115. doi:10.1016/S0047-2727(00)00130-4

Häcki, R., & Lighton, J. (2001). The future of the networked company. *The Mckinsey Quarterly, 3*, 26–39.

Handy, C. (2000). *La organización por dentro*. Madrid: Ed. Deusto

Hansmann, H. (1980). The role of nonprofit enterprise. *The Yale Law Journal, 89*(5), 835–901. doi:10.2307/796089

Kramer, M. R. (2005). *Measuring Innovation: Evaluation in the Field of Social Entrepreneurship.* Boston: Foundation Strategy Group.

Light, P. C. (2007). Searching for Social Entrepreneurs: Who They Might Be, Where They Might Be Found, What They Might Do. *Association for Research on Nonprofit Organizations and Voluntary Action (ARNOVA) Occasional Paper Series—Research on Social Entrepreneurship: Understanding and Contributing to and Emerging Field, 1*(3), 13–37.

Mair, J., & Ignasi, M. (2006). Social Entrepreneurship Research: A Source of Explanation, Prediction, and Delight. *Journal of World Business, 41,* 36–44. doi:10.1016/j.jwb.2005.09.002

Marfleet, J. (2008). Enterprise 2.0 _ What's your game plan?: What, if any, will be the role of the information intermediary? *Business Information Review, 25,* 152. doi:10.1177/0266382108095037

Mckinsey. (2008 July). Building the web 2.0 enterprise. *Mckinsey Quarterly.*

Miles, M. B., & Huberman, A. M. (1994). *Qualitative data analaysis.* Thousand Oaks, CA: Sage.

NCVO. (2002). *The U.K. Voluntary Sector Almanac 2002.* London: NCVO.

OECD. (2003). *The Non-profit Sector in a Changing Economy.* Paris: OECD.

Peredo, A. M., & McLean, M. (2006). Social Entrepreneurship: A Critical Review of the Concept. *Journal of World Business, 41,* 56–65. doi:10.1016/j.jwb.2005.10.007

Perrini, F. (2006). *The New Social Entrepreneurship: What Awaits Social Entrepreneurship Ventures?* Northampton, MA: Edward Elgar.

Seclos, C., & Mahir, J. (2005). *La iniciativa Sekem en Varios: Mejorar la gestión de empresas.* Madrid: McGraw-Hill, IESE.

Skloot, E. (1987). Enterprise and Commerce in Non-Profit Organizations. In W. W. Powell (Ed.), *The Non-Profit Sector: A Research Handbook* (pp. 380–393). Yale University Press, New Haven.

Steinberg, R. (1993). Public Policy and the Performance of Non-Profit Organizations: a General Framework. *Nonprofit and Voluntary Sector Quarterly, 22,* 13–31. doi:10.1177/089976409302200103

Universia Knowlodge Wharton. (2008). *Kiva: Cómo mejorar la vida de las personas con un pequeño préstamo.* Retrieved September 1, 2008, from http://wharton.universia.net/index.cfm?fa=viewArticle&ID=1529

Varadarajan, P., & Menon, A. (1988). Cause-Related Marketing: A Coalignment of Marketing Strategy and Corporate Philanthropy. *Journal of Marketing, 52*(3), 5874. doi:10.2307/1251450

Weisbrod, B. A. (2004). The Pitfalls of Non-Profits. *Stanford Social Innovation Review, Winter,* 40–47.

Wolk, A. (2007). *Social Entrepreneurship and Government.* The Small Business Economy: A Report to the President, 2007.

Zeitlow, J. T. (2001). Social Entrepreneurship: Managerial, Finance and Marketing Aspects. *Journal of Nonprofit & Public Sector Marketing, 9,* 19–43. doi:10.1300/J054v09n01_03

ADDITIONAL READING

Badelt, C. H. (1997). Entrepreneurship Theories of the Non-Profit Sector. *Voluntas, 8*(2), 162–178. doi:10.1007/BF02354193

Boschee, J. (1998). *What Does it Take To Be a Social Entrepreneur?* Retrieved from www.socialentrepreneurs.org/whatdoes.html

Boschee, J., & McClurg, J. (2003). *Toward a Better Understanding of Social Entrepreneurship: Some Important Definitions.* Unpublished paper. Retrieved from http://www.se-alliance.org/better_understanding.pdf

Brinckerhoff, P. C. (2000). *Social Entrepreneurship: The Art of Mission-Based Venture Development.* San Francisco: Jossey Bass.

Chew, C., & Osborne, S. P. (2009, March). Exploring Strategic Positioning in the UK Charitable Sector: Emerging Evidence from Charitable Organizations that Provide Public Services. *British Journal of Management, 20*(1), 90–105. doi:10.1111/j.1467-8551.2007.00554.x

Defourny, J. (2001). Introduction: From Third Sector to Social Enterprise. In C. Borzaga and J. Defourny (Eds.), *The Emergence of Social Enterprise* (pp. 1–28). London: Routledge.

Emerson, J., & Twersky, F. (Eds.). (1996). *New Social Entrepreneurs: The Success, Challenge and Lessons of Non-profit Enterprise Creation.* San Francisco: Roberts Foundation.

Glaeser, E. L., & Shleifer, A. (1998). *Not-For-Profit Entrepreneurs.* NBER Working Paper 8610. Cambridge, MA: National Bureau of Economic Research, Inc.

Glaeser, E. L., & Shleifer, A. (2001). Not-For-Profit Entrepreneurs. *Journal of Public Economics, 81,* 99–115. doi:10.1016/S0047-2727(00)00130-4

Johnson, S. (2003). Social Entrepreneurship Literature Review. *New Academy Review, 2,* 42–56.

Kwon, S., Yang, H., & Rowley, C. (2009, March). The Purchasing Performance of Organizations Using E-Marketplaces. *British Journal of Management, 20*(1), 106–124. doi:10.1111/j.1467-8551.2007.00555.x

Leadbeater, C. (1997). *The Rise of the Social Entrepreneur.* London: Demon.

Leadbeater, C. (2004). *The Co-Creation of Social Value.* A workshop held at The Judge Institute of Management, University of Cambridge.

Martin R. L., & Osberg, S. (2007) Social Entrepreneurship: The Case for Definition. *Stanford Social Innovation Review,* 28–39.

Mort, G. S., Weerawardena, J., & Carnegie, K. (2003). Social Entrepreneurship: Towards Conceptualisation. *International Journal of Nonprofit and Voluntary Sector Marketing, 8*(3), 76–88. doi:10.1002/nvsm.202

Perrini, F. (Ed.). (2006). *The New Social Entrepreneurship: What Awaits Social Entrepreneurship Ventures?* Northampton, MA: Edward Elgar.

Reis, T. K., & Clohesy, S. J. (2001). Unleashing New Resources and Entrepreneurship for the Common Good: a Philanthropic Renaissance. *New Directions in Philanthropic Fundraising, 32,* 109–143. doi:10.1002/pf.3206

Sullivan, G. M., Weerawardena, J., & Carnegie, K. (2003). Social Entrepreneurship: Towards Conceptualization. *International Journal of Nonprofit and Voluntary Sector Marketing, 8,* 76–88. doi:10.1002/nvsm.202

Thompson, J. G., Alvy, G., & Lees, A. (2000). Social Entrepreneurship—a New Look at the People and the Potential. *Management Decision, 38,* 328–338. doi:10.1108/00251740010340517

Young, D. (1986). Entrepreneurship and the Behaviour of Non-Profit Organizations: Elements of a Theory. In S. Rose-Ackerman (Ed.), *The Economics of Non-Profit Institutions: Studies in Structure and Policy* (pp. 161–184). New York: Oxford University Press.

Young, D. (1997). Non-Profit Entrepreneurship. In *International Encyclopedia of Public Policy and Administration* (pp. 1506–1509).

ENDNOTES

[1] Earned income strategies are increasingly used by charities—in 2002, for example, contracts and trading accounted for approximately 33% of total income for charities in the U.K. (NCVO, 2002).

[2] The 1991 law that protects the status of social solidarity cooperative (cooperative di solidarité sociale, divided into type A, cooperative services, or type B social co-operatives insertion) opened the door to social imbued emprenditorialidad the desire to contribute to the welfare of members and society in general. Thus, in late 2003, there were 6159 cooperatives which in turn created approximately 190,000 jobs (about 20,000 insertion cooperatives type B) and mobilized 32,000 volunteers. It is interesting to note that 70% of the human base is made up of women. An additional recognition would hand the law passed in 2006 specifically for social enterprise.

[3] Thus, in 2000 there were about 15,000 social enterprises as companies with limited or guarantee or Industrial and Provident Societies representing approximately 475,000 jobs and 300,000 volunteers. Considering that 88% of these social enterprises, over 50% of the funds come from the sale of goods and services is evidenced by a market orientation of social enterprise in this country.

[4] In Spain, social enterprises have been developed in the form of insertion enterprises. In 2002 there were 147 of this companies employing to 3,550 workers, of whom 2,201 (62%) are employees of insertion and the remaining workers in the trades concerned, responsible for management and technical social support. In its distribution by its legal form the enterprise are divided, almost half, from a formula specific to nonprofits - Associations and Foundations - and the Limited Partnership: 46% of the total, in each case,

adapting the other ways of cooperating, preferably.

[5] Social enterprises can be classified as finishers and companies in transition. The finalists are created by social enterprises to achieve the integration of those who, because of their special difficulties insurmountable, seek to develop their careers in these entities to provide jobs to workers with low labor productivity. They are especially relevant for companies in social groups of people with disabilities.

[6] Workers in insertion usually are between 6 months and 3 years in social insertion enterprise acquiring during this time employ-ability for access to normal enterprises. The reason is simple: there is no intentions that people in insertion remain indefinitely in the same, only the time required to access the labor market. However, this does not mean that there may be contracts of indefinite duration.

[7] Kiva´s founder describe their personal experience; "We went to Africa just before Jessicar would go to the business school" said Flanney. "We were working in Ugada when we had the idea to offer loans by Internet." Jessica, head marketing manager,had worked as a consultant in the recovery area of microloans in an Uganda y Kenia. "My wife adored Africa living as I loved to live in San Francisco with activities in Africa. Thus, my marriage was the trigger to create Kiva" Fuente: Universia Knowledge Wharton (11/06/08) Kiva: Cómo mejorar la vida de las personas con un pequeño préstamo [Online] [Retrieved September 1, 2008, from http://wharton.universia.net/index.cfm?fa=viewArticle&ID=1529>

[8] Kiva only accepts borrowers who go to her through the MIF that have been put under a previous analysis, cancelling the loans done to the MFI whose borrowers have breach high levels of or whose operations seem

sustainable little. When evaluating the MFI, Kiva take into account the data given by the own companies and independent agents. The company created a system of classification of five stars for the MFI, whose evaluation, as well as the profile of the company, is available in its Web.

9   Kiva hopes to make a pursuit of the landlords of liquidation of the loans, and the social impact of the done loans. His executive president Shah Prelah indicates that the company sends volunteers to the field so that they work along with the microfinancers. The volunteers send the obtained data to headquarter and narrate their experience in blogs of the company.

10   The founder of Change.org has been interviewed by Wall Street Journal. The famous American presenter Oprah dedicated part of her well-known television program to Kiva´s experience. Also Nicholas Kristof, New York Times columnist, borrowed money through Kiva and travelling to Afghanistan to know his two personally borrowers - a baker and a specialized technician in the repair of television sets. Recently, even mainstream media outlets such as MSNBC (Facebook Causes), Steven Colbert (DonorsChoose), and CNN (SixDegrees) are covering microphilanthropy.

Section 2
Organization

Chapter 8
Enlisting Online Communicators in Web 2.0

Gianfranco Walsh
University of Koblenz-Landau, Germany & University of Strathclyde Business School, Glasgow, UK

Simon Brach
University of Koblenz-Landau, Germany

Vincent-Wayne Mitchell
City University, London, UK

ABSTRACT

The Web 2.0 has changed the basic marketing communication paradigm in that it forces companies to acknowledge that Internet-based consumer-to-consumer communication can be a powerful success driver. Information dissemination, which can enhance the success of on-line and off-line products, is increasingly outside the realm of influence of companies because in many markets on-line communicators can play a central role in influencing others' purchase decisions. e-Mavens are recognized as a consumer type that engage in on-line communication. Using a sample of more than 2,500 consumers, the authors profile e-Mavens using demographic and psychographic characteristics as well as explore their motives for visiting music web sites. In addition, changes in e-Mavens' music-related consumption behavior are investigated. Next, using cluster analysis, the authors develop a typology of e-Mavens. Implications for both managerial practice and Web 2.0 research are discussed.

INTRODUCTION

The way people are enabled to participate in creating the Internet has undergone a radical change during the last few years. While in the past users were passive consumers of content, they have become active producers of what they consume today. Web 2.0 applications restructured the architecture of the

Internet in a way that turned users into "prosumers". In contrast to traditional Web 1.0 websites where content could only be modified by the owner and where visitors were limited to viewing, websites in the times of Web 2.0 are characterized by user participation and communication. Most Web 2.0 applications can be described as tools for sharing information and communicating with organizations and other end users (Walsh, Hass, & Kilian, 2010). Especially social networks and weblogs are grow-

DOI: 10.4018/978-1-61520-597-4.ch008

ing fast in numbers and traffic – there are almost 190 million weblogs and four of the top 10 US entertainment sites are weblogs (Bernoff, 2009a; technorati.com, 2008). According to a recent Nielson Online (Bausch, & McGiboney, 2009) study, member communities including social networking websites and weblogs are the fourth most popular online activity. There is little doubt amongst experts regarding the word-of-mouth power of social networking websites, blogs or the Internet in general (Brown, Broderick, & Lee, 2007; Duan, Gu, & Whinston, 2008; Muñiz, & O'Guinn, 2001; Sassenberg, & Scholl, 2009; Wenger, 2008).

A growing number of companies is using the enormous potential of electronic word-of-mouth for marketing campaigns. So-called viral marketing strategies are effective ways of promoting new products or services and firms are increasingly approaching influential bloggers to promote products and disseminate product information. For example, when Ford became aware that the well-known blogger Jessica Smith (www.jessicaknows.com) said she planned to buy a new car, Ford offered her to use the Ford Flex free of charge for a week. Jessica Smith wrote a blog post on her experience and uploaded a video and subsequently, Ford offered her the car for a whole year (Bernoff, 2009b).

There is evidence that consumer-to-consumer communication is particularly common, and effective in terms of product dissemination and sales, in an electronic media environment. We can use three examples to exemplify this point.

In the field of politics Barack Obama's campaign for the White House can be seen as an example of the powerful impact of electronic word-of-mouth. Experts argue that without the Internet Barack Obama would still be the junior senator from Illinois. Obama's two-year campaign for the White House largely relied on electronic communications to achieve several goals: organizing volunteers and staff, finding new supporters

and putting them to work, turning out voters on election day and raising large funds – all giving him a crucial edge in the primaries and general election. On the social network site MyBarackObama.com, or MyBO, two million profiles were created. In addition, 200,000 off-line events were planned, about 400,000 blog posts were written and more than 35,000 volunteer groups were created – at least 1,000 of them on February 10, 2007, the day Obama announced his candidacy. Some three million calls were made in the final four days of the 2008 campaign using MyBO's virtual phone-banking platform. On their own MyBO fundraising pages, 70,000 people raised $30 million (Bernoff, 2009a; 2009b; Delany, 2009).

Another vivid example of effective Web 2.0 marketing is the 20th Century Fox movie *Borat*. While it is common practice in the US Film industry to use 50% of the production budget for marketing the movie, 20th Century Fox in promoting *Borat* relied on stimulating word-of-mouth via social media. For example, the studio posted trailers on Youtube to create buzz and used MySpace as their viral marketing hub – members of MySpace were encouraged to add a picture of *Borat* to their list of "8 best friends". Compared to a relatively small production budget of $18m the return of $260m within 6 months after release shows that in times of the Web 2.0 it is possible to attract a big audience without spending millions of dollars.

Another case in point is the British band *Arctic Monkeys*. Because no record label was interested in their music, the young band from Sheffield sold its songs through their website and on Myspace which led to a considerable fan base. After signing a contract with the DIY Record label Domino the band's first single "I Bet you Look good on the Dancefloor", was released on 17 October 2005 and made #1 in the UK single charts. Their debut album "Whatever People Say I Am, That's What I'm Not" sold more copies on its first day alone (118,501) than the rest of the

Top 20 albums combined. It became the fastest selling debut album in UK chart history, selling 363,735 copies in the first week.

The above examples are indicative of the fact that on-line consumer-to-consumer communication is particularly potent in a media context. The importance of so-called e-fluentials is largely undisputed, especially in a viral marketing context. According to Cakim (2006), these people are key in the generation of viral messages because they are active users of email, newsgroups, bulletin boards, listservs and other on-line vehicles and social media when conveying their messages. The literature distinguishes between three relevant e-fluential types – innovators, opinion leaders and market mavens.

In this study, we focus on e-Mavens who are likely to be particularly good allies in on-line word-of-mouth promotion. Indeed, the literature suggest using early adopters and opinion leaders as information providers can be risky for marketers as these consumers can have imperfect information or can pass-on negative product experiences. Because of this, Enis (1979) considers opinion leaders as "unreliable allies of marketers" (p. 56). Market mavens, on the other hand, are relatively well informed and their knowledge is based on other information as well as usage. Unlike innovators and opinion leaders, market mavens are more general opinion leaders, who have a solid overall market-related knowledge and a willingness to disseminate information which is not product specific (Wiedmann, Walsh, & Mitchell, 2001). Previous studies found that some consumers have distinct traits that mark them as mavens (Walsh, Gwinner, & Swanson, 2004). Those traits, especially the tendency to actively and passively disseminate information to other consumers, make them ideal targets of messages in a fast-moving market environment, such as the media market.

Within the media industry the music market stands out in terms of the effects the Web 2.0 had on revenues and business models. As CD sales continue to decrease (minus 20% from 2007 to 2008) record companies are beginning to generate revenues from music on Web 2.0 sites like Youtube and Myspace, for example from fees for streamed videos and music downloads (Sisario, 2008). We argue that media companies should make greater use of on-line communicators to market their products. By enlisting on-line communicators with known traits, such as e-Mavens, media companies can increase the effectiveness of their promotional efforts. For example, music/media companies could enlist e-Mavens to advise consumers about the legality of different music download options, to target special consumer groups that are difficult to reach via conventional communications or to test-market new films and songs. However, before media companies can enlist their help, e-Mavens need to be profiled, which is the aim of this study.

BACKGROUND

Market Mavens

Feick and Price (1987) identified market mavens as a distinct type of 'reference person' and conceptualized market mavens as being, "individuals who have information about many kinds of products, places to shop, and other facets of markets, and initiate discussions with consumers and respond to requests from consumers for market information" (p. 85). That is, they initiate conversations on market information and share their knowledge with others, as well as asking others for information. Some of the reasons for looking at mavenism within the Web 2.0 and on-line music context are; mavens acquire information actively which is much more a kin to the way in which music enthusiasts operate. Also, music enthusiasts are more motivated to help friends and family enjoy music from an altruistic perspective which is a market maven trait (Walsh et al., 2004). As music consumption is changing because of video-sharing websites like Youtube and music downloading is now largely legitimate and legal and no longer new, mavens are more likely to know about it and be more active at disseminating information about it.

Off-line studies have found mavens to have traits which suggest they are likely to use Internet music sources. For example, they are likely to be bargain seeking and smart shoppers (Price, Feick, & Guskey-Federouch, 1988; Wiedmann et al., 2001), which is highly relevant to obtaining free or cheap music on-line. Second, they have larger evoked sets (Lichtenstein, & Burton, 1990) and place a greater importance on brand (or in this context, band) criteria rather than store criteria (Williams, & Slama, 1995), which would make them more willing to use Web 2.0 applications to obtain music. Third, they are more motivated to pass on information to peers (Walsh et al., 2004); something which is characteristic of on-line communities and social media. Previous studies have identified market mavens on the Internet (Walsh, Mitchell, Wiedmann, Frenzel, & Duvenhorst, 2002; Belch, Krentler, & Willis-Flurry, 2005). Drawing on this work, we profile and segment e-Mavens to help companies create more audience-focused and effective online communication strategies.

METHODOLOGY

The Questionnaire and Sample

Market mavens were identified using modified version of the original six-item Market Maven Scale. The wording of items was slightly changed to take account for the special e-music context. Respondents rated the items on a 5-point scale (1 = strongly disagree, 5 = strongly agree). The on-line questionnaire was accessible through a banner link on the homepage of the seven participating Internet firms' web sites. The on-line survey yielded a sample of 2,530. Most respondents aged 20-29, suggesting that many younger people, students

and males are particularly interested in music and use the Internet more.

Identifying Music e-Mavens

The music e-Maven items were subjected to a confirmatory factor analysis and model identification was achieved. The global fit of the model was satisfying (see Figure 1), with GFI = 0.92, RMR = 0.037, CFI = 0.94, RMSEA = 0.08 and the value of the AGFI was 0.84. The scale's Cronbach's alpha was 0.90, indicating that the music e-Maven scale is reliable and generalizable to Internet populations (Nunnally, 1978).

The range of the e-Maven scale was 7 to 35 with an average score of 19.12. Consistent with previous studies (Wiedmann et al., 2001), respondents were categorized into low (< 11; 26.7%), medium (11-24; 46.2%) and high (> 24; 27.1%) e-Mavenism. Those respondents in the high group (n = 685) are referred to as music e-Mavens and those in the low group as non-e-Mavens (n = 676). Respondents from the medium group (n = 1169) were not considered in subsequent analyses. On average, music e-Mavens tend to be: younger than non-e-Mavens (average age 26.8 vs. 31.2 years; $p<.01$); have a lower education than non-e-Mavens and are more likely to be female ($p<.05$). A higher percentage of music e-Mavens than non-e-Mavens were found in the low-income group which is likely to be due to the economic advantages of downloading free music.

Music e-Mavens' Motives for Using Internet Music Sites

First, we examined the motives of e-Mavens for using Internet music sites. Exploratory principal components analysis was used to summarize our items into an underlying set of motives for music site usage. At 0.80, the measure of sampling adequacy (KMO) value was very satisfactory and two factors were identified which accounted for 67% of the variance. With alphas of above

Figure 1. Coefficients of determination on the Music e-maven scale

	Squared Loadings (of CFA)	Mean	
		e-Mavens	Non-e-Mavens
My friends think of me as a good source of information when it comes to new music or Internet music sites.	.77	4.15	1.60
People ask me for information about music styles, bands, songs and Internet music sites.	.73	3.84	1.43
I like helping people by providing them with information about many kinds of music and Internet music sites.	.66	3.90	1.36
If someone asked me which Internet music sites to visit with regard to different music styles, I could tell him which sites to visit.	.64	3.79	1.21
I like introducing interesting Internet music sites to my friends.	.59	3.62	1.27
I like introducing new bands and songs to my friends.	.57	3.79	1.17
Think about a person who has information about a variety of music styles and Internet music sites and likes to share this information with others. This person knows about new music styles, bands, new songs, and Internet music sites, but not necessarily feels he or she is a music expert. How well you say this description fits you?	.48	3.50	1.50

0.70, the scales representing the two factors are stable and internally consistent in the sample (see Figure 2). Factor 1 was Music Information Need. Users scoring highly on this factor appear to be in a constant demand of different kinds of music-related information. Factor 2 was Personal/Professional Interest. Users who score highly on this factor seem to be driven by a combination of private and professional reasons. They visit Internet music sites not only because they seek information that helps them with their job, but also because they can 'meet' other consumers interested in music. As expected, e-Mavens score significantly higher than non-e-Mavens on both motives (p<.01).

Next, we explored in how far the music consumption pattern of e-Mavens and non-e-Mavens has changed as a consequence of using Internet music sites (see Figure 3). e-Mavens have consistently higher means (sig. at p≤.01) than non-e-Mavens across all items capturing changes in music consumption. It appears that using those sites affects not only their communication behavior but also their consumption behavior. Specifically, using Internet music sites appears to make consumers more price sensitive and is negatively associated

with their use of traditional music media. Our findings provide support for the notion that Web 2.0 media replace traditional (off-line) media.

Identifying Music e-Maven Groups

To identify groups of music e-Mavens, a hierarchical cluster analysis followed by a *k*-means analysis was performed. In this study, the aggregated music market e-Maven factor was used to develop the clusters, while demographic variables, motives for using Internet music sites and other variables were used to profile the clusters. Distances between the clusters were calculated with the Euclidean distance measure and aggregation of clusters was performed with Ward's procedure (see Figure 4). We now describe the individual segments.

Segment 1 represents e-Mavens that can be described as music wallowers. These e-Mavens have the highest music e-Maven score and are true music e-Mavens. In particular, friends think of them as a good source of music information. They have the most even balance of male and females of all the segments and are the least educated of all the groups. They are motivated by getting information about tour dates and new releases

Figure 2. e-Mavens' motives for using internet music sites

	Cronbach's α/ Eigenvalue/ Factor loading	Mean (SD)		
Factor 1: Music Information Need	α = .74 Eigenvalue = 3.10	*Total Sample*	*e-Mavens*	*non-e-Mavens*
To get information such as tour dates or new releases of my favorite stars.	0.87	3.52 (1.38)	4.03 (1.09)	2.90* (1.42)
To stay informed about music events such as festivals.	0.82	3.19 (1.36)	3.69 (1.15)	2.64* (1.34)
Because one can get information on new music styles and bands.	0.60	3.24 (1.37)	3.94 (0.99)	2.42* (1.26)
Factor 2: Personal/Professional Interest	α = .71 Eigenvalue = 1.23			
Because I have a job-related interest in Internet music sites.	0.87	1.85 (1.31)	2.47 (1.46)	1.30* (0.78)
Because I am interested in the music industry.	0.80	2.27 (1.38)	3.05 (1.36)	1.58* (0.94)
Because I like to communicate with like-minded in the community areas of such sites.	0.53	2.51 (1.30)	3.15 (1.18)	1.83* (1.05)
* sign. at p ≥ 1%				

Figure 3.

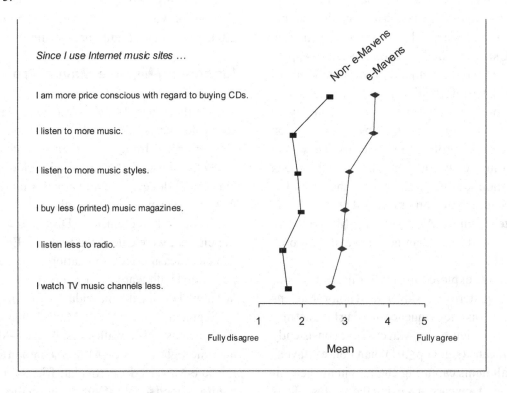

on their favorite artists and are the most likely of all the groups to have a job-related interest in music sites. As a result, they use the Internet at work and home more than other segments and have the highest frequency of visiting Internet music sites with 25% visiting more than once a

Figure 4. Characterization of the e-Maven clusters

	Music Wallowers (n = 188)	Self-serving Music e-Mavens (n = 194)	Hidden music e-Mavens (n = 109)	Weak music e-Mavens (n = 194)
Cluster Results				
e-Maven aggregate	*4.45ᵃ	3.66ᵇ·ᵈ	3.75ᶜ·ᵈ	3.70ᵈ
Cluster Profiles				
Age	26.17ᵃ·ᵇ	26.49ᵃ·ᵇ	25.27ᵃ	27.65ᵇ
Gender				
male	79 (42%)	73 (38%)	38 (35%)	75 (39%)
female	109 (58%)	121 (62%)	71 (65%)	120 (61%)
Education				
Some High School or Less	8 (4.26%)	8 (4.12%)	5 (4.59%)	6 (3.09%)
High School Graduate	19 (10.11%)	16 (8.29%)	3 (2.79%)	13 (6.70%)
Vocational School/Some College	60 (31.91%)	55 (28.39%)	26 (23.89%)	51 (26.25%)
College Graduate	57 (30.32%)	55 (28.39%)	42 (38.53%)	67 (34.54%)
Graduate School	26 (13.83%)	39 (20.16%)	23 (21.10%)	44 (22.68%)
No answer	18 (9.57%)	21 (10.82%)	10 (9.17%)	13 (6.70%)
Factor 1: Information Need	3.94ᵃ	3.47ᵇ	3.19ᶜ	2.52ᶜ
To get information such as tour dates or new releases of my favorite stars.	4.08ᵃ	3.62ᵇ	3.48ᶜ	2.76ᵈ
To stay informed about music events such as festivals.	3.75ᵃ	3.30ᵇ	3.09ᶜ	2.54ᵈ
Because one can get information on new music styles and bands.	3.98ᵃ	3.49ᵇ	3.01ᶜ	2.26ᵈ
Factor 2: Personal/Professional Interest	2.95ᵃ	2.38ᵇ	1.91ᶜ	1.48ᵈ
Because I have a job-related interest in Internet music sites.	2.58ᵃ	1.97ᵇ	1.52ᶜ	1.25ᵈ
Because I am interested in the music industry.	3.11ᵃ	2.42ᵇ	1.98ᶜ	1.46ᵈ
Because I like to communicate with like-minded in the community areas of such sites.	3.15ᵃ	2.76ᵇ	2.21ᶜ	1.73ᵈ
Locus of Internet use				
only privately	82 (44%)	97 (50%)	67 (61%)	91 (47%)
only at workplace	3 (2%)	6 (3%)	3 (3%)	6 (3%)
both	103 (55%)	91 (47%)	39 (36%)	98 (51%)
Time online (hours per week)				
>10 hrs	5 (3%)	3 (2%)	0	3 (2%)

	Music Wallowers (n = 188)	Self-serving Music e-Mavens (n = 194)	Hidden music e-Mavens (n = 109)	Weak music e-Mavens (n = 194)
5-10 hrs	9 (5%)	9 (5%)	7 (6%)	7 (4%)
2-5 hrs	34 (18%)	50 (26%)	23 (21%)	35 (18%)
1-2 hrs	41 (22%)	55 (28%)	27 (14%)	46 (24%)
<1h	99 (53%)	77 (40%)	52 (48%)	104 (54%)
Frequency of visiting Internet music sites				
< once a week	34 (18%)	61 (31%)	40 (37%)	69 (36%)
at least once a week	44 (23%)	74 (38%)	22 (20%)	47 (24%)
several times a week	62 (33%)	33 (17%)	27 (25%)	45 (23%)
at least once a day	27 (14%)	17 (9%)	13 (12%)	23 (12%)
several times a day	21 (11%)	9 (5%)	7 (6%)	11 (6%)
Time online on Internet music sites (per visit)				
>1h	49 (26%)	55 (28%)	39 (36%)	58 (30%)
>45 min < 1h	71 (38%)	75 (39%)	45 (41%)	66 (34%)
30-45 min	35 (19%)	31 (16%)	9 (8%)	34 (18%)
15-30 min	14 (7%)	19 (10%)	7 (6%)	23 (12%)
<15 min	19 (10%)	14 (7%)	9 (8%)	14 (7%)
How do you get to know Internet music sites? (three most frequently mentioned)				
1) Friends and acquaintances	11 (6%)	10 (5%)	8 (7%)	18 (9%)
2) Surfing the net	12 (6%)	7 (4%)	7 (6%)	5 (3%)
3) searching	17 (9%)	21 (11%)	10 (9%)	21 (11%)
4) Topic-related Internet communities	6 (3%)	10 (5%)	7 (6%)	10 (5%)
5) magazines and newspapers	60 (32%)	30 (15%)	23 (21%)	58 (30%)
6) CD cover	31 (16%)	41 (21%)	29 (27%)	40 (21%)
7) e-mail newsletter	51 (27%)	75 (39%)	25 (23%)	43 (22%)

* Mean; within a row, means with the *same* superscript are not significantly (p < .05) different from each other (according to Scheffe LSD test).
Scale: 1 = strongly disagree, 5 = strongly agree

day and spending mainly between 45-60 minutes on each visit. These music e-Mavens get to know about music sites mainly through magazines and newspapers, but very rarely through on-line music communities.

The self serving e-Mavens in segment 2 have a similar overall music e-Maven score to segments 3 and 4. However, they have quite a high need for information and spend the most time on-line of all the groups with 33% of them spending more than 5 hours a week on the Internet. They get to know about Internet music sites mainly via email newsletters and hardly ever surf the net to find music sites.

The hidden music e-Mavens in segment 3 are the smallest and youngest group with an average age of 25 and the best education. One of their defining characteristic is that people rarely ask them for information about music styles, bands, songs and Internet music sites which earns them the descriptor of hidden music e-Mavens. They have the highest proportion of females of any segment (65%) and are not interested in the music industry. They principally use the Internet for private purposes; spend the least amount of time on-line with only 27% spending more than five hours a week and 57% visit music sites once a week or less. Importantly, they get to know about Internet music sites via CD covers and rarely get involved with Internet music communities.

Segment 4 represents one of the largest and oldest segments with an average age of nearly 28. These weak music e-Mavens have the lowest need for information; are not likely to have a job-related interest or an interest in the music industry and are not likely to communicate with other like-minded people. They get to know about music sites from newspapers and magazines and rarely from surfing the net. The amount of time spent on-line does not seem to vary much between the different e-Maven segments, but this could be accounted for by considering that the groups may not be always be engaged in music related activities.

CONCLUSIONS

The research set out to profile e-Mavens and propose an e-Maven typology. All four groups identified seem to have a relatively low income which is likely to make them receptive to price-related information which can help them save money and partly explain their interest in free on-line

music. Indeed, Laroche, Pons, Zgnolli, Cervellon and Kim (2003) show that in the context of sales promotions mavenism has a positive influence on consumers' cost/benefit evaluations and others suggest that deal-prone consumers exhibit market maven tendencies. This is also an important issue for their status as music e-Mavens because while much information can vary in meaning due to it being affected by subjective interpretation (e.g., the music assortment at that web site is poor), price information is objective and transparent. Music e-Mavens could therefore be particularly suitable for disseminating price-related information.

The identification and profiling of music e-Mavens has implications which could help e-marketers in general and music e-marketers in particular in several ways. For example, they can be used to endorse and disseminate Internet addresses of music-related video-sharing sites such as Youtube or of on-line music sites offering commercial file-sharing services and on-line music retailers. Since music e-Mavens are generally knowledgeable on marketing-mix information (e.g., price changes, new subscription services, and temporary special offers) they could be an inexpensive way of communicating short-term messages and be targeted with specific emails tailored to them. In particular, the music wallower seems best placed e-Maven group to help spread word-of-mouth promotional messages and new product ideas. Indeed the ability to use music e-Mavens could become an e-firm's competitive advantage as the Internet becomes more and more cluttered and as consumers experience increasing difficulty in finding and comparing offerings efficiently (Peterson & Merino, 2003). It would be relatively easy for e-companies to identify e-Mavens as the short 7-item questionnaire could be used as part of a more general 'site registration' questionnaire. Another implication, given the interest motives identified, is that new singles or bands could be tested more quickly and less expensively using music e-Mavens. This is particularly the case for the music wallower e-Mavens who are thought to be a good source of new music by their friends. Traditional audience testing for new music has been a costly and labor-intensive task, yielding questionable results.

Also, although the results show that music e-Mavens are distinct from non-e-Mavens, we advise e-marketers against treating them as a homogeneous group whose members have similar preferences. The cluster analysis identified four music e-Mavens sub-groups, which could serve e-marketers in different ways. Marketers could design products and/or communication strategies specifically to target the most useful music e-Mavens segments.

Conventional marketing wisdom holds that Internet firms need effective methods of information dissemination as it becomes increasingly difficult to reach their on-line and off-line target groups. Marketplace influencers, like music e-Mavens, could be useful in enhancing the effectiveness of message and product diffusion in the Web 2.0 era. Indeed, the Internet was originally designed as a social space where consumer-to-consumer communication takes place and where e-Mavenism might flourish (Evans, Wedande, Ralston, & Van't Hul, 2001). Future studies could extend our research by seeking to identify e-Mavens in different Web 2.0 contexts, such as blogging, video sharing or wikis. Another promising avenue of future research would be investigating the customer lifetime value of e-Mavens compared to non-e-Mavens.

Traditionally, marketers treated word-of-mouth as something they could not actively manage. They spent money on marketing communications and expected the message to somehow magically trickle down to the relevant market segment by means of word-of-mouth. The problem with such approaches is that it is difficult to track consumers who actively pass on messages to other consumers and to steer messages to specific audiences. Hence, successful word-of-mouth marketing requires firms to understand the customers they expect to do the word-of-mouth for them. This study hopes to contribute to the growing body of research on on-line consumer-to-consumer communication.

REFERENCES

Bausch, S., & McGiboney, M. (2009, March 9). Social Networks & Blogs now 4th most Popular Online Activity, Ahead of Personal Email. *News Report.* Retrieved http://www.nielsen-online.com/pr/pr_090309.pdf

Belch, M., Krentler, K., & Willis-Flurry, L. (2005). Teen internet mavens: influence in family decision making. *Journal of Business Research, 58,* 569–575. doi:10.1016/j.jbusres.2003.08.005

Bernoff, J. (2009a, February 15). Blogs, Marketing and Trust. *Marketing news, 17.*

Bernoff J (2009b, March 15). Get more than an Ad, get in the conversation. *Marketing News,* 18.

Brown, J., Broderick, A., & Lee, L. (2007). Word of mouth communication within online communities: Conceptualizing the online social network. *Journal of Interactive Marketing, 21*(3), 2–20. doi:10.1002/dir.20082

Cakim, I. (2006). Online opinion leaders: a predictive guide for viral marketing campaigns. In J. Kirby & P. Marsden (Eds.) *Connected Marketing: the Viral, Buzz and Word-of-mouth Revolution* (pp. 107-118). Oxford, UK: Butterworth-Heinemann.

Delany, C. (2009, February 24). Learning from Obama: Lessons for Online Communicators in 2009 and Beyond. Message posted to http://techpresident.com/blog-entry/learning-obama-lessons-online-communicators-2009-and-beyond

Duan, W., Gu, B., & Whinston, A. B. (2008). The dynamics of online word-of-mouth and product sales- An empirical investigation of the movie industry. *Journal of Interactive Marketing, 23*(2), 179–190.

Enis, B. M. (1979). *Personal Selling: Foundations, Process, and Management*. Santa Monica, CA: Goodyear Publ.

Evans, M., Wedande, G., Ralston, L., & Van`t Hul, S. (2001). Consumer interaction in the virtual era: some qualitative insights. *Qualitative Market Research: An International Journal, 4*(3), 150–159. doi:10.1108/13522750110393053

Feick, L. F., & Price, L. L. (1987). The Market Maven: A Diffuser of Marketplace Information. *Journal of Marketing, 51*, 83–97. doi:10.2307/1251146

Laroche, M., Pons, F., Zgolli, N., Cervellon, M. C., & Kim, C. (2003). A model of consumer response to two retail sales promotion techniques. *Journal of Business Research, 56*, 513–522. doi:10.1016/S0148-2963(01)00249-1

Lichtenstein, D. R., & Burton, S. (1990). An Assessment of the Moderating Effects of Market Mavenism and Value Consciousness on Price-Quality Perception Accuracy. *Advances in Consumer Research. Association for Consumer Research (U. S.), 17*(1), 53–59.

Muñiz, A. M. Jr, & O'Guinn, T. C. (2001). Brand Community. *The Journal of Consumer Research, 27*(4), 412–432. doi:10.1086/319618

Nunnally, J. C. (1978). *Psychometric Theory* (2nd Ed.). New York: McGraw-Hill.

Peterson, R. A., & Merino, M. C. (2003). Consumer Information Search Behavior and the Internet. *Psychology and Marketing, 20*(2), 99–121. doi:10.1002/mar.10062

Price, L. L., Feick, L. F., & Guskey-Federouch, A. (1988). Coupon Behaviors of the Market Maven: Profile of a Super Couponer. *Advances in Consumer Research. Association for Consumer Research (U. S.), 15*, 354–359.

Sassenberg, K., & Scholl, A. (2010). Soziale Bindungen von Usern an Web 2.0-Angebote. In G. Walsh, B. H. Hass, & T. Kilian (Eds.), *Web 2.0 - Neue Perspektiven für Marketing und Medien* (2nd ed.). Heidelberg, Germany: Springer.

Sisario, B. (2008, December 31). Music Sales Fell in 2008, but Climbed on the Web. *The New York Times*. Retrieved June 15, 2009, from http://www.nytimes.com

Technorati. (n.d.). *State of the Blogsphere 2008*. Retrieved June 15, 2009, from http://technorati.com/blogging/state-of-the-blogosphere

Walsh, G., Gwinner, K. P., & Swanson, S. R. (2004). What Makes Mavens Tick? Exploring the Motives of Market Mavens' Initiation of Information Diffusion. *Journal of Consumer Marketing, 21*(2), 109–122. doi:10.1108/07363760410525678

Walsh, G., Hass, B., & Kilian, T. *(2010)*. Web 2.0: Neue Perspektiven für Marketing und Medien *(2nd Ed.). Heidelberg, Germany: Springer.*

Walsh, G., Mitchell, V. W., Wiedmann, K. P., Frenzel, T., & Duvenhorst, C. (2002). German eMavens on Internet Music Sites. In W. J. Kehoe & J. H. Lindgren (Eds.), *AMA 2002 Summer Educators' Conference 13: Proceedings: Enhancing Knowledge Development in Marketing* (pp. 435-436). Chicago: American Marketing Association.

Wenger, A. (2008). Analysis of travel bloggers' characteristics and their communication about Austria as a tourism destination. *Journal of Vacation Marketing, 14*(2), 169–176. doi:10.1177/1356766707087525

Wiedmann, K. P., Walsh, G., & Mitchell, V. W. (2001). The German Mannmaven: An Agent for Diffusing Market Information. *Journal of Marketing Communications, 7*(4), 1–17.

Williams, T. G., & Slama, M. E. (1995). Market maven's purchase decision evaluative criteria: implications for brand and store promotion effort. *Journal of Consumer Marketing, 12*(3), 4–21. doi:10.1108/07363769510147218

ADDITIONAL READING

Abbasi, A., Chen, H., & Nunamaker, J. Jr. (2008). Stylometric Identification in Electronic Markets: Scalability and Robustness. *Journal of Management Information Systems*, *25*(1), 49–78. doi:10.2753/MIS0742-1222250103

Amblee, N., & Bai, T. (2008). Can Brand Reputation Improve the Odds of Being Reviewed On-Line? *International Journal of Electronic Commerce*, *12*(3), 11–28. doi:10.2753/JEC1086-4415120302

Awad, N., & Ragowsky, A. (2008). Establishing Trust in Electronic Commerce Through Online Word of Mouth: An Examination Across Genders. *Journal of Management Information Systems*, *24*(4), 101–121. doi:10.2753/MIS0742-1222240404

Barabási, A. (2002), *Linked: The New Science of Networks,* Perseus Publishing.

Bickart, B., & Schindler, R. (2001). Internet Forums as influential Sources of Consumer Information. *Journal of Interactive Marketing*, *15*(3), 31–40. doi:10.1002/dir.1014

Chen, Y., & Xie, J. (2008). Online Consumer Review: Word-of-Mouth as a New Element of Marketing Communication Mix. *Management Science*, *54*(3), 477–491. doi:10.1287/mnsc.1070.0810

Cheung, C., Lee, M., & Rabjohn, N. (2008). The impact of electronic word-of-mouth: The adoption of online opinions in online customer communities. *Internet Research*, *18*(3), 229–247. doi:10.1108/10662240810883290

Cheung, M., Luo, C., Sia, C., & Chen, H. (2009). Credibility of Electronic Word-of-Mouth: Informational and Normative Determinants of On-line Consumer Recommendations. *International Journal of Electronic Commerce*, *13*(4), 9–38. doi:10.2753/JEC1086-4415130402

Chevalier, J., & Mayzlin, D. (2006). The Effect of Word of Mouth on Sales: Online Book Reviews. *JMR, Journal of Marketing Research*, *43*(3), 345–354. doi:10.1509/jmkr.43.3.345

Clemons, E., Gao, G., & Hitt, L. (2006). When Online Reviews Meet Hyperdifferentiation: A Study of the Craft Beer Industry. *Journal of Management Information Systems*, *23*(2), 149–171. doi:10.2753/MIS0742-1222230207

Dellarocas, C. (2006). Strategic Manipulation of Internet Opinion Forums: Implications for Consumers and Firms. *Management Science*, *52*(10), 1577–1593. doi:10.1287/mnsc.1060.0567

Dwyer, P. (2007). Measuring the value of electronic word of mouth and its impact in consumer communities. *Journal of Interactive Marketing*, *21*(2), 63–79. doi:10.1002/dir.20078

Godes, D., & Mayzlin, D. (2004). Using Online Conversations to Study Word-of-Mouth Communication. *Marketing Science*, *23*(4), 545–560. doi:10.1287/mksc.1040.0071

Iyengar, R., Han, S., & Gupta, S. (2009). *Do Friends Influence Purchases in a Social Network?* (Working paper No. 09-123) Boston: Havard Business School Marketing Unit

Keller, E., & Barry, J. (2003), *The Influentials: One American in Ten Tells the other Nine How to Vote, Where to Eat, and What to Buy,* New York: The Free Press.

Mayzlin, D. (2006). Promotional Chat on the Internet. *Marketing Science*, *25*(2), 155–163. doi:10.1287/mksc.1050.0137

Park, D., Lee, J., & Han, I. (2007). The Effect of On-Line Consumer Reviews on Consumer Purchasing Intention: The Moderating Role of Involvement. *International Journal of Electronic Commerce*, *11*(4), 125–148. doi:10.2753/JEC1086-4415110405

Sen, S., & Lerman, D. (2007). Why are you telling me this? An examination into negative consumer reviews on the Web. *Journal of Interactive Marketing*, *21*(4), 76–94. doi:10.1002/dir.20090

Srinivasan, S., Anderson, R., & Ponnavolu, K. (2002). Customer loyalty in e-commerce: An exploration of its antecedents and consequences. *Journal of Retailing*, *78*(1), 5–5. doi:10.1016/S0022-4359(01)00065-3

Thong, J., & Tan, F. (2009). Introduction to the Special Section: Consumption, Influence, and Participation of Web Users. *International Journal of Electronic Commerce*, *13*(4), 5–7. doi:10.2753/JEC1086-4415130401

Trusov, M., Bodapati, A., & Bucklin, R. E. (2009). Determining influential users in internet social networks, Working paper, University of Maryland.

Trusov, M., Bucklin, R. E., & Pauwels, K. (2008). (Forthcoming). Effects of word-of-mouth versus traditional marketing: findings from an internet social networking site . *Journal of Marketing*.

Chapter 9
The Role of Creativity (and Creative Behaviour) in Identifying Entrepreneurs

Debbie Richards
Macquarie University, Australia

Peter Busch
Macquarie University, Australia

Ayse Bilgin
Macquarie University, Australia

ABSTRACT

As the importance of creativity and in turn innovation for individuals, organizations, nations and the global community as a whole becomes recognized, so too does the value of identifying those individuals with the potential to become entrepreneurs. The nature of creative knowledge is such that it draws typically upon both codified and tacit forms of knowledge, to which end an instrument is presented based on workplace scenarios combined with a number of psychometric tests. With opportunities for innovation afforded by the internet, the identification and development of a new breed of individuals known as e-entrepreneurs seems particularly worthwhile. Thus in this study we have focused on scenarios within the field of information and communication technology. Results indicate innovators may present multiple personality styles which offer strengths to entrepreneurial activities. Finally through identification of creative personnel our approach offers a way for organizations to cultivate promising entrepreneurs.

INTRODUCTION

The Internet is providing new opportunities for individuals and businesses to be creative and explore Information and Communication Technology (ICT) ventures in ways not previously possible. As Amit and Zott (2001) note, "business conducted over the Internet (which we refer to as 'e-business'), with its dynamic, rapidly growing, and highly competitive characteristics, promises new avenues for the creation of wealth" (p. 493). This provides incentives for the emergence of a new breed of business people known as e-entrepreneurs.

DOI: 10.4018/978-1-61520-597-4.ch009

Entrepreneurship is closely associated with innovation (Baumol, 1993). Similarly creativity plays an important role in the success of an innovation particularly because it enables individuals to overcome obstacles (Amabile, 1996; 1993) that might have prevented the success. Creativity is a characteristic of particular relevance to e-entrepreneurs as they will need to be able to respond rapidly and in novel ways to an environment in which the only constant is change (Brown, & Eisenhardt, 1998). These changes are "largely driven by new technology and globalization" [resulting in] a competitive landscape with substantial uncertainty (Hitt et al., 2001 pp. 479-480). The importance of innovation for competitive advantage and even survival has been generally recognized (Porter, 1985). In highly competitive and uncertain environments, it logically follows that the success of an ICT venture by an e-Entrepreneur will largely depend on the innovation associated with the venture and ability of the entrepreneur to creatively respond to opportunities and threats.

Many courses, often at the postgraduate level, have emerged over the last decade seeking to develop entrepreneurs and equip students to understand and manage innovation. Interestingly, the study by Zampetakis and Moustakis (2006) found that the study of business courses at university including those intended to promote innovative and entrepreneurial behaviour tended to dampen motivation to pursue this path. Instead, desire to become an entrepreneur was related to a student's self-perception of creativity, in turn largely the product of being exposed to a culture of self-employment within their home environment. Entrepreneurs by definition need to be highly motivated and self-driven individuals. Thus motivation, desire and determination play important roles in achieving success. Innovation is often driven and enabled by technology. ICT ventures provide strong extrinsic motivators to entrepreneurs who are intrinsically motivated to identify and exploit business opportunities.

Given the difficulty of producing entrepreneurs via education and training, this paper is particularly interested in offering a method by which potential e-entrepreneurs can be identified as measured by their creativity and responses to innovation relevant scenarios. As an extension the method can also be used to identify compatible business partners in a joint venture and to identify areas of difference or weakness. In the next section, we review the current psychology-based literature on creativity and present a framework for investigating creative and innovative individuals. We present our methodology followed by data analysis and discussions. The paper concludes with future work and final remarks.

BACKGROUND

The work reported in this paper follows on from our work on ICT innovation and entrepreneurship (Richard, & Busch, 2008). We argue ICT innovation is really just a subset of innovation. We focus here on what it means to be a creative or innovative individual, for creative individuals will tend to be creative regardless of the discipline, just as exemplary tacit knowledge users will be regardless of their domain (Sternberg et al., 1995); and this 'finding' in turn explains why psychometric instruments exist testing for creativity, the ability to innovate and in the case of Sternberg et al. (1995), the ability to maximize use of tacit knowledge. In short, the outcome of the work reported here is a means by which organizations including e-businesses, may either establish the likelihood of innovative ability and entrepreneurialism in individuals, or alternatively provide an opportunity for individuals themselves to determine if they have an 'inventive streak' or possess more general entrepreneurial qualities. The authors are in the ICT domain and their testing to date has largely been with ICT aligned personnel. Of course as Sternberg et al. (1995) implies, much of the testing for knowledge we discuss in this chapter does not have to be domain-specific; the same means of assessment could apply to personnel in other disciplines.

It is generally accepted that creativity involves both convergent and divergent styles of thinking (Eysenck, 1993; Runco, 2004). Here creative thinking resembles dream mentation (e.g., the processes of condensation and displacement), waking fantasy, and even 'play', all of which are connected with primary process thinking (Arieti, 1978; Martindale, & Dailey, 1996; Russ, 1998; Domino, Short, Evans, & Romano, 2002; Boag, 2006a, 2006b). This fluid type of thinking must be inhibited in order to be reality-focused, a view supported by studies examining attentional control mechanisms and psychotic processes (Stavridou, & Furnham, 1996; Langdon, & Coltheart, 2000; Karayanidis, Coltheart, Michie, & Murphy, 2003; McKay, Langdon, & Coltheart, 2005; Boag, 2006a, 2006b; Solms, 1997, 2000). Additionally, Eysenck's (1993) account of personality claims that creativity is related to higher scores on a personality dimension referred to as 'Psychoticism' (or 'P'), which is, at its extremes, said to include psychotic disorders, as well as anti-social and non-cooperative personality styles. These individuals are said to be less conventional in their thinking, and more 'conceptually expansive' than people scoring low on P, and hence more creative. Some research has supported Eysenck's claim here (Zanes et al., 1998; Kaufmann 2002; Abraham et al., 2005), and a robust body of research has indicated that creativity is further linked to reduced Latent Inhibition (LI) (Carson, Peterson and Higgins, 2003) which is the extent to which the brain is able to ignore stimuli outside of the current focus of attention. What this all suggests, then, is that a creative individual is one who to varying degrees can be more inclined towards fantasy and psychosis, and hence, creativity can come at a cost (i.e., the creative individual may be psychosis prone). On the other hand, the innovative person, who is capable of putting creative ideas into practice, may then well be the person

with the sufficient combination of motivational traits to allow fluid thinking, as well as reality-orientation, achievement-motivation and so on. Hence, this demonstrates that research investigating personality factors associated with the creative process must take into account many cognitive, motivational and behavioural factors.

Finding and retaining creative minds is difficult, as innovators often become entrepreneurs of their own companies. In managing an organization's knowledge resources it will be increasingly important for organizations to identify, recruit and nurture employees that have the potential to be innovators and entrepreneurs. The role of organizational psychologists in many modern western corporations is to manage recruitment techniques involving the use of psychometric instruments (such as the Kirton Adaption-Innovation (KAI) (Kirton 2003) Inventory, the Myers-Briggs Type Indicator (MBTI) Creativity index (Gough 1981) or O-C-E-A-N (Openness, Conscientiousness, Extraversion, Agreeableness, and Neuroticism) (Thurstone, 1934) along with techniques such as role-playing, skill tests and scenario analysis. While, these popular tests can be useful in creating a balanced team of different individuals and in helping individuals understand themselves better, their direct relevance to creativity is not clear and they are not instruments currently employed to measure creativity in recent psychological research.

Early management theories focused on traits that made for good managers, later research acknowledged workplace circumstances and training of staff play more pivotal roles in management success (Robbins et al. 2003). Similarly, instead of focusing on the characteristics of innovators, such as personality and decision styles, which may not really be indicators of successful implementation of innovative ideas, this project focuses on capturing their behaviour via their retelling of their innovation-relevant stories in the form of scenarios. Further 'ecological validity' is achieved through expert innovators from the same discipline, ranking and adding their responses to the scenarios of other experts; thus a bank of scenarios is developed, tested and available to ascertain whether the behaviour of a potential employee is similar to that of experts and whether training may be needed in some areas. From here on in we use the term innovator and entrepreneur concomitantly, although technically speaking one may consider the former to be predominant earlier in the design phase and the latter in the later commercialization stage.

Making the right decisions at critical points is essential for a venture to succeed. Research has shown that decisions are arrived at through the combined use of almost equal amounts of tacit and explicit knowledge (Giunipero, Dawley, & Anthony, 1999). Thus we propose an approach that captures knowledge-in-action via scenarios, which can be viewed as cases grounded in the real world, based on experience, which spans both codified (explicit) and practical (tacit) knowledge (Richards, & Busch, 2002). Managing the knowledge related to decision making is a concern of knowledge management researchers. Knowledge management can be defined as the "practice of selectively applying knowledge from previous experiences of decision-making to current and future decision making activities with the express purpose of improving the organization's effectiveness" (Murphy & Jennex, 2006, p. 616). Recognizing the importance of knowledge and the ways in which different individuals utilize that knowledge, in addition to considering personality factors, we are interested in what has been termed practical intelligence. Our approach draws on the work of psychology Prof. Sternberg in this area which considers if patterns of behaviour of creative/innovative individuals can be found. Through the use of scenarios related to innovation (new methods or products) and entrepreneurship (new business) we seek to elicit responses and characterize the behaviour of entrepreneurs versus others. Our approach is also interested in eliciting the motivation for that behaviour since motivation

plays an important role in successful ventures, however, in our data collection to-date we have not explicitly sought participants' motivation for their responses.

To provide a framework for scenario capture and analysis which draws together personality, behaviour and motivation we have adopted the Novelty-Generation-Model (NGM) developed by Schweizer (2004, 2006, 2007) since it recognizes that creativity and innovation are both multi-dimensional and phasic. The NGM is a bio-psycho-social approach which proposes that the first phase of creativity and innovation is novelty seeking, followed by creativity itself, which is broken into novelty-finding and novelty-production, which then may move into the innovative performance phase (see Figure 1).

Different motivational, cognitive and behavioural characteristics are relevant to each distinct phase, and the model recognizes that at an individual level there may be different sufficient factors for any given stage. The NGM recognizes that at a genetic level some people are, for instance, more inclined to look for new problems and able to come up with novel solutions. One body of research that supports this is from the affective neuroscience field (Davis, Panksepp, & Normansell, 2003; Reuter et al., 2005) that has identified a brain system related to the desire for curiosity and novelty. Schweizer's model is used as a framework for the innovation knowledge inventory by capturing scenarios that address each of the personality/cognitive traits and skills; individual behaviours, individual motivations and the behaviour of others as shown in Figure 1.

METHOD

Our methodology combines a number of techniques, one of them being the use of narrative (Polkinghorne, 1988). The approach involves innovators retelling their key "war-stories", identifying a number of possible responses to the

Figure 1. The novelty generation model (Schweizer, 2004).

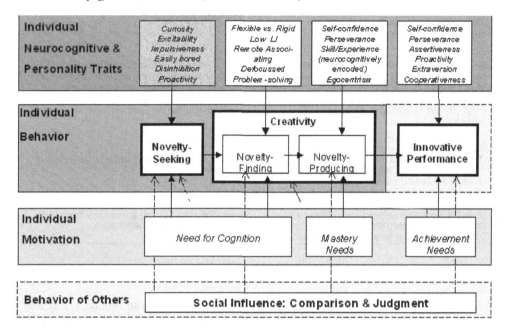

situation and providing a score for each response indicating the merit of such a response. In particular, the scenarios we are interested in concern ICT ventures. One such ICT innovator interviewed was Gordon Bell (Bell, 1991), a pioneer in the field of Computing, after whom Bell's Law was named (Wikipedia, n.d.). Figure 2 provides an example based on a case study in the literature, which was also used in the study by Busch and Richards (2006). The scenarios were developed from case studies in the literature and interviews with recognized ICT innovators. Using an approach adapted from Sternberg et al. (1995), we capture knowledge-in-action via the responses of our participants to the scenarios. We are also interested to capture the motivations behind this behaviour, but to date have not included that in the data we have collected.

This technique builds on the authors previous work (Busch, & Richards, 2005, 2004, 2003) which was developed after extensive review of the literature on the nature of tacit knowledge and research into its measurement and follows on

from the well-reported and accepted work led by Sternberg, in the field of psychology (Wagne, & Sternberg 1991). The scenarios to be elicited cover the phases of the innovation process, described above as part of the novelty-generation model. In future work we will also seek the innovators' motivations and the responses of others to their ideas and behaviours. The goal is to build up a set of innovation experiences for each individual to form a collective repository of patterns of experiences and behaviours. The benefits to the individual are greater self-awareness, potentially leading to learning and change. Again organisations could use the repository to determine whether the behaviour of a (potential) employee is similar to that of experts and whether training may be needed in particular areas. The approach and inventory also becomes a valuable means of exploring questions such as whether there are patterns of behaviour by innovators within and/ or across (sub)fields and the study will provide a rich source of data for discovering the knowledge that expert innovators make use of.

Figure 2. Scenario 2 from the tacit knowledge inventory and answer option 1 (developed from Bell and McNamara (1991) "Ovation: The case of the missing product" pp. 273-276)

Scenario 6

You've come up with innovative new software product. You get a lot of money to start making this product. You start working on developing the software. However it seems that development isn't going as quickly and smoothly as you would wish. Your technology and product development departments are understaffed compared to your marketing and sales departments and you find that while you are making great progress marketing and sales-wise, your product development leaves a lot to be desired. You begin to fear that the product may never actually be completed.

Do you:
a) Cease operations and return any remaining funds to the investors because the technology is inadequate to support the product. **(what Bell suggested)**
b) Reduce the company to a minimal marketing effort until a product can be built.
c) Do nothing and hope the problem resolves itself. **(what Bell suggested)**
d) Hire more technology and product development people.
e) Give the product up for dead and instead concentrate on marketing and sales and spend more money with the hope of generating indeterminate future revenues. **(what Bell actually did (ineffective))**
f) Grab the money and escape to the Bahamas.

The survey procedure we used to collect data is as follows:

1. All participants logged on to the online questionnaire via an information/consent page. To allow for each questionnaire to be linked to the one (unidentified) individual, the user selected their own userId, which was checked for uniqueness to ensure data is not corrupted, lost or merged. This allowed the individual to login again later to complete the questionnaire if they were unable to complete it in one session. If the participant wished to receive a personal report on their results, they could enter an email address to which the report can be sent.

2. Once they have consented, all participants entered various biographic data (Part A – Appendix 1) and their self-assessed credentials as an innovator (Part B – Appendix 2). This is somewhat similar to a Creative Behavior Inventory (Hunaskan, & Callahan, 1995) but focused on externally recognized innovation.

3. Next the participants received the 3 creativity measures (Remote Associates Test (RAT), Alternative Uses Test (AUT), and Visual Creativity Test (VCT)). These tests were seen to require some mental effort and thus we put them near the start before they became fatigued.

4. Participants then were randomly allocated to receive 4 scenarios from our innovation inventory (Part C).

5. Finally, Participants randomly received either the Eysenck Personality Questionnaire (EPQ) or the Affective Neuroscience Personality Scale (ANPS) first, before completing the other.

The time taken to complete the survey was 25-50 minutes. As an enticement to participate in our study we provided each participant with a report based on their results and included the results to the creativity and psychometric tests. Using the self-assessment section (Part B) we placed the participants into three groups: innovators, non-innovators and somewhat innovators. Through incorporating biographical information (Part A) we sought to determine differences in the answering of the scenarios on the basis of gender, or employment seniority, language other than English and so on across the three groups.

We have incorporated 'personality psychology' approaches (RAT, AUT, VCT) and creativity measures (ANPS and EPQ) to complement

Figure 3. Descriptive statistics for psychology and creativity measures by three groups

		N	Mean	Std. Deviation	Std. Error	95% Confidence Interval for Mean		Minimum	Maximum
						Lower Bound	Upper Bound		
SEEK	Innovator	7	29.0	3.1	1.2	26.1	31.9	26	35
	Non-Innovator	22	26.7	3.7	0.8	25.0	28.3	20	33
	Somewhat-Innovator	41	27.9	5.2	0.8	26.3	29.5	18	42
	Total	70	27.6	4.6	0.6	26.5	28.7	18	42
FEAR	Innovator	7	17.6	10.7	4.0	7.7	27.5	3	32
	Non-Innovator	22	23.8	3.8	0.8	22.1	25.5	16	31
	Somewhat-Innovator	41	23.0	4.6	0.7	21.5	24.5	13	35
	Total	70	22.7	5.5	0.7	21.4	24.0	3	35
CARE	Innovator	7	24.7	4.8	1.8	20.3	29.2	17	32
	Non-Innovator	22	25.9	4.8	1.0	23.8	28.0	19	36
	Somewhat-Innovator	41	25.0	5.1	0.8	23.3	26.6	14	38
	Total	70	25.2	4.9	0.6	24.0	26.4	14	38
ANGER	Innovator	7	18.1	8.4	3.2	10.4	25.9	8	32
	Non-Innovator	22	19.3	6.1	1.3	16.6	22.0	5	32
	Somewhat-Innovator	41	20.3	5.1	0.8	18.7	21.9	7	36
	Total	70	19.7	5.7	0.7	18.4	21.1	5	36
PLAY	Innovator	7	29.9	4.4	1.7	25.8	33.9	23	34
	Non-Innovator	22	24.6	4.3	0.9	22.7	26.5	17	34
	Somewhat-Innovator	41	26.0	5.7	0.9	24.2	27.9	16	42
	Total	70	26.0	5.3	0.6	24.7	27.2	16	42
SADNESS	Innovator	7	17.4	8.5	3.2	9.6	25.3	6	29
	Non-Innovator	22	23.5	6.1	1.3	20.8	26.3	13	38
	Somewhat-Innovator	41	21.2	4.8	0.7	19.7	22.7	7	34
	Total	70	21.6	5.8	0.7	20.2	23.0	6	38
SPIRITUALITY	Innovator	7	20.9	7.8	3.0	13.6	28.1	13	32
	Non-Innovator	22	22.4	4.6	1.0	20.3	24.4	17	35
	Somewhat-Innovator	41	19.5	4.6	0.7	18.1	21.0	7	27
	Total	70	20.6	5.1	0.6	19.3	21.8	7	35
Extroversion	Innovator	7	13.4	5.1	1.9	8.7	18.2	5	18
	Non-Innovator	19	11.8	4.4	1.0	9.7	14.0	5	18
	Somewhat-Innovator	40	13.0	4.6	0.7	11.6	14.5	4	21
	Total	66	12.7	4.6	0.6	11.6	13.9	4	21
Neuroticism	Innovator	7	7.6	6.9	2.6	1.2	14.0	0	20
	Non-Innovator	19	13.0	5.2	1.2	10.5	15.5	1	23
	Somewhat-Innovator	40	11.0	5.4	0.9	9.2	12.7	0	23
	Total	66	11.2	5.6	0.7	9.8	12.6	0	23
Psychoticism	Innovator	7	4.6	3.6	1.3	1.3	7.9	0	10
	Non-Innovator	19	6.2	4.0	0.9	4.2	8.1	0	14
	Somewhat-Innovator	40	7.2	4.1	0.7	5.9	8.5	1	17
	Total	66	6.6	4.1	0.5	5.6	7.6	0	17
Social Desirability	Innovator	7	7.4	4.5	1.7	3.3	11.6	3	14
	Non-Innovator	19	9.4	3.5	0.8	7.7	11.0	3	17
	Somewhat-Innovator	40	9.7	3.3	0.5	8.7	10.8	4	18
	Total	66	9.4	3.5	0.4	8.5	10.2	3	18

Schweizer's Novelty-Generation-Model (Steps 3 and 5). Following the NGM, through personality testing of innovators we aim to identify the individual's personality type, degree of novelty-seeking, creativity and innovative type behaviour. This further involves determining whether different combinations of traits (e.g., 'conscientiousness', 'agreeableness', etc.) map onto various phases of the creativity process (the innovation cycle). Participants in our study were 78 Master of IT (MIT) students (enrolled in the units "Biotechnology Innovation and Project Management" and "Information Systems Design and Management"): comprised of 27 females and 51 males, 36 aged 20-24, 22 aged 25-29, 9 aged 30-34, 4 aged 35-39, 4 aged 40-44, 2 aged 45-49 and 1 aged 50-54.

Identifying Innovators – Separating the Cohorts

Identifying potential entrepreneurs/innovators is the key goal of this work. We were interested to see how well the claims of individuals matched

Figure 4. (a) and (b) illustrating ANPS and EPQ for three groups of participants

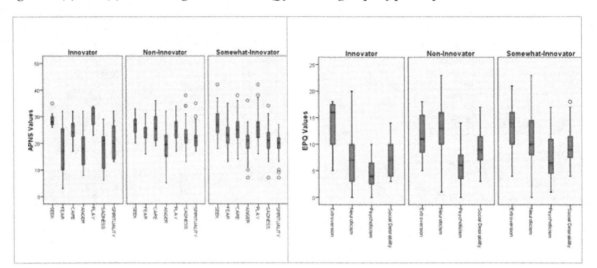

with the scores achieved in the psychometric testing. If self-analysis correlated well with the personality tests, then one or the other would suffice as an indicator. While Part B was not purely subjective but requested evidence of innovation, it is still difficult to validate the existence and importance of the evidence. Based on Part B we identified 3 cohorts: innovators (I), non-innovators (N) and a group that did not clearly belong to either cohort but were somewhat-innovators (S). We were interested particularly in the values for play, seek and psychoticism as they are indicated in the literature as relevant to creativity. Examining Figure 3 and Figures 4a and 4b we see that play and seek are slightly higher for the innovators, but psychoticism is lowest (unexpected) in our innovators. ANOVA for psychology measures show that the mean scores of neither seek (p=0.436) nor play (p=0.73) were statistically significantly different between the three groups. On the other hand, the mean scores of fear (p=0.25) and sadness (p=0.042) were statistically significantly different between the three groups. The boxplots in Figures 4a and 4b display the distribution of ANPS and EPQ values respectively for innovators, non-innovators and somewhat-innovators. These boxes show the first, second (median) and third

quartiles for the observed values while displaying 50% of the data in the box, 25% below and 25% above the box. The circles in the graphs are outlier values.

Figure 4a displays the ANPS values. In these boxplots we observe that innovators had only one outlier (fear values) while non-innovators had two outliers for sadness and spirituality, all being on the upper tails (higher values). In contrast, somewhat-innovators had various outliers both at the lower and upper tails. This is not surprising since somewhat-innovators are more likely to be a less compact group than the innovators and non-innovators. For EPQ values we only observe one outlier (somewhat-innovator, social desirability values).

The outlier for seek would be the cause of the slightly higher values for innovators. The median of seek is 28, 27 and 27 for innovators, non-innovators and somewhat-innovators respectively with the lowest variation for innovators and the highest variation for somewhat-innovators. The medians and variations of fear are very similar for non-innovators and somewhat-innovators where the medians are 24 and 23 while the variation is low (interquantile ranges (IQR) are 4 and 6 respectively) for these two groups. The median of fear for innovators is only 17 with high variation (IQR is 20). The medians of anger are very similar for all three groups, while the variation for innovators is the largest (IQR is 14 for innovators, and only 6 and 5 for non-innovators and somewhat-innovators, respectively). Similarly, the medians of sadness and spirituality are very similar and variation is the largest for innovators.

Even though the variations for play are very similar for the three groups, innovators have slightly higher variation than other two groups as well as having the higher median (31 compared to 25 and 26). The medians and variations were very similar between the three groups for care. The median and the variation of extroversion are slightly higher for innovators compared to the other two groups which had similar values both for median and interquantile ranges. In addition, while these two groups had similar symmetric distributions, the values of extroversion for innovators are skewed to the lower values.

Innovators had the lowest median for neuroticism (7) and the largest variation (IQR is 11 for innovators, and only 6 and 7 for non-innovators and somewhat-innovators, respectively). Similarly, innovators had the lowest median for social desirability (7) and the largest variation (IQR is 10 for innovators compared to 5 for other two groups). In addition, innovators had the lowest median for psychoticism (4), however the variations for all groups were similar (7, 5, & 7).

To describe the cohorts we had identified in this first phase, we applied a number of classification algorithms. We performed rule induction to predict class membership and to identify the most relevant variables for classification by using the Classification and Regression Trees (C&RT) (based on the gini index), C5.0 (based on information gain and entropy) and Neural Networks (feed-forward network) algorithms within SPSS Clementine (Figure 5). In our initial models we found that the outputs of C&RT and C5.0 algorithms provided almost the opposite results. We sought support from the literature in choos-

ing which algorithm might be most appropriate. While some algorithms suggested that *care* (which refers to degree of nurturance and love in your personality) was important in differentiating our participants, from the literature we were unable to find any support for care being related to innovation. On the other hand, *flexibility* seemed intuitively more important for lateral thinking and thus relevant to creativity/innovation. We were also concerned with the high scoring of "social desirability". A problem with questionnaire measures is a greater tendency for some to "lie" based on what they believe they should answer. In many cases these 'lies' are subconscious and based on the individual not having accurate knowledge of themselves. These self-reporting biases are recognised major limitations within the personality and clinical psychology and organisational psychology research. Eysenck's EPQ attempts to minimise this problem by including a 'social desirability' scale, where higher values (than the population norm) indicate that the respondent is prone to providing socially-desirable responses. The fact that social desirability was the third highest factor using the C&R Tree (and also in the first half for the neural network analyses) would indicate that the results are doubtful.

Since our supervised learning techniques were providing very mixed and contradictory results we decided that cluster analysis may help us better identify the cohorts to be found in the data. Using the hierarchical clustering with Ward's method we created a dendogram which suggested two clusters for this data set. Using an alternative cluster analysis method, K-Means, we obtained two clusters. Social desirability was not a distinguishing feature between the clusters and thus self-bias was less of a concern. Using K-means analysis we note that seek, fluency, originality, flexibility, AUT Total and psychoticism were significant factors. Using the clusters identified by hierarchical clustering to reclassify our set of innovators, we reran our classification algorithms (C&R Trees, C5.0 Trees and Neural Networks (NN)), with and without the

Figure 5. (a) illustrating C&RT tree; (b) C 5.0 tree and (c) neural network

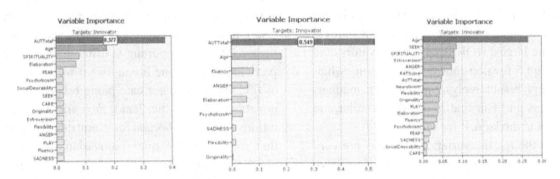

age variable. We note that for C&R Trees and the NN whenever age is included, spirituality is high in importance. We could not find any basis in the literature for age to be related to innovation, and thus believed it could be a factor specific to our sample. While experts will often be older than novices as experience plays a large part in becoming an expert, entrepreneurs seem to be less restricted by age or years of experience. When we removed spirituality and reran the hierarchical cluster analysis, we found that two clusters did not change, confirming further that spirituality was not integral to innovation. In addition, when we removed AUT Total as an input variable, the created clusters became more similar to observed where many of the people who have originally been identified as innovators (as identified by themselves) creating a cluster (which we labelled as the innovators) and others clustering in together in the second cluster; this indicates that their claims have some basis.

The key purpose of the psychometric tests was to assist us to identify who was an innovator and who was not. We sought to align the psychometric results with the classifications assigned based on Part B self assessment. We wanted to identify who was an innovator and who was not so that we could compare and contrast the responses of the two groups to the scenarios we had given them. We examined the results from our questionnaire and identified instances that innovators were differently disposed towards certain concepts than were non-innovators. Some 10 innovators and 19 novices (combined somewhats and non-innovators) answered in this case scenario 9 from our testbank (Figure 6).

As the reader may note, the scenario deals with issues of management in a computer technology firm. The decision of senior management to introduce committees to deal with internal issues is not without ramification. For the above scenario, the following possible responses were suggested.

1. Appoint a committee to find out what's wrong with the company and what can be done to fix it.

2. Do nothing in the hope that everything will work itself out.

3. Decide that the company has become too bureaucratic and centralised and announce a complex reorganisation of the company to decentralize it again. Eradicate the entire committee system and reduce staff where you can.

4. First look at the core design team to ensure it has the right set of resources including leaders, architects and designers. Decouple all the committee from the design team. Address the committee functions after you have a viable project.

5. Quit while you're ahead.

Figure 6. Illustrating a typical scenario from our innovation testbank

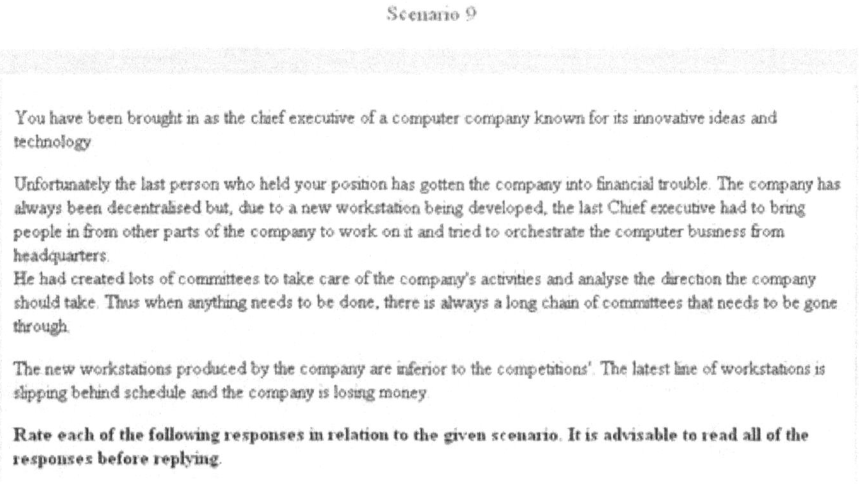

Scenario 9

You have been brought in as the chief executive of a computer company known for its innovative ideas and technology.

Unfortunately the last person who held your position has gotten the company into financial trouble. The company has always been decentralised but, due to a new workstation being developed, the last Chief executive had to bring people in from other parts of the company to work on it and tried to orchestrate the computer business from headquarters.

He had created lots of committees to take care of the company's activities and analyse the direction the company should take. Thus when anything needs to be done, there is always a long chain of committees that needs to be gone through.

The new workstations produced by the company are inferior to the competitions'. The latest line of workstations is slipping behind schedule and the company is losing money.

Rate each of the following responses in relation to the given scenario. It is advisable to read all of the responses before replying.

6. Attempt to merge with a more successful company.

Each of the above questions required an ethical and realistic Likert scale answer value (Figure 7); being those of Extremely Bad, Very Bad, Bad, Neither Good nor Bad, Good, Very Good or Extremely Good.

The first statement is clearly one that relates to deferment of a problem to another group, in this case a committee. The second statement takes a laissez faire approach. The third statement questions the wisdom of committees and indeed the number of staff already extant within the computing firm. The fourth statement separates management issues more so from technical ones; management opinions should then be considered after technical ones have been clarified. The fifth statement relates to giving up altogether. Finally the sixth statement considers a merger with a competitor. Descriptive statistics for each answer option for innovators (count of 10), somewhat innovators (13) and non-innovators (6) are provided in Figures 8-10.

The means for the innovator and novice cohorts can be seen in the following Figure 11. The means represent the values shown on the y axis.

1.0 refers to Extremely Bad, 2.0 Very Bad, 3.0 Bad, 4.0 Neither Good nor Bad, 5.0 Good, 6.0 Very Good and finally 7.0 Extremely Good.

What is immediately apparent is the difference in the response mean for answer 1 (ethical and realistic) and to a lesser extent answer 6. In both cases, but particularly the first answer, issues arise of externality, either externalising the problem thus making it apparent to a committee (answer 1), or merging with another company (answer 6). In both such instances involving externality as a factor, the innovators appear more negatively inclined (mean: ethical response 3.4 and realistic response 2.3 out of 7). Previous research (Busch, 2008) had shown that experts, along the lines of innovators in this instance, were also hesitant to draw in outside personnel when facing many situations, preferring instead to solve issues within the organisation and more specifically the group. In both cases, the novices appear happier to accept outside influences more positively, which is evidenced by their higher means (mean: ethical response 5.1 and realistic response 4.3 out of 7).

What is also interesting is the attitudinal difference between innovators and novices to question 2, doing nothing. The ethical and realistic answers

Figure 7. Illustrating a Likert scale as used in the innovation testbank

Figure 8. Descriptive statistics for innovator respondents

Innovators	1		2		3		4		5		6	
	Ethical	Realistic	Ethical	Realistic	Ethical	Realistic	Ethical	Realistic	Ethical	Realistic	Ethical	Realistic
Mean	3.4	2.3	1.9	1.4	3.7	4.4	5.0	4.8	2.4	3.2	3.6	3.8
Standard Error	0.7	0.7	0.4	0.3	0.5	0.6	0.3	0.5	0.4	0.6	0.3	0.6
Median	3.0	1.0	1.5	1.0	3.5	4.5	5.0	5.0	2.5	3.0	4.0	3.5
Mode	3.0	1.0	1.0	1.0	2.0	6.0	5.0	5.0	1.0	4.0	4.0	3.0
Standard Deviation	2.1	2.3	1.2	1.0	1.7	2.0	0.8	1.7	1.3	1.9	1.1	1.8
Sample Variance	4.5	5.1	1.4	0.9	2.9	3.8	0.7	2.8	1.8	3.5	1.2	3.1
Kurtosis	-0.9	1.4	0.1	7.2	0.1	-0.8	-1.4	-0.2	-2.0	0.5	-0.9	-0.1
Skewness	0.4	1.7	1.2	2.7	0.9	-0.5	0.0	-0.8	0.1	0.8	-0.3	0.2
Range	6.0	6.0	3.0	3.0	5.0	6.0	2.0	5.0	3.0	6.0	3.0	6.0
Minimum	1.0	1.0	1.0	1.0	2.0	1.0	4.0	2.0	1.0	1.0	2.0	1.0
Maximum	7.0	7.0	4.0	4.0	7.0	7.0	6.0	7.0	4.0	7.0	5.0	7.0
Count	10.0	10.0	10.0	10.0	10.0	10.0	10.0	10.0	10.0	10.0	10.0	10.0
Largest(1)	7.0	7.0	4.0	4.0	7.0	7.0	6.0	7.0	4.0	7.0	5.0	7.0
Smallest(1)	1.0	1.0	1.0	1.0	2.0	1.0	4.0	2.0	1.0	1.0	2.0	1.0
Confidence Level(95.0%)	1.5	1.6	0.9	0.7	1.2	1.4	0.6	1.2	1.0	1.3	0.8	1.3

Figure 9. Descriptive statistics for somewhat innovative respondents

Somewhat innovators	1		2		3		4		5		6	
	Ethical	Realistic	Ethical	Realistic	Ethical	Realistic	Ethical	Realistic	Ethical	Realistic	Ethical	Realistic
Mean	5.1	4.0	1.4	2.1	4.2	4.5	5.1	5.3	2.5	2.6	4.2	4.5
Standard Error	0.4	0.5	0.1	0.4	0.5	0.5	0.5	0.3	0.6	0.6	0.4	0.4
Median	6.0	4.0	1.0	2.0	4.0	5.0	6.0	5.0	2.0	2.0	4.0	5.0
Mode	6.0	6.0	1.0	1.0	6.0	5.0	6.0	5.0	1.0	1.0	3.0	5.0
Standard Deviation	1.5	1.6	0.5	1.4	1.8	1.9	1.7	1.0	2.0	2.1	1.5	1.5
Sample Variance	2.4	2.7	0.3	1.9	3.2	3.8	2.7	1.1	3.9	4.4	2.2	2.1
Kurtosis	3.2	-0.7	-2.1	5.3	-1.5	-0.9	-1.0	-0.8	0.6	0.1	-0.7	-0.8
Skewness	-1.6	-0.1	0.5	2.1	0.1	-0.5	-0.7	0.3	1.2	1.2	0.4	-0.8
Range	6.0	5.0	1.0	5.0	5.0	6.0	5.0	3.0	6.0	6.0	5.0	4.0
Minimum	1.0	1.0	1.0	1.0	2.0	1.0	2.0	4.0	1.0	1.0	2.0	2.0
Maximum	7.0	6.0	2.0	6.0	7.0	7.0	7.0	7.0	7.0	7.0	7.0	6.0
Count	13.0	13.0	13.0	13.0	13.0	13.0	13.0	13.0	13.0	13.0	13.0	13.0
Largest(1)	7.0	6.0	2.0	6.0	7.0	7.0	7.0	7.0	7.0	7.0	7.0	6.0
Smallest(1)	1.0	1.0	1.0	1.0	2.0	1.0	2.0	4.0	1.0	1.0	2.0	2.0
Confidence Level(95.0%)	0.9	1.0	0.3	0.8	1.1	1.2	1.0	0.6	1.2	1.3	0.9	0.9

contrast somewhat between both groups. The innovators are marginally more positive about such an option ethically (1.9), as opposed to the novice ethical mean of 1.3, remembering that 1 represents Extremely Bad and 2 Very Bad. Alternatively when it came to doing nothing in practice, that is what one would do in reality, the innovators were more negative (mean 1.4), whilst the novices were marginally more positive (mean 1.9).

Question 3 concerned issues of decentralisation, simplification and downsizing. Both cohorts were again (like question 2) close in their means

Figure 10. Descriptive statistics for non-innovator respondents

Non-Innovators	1		2		3		4		5		6	
	Ethical	Realistic	Ethical	Realistic	Ethical	Realistic	Ethical	Realistic	Ethical	Realistic	Ethical	Realistic
Mean	5.2	5.0	1.2	1.5	3.8	3.0	5.5	5.7	2.7	2.8	4.3	4.2
Standard Error	0.9	0.8	0.2	0.5	0.7	0.5	0.7	0.7	0.5	0.5	1.0	0.9
Median	6.0	5.0	1.0	1.0	4.5	3.5	6.0	6.5	2.5	3.0	4.0	4.0
Mode	6.0	4.0	1.0	1.0	5.0	4.0	6.0	7.0	2.0	3.0	2.0	2.0
Standard Deviation	2.1	2.0	0.4	1.2	1.6	1.3	1.6	1.8	1.2	1.2	2.3	2.1
Sample Variance	4.6	4.0	0.2	1.5	2.6	1.6	2.7	3.1	1.5	1.4	5.5	4.6
Kurtosis	-1.3	-1.2	6.0	6.0	1.2	-0.8	-1.0	-1.2	-1.5	-0.4	-2.4	-2.1
Skewness	-0.9	-0.5	2.4	2.4	-1.4	-0.9	-0.8	-0.9	-0.1	-0.7	0.2	0.2
Range	5.0	5.0	1.0	3.0	4.0	3.0	4.0	4.0	3.0	3.0	5.0	5.0
Minimum	2.0	2.0	1.0	1.0	1.0	1.0	3.0	3.0	1.0	1.0	2.0	2.0
Maximum	7.0	7.0	2.0	4.0	5.0	4.0	7.0	7.0	4.0	4.0	7.0	7.0
Count	6.0	6.0	6.0	6.0	6.0	6.0	6.0	6.0	6.0	6.0	6.0	6.0
Largest(1)	7.0	7.0	2.0	4.0	5.0	4.0	7.0	7.0	4.0	4.0	7.0	7.0
Smallest(1)	2.0	2.0	1.0	1.0	1.0	1.0	3.0	3.0	1.0	1.0	2.0	2.0
Confidence Level(95.0%)	2.2	2.1	0.4	1.3	1.7	1.3	1.7	1.8	1.3	1.2	2.5	2.2

Figure 11. Illustrating means for innovators and novices in their responses to questions 1-6 in Scenario 9.

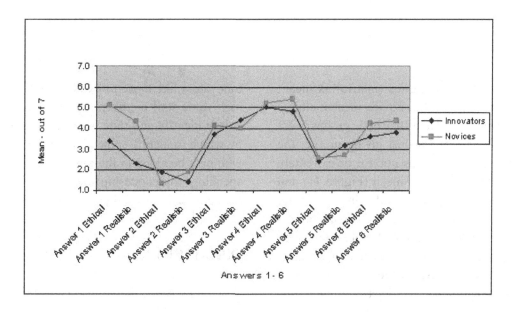

ethically and realistically, but alternated once more in their responses. Novices were noticeably more neutral ethically and realistically (mean: 4.1 ethical, 4.0 realistic), where a mean of 4.0 meant complete neutrality (Neither Good nor Bad) with regard to issues of organisational decentralisation, simplification and downsizing. Innovators on the other hand were ethically slightly opposed to ideas proposed in question 3 (mean 3.7), but somewhat more neutral to positive on these issues in practice (mean 4.4).

Remember question 4 dealt with overcoming technical issues before addressing managerial ones. This question was received noticeably more positively by both innovators (mean: ethical 5.0, realistic 4.8) and more so novices (mean: ethical 5.2, realistic 5.4). The slightly more positive reception by the novice cohort is interesting, particularly in practice (realistic); whether there is an element of naivety at play here is conjectural.

Finally question 5 dealing with giving up altogether was generally regarded as a very bad

Figure 12. Illustrating medians for innovators and novices in their responses to questions 1-6 in Scenario 9.

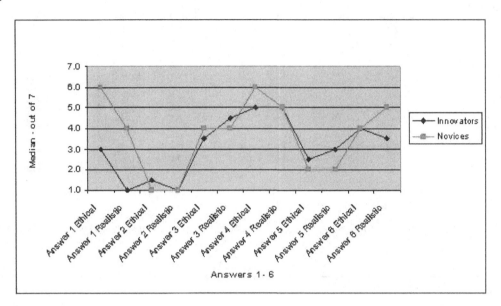

to bad idea by both parties (innovators mean: ethical 2.4, realistic 3.2; novice means: ethical 2.6, realistic 2.7). Note that both groups were not overwhelmingly against giving up, i.e. the mean for the groups was not 1.0 or extremely bad idea. Examining the mean (Figure 11) and median (Figure 12), we note that innovators are more likely to differentiate their behaviour on ethical and realistic grounds. Novices, however, for answer options 2, 3 and 5 did not differentiate at all (Figure 12). Experience may have taught innovators that theory and practice are very different things.

We are able to evaluate all of our scenario answer options along the lines above. What this process allows us to do is determine the closeness of fit between novices and innovators so that an organization might determine which of their novices show innovation potential. A similar approach was adopted by Busch (2008) to determine which novice staff in a number of IT firms showed managerial potential by the closeness of their tacit knowledge questionnaire responses to those of identified experts in the organizations.

Innovators like those of experts are particularly high value staff members to a firm, often difficult to identify and time poor. If a means exists by which to identify potentially innovative staff who may be aided in the innovation process by spending 'apprenticeship time' with an innovator, then our approach will prove useful.

DISCUSSION

When considering entrepreneurship, this research seeks to combine practice (via a knowledge management perspective of innovation as the implementation of a new product or process) with theory (via a psychology-based perspective of creativity) involving factors such as motivation, behaviours and personality types. Our approach aims to capture the way that entrepreneurs think and behave. For example, we are interested in how entrepreneurs: handle risk; incubate, test and persevere with an idea; or recognize when to change tack. Building on our previous work on tacit knowledge measurement, the proposed approach will capture the experiences of recognized innovators by eliciting and validating an inventory of scenarios related to their innovations and set of possible responses and ratings of the goodness or badness of such a response.

A result of Schweizer's Novelty-Generation-Model in combination with the conduct of personality studies, is that we recognize the mixed findings in the literature may simply reflect the fact there may be several factors, all of which are sufficient for creativity, but are not necessary. That is, there is no reason to expect a single cause of creativity, and so the mixed findings may simply indicate such multiple causes. If we view novelty-seeking, creativity and innovative performance as three distinct behaviours, an organization interested in employing "innovative" employees is really seeking to either create a team which comprises of members that exhibit one or more of these behaviours and is able to work with others to provide the behaviours they lack. Or the organization needs to employ people who are a "combination of moderately high novelty-seeking with efficient, organized and persevering behaviour [who] can be expected to be the ideal combination for the production of novelty" (p. 49). For instance, although high psychoticism individuals may be creative (Eysenck, 1993), insofar as they can generate new ideas, they may not actually be innovative individuals (i.e. be incapable of implementing the idea). As Schweizer (2004) notes, "to create something requires a combination of many traits, including the discipline and perseverance to transform new ideas into a product" (p. 47). Thus, innovation would not be expected to be associated with a uni-dimensional personality style, but rather involve a complex of cognitive and motivational dimensions. These views are based on recognition that problem situations are typically complex and there may be a variety of ways of effectively managing a problem; hence there may be a variety of novel ideas that could be generated in response to a situation, as well as a variety of means of realizing those responses.

Rather than assuming, there is a single 'creative and innovative' personality type, we recognize that there may be multiple styles which expert innovators present and this provides a more sophisticated approach than present conceptualizations. Accordingly, our research examined individual responses to determine whether multiple patterns of innovation emerge.

FUTURE RESEARCH DIRECTIONS

To add a biological dimension to the approach, in the future, we propose to conduct neuroimaging studies of creative thinking. Presently, established creativity tests are being designed and tested for functional magnetic resonance imaging (fMRI), including the Remote Associates Test (RAT), which assesses convergent thinking (Schweizer, Deijen, Heslenfeld et al., 2006), and the Alternative Uses Test (AUT), which assesses divergent thinking (Kalis et al. 2008). fMRI scanning is a non-intrusive neuroimaging method that is widely approved by ethics committees since it does not involve radiation and has no other effects on the participant's health. Previous fMRI research suggests that individuals readily participate in such research, especially since they receive an MRIcro version of their brain scan to take home on a CD, which can be viewed on their home computer. After the initial identifying phase, we plan to invite a selection of 20 of the participants, which would exclude the small number of individuals who chose not provide a contact email address, to participate in this last phase of the research (the 10 highest versus the 10 lowest creativity and innovation scorers). These individuals will undertake the neuroimaging creativity tests in the fMRI scanner.

The aim of this last part of the research project is the identification of differences in neural activation between the above-mentioned groups. In contrast to earlier neuroimaging projects on creative cognition, this approach is novel in that the sampling is based on the scores in the battery of creativity tests. Up to now, the approach has been a completely different one: offering the neuroimaging versions to random samples next to a control condition. We believe that our two-stage approach of testing creative performance behaviourally first and designing neuroimaging samples on the basis of the behavioural outcomes is a very fruitful one in learning more about how the brain of exceptionally creative individuals works.

The focus on behaviour and neural activation in addition to personality traits is novel and brings a new dimension to past research on creativity. These views are based on recognition that problem situations are typically complex and there may be a variety of ways of effectively managing a problem; hence there may be a variety of novel ideas that could be generated in response to a situation, as well as a variety of means of realizing those responses.

To allow the approach to be used in other domains and be more specifically valid for a particular organization we propose that an inventory of scenarios be created within the organization seeking to use the technique. Innovators can be identified within the organization using criteria such as the number of patents they have produced, years involved in innovation, number of innovation awards received, whether they have had a startup company, and so on. Scenarios would be acquired via interview as many of the innovators we have had contact with expressed a preference for face-to-face contact. Such an approach fits with the view that tacit knowledge is socially embedded (Keane and Allison 1999) and often best transmitted through face-to-face interaction and repeated contact (Audretsch 1998). The scenarios to be elicited will be structured to fit with and build on the existing body of creativity and innovation literature spanning the psychology, organizational and knowledge management.

CONCLUSION

A study has been conducted using established personality measures to identify 'natural innovators', as measured by 'objective' creativity outcomes. The personality measures were also compared with the scenario outcomes to see whether the personality measures contributed any predictive validity here. This, in itself, is something novel. The general aim is to identify which measures (or subsets thereof) are most appropriate at the various phases of innovation and be the basis of providing tools for industry in terms of predicting potential innovative candidates.

The combined approach concerns the identification of patterns of personality characteristics, behaviour, motivation and corresponding neural activity which emerge, how they fit into the various phases of the innovation process, and how these responses correspond to our current understanding of innovation including the various psychological and knowledge models, instruments and approaches which exist.

The importance of innovation has become increasingly recognized since the 1980s with governments aligning innovation to national core goals. This is true in Australia as reflected in the recent government commissioned Cutler Report "Venturous Australia" (Cutler, 2008) which outlines the role and challenges of innovation in Australia:

It is vital that Australia is well endowed with innovative firms and workplaces. The key to this is deftly enhancing the opportunities and environment for business enterprises to innovate. To do this we must be alert to the hidden realities of business innovation and the changing face of innovation that is no longer the province of the lone inventor or adept technologist. Innovation in the first decades of the 21st century is more open and pervasive, characterized by skill in collaborating and making connections so that knowledge flows and grows, and so becomes available to meet customer and community needs. In such a world innovation policy is a central aspect of economic policy. This requires a significant recasting of Australia's innovation policy to give priority to strengthening innovation at the point where business enterprises and workplaces engage with their markets and customers. Reflected in recommendations for new business innovation and collaboration programs designed for productivity benefits, the end goal is nothing less than innovation-led prosperity for Australia.

The report goes on to identify the critical role of the entrepreneur:

The entrepreneur is the key organizer and agent within the innovation system. The entrepreneur does not, however, operate within a vacuum and it is the context within which the entrepreneur acts which forces us to think about an innovation system. The entrepreneur depends on the backdrop of an education and research system that accumulates and generates both knowledge and ideas and produces talented and creative people. These are crucial prerequisites for an innovative culture. Entrepreneurs also rely on a community of users who are equipped and motivated to think about adopting new product or service offerings (p.17).

Furthermore the report emphasizes that "A truly creative and innovative society requires a broad range of inputs spanning all areas including science, technology and engineering, as well the creative arts (p. 47)" and acknowledges the critical role that the Internet plays in encouraging collaboration leading to innovation.

The approach offered in this paper and the larger project aim to contribute to these goals specifically within the area of ICT ventures by providing a means of identifying creative individuals who also have potential to be innovators and entrepreneurs by bringing together and cross-validating a range of identification techniques including psychometric testing, behavioural responses to ICT innovation scenarios and biographical data

such as their innovations' credentials (patents, awards, start-ups, etc). Our study identifies that there are some individuals who may not even consider themselves to be (potential) innovators but who possess similar characteristics to those with innovation track records. To move ahead in the knowledge economy, innovation needs to become much more widespread and commonplace, challenging many of the existing views of innovation and creativity.

Talk about innovation can be very abstract, but tends to become quite specific and stereotypic when talking about the innovator and entrepreneur — the mad inventor in a lab coat, or the white-shoed commercial hustler. Likewise, there is a tendency to imply that a special 'creative class' of people exists to whom the general population should pay due deference (Cutler, 2008 p. 47).

The tests we administered and reports produced are almost fully automated. They bypass the need for expensive testing and professional intervention, thus, making assessment widely accessible. The approach offers the opportunity for individuals, students, employers or even the wider community, to consider innovation scenarios, consider their own innovation profile and also their levels of creativity. Organizations and educators could use these tools to identify, recruit and nurture budding entrepreneurs. Individuals can use such tools to understand their own potential and increase their awareness of the role that innovation plays within society.

REFERENCES

Abraham, A., Windmann, S., Daum, I., & Güntürkün, O. (2005). Conceptual expansion and creative imagery as a function of psychoticism. *Consciousness and Cognition, 14*, 520–534.

Amabile, T. M. (1983). *The Social Psychology of Creativity*. Berlin: Springer.

Amabile, T. M. (1996). *Creativity in Context*. Boulder, CO: Westview Press.

Amit, R., & Zott, C. (2001). Value Creation in E-Business. *Strategic Management Journal, 22*, 493–520. doi:10.1002/smj.187

Arieti, S. (1978). From primary process to creativity. *The Journal of Creative Behavior, 12*, 225–246.

Audretsch, D. (1998). Agglomeration and the location of innovative activity. *Oxford Review of Economic Activity, 14*(2), 18–29. doi:10.1093/oxrep/14.2.18

Baumol, W. J. (1993). *Entrepreneurship, Management and the Structure of Payoffs*. Cambridge Massachusetts, MIT.

Bell, G., & McNamara, J. F. (1991). *McHigh-Tech ventures: the guide for entrepreneurial success*. New York: Perseus Books.

Boag, S. (2006a). Freudian dream theory, dream bizarreness, and the disguise-censor controversy. *Neuro-psychoanalysis, 8*(1), 5–17.

Boag, S. (2006b). Freudian dream theory, dream bizarreness, & the disguise-censor controversy: Response to Commentaries. *Neuro-psychoanalysis, 8*(1), 60–69.

Brown, S., & Eisenhardt, K. (1998). *Competing on the Edge*. Boston, MA: Harvard Business School Press.

Busch, P. (2008). *Tacit Knowledge in Organizational Learning*. Hershey, PA: IGI.

Busch, P., & Richards, D. (2003). Building and Utilising an IT Tacit Knowledge Inventory. In *Proceedings 14th Australasian Conference on Information Systems (ACIS2003)*, November 26-28, Perth, Australia.

Busch, P., & Richards, D. (2004). Acquisition of articulable tacit knowledge. In *Proceedings of the Pacific Knowledge Acquisition Workshop (PKAW'04), in conjunction with The 8th Pac.Rim Int.l Conf. on AI*, August 9-13, 2004, Auckland, NZ (pp. 87-101).

Busch, P., & Richards, D. (2005). An Approach to Understand, Capture and Nurture Creativity and Innovation Knowledge. In *Proc. 15th Australasian Conference on Information Systems (ACIS2005)*, November 30-Dec 2nd, Sydney, Australia.

Busch, P., & Richards, D. (2006). Innovation Knowledge Acquisition: The Tacit Knowledge of Novices. In Z. Shi, K. Shimohara & D. Feng (Eds.), *Intelligent Information Processing* (IIP'2006), 20-22nd September 2006, Adelaide (pp. 259-268).

Carson, S. H., Peterson, J. B., & Higgins, D. M. (2003a). Decreased Latent Inhibition is associated with increased creative achievement in high-functioning individuals. *Journal of Personality and Social Psychology, 85*(3), 499–506. doi:10.1037/0022-3514.85.3.499

Cutler, T. (2008). *Venturous Australia: Building Strength in Innovation. Report on the Review of the National Innovation System*. Retrieved May 5, 2009, from http://www.industry.gov.au/innovationreview/Documents/NIS_review_Web3.pdf

Davis, K. L., Panksepp, J., & Normansell, L. (2003). The Affective Neuroscience Personality Scales: Normative data and implications. *Neuropsychoanalysis, 5*, 57–69.

Domino, G., Short, J., Evans, A., & Romano, P. (2002). Creativity and ego defense mechanisms: Some exploratory empirical evidence. *Creativity Research Journal, 14*, 17–25. doi:10.1207/S15326934CRJ1401_2

Eysenck, H. J. (1993). Creativity and personality: Suggestions for a theory. *Psychological Inquiry, 4*, 147–178. doi:10.1207/s15327965pli0403_1

Giunipero, L., Dawley, D., & Anthony, W. (1999). The impact of tacit knowledge on purchasing decisions. *Journal of Supply Chain Management.*

Hitt, M. A., Ireland, R. D., Camp, M., & Sexton, D. L. (2001). Guest Editors' Introduction To The Special Issue Strategic Entrepreneurship: Entrepreneurial Strategies For Wealth Creation. *Strategic Management Journal*, *22*, 479–491. doi:10.1002/smj.196

Hunaskar, S., & Callahan, C. (1995). Creativity and Giftedness: Published Instrument Uses and Abuses. *Gifted Child Quarterly*, *39*(2), 110–114. doi:10.1177/001698629503900207

Kalis, A., Mojzisch, A., Schweizer, T. S., & Kaiser, S. (2008). Weakness of will, akrasia, and the neuropsychiatry of decision making: An interdisciplinary perspective. *Cognitive, Affective & Behavioral Neuroscience*, *8*, 402–417. doi:10.3758/CABN.8.4.402

Karayanidis, F., Coltheart, M., Michie, P. T., & Murphy, K. (2003). Electrophysiological correlates of anticipatory and poststimulus components of task switching. *Psychophysiology*, *40*, 329–348. doi:10.1111/1469-8986.00037

Kaufmann, G. (2002). Creativity and Problem Solving. In J. Henry (Ed.), *Creative Management* (pp. 44-63). London: Cromwell Press Ltd.

Kirton, M. J. (2003). *Adaption-innovation: in the context of diversity and change.* London: Routledge.

Langdon, R., & Coltheart, M. (2000). The cognitive neuropsychology of delusions. *Mind & Language*, *15*, 184–218. doi:10.1111/1468-0017.00129

Martindale, C., & Dailey, A. (1996). Creativity, primary process cognition and personality . *Personality and Individual Differences*, *20*, 409–414. doi:10.1016/0191-8869(95)00202-2

McKay, R., Langdon, R., & Coltheart, M. (2005). Sleights of mind: Delusions, defences, and self-deception. *Cognitive Neuropsychiatry*, *10*, 305–326. doi:10.1080/13546800444000074

Murphy, T., & Jennex, M. (2006). Knowledge Management Systems Developed For Hurricane Katrina Response. In B. Van de Walle and M. Turoff, (Eds.), *Proceedings of the 3rd International ISCRAM Conference*, Newark, NJ, May 2006 (pp. 617-624).

Polkinghorne, D. (1988). *Narrative Knowing and the Human Sciences*. New York: SUNY Press.

Porter, M. (1985). *Competitive Advantage: Creating and Sustaining Superior Performance*. New York: Free Press.

Reuter, M., Panksepp, J., Schnabel, N., Kellerhoff, N., Kempel, P., & Hennig, J. (2005). Personality and biological markers of creativity. *European Journal of Personality*, *19*, 83–95. doi:10.1002/per.534

Richards, D., & Busch, P. (2002). Knowledge in Action: Blurring the Distinction Between Explicit and Tacit Knowledge. *Journal of Decision Systems*, *11*(2), 149–164. doi:10.3166/jds.11.149-164

Richards, D., & Busch, P. (2008). Finding and Growing Innovators: Keeping ahead of the Competition. In F. Zhao (Ed.), *Handbook of Research on Information Technology Entrepreneurship and Innovation* (pp. 396-414). Hershey, PA: Idea Group Inc.

Robbins, S., Bergman, R., Stagg, I., & Coulter, M. (2003). *Management* (3rd. Ed). Upper Saddle River, NJ: Prentice Hall.

Runco, M. A. (2004). Creativity. *Annual Review of Psychology*, *55*, 657–687. doi:10.1146/annurev.psych.55.090902.141502

Russ, S. W. (1998). The impact of repression on creativity. *Psychological Inquiry, 9,* 221–223. doi:10.1207/s15327965pli0903_7

Schweizer, T.S. (2004). An Individual Psychology of Novelty-Seeking, Creativity and Innovation. *ERIM Ph.D. Series,* 48.

Schweizer, T. S. (2006). The Psychology of Novelty Seeking, Creativity and Innovation: Neurocognitive Aspects in a Work-Psychological Perspective. *Creativity and Innovation Management, 15*(2), 164–172. doi:10.1111/j.1467-8691.2006.00383.x

Schweizer, T. S. (2007). Neuropsychological Support to the Novelty Generation Process. In: C. Martindale & L. Dorfman (Eds.), *Innovation and Aesthetics.* Cambridge, UK: Cambridge Scholars Press.

Schweizer, T. S., Deijen, J. B., Heslenfeld, D., Nieuwenhuis, S., & Talsma, D. (2006). *Functional magnetic resonance imaging of brain activity during rigid versus creative thought processes in obsessive-compulsive patients.* Poster presented at the Cognitive Neuroscience Society Conference, San Francisco, USA.

Solms, M. (1997). *The neuropsychology of dreams: A clinico-anatomical study.* Mahwah, NJ: Lawrence Erlbaum Associates.

Solms, M. (2000). Dreaming and REM sleep are controlled by different brain mechanisms. *The Behavioral and Brain Sciences, 23,* 843–850. doi:10.1017/S0140525X00003988

Stavridou, A., & Furnham, A. (1996). The relationshiop between psychoticism, trait-creativity and the attentional mechanism of cognitive inhibition. *Personality and Individual Differences, 21,* 1243–153. doi:10.1016/0191-8869(96)00030-X

Sternberg, R., Wagner, R., Williams, W., & Horvath, J. (1995). Testing common sense. *The American Psychologist, 50*(11), 912–927. doi:10.1037/0003-066X.50.11.912

Thurstone, L. L. (1934). The vectors of the mind. *Psychological Review, 41,* 1–32. doi:10.1037/h0075959

Wagner, R., & Sternberg, R. (1991). *TKIM: The common sense manager: Tacit knowledge inventory for managers: Test Booklet.* San Antonio, TX: Harcourt Brace Jovanovich.

Wikipedia. (n.d.). *Bell's Law of Computer Classes.* Retrieved June 30, 2009, from http://en.wikipedia.org/wiki/Bell%27s_Law_of_Computer_Classes

Zampetakis, L. A., & Moustakis, V. (2006). Linking creativity with entrepreneurial intentions: A structural approach. *The International Entrepreneurship and Management Journal, 2*(3), 413–428. doi:10.1007/s11365-006-0006-z

Zanes, J., Ross, S., Hatfield, R., Houtler, B., & Whitman, D. (1998). The relationship between creativity and psychosis-proneness. *Personality and Individual Differences, 24,* 879–881. doi:10.1016/S0191-8869(97)00199-2

Chapter 10
Education and Training for the Entrepreneurial Employee:
Value of ICT-Enabled Learning

Cecilia Hegarty
University of Ulster, Northern Ireland

ABSTRACT

Over the last two decades, computer technology has become an integral part of any business strategy and operation, including non-ICT ventures. In fact technological innovations have very much driven business growth where the capability of companies to embrace, maintain or lead in developing new technologies has shaped contemporary practice. In preparation for entering this dynamic workplace environment, it is necessary to consider how best to educate the entrepreneurial employee and how to expose students and trainees to these newer technologies. A delivery approach that allows for a combination of information communication technologies (ICT) to be used in education and training is termed ICT-enabled learning. Since the modern learner is inclined to engage with a wide range of ICT-enabled technologies, techno-familiarity can create a comfortable learning zone. As a result, ICT-enabled learning can be provided in universities and within modern day firms. This chapter explores entrepreneurship education through the lens of ICT-enabled learning within university education. In the case study presented, learners extol the benefits of ICT-enabled learning on their entrepreneurship module. There are a number of implications for employers and educationalists. In this chapter, the value of entrepreneurship education via ICT-enabled learning is discussed. For the entrepreneurial firm, recommendations are made about providing training in entrepreneurship for employees.

INTRODUCTION

The subject of entrepreneurship education has received much attention over the last three de-cades. Educational establishments have sought to incorporate entrepreneurship within diverse and often non-business curricula. In doing so a variety of methods have been used but there has been a particular reliance on information communication technologies. There is some conflicting evidence

DOI: 10.4018/978-1-61520-597-4.ch010

about the extent to which all students of further education will be exposed to entrepreneurship and enterprise education (Hannon, 2007; Smith, 2008). Yet, from the 1990s onwards demand for entrepreneurship education has been steadily increasing (Hegarty, & Jones, 2008). The entrepreneurship agenda within educational institutions has been somewhat driven by government policies. Increasing amounts of funding have been invested into programmes that are intended to increase levels of entrepreneurial activity in the local economy. In the UK for instance, government has supported university-based initiatives. These initiatives are targeted at raising understanding of enterprise among science, engineering and technology students and at enabling them to develop skills and competence suited to employment within Small and Medium-sized Enterprises (SMEs)[1], large organizations or new ventures. There appears to be an acceptance that university-based entrepreneurship education can prepare graduates for nascent entrepreneurship but equally valuable is its potential to create entrepreneurial employees. Given the decline in traditional sectors, government has also paid increasing attention to developing new technology-based sectors and the role of SMEs in these emergent sectors (Dixon, Thompson, & McAllister 2002). Hence the overarching result has fuelled interest in entrepreneurship and Information Communications Technology (ICT) enabled learning.

In this chapter, we explore ICT-enabled learning as a means of delivering entrepreneurship education and as a means of training in the firm. The premise of this study is similar to Rae and Carswell's (2000). We assert that there is a growing need for entrepreneurship to be taught in schools and further and higher education establishments. A second premise of this study is that the impact of entrepreneurship education cannot be narrowly defined. Whilst entrepreneurship education is directly proportional to entrepreneurial activity, entrepreneurship education is not directly proportional to new business creation. This means

entrepreneurship education has a wide-ranging impact on the local economy in terms of enterprising activity. As a result of entrepreneurship education, graduates may to a greater extent become an entrepreneurial employee and to a lesser extent become an entrepreneur.

The objectives of this chapter are two-fold. Firstly, we aim to investigate the role of entrepreneurship educators in preparing the graduate as an entrepreneurial employee. Secondly, this chapter specifically addresses ICT-enabled learning as a valuable means of supporting entrepreneurship education and of its potential to support training within the firm.

A case study from education will be presented to evaluate the different views towards ICT-enabled entrepreneurship education. The case study follows two lines of enquiry. Firstly, it is argued that ICT-enabled technologies can assist learning within higher education because it enables educators to go beyond the traditional classroom-based boundaries – often essential for entrepreneurial learning. Secondly, through ICT-enabled learning, educators can offer entrepreneurship to more and varied groupings of students. Not only does this serve to better infiltrate university culture for the educator but it can also create dynamism within the learning environment for the learner. Learners who are habituated to ICT-enabled learning may be more likely to successfully engage in further ICT-enabled training programmes as an employee. In summary, the case study seeks to identify the benefits of ICT-enabled learning for entrepreneurship educators and for firms.

BACKGROUND

In the followings sections we firstly explore the changing higher education landscape to show the evolving needs of educators, employers and students. Within a fast-paced society, there is an increasing emphasis on entrepreneurial skills. There is a need to be able to identify emergent opportunities and to adapt to the changes which they present. It is not surprising that there has been a growing interest in entrepreneurship as an area of study and research. The importance of entrepreneurship for today's graduates is also reviewed in this section. The second part of the background literature questions the implications of entrepreneurship education for the SME. If universities are creating entrepreneurial-minded graduates, this has implications for future training needs. Hence the following section also considers the changing SME landscape and scrutinizes the training methods employed within the firm. In summary, below a comparison is made between the changing higher education landscape and the SME landscape to identify the education and training needs for the entrepreneurial employee.

Changing Higher Education Landscape

Undoubtedly higher education is undergoing one of the biggest phases of transition in its history. Universities seek to output entrepreneurial-minded graduates fit to cope with a dynamic and ultra-competitive working environment that is grounded in an ever complex global society. The UK's Higher Education Funding Council (HEFCE, 2000) has implemented measures to ensure university graduates can meet the needs of future employers, for example the introduction of Foundation Degrees. The Foundation Degree is a two-year qualification with a focus on supplying the skills which employers need. Foundation Degrees can function either as pre-entry to employment or as part of a pre-entry to other university courses. In considering these changing course structures, it can be argued that universities are behaving more and more like real businesses. Not only are universities influenced by the requirements of employers, but also by changing government priorities such as the focus on growing high technology companies. Universities also strive to cope with evolving student agendas such as the desire to study and work part-time.

If we look at the most similar and often seemingly separate agendas of enterprise, entrepreneurship, employability, work-based learning and continual professional development, it is likely that universities are engaged to some degree in addressing the components of these agendas through university policy. However there is little rigorous and empirical data to indicate best practice for the university, student or employer (Pittaway & Hannon, 2007). Furthermore some authors suggest there is little conceptual value behind some of these agendas. This is simply because the university can do relatively little to support such an agenda. To illustrate Boud and Symes (2000) believed that "work-based learning is still an idea in search or practice, a pedagogy that is undergoing development as it accommodates itself to the exigencies of the workplace and the university"(p.3). If we consider that there may be a tentative link between education and the SME, how can we strengthen this link through entrepreneurship education? At the time of writing with widespread recognition of the "global downturn", there is a need for SMEs to embrace entrepreneurship to survive. Whilst universities play a vital role in re-training and 'up-skilling' for those that have lost their job, they can also play a critical advisory role for SMEs. It is thought that companies which continue to invest in their people through high quality management education and development will be much better placed than their competitors to benefit from the business opportunities that will inevitably emerge during the upturn. In considering the dot-com bust of 2000-2001, Rae (2008) confirmed that particular downturn had a limited impact on graduate employment and careers.

In summary with the changes in further and higher education as demanded by educators, employers and students, there is a need to explore what entrepreneurship education has to offer today's graduates.

Importance of Entrepreneurship for Today's Graduates

The roles of enterprise and entrepreneurship education in the development of graduate careers and employability have been increasingly explored (Nabi et al., 2006, Rae, 2007; Rae, 2008). Entrepreneurship education has been driven not only by policy concerns but also by the expectations of employers and graduates. In the UK, the Leitch (2006) report comprehensively sets out how higher education provision might meet these expectations which has spurned the use of the term "Entrepreneurial University" (Clark, 1998). Clark's (1998) book examined five European universities which have been working (for at least eight years) to become more enterprising. Clark (1998) suggests that the university-environment relationship is characterized by a deepening asymmetry between environmental demand and institutional capacity to respond. This results in a need for an overall capacity to respond flexibly and selectively to change.

A century later, Rae (2008) also notes that there is thought to be a considerable gap between student, university and employer expectations. This could be influenced to a degree by the re-modelling of the workforce that is occurring in the public services (Edmond et al., 2007). Due to the weakening of traditional job boundaries, job functions and roles are being constantly redefined, and modernized. This is especially visible in education and health sectors if we consider for example allied health care professions where nursing roles have been associated with front office staff. Butt and Lance (2003) in their primary schools study, outline the changing role functions within the education sector. With the blurring of role functions, entrepreneurship education is playing an ever-increasing role in enhancing employability as it encapsulates the notion that the individual who has been exposed to entrepreneurship education is self-aware, can cope with change and can find innovative solutions to workplace problems.

As a result, entrepreneurship when used in its broad sense – rather than the narrow dimension of creating new businesses or self-employment – has considerable drawing power for the educator, student and employer. In addition to preparing graduates for the complex world of work by assisting them in securing advertised employment, entrepreneurship education is also thought to better prepare graduates for non-existing jobs (Bridge et al., 2008). Beyond the employability agenda, entrepreneurship education has a role to play in encouraging graduates to become better citizens by offering their skills to benefit for example art, culture, local community or national government. In effect, entrepreneurship education serves as an umbrella term for many different forms of entrepreneurship within the private or public sector including:

- social enterprise
- project management – renewal/development
- new business activity
- civic engagement
- organizational change or corporate entrepreneurship
- (part-time/self) employability and
- Intrapreneurship[2]

In terms of the 'entrepreneurial skill set' entrepreneurial learning has become recognized as a means to develop student confidence and essential skills such as applied creativity, leadership, innovation, teamwork, communication and problem-solving. These entrepreneurial competencies should assist graduates in acting as change agents and help to foster wider cultural change. The next section evaluates the implications of entrepreneurship education for cultural change within SMEs.

Changing SME Landscape

Previous research within SMEs has consistently emphasized the informality that pervades the management and operational structures of smaller firms – often termed the "gut feel" style of management within flattened hierarchies. Cardon and Stevens (2004) remarked that "we lack much of the theory and data necessary to understand how small and emerging firms train their employees" (p.295). In fact numerous researchers including, Storey (2004), Holden et al. (2006) and Coetzer (2006) all identified that smaller firms were less likely to provide formal training for employees. This suggests graduates may be less aware of the informal learning processes happening in the workplace. It also questions traditional thinking on formal training as the only form of 'real' training.

It would be negligent to ignore that there is a growing body of literature devoted to the scope for informal training and informal learning processes within the SME. These studies denote SMEs as active learning organizations (Rowden, 1995; Walton, 1999; Gibb, 1999; Doyle & Huges, 2004). This compelling body of evidence reaffirms the notion that smaller firms rely on informal modes of skill acquisition. This has even been recognized by government and thus taken into account in Government White Papers (Department for Education and Skills, 2002). Therefore it appears that employers have a role to play in assisting employees to bridge the gap between formal and informal learning.

It is generally accepted that organizations, of all sizes, are willing to engage in learning and view learning as important to survival (Schein, 1993). Some go further and argue that knowledge is critical to competitive positioning and competitive advantage. To illustrate, Awad and Ghaziri (2004) hint that it will be possible to differentiate between firms on the basis of how they manage knowledge. In this context, knowledge is defined as the use of skills and experience, to add intelligence to information. This builds upon earlier notions of the concept of innovation (Drucker 1988) and the process of diffusion (Rogers, 1995).

Harris (2008) informs us that knowledge is critical to developing competency within smaller businesses. Managers that understand how their customers behave and translate that insight into innovative products/services are more likely to succeed. Bahra, (2001) outlines how to do this; identify relevant knowledge, capture it, transfer it and share it to optimize knowledge flows and to manage flows effectively. Bishop (2008) cautions that no two firms operating within the same sector and offering similar products/services (with comparable staffing levels) will adopt the same training programmes (Bishop, 2008). Besides, informality can introduce a differential factor. For instance, Cavusgil et al., (2003) found that tacit knowledge could be obtained from partner organizations due to their frequent and close interactions. Clark (2003) also mentions how email exchanges are used as part of a process of sharing of knowledge. SMEs may contain numerous silos of tacit knowledge but it is thought they commonly fail to convert it to explicit knowledge. This begs the question, are the existing models for learning within SMEs appropriate for the entrepreneurial employee?

Research has proved that employers desire to offer training programmes that are specific and non-transferable in order to ensure their company reaps the benefit of the capital outlay on employee training programmes (Gleeson and Keep, 2004). This type of training programme may also be termed in-house or be-spoke training. Ram (1994) stated that employees may be disadvantaged in the external labor market should they not have been exposed to externally-accredited training programmes. Gorard and Selwyn (2005) are keen to point out that learner engagement is not a simple and objective matter of weighing up economic costs against economic returns. Employees may have very different needs and wants from training programmes than those of their employer (Edmond et al., 2007). If we consider that today's graduates are likely to be exposed to both entrepreneurship education and ICT-enabled learning as part of their university education, this necessitates firm to change their training practices. With government drives to increase the e-readiness of SMEs on the basis that it should increase their competitiveness, firms should also consider offering ICT-enabled training programmes to their employees. Within the education sector, Harris (2008) in his UK study hints that enterprise education can be enhanced through the use of learning technologies. In any virtual learning environment collaborative efforts are required to ensure the learner interacts with people and not simply the computer – both technology and people play a crucial role in the development of SME capability. However, Harris (2008) confirmed that "virtual classrooms were perceived to have only moderate benefits to SMEs, this suggests that simply putting the classroom online is not leading the way on future collaborative learning" (p.682). Sveiby (2001) separates out the technology from the people indicating IT presents knowledge objects whilst people present knowledge processes. In taking a closer look at the role of IT in creating knowledge Sveiby (2001) categorized knowledge management into three phases:

- The first phase (mid-1960s onwards) is the role of information technologies in enhancing productivity
- The second phase (mid- to late-1980s) features the spread of the knowledge-based society and the shift from production driven to market-driven or customer-focused, and;
- The third phase (mid- to late-1990s and into the 21st century) which focuses on harnessing knowledge brought about by technology development.

These three phases provide a key insight into the changes occurring generally within the SME landscape. In the first instance, SMEs tended to engage in IT to enhance productivity. Through time with changing business models, IT offered a means to relate the SME products and services to customers (customer relationship marketing) and more recently also to harness knowledge more effectively within the company. Sveiby (2001) believes a fourth phase could be added which values the role of people, interacting with each other, to unlock knowledge. This means a sharing of knowledge can create new knowledge. In summary, there are shifts in our understanding of knowledge. By collaborating with each other online, albeit having a degree of interdependence, assists in building online communities of practice where knowledge is shared and learning happens. When this becomes integrated with daily business practice, it can give rise to valuable informal learning processes.

In summary, in this section through a comparison between the changing higher education landscape and the SME landscape we can identify a growing need for entrepreneurship education and training but also how ICT-enabled learning might be an appropriate delivery approach. The case study will examine in more detail the provision of entrepreneurship education within the UK university system and how to embrace information communications technology in the delivery approach. The following section outlines the methodology used to generate the case study for this chapter.

METHODOLOGY

Weaver et al. (2006) indicate that there is a widely held assumption that a positive relationship exists between education and entrepreneurial activity. In short, it is an assumption. It has been difficult to accurately measure the impact of entrepreneurship education among sub-groups exposed or not to entrepreneurship education. Longitudinal studies have been proclaimed essential given there are too many uncontrollable factors. On a cautionary note, higher education establishments strive to meet the demands of its key stakeholders amidst clear evidence that there may be no direct link between entrepreneurship education and entrepreneurial activity. In addition to these concerns, from an employer perspective, it is yet unclear as to what extent graduates that have been exposed to entrepreneurship education are better for employers than those that have not. Graduates are rarely an "exact mould fit" for employers. For instance, Greene and Saridakis (2007) revealed that there was a difference between the skills students acquired at university versus what was needed for employment and/or entrepreneurial activity.

Since we aim to investigate the role of enterprise educators and the value of ICT-enabled learning for the subject of entrepreneurship, this investigation focuses on entrepreneurship education within the UK university system. The university under consideration, the University of Ulster, has a clearly articulated entrepreneurship agenda as depicted in its corporate plan. The university offers every learner, regardless of discipline, the opportunity to study a module in entrepreneurship. Given this university-wide approach to delivering entrepreneurship education, ICT-enabled learning has become vital to ensuring learner needs are satisfied. The University of Ulster has four regional campuses dispersed throughout Northern Ireland. The Northern Ireland economy is known to be over-dependent upon the public sector. There is a general recognition that there is a need to create more micro-scale ventures and SMEs and to improve the competitiveness of existing SMEs. To this extent, there has been much government support for entrepreneurship education throughout the entire education system, from primary school level to further and higher education.

The following case study helps to illustrate how educators can design taught delivery programmes for the subject of entrepreneurship at undergraduate and postgraduate level; herein there are reper-

cussions for SME training. The case highlights the views of learners with regards to the perceived value of entrepreneurship education.

The significant contributions of this case study to the body of knowledge include:

- Distinguishing between the possible outcomes of enterprise education
- Providing insights into the evolving entrepreneurship agenda within education
- Identifying with the entrepreneurial skills set
- How to create an ICT-enabled learning environment, and
- The difference between learner needs in education and in the SME environment.

The following section outlines the case study by introducing UK university policy and University of Ulster policy on entrepreneurship education. The undergraduate sample cohort is then outlined before presenting the findings. The findings underline the conceptual framework for embedding entrepreneurship education and the benefits of ICT-enabled learning.

CASE STUDY

Approach

We suggest there are four broad aims associated with any entrepreneurship education programme [See Figure 1]. A common misperception of entrepreneurship is becoming an actual entrepreneur and this forms the narrowest dimension. UK research undertaken by the National Council for Graduate Entrepreneurship (Hannon et al., 2005) has shown few are entrepreneur-ready; only a minority will become graduate entrepreneurs. It is more likely that the vast majority of graduates will work within an existing organization. The widest dimension would be that entrepreneurship education should equip students to become

Figure 1. Broad aims of entrepreneurship programmes

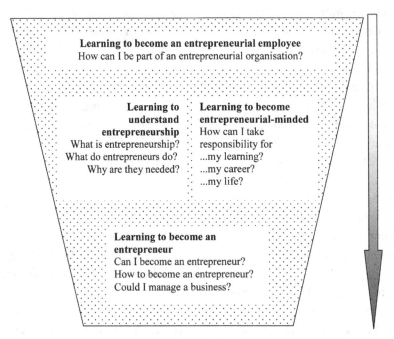

entrepreneurial employees. In between these two extremes the objective of entrepreneurship programmes might be to develop student understanding of what entrepreneurial people do, how we perceive them and why they are important in society. Lastly, entrepreneurship education could aim to find out how students as individuals be entrepreneurial and practice being entrepreneurial-minded in non-business aspects of their life, for example, cope with change or societal problems [See Figure 1].

Introducing entrepreneurship education into the University of Ulster through the Northern Ireland Centre for Entrepreneurship (NICENT) sought to:

- Create a great appreciation and understanding of entrepreneurship
- Recognize the value and contribution it makes to economic and social growth, and
- Encourage entrepreneurship to be seen as viable in any career option.

NICENT was initially funded by the government in 2000 to embed entrepreneurship in the science, engineering and technology faculties. In May 2007 the Centre was refunded to expand its activity across all university faculties. There are two sub-agendas focusing the university's provision of entrepreneurship education: 'enterprise for life' that seeks to develop a range of vital soft skills, core to any degree/training programme and aligned to life-long learning and; 'new venturing' in the wide sense of the word to assist learners in new venturing projects community/enterprise renewal/development and/or management.

Sample

Investigations were carried out using student data from the Department of Hospitality and Tourism Management at the University of Ulster. A largely qualitative research methodology, including focus groups and surveys, was used to investigate learner perceptions towards entrepreneurship education. The Northern Ireland Centre for Entrepreneurship also investigated the learning processes and the learning experiences of students since the key themes identified would be critical to shaping the future direction of the Centre in using ICT-enabled learning for entrepreneurship education. The data would also be recorded for the purposes of longitudinal study collection to assess the longer-term implications of the work of NICENT and the University of Ulster in providing entrepreneurship education to meet emerging industry needs.

The student sample (n=45) was derived from three separate degree programmes two final year groups and one first year cohort within the Department of Hospitality and Tourism Management. The entrepreneurship web-based content was provided by the Northern Ireland Centre for Entrepreneurship (NICENT) and depending on the degree programme; the e-module was either a core or elective 10-point credit module on *Entrepreneurship Awareness* or *Entrepreneurship Applied*. The first year cohort had undertaken an awareness module as a core option whilst one final year cohort had undertaken a core awareness module and another an elective applied module.

The students participated in two surveys, a survey before they undertook the e-module and the same survey instrument was used post-completion of the e-module. These surveys were completed anonymously online. A user generated code identified and matched the pre-survey response with the post-survey response. In the first part of these surveys, the students were questioned about their entrepreneurial skills set. Therefore the first purpose of the pre- and post-surveys was to identify any self-evaluated improvement in their skills. To avoid response bias large samples are preferable. In the second part of the survey, students were asked to define their understanding of some key entrepreneurship terms. The second part of the surveys therefore identified the individual motivations of the learner for studying entrepreneurship and the starting basis for knowledge acquisition. The information gathered from the second part of the survey also serves to

help the enterprise educator to identify learner needs and the level of support material required. For example, in considering the module design the educator might decide to provide additional information (clouds) or case studies within the ICT-enabled learning environment to support those learners who require further information on a particular topic. The final part of the survey covered aspects of IT competency.

After both pre- and post-surveys were completed focus groups were carried out. Focus group activity introduced more detailed discussion into, but not limited to, the following six themes:

- The importance of entrepreneurship education as part of their study programme
- The value they placed on the entrepreneurial skills set
- What possibilities did entrepreneurship education open up/create for them
- How they would use entrepreneurship education in the future (includes in the workplace, in the community or with friends and family)
- How they would continue their entrepreneurship education in the future, and
- What they liked/did not like about the ICT-enabled learning environment

In summary the data collected is largely qualitative. Note, where quantitative data is presented, significant differences are at 0.05 but it is recognized the small sample size affects statistical reliability. The sample provides data from three different undergraduate cohorts within the same discipline area. The findings are thought to be reflective of the undergraduate population and whilst they are not representative of all disciplines there will be common elements for students in a multi-disciplinary context and it is in this context that these findings are presented. Since the Northern Ireland Centre for Entrepreneurship has a university-wide agenda to embed entrepreneurship education in all University of Ulster courses,

Figure 2. Introducing entrepreneurship education into higher education

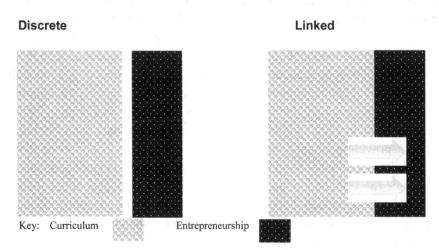

known factors that differ across disciplines can be highlighted.

Findings

A Conceptual Framework for Embedding Entrepreneurship

The University of Ulster provided entrepreneurship education before the introduction of Northern Ireland Centre for Entrepreneurship but only discretely and as part of business curricula. This approach excluded students from non-business disciplines from studying entrepreneurship as a subject [See Figure 2]. However with a dedicated entrepreneurship agenda, entrepreneurship became more and more entwined with existing curricula. As illustrated to the left in Figure 2, the University of Ulster provided entrepreneurship as a modular study within the business faculty. However, with the launch of the Northern Ireland Centre for Entrepreneurship resources became available to design course materials and to advise staff in different subject areas on how to embed enterprise education within their course. Note, prior to May 2007, the work of the Centre was targeted outside the business faculty.

In effect, the Centre worked with faculties such as computing and engineering, life and health sciences and the built environment to embed entrepreneurship education. As a result entrepreneurship became extrinsically linked to the curriculum as illustrated to the right of Figure 2. With the growing interest for entrepreneurship education, the University sought to meet the increased demand through an integrated approach. The integrated approach was achieved via ICT-enabled learning [See Figure 3]. As the left of Figure 3 shows by using ICT-enabled learning, entrepreneurship could now be studied as part of an integrated course structure. This means an entrepreneurship e-module could be taken as a core part of the course teachings.

When entrepreneurship education is not perceived as "a bolt-on" it can be effectively integrated within year 2 modules which set out to develop generic skills of the graduate that provide the foundation for later subject-specific skills. With the essentials covered in an earlier module, there are additional opportunities to embed entrepreneurial learning in subsequent parts of the course, as illustrated by an embedded approach, in the middle of Figure 3. For example this may include a further module study on entrepreneurship. The University of Ulster top-up exists of a further module in entrepreneurship applied and it is often used by educators as a grounding in the

Figure 3. Integrating and embedding entrepreneurship education into higher education

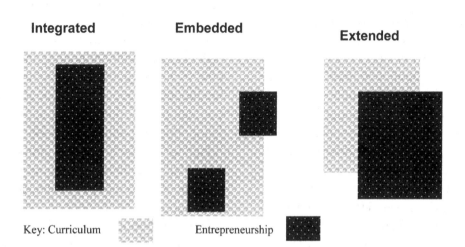

second semester of year 2 to better prepare students for year 3 placement activity. Alternatively educators might prefer to bring in elements of entrepreneurship to an existing course element relating to continual professional development or personal development planning, others may introduce further entrepreneurship content and how it applies within a subject-specific module at a later stage in the learner lifecycle – as in this case study.

Additionally educators on behalf of students may also seek ways to continue their entrepreneurship education through identified training opportunities such as business plan competitions, residential enterprise programmes, enterprise networks and societies.

This is demonstrated in the middle of Figure 3 by the entrepreneurship box extending out of the curriculum, there may be additional opportunities outside the curriculum but nevertheless associated with the opportunities created through studying within the curriculum. Therefore entrepreneurship education can be studied in various modules and outside those modules leading to a fully embedded approach.

Finally, when entrepreneurship education shifts onto the stage of extending beyond the curriculum

and having a life of its own if the student desires, this can be described as an extended approach as illustrated to the right of Figure 3. Hence entrepreneurship can extend beyond the boundaries of course provision and students can drive their own involvement in extra-curricular activities for entrepreneurship [See Figure 3].

At the University of Ulster, approximately 3,500 students each year undertake the ICT-enabled modules. Web-based learning materials have expanded the delivery of entrepreneurship throughout 300 programmes each year. Online delivery has proved a fast and effective way to infiltrating University culture. In summary, NICENT has had substantial success in embedding entrepreneurship learning materials into the curriculum within higher education. This success can be somewhat attributed to the approach adopted, that is ICT-enabled learning as the delivery mechanism.

Entrepreneurship Education Through ICT-Enabled Learning

ICT-enabled learning underpins the role of new technology in providing high quality teaching and learning experiences. Electronic-based entrepreneurship education can empower individuals, both educator and learner, and should meet the needs of modern learners in a broad range of disciplines thereby expanding the study of entrepreneurship beyond the traditional boundaries and assisting to build online communities of practice. In this study ICT-enabled learning generally consists of guidance notes for educator and learner including the rationale for study and a repository of dedicated content on the fit between the entrepreneurial individual, the opportunity and the resources. The highly interactive materials are offered within a secure learning environment and are accompanied by a suite of tools to communicate with e-peers; and interactive exercises e.g. Entrepreneur TV™ and inbuilt assessments. At the University of Ulster, the ICT-enabled learning portfolio includes three modules. The first e-module is *Entrepreneurship Awareness*. It develops understanding of the entrepreneurial process and the entrepreneur's environment. Learners should develop basic market research and financial accounting skills. The second e-module is *Entrepreneurship Applied* and allows application in real time supporting learners through the action areas of researching, feasibility checking and planning as well as preparing learners for the next steps, launching themselves as an entrepreneurial individual. The third e-module is *Advanced Entrepreneurship*, an e-learning offering that combines the two modules (awareness and applied) and is pitched at postgraduate level. The portfolio of e-modules can be readily adapted to operate in various virtual learning environments through different technology platforms. E-module content can also be readily adopted by the educator. It can be customized as appropriate to meet the learning criteria and in agreement with accreditation bodies.

Benefits of ICT-Enabled Entrepreneurship Learning

Upon examining the survey feedback, and the difference between pre- and post-surveys students

rated their capability level higher in entrepreneurship-type skills, there was less improvement in some of the generic skills. However, the focus group activity highlighted that students tended to take generic skills for granted and they were of the view that educators, employers and peers were best placed to evaluate those generic skills. Note that generic skills tended to be evaluated during placement activity, drawing attention to the fact that the use of pre- and post-surveys can have added value in addressing skills needs and skill gaps when considered in conjunction with additional survey instruments and stakeholders.

From the students surveyed in this investigation, there was no statistically significant change in the propensity to act as an entrepreneur because 84% who thought "I would like to be an entrepreneur" before taking the entrepreneurship course still wanted to be an entrepreneur after completing the course. In fact the desire to be self-employed increased by 11%. This difference between the desire to be entrepreneurial versus wanting to be self-employed could suggest two things. Firstly, entrepreneurship has different meanings for each individual, and some students found that the term entrepreneurship "was too aspirational" and they considered self-employment as an option. Secondly, students recognized that entrepreneurship was about more than employability and they preferred to be entrepreneurial. Whilst the sample is small, entrepreneurship education does not, in the immediate term anyway, create entrepreneurs. Student ability to be entrepreneurial-minded as defined by competency in entrepreneurial skill areas had increased over the duration of the course [See Table 1]. Students had improved their ability to try new ideas and new ways of doing things – their capacity to act as change agents had increased. There was a rational thought process behind the changes and students learnt to plan and organize tasks in order to implement change as shown in Table 1.

If we specifically deal with the core business skills, it seems entrepreneurship education for

Table 1. Entrepreneurship education increases entrepreneurial competency

Competency	Percentage increase (%)
Risk-taking	21.2
Problem-solving	21
Taking initiative	15.8
Organising	26.3
Implementing a plan	21
Willingness to try new ideas	26.3

these hospitality and management students equally assisted in developing their business knowledge. For instance, in the pre-surveys, 5.3% admitted having "limited knowledge of market research including opportunity identification" yet in the post-surveys students felt they had above average or good knowledge. We find similar trends for knowledge of business planning and raising finance. In terms of developing competency in costing, pricing and cash flow, the results are less clear cut but most admit to having developed increased knowledge (by one Likert Scale point higher) after completing the course.

In the second part of the survey, where students were asked to define their understanding of some key entrepreneurship terms, students were better able to put the key terms into context and apply them to their own career path in the post-surveys. In contrast to the pre-surveys students were able to make highly accurate judgment statements on the knowledge they had acquired throughout the module. For example, students may have highlighted how they lacked an understanding of the entrepreneurship process before studying the module and that prior to study they were only familiar with the entrepreneur as an individual – media speculation had created the term entrepreneurship for them. For two out of the three cohorts studied, the module was a core module of their course provision. Yet, the data set was too small for any statistical comparison to be made between the motivations of individual students on the core programme versus students who had

chosen the elective module. In general students were motivated by:

- A willingness to embrace a new subject – try something new
- A desire to learn more about the entrepreneurship process, and;
- Learning within a virtual learning environment – use ICT-enabled learning.

All three cohorts indicated that ICT-enabled learning formed part of their overall course design since they communicated using other technologies with their peers and educators. They had been exposed to a range of multi-media tools in existing course provision especially media-supported (example, PowerPoint) lectures and computer-based researches. However, the students did not have the opportunity to study completely online instead of in the lecture theatre or classroom. Therefore ICT-enabled learning in this new context of a virtual learning environment had selling power for the entrepreneurship module.

In considering the qualitative data collected during focus group activity. As Table 2 below shows students were generally positive about incorporating entrepreneurship education within their courses.

Not only did they find the subject interesting, they realized they had poor knowledge of the subject. The student response indicated that the subject may have relevance to other parts of the course, hence the reliance on the educator to build

Table 2. Emergent views of learners on entrepreneurship education

Thematic area	Emergent data
Importance of entrepreneurship education	Entrepreneurship is worthwhile as a core module I realized how little I knew about entrepreneurship It could be (more) relevant to other course subjects It could assist me when I leave university
Importance of entrepreneurial skills set	It makes you more self-aware It gives you an understanding of what you need to aim for It highlights where you need to make improvements It indicates why you could (not) be an entrepreneur
Possibilities of entrepreneurship in individual life story	It is good to be introduced to the subject early on in the course It makes you evaluate your starting position It makes you think through your options It makes you a better learner – open to possibilities
Future of entrepreneurship in individual life story	Being entrepreneurial is for me Being entrepreneurial can secure job happiness and personal satisfaction (e.g. contribute to local sports club) It is possible to be an entrepreneur someday
Further education or training and entrepreneurship	I would consider further study/training in subject I would consider getting experience within an entrepreneurial environment (e.g. placement) I would consider entrepreneurship within my workplace I have a desire for training in my future job
Advantages/ disadvantages of ICT-enabled learning	ICT-enabled learning is appropriate for the subject Interacting with peers in formal online environment helps to develop appropriate online skills/behaviours for the workplace Tendency to rely on other ICT to communicate with peers ICT-enables learning is a great flexible way for me to learn

on the subject in other course areas – this finding gives some indication of how students preferred an integrated approach towards entrepreneurship education [See Figure 3]. Finally students were not yet in a position to accurately assess the value of entrepreneurship education for them but speculated it could be helpful when they exit the education system.

When asked about developing the entrepreneurial skills set, there were opposing views on the extent to which an individual could become an entrepreneur – some felt they could be an entrepreneur, others felt they could not. Nevertheless students generally agreed there was value in understanding your particular skills and areas for improvement but also the need to have critical and often task-specific feedback from the educator or e-peers throughout the module. When we examined the possibilities of entrepreneurship these remained largely unknown for the student

cohorts as shown in Table 2. This is thought to be reflective of the stage in the learner lifecycle, especially for year 1 students. Nevertheless, the positive views which students harbored towards the subject provide some proof for educators that the subject is appreciated by students. Students admitted it could make them better "all-round learners". As revealed in Table 2, when the learners were asked about how they would use entrepreneurship education in the future, they showed a genuine interest that it could be used in the future in different contexts – work, life and family. Some even went further to suggest that maybe one day they could be an actual entrepreneur – the narrow view of entrepreneurship becomes secondary to being entrepreneurial [See Figure 1]. Given the context of this case study within Northern Ireland where there is a weak private sector and an over-reliance on the strong performing SMEs, these findings indicate the need for educators to "sow the seeds of entrepreneurship" among the young population.

The qualitative data collected on the future of education and training in general and in respect to entrepreneurship [See Table 2] confirmed that students at this stage of the learner lifecycle were less aware of training issues in the workplace environment. Whilst they may desire future on the job training (showing an awareness of life-long learning), they did not stipulate what type of training would be desired. This could be taken to be proof that a gap exists between education and training. The most revealing finding was that students were now aware of how entrepreneurship could apply within the workplace environment. Finally, in terms of the advantages and disadvantages of ICT-enabled learning students identified more benefits that drawbacks to the technology. This said there were technology problems that were solved in due course by the educator. Since the particular cohorts in this case had not been habituated to a virtual learning environment, introductory sessions were necessary. Throughout the module in addition to the educator responding to student issues on understanding of content and technical problems, e-peers were as helpful to each other – even during tasks when learners were outside their learning sub-group. The drawback of the ICT-enabled learning being new to the learner is that there is a tendency to rely on existing ICT [See Table 2] such as mobile phone, personal email systems which can detract from interaction within the online environment. Educators need to ensure they use the full suite of interactive tools at their disposal to encourage interaction within the formal online environment. Since ICT-enabled learning was one of the motivating factors for studying this module, it had lived up to their expectation and they were enthusiastic about using ICT-enabled learning in the future – both in education and in the workplace.

DISCUSSION

By exploring entrepreneurship education within tourism and hospitality courses offered at the University of Ulster using the university's portfolio of ICT-enabled courses, we arrive at a number of discussion items for the impacts of ICT-enabled learning for entrepreneurial employees. Whilst today's graduates may be more experienced in the use of ICT, for them there will be significant differences between learning in education and in the SME. In the cocoon of education, the curriculum is fixed but in the SME it is likely to be more open although there is likely to be more one-to one guidance than in education. SME training may also be guided by company-driven practical tasks whereas in education it was more likely to be theoretically driven. Whilst the educator is duty bound to provide timely formal feedback to the learner, in the SME, informal feedback (from different parties) should also be taken into consideration by the learner. In summary today's graduate may initially need further guidance to respond to the real needs of workplace learning and may prefer to engage in project-based learning which blends learning in education with learning in the SME. The challenge is to design appropriate ICT-enabled learning within the SME environment that will satisfy both entrepreneurial employee and employer. Within virtual learning environments there are opportunities for co-creating the learning content thereby increasing the practical focus of SME training.

It must be stated that there will be varied levels of user confidence when education and/or training programmes are ICT-enabled. Firms need to take this into consideration when providing training programmes because ICT-enabled learning can be readily provided within any company provided there is a computer and Internet connection. When the "fear of the technology" and the technical issues are surmounted, this study has shown that learners generally have positive views and perceptions of ICT-enabled learning.

In time, learners grow to appreciate the flexibility it provides as well as the real time interaction it allows not only with the educator but with their peers. Both learner and educator are observed to be the knowledge providers. This finding may have even more significance in the SME where work tasks and training assessments are a product of team effort. This study presents a strong case that web-based technologies are apt for exposing learners to the subject of entrepreneurship since attitude to change, change management and new venturing are core principles to the study of the entrepreneurship process. On a cautionary note, if we consider that entrepreneurship education seeks to imitate real entrepreneurial behaviour; ICT-enabled learning may be well-received due to the subject discipline.

In summary to accommodate the growing interest in making workplaces into effective learning environments (Eraut 2004), ICT-enabled learning is proposed as a viable means especially for entrepreneurship training. The following section outlines the possible lessons to be learnt from providing entrepreneurship education within higher education through the use of ICT-enabled learning. These lessons have implications for SMEs considering how to implement training programmes and how to make appropriate use of ICT-enabled learning within the SME environment.

LESSONS LEARNT

In this section, we attempt to provide some answers to SMEs interested in harnessing the knowledge of entrepreneurial graduates and in stepping up their use of ICT. There is an onus on firms to demonstrate leadership in terms of engaging with leading edge technology and showing an interest in staff developing expertise in newer technologies. Technologies pervade working and social environments and employers should be able to use this to their advantage, that is, to the extent that work seems like play. It is also suggested firms

make some effort to gauge employee attitude, engagement and response to newer technologies. It is likely that recent graduates will engage in informal training without being aware that informal learning processes are happening. Firms might consider providing a mentor for new graduates to ensure they are aware of learning progress with tasks or encourage recent graduates to keep a record of learning activity. These records can be used to identify areas for improvement but as valuable can identify how firms could do things differently and better.

Whilst graduates can effectively engage with ICT-enabled learning, other employees may not. There are a number of wide-ranging solutions to counteract the unwillingness of management and staff to embrace ICT-enabled learning; these have been tested in the education sector when individuals do not have an affinity for ICT-enabled learning. To illustrate these may include providing:

- A face-to-face introductory workshop to alleviate concerns about the technology
- A one-to-one walk through the programme addressing frequently asked questions
- A safety net where employees would be partnered with a learning pal, a trusted work colleague
- A means for employees to design/dictate programme content, and;
- A choice of programme assessment

Employers need to be make employees aware that there is supported guidance throughout the training programme and secondly they need to communicate the benefits of ICT-enabled learning for the learner rather than a singular focus on the expected impacts of training for the SME. To this end, companies are encouraged to investigate their approaches to formal and informal training including recognition and reward systems for employees. For example, if an entrepreneurial employee found a solution to a problem faced by their company, the company could guarantee that the employee could lead the implementation process to solve the problem and/or they could receive some type of financial reward. On a cautionary note, only those willing to explore new frameworks of knowledge transfer and development will be suited to ICT-enabled learning since entrepreneurial e-learning does not fit within the traditional reductionist paradigm of business and management education. By engaging in ICT-enabled learning of entrepreneurship, users are practicing risk-taking behaviour as each individual learner takes control of their own learning experience.

In this way, ICT-enabled learners can critically analyze their experience based on past experience, educational attainment and interaction with their peers – therefore mimicking the real world entrepreneur. Finally it should be noted that the findings of this study may have implications beyond our understanding of the social construction of training in the small firm.

FUTURE RESEARCH DIRECTIONS

As other researchers that have gone before (see for example Greene and Saridakis 2007), the author warns against the misuse of the term entrepreneurship within academia and the misconceptions harbored towards an entrepreneurship agenda and what it can realistically achieve. A useful metaphor to illustrate the abuse of the word entrepreneurship can be presented using the 'Ikea-ised model'. Whilst it may be convenient for some to use the term entrepreneurship to meet targets and objectives, they would not necessarily know how to go about building the "Ikea flat pack". Entrepreneurship is by no means flat. Enterprise and entrepreneurship education remains a nebulous concept for some in education. As this study shows, if we consider the student views in this investigation, entrepreneurship remains a cumbersome term and often means different things to different people. Nevertheless universities with the support of organizations external to the universities (for example

in the UK, the National Council for Graduate Entrepreneurship and Enterprise Educators UK) have a responsibility to find ways to communicate in the same language what entrepreneurship means and how it can apply over time within the different subject disciplines. By the same token, the business world is not static and this offers opportunities for synergy between education and industry. It offers a means of ensuring there is a supply of entrepreneurial-minded graduates capable of coping with the technological advances of the time and the demands of employers within the entrepreneurial firm.

This study deals with the trends in enabling technologies that contribute to change in learner requirements within the education sector and within the workplace or SME environment. Whilst this study dealt with ICT-enabled learning, it may provide a useful comparison for others that are using social technologies such as Web 2.0 for the purposes of education and training. With more of today's graduates exposed to entrepreneurship the likelihood of employees behaving entrepreneurially has increased. This could spur the development of new business models. Thus, there are implications for all ventures, including non ICT-ventures and there are challenges for policy makers following from these influences in the wider operational environment.

CONCLUSION

In conclusion, there has been increased emphasis on entrepreneurship and entrepreneurial behaviour in diverse sectors within governments, local to central. It is thought that industry will be driven by entrepreneurial behaviour practiced across many SMEs. Subsequently, universities must remain focused on providing opportunities for "real" learning and application of tacit knowledge. It is concluded that entrepreneurship education delivered with the use of information communication technologies, should not be overlooked. The creation of learning partnerships and online synergies should remain steadfast in entrepreneurial practice especially for smaller firms reliant upon sharing knowledge to develop successfully. As a consequence, ICT-enabled or 'e-entrepreneurship' education must embrace unique characteristics of people to seek-out original and viable business and market opportunities and have the vision to make new opportunity-resource connections. This is particularly salient if we consider the economic rewards that can be reaped from nurturing and fostering an entrepreneurial spirit.

Entrepreneurship education should also accommodate the notion that implementing business ideas is often without assurances of the rewards – this is the stuff of real-life firms, not the stuff of dreams. Perhaps SMEs have yet a distance to travel in terms of allowing today's graduates to be entrepreneurial within their organization? Herein, we can detect value in longitudinal studies to assess the impact of entrepreneurship education. The next stage of this study would involve feedback from SMEs and employers.

Finally, not only is 'what' we deliver important but 'how' we deliver it. Entrepreneurship education should be grounded in an emotive-based philosophy that covers dimensions of sustaining the dream (keeping the dream alive) and growing the organization beyond the expectations of employer, employees or customers. Inherent in this study is the notion that training for the entrepreneur is very different to education for the entrepreneurial employee.

This chapter is a tentative effort to identify factors that influence entrepreneurship education and factors that dictate interest in ICT-enabled learning. Part two of this study would be to incorporate employer attitudes towards learning and understanding of employee learning processes. This is likely to provide insight into the particular importance given to individual thought and action within the small firm. We would find out the level of control individuals have in influencing and shaping organizational policy and strategy.

That is we would find how accommodating the SME environment is for the entrepreneurial employee. Bishop (2008) thinks the small firm approach to participation in training is deeply affected by the subjective orientation towards education and learning held by those who work within it. This emphasizes the importance of the social environment for education and training which, as demonstrated in this study, can be readily provided through ICT-enabled learning where there is an appropriately designed virtual or collaborative learning environment. There are implications here also for the use of Web 2.0 in learning processes.

In final conclusion, the full impact of knowledge development and management for the next generation of scholars and practitioners will be diminished if effective classroom teaching strategies are not in place. Hence there is a valuable role for web-based technology and newer technologies that have not yet been fully explored, to create opportunities for ICT-enabled learning within education and within the entrepreneurial firm.

REFERENCES

Awad, E., & Ghaziri, H. (2004). *Knowledge Management*. Upper Saddle River, NJ: Pearson Education.

Bahra, N. (2001). *Competitive Knowledge Management*. Basingstoke, UK: Palgrave Macmillan.

Bishop, D. (2008). The small enterprise in the training market. *Training and Education, 50*(8/9), 661–673. doi:10.1108/00400910810917046

Boud, D., & Symes, C. (2000). Learning for real: work-based education in universities. In Symes, C., & McIntyre, J. (Eds.), *Working Knowledge: The New Vocationalism and Higher Education*. Buckingham, UK: SHRE and Oxford University Press.

Bridge, S., Hegarty, C., & Porter, S. (2008). *Rediscovering Enterprise: Exploring Entrepreneurship for Undergraduates*. Institute for Small Business and Entrepreneurship 31st Conference, Conference Proceedings. Belfast, Ireland: ISBE.

Butt, G., & Lance, A. (2005). Modernising the roles of support staff in primary schools: changing focus, changing function. *Educational Review*, *57*(2), 131–137. doi:10.1080/0013191042000308314

Cardon, M. S., & Stvens, C. E. (2004). Managing human resources in small organizations: what do we know? *Human Resource Management Review*, *14*(3), 295–323. doi:10.1016/j.hrmr.2004.06.001

Cavusgil, S. T., Calantone, R. J., & Zhao, Y. (2003). Tacit knowledge transfer and firm innovation capacity. *Journal of Business and Industrial Marketing*, *18*(1), 6–21. doi:10.1108/08858620310458615

Clark, B. R. (1998). *Creating Entrepreneurial Universities: Organizational Pathways of Transition*. Oxford, UK: IAU Press, Elsevier.

Clark, D. (2003). *Epic survey 2003: the future of e-learning*. Retrieved February 2009 from http://www.epic.co.uk

Coetzer, A. (2006). Managers as learning facilitators in small manufacturing firms. *Journal of Small Business and Enterprise Development*, *13*(3), 351–362. doi:10.1108/14626000610680244

Department for Education and Skills. (2002). *Skills: Getting on in Business: Getting on in Work, White Paper*. Norwich, UK: HMSO.

Dixon, T., Thompson, B., & McAllister, P. (2002). *The Value of ICT for SMEs in the UK: A Critical Literature Review*. Report for Small Business Service Research Programme, Reading: College of Estate Management.

Doyle, L., & Hughes, M. (2004). *Learning without lessons: Supporting Learning in Small Businesses*. London: LSDA.

Drucker, P. (1988). The Coming of the New Organization. *Harvard Business Review*, *66*(1), 45–53.

Edmond, N., Hillier, Y., & Price, M. (2007). Between a rock and a hard place: The role of HE and foundation degrees in workforce development. *Education and Training*, *49*(3), 170–181. doi:10.1108/00400910710749305

Eraut, M. (2004). Informal learning in the workplace. *Studies in Continuing Education*, *26*(2), 247–273. doi:10.1080/158037042000225245

Gibb, A. A. (1997). Small firms' training and competitiveness. Building upon small business as a learning organization. *International Small Business Journal*, *15*(3), 13–29. doi:10.1177/0266242697153001

Gleeson, D., & Keep, E. (2004). Voice without accountability: the changing relationship between employers, the State and education in England. *Oxford Review of Education*, *30*(1), 37–63. doi:10.1080/0305498042000190050

Gorard, S., & Selwyn, N. (2005). What makes a lifelong learner? *Teachers College Record*, *107*(6), 1193–1216. doi:10.1111/j.1467-9620.2005.00510.x

Greene, F. J., & Saridakis, G. (2007). *Understanding the Factors Influencing Graduate Entrepreneurship* [Research Report No. 1/2007]. Birmingham, UK: National Council for Graduate Entrepreneurship.

Hannon, P. (2007). Enterprise for all? The fragility of enterprise provision across England's HEIs. *Journal of Small Business and Enterprise Development*, *14*(2), 183–210. doi:10.1108/14626000710746646

Hannon, P., Collins, L. A., & Smith, A. J. (2005). Exploring graduate entrepreneurship: A collaborative co-learned based approach for students, entrepreneurs and educators. *Industry and Higher Education, 19*(1), 11–24.

Harris, R. (2008). Developing a collaborative learning environment through technology enhanced education (TE3) support. *Education and Training, 50*(8/9), 674–686. doi:10.1108/00400910810917055

Hegarty, C., & Jones, C. (2008). Graduate Entrepreneurship: More than Child's Play. *Education and Training, 50*(7), 626–637. doi:10.1108/00400910810909072

Higher Education Funding Council for England (HEFCE). (2000). *Foundation Degree Prospectus*. London: HEFCE.

Holden, R., Nabi, G., Gold, J., & Robertson, M. (2006). Building capacity in small businesses: tales from the training front. *Journal of European Industrial Training, 30*(6), 424–440. doi:10.1108/03090590610688816

Leitch, S. (2006). *Review of Skills: Prosperity For All in the Global Economy – World Class Skills*. Norwich, UK: HMSO.

Nabi, G., Holden, R., & Walmsley, A. (2006). Graduate Career-making and business start-up: a literature review. *Education and Training, 48*(2), 373–385. doi:10.1108/00400910610677072

Pittaway, L., & Hannon, P. (2007). Institutional strategies for developing enterprise education. *Journal of Small Business and Enterprise Development, 15*(1), 202–226. doi:10.1108/14626000810850937

Rae, D. (2007). Connecting enterprise and graduate employability: challenges to the higher education culture and curriculum? *Education and Training, 50*(8/9), 605–619. doi:10.1108/00400910710834049

Rae, D. (2008). Riding out the storm: graduates, enterprise and careers in turbulent economic times. *Education and Training, 50*(8/9), 748–763. doi:10.1108/00400910810917118

Rae, D., & Carswell, M. (2000). Using a life-story approach in researching entrepreneurial learning: the development of a conceptual model and its implications in the design of learning experiences. *Education & Training, 42*(4/5), 220–227. doi:10.1108/00400910010373660

Ram, M. (1994). *Managing to Survive: Working Lives in Small Firms*. Oxford, UK: Blackwell Publishing.

Rogers, E. (1995). *Diffusion of Innovations* (4th Ed.). New York: Free Press.

Rowden, R. W. (1995). The role of human resource development in successful small to mid-sized manufacturing businesses: a comparative case study. *Human Resource Development Quarterly, 6*(4), 355–373. doi:10.1002/hrdq.3920060405

Schein, E. H. (1993). How can organizations learn faster? The challenge of entering the green room. *Sloan Management Review, 34*(2), 85–92.

Smith, K. (2008). Embedding enterprise education into the curriculum at a research-led university. *Education and Training, 50*(8/9), 713–724. doi:10.1108/00400910810917082

Storey, D. (2004). Exploring the link, among small firms, between management training and firm performance: a comparison between the UK and other OECD countries. *International Journal of Human Resource Management, 15*(1), 112–130. doi:10.1080/0958519032000157375

Sveiby, E. K. (2001). What is Knowledge Management? Retrieved February 2009, from www.sveiby.com/articles/KnowledgeManagement.html

Walton, J. (1999). *Strategic human resource development*. London: Prentice Hall.

Weaver, M., Dickson, P., & Solomon, G. (2006). Entrepreneurship and education: what is known and not known about the links between education and entrepreneurial activity? *The Small Business Economy for Data Year 2005: A Report to the President*. Washington, DC: United States Government Printing Office.

ADDITIONAL READING

Alexander, S. (2001). E-learning developments and experiences. *Education and Training, 43*(4/5), 240–248. doi:10.1108/00400910110399247

Athayde, R. (2000 March). Measuring Enterprise Potential in Young People. *Entrepreneurship Theory and Practice*, 481-500.

Campbell, J. (2000). Using Internet technology to support flexible learning in business education. *Information Technology and Management, 1*(1), 351–362. doi:10.1023/A:1019193513024

Carter, S., & Jones-Evans, D. (2006). Enterprise and Small business Principles, Practice and Policy (2nd Ed.). London: Prentice Hall.

Coulson-Thomas, C. (2000). Developing a corporate learning strategy. *Industrial and Commercial Training, 32*(3), 84–88. doi:10.1108/00197850010381232

Davies, J., Hides, M., & Powell, J. (2002). Defining the development needs of entrepreneurs in SMEs. *Education and Training, 44*(8/9), 406–412. doi:10.1108/00400910210449240

Gunasekaran, A., McNeil, R., & Shaul, D. (2002). E-learning Research and Applications. *Industrial and Commercial Training, 34*(2), 44–53. doi:10.1108/00197850210417528

Jiwa, S., Lavelle, D., & Rose, A. (2004). Netpreneur simulation: enterprise creation for online economy. *International Journal of Retail and Distribution Management, 32*(12), 587–596. doi:10.1108/09590550410570082

Kuratko, D. F. (2006). The emergence of entrepreneurship education: development trends and challenges. *Entrepreneurship Theory and Practice, 29*(5), 577–597. doi:10.1111/j.1540-6520.2005.00099.x

Martin, L., & Matlay, H. (2003). Innovative use of the Internet in established small firms: the impact of knowledge management and organizational learning in accessing new opportunities. *Qualitative Market Research: An International Journal, 1*, 18–26. doi:10.1108/13522750310457348

Morrison, A., & Johnston, B. (2003). Personal creativity for entrepreneurship, teaching and learning strategies. *Active Learning in Higher Education, 4*, 145–158. doi:10.1177/1469787403004002003

Nabi, G., Holden, R., & Walmsley, A. (2006). Graduate Career-making and business start-up: a literature review. *Education and Training, 48*(2), 373–385. doi:10.1108/00400910610677072

Packham, G., Jones, P., Miller, C., & Thomas, B. (2004). E-learning and retention: key factors influencing student withdrawal. *Education and Training, 46*(6/7), 335–342. doi:10.1108/00400910410555240

Pittaway, L., & Cope, J. (2007). Entrepreneurship Education: A Systematic Review of the Evidence . *International Small Business Journal, 25*, 479–510. doi:10.1177/0266242607080656

Shim, J., Shropshire, J., Park, S., Harris, H., & Campbell, N. (2007). Podcasting, e-learning, communication and delivery. *Industrial Management & Data Systems, 107*(4), 587–600. doi:10.1108/02635570710740715

Thompson, P., & Randall, B. (2001). Can E-learning spur Creativity, Innovation and Entrepreneurship? *Educational Media International, 38*(4), 289–292. doi:10.1080/09523980110105105

Zampetakis, L., & Moustakis, V. (2006). Linking creativity with entrepreneurial intentions: A structural approach. *Entrepreneurship Management, 2*, 413–428. doi:10.1007/s11365-006-0006-z

Zhao, F. (2008). *Information Technology Entrepreneurship and Innovation.* New York: IGI Global.

ENDNOTES

[1] SME is the recognized abbreviation for Small and Medium Sized Enterprises. The majority of the workforce is employed by SMEs. There is no singular definition for SMEs either nationally or internationally.

[2] Entrepreneurship can be defined as the practice of employees within an existing organization. Entrepreneurs can use entrepreneurial skills without taking on the risks or accountability associated with entrepreneurial activities.

Chapter 11

Open Scientific Entrepreneurship:
How the Open Source Paradigm can Foster Entrepreneurial Activities in Scientific Institutions

Harald von Kortzfleisch
University of Koblenz-Landau, Germany

Mario Schaarschmidt
University of Koblenz-Landau, Germany

Philipp Magin
University of Koblenz-Landau, Germany

ABSTRACT

The objective of this article is to conceptually transfer the concept of open source software (OSS) development to scientific entrepreneurship and to hypothetically discuss the support potentials of this rather new development philosophy for what we than call open scientific entrepreneurship. Therefore, at first the authors will go into conceptual details of scientific entrepreneurship and than of OSS development. Following, the main thrust of the article presents open scientific entrepreneurship from two points of origin: first of all, OSS development as a specific form of scientific e-entrepreneurship and further on potential benefits of opening "traditional" scientific entrepreneurship up by looking at specific action fields. These action fields are theoretically based on the process and competence perspective of scientific entrepreneurship. Finally, the general benefits as well as downsides of the concept of openness are discussed on a generic level. It becomes obvious that there is need for balancing the tensions between an open and closed design pattern for scientific entrepreneurship with a general emphasis on the open design perspective.

DOI: 10.4018/978-1-61520-597-4.ch011

INTRODUCTION

During the last years, open source software (OSS) development has become a major industry trend (Weber, 2005). OSS refers to software products distributed under terms that allow to use the software, modify it, and redistribute the software without the requirement of paying the copyright holding authors of the software. What started as an ideology with the aim to provide free access to everyone, evolved to a highly complex (eco)-system of voluntary programmers, sponsoring firms, implicit and explicit governance structures, and simple economics (Lerner, & Tirole, 2002). One of the most well-known examples of OSS are the Linux operating system, the Apache web server, or the Mozilla web browser. In the meantime, the open source concept has not only been applied to software development but also to the open design and engineering of hardware products like mobile phones, furniture or even cars (e.g., www.opendesign.org).

Against this background, the transfer of this rather new development philosophy to scientific entrepreneurship seems to be very paradoxical at first glance. By scientific entrepreneurship we mean the application of principles, methods and instruments in respective entrepreneurship-related action fields in order to systematically and holistically support entrepreneurial activities within the academic community (Magin, & von Kortzfleisch, 2008; for more details and references see the background chapter). The paradox in this context results from intellectual property (IP) as the outcome essence of scientific work and as primarily being something which needs to be protected against other researchers' publication desires in principle (Murray & Stern, 2005). Scientific entrepreneurs, as well as producing companies usually build new businesses through the development and the commercialization of incremental or even better, radical innovations. As these innovations require large investments in R&D it is most likely that both, entrepreneurs as well as existing companies tend to protect their investments in IP by using trade secrets, copyrights, trademarks or patents (Lichtenthaler, 2009). Following the logic that technological features themselves have no benefit without a business model which transforms technology into economic value, copyright holders usually generate their revenue through the sale of owned IP in the form of (technological) products or services.

With regard to the paradoxical situation described above however, besides the OSS development movement another concept might support our idea of transferring the OSS development philosophy to entrepreneurship, i.e. the concept of open innovation (Chesbrough et al., 2008). Also this concept proclaims the benefits of openness and at the same time it is closely related to entrepreneurship by focusing on new knowledge creation, too. Open innovation at its core is the increasing usage of external sources for creating and developing new ideas which lead to innovation. In contrast to a closed innovation paradigm, firms try to include customers, users, universities and even competitors in different stages of their new product development processes (Chesbrough, 2003). The change from a closed to a more open development paradigm includes a change of the underlying mental models as well. In a closed innovation environment, firms try to hire the smartest people to work for them, they rely heavily on internal research and development (R&D) activities, and try to control and to protect their IP. In contrast, in an open innovation environment firms are trying to work with smart people from inside and outside the company, are recognising internal R&D activities as only a part of an innovation process, and are buying IP from outside whenever it is needed and suitable for the current business model (Lichtenthaler, 2009).

In recent years, many firms opened several parts of their innovation processes for external participation. Most activities can be observed in integrating users or customers especially in early and late phases of the innovation process – like making use of lead users or mass customizing products and services (von Hippel, 1994; Piller, & Walcher, 2006). On the contrary, openness in the sense of integrating external individuals or even competitors in core development activities is rarely to be found. Providing internally developed IP to external participants is always a matter of trust. In the past, firms mainly decided to build inter-firm R&D consortia and joint ventures which generally require formal agreements (de Rond, & Bouchikhi, 2004; Singh, 2008) – without integrating further external participants. However, the intensified commercialization of OSS products in recent years leads to the stimulus of rethinking the role of external sources in firm-driven development (Dahlander et al., 2008; West, & Lakhani, 2008). As every OSS innovation process is based on the desire of integrating external knowledge, it is not astonishing that OSS development is often referred to the open innovation paradigm (Dahlander et al., 2008; West, & Gallagher, 2006; West, & Lakhani, 2008) and extended by us to the idea of open scientific entrepreneurship.

The objective of this article is to conceptually transfer the concept of OSS development to scientific entrepreneurship and to hypothetically discuss the support potentials of this rather new development philosophy for what we than call open scientific entrepreneurship. This article is then structured as follows: In the background chapter, firstly we will go into details of scientific entrepreneurship and secondly of OSS development. Following, the main thrust of the article presents open scientific entrepreneurship from two points of origin: (1) OSS development as a specific form of scientific e-entrepreneurship and (2) potential benefits of opening "traditional" scientific entrepreneurship by looking at specific action fields. In addition, the general benefits as well as downsides of the concept of openness are discussed on a generic level. Future research directions and conclusions are provided at the end of the article.

BACKGROUND

Scientific Entrepreneurship

The increasing interest in entrepreneurship as a research discipline of its own initially referred to the traditional mission of universities as sources of knowledge creation and dissemination (Bok, 2003; Geisler, 1993). Although academic thinking about entrepreneurship resulted in a huge body of theoretical knowledge about various related phenomena, it did not contribute to the enforcement and support of entrepreneurial activities themselves. A first step into this direction was the transfer of theoretical knowledge from academia into (existing) businesses (Siegel et al., 2003; David, 1997). This was a kind of "third mission" (Braunerhjelm, 2007; Miner et al., 2001; Feller, 1990) complementing research and education. A major step, however was taken by some U.S. universities during the 1970s which started to add the missing practical perspective to entrepreneurship (Anderseck, 2004; Vesper, & Gartner, 1997). Their main objective was to enable and support the commercialization of academic knowledge by awaking the target groups' attention, arousing interest in starting-up own companies, and by teaching specific entrepreneurship related skills (Klandt, & Volkmann, 2008).

Since the middle of the 1990s also European universities began to adopt such approaches and concentrated on the development of appropriate measures to integrate the practice of entrepreneurship into the academic community (Anderseck, 2004). At this time also governmental institutions perceived the importance of entrepreneurial activities from the academic community and established related publicly-funded programs. One example of such governmental initiatives is the EXIST program, founded by the German Federal Ministry of Economics and Technology. The main reason of all of these programs and initiatives is the enormous importance of technology-oriented and knowledge-based foundations for the prosperity and lasting economic development in today's technology-driven knowledge societies (Braunerhjelm, 2007; Etzkowitz, 2002; O'Shea et al., 2004).

With regard to the initiatives and programs mentioned above, we can differentiate between the development of specific supportive institutional settings, which are required in this context on the one side and the concrete activities of supporting entrepreneurship by specific measures on the other side. The latter is a rather functional perspective on entrepreneurship whereas the former represents an institutional view. The institutional view on entrepreneurship is often defined as academic entrepreneurship (for a review of the literature on academic entrepreneurship see O'Shea et al., 2004). Since today, scholars have mainly focused on this perspective and investigated the entrepreneurial university as a specific institutional setting. In contrast to the institutional view, the rather functional perspective is considerably less investigated in the literature. The so-called "Sylter Runde" (www.sylter-runde.de), a German group of entrepreneurship researchers under the direction of Norbert Szyperski, labeled the rather functional perspective as scientific entrepreneurship. They define the scientific entrepreneur as "an entrepreneurial oriented promoter in the academic community, who creates or modernizes institutional structures through invention, innovation and transformation by using specific methods and instruments" (Sylter Runde, 2007 (translated by the authors); see also Magin, & von Kortzfleisch, 2008). Compared to the field of academic entrepreneurship, the functional research stream of scientific entrepreneurship lacks on systematic and comparative studies (Klandt, & Volkmann, 2006). Also, it lacks on the necessity of identifying, investigating, and evaluating the determinants of successful supporting initiatives for scientific entrepreneurship (Teasley, & Lockwood, 2009).

In response to the lack of systematization and the rather unrelated development of approaches to support scientific entrepreneurship, Magin and von Kortzfleisch (2008) categorize the different theoretical backgrounds of scientific entrepreneurship initiatives into four main approaches. Each of these four approaches stands for the description of rather implicit heuristics than comparable, well-conceptualized and evaluated theories. The aim of this categorization is not to evaluate and compare the different approaches against one another, but to make these different perspectives transparent and to learn from them in order to address scientific entrepreneurship effectively. At the same time, these different perspectives can be understood as a starting point for the integration of so far unrelated initiatives to support scientific entrepreneurship.

The first approach to support scientific entrepreneurship is named the task-role-matching approach (EFER, 2006). Initiatives are conceptualized by matching essential tasks with different roles, which again are assigned to different actors. This approach is based on the idea of division and specialization within multitask distributed initiatives. Another heuristic is made transparent by the deficit-oriented approach (Twaalfhoven, 2004). The first step here is to evaluate the initiatives and identify the current deficits. Based on this evaluation, opportunities for improvement are developed and can be implemented. The contributions which can be assigned to this rather theoretical approach do not refer to the conceptualization of single initiatives -like the task-role-matching approach does-, but to the more general aim of evaluating scientific entrepreneurship on aggregated levels like countries or educational systems (Twaalfhoven, 2004). A third approach is based on the idea of process-orientation. Measures within the initiative are dynamically ordered and built on top of one another. One example for this approach is the entrepreneurship education process developed by Ashmore (2005) and implemented by the Consortium for Entrepreneurship Research in the U.S. Based on the general management resource-based view of the firm within the economic context

(Penrose, 1959), the fourth approach adopts this principle to the context of scientific entrepreneurship. The underlying assumption of this approach is the possibility to characterize a company with regard to its resource combination. These resource combinations are assumed to be unique for each company and lead to respective competitive advantages. For scientific entrepreneurship this logic implies that initiatives which aim to support commercialization intentions among academics should focus on building unique resource combinations. Therefore the conceptualization of initiatives is based on the identification of central resource-fields and the implementation of specific measures and instruments to support startup teams in each of these fields (Volery, 2005; Burshtein, & Brodie, 2006).

As a summary, we will use the process-oriented as well as the competence-focused approach to scientific entrepreneurship when we distinguish between certain action fields for scientific entrepreneurship in the main thrust of this paper. The two other approaches become either an integral part of our chosen two approaches (like the role of a mentor by emphasizing the activity of mentoring) or the deficits are covered by the holistic characters of the examined action fields based on the two chosen approaches.

Open Source Software (OSS) Development

A few years ago researchers had a common understanding of OSS development as an activity mainly driven by altruistic programmers who voluntarily contribute to software projects. Meanwhile, it is more demanding to provide a common understanding due to OSS research activities in many areas like individual developer motivation, organization of communities, elaboration of business models, and firm involvement (Bonnaccorsi et al., 2006; Dahlander, & Wallin 2006; Fosfuri et al., 2008; Hertel et al., 2003; Krishnamurthy, 2005; Wu et al., 2007). Especially the advocacy

of firms in OSS development projects lead to new questions for both researchers and practitioners (Alexy, 2009; Fosfuri et al., 2008; Schaarschmidt, & von Kortzfleisch, 2009; von Krogh, & Spaeth, 2007).

Due to the radical change in how to produce software compared to established models, the first OSS projects like the Linux operating system attracted a lot of attention. Traditionally, software producing firms try to get their revenue by demanding monetary compensation for the use of their products -and therefore their intellectual property (IP)- through licensing agreements (Teece, 1986; de Paoli et al., 2008; Lichtenthaler, 2009). In contrast, open source licences allow every licensee not only to use the software but also to look into the source code and to manipulate it (Chen et al., 2007). This enables every user to contribute to the ongoing development of the product either by reporting bugs or by adding new functionalities.

Not only software developers were interested in this new phenomenon, also management science had a deep interest in why people participate and how those development processes work (Bitzer et al., 2007; Hertel et al., 2003; Iannacci, 2005; Lakhani, & von Hippel, 2003; O'Mahony, & Ferraro, 2007; Shah, 2006). Early research on OSS development focused on the question why people voluntarily contribute to software projects (Bagozzi, & Dholakia, 2006; Hertel et al., 2003). Accordingly, the main drivers originate in the open source ideology, the desire to satisfy own needs, career opportunities or reputation and status in a community (Franke, & von Hippel, 2003; Roberts et al., 2006; Shah, 2006). Similar aspects can be found in the literature on collective invention and user generated content (Piller, & Walcher, 2006; Osterloh, & Rota, 2007; von Hippel, & Katz, 2002; von Krogh, & Spaeth, 2007). Additionally, Lakhani & Wolf (2005) found out that not all of the so-called voluntary committers are just intrinsically motivated. According to their study 40% received direct or indirect financial compensation. It became obvious that firms play an important role in OSS development either as a hidden donator or as an active supporter (Dahlander, & Wallin, 2006; West, & O'Mahony, 2008).

At this point, the link to e-entrepreneurship (Kollmann, 2009) becomes obvious because firms play suddenly a specific role in otherwise self-organized communities of voluntary committers. Therefore, the following first part of the main thrust of our article will deal with OSS e-entrepreneurship.

OPEN SCIENTIFIC ENTREPRENEURSHIP

Issues, Controversies, Problems

OSS e-Entrepreneurship

The success of the OSS model in commercial settings encourages more and more firms to open their products which they formerly developed in a conventional way (Dahlander, 2007; Fosfuri et al., 2008; Lee & Cole, 2003; Lee et al., 2009). As argued before, firms are releasing their in-house developed software code to an open source community for several reasons; some of them in order to reduce costs, some of them to increase their creative potential, and others due to strategic and competitive reasons such as extending product lifetimes (Alexy, 2009; Fitzgerald, 2006; Fosfuri et al., 2008; Lerner, & Tirole, 2002; West, & Gallagher, 2006). Especially the latter case offers new ways to deal with rivalry.

Oftentimes, software producers face the problem that they still own IP but are unable to generate revenue anymore. Instead of shutting down all activities and leaving the market to competitors, with OSS firms are able to reveal their code to the public as in the case of Netscape and Mozilla or IBM and Eclipse. Using OSS in that way offers the potential to gain momentum again and prevents direct competitors to increase their market shares. Admittedly, this is only

suitable for firms with a large stock of IP, e.g. treasured in hard- or software patents (Fosfuri et al., 2008). Additionally, many projects which started as non-profit activities of small groups of software programmers were either supported or taken over by large software vendors. For example, IBM has contributed more than $ 1 billion to the development and promotion of Linux (Iansiti, & Richards, 2007). However, our hypothesis is that also scientific entrepreneurs who are active in software development can use the OSS model in order to release their innovative software code to an open source community for the reasons already mentioned before in order to commercialize on the basis of complementing business model. The presence or absence of a strong community -either a "user" or a "developer" community- has a deep impact on the question of how to benefit as an entrepreneur from freely revealing. West and Gallagher (2006) therefore distinguish between four major types of OSS commercialization, namely pooled R&D, spinouts, selling complements, and donated complements which here is transferred to e-entrepreneurship.

Pooled R&D is close to what other bodies of literature call R&D alliances or consortia (Kalaignanam et al., 2007; Mowery et al., 1996; Sampson, 2005; O'Mahony, & Vecchi, 2009; Vanhaverbeke et al., 2002). In the latter case, at least two firms are putting together their R&D effort to develop products according to their needs (Arranz, & de Arroyabe, 2004; Simonin, 2004; Singh 2008). Recent research shows that firms not only cooperate to save costs but also in cases of strong vertical relationships and high technological uncertainty (Sakakibara, 2002; West, & Gallagher, 2006). Moreover, firms donate money and/or development capacities to open source projects in order to boost the sales of related products. Typically, this kind of OSS donation concentrates on software designed for lower levels of the OSI reference model, like operating systems or web servers. The generation of revenue is realized through sale of applications built on top. Furthermore, using

OSS in the sense of pooled R&D helps to define open standards and to avoid incompatibility in inter-firm collaboration. However, pooled OSS R&D differs fundamentally from typical R&D consortia with regard to the non-controllability of evolved knowledge and the coordination challenge of integrating contributions from external participants.

In some cases, technology is no longer of use for a firm, especially when it does not contribute to the firm's performance or does not fit in the corporate strategy. Firms then stop maintaining a product and leave it to those who developed it. Freed from firms' stranglehold these spinoffs oftentimes are able to perform well as observable in the case of Xerox and Adobe (Chesbrough, 2003). If a firm continues to support the technology, it is possible to remain control and generate demand for related products or services. West and Gallagher (2006) call this kind of OSS approach "spinout".

Selling complements means that firms are giving away innovations for free to generate revenue from complementary goods (Boudreau, 2008; Eisenmann et al., 2008). With regard to literature on marketing, this is nothing fundamentally new. Razor blades as well as ink cartridge generate more revenue than the printer or the shaver, respectively. Firms use two-sided pricing strategies and lose money on the hardware to profit from the complementary good. In the case of separated target groups, like the video game or web server industry where firms address consumers as well as developers, a two-sided pricing strategy can increase the overall profit although "consumers of one segment in a two-sided market need never acquire the complement" (Gallaugher, & Wang, 2002, p. 307). Economides and Katsamakas (2006) show that especially in the case of open platforms the preference for application variety determines the industry's success and provide an explanation for Microsoft's dominance in the operating systems market.

Closely related to the concept of selling complements is the concept of *donated complements*. Although firms do not receive direct revenues neither through the core product nor by selling complementary goods, they can focus on customer loyalty by open their products for user adjustments. As it is not possible to gain from the openness directly, firms create an infrastructure to invite people to participate and hoping for increased publicity (West, & Gallagher, 2006).

To sum up, all four of these above mentioned approaches to OSS commercialization can also be used by scientific entrepreneurs who want to be active in the context of OSS software development.

Scientific Entrepreneurship Opened Up

The four theoretical approaches to scientific entrepreneurship which we described above each of them explains scientific entrepreneurship from just one point of view. To enable improvements in the direction of getting an in-depth access to certain potential fields of action, it is necessary to integrate these perspectives in a single framework. Magin and von Kortzfleisch (2008) propose such an integrative framework, based on the process and competence perspective (as argued above) and then based on a qualitative text analysis of the self-description of more than 120 initiatives in German-speaking Europe (see figure 1). This framework includes 13 action fields which than allow to put respective methods and tools in place in order to support scientific entrepreneurship. These 13 action fields are also our starting point so as to systematically think about the potentials to open the activities within these action fields up.

In order to discuss the potentials of an (more) open perspective for scientific entrepreneurship, it is useful to firstly provide an access to the concept of openness, hereby looking at the underlying principles of OSS development. Then, we will use these insights in order to hypothetically provide

Figure 1. Integrative approach to scientific entrepreneurship

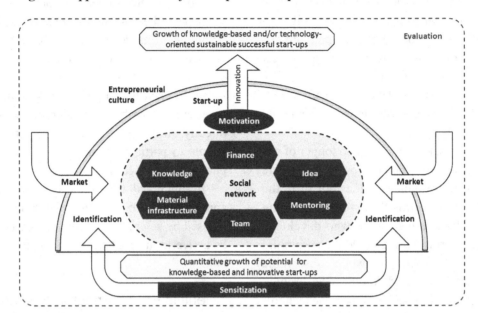

recommendations for rethinking the activities for the single actions fields of scientific entrepreneurship (Magin, & von Kortzfleisch, 2008) under the perspective of openness.

The basic principle which stands behind OSS development is the paradigm of openness per se (for references see the second part of this main thrust of the article). More precisely, as a first approximation it stands for certain characteristics inspired by related terms like permeability, unfinishedness, collaboration and exchange or boundlessness (Weber, 2005). These characteristics lead to certain must-haves of software products, i.e. for example they must be accessible and described in a manner that they are comprehensible and understandable, it must be possible that they can be copied, distributed and used unboundedly and mainly without costs, and that they can be modified and then shared again in this new altered form free of any restrictions. These must haves do not only stand for a generic OSS approach but represent also an open learning process for both, active co-developers and users. In the following, these characteristics of openness in OSS development

are implicitly used in order to rethink the action fields of scientific entrepreneurship.

Sensitizing students or researchers for entrepreneurship is widely accepted as a strategic need for universities and other schools of higher education or research institutions, supported by respective political will and initiatives. In a broader sense, these initiatives suggest the establishment of what they call an entrepreneurship culture in order to foster the positive values and believes of entrepreneurship and to make it visible also for the purpose of sensitization. Although sensitization per se has implicitly build-in the strategy of being open, still there are possibilities to further open these initiatives. Two recommended directions in order to open sensitization in addition are, firstly a more active participation from the side of the target groups with regard to the design of the respective initiatives and secondly a more holistic approach in order to comprehensively address marginal groups like women, migrants, handicapped person or university departments of faculties with just little nearness to the idea of starting own companies. The first recommendation can for example be supported by Web 2.0-based platforms in the pure sense of open innovation, the second would need to identify the generic structure which all of these marginal groups have in common in order to overcome the patchwork of single initiatives as we can find them today.

With regard to identification, there is an obvious need for systematically identifying potential ideas which might become a business success. Normally, so-called idea scouts follow a strict sequence of activities, starting with personally talking to students or researchers with the aim to detect and discuss potent ideas, than involving experts like patent attorneys if necessary, than involving technology transfer departments and further specialists with technology or branch expertise, and finally integrating other network resources which can support the entrepreneurial process. From the open point of view, we like to suggest that this procedure should be more agile and incremental allowing for circular rebounds and more version-oriented acting instead of planning. Also and again, the community of idea owners should be motivated and enabled to "talk" about their ideas by themselves, e.g. on open Web 2.0-based platforms.

Potent **ideas** are based on the creativity of students and researchers within a field of tensions between degree of innovation and market risk. Normally, especially researchers have to be creative and innovative considering their topics because otherwise they do not get any additional resource funding to work on their hypothesis or they have no possibility to publish their scientific insights as being unique. Typically, they are working in an ivory tower which guarantees their absolute expertise. Here, we see a lot of potential to open this working attitude towards true interdisciplinary research. Then, this interdisciplinary research approach can also be assigned to the study and work of students. Finally, an open discussion of the **innovation** potentials could lead to a more reflective appraisal of market success.

Sound **teams** are the basis for successful start-ups. Most often, potential team member use well established contacts in order to build a team accrue from stable friendship-based relationships or family connections. Without questioning the positive effects of trust-based close relationships, we like to recommend a more open perspective also here because we see a huge gap between what is used as contacts and what could be used. Therefore, our recommendation again goes into the direction of using Web-based matching platforms in order to systematically bring team members together. A prerequisite for team matching are profiles of potential team members and respective profiles of the demands on the searching side.

Social networks are open by definition. As we all know, everybody has his or her own private or business social network connecting people by mutual personal characteristics or interests. Also, there are many Web 2.0-based platforms on the internet which facilitate potential social communication and network access and extension, like facebook, studiVZ oder XING just to name a few. What is missing, however are dedicated open networks for entrepreneurship. Again, entrepreneurship related networks do exist but they are either informal or very much specialized, e.g. on business plan competitions, venture capitalists or alike. Our recommendation here is to virtually bring more and especially more different entrepreneurship related stakeholders together by using the potentials which the internet offers today. This includes also the necessary task of mentoring or coaching, respectively.

Looking at necessary competencies in order to start companies brings with it the need to provide platforms for education and training. Many universities or other institutions of higher education have these platform for scientific entrepreneurship in place because it is part of their business. What is also observable is that content and tools which are offered are very similar and that a high degree of redundancy can be found with regard to institutions and regions. Also, potential entrepreneurs often do not know what kind of institution offers what type of educational service or support. Our recommendation in terms of openness goes into the direction of more transparency over the existing contents and tools on the one hand side and more coordination of offerings on the other side. In addition, we suggest an open evaluation of all these measures so that improvements are made possible, e.g. again by using Web 2.0-oriented platforms.

What was written about necessary competencies holds also true for access to financial resources as another absolute condition in order to act entrepreneurial and also for access to rooms: The respective offers are widely distributed, redundant and sort of similar out of which the need for more transparency and coordination becomes obvious from the view of potential founders.

From a behavioral perspective, motivation is the absolute condition in order to start companies. Especially, the process of purposive striving which is called volition (Kielhofner, 2008) is a particular challenge for entrepreneurs always facing uncertainty and with it potential failure. In order to keep the level of willpower or commitment high, several psychological instruments can be used like negative and positive emotional control or cognitive control (Gollwitzer, 1999). These instruments allow for crossing the threshold of uncertainty which impedes the necessary entrepreneurial course of action. The commitments to these courses of action are even more important with regard to successful entrepreneurship in comparison to the traceable wish for uncertainty reduction as the theory of effectuation clearly points out (Sarasvathy, 2008). Since all of the above mentioned behavioral concepts, i.e. motivation, volition and effectuation are strongly related to sensitization and entrepreneurship culture our respective recommendations in terms of openness need also to be considered here. Beyond that we suggest to expand the usefulness of social networks with regard to their motivational effects

by making visible that others are really "doing it", i.e. founding companies.

To summarize, the generic characteristics of OSS development provide major hints in order to rethink action fields of scientific entrepreneurship and to point to certain benefits of opening-up. What needs to be discussed at the end of the main thrust of this article, however are the implications of a more reflective in-depth investigation of the concept of openness and its benefits but also its downsides which mark the tensions between an open or closed design perspective in general (von Kortzfleisch, 2003).

Solutions and Recommendations

Openness as a general concept can be found in diverse research disciplines like psychology, pedagogy, politics, mathematics or systems theory. Within all of these research disciplines openness is always demarcated to the opposite concept of closeness, i. e. attempts to specify the qualities of openness are throughout relative.

Tensions Between an Open and Closed Design Pattern

In order to identify relative distinguishing marks of openness, we substantiate the distinction between an open design pattern and a closed design pattern by following Popper's (1962; 1968) sociological differentiation between the "open society" and "closed society". Basic assumptions and distinguishing characteristics of both positions are then elaborated as follows (see also von Kortzfleisch, 2003): firstly from a sociological point of view, secondly, from the view of philosophy of science; finally, from the perspective of learning or knowledge transfer, respectively. The sociological substantiation extends on Popper's argumentation. The substantiation form the philosophy of science perspective looks for the underlying basic assumptions of the two opposing concepts. The knowledge transfer perspective acknowledges

Figure 2. Distinguishing marks from the perspective of sociology

Downsides (closed)	Benefits (closed)	Basic assumptions of closed society	Distinguishing marks (sociology)	Basic assumptions of open society	Benefits (open)	Downsides (open)
Isolated groups Oppressing hierarchy Discrimination of minorities	Stable roles Elites	*Imparity*	**Valance**	*Parity*	Equal treatment Liberty Equal opportunities	Unclear role allocation Egalitarianism
Stagnation Manipulation	Rest Low adjustment efforts Unity Trust	*Uniformity of interests*	**Nature of interest**	*Diverseness of interests*	Progress over time Creativity thru acceptance of different opinions	Disquietness High coordination demands Conflicts Distrust
Compulsion Narrowing	Exterior safety Orientation Sense of well-being in solidarity	*Collective*	**Social orientation**	*Individual*	Free will Independence	Selfishness Disorientation Solitude

that knowledge and its transfer become a common reference point for the positive connotation of openness in the before mentioned context as being also an open learning process.

With a first view on the sociological substantiation, Popper's (1962; 1968) idea of the open society is mainly influenced by the critical philosophy of Immanuel Kant. At the same time, he criticizes Platon's descriptive sociology which in Popper's view represents the closed society as the enemy of the open society. Distinguishing marks of both societies are valency, nature of interest, and social orientation (Boener, & Gebert, 1999). The corresponding basic assumptions of the closed society and the open society facing each other and the respective benefits and downsides on both sides are summarized in Figure 2.

Looking at the substantiation from the philosophy of science perspective researchers consciously or unconsciously, explicitly or tacitly lay certain basic beliefs under their research efforts. These basic beliefs can be differentiated into ontological, epistemological, and methodological assumptions (Guba, & Lincoln, 1994; Orlikowski, & Baroudi, 1991). Ontology comprises knowledge about the nature, the essence of reality or being. Epistemology aims at criterions of the design and evalua-

tion of valid knowledge. Finally, methodology scrutinizes the suitability of research methods and instruments with a view of the knowledge researchers expect to find out about. The corresponding basic assumptions of the closed design pattern and the open design pattern facing each other and the respective benefits and downsides on both sides are summarized in Figure 3.

Referring to the distinction between an individual and an organizational knowledge basis (Kim, 1993) interaction processes within the scope of knowledge transfer can be distinguished according to the individual, group and (inter-) organizational learning level. The analysis of knowledge transfer on the individual level is guided by three main streams in the field of learning psychology (Bower, & Hilgard, 1997), i.e. behaviorism, cognitivism and constructivism. From the perspective of behaviorism, learning takes place as passive absorption of knowledge. Within the well-known stimulus-organism-response (SOR) model, the organism remains a black box. In contrast to the explication of learning as stimulus-response-connections, cognitivism literally opens the black box. In the foreground of interest stand the internal cognitive processes of the human brain. Learning takes place as active processing of knowledge.

Figure 3. Distinguishing marks from the philosophy of science perspective

Downsides (closed)	Benefits (closed)	Basic assumptions of closed science	Distinguishing marks (philosophy of science)	Basic assumptions of open science	Benefits (open)	Downsides (open)
Fixed adherence Immovability Consolidation of powers	Durability Stability Identity	*Predetermined legalities*	**Ontology**	*Will as principle of being*	Flexibility Selfliberation	Impermanence Mess Arbitrariness Loss of identity
Implementation bondage of ideas Scientificially conditioned doctrine	Clearness Guarantee Certainty Finality	*Error-freeness of knowledge*	**Epistemology**	*Error-proneness of knowledge*	Permeability for new ideas Critical rationality	Ambiguity Uncertainty Fear Tentativeness
Ignorance Distance	Concentration Certainty	*Observation*	**Methodology**	*Participation*	Joining in Nearness Exchange of thoughts	Being mixed up Distraction Giving up on own objectives

Constructivists however show the way to a much more open pattern of learning than behaviorists and also cognitivists do. From a constructivist's perspective learning takes place as an active blueprint or design of knowledge, based on personal interpretations of reality by the individual learners (Duffy, & Jonassen, 1992).

Knowledge transfer on the group level is a process of socialization between an individual and a community (Berry et al., 1992). By this process, the human being gets the disposing capacity to become a social personality by learning the way of thinking and acting of a society. From the perspective of a closed design pattern, this process is just one-sided from the community or group towards the individual. However from the viewpoint of an open design pattern, this process is reciprocal.

Finally, knowledge transfer on the (inter-) organizational level assumes transfer between collective knowledge bases and is also designated as acculturation. "Acculturation comprehends those phenomena which result when groups of individuals having different cultures come into continuous first-hand contact, with subsequent changes in the original cultural patterns of either or both groups" (Redfield et al., 1936, p. 149). Processes of acculturation follow three phases

according to Berry (1980): Contact, conflict, and consolidation. These three phases are influenced by (a) the readiness of the partners to collaborate and (b) the respective intentions to get one's own values and mental frameworks through. As a result, the closed design pattern or "deculturation" is characterized by partners who are not willing to collaborate. They give up a common knowledge base. Problem solutions will become individualized. Existing levels of knowledge are defended. On the other hand the respective intentions to get one's own values and mental frameworks through are low. The open design pattern or "integration" is characterized by a high niveau of readiness to collaborate. Furthermore, the respective intentions to get one's own values and mental frameworks through are high. This is only possible if parts of a new sub-culture are created without getting totally rid of the respective existing cultures of each of the partners.

To sum up, the corresponding basic assumptions of the closed design pattern and the open design pattern facing each other and the respective benefits and downsides on both sides with a view of knowledge transfer are summarized in Figure 4.

Against the backdrop of benefits of the open design pattern and benefits of the closed design

Figure 4. Distinguishing marks from the knowledge transfer / learning perspective

Downsides (closed)	Benefits (closed)	Basic assumptions of closed learning	Distinguishing marks (learning theory)	Basic assumptions of open learning	Benefits (open)	Downsides (open)
Linearity of learning Non-consideration of different knowledge types Little consideration of social environment and of learner individuality	Fast progress at learning facts Observable and partly explainable input-output-relations Possibility of knowledge transfer to similar issues	*Knowledge absorption and processing*	**Individual learning**	*Knowledge production and construction*	Networked and holistic thinking Creation of complex problem solution competences Strong consideration of personal differences of learners and of environmental connectedness	High complexity of designing respective learning environments Responsibility shift from teachers to learners
Disappointment of individual expectations against group behaviour	Completion of individual expectations against group behaviour	*One-sided*	**Group learning**	*Reciprocal*	Completion of individual and group expectations	Disappointment of individual and group expectations
Little possibility for jointly developing new ideas Future collaboration is not likely to happen	Little duration of negotiation between partners	*Deculturation*	**(Inter-) Institutional learning**	*Integration*	Common development of new ideas Future collaboration is likely to happen	High duration of negotiation between partners

pattern, the desire to implement a design pattern which will take advantage of the benefits of a completely open and closed design pattern at the same time becomes obvious. Such a desire, however would try to dialectically combine irreconcilable facts. Therefore, in the following it will be focused on finding agreements via reciprocal concessions between the open and the closed design pattern in the sense of "trialectic" (Ford, & Ford, 1994) compromises.

Tension Balancing Strategies Between an Open and Closed Design Pattern

Each of the two design patterns facing each other comprise benefits and downsides. From the perspective of downsides of each pattern, the respective other pattern becomes very attractive because of its benefits. Within this "logic of attraction" (Ford, & Ford, 1994), balancing can be interpreted as "active circulation of energy, rather than a static state of balance" (Ford, & Ford, 1994, p. 766). It is the recurring balance of tensions between benefits and downsides of each of the patterns which comes to the fore as a necessity for scientific entrepreneurship design.

At least four balancing strategies for scientific entrepreneurship can be distinguished (von Kortzfleisch, 2003): The first balancing strategy (1), the complete change between the open and closed design pattern in succession for the hole field of scientific entrepreneurship has to be rejected. The reason is that the purer one design pattern is implemented, the more the other pattern becomes attractive which will mobilize destroying forces in order to change the prevailing pattern into the attractive one. The second balancing strategy (2) considers the open and closed design pattern at the same time, however distributed in different action fields of scientific entrepreneurship. This strategy also has to be rejected for the same reason as the first strategy because it would only shift the problem to lower levels of analysis. The third balancing strategy (3) implements cut down parts of the open and closed design pattern at the same time in certain action fields of scientific entrepreneurship. The problem is that one has to compromise on the full potential of each of the two design patterns in terms of realizing all respective benefits, highly. The fourth balancing strategy (4) combines selected bundles of basic assumptions of the open design pattern with selected bundles of basic assumptions of the closed design pattern at the same time. The selection of bundles of basic assumptions follows the distinction between sociology, philosophy of science, and knowledge transfer. This strategy seems to be the most successful. Universites, for example might try to implement benefits of the open design pattern for scientific entrepreneurship in their incubating departments from the sociological perspective, like freedom, further development, or independence and from the knowledge transfer perspective like individuality, support for the group and collaboration interest in order to reach the objective of innovation leadership. At the same time they might also try to implement opportunities of the closed design pattern from the philosophy of science perspective, like durability, clearness, and concentration in order to provide a certain orientation and constancy for creative entrepreneurial development processes. However, there still remains a high potential for tensions because within each of the bundles of basic assumptions, the opportunities will not only be realized to the extreme but also the downsides become more attractive (see also the first balancing strategy).

As a consequence, an extension of the fourth balancing strategy is suggested here (5) to disintegrate each of the three bundles of basic as-

sumptions from the perspectives of sociology, philosophy of science, and knowledge transfer and to consider the balancing potential of each of the basic assumptions, separately for scientific entrepreneurship. In principal, we emphasize the benefits of the open design pattern following a "conception of the good", for example in the sense of the political liberalism of Rawls (1993), which obviously marks a normative position which cannot be justified for good. This normative position comes close to the "jazz metaphor" which Orlikowski and Hofman (1997) named the "improvisational model for change management." At the same time we are aware that we have to integrate some benefits of the closed design pattern in order to stabilize and not falling into the trap of the first balancing strategy. The nucleus of this fifth balancing strategy is to make quantitative and/or qualitative adjustments between both design patterns, still trying to realize –quantitatively and/or qualitatively– more benefits of the open design pattern than of the closed design pattern for scientific entrepreneurship.

FUTURE RESEARCH DIRECTIONS

The remaining question of how much openness and closeness and in which quality cannot be answered at this stage of the research because it needed respective measurement criteria which are not available, at the moment and in-depth empirical validation. Still, balancing also means carefully approaching compromises which can only be tried out individually within the practice of scientific entrepreneurship itself. The framework suggested here can be looked upon as a first starting point for providing systematic access to potential efficiency criteria and related empirical investigations.

The need for a tension-balancing management for scientific entrepreneurship is motivated by the fact that the tensions between the open design pattern and the closed design pattern are not so obvious in scientific entrepreneurship practice as they were elaborated before. In order to establish the needed transparency, the following demands of a tension-balancing scientific entrepreneurship management have to be fulfilled: Firstly, to perceive scientific entrepreneurship as fundamentally und permanently tense (Quinn, & Cameron, 1988; Van de Ven, & Poole, 1995); secondly, to recognize the tensions as attracting forces of the respective benefits and downsides of the open design pattern and the closed design pattern facing each other; thirdly, to sufficiently argue the advantages of the open design pattern against the downsides of this pattern in order to realize the related entrepreneurship-related benefits but also to be aware of that one has to pay "prices" (in terms of potential downsides) in order to realize these opportunities; fourthly, to work out the opportunities of the closed design pattern as a tensions-reducing stabilizer for the open design pattern; fifthly, to realize the potential downsides of the also attractively looking closed design pattern in order to reduce the attractiveness of this pattern; finally, to integrate actual trends in scientific entrepreneurship into the respective benefits and downsides of both design patterns in order to potentially influence their implementation and to be aware of potential change. In connection with the sixth demand, Robey, Whishart and Rodriguez-Diaz (1995), for example compare the closed concept of business process reengineering with the open concept of organizational learning and suggest the stabilizing integration of business process reengineering into the dominating concept of organizational learning. A dominant open learning perspective for scientific entrepreneurship would initiate the analog and could provide a new theoretical orientation for future research on open scientific entrepreneurship.

CONCLUSION

This article brought together two relevant research streams under the roof of openness: software development and scientific entrepreneurship. Open software development leads to the OSS development approach which by itself broaches the issue of scientific entrepreneurship in the sense of e-entrepreneurship. Open scientific entrepreneurship is motivated by the potential benefits of openness for the identified 13 relevant action fields supporting the foundation of new companies in the academic community. The general and in-depth discussion of openness shows that openness per se not only leads to benefits but also to potential downsides. In so far it is necessary from the perspective of successful scientific entrepreneurship management to decide on a balancing strategy between the open and closed design pattern. Overall, we still suggest a primarily open design approach for scientific entrepreneurship but we also acknowledge that stabilizing elements of a closed design pattern are necessary in order to efficiently balance the tensions between these two design models for the success of scientific entrepreneurship at the end.

REFERENCES

Alexy, O. (2009). *Free Revealing. How Firms Can Profit From Being Open*. Wiesbaden, Germany: Gabler.

Anderseck, K. (2004). Institutional and Academic Entrepreneurship: Implications for University Governance and Management. *Higher Education in Europe*, *29*(2), 193–200. doi:10.1080/0379772042000234820

Arranz, N., & de Arroyabe, J. (2008). The choice of partners in R&D cooperation: An empirical analysis of Spanish firms. *Technovation*, *28*, 88–100. doi:10.1016/j.technovation.2007.07.006

Bagozzi, R. P., & Dholakia, U. M. (2006). Open Source Software User Communities: A Study of participation in Linux user groups. *Management Science, 52*(7), 1099–1115. doi:10.1287/mnsc.1060.0545

Berry, J. W. (1980). Acculturation as Varieties of Adaption. In A. M. Padilla (Ed.), *Theory, Models and Some Findings* (pp. 9-25). Boulder, CO: Westview Press.

Berry, J. W., Poortinga, Y. H., Segall, M. H., & Dasen, P. (1992). *Cross-Cultural Psychology: Research and Applications*. Cambridge, MA: Cambridge University Press.

Bitzer, J., Schrettl, W., & Schröder, P. J. H. (2007). Intrinsic Motivation in Open Source Software Development. *Journal of Comparative Economics, 35*, 160–169. doi:10.1016/j.jce.2006.10.001

Boerner, S., & Gebert, D. (1999). The Open and the Closed Corporation as Conflicting Forms of Organization. *The Journal of Applied Behavioral Science, 35*(3), 341–359. doi:10.1177/0021886399353006

Bok, D. (2003). *Universities in the Marketplace: The Commercialisation of Higher Education*. Princeton, NJ: Princeton University Press.

Bonaccorsi, A., Giannangeli, S., & Rossi, C. (2006). Entry Strategies Under Competing Standards: Hybrid Business Models in the Open Source Software Industry. *Management Science, 52*(7), 1085–1098. doi:10.1287/mnsc.1060.0547

Boudreau, K. (2008). Opening the platform vs. opening the complementary good? The effect on product innovation in handheld computing. *Social Science Research Network*, abstract 1251167. Retrieved August 24, 2008, from http://papers.ssrn.com/sol3/papers.cfm?abstract_id=1251167&CFID=12533725&CFTOKEN=38798633

Bower, G. H., & Hilgard, E. (1997). *Theories of Learning*. Upper Saddle River, NJ: Prentice-Hall.

Braunerhjelm, P. (2007). Academic entrepreneurship: social norms, university culture and policies. *Science & Public Policy, 34*(9), 619–631. doi:10.3152/030234207X276554

Burshtein, S., & Brodie, S. (2006, July). *Developing a modular entrepreneurship education program: The MILK Framework*. Paper presented at the Intent2006 Conference, Sao Paulo, Brazil.

Chen, M. X., Iyigun, M., & Maskus, K. E. (2007). General Public Licensing and the Intensity of Aggregate Software Development. *Economics of Innovation and New Technology, 16*(5-6), 451–466. doi:10.1080/10438590600914452

Chesbrough, H. (2003). The Logic of Open innovation: Managing Intellectual Property. *California Management Review, 45*(3), 33–58.

Chesbrough, H. W., Vanhaverbeke, W., & West, J. (2008). *Open Innovation: Researching a New Paradigm*. New York: Oxford University Press.

Dahlander, L. (2007). Penguin in a new suit: A tale of how de novo entrants emerged to harness free and open source software communities. *Industrial and Corporate Change, 16*(5), 913–943. doi:10.1093/icc/dtm026

Dahlander, L., Frederiksen, L., & Rullani, F. (2008). Online Communities and Open Innovation: Governance and Symbolic Value Creation. *Industry and Innovation, 15*(2), 115–123. doi:10.1080/13662710801970076

Dahlander, L., & Wallin, M. W. (2006). A man on the inside: Unlocking communities as complementary assets. *Research Policy, 35*, 1243–1259. doi:10.1016/j.respol.2006.09.011

David, P. (1997). The knowledge factor: A survey of universities. *The Economist, 4*(10), 13–17.

De Paoli, S., Teli, M., & d'Andrea, V. (2008). Free and Open Source Licences in Community Life: Two empirical cases. *First Monday, 13*(10). Retrieved July 24, 2009, from http://www.maurizioteli.eu/publications/DePaoliTeliDandreaIn-Progress.pdf

De Rond, M., & Bouchikhi, H. (2004). On the Dialectics of Strategic Alliances. *Organization Science, 15*(1), 56–69. doi:10.1287/orsc.1030.0037

Duffy, T. M., & Jonassen, D. H. (Eds.). (1992). *Constructivism and the Technology of Instruction: A Conversation.* Hillsdale, NJ: Erlbaum.

Economides, N., & Katsamakas, E. (2006). Two sided competition of proprietary vs. Open source technology platforms and implications for software industry. *Management Science, 52*(7), 1057–1071. doi:10.1287/mnsc.1060.0549

EFER (Ed.). (2006). *20 Centers of Dynamic Entrepreneurship.* München, Germany: EFER.

Eisenmann, T. R., Parker, G., & Van Alstyne, M. (2008). *Opening platforms: How, when and why?* (Working Paper Series 09-030). Cambridge, MA: University of Cambridge, Harvard Business School.

Etzkowitz, H. (2002). *MIT and the Rise of Entrepreneurial Science.* London: Routledge.

Feller, I. (1990). Universities as engines of growth: they think they can. *Research Policy, 19,* 335–348. doi:10.1016/0048-7333(90)90017-Z

Fitzgerald, B. (2006). The Transformation of Open Source Software. *MIS Quarterly, 30*(3), 587–598.

Ford, J. D., & Ford, L. W. (1994). Logics of Identity, Contradiction, and Attraction in Change. *Academy of Management Review, 19*(4), 756–785. doi:10.2307/258744

Fosfuri, A., Giarratana, M., & Luzzi, A. (2008). The Penguin Has Entered the Building: The Commercialization of Open Source Software Products. *Organization Science, 19*(2), 292–305. doi:10.1287/orsc.1070.0321

Franke, N., & Von Hippel, E. (2003). Satisfying heterogeneous user needs via toolkits: The case of the apache security software. *Research Policy, 32,* 157–178. doi:10.1016/S0048-7333(02)00006-9

Gallaugher, J., & Wang, Y.-M. (2002). Understanding Network Effects in Software Markets: Evidence from Web Server Pricing. *MIS Quarterly, 26*(4), 303–327. doi:10.2307/4132311

Geisler, R. L. (1993). *Research and Relevant Knowledge: American Research Universities since World War II.* Oxford, UK: Oxford University Press.

Gollwitzer, P. M. (1999). Implementation intentions: Strong effects of simple plans. *The American Psychologist, 54*(7), 493–503. doi:10.1037/0003-066X.54.7.493

Guba, E. G., & Lincoln, Y. S. (1994). Competing Paradigms in Qualitative Research. In N. K. Denzin & Y. S. Lincoln (Ed.), *Handbook of Qualitative Research* (pp. 105-117). Thousand Oaks, CA: Sage.

Hertel, B., Niedner, S., & Herrmann, S. (2003). Motivation of software developers in open source projects: An Internet-based survey of contributions to the Linux kernel. *Research Policy, 32,* 1159–1177. doi:10.1016/S0048-7333(03)00047-7

Iannacci, F. (2005). Coordination processes in open source software development: The Linux case study. *Emergence: Complexity and Organization, 7*(2), 20–30.

Iansiti, M., & Richards, G. (2007). The Business of Free Software: Enterprise Incentives, Investment and Motivation in the Open Source Community (Working Paper Series 07-028). Cambridge, MA: University of Cambridge, Harvard Business School.

Kalaignanam, K., Shankar, V., & Varadarajan, R. (2007). Asymmetric New Product Development Alliances: Win-Win or Win-Lose Partnerships? *Management Science, 53*(3), 357–374. doi:10.1287/mnsc.1060.0642

Kielhofner, G. (2008). Volition. In G. Kielhofner (Ed.), *Model of Human Occupation: Theory and application* (pp. 33-509). Baltimore, MA: Lippencott Williams & Wilkins.

Kim, D. H. (1993). The Link Between Individual and Organizational Learning. *Sloan Management Review, 35*(1), 37–50.

Klandt, H., & Volkmann, C. (2006). Development and Prospects of Academic Entrepreneurship Education in Germany. *Higher Education in Europe, 31*(2), 195–208. doi:10.1080/03797720600940880

Kollmann, T. (2009). E-Entrepreneurship: *Grundlagen der Unternehmensgründung in der Net Economy.* Wiesbaden, Germany: Gabler.

Krishnamurthy, S. (2005). An Analysis of Open Source Business Models. In J. Feller, B. Fitzgerald, S. A. Hissam, & K. R. Lakhani (Eds.), *Perspectives on Free and Open Source Software* (pp. 279-296). Cambridge, MA: MIT Press

Lakhani, K. R., & Von Hippel, E. (2003). How Open Source software works: "Free" User-to-User Assistance. *Research Policy, 32,* 923–943. doi:10.1016/S0048-7333(02)00095-1

Lakhani, K. R., & Wolf, R. G. (2005). Why Hackers Do What They Do: Understanding Motivation and Effort in Free/Open Source Software Projects. In J. Feller, B. Fitzgerald, S. A.Hissam, & K. R. Lakhani (Eds.), *Perspectives on Free and Open Source Software* (pp. 279-296). Cambridge, MA: MIT Press.

Lee, G., & Cole, R. (2003). From a Firm-Based to a Community-Based Model of Knowledge Creation: The Case of the Linux Kernel Development. *Organization Science, 14*(6), 633–649. doi:10.1287/orsc.14.6.633.24866

Lee, S.-Y. T., Kim, H.-W., & Gupta, S. (2009). Measuring open source software success. *Omega, 37*(2), 426–438. doi:10.1016/j.omega.2007.05.005

Lerner, J., & Tirole, J. (2002). Some simple economics of open source. *The Journal of Industrial Economics, 50*(2), 197–234.

Lichtenthaler, U. (2009). (forthcoming). Intellectual Property and Open Innovation: An Empirical Analysis. *International Journal of Technology Management.*

Magin, P., & Von Kortzfleisch, H. F. O. (2008, December). *Scientific Entrepreneurship engineering: Exploratory Study and Conceptual Framework for Methods and Tools to Support Entrepreneurial Activities in Universities.* Paper presented at the International Innovation Conference in Complex Social Systems, Dublin, Ireland.

Miner, A., Eesley, D., Devaughn, M., & Rura-Polley, T. (2001). The magic beanstalk vision: commercializing university inventions and research. In C. Schoonhoven, & E. Romanelli (Eds.), *The Entrepreneurial Dynamic* (pp. 109-146). Stanford, CA: Stanford University Press.

Mowery, D., Oxley, J., & Silverman, B. (1996). Strategic Alliances and Interfirm Knowledge Transfer. *Strategic Management Journal, 17,* 77–91.

Murray, F., & Stern, S. (2005). *Do Formal Intellectual Property Rights Hinder the Free Flow of Scientific Knowledge? An Empirical Test of the Anti-Commons Hypothesis.* (NBER Working Paper No. 11465). Cambridge, MA: University of Cambridge, National Bureau of Economic Research, Inc.

O'Mahony, M., & Vecchi, M. (2009). R&D, Knowledge Spillovers and Company Productivity Performance. *Research Policy*, 38, 35–44. doi:10.1016/j.respol.2008.09.003

O'Mahony, S., & Ferraro, F. (2007). The emergence of Governance in an Open Source Community. *Academy of Management Journal*, 50(5), 1079–1106.

O'Shea, R., Allen, T. J., O'Gorman, C., & Roche, F. (2004). Universities and Technology Transfer: A Review of Academic Entrepreneurship Literature. *Irish Journal of Management*, 25(2), 11–29.

Orlikowski, W. J., & Baroudi, J. J. (1991). Studying Information Technology in Organizations: Research Approaches and Assumptions. *Information Systems Research*, 2(1), 1–28. doi:10.1287/isre.2.1.1

Orlikowski, W. J., & Hofman, D. J. (1997). An Improvisational Model for Change Management: The Case of Groupware Technologies. *Sloan Management Review*, 38(2), 11–21.

Osterloh, M., & Rota, S. (2007). Open Source development – Just another case of collective invention? *Research Policy*, 36, 157–171. doi:10.1016/j.respol.2006.10.004

Penrose, E. T. (1959). *The Theory of the Growth of the Firm*. New York: Wiley.

Piller, F. T., & Walcher, D. (2006). Toolkits for idea competitions: a novel method to integrate users in new product development. *R & D Management*, 36(3), 307–318. doi:10.1111/j.1467-9310.2006.00432.x

Popper, K. R. (1962). *The Open Society and Its Enemies: Volume 1: The Spell of Plato*. London: Routledge.

Popper, K. R. (1968). *The Open Society and Its Enemies: Volume 2: The High Tide of Prophecy: Hegel, Marx and the Aftermath*. London: Routledge.

Quinn, R. E., & Cameron, K. S. (1988). Paradox and Transformation: Toward a Theory of Change in Organization and Management. Cambridge, MA: Ballinger.

Rawls, J. (1993). *Political Liberalism (The John Dewey Lectures in Philosophy)*. New York: Columbia University Press.

Redfield, R., Linton, R., & Herskovits, M. (1936). Memorandum for the Study of Acculturation. *American Anthropologist*, 38, 149–151. doi:10.1525/aa.1936.38.1.02a00330

Roberts, J. A., Hann, I. H., & Slaughter, S. A. (2006). Understanding the motives, participation, and performance of open source software developers: A longitudinal study of the Apache project. *Management Science*, 52(7), 984–999. doi:10.1287/mnsc.1060.0554

Robey, D., Wishart, N. A., & Rodriguez-Diaz, A. (1995). Merging the Metaphors for Organizational Improvement: Business Process Reengineering as a Component of Organizational Learning. *Accounting . Management & Information Technology*, 5(1), 23–39. doi:10.1016/0959-8022(95)90012-8

Runde, S. (2007). *Memorandum der 18. Sylter Runde: Scientific Entrepreneurship: Was sollen Wissenschaftler noch alles richten?* Retrieved from http://www.sylter-runde.de

Sakakibara, M. (2002). Formation of R&D Consortia: Industry and Company Effects. *Strategic Management Journal*, 23(11), 1033–1050. doi:10.1002/smj.272

Sampson, R. C. (2005). Experience effects and collaborative returns in R&D alliances. *Strategic Management Journal*, 26(11), 1009–1031. doi:10.1002/smj.483

Sarasvathy, S. D. (2008). *Effectuation: Elements of Entrepreneurial Expertise*. Cheltenham, UK: Edward Elgar.

Schaarschmidt, M., & Von Kortzfleisch, H. F. O. (2009, December). *Divide et Impera: The Integration of External Knowledge in Firm-Driven OSS Development - An Empirical Investigation*. Paper submitted to the International Conference on Information Systems (ICIS), Phoenix, Arizona.

Shah, S. (2006). Motivation, Governance, and the Viability of Hybrid Forms in Open Source Development. *Management Science, 52*(7), 1000–1014. doi:10.1287/mnsc.1060.0553

Siegel, D. S., Waldman, D., Atwater, L., & Link, A. (2003). Commercial knowledge transfers from universities to firms: Improving the effectiveness of university industry collaboration. *The Journal of High Technology Management Research, 14*(1), 111–133. doi:10.1016/S1047-8310(03)00007-5

Simonin, B. (2004). An Empirical Investigation of the Process of Knowledge Transfer in International Strategic Alliances. *Journal of International Business Studies, 35*(5), 407–427. doi:10.1057/palgrave.jibs.8400091

Singh, J. (2008). Distributed R&D, cross-regional knowledge integration and quality of innovative output. *Research Policy, 37*, 77–96. doi:10.1016/j.respol.2007.09.004

Teasley, R., & Lockwood, F. (2009, March). *Unlocking Academic Entrepreneurship: The Role of Technology Maturation*. Paper presented at the workshop on Centers, Universities, and the Scientific Innovation Ecology, Arlington, Virginia.

Teece, D. J. (1986). Profiting from technological innovation: Implications for integration, collaboration, licensing and public policy. *Research Policy, 15*, 285–305. doi:10.1016/0048-7333(86)90027-2

Twaalfhoven, B. W. M. (2004). *Red Paper on Entrepreneurship*. Hilversum, The Netherlands: European Foundation for Entrepreneurship Research (EFER).

Van de Ven, A. H., & Poole, M. S. (1995). Explaining Development and Change in Organizations. *Academy of Management Review, 20*(3), 510–540. doi:10.2307/258786

Vanhaverbeke, W., Duysters, G., & Noorderhaven, N. (2002). External Technology Sourcing Through Alliances or Acquisitions: An Analysis of the Application-Specific Integrated Circuits Industry. *Organization Science, 13*(6), 714–733. doi:10.1287/orsc.13.6.714.496

Vesper, K. H., & Gartner, W. B. (1997). Measuring Progress in Entrepreneurship Education. *Journal of Business Venturing, 12*(5), 403–421. doi:10.1016/S0883-9026(97)00009-8

Volery, T. (2005). Ressourcenorientierter Ansatz von Entrepreneurship: Ressourcen sind der Kern des Wettbewerbsvorteils. *KMU Magazine, 9*, 12–14.

Von Hippel, E. (1994). Sticky Information and the Locus of Problem Solving. *Management Science, 40*, 429–439. doi:10.1287/mnsc.40.4.429

Von Hippel, E., & Katz, R. (2002). Shifting Innovation to Users via Toolkits. *Management Science, 48*(7), 821–833. doi:10.1287/mnsc.48.7.821.2817

Von Kortzfleisch, H. F. O. (2003). *Organizational Design of Information Technology in the Context of E-Business: Methodology for Balancing Tensions between Benefits and Drawbacks*. Paper published on CD-ROM, in Proceedings of the Thirty-Sixth Annual Hawaii International Conference Systems Sciences, HICCS-36.

Von Krogh, G., & Spaeth, S. (2007). The open source software phenomenon: Characteristics that promote research. *The Journal of Strategic Information Systems, 16*, 236–253. doi:10.1016/j.jsis.2007.06.001

Weber, S. (2005). *The Success of Open Source*. Boston, MA: Harvard University Press.

West, J., & Gallagher, S. (2006). Challenges of open innovation: The paradox of firm investment in open source software. *R & D Management*, *36*(3), 319–331. doi:10.1111/j.1467-9310.2006.00436.x

West, J., & Lakhani, K. (2008). Getting Clear About Communities in Open Innovation. *Industry and Innovation*, *15*(2), 223–231. doi:10.1080/13662710802033734

West, J., & O'Mahony, S. (2008). The Role of Participation Architecture in Growing Sponsored Open Source Communities. *Industry and Innovation*, *15*(2), 145–168. doi:10.1080/13662710801970142

Wu, C.-G., Gerlach, J. H., & Young, C. E. (2007). An Empirical Analysis of Open Source Software Developers' Motivations and Continuance Intentions. *Information & Management*, *44*, 253–262. doi:10.1016/j.im.2006.12.006

ADDITIONAL READING

Alves, J., Marques, M., Saur, I., & Marques, P. (2007). Creativity and Innovation through Multidisciplinary and Multisectoral Cooperation. *Creativity and Innovation Management*, *16*(1), 27–34. doi:10.1111/j.1467-8691.2007.00417.x

Andersen, B., & Konzelmann, S. (2008). In a search for a useful theory of the productive potential of intellectual property rights. *Research Policy*, *37*, 12–28. doi:10.1016/j.respol.2007.02.024

Ashmore, C. (2005). *Entrepreneurship Everywhere: The Case for Entrepreneurship Education*. Columbus, OH: The Consortium for Entrepreneurship Education.

Bullinger, H.-J., & Scheer, A.-W. (Eds.). (2002). *Service Engineering*. Berlin, Germany: Springer.

Dahlander, L. (2005). Appropriation and appropriability in open source software. *International Journal of Innovation Management*, *9*(3), 259–285. doi:10.1142/S1363919605001265

Dahlander, L., & Magnusson, M. G. (2008). How do make Firms Make Use of Open Source Communities? *Long Range Planning*, *41*, 629–649. doi:10.1016/j.lrp.2008.09.003

Deetz, S. (1996). Describing Differences in Approaches to Organization Science: Rethinking Burrell and Morgan and their Legacy. *Organization Science*, *7*(2), 191–207. doi:10.1287/orsc.7.2.191

El Sawy, O. A., Malhotra, A., Gosain, S., & Young, K. M. (1999). IT-Intensive Value Innovation in the Electronic Economy: Insights from Marshall Industries. *Management Information Systems Quarterly*, *23*(3), 305–335. doi:10.2307/249466

Fershtman, C., & Gandal, N. (2007). Open Source Software: Motivation and restrictive Licensing. *Journal of International Economics and Economic Policy*, *4*(2), 209–225. doi:10.1007/s10368-007-0086-4

Fleming, L., & Waguespack, D. (2007). Brokerage, Boundary Spanning, and Leadership in Open Innovation Communities. *Organization Science*, *18*(2), 165–180. doi:10.1287/orsc.1060.0242

Gao, Y., & Madey, G. (2007). Network Analysis of the Sourceforge.net Community. In J. Feller, B. Fitzgerald, W. Scacchi, & A. Sillitti (Eds.), *Open Source Development, Adoption and Innovation* (pp. 187-200). Boston, MA: Springer.

Grewal, R., Lilien, G. L., & Mallapragada, G. (2006). Location, Location, Location: How Network Embeddedness Affects Project Success in open Source Systems. *Management Science*, *52*(7), 1043–1056. doi:10.1287/mnsc.1060.0550

Haeflinger, S., Von Krogh, G., & Spaeth, S. (2008). Code Reuse in Open Source Software. *Management Science*, *54*(1), 180–193. doi:10.1287/mnsc.1070.0748

Katz, J. A. (2003). The Chronology and Intellectual Trajectory of American Entrepreneurship Education 1876-1999. *Journal of Business Venturing*, *18*(2), 282–300. doi:10.1016/S0883-9026(02)00098-8

Keller, R. T. (2001). Cross-Functional Project Groups in Research and New Product Development: Diversity, Communications, Job Stress, and Outcomes. *Academy of Management Journal*, *44*(3), 547–555. doi:10.2307/3069369

Laursen, K., & Salter, A. (2006). Open for Innovation: The role of Openness in Explaining Innovation Performance among U.K. Manufacturing Firms. *Strategic Management Journal*, *27*, 131–150. doi:10.1002/smj.507

Miller, D. J., Fern, M. J., & Cardinal, L. B. (2007). The Use of Knowledge for Technological Innovation within Diversified Firms. *Academy of Management Journal*, *50*(2), 308–326.

Mockus, A., Fielding, R., & Herbsleb, J. D. (2002). Two case studies of open Source software development: Apache and Mozilla. *ACM Transactions on Software Engineering and Methodology*, *11*, 309–346. doi:10.1145/567793.567795

Nonaka, I., & Takeuchi, H. (1995). *The Knowledge-Creating Company: How Japanese Companies Create the Dynamics of Innovation*. Oxford, UK: Oxford University Press.

O'Mahony, S., Cala Diaz, F., & Mamas, E. (2005). *IBM and Eclipse* [Working Paper Series 9-906-007]. Cambridge, MA: University of Cambridge, Harvard Business School.

O'Shea, R., Allen, T. J., Morse, K. P., O'Gorman, C., & Roche, F. (2007). Delineating the anatomy of an entrepreneurial university: the Massachusetts Institute of Technology experience. *R & D Management*, *37*(1), 1–16. doi:10.1111/j.1467-9310.2007.00454.x

Robey, D., & Boudreau, M.-C. (1999). Accounting for the Contradictory Organizational Consequences of Information Technology: Theoretical Directions and Methodological Implications. *Information Systems Research*, *10*(2), 167–185. doi:10.1287/isre.10.2.167

Stewart, K. J., & Gosain, S. (2006). The Impact Of Ideology On Effectiveness In Open Source Software Development Teams. *Management Information Systems Quarterly*, *30*(2), 291–314.

Timmons, J. A., & Spinelli, S. (2003). *New Venture Creation, Entrepreneurship for the 21st century*. Boston, MA: McGraw Hill.

Von Krogh, G., Spaeth, S., & Lakhani, K. R. (2003). Community, joining, and specialization in open source software innovation: A case study. *Research Policy*, *32*, 1217–1241. doi:10.1016/S0048-7333(03)00050-7

Chapter 12
Open Source:
Collaborative Innovation

Avi Messica
The College of Management, Rishon-Lezion, Israel

ABSTRACT

This chapter reviews the current status of Open Source (OS) and provides new insights into the prerequisites of the OS process as well as the profile of OS contributors. Moreover, it extends the scope of possible business models such to augment those that exist or were already discussed in the past. While the term OS was coined in the context of software development and redistribution, this chapter presents and discusses the concept of OS to include any Open Collaborative Innovation in both software and hardware.

INTRODUCTION

The term Open Source (OS) was coined, as implied, to represent a software code that is usually distributed in the form of a high level programming language – in contrast to machine, compiled, code – and is freely copied, redistributed as well as modifiable by users at no cost. This description differentiates OS software from Freeware software that can be freely copied/ downloaded from the web for personal use but is distributed as (binary) executable machine code and most commonly restricted to personal use. It also differs from public

domain software that is available to the public and is uncontrolled (more formal definition is available at http://www.opensource.org/docs/osd). The purpose of this chapter is to review the current status of OS and to provide new insights into the prerequisites of the OS process as well as the profile of OS contributors. I also extend the scope of possible business models such to augment those that exist or were already discussed in the past. While the term OS was coined in the context of software development and redistribution, in this chapter I will present and discuss the concept of OS to include any Open Collaborative Innovation in both software (SW) and hardware. Having said that, the vast majority of examples still come from software applications

DOI: 10.4018/978-1-61520-597-4.ch012

although few nineteenth's century examples of HW collaborative invention were discussed by Allen (1983). Note that I make the distinction between invention and innovation. Formally speaking, invention is the first conception or occurrence of a new idea of a product, a process or a service while innovation is the realization of an invention. Open source relates to the latter process and should be clearly distinguished from invention. It is involved with the use of existing framework for the development of new products or services rather than inventing such.

Open source have already penetrated our lives far more than most of us perceive. There are examples in business (Linux, MySQL) finance (XBRL reporting format), information technology and communications (ITC) including the Internet (from Apache web server to Facebook widgets) and mobile communications (e.g. Iphone's App-Store, Moblin.org), image editing (GIMP), R&D and services (e.g. Utest's quality assurance community) and more. The LAMP (Linux, Apache, MySQL, PHP/Python/Perl) stack can be viewed as the spearhead of OS products but OS sparks are spread all over. In the arts front we find OS examples in video (e.g. Xvid compression format), animation creation (blender.org, artis.imag.fr etc.), music making (digitalmuiscian.net for online collaboration real-time music recording), collaborative knowledge development and learning (Knownet.com), movie making (Drupal.org) and screen writing (plotbot.com). In game development, Acclaim.com have opened its multi-player PC game design process to the OS community and claims to harness the brainpower of 60,000 individuals for development. Open source in hardware is by far more difficult to develop since real objects cannot be redistributed over the Internet. However, hardware designs can be shared and improved by a collaborative process. Such example is the Arduino USB board. Moreover, there are many forums on the web in which users present discuss and improve hardware designs that range from electronic circuit design (e.g. forums.

parallax.com) to mechanical design and naturally to hardware-dedicated software (www.arduino.cc for example).

In general, variety of restrictions might be placed on the usability and distribution of an OS product and these depend on the license dictated by the originator. Such restrictions are not limited only to the use or distribution of the code but also to other relevant issues such as documentation, support, warranty, user interface, backward compatibility and the like. The web site freshmeat.net lists 46,000 OS projects, 410,000 registered users and about 60 types of OS licenses. SourceForge.net lists 180,000 projects and roughly two million registered users. The most common OS license is the General Public License (GPL) that permits the copying and distribution of OS software, modifying it or a portion of it, making derivatives or embedding it under a Reciprocity/Copyleft license that conveys all rights to any other recipient of the software. Namely, any person who redistributes software under GPL – with or without modifications - cannot add restrictions to deny other people the above-mentioned central freedoms and must pass along the freedom to further copy, modify and redistribute the software. The motto of the OS movement is free in the context of freedom and should not be confused with free of charge. The legal aspects of OS are presented and more broadly discussed toward the end of the chapter.

Naturally, OS projects are expected to flourish in ITC-software related environments because they can leverage on connectivity to result in voluntary collaborative innovation. As such, OS collaborative innovation relies on and comprises of three components: knowledge sharing, active contribution and distribution. By active contribution I specifically refer to code origination or modification. Passive contributors may also play an important role. A passive contributor might, for example, provide a wish list of features (therefore he/she helps in defining product specifications and actually takes a product management role), report about bugs (testing and quality assurance), send it to a colleague or a friend (distribution channels) or post it on his/her web site or blog etc. OS collaboration is a relatively new form of collaborative innovation that extends the conventional boundaries of knowledge sharing. Knowledge sharing is categorized into three categories. These are: Knowledge Dependence (where individuals are knowledge lacking in order to accomplish tasks), Knowledge Independence (where individuals can access other individuals knowledge) and Knowledge Interdependence (where individuals actively share their knowledge and collaborate with other individuals). OS extends beyond these definitions to deliver a collaborative effort that results in a realization of a new application, a product, an expression of art and the like. As such, OS may be viewed as a new level of knowledge sharing that manifests in the active generation of a usable product, process or service. In this sense, one can refer to – and make the distinction between mere knowledge sharing to collaborative innovation – passive vs. active OS contributors that might be considered as a reference. Namely, OS is characterized by the voluntary willingness of contributors to actively invest the time and efforts that are required in order to realize a usable product than merely spreading and sharing knowledge. It is this voluntary motivation that pushes collaborative innovation beyond the realm of software coding to the hardware environment and products as well.

The History of Open Source

Many OS researchers have traced back the origins of OS, as a form of collaborative software development, to the late sixties of the last century in academic institutions such as MIT and Berkeley as well as in large corporate research facilities such as Bell Labs and Xerox. It is true that at that time, a time in which software development was at infancy, programmers did share their code with colleagues from other organizations. However, it is safe to say that the cornerstone of OS in its present form was set by MIT's Richard Stallman's Free Software Foundation (FSF). Frustrated by AT&T's increasing enforcement of its intellectual property (IP) rights over UNIX in the early eighties, Stallman (2007), back then with the Artificial Intelligence Lab at MIT, had founded the FSF as a counter reaction to the then rising trend of corporations to establish a business model based on a closed source. Stallman founded the FSF in order to support and promote the development of free software that is viewable and modifiable by users. Moreover, the foundation's charter was to promote the development and distribution of free software at nominal cost or no cost at all. As such the FSF introduced a formal license dubbed General Public License (GPL is also known as copyleft, www.gnu.org) that was aimed to prevent potential claims for intellectual property rights on collaboratively developed software, as many programmers felt at the time that AT&T did with Unix.

One of the first applications of the GPL was for the GNU operation system in 1983 (GNU is a recursive acronym that stands for "GNU is Not Unix"). The condition for a user to be allowed to improve, modify and distribute GNU was that he/she had to agree and abide by the GPL license. The GPL reciprocity/copyleft principle that allows for users to copy, modify, enhance and redistribute OS software while replicating the license terms is one of the first demonstrations of viral propagation among software users. Moreover, the GPL is strict in the sense that even if the original OS code is integrated with or embedded in another proprietary code then the new code should be redistributed under the GPL license. Namely, the user cannot impose any restriction on following users and he/she has to redistribute and license the new code as an OS code and under the GPL terms. The GPL license was instrumental in harnessing the contribution of many individuals by setting up a framework in which software developers send a project leader or a program management group their software modifications or bug fixes of the OS code. These are then reviewed, approved and integrated into the official version of the OS code.

In 1985 Stallman published his GNU manifesto (www.gnu.org) asking developers to participate and support the GNU operating system (Unix compatible), providing the motivation and incentive for users to contribute by listing a long list of justifications and describing the benefits that all computer users will gain from the project. However, it was not until the early nineties, in which there was a dramatic growth in OS activity, that OS projects started taking off. Most known is the GPL Linux operating system that was developed by Linus Torvalds in 1991 (utilities and libraries were taken from GNU) and that was already adopted by commercial companies in 1993 (Redhat. com). Torvalds still continues to lead the further development of the Linux kernel and Stallman still heads the Free Software Foundation that supports GNU components. Furthermore, contributors and corporations routinely develop new components that deliver complementary functionality to both the Linux kernel or to user applications and libraries. There are commercial Linux vendors (Redhat. com) that distribute the Linux kernel and either sell complementary components or provide support and management services that are based on OS code. In view of the dominance of Linux in the OS world then the FSF have gained monopolistic position that is equivalent to Microsoft's dominance in the closed source world or that of Google's in the web (GPL comprises about 60% of all licenses types, www.freshmeat.net).

Recent years have put OS software in the mainstream side-by-side to closed source code and pushed OS code to the forefront of business and commercial arenas. On November 2006 Sun Corporation announced that its popular JAVA programming language, its compiler, libraries, development kit (JVM) and associated tools would be available as OS under the second version of the GPL license (GPL-v2). At the same time Microsoft and Novell have signed a deal (with respect to patents) aimed at permitting users of Novell's open-source products to run on both Windows and Linux-based systems. Other giant corporations have also joined the OS world. For example, Oracle lists more than fifty OS projects (http://oss.oracle.com/projects/) on its web site and its open-source scripting language (PHP) is one of the world's most popular Web applications programming languages. Oracle has also committed to helping the PHP community by delivering stable production environments, native integration with the Oracle database as well as PHP support in the Oracle application server.

Lastly, on December 2008, several hundreds of OS contributors have met at Google's HQ in Mountain View California to discuss how to further develop and promote the four years old Linux-based Ubuntu operating system that is threatening Microsoft dominance in the developing countries (more than ten million users). Linux-based Ubuntu is challenging Microsoft's Windows by addressing the home computers market in contrast with the traditional approach of Linux-based operating systems that target the servers market. Roughly half of Google's employees use Ubuntu that, needless to point out, is free of charge. Dell has already started shipping Ubuntu installed computers in 2007 and IBM has decided to deliver an Ubuntu-based package that will compete directly with Microsoft. There are about 5,000 volunteers who distribute information about Ubuntu over the web and 38,000 contributors have committed to translate it to different languages. International Data Group (IDC) research estimates that about 11% of American businesses use Ubuntu. In Europe, the Ministry of Macedonia provides 180,000 copies of the operating system to pupils and the Spanish education system uses 195,00 copies. The French police as well as National Assembly installed 80,000 copies of Ubuntu. Since Ubuntu is based on an earlier version of a Linux-based operating system, Debian, then it is also supported by a thousand contributors that work on the Debian project. Linux-based Ubuntu represents the first significant threat on Microsoft's Windows hegemony at home computers.

THE PREREQUISITES FOR OPEN SOURCE

Prerequisites

The tribal campfire has gone global and interactive. However, OS activity should not be taken for granted. For an OS project to conclude successfully there are several prerequisites that have to be met. Based on literature analysis as well as interviews with industry professionals it is possible to draw upon and compile the following prerequisites.

Literature Review

Even though many OS researchers trace back the origins of OS to the late sixties of the last century, OS in its present form of a computer-network based collaborative development process is less than thirty years old.

An extensive discussion about the incentives and motivation of OS contributors is available. The vast majority of OS contributors are volunteers and only few are actually employed for working on OS projects (e.g. by firms like Red Hat, Novell or in the academy). Lerner and Tirole (2002) extensively discussed what motivates skilled programmers to dedicate time and efforts for no immediate monetary reward. Economic answers to this question have been put forth also by some non-economic commentators and include altruism, fun, intellectual challenge, or making political statement. Lerner and Tirole point out that the altruism hypothesis does not explain voluntary contribution and why free riding would be less prevalent in OS than in other industries. They point out that we should be skeptical of these explanations since it is unclear why contributors cannot find these challenges in paid employment. They emphasize the existence of delayed payoffs

from open source projects and classify them into two different incentives: the career concern incentive, which relates to future job offers or future access to the venture capital market, and the ego gratification incentive, which stems from a desire for peer recognition. Holmstrom (1999) and von Engelhardt (2008a) provide useful insights in this regard, also based on economic theory. Johnson (2001) presents a game-theoretic model of behavior that borrows from the theory of private provision of public goods. His model explains why purely self-interested programmers may wish to improve an OS program even when they are aware that there are other programmers who may make the same improvement and even when they cannot coordinate their actions. Lerner and Tirole (2002), Ghosh and Prakash (2000) and Ghosh (2004) try to portray a profile of an OS contributor but they do not clearly make the distinction of an active contributor (i.e. one that rewrites the code) from a passive contributor (e.g. on that reports bugs). The elitist view is discussed by Mockus et al. (2002) with respect to the development of the Apache server. There is evidence that OS contributors are driven by social signaling among the OS community (Dempsey et al., 1999). Von Hippel and von Krogh (2003) propose that OS presents a novel innovation model, they dubbed private-collective, in which economic players invest their own private resources to produce public goods. These contributors gain benefits through extended functionality either as user innovators or as lead users who tailor the software according their own need. Baldwin and Clark (2006) put their finger on the intangibility of information technology (IT) products, their lack of economics of scale and that with IT there is no rivalry in consumption. These aspects allow for OS ITC products to be developed and distributed at relatively low costs and moreover contribution does not preclude consumption on part of the contributor. On the contrary, given an active OS community, a contributor will be rewarded in variety of aspects. Hars and Ou (2001) and Osterloh and Frey (2000) apply a generalized approach by classifying motivation into intrinsic (immediate need satisfaction) and extrinsic (mostly monetary). Intrinsic motivation was also studied by Tyler and Blader (2000) with respect to pro-social motivation. In this context Faraj and Wasko (2001) and Wellman and Gulia (1999) view the OS community as a gift-culture vs. the more common exchange-culture that we are used to. This is also in parallel with intrinsic motivation in which contributors perceive coding or debugging as fun (Csikszentmihalyi 1996; Lakhani et al. 2005). Reputation motives were analyzed by Lerner and Tirole (2002) and Moon and Sproull (2000) who found that contributors can gain monetary compensation by signaling their expertise and skills set through working on OS projects. These are in sync with commercial motives on part of companies such as Red Hat, Novell, Sun and the like (Kogut and Metiu, 2001). The co-existence of intrinsic and extrinsic incentives is vital to the success of OS as pointed out by Franck and Jungwirth (2002).

Raymond (2000) identifies seven different business models that range from selling complementary software or services to OS code to selling content generated with an OS platform, these models will be listed and discussed in the following. However, very little theoretical or empirical work has been done on corroborating the viability of these business models, the competition between firms and the effect of firms using these business models on existing closed source software firms. An economic analysis of the interaction between a closed source monopolist and an open source community is provided by Mustonen (2003) who analyzed the case of an OS program that is a substitute for a program provided by a profit-maximizing monopolist. A more heuristic analysis of the economical effects of the open source movement on closed source firms is provided by Lerner et al. (2006). Advocates of OS such as Raymond (2000) argue that it is a superior model of software development in terms of the speed of development and bugs fixing due to the

large number and highly motivated programmers. Lerner and Tirole (2002) discussed the extent to which closed source firms can emulate the incentives structure provided by OS and conclude that closed source firms will never be able to replicate the visibility of performance of open source and that will always reduce the incentives and motivation of programmers in closed source firms. Acs and Audretsch (1987) as well as Fink (2003) provide a detailed discussion about OS in the context of innovation, firms' business activity and market transformation from economic perspective. Fink's key point is that the value of closed source software diminishes over time due to erosion by competition and adopts the Schumpeterian view of creative destruction (Schumpeter, 1975). Open source software (OSS) further accelerates this creative destruction process. The merits of OSS development are that there is no upfront sunk cost, distribution is at marginal cost or even zero and the development time is shortened in comparison with closed source. Lerner and Tirole (2002) also provide a thorough discussion of the OS business model. An interesting account, as well as refreshing, of OS economy vs. closed source is presented by Raymond (2000) based on his observations of the Linux kernel development process and his experience in managing the fetchmail OS project. Raymond contrasts two different OS development models. The Cathedral model in which source code is available with each software release but the code is developed between releases and restricted to an exclusive group of developers such as was the case in the GNU Emacs development and the *Bazaar* model in which the code is developed over the World Wide Web (WWW) and is publicly accessible. The most common OSS-based business model is the provision of complementary services and products, mostly in the form of software management and maintenance (e.g. Red Hat, Novell) that are not provided by the OS community. Another business model for commercial firms is to take an active role in OSS development as was engaged by HP in the adoption of Linux to its Reduced Instructions Set Code operating system (RISC) architecture in order to increase product penetration and usage. Another model also used by HP was to release the code of its Razor Blade server and rely on generating additional revenue from consulting services. Sun release of Java was also a move in this direction and there are more. Lastly, there is also a model of selling complementary products to the OSS (e.g. components, add-ons, libraries and the like) including hardware (e.g. VA Linux). It is interesting to note that in a recent survey among 300 OS developers (Redmond Developer News, January 20 2009) it was found that many of them plan to distribute their OSS as services over the web (Internet cloud) via Google's App engine, Amazon's cloud platform, Microsoft's or IBM's clouds. Moreover, the vast majority of OSS products – roughly seventy percents – were for the enterprise (thirty percents reported their products as "other") such as business applications, development tools, software infrastructure and system management. It is also reported that in the virtualization front more than half of the OS developers rely on a Linux-based operating system and so is for their database choice (more than fifty percents choose MySQL).

Von Hippel (2001) discussed the must-have conditions for the formation and the characteristics of an OS process. It is usually related to IT products (non-physical products). There must be a community of contributors that holds the power and talent to innovate (Harhoff et al., 2003) and project modularity (Baldwin and Clark, 1997) is of necessity in view of the distributed nature of the development process as discussed by Langlois (2002), Narduzzo and Rossi (2005) and Sanchez and Mahoney (1996). OS development was described as collective invention by Meyer (2003), Nuvolari (2002) and others. However, OS development does not meet the criteria of *invention* and as such is actually less restricted by definition. As Narduzzo and Rossi (2005) state, OS is clearly related to the stage of realization

and most OS projects have clearly avoided the realm of new architectural designs and adopted existing architectures. They also point out that the modularity characteristic is evidential of a non-exploratory phase and that in fact OS can flourish only in a very well understood development environment. This understanding is also supported by studies of Langlois (2002) and Ethiraj and Levinthal (2004).

Del Amo's (2007) thesis is an excellent account of variety of OS licenses. It provides a thorough review of the main features of most popular open source licenses, the consequences of using them and a discussion about controversial issues (the thesis itself is licensed under the Creative Commons license). In general, the broad spectrum of licensing ranges from copyleft (free) to copyright (proprietary). However, OS distribution licenses (Frost et al., 2005) can be classified into two major classes of either reciprocity (namely, a GPL-based work must be redistributed under a GPL) type or permissive type (redistribution of a work night be on terms that are more restrictive than those of the original license). The Berkeley Software Distribution License (BSD) is the dominant permissive type. It is tolerant to derivative work that is based on a BSD protected code and imposes no further legal constraints (older versions of the BSD license required that a derivative work would place a credit note to UC Berkeley). The key feature of the BSD license is that any code that is derived from a BSD protected code can be distributed as proprietary and as such opens the door for the derived code to be sold and protected commercially (Weber, 2003). The General Public License is of the reciprocity/copyleft type. It was conceived (in 1983) under the notion that a source code should always be accessible and modifiable in order to nurture and facilitate collaborative innovation. The key feature of the GPL license is the requirement that all subsequent developments that are based on a GPL protected code will also be distributed under the GPL license and terms (reciprocity). Therefore developers are effectively being forced to forego a majority of their potential benefits and they are only able to gain benefits or compensation from complementary goods (Frost et al., 2005; Fink, 2003). Noteworthy, the term *derivative work* refers to any program that is either integrated, embedded or bundled with the GPL protected code. However, it is possible to code standalone software (e.g. ASP, SaaS) that interacts with a GPL protected code but is not part of it (Frost et al., 2005) and therefore is not subjected to the GPL terms. The flip side is that any enhancement, improvement, modification etc. of GPL protected code is subjected to the GPL license terms. The GPL license enforces democratization among subsequent generations of developers on equal rights basis. Namely, when a contributor contributes his/her IP rights to an OS code he/she is protected forever and assured that followers will not take possession over his/her contribution. Moreover, others will not be able to exploit his/her contribution for commercial purposes thus eliminating free riders and ensuring that the contribution made was for the good of the public. Moreover, GPL established the fruitful coexistence between commercial organizations and OS contributors by defining a No-Entry IP zone such that the former will not take advantage of the goodwill of OS developers (Franck, & Junqwirth, 2002; von Engelhardt 2008b).

Connectivity

Connectivity is a must-have in order to accomplish any collaborative innovation task. It is an enabling factor that is by far more important than any other prerequisite. Connectivity enables us to reach and discover talent. The evolution of the Internet has facilitated the public exposure of extremely talented individuals such as Norwegian Jon Johansen, a self-trained software engineer who quit high school to spend time on a DeCSS code and whom published the first DeCSS descrambler (DeCSS is a computer code that provides method of decrypting CSS-encrypted DVDs, cracking the encryption allows for converting a large DVD file into compressed MPEG-4 or DivX files that can be transmitted over the Internet) and opened a Pandora box with respect to DVD protection. In the absence of connectivity, it is quite certain that none of the works of extremely talented individuals that live somewhere on the globe would have gone public (in variety of fields as well and not necessarily limited to OS). So the importance of connectivity is twofold. First, it allows the discovering of and connecting with talented individuals all around the globe and as such greatly extends the pool of talents that is available thereby lifting a geographical constraint. Second, it allows for the public distribution of the work of these individuals. So connectivity provides accessibility to human talent on top of serving as a distribution channel for the work of that talent. Philosophically speaking, creativity leverages on connectivity for a viral distribution of itself.

Environment

In a manner similar to a formal (that is, paid) software development environment that may include support programs, code libraries, and the like a suitable OS environment should be available to contributors. Such environment should provide the required tools for programmers such as source code editor, compiler/interpreter, build automation tools, debugger etc. In formal software development an Integrated Software Development (IDE) is designed to maximize programmers' productivity by providing a features set that most closely matches the programming needs of developers. A similar infrastructure should be available for OS contributors as well in order to remove potential barriers for contribution.

Contributor Costs

A major factor for the buildup of an active OS community is cost. This factor is also one of the factors that act as barrier for the progress of collaborative innovation in hardware as well as other types of projects. From an OS programmer perspective, software development should bear either zero or negligible costs. In fact, it is benefits non-deprivation that an OS contributor is concerned with rather than costs. However, focusing on costs, an OS project software development is characterized by time, skill and intellectual property contributions. Namely, a contributor devotes both her time and skills\talent and occasionally original IP. These contributions may be viewed as "soft money" contribution in the sense that a contributor does not invest his/her own out-of-pocket money – referred to as "hard money" – in the project. However, he/she does insist on the benefits non-deprivation principle (either consciously or unconsciously). Namely, he/she would not like his/her contribution to generate monetary compensation, commercial or other material benefits for another person or organization without his/her being compensated as well. Enters Stallman and the FSF with the GPL. The cornerstone of the GPL License is the prevention of the violation of the benefits non-deprivation principle from materializing in OS projects. It is the protection of this principle that assures an OS contributor that others will not exploit his/her voluntary contribution of time and efforts for profit making at his/her expense. Moreover, GPL not just assures contributors that their contribution will not get commercially exploited but that any derivative of their contribution or next generation development will maintain the benefits non-deprivation principle as well. Relieving this uncertainty removes doubts and barriers that an OS contributor might have. He/she is "insured" that his/her contribution will be for the public good and his/her opportunity cost is not exploited by others.

Distribution Cost

Even though transportation costs have greatly diminished over the past twenty years, product distribution is still an issue and certainly when mass distribution is concerned. This naturally puts a high barrier for collaborative innovation on hardware projects that cannot be transported among users with no cost. Software projects however, can. Since all users pay for an Internet connection for purposes other than collaborative innovation, than those who are OS contributors can readily distribute their contribution at practically no cost. In the absence of distribution cost then the last barrier for collaborative innovation has been removed as far as digital files are concerned. There is emerging evidence for collaborative innovation in music composing, film scripting, animation creating, video filming and editing, remote education and knowledge sharing, PC/Web games development and more. The OS framework of product development is extremely suitable to any ITC product that can be converted into a digital file. With the advent of Internet storage, users can now store their works on remote servers, in many cases free of charge. The proliferation of cable/ADSL broadband networks is also of importance. The combination of fast distribution with storage capacity of digital file-based ITC products has no equivalence in other sectors such as the automobile industry, robotics & automation, consumer electronics and the like. As such, OS has a much deeper impact on the ICT sector than other sectors and collaborative innovation spreads and gains recognition in the ITC sector more than any other sector as well.

Community

The existence of community of professionals and non-professionals that can either develop or use the OS product is a must-have. When there exists a large community of users, then an OS project initiator can draw enough contributors out of it. This relies merely on a law of large numbers. The more users there are, the larger the pool of talent and the higher the number of volunteers. Given that the probability that a user, be it professional or non-professional, will act and voluntarily contribute to a project is relatively low, then the larger the users population is, the larger the OS community is. Volunteering is culture related. Therefore, if it was geographically constrained then each project might have been country-dependent and limited. However, having connectivity allows for ITC projects to leverage on pooling of global talent and overcome local cultural barriers by going global. Having roughly one billion of Internet users, this means that it is possible to form large communities (e.g. Ubuntu) and harness the brainpower of masses of individuals to an extent never done before and moreover far beyond the reach of any single organization. Namely, attracting several thousands of programmers to voluntarily contribute to a code is not out of the ordinary. Taking the average global entrepreneurship rate (7%-10%) as representative for voluntary spirit it is possible to estimate the potential global OS community to range from seventy to one hundred million contributors. Among these, only a small fraction possesses programming capabilities. If only one of thousand individuals has a programming capability then communities as large as 100,000 contributors may exist (Acclaim.com may serve as good example).

The above listed prerequisites are central to the formation of collaborative innovation. The list also addresses the general question raised by Lerner and Tirole (2002) whether the OS model can be transferred to other industries. There are examples of co-development of technology or products between for-profit and non-profit organizations in a spectrum of models that range from innovation networks to joint ventures (e.g. the European Union's FPx or the American DARPA programs). There are also examples for user-driven (open) innovation. However, Lerner and Tirole (2002) illustrate the difficulty of replicating the OS model in other industries by considering the case of Biotechnology. They conclude that the tasks that are involved in developing a biotech product are costs and managerial prohibitive. They

also add that projects that require large capital investment are also likely to be excluded from the collaborative innovation framework. This case analysis as well as other conclusions is explained by the discussed prerequisites list.

The Profile of an OS Contributor

As pointed out by Frost et al. (2005), programmers consider coding as a form of expression. This is in contrast to Lerner and Tirole's (2002) analysis that tries to frame an OS contributor in an economical context. In order to further drill down into the nature of OS contributors I used the hackers community as benchmark. Even though hackers and crackers act on the dubious side of the OS world, their motivation nonetheless seems to parallel that of OS contributors. Frost et al. point to a Boston Consulting Group survey (BCG, 2001) that examined eleven main motivational factors of OS contributors and concluded that more than forty percents of the respondents chose "Intellectual Stimulation" and "Improving skill" as the two most popular choices. The third motivational factor was ideological in nature and was the belief that all code should be freely shared (about thirty five percent of respondents have marked this their third choice). In the case of OS software, the classic economic model of producers and consumers is blurred since single individuals take both roles. The users of OS software are also the ones producing it.

Raymond (2000) argues that the driver of OS programmers, in contrast to a free-rider approach of just waiting for the desired code to magically spring forth from the community, is personal. They just do not want or cannot wait the time. The answer to the question why do not programmers keep their modifications to themselves seems to be that by making the modification publicly available then costs are reduced to the individual and to the community as well. Another plausible explanation along these lines is that by making a modification publicly available a contributor further incentivizes other contributors to make their contribution to result in better software for the community as a whole. The latter is supported by a study of Dempsey et al. (1999) who analyzed the archive of Linux postings and concluded that OS projects are driven by signaling. The notion that OS is an ideological movement seeking to "beat the system" (of closed source) is not supported by BCG's survey. This choice was ranked almost last which debunks such notion. The web site nfodb. org provides access to "NFO" files of hacked or cracked software. NFO files are small text files that are attached to cracked software by crackers. These files contain a description of the cracked software, information about the encryption method that was cracked and installation instructions. Moreover, these NFO files most often also contain some text from the crackers themselves. This may include a motto (e.g. "Sharing is Caring", "Try before you Buy" and the like), a unique logo, statements of personal beliefs etc. The following text is an illustrative excerpt of such NFO file provided by a group/cracker nicknamed "EMBRACE".

I analyzed eighty-five NFO files from different crackers/groups and variety of software in order to compile a generic personality profile of an active OS contributor. The textual analysis included semantic, lexical and commonality analysis of outline/format, themes, style, rhetorics and figurative phrasing. The conceptual analysis included commonality of self-perception, attitude, ideology and justification as well as subjective "feel" of the text.

Valloppillil (1998) has found that the active to passive contributors ratio is 1:5. Namely on every individual that makes a code contribution there are five that merely report bugs. The hackers group named EMBRACE NFO file is quite representative as far as mindset; self-perception, conduct and ethical code are considered. Apart from the taken-for-granted proficiency in coding, OS contributors seem to be individuals with a highly developed sense of community as well as high sense of justice, fairness and equality seek-

ing. They exhibit pride in their work and seek the recognition of colleagues and peers. This leads them to adopt and adhere to some personal code of conduct and ethics as well as to the rules of the OS community as they seek to gain recognition from other fellow individuals. OS contributors are highly aware of their skills and talent and there is a show-off element in their contribution. This in part explains Ghosh and Prakash (2000) findings - when analyzed 25 million lines of OS code - that the vast majority of OS contributors (more than three quarters) make a single contribution. Namely, once a contributor has demonstrated his/her skills he/she has no incentive to make further contributions. As Ghosh and Prakash (2000) found, only four percents of OS contributors made more than five contributions and the two top deciles accounted for more than eighty percents of the code.

On the professional side, OS contributors seem to be highly self aware with high self esteem. They are well informed about their professional environment and moreover very proud of their contribution. In marketing terms, OS contributors may be considered as leading edge consumers, namely early adopters, because they are willing to take the risk of using immature product as well as making a contribution to its development or improvement. The vast majority of OS contributors are most likely mainstream software professionals in the academy or the ITC industry making living of a daytime job and devoting a finite and limited amount of their spare time for OS projects that are in the domain of their expertise. As such they need or require no monetary compensation and make their contribution for pure fun, on a voluntary non-profit basis and under the benefits non-deprivation principle that was discussed in the contributor cost section. This does not mean that the net benefit model is not valid in this context (Lerner and Tirole 2002). It is just that a contributor receives an immediate compensation (i.e. fun) and the delayed compensation is likely to be peers recognition rather than any material compensation. The only material compensation

Table 1.

```
From the sky we will
rise and we will
conquer as we did so
many times before, we
will show the spirit
of ...⌐
E M B R A C E
Embrace proudly presents…
Software name censored by the author
supplier.: TEAM EMBRACE
date.......: 09, feb 2008
cracker..: TEAM EMBRACE
size.......: 01 disks/5.00 MB
tester...: TEAM EMBRACE
OS.........: WinAll
packer...: TEAM EMBRACE
language...: English
type.......: Util
protection.: Serial
release....: Keymaker
[ RELEASE INFO ]
Use our included keygen to register ...
```
EMBRACE has been around since October 2000, and most of its members for much longer. We exist to serve the scene with quality releases, and to help the scene maintain some vestige of its former self.

5000 fully working releases, and we're still dedicated to what we do best, bringing u quality keygens, in style! We've been around for over 6 years now, and we aren't planning on leaving anytime soon.

Times have changed since we first started doing this, and so have we, but we're still here. It is however, time that the scene itself starts embracing some of this change as well, instead of dwelling on the past Because of this, we would like to ask all our fellow sceners to consider the following:

STOP FLOODING OUR SITES WITH CRAP!

We have enforced a 1-month MU rule on our own releases, and we would like YOU to follow our lead. Everyone is tired of releasing/ testing/trading the same releases over and over again, and it's up to *us* to change this. There are plenty of uncracked, useful applications out there, begging for some attention. So stop wasting your time on crap just because it updates a lot and it serves in boosting the number of releases your group does. We know that we've done similar things in the past, as most groups, but this doesn't dismiss the truth in this

message, it's never too late to change.

In light of this same issue, we would also like to encourage everyone to TEST your releases! We spend *a lot* of time to make sure everything we pre WORKS, and so should you!

Remember, *WE* ARE the SCENE and we SHOULD enforce some standards on ourselves! ☐°☐ ☐°☐

You don't agree? Fine, we'll keep doing what we feel is right anyway, and the end-user can continue to expect quality over quantity from us.

☐°☐ ☐°☐

As a final note, I would like to send out greetings to all our past and present members for making this group of ours what it is. I love you all!

☐°☐ -(e)- ☐°☐

"once you've tried it, you'll never want anything else" EMBRACE does this for fun, not for profit.

that most of the OS contributors get is better software. There is mentioned in the literature of career incentive as a driver. For the vast majority of contributors it is hardly likely that having a credit posting – code credit - in an OS project will dramatically affect their career not to say get them a job. The results of the NFO files analysis are in congruence with the elitist view that is presented in Mockus et al. (2002) study of the development of the Apache server. Empirical evidence points out that for most OS contributors (more than seventy percents) making a contribution to an OS project is a one-time fun task and only few are significantly committed to it. There is strong empirical evidence that the drivers of OS contributors are fun, self-esteem (namely, proving to one self that he/she can write a code) and peer recognition (positive feedback from fellow programmers). The profile portrayed has some important practical implications for organizations that seek to build upon collaborative innovation for either commercial or non-commercial projects. For example, an organization may incentivize potential OS contributors by dividing the OS project into small modules or components and publish these tasks as a reverse-auction type of offering. By attaching and publishing the names of individuals who undertook a task, the OS project coordinator provides contributors with a desired sustained visibility resulting in peer recognition immediately rather than delayed. Based on the OS profile presented, other techniques may be derived to attract contributors and manage the community for improved, as well as sustainable, productivity.

Examples of Collaborative Innovation Products

The Apache server is one of the most famous OS products. The wide spread of the Apache server was very dramatic. It is currently installed on a large fraction of public Web servers. Perl (Practical Extraction and Reporting Language) that was created by Larry Wall in 1987 is another well-known example of an OS product. Linux is probably the most successful OS product. Its market is growing rapidly with estimated total revenue of $35B (in 2008) generated from servers, desktops, and packaged software. These products were followed by programs such as the GIMP image editing, Sun's Java programming language or MySQL database that have become the standards of their field. New entrant products such the Firefox web browser, Open Office Suite etc. penetrated the strongholds of well entrenched companies and gained ground.

The OS web site freashmeat.net lists the top twenty most popular OS products. First ranked is MPLayer, a media player that seems to outper-

form by far all media players, both OS and closed source. Its video player can play any known video format as well as compressed files (Windows or Mac). Its user interface is straightforward and allows users for easy control and usable features of video & audio playback, subtitles and more. Other top-notch products that are listed are CDRTools, a tool for creating CDs and DVDs, VLC Media Player (A multi-platform multimedia player and server), Clam Anti-Virus for Unix-based systems, PostgreSQl (advanced mature object-relational DBMS), Wine (an Emulator of the Windows 3.x and Win32 APIs) and more. Just recently Mozilla (Firefox, OS browser) has teamed up with Wikimedia (OS media aggregator) to further accelerate the OS video format, named Ogg, in order to fight the dominance of Adobe's Flash on web video. Global OS groups are accelerating the Ogg Theora video format development that is coordinated by Wikimedia over the first six months started on January 2009. This new race between OS developers and the closed source vendors Adobe (Flash) and Microsoft's (Silverlight) will determine how users will consume, use, and handle video on the web in the future.

THE DEVELOPMENT OF OPEN SOURCE CODE

OS software development is an unstructured process even when there are development tools available. However, there are key principles that are similar among OS development projects. OS development can be categorized into several phases. These are listed and reviewed in the following paragraphs.

Development Phases

Project Initiation

The first stage of OS development starts with a problem or a need identification. The project initiator, or leader, can be an individual, a group of programmers and even commercial organization. This stage is equivalent to the market requirements survey of closed source development. The project leader should be able to describe the problem such that it can be clearly communicated to others. Already at this stage, the project leader should have a good estimate of the potential of OS contributors that are available.

Community Formation

This is the stage where a community is formed. The project leader approaches potential contributors via web boards, forums, dedicated OS web sites, intermediaries, newsgroups, mailing lists and the like. Commercial organizations usually list their OS projects on their web site. The project leader must have some core programming capabilities such that the project can be defined and kicked off without the initial contribution of OS programmers. However, if a project leader gets a good response then the project leader/coordinator might involve some of the contributors in the software design process itself. This stage is equivalent to assembling the development team in closed source development. However, apart from a core team (i.e. the initiating group) there is no formally committed development team here. Programmers may be spread around the globe.

Work Plan

After getting some response from potential contributors it is possible to come up with a tentative work plan. This can also be accomplished already at the first stage (relying on the core competence of the initiating team) but knowing the extent of the coding power is desirable and moreover may lead to a shorter development time. It is important to provide a time lined work plan to the community so to synchronize everybody to the development phases as well as the release target

date. This process is equivalent to deciding upon the work breakdown structure (WBS) and Gantt chart in closed source projects. At the end of this stage, a review is performed to ensure that the project is correctly set to accomplish its objectives as planned.

Source Coding

At this stage, the core coding is performed by the project leader and a fraction of the OS community. Noteworthy, OS contribution may not be in sync with the work plan. However, it is quite often that the leading team and some seriously committed contributors conclude the core code. Contributions may stream on an occasional basis to the leading team as well as bug reports.

Code Review and Approval

The leading team receives lines of code from OS contributors. These modules, routines, and code lines are reviewed and approved to acceptance. This process might be iterative. Once approved, a piece of code becomes part of the source code that will be released. Noteworthy, documentation is weak in OS projects. OS contributors are usually weak (no fun!) in providing a detailed documentation about their code. It is the responsibility of the project leader to take care of this aspect of the project.

Code Release

The last stage of the development is off course code release. However, contributors may keep sending bug reports and modifications after the release date. So in principle OS development may be considered as a never-ending process. The project leader may review these modifications or bug reports and accept them into the next release.

Legal Aspects

The legal aspects of OS development should be addressed already, or even before, at the project design stage in order to avoid commercial issues that usually stem from the lack of understanding of OS and copyright laws and consulting with a professional legal entity is strongly advised. In contrast to intuition, OS licenses are well rooted into copyright laws. In fact, in the absence of copyright laws there would be no OS possible. In a manner identical with closed software licenses, users must legally abide to OS licenses. In the historical review I have presented and discussed the basic aspects of the GPL and its derivatives as well as the BSD and the CC licenses. The same as with commercial software licensing, OS contributors can choose how to license their code. However, the fact that the code is publicly available does not necessarily mean that it is liability excluded. Therefore, it is important for OS contributors to decide upon the terms under which the recipient of the code can use it (Frost et al., 2005; Lerner and Tirole, 2005). The purpose of licensing is not just to perpetuate the availability of the code but also to place reservations as well as protection provisions (for the programmer) upon its use. A programmer that does not want his/her code to be used within a proprietary product can choose an OS license that enforces that any future derivative work of the code under license (e.g. GPL) must be under the same terms. The phrasing of OS terms determines their extent and scope of enforcement, what a recipient of the licensed code can and cannot do (Gomulkiewicz, 1999). The Open Source Initiative (opensource.org) definition of OS code lists ten key terms that when introduced into a license designate it as OS. Of these, the most important are *free redistribution*: (recipient of the program can distribute it to others and at no cost), *code is open* (the code is readable and modifiable), *allowed derived works* (the same licensing terms are applied to a derived code) and *no liability* (licensor warrants no liability for any

harm or damage that the recipient may experience upon the use of the licensed code). Noteworthy, GPL's self-perpetuating term (Copyleft) is not listed among these ten key terms.

In 1995 the GPL license was found to be too strict even among the OS community. It was argued that OS projects should be viral distribution-wise but that the license should not infect the whole code, proprietary code specifically. One of the organizations that were set out to distribute Linux, Debian (debian.org), published modified OS guidelines – later termed as OS definition - that allowed licensees greater freedom with respect to bundling of OS code with proprietary code such that the OS license will not impose restrictions on other software that is distributed with it (opensource.org). This modification allowed for the commercial proliferation of OS code since under this license licensees were not forced to transform their proprietary code into an OS code upon compiling with it. Aware of this drawback, the FSF has updated the GNU license to a Lesser General Public License (LGPL) that is a less strict version of the GPL. The LGPL imposes copyleft restrictions on the OS code itself but does not impose these restrictions on other proprietary software that is bundled with it. The LGPL was originally intended for software libraries but it is now also used for standalone applications such as Mozilla's Firefox. There is also a GNU Free Documentation License (GFDL) that was originally intended for the documentation of GNU but has also been adopted for other uses in content creation and management such as the Wikipedia project. The GFDL has turned out to be a cumbersome restricting license that places serious limitation upon users (e.g. keeping a log of all changes, publishing any created derivative under GFDL, inclusion of the GFDL copy in any distribution, etc.) and moreover irreversible. Namely, once an application, content and the like were created under the GPL licensing family it is practically impossible to switch to another type of license. Most notable is the Wikipedia

227

case that was resolved when the FSF released its third version of GFDL (November 3 2008) that allowed Wikipedia to relicense its content under the Creative Commons license.

In 1998 Eric Raymond (2000) and Bruce Perens (1999) have founded the Open Source Initiative (OSI) as a non-profit corporation formed to educate about and advocate for the benefits of open source and to build bridges among different constituencies in the open source community. Raymond & Perens considered OS a development method for software that harnesses the power of distributed peer review and transparency. The promise of open source is better quality, higher reliability, more flexibility, lower cost and no vendor lock-in (opensource. org). OSI acts as a standards institute for licenses by applying an approval process for licenses that comply with its OS Definition. OSI parallels with the FSF. However, not all the FSF licenses have been approved by OSI and vice versa.

The Creative Commons (CC) license was issued by the Creative Commons non-profit organization that was founded by Lawrence Lessig in 2001 in order to expand the range of original creative works that can be available for the creative use of other users legally. It is mostly applicable to content creation and management in the arts such as music composing, writing, filming, animation and the like. The organization has released several copyright licenses under the Creative Commons title that allow creators to determine and communicate which rights they reserve and which rights they waive for the benefit of the public. In the digital era, GFDL is perceived as totally anti Digital Rights Management (DRM) while CC is perceived as bridging between the two. The lack of standardization and the incompatibility between GFDL and CC creates severe problem for OS creativity as far as content creation is concerned (currently it is not possible to combine a CC licensed work with a GFDL licensed work, legally wise).

Recently users have identified a loophole in GPL in the form of application service (ASP) or Software-as-a-Service (SaaS). In ASP/SaaS a provider charges users for granting them access to programs online, thereby eliminating the need for code installation and running software on a local PC. Since GPL-v2 only covers cases of distribution of a derived work then users who use GPL-based programs in this context are not bound by any of its terms. Dynamic linking, (CORBA) is not covered within GPL. However, the FSF did not try closing this loophole as Stallman considered such a move an anti-business. On November 2007 the FSF has released the third version of GPL (GPL-v3) trying to address some of the difficulties that arose along the years, most notably resolving some of the compatibility issues with permissive licenses such as the Apache and Xfree86 (www.fsf. org/licensing/licenses/quick-guide-gplv3.html). GPL-v3 also addresses globalization issues by rephrasing its terms in order to address Lex Fori issues. That is to say, the FSF acknowledges that local courts as well as copyright laws in countries other than the US may use the same word but give it different meanings. Because of this, a judge in such a country might analyze the former GPL-v2 differently than a judge in the United States. GPL-v3 comes to address these issues. GPLv3 has also adjusted the definition of system library to include software that may not come directly with the operating system but that users of the software may reasonably expect to have. For example, it now also includes the standard libraries of common programming languages such as Python, Ruby and more.

A full account of the legal aspects of OS is beyond the scope of this chapter and deserves special attention of its own. Del Amo's (2007) thesis at the Norwegian University of Science and Technology presents a detailed survey and discussion of OS licensing. Del Amo lists the top twelve leading licensing models, as well as more exotic ones, and discusses their advantages and disadvantages. He also points out to the implications of the differences in licensing terms that may be quite significant for commercial firms.

Even though OS licenses share some common characteristics they may differ in the rights that they grant to the recipients who accept the terms of usage. A business that intends to use an OS code and misinterprets its license may experience serious consequences. A business can also be damaged due to, for example, the rights allowed to competitors. When considering under which license to release a product, the marketing aspect of the software should be the most important factor in affecting OS license selection. If the product is aimed at end-users then the benefits of choosing an OS license for the product are negligible and therefore the license can be of the commercial type. On the other hand, if for example the target platform is Linux or some other free operating system where most of the competing products are under OS licenses then an OS license might be the right choice to allow for contributors and other third parties to support the product. A best of breed strategy might be to release the software under persistent license and also sell the same software under a commercial license to those who do not want to be bound by the terms of the OS license (dual licensing). Lastly, there may also be substantial switching costs when a commercial organization wants to changes its licensing policy and switch from an OS license to a commercial license or vice versa (including code rewrite).

THE BUSINESS AND ECONOMICS OF OPEN SOURCE

The following four models (Raymond, 2000) are the most common business models for OS software.

- Complementary Software (a firm uses OS software as complementary to the offering of its proprietary software).
- Accompanying Hardware (a firm sells hardware with OS software).
- Services (a firm provides services and support to the OS software).

- Add-ons (a firm provides add-on components to the OS software).

There are attempts of some commercial firms to unlock their proprietary software and release it as an OS but this approach has not proven successful as far as OS contributors are concerned. Still, there are additional business models that did not get the appropriate attention in OS literature. Naturally, the focus of most research is on new code development and distribution. However, there is room for OS strategies toward the end of product's life cycle in which sales significantly decline in order to slow down the decline or even inhibit it such that further revenue can be sustained at the tail. Such additional feasible business models are as follows:

- Life extension - a company (either hardware or software) can open the source code of old products upon introducing a new, significantly different, version or model thereby extending the value and the life span of such products maintenance-wise while releasing expensive engineering and support resources for newer products (Raymond, 2000).
- Resurrection - a company can open the source code of a discontinued product thereby allowing for the users to keep it alive as long as it does not significantly affect the replacement rate.
- Dual Licensing - some commercial firms prefer to purchase a proprietary license rather than an OS license, mostly happens when GPL is involved, so the same software can be sold under either type of license (can be applied at any stage).
- Product sales promotion - providing a stripped/basic version opened and charging for a pro/enterprise version or upgrade plus professional services.

Other, more difficult to realize business models might be:

- Advertisement - when software-as-a-service will turn significant then an application specific provider that funds an OS project might be willing to pay for customers' leads as well as traffic that is referred from OS contributors that are working on that OS project.
- Branding - a firms sells developers the compatibility of its OS software with other products of the same brand, namely compatibility certification, (Raymond, 2000).
- Unlocking - a firm sells a proprietary software that will switch into an OS license after some period.
- Content generation - a firm sells an OSS for the sake of User-Generated-Content – UGC- and either sells the content or leverages on it via advertising and the like, e.g. MySpace, YouTube etc. (Raymond, 2000).

Mustonen (2003) studied the interaction between a closed source monopolist firm and an OS product. Under his game theory setting, substitutive OS software competes with commercial software that is sold by a profit-maximizing monopolist. Bitzer and Schröder (2005) as well as Lerner and Tirole (2002) provided descriptive analysis of the effects of the open source movement on closed source firms in symbiotically context. One overlooked fact is that the emergence and entrance of an OS product into a market segment of an entrenched commercial vendor leads to sales cannibalization of the latter. As such, OS products pose a threat to commercial companies. Companies have applied different strategies that try to leverage on the OS movement such as providing complementary services or products but do not have a good solution for direct competition. OS software has already gained ground among many commercial, governmental, and institutional organizations. The most common reason for choosing an OS product is costs reduction. However, many governmental and institutional organizations point out to vendor lock-in as the main reason for using OS software. Such organizations, especially public organizations, who wish to save tax payers' money are not comfortable of being captive by a commercial vendor that forces them to costly upgrades or arbitrarily raises prices. This reluctance to bear, sometimes unnecessary, extra costs has led to the popularity of OS software among public organizations. Using OS to weaken rivals is another strategy that was adopted by commercial firms as well as migrating to the OS arena in order to weaken dependency on supplying vendors or business partners. There is the free-rider issue that is often discussed in the economics of OS that limits the potential funding that OS projects can receive from commercial companies because competitors can benefit from the investment made by such companies. On another note, the fact that a commercial company may not be able to credibly commit to keeping all source code free opened the door for intermediaries such as Collab.Net (an organization that manages OS projects for companies who wish to develop part of their software in this manner). In the case of Collab.net, the visibility to the OS community is achieved through well-known OS figures (e.g. founder Brian Behlendorf is a former director and president of the Apache project and currently serves at Mozilla's board of directors) and the engagement with O'Reilly (a technical book publisher with strong ties to the OS community). There are cases in which it is advantageous for a commercial company to unlock proprietary code and release it under an open source license. The drivers for such a move might be that a company can increase its profit in a complementary segment or when the increase in the complementary segment will more than compensate for profits that would have been made by selling it in as proprietary software in the primary segment. In addition, when a company is too small to commercially compete in a primary segment there is logic in unlocking the product and generating revenue from an OS business model.

In general Del Amo (2007) points out to the following criteria about whether to use an OS license or not. Market focus (for end-users the license terms may be restrictive but for developers rather permissive), Software patenting (GPL and LPGL licenses are incompatible with software patents), Competition and leadership (the risk with a open license is that if the project does not have strong leadership it may be taken over by a competitor), Third party developers (GPL is incompatible with most types of commercial add-on products) and Rights clearing (clearing an OS code may require re-writing it).

FUTURE RESEARCH DIRECTIONS

Unisys Inc. predicts that OS will start to predominate when mature and established mainstream enterprises will recognize the need for holistic architecture. Enterprises will turn to systems integrators who can create and manage an infrastructure that integrates OS software elements that are optimized for their performance. It is expected that in the near future OS offering will further evolve to offer more differentiated OS stacks (other than or augmenting the LAMP stack, i.e. the Linux, Apache, MySQL, and one Scripting language such as PHP or Perl) for specific purposes such as business intelligence, content management etc. A plug-and-play configuration is expected to penetrate into OS as much as it did in closed source (essential to ITC management). The semantic web is expected to accelerate the assimilation of OS products as business intelligence (BI) and content management will converge (BI and content convergence). Work-in-process standardization will help bridging compatibility and interoperability issues that exist between Legacy systems and OS systems and that is expected to results in an optimal mixture of reduced costs and enhanced functionality. For example, the Norwegian government has not just adopted the Open Office software package (a packages that is based on Sun's Star Office) but also promotes its use in its private sector through the Norwegian National Center for Open Source. It has recently allocated two million krones (roughly a quarter of million of US dollars) to solve compatibility issues between Open Office and MS Word in order to encourage the private sector to migrate to Open Office.

The more the OS movement adapts to industry standards the more value its products will be able to deliver as far as integration of transactions, processes and data are concerned and especially in complex areas where integration between heterogeneous platforms is required. Apart from direct distribution, one avenue of product distribution for OS vendors is through industry credible systems integrators and vertical-solutions providers in a manner that high technology startup companies accomplish through original equipment manufacturers (OEM). Value added resellers (VARs) as well as independent software vendors (ISVs) are also a way to go to the market as OS products mature. The basic value proposition, and message, of OS vendors to their customers is still likely to be the theme of cost reduction and non-captivity for the next decade.

REFERENCES

Acs, Z., & Audretsch, D. (1987). Innovation, Market Structure, and Firm Size. *The Review of Economics and Statistics, 69*, 567–574. doi:10.2307/1935950

Allen, R. C. (1983). Collective Invention. *Journal of Economic Behavior & Organization, 4*(1), 1–24. doi:10.1016/0167-2681(83)90023-9

Baldwin, C. Y., & Clark, K. B. (1997). Managing in the age of modularity. *Harvard Business Review, 75*(5), 84–93.

Baldwin, C. Y., & Clark, K. B. (2006). Clark The Architecture of Participation: Does Code Architecture Mitigate Free Riding in the Open Source Development Model? *Management Science, 52*(7), 1116–1127. doi:10.1287/mnsc.1060.0546

Bitzer, J., & Schröder, P. J. H. (2005). *The Impact of Entry and Competition by Open Source Software on Innovation Activity.* Industrial Organization 0512001, EconWPA.

Csikszentmihalyi, M. (1996). *Creativity: Flow and the psychology of discovery and invention.* New York: Harper Perennial.

Del Amo, M. Q. (2007). *Critical review of scientific literature and other sources.* Retrieved May 10, 2009, from http://www.idi.ntnu.no/grupper/su/su-diploma-2007/dipl07-queroldelamo.pdf

Dempsey, B., Weiss, D., Jones, P., & Greenberg, J. (1999). *A quantitative profile of a community of open source Linux developers.* SILS Technical Report # TR-1999-05, School of Information and Library Science, University of North Carolina, Chapel Hill, NC. Retrieved February 10, 2009, from sils.unc.edu/research/publications/reports/TR-1999-05.pdf

Ethiraj, S. K., & Levinthal, D. (2004). Modularity and Innovation in Complex Systems. *Management Science, 50*, 159–174. doi:10.1287/mnsc.1030.0145

Faraj, S., & Wasko, M. (2001). The web of knowledge: An investigation of knowledge exchange in networks of practice. *MIT - Open Source Research Community.* Retrieved February 10, 2009, from http://opensource.mit.edu/papers/Farajwasko.pdf

Fink, M. (2003). *The Business and Economics of Linux and Open Source.* Upper Saddle River, NJ: Prentice Hall.

Franck, E., & Jungwirth, C. (2002). Reconciling investors and donators - The governance structure of open source, Working Papers 0008, University of Zurich, Institute for Strategy and Business Economics (ISU). Retrieved February 10, 2009, from http://econpapers.repec.org/paper/isowpaper/0008.htm

Frost, J. (2005). *Some Economic & Legal Aspects of Open Source Software.* University of Washington. Retrieved February 10, 2009, from opensource.mit.edu/papers/frost.pdf

Ghosh, R., & Prakash, V. V. (2000). The Orbiten Free Software Survey. *First Monday, 5*(7). Retrieved May 10, 2009, from http://firstmonday.org/issues/issue5_7/ghosh/index.html

Ghosh, R. A. (2004). Economic Foundations of Open Source, In J. Feller, B. Fitzgerald, S. Hissam, & K. R. Lakhani. (Ed.), *Making sense of the Bazaar: Perspectives on Open Source and Free Software.* Sebastopol, CA: O'Reilly & Associates.

Gomulkiewicz, R. W. (1999). How Copyleft Uses License Rights to Succeed in the Open Source Software Revolution and the Implications for Article 2B. *Houston Law Review, 36.*

Harhoff, D., Henkel, J., & von Hippel, E. (2003). Profiting from voluntary information spillovers: How users benefit from freely revealing their innovations. *Research Policy, 32*, 1753–1769. doi:10.1016/S0048-7333(03)00061-1

Hars, A., & Ou, S. (2001). Working for free? - Motivations for participating in open source projects. *International Journal of Electronic Commerce, 6*(2), 25–39.

Holmstrom, B. (1999). Managerial incentive problems: A dynamic perspective. *The Review of Economic Studies, 66*, 169–182. doi:10.1111/1467-937X.00083

Johnson, J. P. (2001). *Economics of open source software*. Retrieved February 4, 2009, from http://opensource.mit.edu/papers/johnsonopensource.pdf

Kogut, B., & Metiu, A. (2001). Open-source software development and distributed innovation. *Oxford Review of Economic Policy, 17*(2), 248–264. doi:10.1093/oxrep/17.2.248

Lakhani, K. R., & Wolf, R. G. (2005). Why Hackers Do What They Do: Understanding Motivation and Effort in Free/Open Source Software Projects. In J. Feller, B. Fitzgerald, S. Hissam, & K. R. Lakhani (Eds.), *Perspectives on Free and Open Source Software*. Cambridge, MA: MIT Press

Langlois, R. N. (2002). Modularity in technology and organization. *Journal of Economic Behavior & Organization, 49*(1), 19–37. doi:10.1016/S0167-2681(02)00056-2

Lerner, J., Pathak, P. A., & Tirole, J. (2006). The Dynamics of Open Source Contributors. *The American Economic Review, 96*(2), 114–118. doi:10.1257/000282806777211874

Lerner, J., & Tirole, J. (2002). Some simple economics on Open Source. *The Journal of Industrial Economics, 50*(2), 197–234.

Lerner, J., & Tirole, J. (2005). The Economics of Technology Sharing: Open Source and Beyond. *The Journal of Economic Perspectives, 19*(2), 99–120. doi:10.1257/0895330054048678

Meyer, P. B. (2003). Episodes of Collective Invention, Working Papers 368. *U.S. Bureau of Labor Statistics*. Retrieved February 10, 2009 from http://ssrn.com/abstract=466880

Mockus, A., Fielding, R. T., & Herbsleb, J. D. (2002). Two case studies of open source software development: Apache and Mozilla. *ACM Transactions on Software Engineering and Methodology, 11*(3), 309–346. doi:10.1145/567793.567795

Moon, J. Y., & Sproull, L. S. (2000). Essence of Distributed Work: The Case of the Linux Kernel. *First Monday, 5*(11). Retrieved February 10, 2009, from http://www.informatik.uni-trier.de/~ley/db/journals/firstmonday/firstmonday10.html.

Mustonen, M. (2003). Copyleft – the economics of Linux and other open source software. *Information Economics and Policy, 15*(1), 99–121. doi:10.1016/S0167-6245(02)00090-2

Narduzzo, A., & Rossi, A. (2005). The role of modularity in free/open source software development. In S. Koch (Ed.), *Free/open source software development*. Hershey, PA: Idea Group Publishing.

Nuvolari, A. (2002). The 'Machine Breakers' and the Industrial Revolution. *The Journal of European Economic History, 31*, 393–426.

Osterloh, M., B., & Frey, S. (2000). Motivation, knowledge transfer, and organizational firms. *Organization Science, 11*(5), 538–550. doi:10.1287/orsc.11.5.538.15204

Perens, B. (1999). *Open Sources: Voices from the Open Source Revolution*. Sebastopol, CA: O'Reilly Media.

Raymond, E. (2000). *The Cathedral and the Bazaar*. Sebastopol, CA: O'Reilly & Associates.

Redmond developer news. (2009). Retrieved January 20, 2009, from http://www.reddevnews.com

Retrieved February 10, 2009, from http://www.houstonlawreview.org/1999/05/15/volume-36-number-1-symposium-1999/

Sanchez, R., & Mahoney, J. (1996). Modularity, flexibility, and knowledge management in product and organization design. *Strategic Management Journal, 17*, 63–76.

Schumpeter, A. J. (1975). *Capitalism, Socialism and Democracy*. New York: Harper.

Stallman, R. (2007). *Why Open Source Misses the Point of Free Software: Open Source is a development methodology; free software is a social movement.* Retrieved February 9, 2009, from http://www.gnu.org

The Boston Consulting Group/OSDN hacker survey, Release 0.73 (2002). Retrieved February 10, 2009, from flosscom.net/index.php?option=com_docman&task=doc_view&gid=45.

Tyler, T. R., & Blader, S. L. (2000). Cooperation in Groups: Procedural Justice, Social *Identity and Behavioral Engagement.* Philadelphia, PA: Psychology Press.

Valloppillil, V. (1998). Open Source Software: A (New?) Development Methodology, Unpublished working paper. *Microsoft Corporation.* Retrieved February 9, 2009 from http://edge-op.org/iowa/www.iowaconsumercase.org/011607/6000/PX06501.pdf von Engelhardt, S. (2008a). The Economic Properties of Software. *Jena Economic Research Papers, 2,* Number 2008-045. Retrieved February 10, 2009, from http://zs.thulb.uni-jena.de/receive/jportal_jparticle_00101440

von Engelhardt, S. (2008b). Intellectual Property Rights and Ex-Post Transaction Costs: the Case of Open and Closed Source Software, Jena Economic Research Papers 2008-047. Retrieved February 10, 2009, from http://zs.thulb.uni-jena.de/receive/jportal_jparticle_00101864.

von Hippel, E. (2001). Innovation by User Communities: Learning from Open-Source Software. *MIT Sloan Management Review, 42*(4), 82.

von Hippel, E., & v. Krogh, G. (2003). Open Source software and the private-collective innovation model: Issues for organization science . *Organization Science, 14*(2), 209–223. doi:10.1287/orsc.14.2.209.14992

Weber, S. (2003). The Success of Open Source. Cambridge, MA: Harvard University Press.

Wellman, B., & Gulia, M. (1999). The network basis of social support: A network is more than the sum of its ties. In B. Wellman (Ed.), *Networks in the Global Village: Life in Contemporary Communities.* Boulder, CO: Westview Press.

Chapter 13
Enterprise Resource Planning:
An E–Entrepreneurial Challenge

John Douglas Thomson
RMIT University, Australia

ABSTRACT

The Enterprise Resource Planning (ERP) entrepreneurial venture challenge for the innovators was to develop an ERP database using standard generic database software within existing resources and available data at lowest cost in minimum time. The generic ERP database model so developed was completed as a part time task by two innovative entrepreneurs over twelve months for the Australian Department of Defense. They used standard generic database software, existing data, with no additional resources or external consultants. This action research was undertaken on a longitudinal basis by the two entrepreneurs networking closely with the many internal and external stakeholders. The Australian Department of Defense is a complex, high tech Australian Federal Government Department of around 90,000 employees. In 2008-09 the Australian Department of Defense will spend more than $9.6 billion acquiring and sustaining military equipment and services, and will employ over 7,500 people in more than 40 locations around Australia and overseas (Department of Defense, 2009). This comprises the procurement of defense capability products (goods and services) and their support and maintenance from almost every industry sector, on a global basis. Hundreds of small to large enterprises are dependent on the Australian Department of Defense for such orders. The anticipation of the developers of the ERP database was that this entrepreneurial venture could not only help the Australian Department of Defense become an inclusive knowledge based learning society, but subsequently provide an inexpensive database model for other organizations, large or small.

INTRODUCTION

Enterprise resource planning (ERP) is an organization wide computer software system used to manage and coordinate all the resources, information and functions of a business from shared data stores (Esteves, & Pastor, 2004). An ERP system can facilitate the smooth flow of common functional information and reduce cycle times. However, without top management support having an appropriate business strategy, plan and vision, busi-

DOI: 10.4018/978-1-61520-597-4.ch013

ness processes, effective project management, user involvement and education and training, organizations cannot embrace the full benefits of such complex system and the risk of failure might be at a high level (Al-Fawaz, Zahran, & Tillal, 2008). Due to the complexities of most ERP vendor systems and the negative consequences of a failed ERP vendor implementation, most ERP vendors have included 'best practice' into their software. These are what the ERP vendor deems as best practice to carry out a particular business process in an integrated enterprise-wide system (Monk, & Wagner, 2009) – that is, from the ERP vendors point of view.

An ERP study conducted by Lugwigshafen University of Applied Science (2004) surveyed 192 companies. It concluded that companies which implemented SAP's industry best practices decreased mission-critical project tasks such as configuration, documentation, testing and training – but how objective was such research? There is but limited, recent, rigorous, objective literature on ERP. Much of the literature is sourced from and based upon evidence provided by the ERP vendors themselves, their data, their perspectives and their advice. ERP vendors have designed their systems around standard business processes, based upon their perceptions of best business practices. Different ERP vendors have different types of processes but all are of a standard, modular nature. Some of these may well be suited to many organizations, but which one suits which organization best?

Firms that want to implement ERP vendor systems may be consequently forced to adapt their organizations to the ERP vendor's standardized processes or adapt the ERP vendor's package to the organization's existing structure, systems and processes (Turban, 2008). Neglecting to map current business processes prior to starting ERP implementation is a main reason for failure of ERP projects (Brown, & Vessey, 2003).

It seems necessary for organizations to perform a thorough business process analysis before selecting an ERP vendor and undertaking ERP implementation. Such analysis should map current structures, organization, systems and operational processes to enable the selection of an ERP vendor whose standard modules are most closely aligned with the established organization (King, 2005; Yusuf, Gunasekaran, & Abthorpe, 2004). ERP implementation is difficult and politically charged in organisations structured into nearly independent business units because they may each have different processes, business rules, data semantics, authorization hierarchies and decision centres (Daneva, & Wieringa, 2008). ERP implementation can cause significant centralization of arrangements, such that once implemented may then limit the freedom and flexibility or needs of the organization to adapt quickly to environmental changes in the organization's situation without incurring significant costs, lengthy duration and significant change management and organizational turmoil.

BACKGROUND

ERP vendor solutions often include significant change management requirements coordination. A disadvantage usually attributed to ERP is that business process redesign to fit the standardized ERP vendor modules can lead to a loss of existing competitive, quality, or efficiency and effectiveness advantages. While documented cases exist where this has occurred, other cases show that following thorough process preparation, ERP systems can increase sustainable competitive advantage (Turban, 2008; Dehning, & Stratopolous, 2003). Koch and Wailgum (2007) suggest that ERP attempts to integrate all departments and functions across an organization onto a single computer system that can serve different individual's particular needs. Individuals should all be able to see the same information.

Most ERP vendor systems were designed to be used by discrete manufacturing companies rather than process manufacturers, other private sector industries, the public or not for profit sectors. While this is changing, each of these industries and sectors has struggled with the different ERP vendors to modify core ERP vendor programs to their needs. To help address such industry-specific problems and customization needs, ERP vendors have only recently begun to offer specially tailored ERP application sets, but there is still much customization work to do. Packaged applications now target such industries as retail, media, utilities, high-tech, public sector, higher education and banking. In addition, ERP vendors have tailored applications to address the individual concerns within the broad manufacturing space. The issue here is that the ERP vendors are both the researchers and the applicators, so can research based on ERP vendor information be deemed rigorous or objective?

It is critical for public, private and not for profit organizations (not just some private sector industries to which most of the literature is targeted) to determine if their way of doing business will fit a standard ERP vendor package before contracts are signed. There are options - they can change their business structure, systems and processes to accommodate the software, or they can modify the software to fit their processes. ERP vendors argue that the latter will 'slow down the project, introduce dangerous bugs into the system and make upgrading the software to the ERP vendor's next release excruciatingly difficult because the customizations will need to be torn apart and rewritten to fit with the new version'.

A Meta Group (now Gartner) (2002) ERP vendor total cost of ownership study investigated hardware, software, professional services and internal staff costs. Costs included initial installation and the two year period that followed Among the 63 companies surveyed - including small, medium and large companies in a range of industries - the average total cost of ownership was US$15m (the highest was US$300m and lowest was US$400,000). The total cost of ownership

for a single user over that period was US$53,320. This study also found that it took eight months after the new system was in (31 months total) to see any benefits. Results from a 2007 Aberdeen Group survey (Jutras, 2007) of more than 1,680 manufacturing companies of all sizes found a correlation between the size of an ERP vendor deployment and the total costs. For example, a company with less than US$50m in revenue should expect to pay an average of US$384,295 in total ERP vendor costs, according to the survey results. A mid-market company with US$50m to US$100m in revenues can expect to pay (on average) just over US$1m in total costs; a much bigger mid-market company, with US$500m to US$1b in revenues, should expect to pay just over US$3m in total costs. Companies with more than US$1b in revenues can expect to pay, on average, nearly US$6m in total ERP vendor costs.

The hidden vendor costs of ERP most likely to result in budget overrun are training (expensive); integration and testing (high risk); customization (expensive); data conversion (from old systems to new ERP vendor systems); data analysis (combined with data from external systems for analysis purposes); consultants (ad infinitum); retaining the organization's trained ERP employees; implementation (never stops); waiting for the organization's ROI; post-ERP depression; and adjusting to the new ERP vendor system. In a Deloitte Consulting survey of 64 Fortune 500 companies (Deloitte, 2008; Khosrow-Pour, 2006; Saleh, Abdulaziz, & Alkattan, 2006), one in four admitted that they suffered a drop in performance when their ERP vendor system went live - the most common reason for the performance problems was that everything looked and worked differently from the way it did before, which occurs when people can't do their jobs in the familiar way and haven't yet mastered the new way. Implementing ERP vendor systems is a difficult and costly process that has caused serious business losses because the planning, development and training necessary to re-engineer their business processes were underestimated. The training of end users is also a key success factor to achieving benefits.

For example, according to Gray (2003), RMIT University's PeopleSoft ERP implementation was the subject of a Victorian Government Auditor General's (2003) report following the ERP vendor system's failure to deliver. The system was to integrate basic student administration (and related financial) tasks with Web-enrolments, the alumni system and other peripheral tasks. It went live in October 2001. The problems that followed cost RMIT University more than AU$47m, or 3.7 times the original budget (Victorian Auditor General, 2003), and ultimately the resignation of the University's Vice Chancellor. The structural and process changes required were underestimated, as was the time allowed for implementation. The system went live at a time when, from both a technology perspective and a business ready perspective, it wasn't ready and there wasn't a fallback position. There was an expectation that the early issues were technology problems that would be fixed fairly quickly. By the time the University realised how committed it was, it was too late to revert to the previous system.

The ICT industry as a whole has a tendency to oversell, creating a perception of software readiness and proficiency to meet a customer's needs rather than the reality. An example of this is another estimated AU$65m ERP vendor implementation failure in 2002 which involved 14 major Australian corporations as Founding Shareholders (Amcor, AMP, ANZ, Australia Post, BHP, Coca-Cola Amatil, Coles Myer, Fosters, Goodman Fielder, Orica, Pacific Dunlop, Qantas, Telstra and Wesfarmers) with Price Waterhouse Coopers as consultants for the development of a regional ERP entrepreneurial venture, corProcure, based in Melbourne, Australia. This was to provide an e-marketplace for electronic trading across buyers and sellers, and the integration and provision of other ERP services and processes. After 18 months of intensive and expensive development, the project failed and the entity was sold off to one of the Founding Shareholders, Australia Post, for $1 (Head, 2003).

Similar examples abound. Gray (2003) suggests that rather than trying to modify the ERP vendor software systems to suit an organization's business processes, there is a need to look at ways of modifying the business's processes to suit the ERP vendor system. However, this may lead to other acute and expensive complications in writing software variations and revising and adjusting business structures and processes. Is this 'the tail wagging the dog'? Is an ERP system a tool of management or vice versa?

Why do ERP projects fail so often? At its simplest level, Koch and Wailgum (2007) suggest that ERP is a set of best practices for performing different functions including procurement, logistics, finance, HR, and other processes. To get the most from the ERP vendor software, they argue that employees need to adopt the work methods outlined in the software. If the people in the different departments that will use ERP don't agree that the work methods embedded in the software are better than the ones they currently use, they will resist using the software or will want IT to change the software to match the ways they currently do things. This can be where ERP vendor projects break down. Political fights break out over how, or even whether, the ERP vendor software should be installed. IT becomes involved in long, expensive customization efforts to modify the ERP vendor software to fit the business requirements. Customizations make the software more unstable and harder to maintain when it is implemented. Because ERP covers so much of what a business does, a failure in the software can bring an organization to a halt.

However, every business is different with unique work methods that an ERP vendor cannot account for when developing its software. Further, changing employee's work processes and habits will also create difficulties, and getting employees to use the ERP vendor's software to improve the ways they do their jobs may be a harder challenge, particularly if it means that on success, many of the employees will lose their jobs. If the organization is resistant to change, then an ERP project is more likely to fail. For example, the US waste-disposal company Waste Management announced in March 2008 that it was suing SAP, seeking the recovery of US$100m in project expenses that related to a failed ERP vendor implementation started in 2005. In the complaint, Waste Management alleges that SAP executives participated in a fraudulent sales scheme and that SAP's Waste and Recycling ERP product was actually fake software that was still not ready for Waste Management's use by Spring 2008 (Finkle, & Chernikoff, 2008).

THE E-ENTREPRENEURIAL CHALLENGE

Literature Review

Senior management in public, private and not for profit organizations who are seeking cost savings and improved effectiveness and efficiency may wish to review their current data arrangements. Large, medium and small organizations around the world are considering or reconsidering enterprise resource planning (ERP), and are looking for guidance as to how ERP can be used with highest amenity at lowest cost. They have variously considered ERP as a pervasive organization wide tool for coordinating many activities such as procurement, HR, project management, finance, and budgeting. This adoption has been because downsizing and outsourcing pressures to reduce costs have been and will continue to be intense. While the adoption of ERP has been viewed as a means of reducing costs, in practice such implementation often increases costs (Cordella, & Simon, 1997; Cordella, 2006; Cordella, 2001). Such costs vary from country to country. The ICT Development Index provides comprehensive benchmarking information across nations indicat-

ing that 'large disparities remain among countries' (ITU, 2009). Low income countries are low on the index, with an important element being 'the cost of ICT services' (ITU, 2009).

There is much organizational information associated with ERP functions. For example, e-sourcing can represent up to 60% of an organization's annual spend – and so it is rich in information on how an organization's strategy and operations are being achieved. Rarely is this data used in organizational performance prediction as leading indicators of performance, or measurement as lagging indicators. But the entrepreneurial conversion of e-sourcing and other data to organizational intellectual capital could be beneficial. For an organization to access and orchestrate the use of such data, there is a need to establish a repository for the data i.e. an ERP data base. However, ERP data is often spread throughout different organizational functions such as accounting, project management, purchasing and procurement, and supply logistics. Wittmann and Cullen (2000) suggest that such data is a key value driver. In many organizations it remains an untapped source of core business data. It could be that this is because its value is not recognized by management, or that some or all of these functions have been outsourced to an external provider and so have become opaque to management. By outsourcing such a core function, organizations become dependent upon external, often rent seeking, service organizations. Such rent seeking can take the form of system and software adoption and subsequent upgrades, specialist training for staff, ongoing license fees on an annual per user basis, consultancy fees, special service fees and so on. Once committed to such ERP arrangements, it is difficult for any organization to break out of such contracts without suffering heavy expense, but to remain in the arrangement is also very expensive – it becomes a most effective monopoly.

ERP enables masses of information, previously dispersed and fragmented, difficult and expensive to bring together manually in a timely way, to be brought together and interrogated in seconds (Wilgum, 2007). This contributes to improved organizational efficiency and effectiveness, and to a lowering of an organization's transaction costs and environmental impacts. Because ERP can be used to collect, correlate, track and aggregate electronic transactions quickly and easily, it has the potential to become a valuable source of strategic and operational knowledge with cost saving and performance management potential. ERP can encompass activities across the back office of an organization, as well as other areas. For example, an ERP supply management system enables various data from functions such as accounting, finance, logistics, procurement, and project management to be collected, collated, coordinated, and disseminated. ERP systems may be designed to record and hence provide the data for measuring critical aspects of 'core' business operations across an organization's back office, from strategy development, planning and execution, to management, operations, and control. They can do this by providing data to management which can be used to measure and hence evaluate organizational processes and functions that were previously disparate and disjointed (Bouret, 2005). Through these means, an ERP data base can help in the facilitation of more efficient completion of day-to-day tasks; reduce redundant and overlapping activities that waste time and resources by standardizing 'core' processes and procedures; eliminate data silos by creating a single, central repository of timely, accurate data; and enable more effective resource allocation and management (Business Software, 2008).

ERP databases and systems are core business for any organization, yet they are often outsourced to ERP vendors at considerable capital set up costs and subsequent ongoing service and maintenance costs. This outsourcing then leaves them vulnerable to activities over which they have no control, including virus infections to the ERP vendor or ISP, and 'ghost net' activities (Markoff, 2009). Organizations often attempt to modify their operations to suit the software of the ERP vendor. Alternatively, if an organization does require the ERP vendor's software to be modified, the organization is usually required to provide the funding and other resources for this to be undertaken and often does not own the intellectual property so developed which is claimed by the ERP vendor. The ERP vendor may then use it with the organization's competitors. During any demanding or difficult periods, an organization may need to wait in queue for service from the ERP vendor.

So rapid have been software and hardware improvements that decision making senior management is sometimes unaware of the inherent latent usable potential available to prosecute their interests. In some organizations ICT expertise and materiel may not be realized or valued. But since 2000, there have been significant improvements in the lowering of energy use and the increase in computing power of generic software database tools for which there are 'at no cost' upgrades. Inexpensive training in the use of generic database software is accessible on line. Such is the skill and curiosity of ICT entrepreneurs that often no training is necessary. These skills are readily applied to innovative entrepreneurial challenges such as ERP databases. Such entrepreneurial opportunities are dormant, and there to be realized.

The Purpose

The ERP entrepreneurial venture challenge for the innovators was to develop an ERP database using standard generic database software using existing resources and data at lowest cost in minimum time.

This evidence based research is about the innovative and entrepreneurial challenge to develop and implement an ERP database model within a large organization, the Australian Department of Defense (DoD). The Australian DoD is a complex, high tech Australian Federal Government Department of around 90,000 employees. In 2008-09 the

DoD will spend more than $9.6 billion acquiring and sustaining military equipment and services, and will employ over 7,500 people in more than 40 locations around Australia and overseas (Department of Defense, 2009). This comprises the procurement of products (goods and services) and their support and maintenance from almost every industry sector, on a global basis. Hundreds of small to large enterprises are dependent on the DoD for orders, so whatever software is adopted by a large organization such as the DoD will have an impact on them also. The anticipation was that this entrepreneurial venture could not only help the organization become an inclusive knowledge based learning society, but subsequently provide an inexpensive database model for other organizations, large or small, for example, in developed or under-developed countries (ITU, 2009).

Twelve Months, Two Entrepreneurs Part Time, Develop an ERP Data Base

The generic ERP database model was developed part time by two innovative entrepreneurs over twelve months for the Australian Department of Defense (DoD) using standard generic database software, existing data, and no additional resources. This action research was undertaken on a longitudinal basis with the two entrepreneurs networking closely with the many stakeholders. One of the entrepreneurs was an experienced senior executive and project manager/engineer, the other a computer scientist/logistician. They also had the use of an administrative assistant on a part time basis. No formal DoD management tasking of this entrepreneurial team took place, or was necessary. MS Access software selection took place only because the DoD was already committed to generic Microsoft software as its standard, and the researchers had no choice but to keep development costs to a minimum. But any other current database software such as IBM DB2,

Oracle, Sybase, MySQL, PostgreSQL is likely to be satisfactory (ALTOVA, 2009).

Performance Criteria

The performance criteria set by the entrepreneurs for DoD's ERP database were several:

Firstly, it had to be simple, reliable, accurate and timely and kept up to date with new data entry as ERP transactions occurred;

Secondly, it had to meet the internal customer's many and varied needs on an established work priority basis but be capable of modification or adjustment should these needs change;

Thirdly, it had to be user friendly, easy and intuitive to use, simple to understand in concept and structure, and be perceived and accepted by the users as of value and not as a threat to their jobs; and

Finally, it needed to be developed, installed and maintained using existing data and resources at no additional transaction or capital cost to the organization.

Database Model Capacity and Boundaries

To achieve these performance criteria, the boundaries of the model were based on existing financial data for each financial year's transactions. This data was readily available, but spread throughout the DoD in various functional areas such as accounting, project management, procurement and supply logistics. Initial exploratory research found there were around 250,000 electronic procurement transactions per annum, around 200,000 of which were under AU$2,000 in individual value. The ERP data for these less than AU$2,000 commodity purchases, large in number but individually very small in value, was already available through bank card statements and could be added to the database later if necessary. Details of the remaining (approximately) 50,000 ERP transactions, each above the DoD bank card delegation of AU$2,000, were publicly available and formed the basis of the initial generic ERP database.

One Unique Field Required

For database development, a unique attribute common to every transaction is necessary and was identified. This unique field, the DoD Purchase Order number, provided the means by which data within and across each financial year was identified. This unique attribute thus provided the basis for the individual records of related data to be selected, interrogated, dissected, grouped and extracted in many shapes and forms. A 'flat file' transparent approach made access to all data in the database easy and quick to access by people with very limited training. This approach ensured each individual employee was able to intelligently determine the usefulness of the database to their own particular needs. Any masking of the 'flat file' data restricts and limits the usefulness of the database. ERP vendors do not advocate this. The simple MS Access relational database 'flat file' structure used did not overload or make the database complicated or difficult to interrogate by users. Relational database fields were subsequently added as 'pull down' menus, such as Zip Codes and industry codes (ANZIC). Pull down menus for buyer and seller attributes, such as address, contact person, email addresses, telephone numbers and so on were also added. Procurement and supply reports were structured to meet a variety of management needs at the various organizational levels, for example, strategic, tactical, operational or for other specific needs. Other tailored reports were designed and developed as necessary.

Intuitive Use of Comprehensive Data

The structure of the extended relational database fields with each individual record tied to its unique Purchase Order (P/O) number was based on the chronology of the DoD capability acquisition i.e. in the order in which the processes occurred - from the DoD buyer to product/price to seller to delivery to final location – no changes to existing DoD systems or processes were required. This included fields for the buyer's name, buyer's address and contact details, contract, contract type, account number, purchase order number and date, portfolio, department, division, branch, agency, and postcode, and details of payment arrangements and progress; product description and ANZIC industry code (Australian Bureau of Statistics, 1998), value and industry sector; seller company number, name and address, and contact details. Other data required by specialist DoD areas could be added as required. In this format, the data was able to be intuitively understood and interrogated by users of the database, who were able to draw upon accurate and timely procurement, financial, project and supply records continuously updated with new information at the end of each month. Thus the DoD's AU$3b to AU$4b per annum history of strategic capability acquisition over six financial years was established on a part time basis by the two technology entrepreneurs over a twelve month period. Good relations with all stakeholders were maintained during the development period, no consultants, or expensive vendor software, or special training or ongoing license fees were necessary in the development and establishment of this ERP database. Some of the many possible fields used in the database are shown in Table 1. These fields reflect the nature of the ERP business of the DoD organization. The 'flat file' database structure can be readily and rapidly 'cut and diced' by any user to obtain desired data. No change management or adjustments to systems or processes were required, no changes to the DoD organization or structure, and no threat of job losses to employees.

Table 1. An example of some few of the possible database attributes (columns) and records (rows).

P/O no	Date 2008	Value (AU$K)	A/C to date AU$K)	DoD Cost Centre	Supplies description	Qty	Supplier
446	18Dec	9,103	8,197	DCPM	PINTAIL radios	20	Stanilite Electronic
447	25Dec	7,557	6,000	DNSDC	Lep'chaun lease	1	Dan Murphy
448	01Jan	6,320	0	MM	Goods	65	Disney Land

One Database, Many Users, Many Uses

An important issue was the accessibility of the ERP database information to general and specialist users, and the ability of these users to easily interrogate the information. Many users were already familiar with MS Access and so had few difficulties. Others not so familiar could take a short training program with an MS Access training organization at minimum cost. The data was made available to authorized users on a 'flat file' basis, that is, all attributes and individual records were made available to all authorised users all of the time. Thus the same up to date ERP database information was accessible across the DoD organization. Because of this easy access, employees were able to quickly and accurately answer questions however these were framed, provide formatted regular reports or develop specific reports themselves using the one central database of up to date information i.e. one database, many users and uses.

The database was designed to be responsive, intuitive, easy to use, and adaptable – and this proved to be the outcome. For example, typical and unpredictable questions included Questions With/Without Notice from Australian Federal Parliament Government Ministers requesting advice on DoD related industry located in a Minister's electorate, how much was being spent there, with which company, when, for what and so on; what spend did the DoD have with a particular company or country; or what was the DoD's contractual arrangements and their state of completion with certain suppliers. Other examples included DoD's specific exposure across a wide range of contracts to companies whose financial status was uncertain or deteriorating. In being able to access the ERP database, reports and responses to government or other stakeholder questions could be easily, quickly and accurately addressed by few staff, thus significantly reducing the transaction costs and lengthy time previously associated with responding to these questions, in particular coordination costs and time.

Corrupt Practices

With this ERP database, the coordination and knowledge management problems associated with incomplete supply and transaction information and corporate governance issues are reduced. With accurate scrutiny of historical e-sourcing data over several financial years, an organization is better able to choose the most efficient and effective arrangements so reducing its transaction costs. It is also able to better synchronize the motivation of the organization and its suppliers by reducing the differences of interest and information between the two, with ever increasing transparency and trust so reducing the opportunities for rent seeking activities. The ERP database could immediately provide accurate details of each product (good or service) purchased, by whom and from which supplier in which industry, when and where, at what cost, as well as the current status of the account. This transparency in itself reduces the potential for, or possibility of, corrupt practices.

Table 2. Value and number of DoD transactions

Value Bracket	F/Y 1: No of transactions	F/Y 1: Value AU$m	F/Y 2: No of transactions	F/Y 2: Value AU$m
$150m and over	4	1404	2	1515
$100m to $150m	nil	nil	nil	nil
$50m to $100m	3	178	4	306
$20m to $50m	7	195	6	187
$10m to $20m	18	241	12	177
$5m to $10m	28	191	28	197
$1m to $5m	193	395	253	549
$100k to $1m	2221	590	2205	583
$30k to $100k	4746	250	4410	231
$2k to $30k	43769	327	42035	309
Less than $2k	200,000	50	200,000	50
Greater than $2k	50,989	3,768	48,955	4,054

Need to Know, Now

Organizations for a wide range of reasons need to know with whom they are doing business, what business, and what financial exposure they have at any particular point of time. They need to know now, not in a month, or a week, or tomorrow, but now. Access to this ERP database enabled the DoD to know immediately the number and value of transactions, and with whom the DoD was doing business over the six financial years the database covered. This is demonstrated across two financial years of the DoD ERP database (Table 2). Each of the transactions comprising the data can be individually sourced. The DoD ERP database provided an immediate, accurate, and timely summary of such information. Without the database, it was difficult, slow and costly to obtain up to date data or historical data from the various DoD functional departments such as accounting, project management or logistics.

Benchmark Buyer Delegation Limit

Table 3 provides a typical summary extract from two financial years of the DoD ERP database.

This extract demonstrates the number of notifications of value greater than the (then) DoD bank card delegation limit of AU$2,000 and the total value of the notifications in this category. This information is useful if the level of delegations is to be reconsidered, particularly as each product (good or service) comprising the data can be identified. Such information can also be used to benchmark a division's or business unit's performance intra or inter organizationally, regionally or internationally.

Strategic Sourcing Policy: International Technology Transfer

Major DoD capability contracts, often high tech projects, were a focus of the DoD's strategic management policy because of the potential for technology transfer and local high tech industry development and the national benefits derived therefrom. The Table 4 example summary, quickly and easily extracted from the DoD ERP database, provides an indication of whether a local high tech strategic sourcing policy was working or not. Detailed investigation of each contract from the ERP database gave information on the technol-

Table 3. DoD e-sourcing statistics – Global summary

Financial Year	FY1	FY2
Number of DoD Notifications >AU$2,000	50,989	48,995
Value of Notifications >AU$2,000 (then year prices)	3768.06	4054.03
Value of Notifications (AU$m) at constant prices	3768.06	4159.94

Table 4. E-sourcing contracts greater than $5m

F/Y	Total value (AU$m)	Number of contracts	Value to local suppliers ($m)	Total number of contracts awarded to local suppliers
1	2208.7	60	1074.1	52
2	2382.8	52	1528.3	43

ogy, performance, supplier details and much other information of national strategic and operational importance. Such information gave a very good indication of the breadth and depth of high technology transfer, innovation and entrepreneurship being undertaken in Australia. For example, in FY1, out of the total value of AU$2208.7m, each contract greater than AU$5m, AU$1074.1m was spent with Australia based suppliers. In the following F/Y, this increased to AU$1528.3m, indicating an increase of AU$454.2m in local spend with Australia based industry. This indicated that from a value perspective, strategic insourcing policies were being successfully applied. With instant access to each contract's details through the ERP database, it was also possible to confirm the nature, quality, value and content of the technology transfer.

Offshore Capability Sourcing

The DoD was interested in its offshore capability delivery vulnerability and spend. If there is a major disaster such as a tsunami, earthquake or epidemic (or spare us, war), then it is necessary for the DoD to be quickly aware of the effect on its offshore suppliers i.e. with whom, for what, when. Table 5 provides an example of aggregated data of country of origin from which the DoD was

obtaining supplies over one financial year, with the specific details of each individual transaction comprising the summary data being able to be identified instantly from the ERP database:

Business Centre Comparative Performance

Compilation of summary data by each of DoD's Business Centres for each financial year was also easily, accurately and quickly obtained (Table 6). This summary of the activities being undertaken by each DoD business unit each financial year can be used by management to review the human resources allocated to each cost centre, and their performance commensurate with the type of procurements being undertaken and their location. Resourcing equity across Business Centres was a key issue for DoD management because it could provide the basis for resource allocation so affecting the efficiency and effectiveness of program budgeting and capability delivery.

Top Ten Principal Industry Sectors

The DoD sources its capabilities across most UN/NATO/ANZ Industry Sectors. Each sourcing can be placed in an industry sector. In summary, Table 7 provides an example of the top ten principal

Table 5. Australian DoD e-sourcing greater than $100,000 from non local suppliers

Country of Origin	F/Y1: Number of suppliers	F/Y1: Value
Belgium	5	$2,121,098
Canada	7	$40,493,060
Denmark	1	$7,271,003
Fiji	1	$670,000
France	4	$2,603,403
Germany	3	$548,256
Greece	nil	nil
Indonesia	1	$200,000
Ireland	1	$173,040
Israel	2	$416,963
Italy	2	$333,379
Netherlands	2	$375,028
Norway	nil	nil
NZ	12	$5,196,147
Singapore	1	$152,480
Spain	1	$127,001
Sweden	2	$1,466,168
Switzerland	6	$1,207,153
UK	33	$14,770,414
USA	126	$1,1444,801,682
Total	210	$1,222,926,275

Table 6. DoD e-sourcing by business unit

DoD Program (Business Centre)	Number of Notifications (each > AU$2,000)	Value of Notifications (AU$m)
Forces Executive	1532	40.37
Navy	6734	359.77
Army	11845	342.57
Air Force	14251	452.51
Strategy and Intelligence	211	10.25
Acquisition	2778	1660.40
Budget and Management	7589	731.31
Science and Technology	3308	62.59
London	973	33.25
Washington	1496	72.61
Unstated	272	2.42
Total Organization (DoD)	50989	3768.06

Table 7. Top ten DoD industry sector e-sourcing over one F/Y

Industry Code	Industry Sector Title	No of Notifications	Value (AU$m)	% by value
15	Transport equipment	4457	1380	37
22	Construction and Construction services	4889	729	19
27	Consultancy, Property and Business services	6313	477	13
18	Computer, office Equipment and Electrical equipment not elsewhere classified	7196	422	11
11	Chemicals, Petroleum and Coal Products	2332	146	4
19	Industrial machinery and equipment	2507	108	3
17	Electrical equipment,hardware,household appliances	3846	91	2
16	Photographic, Professional and Scientific equipment	2398	56	1
8	Textiles, clothing and footwear	1366	49	1
25	Communication services	435	47	1
Total		35739	3505	93

industry sectors within which the DoD invested its sourcing activities. This information, drawn instantly from the ERP database, is valuable for a multitude of DoD purposes, and particularly for the development of DoD industry policy. The specific details supporting each of the contributing transactions can be made immediately available.

Top Ten Suppliers by Value

A summary of the top ten DoD suppliers by value each F/Y is also readily available from the ERP database. For the DoD, this data is of significance from industrial, national and international perspectives (Table 8).

Table 8. Top ten DoD e-sources by value

No	Supplier	No of procurements	Value (AU$m)	% by value
1	Lockheed Martin	14	916	24
2	Civil and civic	9	239	6
3	NQEA	36	188	5
4	ADI	646	165	4
5	Raytheon	3	156	4
6	DAS	1730	99	3
7	Rockwell	55	91	2
8	CSP	26	77	2
9	Forgacs	4	63	2
10	Shell	490	50	1
	Total top ten suppliers	2987	2046	54
	Other suppliers	48002	1723	46
	Total suppliers	50989	3768	100

Price Setting and Competitive Bids

ERP data is able to be used for strategic procurement and supply development purposes. For example, supplier data can quickly reveal different or in some cases the same suppliers supplying an organization with the same 'off the shelf' product at significantly different prices. This knowledge can be used to re-arrange competitive bids by fewer suppliers at better prices and so lower overall prices and transaction costs. Alternatively, because ERP data is accurate, timely and easy to access, there may be no need to limit the number of suppliers of a particular product but price setting may be to a buyer's and seller's advantage. Such technological innovation enables an organization to review, revise and renew its existing buyer-supplier strategic sourcing relationships.

FUTURE RESEARCH DIRECTIONS

Future research directions will be to case study adoptions of this generic ERP database model by entrepreneurial organizations, and to research non-vendor ERP models successfully developed and adopted by e-entrepreneurs in other organizations.

CONCLUSION

This strategic management entrepreneurial venture by two part time entrepreneurs over a twelve month period gave rise to the innovation of an inexpensive generic ERP database. The ERP database did not require any adjustment of existing (or any future) organization structures, systems or processes, or any additional resources or change management. This model, which can be considered by other e-entrepreneurs for implementation, was based on the DoD's AUD2.3bn sourcing of its strategic capability across almost all industry sectors. The model, implemented with a major high tech organization, may be adopted by other not so complex large and small organizations and in particular by developing countries and organizations with limited resources. It provides both centralized and decentralized functionality, high amenity, search sensitivity and speed to users. It is a systematic, logical, high quality and ultimately a routine basis for the collection, collation and dissemination of both strategic and detailed data, and this through the establishment of one central ERP database using available generic database software. This ERP database enables the unhindered networking of information sharing both inside and outside an organization, and provides an accurate historical corporate memory which can be used for many strategic and operational purposes.

REFERENCES

Al-Fawaz, K., Zahran, A., & Tillal, E. (2008, May). *Critical Success Factors in ERP Implementation: a Review*. Paper presented at the European and Mediterranean Conference on Information Systems, Dubai, United Arab Emirates.

ALTOVA. (2009). *Database mapping*. Retrieved March, 2009, from http://www.altova.com/products/mapforce/xml_to_db_database_mapping.html

Australian Bureau of Statistics. (1998). *1291.0 - A Guide to Major ABS Classifications*. Retrieved July, 2009, from http://www.abs.gov.au/AUSSTATS/abs@.nsf/DirClassManualsbyTopic/F19DB188D50D978ACA2570B30006A35D?OpenDocument

Bourret, R. (2005). *XML and Databases*. Retrieved July, 2009, from http://www.rpbourret.com/xml/XMLAndDatabases.htm

Brown, C., & Vessey, I. (2003). Managing the Next Wave of Enterprise Systems: Leveraging Lessons from ER. *MIS Quarterly Executive, 2*(1), 65–77.

Business Software. (2008). *Top 10 ERP Vendors – 2008 Profiles of the Leading Vendors*. Retrieved from http://www.BusinessSoftware.com

Centre for Environment and Sustainability. (2002). Technology and Policy for Sustainable Development. *Chalmers University of Technology and the Göteborg University, 5*(February), 4.

Cordella, A. (2001, June). *Does Information Technology Always Lead to Lower Transaction Costs?* Paper presented at the 9th European Conference on Information Systems, Bled, Slovenia.

Cordella, A. (2006). Transaction costs and information systems: does IT add up? *Journal of Information Technology, 21*, 195–202. doi:10.1057/palgrave.jit.2000066

Cordella, A., & Simon, K. A. (1997, August). *The Impact of Information Technology on Transaction and Coordination Cost.* Paper presented at the Conference on Information Systems Research, Oslo, Norway.

Daneva, M., & Wieringa, R. (2008). *Requirements Engineering for Cross-organizational ERP Implementation: Undocumented Assumptions and Potential Mismatches.* Presented at University of Twente.

Dehning, B., & Stratopolous, T. (2003). Determinants of a Sustainable Competitive Advantage Due to an IT-enabled Strategy. *The Journal of Strategic Information Systems, 12*(1), 7–28. doi:10.1016/S0963-8687(02)00035-5

Deloitte. (2008). *In fighting shape? 2008 survey of cost-improvement trends in the Fortune 500.* Deloitte.

Department of Defence. (2009). *Defence Materiel Organization.* Australian Government, Australia.

Esteves, J., & Pastor, J. (2004). Enterprise Resource Planning Systems Research: An Annotated Bibliography. *Communications of AIS, 7*(8), 2–54.

Finkle, J., & Chernikoff, H. (in press). Waste Management sues SAP over software quality. *Reuters.*

Fukuyama, F. (1999). *The Great Disruption.* London: St Edmundsbury Press.

Gray, P. (2003, September 30). In depth: RMIT's PeopleSoft disaster. *ZDNet Australia.*

Head, B. (2003). *Exchange of Pace.* Retrieved July, 2009, from http://www.theage.com.au/articles/2003/04/07/1049567609043.html

International Association for Impact Assessment. (1999). *Principle of Environmental Impact Assessment Best Practice, European Union.*

ITU. (2009). *Measuring the Information Society: The ICT Development Index.* International Telecommunication Union, Geneva, Switzerland.

Jutras, C. (2007). *The Total Cost of ERP Ownership in Mid Sized Companies.* Boston, MA: Aberdeen Group.

Khosrow-Pour, M. (2006). *Emerging Trends and Challenges in Information Technology Management.* Hershey, PA: Idea Group Inc.

King, W. (2005). Ensuring ERP implementation success. *Information Systems Management, 22*(3), 83–84. doi:10.1201/1078/45317.22.3.20050601/88749.11

Ludwigshafen University of Aplplied Sciences. (2004). *Enhanced Project Success Through SAP Best Practices – International Benchmarking Study.* Ludwigshafen, Germany: Ludwigshafen University.

Markoff, J. (in press). Worm Infects Millions of Computers Worldwide. *The New York Times.*

Markoff, J. (in press). Vast Spy System Loots Computers in 103 countries. *The New York Times*.

Monk, E., & Wagner, B. (2009). *Concepts in Enterprise Resource Planning* (3rd.ed.). Boston, MA: Course Technology Cengage Learning.

Petts, J. (1999). *Handbook of Environmental Impact Assessment*. Oxford: Blackwell.

Porter, M. (2008). *On Competition*. Harvard Business School Publishing Corporation.

Saleh, K., Abdulaziz, A., & Alkattan, I. (2006). A Services – Oriented Approach to Developing Security Policies for Trustworthy Systems. In *Emerging Trends and Challenges in IT Management*. Hershey, PA: Idea Group Inc.

Selsky, J., Goes, J., & Oguz, B. (2007). Contrasting Perspectives of Strategy Making: Applications in 'Hyper' Environment. *Organization Studies*, *28*(1), 71–94. doi:10.1177/0170840607067681

Thompson, G., Frances, J., Levavic, R., & Mitchell, J. (1991). *Markets, hierarchies and networks: the coordination of social life*. Thousand Oaks, CA: Sage.

Turban, A. (2008). *Information Technology for Management, Transforming Organizations in the Digital Economy*. Hoboken, NJ: John Wiley & Sons, Inc.

Victorian Auditor General. (2003). *Report of the Auditor General on RMIT's Finances*. State Government of Victoria, Australia.

Wailgum, T. (2007). *ERP: Definitions and Solutions*. Retrieved July, 2009, from http://www.ambriana.com/C298_website/ERP_CIO.pdf

Williamson, O. E. (1991a). Comparative Economic Organization: The Analysis of Discrete Structural Alternatives. *Administrative Science Quarterly*, *36*(June), 269–296. doi:10.2307/2393356

Williamson, O. E. (1991b). Economic Institutions: Spontaneous and Intentional Governance. *Journal of Law Economics and Organization*, *7*(Special Issue), 159–187.

Williamson, O. E. (1996). *The Mechanisms of Governance*. New York: Oxford University Press.

Williamson, O. E. (2002a). *The Lens of Contract: Private Ordering*. Berkley, CA: University of California.

Williamson, O. E. (2002b). *The Theory of the Firm as Governance Structure: from Choice to Contract*. Berkley, CA: University of California.

Williamson, O. E. (2002c). Empirical Microeconomics: Another Perspective. In M. Augier & J. March (Eds.), *The Economics of Choice, Change and Organization*. Brookfield, VT: Edward Elgar.

Wittmann, C., & Cullen, M. (2000). *B2B Internet*. First Union Securities.

Yusuf, Y., Gunasekaran, A., & Abthprpe, M. (2004). Enterprise Information Systems Project Implementation: A Case Study of ERP in Rolls-Royce. *International Journal of Production Economics*, *87*(3), 251–266. doi:10.1016/j.ijpe.2003.10.004

ADDITIONAL READING

Australia Post. (2003). *Business Magazine, Australia Post*. Retrieved March, 2009, from http://www1.auspost.com.au/priority/index.asp?issue_id=30&area=features&article_id=632

Puschmann, T., & Alt, R. (2005). Successful use of e-procurement in supply chains. *Supply Chain Management: an International Journal, (2)*, 122-133.

Chapter 14
Delivery in the Net Economy

Anthony Scime
State University of New York, USA

Anthony C. Scime
Purdue University, USA

ABSTRACT

Firms need to deliver their products. In the Net Economy, delivery often has to leave the Net and be provided through traditional means. The firm's delivery mechanism influences the design of the firm's Net presence. This chapter examines the pursuit of e-entrepreneurial ventures by existing businesses with specific attention on the architecture of Web portals and the delivery mechanisms of products. Additionally, outlined are features and facets of Web portals necessary to sell and deliver mark-up based and production based products and services in the B2C sector of the Net Economy. Specifically, three case studies are examined: a catalog sales/brick-and-mortar business, a financial service institution, and a travel provider.

INTRODUCTION

The Net Economy encompasses all transactions and transfers that utilize the Internet and World Wide Web technologies. Commonly, these activities can be classified as business to business (B2B), consumer to consumer (C2C), and business to consumer (B2C). All of these relationships have existed, of course, outside the Net Economy for centuries. The use of information technology provides opportunities for businesses to establish a presence as an e-

entrepreneur in the Net Economy (Kollmann, 2006). It is the establishment of electronic connections that has changed, and is changing the conduct of business (Laugero, & Globe, 2002). In the United States the Net Economy is the fastest growing sector of the economy (Mesenbourg, 2008). Despite this progress to electronic connections, there is one aspect that the 'Net' cannot always provide – delivery.

There is a relationship between the product, the product's delivery, and the product's presentation in the Net Economy (Phau, & Poon, 2000; Smith, & Brynjolfsson, 2001). Products are presented on the Web through Web portals. The portal facilitates

DOI: 10.4018/978-1-61520-597-4.ch014

Table 1. Product and delivery

Product Type	Delivery Mechanism
Physical Service	Traditional Delivery
Physical Item	Traditional Delivery
Digital Service	The 'Net'
Digital Item	The 'Net'

the execution of a transaction for the product that varies according to the product type. Products may be a physical service, a physical item, or with the advent of the Net Economy, a digital service or digital item (Basu, & Muylle, 2002; Kiang, Raghu, & Shang, 2000). Services are things the provider does for the receiver without there being a residual artifact. Physical products move as a result of the exchange from the provider to the receiver and continue to exist with the receiver after the exchange. Digital products (Choi, Stahl, & Whinston, 1997) exist solely within automated systems, move from provider to receiver, but seldom leave the digital form. Importantly, digital products and digital services can be entirely exchanged in the Net Economy; whereas, products and services with a physical component require an additional mode of transfer for delivery (see Table 1).

While Business to Business (B2B) and Consumer to Consumer (C2C) e-operations exist on the Web, the business to consumer processes are the transactions in which delivery may be a onetime small volume activity and the technology expertise may exist on only one side of the transaction. In a B2B transaction the firms behave as partners and delivery may be made continuously and in bulk. On both sides of the transaction information technology professionals are employed to establish the physical and logical connections necessary, and for transfer of data to and from each organization's internal business systems. In Web based C2C transactions the seller places the advertisement on a Web site designed especially for that purpose. Often neither the buyer nor the seller is an information technology professional.

The Web site's information technologists provide the necessary mechanism to initiate the transaction. Delivery is typically accomplished one time by a third party service (Reynolds, 2010; Stair, & Reynolds, 2008).

E-commerce B2C transactions are possible because of the Web. Web technology provides the venue for the business and consumer to meet, the ability to initiate the transaction, and complete all or part of the transaction (Reynolds, 2010; Stair, & Reynolds, 2008). The business has the information technologists that establish the business' Web site. The consumer only needs information literacy skills sufficient to navigate the firm's Web portal. Delivery varies according to the type of product or service, but the firm makes many deliveries over time to many individual consumers. Because of the imbalance of skills and delivery on opposite sides of the B2C transaction, the Net presence and delivery mechanism of the firm must be easily understandable and workable by the novice consumer.

In terms of product delivery, there are three 'modus operandi' for B2C businesses in the Net Economy.

1. The business may be extending their 'brick-and-mortar' operation, providing ordering of their physical product through the Web followed by physical delivery. Consumers previously purchased these products by visiting a store or by mail from a catalog. In 2006 e-commerce sales requiring physical delivery was over $101.2 billion of the US economy, or 5.4 percent of total retail

sales, and a 21.7 percent increase over 2005 (Mesenbourg, 2008).

2. The business provides a product, which is orderable through the Web, but requires the consumer's presence to obtain. These type of service sales accounted for $75 billon, 6.6 percent of total service sales in 2006. This is an 18 percent increase from 2005 (Mesenbourg, 2008). These are service products such as travel, which accounted for 27.2 percent of this type of sale (Mesenbourg, 2008). These service industries provide a different type of product and therefore have different requirements in connecting with, and completing transactions with consumers (Chariton, & Choi, 2006).

3. The business may have a product deliverable through the Net, such as software, music, and movies. These are products that are ideal for the Net Economy, the entire transaction can occur in one session, from product selection through payment and delivery. The $5.3 billion in 2006 sales for these products is 12.2 percent of total sales of software, music, and movies; over a 26.2 percent increase from 2005 (Mesenbourg, 2008; Mesenbourg, 2007). For this type of product, consumers want flawless, real-time access at reasonable cost (Raciborski, 2004).

Before delivery can take place the product must be sold. This requires the consumer to enter the business' store. The Net Economy's store is the Web portal. The Internet and e-commerce has evolved tremendously since the beginning of e-commerce. Starting out as static Web pages that advertised a firm's products to today where a firm provides its customers a portal into the company, its products, and complimentary information about the industry and domain in which the firm operates.

The domain in which a firm operates drives the features the firm uses on its Web portals. The selection and use of the appropriate technology is a business manager's responsibility as they seek to increase productivity, profitability, and growth (Laugero, & Globe, 2002; Pinker, Seidmann, & Foster, 2002).

Electronic commerce and online shopping depend to a great extent upon the firm's Web portal and how people interact with the computer (Lohse, & Spiller, 1998). These Web portals are much more than simple Web sites. In addition to providing product purchase capability, the portal remembers the customer, their preferences, and past actions. The Web portal provides advice and information to the user, whether they are customers or not, that helps the user to participate in the areas of interest shared with the firm. This record of customer information and advice on shared interests are provided, of course, to stimulate sales.

Sales are the ultimate reason for the e-commerce Web portal. There are four components to Web portals that add value – search, evaluation, problem-solving, and transaction activities (Lumpkin, & Dess, 2004). Search is the ability to find information and, in the case of e-commerce, purchase options. Evaluation is the ability to compare options in terms of costs and benefits. Problem-solving is the process of identifying needs and developing courses of action to meet those needs. A transaction is the activity of negotiating and agreeing on a sale, making payments, and taking delivery. The eventual transaction provides value to the firm, but it is search, evaluation, and problem-solving that makes the Web portal of value to the customer.

There are a number of business models that operate in the Net Economy: commission-based, advertising-based, referral-based, subscription-based, fee-for-service-based, markup-based, and production-based (Lumpkin, & Dess, 2004). Most firm Web portals use a combination of these basic models. It is markup-based and production-based models that that deliver end products to the consumer.

The markup-based model is the reselling of merchandise. It involves the selection and distribution of a product. An effective Net Economy firm using this model needs to provide its customers with search and transaction capabilities (Lumpkin & Dess, 2004).

A firm using the production-based model sells its own manufactured goods and services. A firm with this model uses search and problem-solving components on its Web portal. It depends on capturing customer preferences and improving customer service to be successful (Lumpkin, & Dess, 2004).

Regardless of the type of transaction and delivery, the Net Economy's technologies are available to all. However, the selection of a particular technology and its use varies depending on the type of exchange and the type of product.

As an e-entrepreneur begins to develop plans involving the creation of a Web portal on which to conduct business, they must consider their product, how it will be presented, and how it will be delivered. This chapter provides background on e-transactions and delivery in the Net Economy as well as on each of the example firms. The chapter discusses how the architecture of a Web portal relates to products and delivery, provides detailed descriptions of three example Web portals, and offers recommendations for future research. The Web is a dynamic environment. Web pages are constantly changing and being improved. As a result, the Web portals discussed are meant as exemplars of typical Web portals and the facets of portal architecture.

BACKGROUND

The automobile created freedom. It provided consumers with the ability to travel to work and the store. Consumers no longer needed to live within walking distance of both their place of employment and the marketplaces in which they shopped. When the consumer moved into the suburbs, the stores followed and established new marketplaces – the mall. Another phenomenon

developed to service the rural population, even before the automobile – mail-order. Now with the growing speed of home Internet connections and the relatively low cost of personal computers, the Net Economy has emerged. Companies and other organizations know they can reach a large part of their customer base through this Net Economy (Lucas, 2001).

The Net Economy works even for business domains in which customers have traditionally felt that physical presence of the product is necessary prior to purchase (Lucas, 2001). This is a legacy from mail order where "a reputation for quality and offering the option of free returns, succeeded in luring millions of American consumers out of stores" (Lucas, 2001).

While the mail order legacy of product quality carried over from mail order, placing an order can be more complex on-line than through a catalog book and simple mail-in order form. Lohse & Spiller (1998) found consumers had serious concerns about the deficiencies in e-commerce sites at the end of the 20th Century. Problems existed in product variety, the ability to find products, navigation around the on-line store, and understanding product advertisements. Shopping on-line was not the same experience as it was in-store or by the book catalog where products are easy to find. In stores, information directories are often found at entrances, or sales people can be asked for help. In book catalogs tables of contents, the index, and color coding are used to direct users to products. B2C Web portals need to replicate the in-store experience as much as possible (Lohse, & Spiller, 1998).

E-commerce business to consumer transactions are possible because of the Web. Web technology provides the venue for the business and consumer to meet, the ability to initiate the transaction, and complete all or part of the transaction. The Web portal's information technologies provide the necessary mechanisms to initiate the transaction. Buyers need to only have sufficient information literacy skills to interact with the Web portal. The portal developer has the responsibility to ensure that even users with minimal computer skills can complete a transaction. Since the transaction takes place electronically through the Web portal, the buyer may be anywhere in the world, and the delivery may need to be made anywhere.

In all transactions customers want to know they can trust the firm to deliver a quality product. Communication technologies can help the firm gain the consumers trust in the business (Basso et al., 2006). In the brick-and-mortar world, businesses developed trust by knowing their customers. In the store environment, the sales clerk becomes a person of trust to the regular customer. The sales clerk may know the customer by name or product preferences. They develop a communications channel based mutual interests and friendliness. This level of service can be replicated on the Web portal through the use of access to live sales representatives, a frequently asked questions page, assurance about payment security, company policies on product return, shipping details and costs, statements about product quality, and selection help (Lohse, & Spiller, 1998).

The Net Economy is based on the technologies of the internet. These technologies provide the capability for selection and payment for products and services from the customer's home. Web portals of the Net Economy or the e-commerce portions of firms can accommodate the selection of their products by displaying pictures, providing descriptions, and helping customers in making a wise choice among product alternatives. Payment for the products is easily accomplished by credit card or other electronic means.

Delivery is a different matter. Product delivery depends upon the type of product. Physical products cannot be delivered through the Internet. They must be delivered or picked-up. The product provider, the customer, or a third party delivery service, acting as the agent of either the product provider or the customer, must accomplish delivery or pick-up. Products that are digital, that are not a physical entity, can be delivered over the internet. This can be done by allowing the consumer to download the product or emailing the product.

There is a class of physical products that are not a physical entity nor are delivered digitally. These products are often services. These products require either the product provider or, more commonly, the customer to go to a specific place to utilize the product. Figure 1 provides an example of three Net Economy firms as they apply to the possible product types and delivery modes.

To understand the types of retailers in the Net Economy it is necessary to understand the history of the companies. Three types of companies are evaluated in this paper – a traditional catalog sales/brick-and-mortar retailer, a financial services company, and a travel service provider. They provide physical products, software products,

Figure 1. Net economy firms, product type, and delivery mode

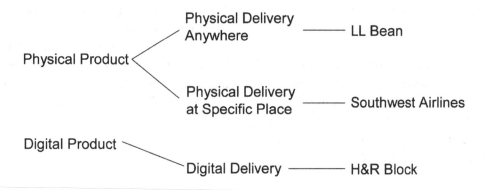

or a service, respectively. All these firms existed before the advent of the Net Economy, but all have taken advantage of the opportunities the Net Economy presents.

A Traditional Retailer – LL Bean (http://www.llbean.com/)

L. L. Bean is a catalog sales/brick-and-mortar firm, founded in 1912 as an outdoor mail order apparel company. L. L. Bean quickly grew a reputation for quality goods and service. Expansion in 1951 brought a 24 hour 365 days a year factory store in Freeport, Maine. This allowed customers to visit on the way to camping and hunting. Significant expansion occurred with the automation of the mailing lists in the late 1960s, the acceptance of credit cards in 1976, and the introduction of a full color catalog in 1979. Shopping by phone became possible in 1985 with the addition of toll free numbers. In 1988 outlet stores began to open in the Northeast US, and an international store in Japan in 1992. L. L. Bean entered the Net Economy in 1995 by launching llbean.com, five years before opening its first full service retail stores in the United States. Internet sales exceeded phone orders in late 2006 (About L.L. Bean, 2009).

Currently, L. L. Bean has world-wide annual sales of over $1.62 billion with over 5,300 year-round and 12,000 seasonal employees. In addition to the Web portal, they produce 54 catalogs which are distributed to customers world-wide. The Web portal, catalogs and stores carry over 20,000 different items. Nearly 15 million customer contacts are received annually. Over 98,000 L. L. Bean orders were placed online in a single day in December 2007. This level of sales results in eighteen million packages shipping annually.

From the Web portal customers can purchase outdoor and clothing products, such as sporting goods, home furnishings and casual and active clothing (About L.L. Bean, 2009).

The llbean.com Web portal provides interactive shopping guides, 24-hour live customer service and features such as order tracking, up-to-date product availability and customer order history. As an added service to their customers L. L. Bean provides information on state, national and international parks, their sponsored Outdoor Discovery Schools, as well as, email access to customer service representatives and directions to the stores (About L.L. Bean, 2009).

A Travel Service Provider – Southwest Airlines (www. southwest.com)

Beginning in 1971 as a regional airline, the travel provider Southwest Airlines has become one of the largest airlines in the United States. They fly over 104 million passengers to 64 US cities annually with more than 3,400 daily flights. By 1974, Southwest carried one million passengers and five million by 1977. A leader in customer service and the use of technology Southwest introduced self-ticketing machines in 1979, their frequent flyer program in 1987, and ticketless travel in 1994 (Southwest.com, 2009).

Southwest's internet presence and online ticketless travel began in 1995 and 1996, respectively. In 2000, Southwest launched an automated tool to help company travel managers make bookings and track travel made through the Southwest Web portal. Self-service flight check-in came in 2002, this service increased speed and efficiency for passengers in the airports. Improvement in 2004 gave the ability to print boarding passes prior to arriving at the airport. Southwest gained access to customer's computer desktops with the implementation of DING!. This software agent delivers live updates that are customized to the customer's travel needs (Southwest.com, 2009).

A Financial Services Company – H&R Block (www.hrblock.com)

Founded in 1955 in Kansas City, MO as the IRS stopped providing income tax preparation, H&R Block has become the largest financial and tax services company with subsidiaries offering a full range of software, online, and in-office tax solutions. It services 23.5 million clients in more than 13,000 retail offices and through its digital tax solutions. Seven branch offices opened in New York City in 1956, later becoming the first franchise offices. (New York was the next city the IRS discontinued tax preparation services.) By 1962 there were 206 offices approaching $800,000 in revenues. (H&R Block – Press Center, n.d.)

In 1986 H&R Block began electronic filing of tax returns through sites at Sears stores. In the first year 22,000 returns were electronically filed from two sites – Cincinnati and Phoenix. Electronic filing reduced the time required to receive a refund and reduced errors. Over 16 million returns were filed electronically in 2003 (H&R Block – Press Center, n.d.).

WEB PORTAL ARCHITECTURE, PRODUCT TYPE, AND DELIVERY

Every Web portal is constructed of architectural features. These architectural features facilitate navigation connecting the pages in a way that eases the customer's ability to find products. E-commerce portals are constructed to sell something. They must accommodate the execution of a transaction. Finally, most Web portals provide some service and general information, either to help use the portal, information about the company, or information in the domain in which the firm operates (Jakob et al., 2006; Lohse, & Spiller, 1998).

This section begins with an introduction to the features and facets of Web portals and then discusses the relationship to delivery of product types. The Web portal specifics of the three example companies are outlined - L. L. Bean, a catalog sales/brick-and-mortar firm; H&R Block, a financial services institution; and Southwest Airlines, a travel provider. The section concludes with a comparative analysis of each example company's portal architecture and delivery mechanism, and discussion about other firms and their unique delivery mechanisms.

Regardless of the business model, whether it is the mark-up or production-based model, Web applications all have the basic components of content, navigation, presentation, and application logic (Jakob et al., 2006). The application logic includes the functionalities of shopping carts, search, personalized recommendations, and the sorting of products to the user's specification (Jakob et al., 2006).

Navigation features are ultimately designed to direct the customer to products (Lohse, & Spiller, 1998). Web portals that have pages based on templates are easier for a user to follow and understand. Using a template for Web pages provides consistency throughout the portal. A breadcrumb trail is a record on the Web page of the path taken, i.e. links to the pages used to arrive at the current page. This trail provides the customer a history of how they navigated to the current page. They allow users to return to a specific previous page. They are especially useful if the page hierarchy is deep or is very interconnected. Horizontal navigation bars often appear at the top of Web pages and provide top-level menus for the entire portal, or a major section of it. They are especially appropriate when the number of portal sections is limited to six or seven. Tabs and tab cards are specialized horizontal navigation bars. The tabs are mutually exclusive, and often bring into the current page a content information window without leaving the current page. Expansion boxes are similar to tabs. Here when the box title is clicked-on or rolled-over a content box appears below the title.

Navigation bars with drop-downs contain top menu items which display a multiple-item sub-menu either one-click or roll-over. This feature allows the hiding and displaying, on need, of a large number of menu choices. Multi-level trees are menu systems that display all or part of the hierarchy of the portal. Often the multi-level tree is used on the left side of a page, highlighting the user's current location and the location's relationship to other pages. Typically, these trees are used in another navigation device, the site map. Site maps show the entire hierarchical structure of the Web portal, with links to each individual page.

Paging is the technique of dividing information among Web pages and indicating the pages exist by providing a row of numbers as links to the other pages. It is useful when the page becomes very long. Often this technique is used with sort results. Cross links are used on Web pages so that users need not have to return to the top of a hierarchy to go to a related page. Search capability allows the knowledgeable user to quickly find specific Web pages, or products. Search may be based on text boxes, where the user types in a keyword on which to search. As an alternative, the search may be limited by the use of drop down boxes to define the search terms. Use of drop down boxes forces the users to define the search query in a manner the portal is sure to understand. Drop down boxes are especially useful when the query values can be defined; and they can be dynamic, providing only permissible query values based on other query values already selected. After all, if the consumer cannot easily find the products, they will not buy.

The purpose of the Web portal is to sell the product. Due to navigation hierarchies, this product content can be buried deep in the portal. The brick-and-mortar store has its front windows and end-of-the-aisle caps to display featured products. This same effect can be achieved on a portal through advertising that directs the customer to featured products. The ads may be banners, rectangular ads on the top or bottom of a Web page, spotlight ads that feature images, or lists of 'hot' products (Lohse, & Spiller, 1998).

When making product selection the on-line consumer undergoes a decision process slightly modified from Simon's intelligence, design, and choice. Also important to the consumer is cost and time savings (Kohli, Devaraj, & Mahmood, 2004). Search results based on price, size, or other characteristics can help customers find the product and sorting can save time finding the least cost product.

Recommendations can be key in e-commerce. The customer may not know specifically what product to purchase. A recommendation of a product or a rating of the product by previous customers can help in the customer's decision process. Another product based decision selection feature is pictures. Pictures of products give the customer a sense of the physical product. Zoom or color changing capability added to pictures enhances the experience. Inventory status and back ordering allows the customer to understand when they may receive the product, and allows them to decide if they should wait or choose something else.

Selected products are often collected in an electronic shopping cart (Jakob et al., 2006). The shopping cart is a tool that keeps track of the customer's intended purchases. Once products are selected, the customer and firm must complete the transaction. This involves the exchange of money for the product. Discounts in the form of coupon codes can sometimes be applied as part of the payment. Of course, there is a need to accept the payment, usually in the form of a credit card. This payment needs to be conducted using a secure server to protect the customer.

After selecting and purchasing a product, delivery follows. Delivery is either physical or digital. With physical delivery, the delivery address is needed, and it may be different from the credit card billing address, there may even be multiple addresses. Physical products are sometimes purchased as gifts; in this case gift wrapping may be available at an extra cost. The customer needs assurance delivery will occur. In the case of physical delivery the order status and a connection to the shippers tracking system can be provided. E-mail notification of the order and its shipment also assure the customer. With digital products and delivery, the customer needs to be sure that if the download or their computer fails they will be able to recover the product without added cost.

Net Economy Web portals also have the luxury of providing users with services specific to their purchases, information about the firm, and information in the firm's industry in general. Such services help to ensure the customer that the business is viable and has some creditability. Customer computer based notifications require the customer to down-load an application and install it on their computer. The Web portal can then send the application announcements of specials. Services about customers and their purchases are held by the portal in a customer account (Lohse, & Spiller, 1998). Account information stored often includes customer characteristics such as name address, phone, credit card information, and previous purchases. Help in making a purchase, if needed, can be provided by telephone, internet chat, or email. Email help can come by providing an email address, or be Web form based. In the case of customers that may be away from their computers the portal may even provide mobile access.

These architectural features do not all appear on every Web portal. Depending on the firm's business model different features are necessary on the Web portal.

L. L. Bean Portal Architecture

As a catalog sales/brick-and-mortar firm, L. L. Bean primarily uses a mark-up based business model. They specify but do not manufacture most of their products. Similar items can be purchased elsewhere. The L. L. Bean Web portal is designed to support this retail mark-up operation.

The L. L. Bean Web portal is designed as a template which most of the portal's Web pages follow. This template contains horizontal bars at the top and bottom of the page. The top most horizontal bar announces the company name and tag line and provides links for logging in, accessing the customer's account, and the shopping cart. The second horizontal bar is a single link to a current discount promotion. The third horizontal bar provides search by item number or keyword, a quick search link based on catalog number, a link to credit card sign up, and a link to gift card information. A static ordering toll free phone number is also provided. The toll free number is answered by a customer service representative in Maine. The fourth horizontal bar is a menu system with the top level of eight categories of products. These top level categories provide menu selections upon roll over. The menu selections are links to sub-category Web pages. It is the middle of the template page that changes content. The bottom of the page contains service information. It begins with a horizontal bar providing navigation to common customer service needs, such as order tracking and returns. A customer service detailed site map follows. Below the customer service information is another single link to the current discount promotion. Finally, the page ends with links to the Web portal's privacy and security notices, the firm copyright and trademark declaration, and a special link to product recall notices.

Arrival at www.llbean.com is greeted by a three-slide slide show across 2/3rds the browser width promoting discounts and products. The remaining third features a promotion for the L. L. Bean credit card. The next portion of the opening portal page contains advertisements and links to on sale products and services. This page is topped and bottomed with the template horizontal bars. This portal home page is the front door and display windows of the portal store.

All pages after the portal home page contain a fifth horizontal bar at the top with a breadcrumb trail indicating the navigation path used to that current page. There are also additions to the template as the pages functionality changes. The product category pages extend the template by adding a left side column with marketing ads for the category. A top middle section displays pictures and links to featured category items, the first of which is also displayed with a larger picture. The center content is a site map for the category, providing links to sub-categories (2nd level) and 3rd level pages.

The sub-category pages add to the template a left side column one level navigation tree for the category expanded for the sub-category. The sub-category is divided into a 3rd level. Each 3rd level is represented on the sub-category page with up to 4 specific products on a row and a link to the 3rd level page.

The 3rd level pages also have the same left side navigation tree as its parent level and an advertisement banner on top. The center contains the individual products in this 3rd level. Products may be assigned to more than one category, sub-category, or 3rd level. The 3rd level pages may continue on additional pages and the template now includes a sort capability. Sorting can be done on price (either highest to lowest or lowest to highest), customer rating, alphabetically, newness to L. L. Bean, or recommendation. Each product is displayed with a picture, name, and link to its individual page. There is also a link for each product to a pop-up window that provides additional information and a link to the product's page.

The product page template changes again with the loss of the left side navigation tree. The product page template has a zoom-able picture of the product that includes color changing capability. An email a friend link opens a new window where the customer can send a personal email about the product. The email generated and sent to the customer and up to three friends contains a complete description of the product to include a picture, price, size, a personal message, and a link to the product page. The right column contains an order block that includes a log-in link, option selection drop down boxes, such as for color and size, an order quantity box, and a check availability link. The availability link opens a pop-up window with the in stock status, which is linked back to the product picture for color and size. Finally, this order block contains a link to place the item in the shopping cart, which L. L. Bean refers to as a shopping bag. Below the product information is a tab card display with an overview of the product, key features, customer comments, and the ability to access an expert by phone, internet chat, email, or finding a store to visit. Below this display and above the template's bottom horizontal bars are links and pictures of recommendations of three similar items and the last three recently viewed items.

Adding the product to the shopping cart brings the customer to a summary page again identifying the product just added and the number of items and dollar amount in the shopping cart. Also identified are three products that other customers who bought this item also bought and listings of recently viewed products by this customer. The left menu column continues to be displayed as well as a right side column with marketing and customer service links. The "Continue Shopping" button returns the customer to the product page. The "Check Out Now" button takes the customer to the shopping cart.

The shopping cart lists the items selected as well as links and pictures to other products to consider. Each item includes a picture and a link back to the product's page. There is the opportunity to change the quantity ordered, save the item for later, which requires logging in, or removing the item completely from the shopping cart. A different shipping address can be established for each item. Gift boxing is available. Separate pages allow the customer to gift box items together in any combination. A summary of cost is provided including tax and shipping.

Proceeding to check out the customer is taken to a secure Web site with a link to the VeriSign certificate. Here the customer can either log into their account, establish an account, or continue as a guest. Help access is also provided through a telephone number, on line chat, or email. An international help link leads to a frequently asked questions page, which can be viewed in five languages.

The second page of check out asks for credit card billing and shipping information. Shipping information is verified and if believed incorrect editing or acceptance is necessary. It provides the same help links. The third page lists all the items and shipping and billing information, which is editable. The shipping method can be upgraded, here. There is a link to a page for redeeming coupons, promotions, and gift cards. The bottom left column contains the help access links and customer service links. The top left side of the page asks for the credit card number. This is the point at which the credit card is charged.

Following order placement, a confirmation page is displayed and an email sent to the customer.

H&R Block Portal Architecture

Today financial service institutions provide a Web presence as well as traditional offices. At H&R Block, offices and Web portal provide tax advice, access to software, and other financial services. Although the actual programming of their software may be done by a third party, and other firms produce similar applications, H&R Block is selling a product they are responsible for producing. While there are small variations in features among three product choices, there is really only one product. Their Web portal needs to support this production-based model.

The H&R Block Web portal is based on a template with top and bottom horizontal bars. The top of the page contains the company name and logo; and a link to their instructions on how to find your tax refund status, an H&R Block office search based on zip code, and a site search

capability. The horizontal bar immediately below this header is the menu bar, which takes the user to the major product and customer service sections of the Web site. These sections include the ability to complete the IRS tax return online and to purchase the H&R Block tax preparation software. The bottom of the template contains another menu to the customer service and company information areas of the site. This is followed with a section of legal disclosures, patent, copyright, and portal specific information and links.

The center of the home page contains a 3-slide automatically looping, flash slide show advertising products and services. This is followed by four static ads in a row. Again, these are the equivalent of the display window.

The sections of products cover all the services provided by the company. The Offices section allows zip code based look up of H&R Block offices and individual tax specialist. The Tax Tips section provides customized advice on tax topics, deductions, and planning through a question asking session. It is a service provided to visitors of the portal. The calculator section is another service that will complete various tax calculations. The Emerald Card (debit card), Investments, Banking, and Loan sections provide non-tax services to the customer. The section Online contains access to six products with varying levels of service to complete, file, and maintain tax returns on the site. This service ranges from completing a basic return and electronically filing it to having a tax professional prepare the return and provide year round tax advice. The Software section provides four versions of the H&R Block TaxCut software program.

Software is available for the PC and Mac. It can be delivered as a CD through a delivery service (US Postal Service or United Parcel Service) or it can be down loaded directly by the customer over the internet. Regardless of the delivery mode, the selected product is placed in a shopping cart, which is on a secure server using secure socket layer technology. The shopping cart allows the customer to apply a discount coupon code, order a back up CD of the software, order download protection, and select the shipping provider and the destination country for CD shipments, all of which can increase the cost. The next page after the shopping cart is payment information. Payment can be made by credit card, check or wire transfer. A password is also created to allow the customer to view order and account status at a later date. The page also includes a toll free phone number to H&R Block.

The ordering and delivery of software to be downloaded is actually outsourced by H&R Block to Digital River. This software company specializes in providing e-commerce services. They provide site development and hosting, order management, fraud prevention, export controls, tax management, physical and digital product fulfillment, multi-lingual customer service, advanced reporting and strategic marketing services. Founded in 1994, Digital River is a world-wide, Net Economy company headquartered in Minneapolis, Minnesota (www.digitalriver.com).

Southwest Airlines Portal Architecture

As a travel provider, the Southwest Airlines Web portal does more than just air travel reservations. It provides access for making reservations for a complete business or leisure trip. They provide air travel services and although this is not a product, the airline is solely responsible for producing the services. In this production-based portal, the consumer is interested in finding the specific service they require.

The Southwest Airlines Web portal home page begins with two horizontal bars at the top of the page. The first contains right side links to company information, help, the Spanish version of the Web portal, and a link to the account login screen. The second and main menu horizontal bar links to portions of the portal that are of interest to the traveler – booking travel, special offers, travel

tools, the frequent flyer program Rapid Rewards and back to the home page. These two horizontal bars form a template and appear on most of the remaining portal pages.

Following the navigation bars, a two-thirds screen size advertisement and a vertical list of expansion boxes for air flight reservation details – booking, checking in, checking flight status, and changing a flight. These expansion boxes allow the customer to begin one of these processes and cross linking to the appropriate page. The rest of the page contains smaller ads for special deals, and cross linking menus for travel services and company information.

The main menu horizontal bar choices lead to the selected portion of the portal. These sections are organized with a template that includes the same top horizontal bars as the home page, a left side one level navigation tree for that section, and a bottom listing of cross links for other travel services and company information.

There is an important exception to the above page structure. The Book Travel section contains only the top horizontal bars followed by a set of tab cards for air travel, car rental, hotel reservations, cruise reservations, vacation packages, and a travel summary. Each tab card provides selection boxes and text boxes for the traveler to use in selecting that portion of their trip. The selection boxes are dynamic; for example, the selection of arrival airports changes as the traveler chooses different departure airports. The selection and text boxes for rental car and hotels are repeated on the bottom of the air travel tab card. The travel summary page provides one location for displaying all the travel features selected.

For air travel, after the selection is made the traveler has the opportunity to enter discount codes, which may affect the prices displayed on the next page. The next page displays the available flights and cost based on level of service. There is also the opportunity to modify flight time or airports. After selection of a specific flight, an air itinerary is provided with a breakdown of cost (fare, taxes, fees). The final page is the purchase page. This page is on a secure server. The traveler may pay by a combination of credit card, gift card, travel voucher, or funds from a previously canceled ticket. A ticketless travel receipt is emailed to the traveler. This receipt contains the itinerary and a reservation number, which can be used to actually take the flight. There is also an opportunity to email the itinerary to up to four friends by providing their email address. The rental car, hotel reservation, cruise, and vacation packages tab cards behave in a similar manner. With the vacation packages tab card after the initial selection of dates and location the main menu horizontal bar changes to specific vacation package links.

The section of the portal on special offers provides quicker access to the same pages as the book travel section. The travel tools section provides links to pages to check or modify existing reservations.

Travel tools is a key resource for familiar customers to use to gain quick results from the portal without having to follow the progression of links. It also has links to company policies, airport, and airport shuttle information. At selected airports, a traveler can order shuttle bus service through Southwest. Travel tools is a collection of short cuts to the navigation of the portal. Travel tools include such actions as reserving a flight, requesting a refund, establishing and managing an account, flight check-in and printing a board-

ing pass, viewing available voucher, gift card, or cancelled reservation balances held by Southwest, viewing frequent flier status and balance, purchasing and managing Southwest gift cards (which can be emailed or delivered), establishing wireless access to the portal, and downloading DING! DING! is an application which runs on the traveler's computer. It provides access to the Southwest portal pages and accepts messages from Southwest. These messages are special offers customized to the traveler's selection of up to ten cities.

Southwest Airlines Wireless Access allows the traveler to access key components of the Southwest portal from a Web-enabled mobile device. The traveler is able to check flight schedules, check-in for a flight, and receive flight status information.

Architecture and Delivery

The features of catalog sales/brick-and-mortar, financial and software services, and travel providing Web portals have a number of similarities and differences. Tables 2-5 summarize the architectural features of the three example firms with respect to navigation, product, transaction, and service, respectively. Note that the features of the portals are not all the same. The features of each depend on the products and product variety offered. L. L. Bean has a large selection of products, all of

Table 2. Navigation features of portals

LL Bean	H&R Block	Southwest Airlines
Templates	Templates	Templates
Bread crumb trails		
Cross links to products		Cross links to products
Tab cards		Tab cards
		Expansion Boxes
Paging		
Search - Text box	Search - Text box Zip Location lookup	Search – Dynamic Selection

Table 3. Product selection features of portals

LL Bean	H&R Block	Southwest Airlines
Sort		
Recommendation of items		
Customer rating of products		
Products pictures w/zoom & color		
Recently viewed items		
Other customer also purchased items		
Inventory status		
		Notification application

which are physically delivered. This requires navigation, search, and selection to help the consumer, more so than the limited products of H&R Block and Southwest Airlines. Both H&R Block and Southwest have digital delivery of their limited products. Selection features are nearly non-existent (The only selection feature being Southwest's DING! application.) The consumer's need is well defined, so selection assistance is not as critical for these products.

The physical delivery requirement for L. L. Bean products also requires additional transaction features, delivery location from the consumer and delivery process information from L. L. Bean.

Digital delivery of software (H&R Block) or use authorization (Southwest Airlines) requires at most an e-mail address beyond the capability to place the order. In both product delivery cases (L. L. Bean and H&R Block), delivery is handled by a third party service. H&R Block will also handle the onward delivery of the completed tax forms to the IRS. In this case, H&R Block is the third party service provider.

Note that the product type determines the delivery mechanism; and both product type and delivery mechanism determine the architecture of the Web portal. The business model (mark-up based and production-based) is less significant in

Table 4. Transaction features by firm

LL Bean	H&R Block	Southwest Airlines
Order status	Order status	Reservation status
Shipper's tracking system		
Email notification		
Item shipping addresses		
Combined items gift boxing		
Secure shopping cart	Secure shopping cart	Summary of purchases
Secure check out	Secure check out	Secure check out
Application of discounts	Application of discounts	Application of discounts
Product physical delivery	Digital delivery – Third party	Email of authorization to use service/ receipt
	Back up service	Record of Transaction
	Tax e-file service	

Table 5. Service features by firm

LL Bean	H&R Block	Southwest Airlines
Storage of account information including wish lists		Storage of account information including funds available
Email a friend		Email a friend
Help by phone	Help by phone	Help by phone - hard to find
Help by email – Web form		
Help by chat		
		Access by mobile device
Information about LL Bean	Information about H&R Block	Information about Southwest Air
Customer helpful information on outdoor parks	Customer helpful information from the IRS	Customer helpful information about air travel and airports

the portal design. A production-based firm producing a unique physical product would need a Web portal similar to L. L. Bean. Likewise, a distributor of varying and different software (mark-up based) may have a portal with navigation and selection features similar to L. L. Bean, transaction features similar to H&R Block, and perhaps service similar to Southwest Airlines.

Other entrepreneurs have been using the delivery methods and Web portal architectural features discussed. These innovations in the Net Economy are changing the world economy. In the past, distribution of books has been a controlled activity, controlled by publishers, book distributors, and bookstores. The Internet has changed the entire process. The distribution of books can be accomplished over the Web. Amazon.com's kindle and kindle service is a digital book delivery method. With a kindle, a specialized computer, a consumer can download and then read any one of 270,000 titles from Amazon.com. The kindle computer is no bigger in size or weight than a paperback book (Amazon.com, 2009). But, one of the more difficult activities for an author is to get published. They must pass through and gain the approval of editors and publishers. A technology entrepreneur, Bob Young, has developed a publishing business on the Web. At Lulu.com an aspiring author can write a book by uploading the manuscript and

control the look and feel of the completed book. Lulu markets the book on the Web portal and will either physically print and deliver the completed book as a paperback or digitally deliver the book as a file, as specified by the author and as desired by the consumer (About Lulu, 2009).

Delivery depends on the type of product and both product and delivery mechanisms have their B2C limitations. Clearly, products digitally delivered are more suitable in the Net Economy. One limitation is physical products with short shelf lives. They must be delivered quickly. Food delivery is an example; in England the Tesco stores have a Net Economy presence with a Web portal allowing ordering of the same food found in their stores. The shelf life problem is handled by having the customer specify the day and time of delivery, limiting delivery geographically to locations close to a store, and only allowing a limited number of deliveries each day. Product picking and delivery is done on delivery day by a Tesco employee (Tesco, 2009).

Commercial enterprises are not the only use of Web portals with the delivery options and architectural features discussed in this chapter. As public and non-profit institutions make use of the Web they too will develop Web portals. E-government portals such as the US Department of Defense (DefenseLINK, 2009), the US Internal

Revenue Service (Internal Revenue Service, 2009) or other social services agencies have similar considerations concerning delivery and portal design. In addition to e-commerce, countries such as Sweden (Hansen, 2008), Latvia (EPS, 2009) and Malta (CYB Newslog, 2009) have developed major e-government initiatives, which have the same architectural facets and delivery issues discussed.

FUTURE RESEARCH DIRECTIONS

Malls followed the automobile to the suburbs. Rural consumers accessed products through mail-order. The Net Economy is replacing both. The Net Economy's e-commerce will in-turn be augmented by mobile commerce (m-commerce). As mobile computing becomes more prevalent with Web enabled PDAs and cell phones e-commerce will become m-commerce (Lucas, 2001). M-commerce has some limitations not felt by e-commerce. Band width, storage capacity, and the human-computer interface are just some of the areas of research in m-commerce.

Delivery in m-commerce becomes an issue for physical delivery. Digital delivery can be handled much the same – through the Net. Physical delivery requires matching the location of the consumer with the product. In m-commerce, the consumer may be in motion. Speedy delivery becomes critical. Should the product be warehoused in strategic locations? Can the delivery services be mobilized quickly enough? Technologies such as global positioning systems will help, but technology to anticipate demand, preposition products and calculate intercepts may be key.

Delivery itself is an issue that can be further considered. Are there other ways to deliver goods and services beyond physically and digitally? As new delivery methods are developed how will they fit into the Net Economy?

Although Web portal and delivery issues are common there is the possibility in the worldwide Net Economy that culture become an issue. An interesting area of research is the impact of cultural differences on portal design and delivery. Prior research shows that the effectiveness of simple items such as Web page color combinations and page layout is dependent on culture (Chakraborty et al., 2008). Similar research is needed to investigate the variation in delivery preferences across cultures.

CONCLUSION

This chapter has identified the relationship between product, delivery, and the Web portal. In the process of identifying this relationship, outlined are some features and facets of Web portals necessary to sell and deliver mark-up based and production-based products and services in the B2C sector of the Net Economy.

Although anything can be sold in the Net Economy, delivery mechanism varies by product type. Product type also drives the architecture of the firm's Web portal. The three example firms in this chapter show how a firm delivering a physical product, a firm delivering software, and a firm providing a service need different features in their Web portals to sell and deliver their products and services, tangibility of offering and delivery mechanism drives how firms operate in the Net Economy.

Successful B2C commerce ultimately depends on getting the product to the consumer. The business' Web portal features and structure are designed to help the consumer in product selection. The simpler the selection process, the simpler the portal.

Delivery methodology, physical or digital, also drives the complexity of the business' portal. Physical delivery requires a more expensive Web portal including tracking of the physical product to its destination. Digital delivery is much easier and quicker. Assurance need only be provided that delivery was complete.

REFERENCES

About, L. L. Bean. (2009). *Company Information*. Retrieved December 9, 2008, from http://www.llbean.com/customerService/aboutLLBean/background.html?nav=ln

About Lulu. *Corporate Profile*. (2009). Lulu.com. Retrieved April 30, 2009, from http://www.lulu.com/en/about/index.php

Amazon.com. (2009). *Kindle 2: Amazon's New Wireless Reading Device (Latest Generation)*. Amazon.com, Inc. Retrieved April 30, 2009, from http://www.amazon.com/Kindle-Amazons-Wireless-Reading-Generation/dp/B00154JDAI/ref=sa_menu_kdp23_gw/188-4117823-4045537?pf_rd_m=ATVPDKIKX0DER&pf_rd_s=left-nav-1&pf_rd_r=1NS368NYM5RE5CNX6QT2&pf_rd_t=101&pf_rd_p=328655101&pf_rd_i=507846

Basso, A., Goldberg, D., Greenspan, S., & Weimer, D. (2001). First Impressions: Emotional and Cognitive Factors Underlying Judgments of Trust in E-Commerce. In *Proceedings of the 3rd ACM Conference on Electronic Commerce*, (pp. 137-143).

Basu, A., & Muylle, S. (2002). Online Support for Commerce Processes by Web Retailers. *Decision Support Systems*, *34*(4), 379–395. doi:10.1016/S0167-9236(02)00065-9

Bergeron, F., & Raymond, L. (1992). The Advantages of Electronic Data Interchange. *Database*, *23*(4), 19–31.

Chakraborty, J., Hansen, L., Denenberg, D. A., & Norcio, A. F. (2008). Preliminary Investigation into the Internationalization of User Interfaces. In *Proceedings of the Applied Human Factors and Ergonomics 2nd International Conference*, Las Vegas, Nevada.

Chariton, C., & Choi, M.-H. (2002). User Interface Guidelines for Enhancing Usability of Airline Travel Agency E-Commerce Web Sites. In *Proceeding of the Conference on Human Factors in Computing Systems*, (pp. 676 – 677).

Choi, S.-Y., Stahl, D. O., & Whinston, A. B. (1997). *The Economics of Electronic Commerce*. Indianapolis, IN: Macmillan Technical Publishers.

Defense, L. I. N. K. (2009). *US Department of Defense*. Retrieved April 30, 2009, from http://www.defenselink.mil/

EPS. (2009). *Secretariat of Special Assignments Minister for Electronic Government Affairs*. Retrieved April 29, 2009, from http://www.eps.gov.lv/index.php?&93

Hanson, W. (2008). Sweden Tops 2008 E-Government Readiness Report, U.S. Drops to Fourth. *Government Technology*, Retrieved April 29, 2009, from http://www.govtech.com/gt/articles/244097.

Hevner, A. R., Collins, R. W., & Garfield, M. J. (2002). Product and Project Challenges in Electronic Commerce Software Development. *ACM SIGMIS Database*, *33*(4), 10–22. doi:10.1145/590806.590810

H&R Block – Press Center. (n.d.). *Henry W. Bloch*. Retrieved November 28, 2008, from http://www.hrblock.com/presscenter/about/hbbio.jsp

Internal Revenue Service. (2009). *Internal Revenue Service, United States Department of the Treasury*. Retrieved April 30, 2009, from http://www.irs.gov/

Jakob, M., Schwarz, H., Kaiser, F., & Mitschang, B. (2006). Modeling and Generating Application Logic for Data-Intensive Web Applications. In *Proceedings of the Sixth International Conference on Web Engineering* (ICWE'06) (pp. 77-84).

Kiang, M. Y., Raghu, T. S., & Shang, K. H.-M. (2000). Marketing on the Internet — Who Can Benefit from an Online Marketing Approach? *Decision Support Systems*, *27*, 383–393. doi:10.1016/S0167-9236(99)00062-7

Kohli, R., Devaraj, S., & Mahmood, M. A. (2004). Understanding Determinants of Online Consumer Satisfaction: A Decision Process Perspective. *Journal of Management Information Systems*, *21*(1), 115–136.

Kollmann, T. (2006). What is e-entrepreneurship? – Fundamentals of Company Founding in the Net Economy. *International Journal of Technology Management*, *33*(4), 322–340. doi:10.1504/IJTM.2006.009247

Laugero, G., & Globe, A. (2002). *Enterprise Content Services: Connecting Information and Profitability*. Boston, MA: Addison-Wesley Longman.

Li, W.-S., Hsiung, W.-P., Po, O., Hino, K., Candan, K. S., & Agrawal, D. (2004). Challenges and Practices in Deploying Web Acceleration Solutions for Distributed Enterprise Systems. In *Proceedings of the 13th International Conference on World Wide Web* (pp. 297-308).

Lodish, L., Morgan, H., & Archambeau, S. (2007). *Marketing that Works: How Entrepreneurial Marketing can Add Sustainable Value to Any Sized Company* (1st Ed.). Philadelphia, PA: Wharton School Publishing.

Lohse, G. L., & Spiller, P. (1998). Electronic Shopping. *Communications of the ACM*, *41*(7), 81–88. doi:10.1145/278476.278491

Lucas, H. C. (2001). Information Technology and Physical Space. *Communications of the ACM*, *44*(11), 89–96. doi:10.1145/384150.384167

Lumpkin, G. T., & Dess, G. G. (2004). E-Business Strategies and Internet Business Models: How The Internet Adds Value. *Organizational Dynamics*, *33*(2), 161–173. doi:10.1016/j.orgdyn.2004.01.004

Mesenbourg, T. L. (2007). *E-Stats*. US Census Bureau.

Mesenbourg, T. L. (2008). *E-Stats*. US Census Bureau. Gasson, S. (2003). The Impact of E-Commerce Technology on the Air Travel Industry. In *Annals of Cases on Information Technology* (pp. 234 – 249). Hershey, PA: IGI Publishing.

Newslog, C. Y. B. (2009). *E-Government in Malta*. ITU-D ICT Applications and Cybersecurity Division. Retrieved April 29, 2009, from http://www.itu.int/ITU-D/cyb/newslog/EGovernment+In+Malta.aspx

Phau, I., & Poon, S. M. (2000). Factors Influencing the Types of Products and Services Purchased over the Internet. *Internet Research*, *10*(2), 102–113. doi:10.1108/10662240010322894

Pinker, E. J., Seidmann, A., & Foster, R. C. (2002). Strategies for Transitioning 'Old Economy' Firms to E-Business. *Communications of the ACM*, *45*(5), 77–83. doi:10.1145/506218.506219

Qu, Z. (2007). Advance Selling and Internet Intermediary: Travel Distribution Strategies in the E-Commerce Age. In *Proceedings of the Ninth International Conference on Electronic Commerce* (pp. 177-184).

Raciborski, N. (2004). Digital Delivery Considerations for Entertainment Media. [CIE]. *Computers in Entertainment*, *2*(4), 8. doi:10.1145/1037851.1037864

Reynolds, G. W. (2010). *Information Technology for Managers*. Boston: Course Technology.

Schonberg, D., & Kirovski, D. (2004). Fingerprinting and Forensic Analysis of Multimedia. In *Proceedings of the 12th Annual ACM International Conference on Multimedia* (pp. 788-795).

Smith, M. D., & Brynjolfsson, E. (2001). Consumer Decision-Making at an Internet Shopbot: Brand Still Matters. *The Journal of Industrial Economics, 49*(4), 541–558.

Southwest.com. (2009). *We Weren't Just Airborne Yesterday*. Retrieved November 28, 2008, from http://www.southwest.com/about_swa/airborne.html

Spiller, P., & Lohse, Gerald L. (1997). A Classification of Internet Retail Stores. *International Journal of Electronic Commerce, 2*(2), 29–56.

Stair, R. M., & Reynolds, G. W. (2008). *Fundamentals of Information Systems: A Managerial Approach* (4th ed.). Boston: Thomson Course Technology.

Stomper, A. (2006). A Theory of Banks' Industry Expertise, Market Power, and Credit Risk. *Management Science, 52*(10), 1618–1633. doi:10.1287/mnsc.1060.0559

Tesco. (2009). *Tesco PLC*. Retrieved April 30, 2009, from http://www.tesco.com/

Ting, M. P., Seth, V., & Gao, J. (2004). The e-Salesman System. *Proceedings of the International Conference on Information Technology: Coding and Computing* (ITCC'04) (Vol. 2, p. 277).

Werthner, H., & Fodor, O. (2005). Harmonise: A Step Toward an Interoperable E-Tourism Marketplace. *International Journal of Electronic Commerce, 9*(2), 11–39.

Werthner, H., & Ricci, F. (2004). E-commerce and Tourism. *Communications of the ACM, 47*(12), 101–105. doi:10.1145/1035134.1035141

ADDITIONAL READING

Amit, R., & Zott, C. (2001). Value Creation in E-Business. *Strategic Management Journal, 22*(6/7), 493–520. doi:10.1002/smj.187

Austin, R. D., & Nolan, R. L. (2007). Bridging the Gap Between Stewards and Creators. *Sloan Management Review, 48*(2), 28–36.

Bharati, P., & Chaudhury, A. (2007). SMEs and Competitiveness: The Role of Information Systems. *International Journal of E-Business Research, 5*(1), 1–8.

Brenner, W., & Hamm, V. (1996). Information Technology for Purchasing in a Process Environment. *European Journal of Purchasing & Supply Management, 2*(4), 211–219. doi:10.1016/S0969-7012(96)00017-2

Chesbrough, H. (2007). Business Model Innovation: It's Not Just About Technology Anymore. *Strategy and Leadership, 35*(6), 12–17. doi:10.1108/10878570710833714

Cordella, A. (2001). Does Information Technology Always Lead to Lower Transaction Costs? In *Proceedings of The 9th European Conference on Information Systems*, Bled, Slovenia, June 27-29.

Cordella, A. (2006). Transaction Costs and Information Systems: Does IT Add Up? *Journal of Information Technology, 21*(3), 195–202. doi:10.1057/palgrave.jit.2000066

Cordella, A., & Simon, K. A. (1997). The Impact of Information Technology on Transaction and Coordination Cost. *Proceedings of the Conference on Information Systems Research in Scandinavia*, Oslo, Norway, August 9-12.

Dehning, B., Richardson, V. J., Urbaczewski, A., & John, D. W. (2004). Reexamining the Value Relevance of E-Commerce Initiatives. *Journal of Management Information Systems, 21*(1), 55–82.

Franquesa, J., & Brandyberry, A. (2009). Organizational Slack and Information Technology Innovation Adoption on SMEs. *International Journal of E-Business Research, 5*(1), 25–48.

Gladwell, M. (2000). *The Tipping Point: How Little Things Can Make a Big Difference*. New York: Little, Brown and Company.

Hall, J., & Saias, M. A. (1980). Strategy Follows Structure! *Strategic Management Journal, 1*(2), 149–163. doi:10.1002/smj.4250010205

Krishnamurthy, D., & Rolia, J. (1998). The Internet vs. E-commerce Servers: When Will Server Performance Matter? In *Proceedings of the 1998 Conference of the Centre for Advanced Studies on Collaborative Research*, Toronto, Ontario, Canada, November 30-December 03.

Looney, C. A., & Jessup, L. M., & Valacich, Joseph S. (2004). Emerging Business Models for Mobile Brokerage Services. *Communications of the ACM, 47*(6), 71–77. doi:10.1145/990680.990683

Mahmood, M. A., Kohli, R., & Devaraj, S. (2004). Measuring Business Value of Information Technology in E-Business Environments. *Journal of Management Information Systems, 21*(1), 11–16.

Qureshil, S., Kamal, M., & Wolcott, P. (2009). Information Technology Interventions for Growth and Competitiveness in Micro-Enterprises. *International Journal of E-Business Research, 5*(1), 117–140.

Rappa, M. A. (2004). The Utility Business Model and The Future Of Computing Services. *IBM Systems Journal, 43*(1), 32–42.

Salomann, H., Dous, M., Kolbe, L., & Brenner, W. (2007). Self-service Revisited: How to Balance High-tech and High-touch in Customer Relationships. *European Management Journal, 25*(4), 310–319. doi:10.1016/j.emj.2007.06.005

Schlemmer, F., & Webb, B. (2009). The Internet as a Complementary Resource for SMEs: The Interaction Effect of Strategic Assets and the Internet. *International Journal of E-Business Research, 5*(1), 1–24.

Teece, D. J. (1993). Profiting from Technological Innovation: Implications for Integration, Collaboration, Licensing and Public Policy. *Research Policy, 22*(2), 112–113. doi:10.1016/0048-7333(93)90063-N

Timmers, P. (1998). Business Models for Electronic Markets. *Electronic Markets, 8*(2), 3–8. doi:10.1080/10196789800000016

Utterback, J. M. (1994). *Mastering the Dynamics of Innovation: How Companies Can Seize Opportunities in the Face of Technological Change*. Boston, MA: Harvard Business School Press.

Venkatraman, N. (1994). IT-enabled Business Transformation: From Automation to Business Scope Redefinition. *Sloan Management Review, 35*(2), 73–87.

Voelpel, S. C., Leibold, M., & Tekie, E. B. (2004). The Wheel of Business Model Reinvention: How to Reshape your Business Model to Leapfrog Competitors. *Journal of Change Management, 4*(3), 259–276. doi:10.1080/1469701042000212669

Zhu, K. (2004). The Complementarily of Information Technology Infrastructure and E-Commerce Capability: A Resource-based Assessment of Their Business Value. *Journal of Management Information Systems, 21*(1), 167–202.

Section 3
Technology

Chapter 15
Web 1.0, Web 2.0 and Web 3.0:
Revealing New Vistas for E–Business Founders

Tobias Kollmann
University of Duisburg-Essen, Germany

Carina Lomberg
Ecole Polytechnique Fédérale de Lausanne, Switzerland

ABSTRACT

Both Web 1.0 and Web 2.0 were linked directly to new stages in the development of e-business. Whereas the distinction between Web 1.0 and Web 2.0 became widely accepted in literature and practice, we are merely at the beginning of the possibilities arising from current trends culminating in our information society. Information emerges increasingly as a major factor of production, allowing the activation of innovative business opportunities. However, over the past years, a sheer explosion of supplies has taken place. This development is both a blessing and a curse as it leads to an oversupply of information within the World Wide Web. Thus, the time needed for finding required information may take longer eventually. Therefore, a next generation technology is needed being capable to cope with these challenges. Due to the logic of this chain of ideas, Web 3.0 technologies are characterized particularly by demand-orientated systems, i.e. demand for objects and services are at the centre. Starting point are demand-driven registration and specification systems. The consumer is at the centre of these processes and will gain individual help, comparable to an information desk. Not only information but also individual products and services may be released (customized products). Against the background of an increasing information overload, the question to be asked is how technological and market-oriented future developments will cope with these challenges. This chapter aims at clarifying this overall development with the objective of giving impulses for the 3rd generation of e-business. For this purpose, the characteristics of each generation (Web 1.0, Web 2.0, and Web 3.0) are clearly highlighted.

DOI: 10.4018/978-1-61520-597-4.ch015

INTRODUCTION

Internal and external information and communication processes at enterprises across almost every industry sector have been increasingly supported by electronic information technologies. The constant and rapid development of technology in the accompanying Net Economy has inevitably had a significant influence on various possibilities for developing innovative business concepts based on electronic information and communication networks and realizing these by establishing a new company (e-ventures). Above all, internet-related technologies have produced new possibilities with respect to how enterprises create value for their customers. By offering physical and digital products and services via the World Wide Web, customer value are no longer be created on a physical level only, but also on an electronic level (Weiber, & Kollmann, 1998; Amit, & Zott, 2001; Lumpkin, & Dess, 2004). In fact, an entirely new business dimension which may be referred to as the Net Economy has emerged (Matlay, 2004; Kollmann, 2006) significantly influencing on various possibilities for developing innovative business concepts and realizing these by establishing entrepreneurial ventures that generate revenue and profits independent from a physical value chain. Against this background, the term 'e-entrepreneurship' was established (Matlay, 2004). E-entrepreneurship refers to establishing a new company with an innovative business idea within the Net Economy, which, using an electronic platform in data networks, offers its products and/or services based upon a purely electronic creation of value. Essentially, this value offer was only made possible through the development of information technology (Kollmann, 2006).

Directly linked to these new stages of e-business is the development Web 1.0 and Web 2.0. However, over the past years, a sheer explosion of supplies has taken place. This development is both a blessing and a curse as it leads to an oversupply of information within the World Wide Web. Thus,

the time needed for finding required information may take longer eventually. Therefore, a next generation technology is needed being capable to cope with these challenges. Due to the logic of this chain of ideas, Web 3.0 technologies are characterized particularly by demand-orientated systems, i.e. demand for objects and services are at the centre. Starting point are demand-driven registration and specification systems. The consumer is at the centre of these processes and will gain individual help, comparable to an information desk. Not only information but also individual products and services may be released (customized products). Against this background, we proceed this article with highlighting the development from Web 1.0 to Web 3.0, pointing out business opportunities for each phase.

BACKGROUND

One of the central characteristics of the post-industrial computer society is the systematic use of information technology (IT) as well as the acquisition and application of information that complements work-life and capital as an exclusive source of value, production and profit. Information became an independent factor of production (Porter, & Millar, 1985; Weiber, & Kollmann, 1998) and thus established the information economy (see Figure 1). From a historical perspective, initially only the product characteristics (quality) and corresponding product conditions (e.g. price, discount) determined if a product was successful (Kirzner, 1973; Porter, 1985). At that point it was important to either offer products or services to the customer that were either cheaper than (cost leadership) or qualitatively superior (quality leadership) to the competitor's product. Thereafter the first major successes, two additional factors joined the scene–time (speed) and flexibility (Meyer, 2001; Stalk, 1988). At this point, it was important to offer products/services at a certain point in time at a certain place (availability lead-

Figure 1.

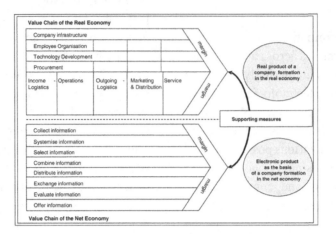

ership). Additionally it became crucial to allow for customer-oriented product differentiation of important product characteristics (demand leadership). Information technologies have now created an environment in which information is more easily accessible and can be increasingly used for commercial purposes. The source of a competitive advantage is determined as a result of the technological development presented here, by achieving knowledge and information superiority over the competition (information leadership). The growing relevance of IT and the expansion of electronic data networks have created a new commercial/business dimension that can be called the network economy or the Net Economy (see Figure 1). It is especially influenced by the area of electronic business processes that are concluded over digital data pathways (Kollmann, 2001; Taylor, & Murphy, 2004; Zwass, 2003). Due to the importance of information as a supporting and independent competitive factor, as well as the increase in digital data networks, a division of the relevant trade levels on which the world does business emerged (Weiber, & Kollmann, 1998): in addition to the real level of physical products and/or services (Real Economy), an electronic level for digital data and communication networks (Net Economy) evolved.

The commercial possibilities resulting from this development can be called, in this context, e-business (see Figure 1), which means the use of digital information technologies for supporting business processes in the preparation, negotiation and conclusion phases (Kollmann, 2001). The necessary building blocks, including information, communication and transaction are in this case transferred and respectively concluded between the participating trade partners over digital networks (Kollmann, 2004).

The growing relevance of electronic data networks such as the Internet has created a new business dimension. It is especially influenced by the area of electronic business processes that are concluded over digital data pathways (Kollmann, 2001; King et al., 2002; Zwass, 2003; Taylor & Murphy, 2004). Due to the importance of information as a supporting and independent competitive factor, as well as the increase in digital data networks, it must be assumed that there will be two relevant trade levels on which the world will do business in the future. In addition to the level of real, physical products and services (Real Economy), an electronic trade level for digital products and services (Net Economy) is evolving. "The Net Economy refers to the commercial use of electronic data networks, that is to say, a digital network economy, which, via various electronic platforms, allows the conclusion of information, communication and transaction processes" (Kollmann, 2006, p. 326).

The value chain of the Real Economy (Porter, 1985) divides a company into strategically relevant activities and identifies value activities that can be differentiated physically and technologically. The customer is prepared to pay for a valuable product that is based on these value activities. This product can then form the basis for establishing an enterprise in the Real Economy. In this model, the individual steps of a sequence of value generating or value increasing activities are analyzed in order to efficiently and effectively develop primary processes (for instance, in the areas of incoming logistics, operations, and outgoing logistics) and supporting processes (for instance, in the areas of technology development and procurement). Even here, information is extremely important when striving to be more successful than the competition. Information can be used to improve analysis and monitoring of existing processes. The crucial point is that information has previously been regarded as a supporting element only, but not as an independent source of customer value.

With the establishment of the Net Economy and the newly created dimension of information as an independent source of competitive advantage, value can be created through electronic business activities in digital data networks independent from a physical value chain as they are predominantly performed by the underlying information systems and do not include physical production machinery or personnel (Amit, & Zott, 2001; Lumpkin, & Dess, 2004; Weiber, & Kollmann, 1998). These electronic value added activities are thus not comparable to the physical value creation activities presented by Porter (1985), as they are rather characterized by the way information is used. Such value activities might include, for example, the collection, systemization, selection, combination and distribution of information. Through these specific activities of

creating value within digital data networks, an electronic value chain manifests itself (Figure 1). Based on this new value creation level, innovative business ideas evolve through the use of the various platforms and new digital products and Internet-based services are created. As customers are willing to pay for the value created by such an electronic product, it can form the basis for founding an electronic venture (e-venture) in the Net Economy (Kollmann, 2006).

Information emerges increasingly as a major factor of production, allowing the activation of innovative business opportunities. Both, Web 1.0 and Web 2.0 were linked directly to new stages in the development of e-business. However, against the background of an increasing information overload, the question to be asked is how technological and market-oriented future developments will cope with these challenges. Aiming at clarifying this overall development with the objective of giving impulses for the 3rd generation of e-business, the characteristics of each generation (Web 1.0, Web 2.0, and Web 3.0) will be clearly highlighted in the following.

Web 1.0: E-Procurement, E-Shop and E-Marketplace Systems

Web 1.0 describes supply-orientated information-, communication- and transaction processes within the Net Economy. Due to these processes, the supplier and the supply via object-orientated databases constitutes the starting point for related e-offer-, e-sales-, and e-trading-processes predominantly carried out by means of e-procurement, e-shop, and e-marketplace platforms. Web 1.0 is particularly characterized by supply-orientated systems, i.e. supply of objects and services is vital. Consequently, private or commercial suppliers try to use the internet as an additional distribution channel in order to provide products to the market using supply-orientated database systems as a starting point, yielding in three potential business opportunities:

E-Procurement-Systems

E-procurement enables the electronic purchasing of products and services from a company via digital networks using the integration of innovative information and communication technologies to support and conclude both operative and strategic tasks in the area of procurement (Kollmann, 2006). As a matter of principle, e-procurement represents a collective term for electronically supported procurement. The basic idea of electronic procurement refers to the procurement-relevant activities between an entrepreneur (procurement-manager) and a distributor (vender).

Key drivers for e-procurement are multifaceted problems of real purchase, which may be resolved by the means of electronic information processing. Regarding these problems, the following aspects are relevant (Dolmetsch, 2000):

- **Routine work:** The purchase department spends a lot of time for recurring assignments, e.g. filing an application for procurement, requesting supplier catalogues and manually conducting searches for suppliers and products. Studies reveal that almost 70% of all purchasing activities belong to recurring assignments. Correspondingly, there is barely time for assignments with higher added value such as negotiations with suppliers.
- **Purchasing regulation:** Up to one third of all procured goods and services are purchased beyond the formal procurement process and are thus detached from legal regulations. Despite negotiated contracts, employees often procure products from companies without any agreement in advance. Partially, there are no regulations for procurement. In these cases the decisions are made on a by-case basis.
- **Procurement lead time:** The actual procurement process requires a vast amount of time resources, because each step is carried out by an employee. This applies to the notification of demand, the approval procedure, and the order processing itself (e.g. supplier selection and receiving inspection). Investigations indicate that real procurement processes can last up to nine days.
- **Procurement costs:** The actual procurement process is relatively expensive. These costs are reasonable regarding the fact that approx. 50% of all orders are paper-based. In an international environment, research reveals that the procurement costs for a $ 5-item and a $ 4000-item are comparably, whereas total costs for each procurement transaction add up to $ 70 - $ 300.

E-Shop Systems

An e-shop is a company's virtual salesroom, allowing the electronic selling of products and services using digital networks. Thus, innovative information and communication technologies may be used supporting and concluding operative and strategic tasks for the buying process (Kollmann, 2006). The increasing acceptance of electronic media by customers goes along with a rising supply of products and services being partially or exclusively distributed by "virtual shops" via the internet. The basic idea of electronic sale refers to the relationship and the sale-relevant activities between entrepreneurs (suppliers) and consumers. Electronic sale consists of three fundamental aspects transferred from the actual sale (Choi et al., 1997): First, the shop owner himself aims at distributing products via the internet whereas traditionally, the seller is physically present in a shop. Second, contact merely takes place virtually, and selling from a customer's perspective is executed by the means of machine transactions. Finally, the product is either available in physical (e.g. computer) or in digital (e.g. software) form, which affects the buying process. If the product is available physically, the virtual sale will be combined with an actual distribution whereas digital products may be delivered electronically.

Once again, key drivers for e-shops are numerous issues of the actual sale which may be resolved by the means of electronic information processing. Concerning these problems, the following aspects are of relevance (Kollmann, 2008):

- **Capacity restrictions:** The sales area of a real shop is restricted by areal circumstances and related limitations. Out of respect for the limited sales area, the seller has to select a range of products which he intends to present in his shelves.

- **Trade structures:** In most branches of trade, there is no direct contact between the supplier or producer of goods and a particular customer. Multi-stage trade structures (e.g. relationship between wholesale traders and/or retail traders) intervene direct consumer communication and hinder an unfiltered communication in both directions. This affects both pace and efficiency of market cultivation.

- **Market anonymity:** In traditional mass markets, communication between manufacturer and customer is often anonymous. Correspondingly, e.g. identical advertising messages are sent to a variety of customers. Thus, individuality and the personal addressing of valuable customers are hardly possible.

- **Impenetrability:** Actual trade consumers have no insight into activities within the trade structure itself. Consequently, there is an apparent lack of transparency for those processes being behind the actual act of sale. Moreover, keeping track of the market structure is one of the most difficult tasks for customers.

E-Marketplace Systems

An e-marketplace allows for electronic trade with products and/or services via digital networks (Pavlou, & Gefen, 2005). Moreover, this represents the integration of innovative information and communication technologies to support and conclude, respectively, the matching process of supply and demand sides (Kollmann, 2006). Whereas actual marketplaces are characterized by local circumstances (e.g. tradeshows or weekly farmers' markets), electronic marketplaces focus on the digital networking of their market participants (Kollmann, 2009b). Participants may electronically access any e-marketplace from any digital access point without actually being present at a particular place at a particular moment, since e-marketplaces are permanently accessible. Supplier and consumer do not meet personally to settle a transaction but conclude contracts via digital data paths. The e-marketplace concept refers to a digital meeting place in which suppliers and consumers are connected by the means of electronic data processing to close business transactions. The transaction itself is detached from actual restrictions such as location-based limitations and is facilitated by a higher market instance (market operator), who actively coordinates transaction requests (Kollmann, 2005).

Once again, key drivers for e-marketplaces are numerous issues of the actual trade which can be resolved by means of the electronic information processing. Regarding these problems, the following aspects are of relevance (Kollmann, 2008):

- **Capacity restrictions:** Retail spaces of actual marketplaces are limited by areal circumstances and limitations.

- **Intermediation-related limitations:** Usually, the intermediate provides the retail space. The actual trade intermediation function focuses on the possibility of providing an overview of trade partners and trade objects without responding to individual transaction requests. Thus, a particular intermediation function for a single transaction object cannot be guaranteed.

- **Market transparency:** Due to many players on both sides, (opportunity) costs for gaining an overview are comparatively high. This undermines an effective price competition amongst competing suppliers, forcing the consumers to accept transactions at high price levels.

- **Coordination inefficiencies:** Usually, no direct contact between all consumers and all suppliers is in place, e.g. a consumer is not able to solicit a bid from every single supplier and to ensure that he or she receives a favorable price. Consequently, often suboptimal objects are purchased.

Summing up these aspects, Web 1.0 has offered a wide range of business opportunities in the past, overcoming limitations from the actual trade. However, with increasing recipients, benefits of web 1.0 decline whereas the opportunities Web 2.0 offers in readiness become the focal point of interest.

Web 2.0: E-Community Systems

As opposed to Web 1.0 technologies, Web 2.0 is characterized by networking systems being supposed to connect private or commercial users over the internet, setting up social networks. Web 2.0 describes membership-orientated information-, communication-, and transaction processes within the Net Economy. Due to these processes, the network via profile-orientated databases represents the starting point for related e-networking-processes predominantly carried out by means of e-community platforms. Web 2.0 emphasizes communication via the e-networking process, occurring on so-called e-community platforms. Therefore, contact between users is the utmost concern. Contact is easily conceivable for private

as well as for commercial purposes. Correspondingly, the community-thought comes forward, providing the basis for various new business ideas that were unconceivable a few years ago. Accordingly, the economic potential of these business ideas illustrates the high-volume going public of YouTube (1.65 billion U.S. dollars). However, Web 2.0 technology offers even more than mere successful business ideas: By means of concepts like wikis, blogs, and mashups, companies are able to enter even closer into dialogue with their customers (O'Reilly, 2005). Social capital has a great impact on the latest e-business developments and since there are a lot of common goals and interests in connecting people, the web of companies became a web of people (Wahlster, & Dengel, 2006).

An e-community may be considered as structure of organized communication within an electronic contact network. More specifically, an e-community accounts for the supply of a technical platform in order to enable interaction between individuals (Kollmann, 2009b). Relationships between individuals may be characterized thematically by communication contexts but also by the social or professional status of community members. Focusing on social interaction, the exchange of information is individually generated, i.e. user-generated content. Accordingly, individuals possess common ideas in terms of interests, goals, or activities, and attend at least occasionally common places in terms of electronic platforms. Via these platforms, individuals are able to communicate with each other for a longer period (O'Reilly, 2005), and mutual communication is particularly affected by the asynchronous and location-independent character of the electronic information exchange. Thereby, the e-community supports members in two directions: On the one hand by assuring information- and communication exchange between members and on the other hand by managing the emerging social network between the members. Thus, support is usually provided

Figure 2.

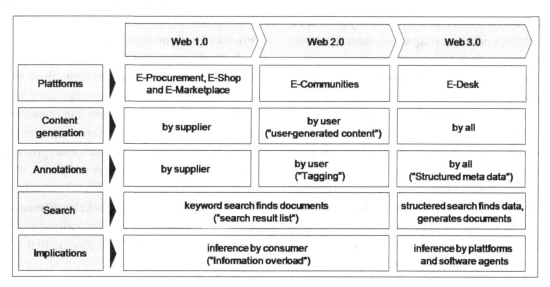

by common rules, values and standards (Farrell, & Saloner, 1985), determining the conditions of participation.

Summing up, Web 2.0 technology offers the opportunity to provide and access information at any time and place for companies as well as private persons. However, without knowing about the availability of particular information, users cannot utilize them. Additionally, current search engines are no longer capable of solving information problems efficiently and effectively. The fact that information seekers are increasingly overburdened with information overloads leads to an increased time being required for discovering particular information. Therefore, further development of technology is necessary being capable of coping with these challenges primarily characterized by information efficiency issues.

WEB 3.0: E-DESK SYSTEMS

Accordingly, Web 3.0 is characterized particularly by demand-orientated systems, i.e. demand for objects and services is vital. Web 3.0 describes

demand-orientated information-, communication-, and transaction processes within the Net Economy. Due to these processes, the consumer and the demand via individual registration-, and specification systems represent the starting point for related e-request-, and e-customization processes predominantly carried out by means of e-desk (request) or modified e-shop platforms. Starting point are demand-driven registration and specification systems. The consumer is central to these processes and may get individual help comparable to help from an information desk. Figure 2 illustrates the transition from Web 1.0 over Web 2.0 to Web 3.0. Not only information but also individual products and services may be released (customized products).

E-Request Systems

Web 2.0 and semantic web are growing together slowly. Thereby, potential methods of resolution for coping with information overloads advance. However, evolution processes require time. A variety of user information issues are yet to be resolved. Despite the increased spread of tags and metadata, software systems can hardly respond to further issues such as automatically generated answers to personalized requests. Customers, however, need a demand tailored (mobile) e-business solutions instead of searching for a matching object on several distinct platforms. Hence resulting, business opportunities will arise from the identification of costumers' information needs. New business concepts allow for the individualization of existing products and services. For recording customers' demand, demand-orientated platforms and e-request systems facilitated by intelligent and user-friendly (e.g. Ajax-based) interfaces are required. Consequently, objects matching particular user demand are not merely generated by the information overloaded web but rather by the means of human references from a well-structured pool of a partner companies, charging commission for the mediation function (Kollmann, 2009a). One example of a demand-oriented platform is *askerus*, being a portal for holiday seekers.

The proverb '*seek, and you shall find*' does not necessarily apply to the context of searching for trips and booking holidays over the internet anymore, due to the information overload that hinders consumers to find what they are actually looking for. Along with this, the information overload reduces the recognition value for travel businesses since overlooking particular companies becomes more and more likely. In contrast to this, *askerus* focuses on counseling services. Travelers may configure individually their vacation demands via a particular template and may then request associated travel agencies to send up to 15 matching offers. Thus, the focus is on the customer, who uses the web of the future to actively communicate demands. Moreover, this is advantageous for travel businesses as well since clientele and customer frequency increase, while acquisition costs decrease (e.g. for paper catalogs, electronic supplier marketplaces, telephone sessions, costly field workers).

E-Customization Systems

Product configuration attempts to provide individualization options for customers, allowing for customization in alignment with their product demands. For this purpose, particular product characteristics are selectable facilitated by option menus. Choosing particular options allows customers to generate own individual products out of predefined sets of product variations, whereas the provider additionally generates useful information about demanded product characteristics. An explicit personalization is the option for customers to configure products according to their own desires, based on product-specific parameters being defined by the supplier himself. For possible product configurations, individualization and personalization become essential components of electronic business ideas and an upward trend can be observed for so-called e-customization systems (Kollmann 2009a). *Dell* can be regarded as a pioneer for product configuration options where the customer gets the ability to individually arrange the components of his laptop (e.g. processor, RAM, video card). Moreover, as well within the sector "food", a variety of young start-up companies emerged recently based on the business idea of product configuration (e.g. mycornflakes. com). The product analysis includes three main issue areas:

- **The main component:** The number of individual components of the end product, being supposed to be sold in an e-shop, may vary depending on complexity. Many business models emphasize one particular main component. Contrastingly, components depend on customers' demands and can be adjusted. In contrast, other business models attempt to attain a new, individual end product by combination of several individual products, e.g. mycornflakes. com. Besides the basic product, customers may further select cereal ingredients (nuts,

Figure 3.

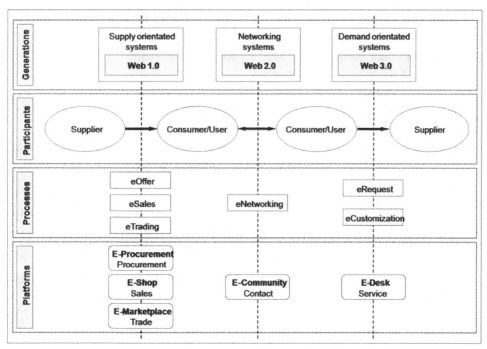

seeds, fruits) for their individual purchasable product.

- **Alternatives:** Nature and number of variations (such as diverse nuts- or fruit types) have to be taken into account for the analysis of product configuration business models. Merely one predominant ingredient allows for the focusing on offering as many variations and types as possible for covering a wide range of individual tastes. A different way is to offer a wide variety in single products. However, this has to be regarded bearing content and profitability in mind - the more variations the more effort and costs for the process of composition.
- **Share volume and price:** An important criterion for product analysis is the identification of proportions of several components as well as pricing. If customers are allowed the possibility to configure a product by themselves, the impact of each step (e.g. selection of a type) needs to be apparent,

e.g. the customer needs to be immediately able to find out how the final price changes by adding or removing ingredients.

Summing up, when information overloads will be reduced by the means of Web 3.0 technologies, new competitive advantages will open up (Figure 3).

FUTURE RESEARCH DIRECTIONS

In this paper we highlight the development from Web 1.0 to Web 3.0, pointing out business opportunities for each phase. Future studies should consider this as a starting point for conducting further research regarding opportunities provided by all web technologies. The creation of new ventures plays a decisive role for the social and economic development of every country. This is due to the fact that with each new venture created, a market participant comes into existence, which potentially stimulates the competition and drives the economy further. The founding of electronic ventures within the Net Economy is therefore a key topic for every national industry. As the significance of Internet-based technologies has triggered a technological and societal development that is irresistible, e-entrepreneurship can be expected to gain further importance in the future. The pervasiveness of digital technologies and changes in customer behavior are increasingly blurring the borders between electronic and physical trade levels. Real Economy and Net Economy are merging. Particularly in this context, the need for a complementary utilization of physical and electronic value creation activities can be expected, as customers will increasingly use online and offline channels contemporaneously (Kollmann, & Häsel, 2006). Researchers will have to further elaborate the concepts presented here in order to explain the full range of commercial activities that future technologies will allow and future customers will ask for.

CONCLUSION

With the dawn of the Internet in the last decade of the twentieth century, a structural change in both social and economic spheres was induced. Information technology has become an integral part of daily life and its influence on the transfer of information has become ubiquitous. The fundamental advantages of Internet-related technologies, especially in regard to their efficiency and effectiveness, assure that its diffusion in society and in most industries will continue. It should have become apparent that all three web-forms offer a wide range of opportunities to found electronic ventures. To fully exploit the potentials of internet-related technologies, however, founders need to approach e-entrepreneurship in a systematic and precautious way that is backed by sound strategy. Regardless of which technology is implemented to cope with those issues, taking advantage of

current challenges, only one conclusion is possible: We are just at the beginning – the future of the World Wide Web holds lots of business opportunities ready.

REFERENCES

Amit, R., & Zott, C. (2001). Value Creation in E-Business. *Strategic Management Journal, 22*(6/7), 493–520. doi:10.1002/smj.187

Choi, S.-Y., Stahl, D. O., & Whinston, A. B. (1997). *The economics of electronic commerce*. Indianapolis, IN: Macmillan.

Farrell, J., & Saloner, G. (1985). Standardisation, compatibility and innovation. *The Rand Journal of Economics, 16*(1), 70–83. doi:10.2307/2555589

King, D., Lee, J., Warkentin, M., & Chung, H. (2002). *Electronic Commerce: A Managerial Perspective*. Upper Saddle River, NJ: Pearson Education International.

Kirzner, I. M. (1973). *Competition and Entrepreneurship*. Chicago: University of Chicago Press.

Kollmann, T. (2001). Measuring the acceptance of electronic marketplaces. *Journal of Computer Mediated Communication, 6*(2). Retrieved July 23, 2009, from http://jcmc.indiana.edu/vol6/issue2/kollmann.html

Kollmann, T. (2005). The matching function for electronic market places – determining the probability of coordinating of supply and demand. *International Journal of Electronic Business, 5*(3), 461–472. doi:10.1504/IJEB.2005.008520

Kollmann, T. (2006). What is e-entrepreneurship? – Fundamentals of company founding in the net economy. *International Journal of Technology Management, 33*(4), 322–340. doi:10.1504/IJTM.2006.009247

Kollmann, T. (2009a). *E-Entrepreneurship* (3rd Ed.). Wiesbaden, Germany: Gabler.

Kollmann, T. (2009b). *E-Business* (3rd Ed.). Wiesbaden, Germany: Gabler.

Kollmann, T., & Häsel, M. (2006). *Cross-Channel Cooperation: The Bundling of Online and Offline Business Models*. Wiesbaden, Germany: DUV.

Kollmann, T., & Häsel, M. (2007). *Web 2.0*. Wiesbaden, Germany: Gabler.

Lumpkin, G. T., & Dess, G. G. (2004). E-Business Strategies and Internet Business Models: How the Internet Adds Value. *Organizational Dynamics*, *33*(2), 161–173. doi:10.1016/j.orgdyn.2004.01.004

Matlay, H. (2004). E-entrepreneurship and small e-business development: towards a comparative research agenda. *Journal of Small Business and Enterprise Development*, *11*, 408–414. doi:10.1108/14626000410551663

Meyer, C. (2001). The second generation of speed. *Harvard Business Review*, *79*(4), 24–26.

O'Reilly, T. (2005). *What Is Web 2.0. Design patterns and business models for the next generation of software*. Retrieved March 30, 2009, from http://www.oreillynet.com/pub/a/oreilly/tim/news/2005/09/30/what-is-web-20.html

Pavlou, P. A., & Gefen, D. (2005). Psychological contract violation in online marketplaces: Antecedents, consequences, and moderating role. *Information Systems Research*, *16*(4), 372–399. doi:10.1287/isre.1050.0065

Porter, M. E. (1985). *Competitive Advantage*. New York: Free Press.

Porter, M. E., & Millar, V. E. (1985). How information gives you competitive advantage. *Harvard Business Review*, *63*(4), 149–160.

Stalk, G. Jr. (1988). Time – the next source of competitive advantage. *Harvard Business Review*, *66*(4), 28–60.

Taylor, M., & Murphy, A. (2004). SMEs and e-business. *Journal of Small Business and Enterprise Development*, *11*(3), 280–289. doi:10.1108/14626000410551546

Wahlster, W., & Dengel, A. (2006). Web 3.0: Convergence of Web 2.0 and the semantic web. *Technology Feature Paper Edition*, *II*, 2–22.

Weiber, R., & Kollmann, T. (1998). Competitive advantages in virtual markets–perspectives of Information-based Marketing in cyberspace. *European Journal of Marketing*, *32*(7/8), 603–615. doi:10.1108/03090569810224010

Zwass, V. (2003). Electronic commerce and organizational innovation: aspects and opportunities. *International Journal of Electronic Commerce*, *7*(3), 7–37.

ADDITIONAL READING

Adomavicius, G., & Tuzhilin, A. (2005). Toward the next generation of recommender systems: survey of the state–of–the–art and possible extensions. *IEEE Transactions on Knowledge and Data Engineering*, *17*(4), 734–748. doi:10.1109/TKDE.2005.99

Berners-Lee, T., Hendler, J., & Lassila, O. (2001). The semantic web. *Scientific American*, *5*(5), 34–43. doi:10.1038/scientificamerican0501-34

Cayzer, S. (2004). Semantic blogging and decentralized knowledge management. *Communications of the ACM*, *49*(11), 40–45.

Daconta, M., Obrst, L., & Smith, K. (2003). *The semantic web – A guide to the future of XML, web services, and knowledge management*. Indianapolis, IN: Wiley & Sons.

Duffy, G., & Dale, B. G. (2002). E-commerce processes: a study of criticality. *Industrial Management & Data Systems*, *102*(8), 432–441. doi:10.1108/02635570210445862

Farrell, J., & Saloner, G. (1986). Installed base and compatibility: Innovation, product, preannouncement and predation. *The American Economic Review, 76*(5), 940–955.

Fensel, D., Hendler, J., Lieberman, H., & Wahlster, W. (2003). Introduction to the semantic web. In D. Fensel, J. Hendler, H. Lieberman, & W. Wahlster (Eds.), *Spinning the semantic web. Bringing the World Wide Web to its full potential* (pp. 1–25). Cambridge, MA: MIT Press.

Galanxhi-Janaqi, H., & Fui-Hoon Nah, F. (2004). U-commerce: Emerging trends and research issues. *Industrial Management & Data Systems, 104*(9), 744–755. doi:10.1108/02635570410567739

Hagel, J., & Armstrong, A. G. (1997). *Net gain.* Boston, MA: Harvard Business School Press.

Hendler, J. (2001). Agents and the semantic web. *IEEE Intelligent Systems, 16*(2), 30–37. doi:10.1109/5254.920597

Ibeh, K. I. N., Luo, Y., & Dinnie, K. (2006). E-branding strategies of internet companies: Some preliminary insights from the UK. *Journal of Brand Management, 12*(5), 355–373. doi:10.1057/palgrave.bm.2540231

Katz, M. L., & Shapiro, C. (1985). Network externalities, competition, and compatibility. *The American Economic Review, 75*(3), 424–440.

Kollmann, T. (2000). Competitive strategies for electronic marketplaces. *Electronic Markets*

Kollmann, T. (2006). What is e-entrepreneurship? – Fundamentals of company founding in the net economy. *International Journal of Technology Management, 33*(4), 322–340. doi:10.1504/IJTM.2006.009247

Kollmann, T., Stöckmann, C., & Schröer, C. (2009). The Diffusion of Web 2.0 Platforms: The Problem of Oscillating Degrees of Utilization. In J. Xu & M. Quaddus (Eds.), *E-business in the 21st Century: Realities, Challenges, and Outlook.* Hackensack, NJ: World Scientific Publishing.

Laudon, K. C., & Traver, C. (2002). *E-Commerce: Business, Technology, Society.* Boston, MA: Addison Wesley.

Lee, H. G., & Clark, T. H. (1996). Impacts of the electronic marketplace on transaction cost and market Structure. *International Journal of Electronic Commerce, 1*(1), 127–149.

Lumpkin, G., & Dess, G. (2004). E-business strategies and internet business models: how the internet adds value. *Organizational Dynamics, 33*, 161–173. doi:10.1016/j.orgdyn.2004.01.004

Pavlou, P. A., & Fygenson, M. (2006). Understanding and predicting electronic commerce adoption: An extension of the theory of planned behavior. *MIS Quarterly, 30*(1), 115–143.

Powell, T. (2006). AJAX is the future of web app development. *New World (New Orleans, La.), 23*(2), 35.

Rogers, E. M. (2003). *Diffusion of Innovations* (5th ed.). New York: Free Press.

Sheth, A., Verma, K., & Gomadam, K. (2003). Semantics to energize the full service spectrum – Using an ontological approach to better exploit services and the technical and business levels. *Communications of the ACM, 49*(7), 55–61. doi:10.1145/1139922.1139949

Silver, M. (2006). Browser-based applications: Popular but flawed? *Information Systems and E-Business Management, 4*(4), 361–393. doi:10.1007/s10257-005-0024-3

Soliman, F., & Youssef, M. A. (2003). Internet-based e-commerce and its impact on manufacturing and business operations. *Industrial Management & Data Systems, 103*(8), 546–552. doi:10.1108/02635570310497594

Chapter 16
OpenSocial:
Structured Partnerships in the Context of Social Networking Platforms

Matthias Häsel
XING AG, Germany

ABSTRACT

Building on the OpenSocial API suite, developers can create applications that are interoperable within the context of different social networks. Because social applications have access to a network's social graph, messaging systems and update feeds, the OpenSocial standard enables Internet-based businesses to create new kinds of value-creating partnerships without extending themselves beyond their own means or competencies. This chapter argues that by entering structured partnerships, e-ventures and social networks can gain sustainable competitive advantage by integrating their highly complementary resources and capabilities. Building on the Resource-based View (RBV) of the firm and the concept of core competencies, it is shown that both partners can significantly benefit from the technology-induced possibilities that arise from the OpenSocial standard.

INTRODUCTION

The dawn of the Internet in the last decade of the twentieth century induced a structural change in both social and economic spheres. By now, a significant portion of our social interaction happens on the Web (Raman, 2009). At the same time, new possibilities emerged with respect to how enterprises create value. An enterprise can create customer value not only by its physical activities, but also through the

creation of value on an electronic level (Weiber, & Kollmann, 1998; Amit, & Zott, 2001; Lumpkin, & Dess, 2004). An entirely new business dimension which may be referred to as the Net Economy has emerged (Kollmann, 2006). It is characterized by numerous entrepreneurial e-ventures that generate revenue and profits independent from a physical value chain (Matlay, & Westhead, 2005) – often referred to as e-ventures (Kollmann, 2006; Kollmann & Häsel, 2007).

When e-ventures introduce their new business ideas to the market, entering partnerships with

DOI: 10.4018/978-1-61520-597-4.ch016

other Internet-based enterprises is a promising strategy as it enables the partners to create more attractive product offers and represents a basis for more efficiently and effectively communicating and distributing their products (Kollmann, 2006; Kollmann & Häsel, 2007). With the establishment of the Net Economy also the collaboration between enterprises reached a new level of quality. The wide, open and cost-effective infrastructure of the Internet allows a simple, fast exchange of data and thus a synchronisation of business processes over large distances (Kollmann & Häsel, 2008). In particular, URL addressable Application Programming Interfaces (APIs) which have become an integral part of the Web in the past years (Raman, 2009) induce new forms of structured collaboration between Internet-based enterprises and enable technology-orientated growth strategies (Volkmann & Tokarski, 2006).

Intensified attention is currently gained by APIs that allow for creating applications that can exist within the context of social networks, such as OpenSocial (OpenSocial Foundation, 2009). Social networks such as MySpace, Facebook or XING are all examples of very successful online communities with several millions of users. Technically, they are accommodated through networking software that maps a social graph. This enables individual members to create and maintain personal profiles and to manage their connections to other members within a network community (e.g. to friends, colleagues or business contacts). Social networks often permit the sending and receiving of messages, in addition to supporting so-called update feeds, which let users know about their contacts' activity within a given network.

By means of the OpenSocial API suite, a social network may grant third-party products access to its social graph (i.e., profile and contact data), as well as to any messaging systems or update feeds. Used by collaborating people, these products then create a far richer user experience than any product that exists outside a social graph context (Raman,

2009). In this chapter, it is argued that OpenSocial can be seen as an enabler for new kinds of value-creating partnerships between e-ventures and social networks. Building on the Resource-based View (RBV) of the firm and, in particular, the concept of core competencies, it is shown that both e-ventures and social networks can significantly benefit from the technology-induced possibilities that arise from the OpenSocial standard.

BACKGROUND

The OpenSocial API suite defines a set of programming interfaces for developing social applications that are interoperable on different social networking sites which are referred to as containers in this context. Different than applications that have been developed for proprietary environments such as the Facebook Platform (Graham, 2008), OpenSocial applications are interoperable within the context of multiple networks and build on standard technologies such as HTML and JavaScript.

Until it was made public in November 2007, the OpenSocial standard was driven primarily by Google. However, the standard was not suited for productive use at that time as there have been several shortcomings with respect to user interface and security. By now the specification is managed by the non-profit OpenSocial Foundation and has reached a stable state suitable for commercial use. In April 2009, more than 20 large social networking sites (amongst others MySpace, hi5, and orkut) have been using the OpenSocial standard to provide their users with social applications (OpenSocial Foundation, 2009).

Social applications are based on the gadget architecture originally developed by Google, which has been expanded on by interfaces which enable access to the social data found in the context of any given container. Gadgets are XML documents containing HTML and JavaScript code along with metadata. The XML specification of a gadget is rendered by the container and integrated into its own website. Communication between the gadget and the container operates in such instances via standardized Ajax requests (Garrett, 2005).

From a user's perspective, first-time usage of a social application usually involves some kind of installation process whereby the user explicitly gives permission for the application to access the data in their personal user profile. The developer can enter optional URLs in the gadget specification, to which the container reports user-related events – such as the adding or deleting of the gadget to or from the user account. Once the gadget has been added to the user account, the user can then interact with this gadget. Containers can support several different locations where gadgets may be rendered. These locations are formally known as views. A gadget can request through the API which views are supported by the container and in which view it is currently being rendered:

- **Profile View:** The gadget is rendered with other gadgets as part of the user profile. This is particularly useful when users have generated content within the application that they wish to present to other users in their own profile.
- **Canvas View:** The gadget is rendered here by itself in a full-screen view. The canvas view is therefore the main place where users interact with the application and create content.
- **Home View:** The gadget is rendered on the start page of the container here. Several gadgets are usually rendered alongside one another, giving users an overview of new developments in their own information space.
- **Preview View:** This view allows a user to preview the gadget's functionality. It is therefore used particularly often if the user hasn't yet installed the gadget (e.g. on a purely informative page).

The OpenSocial JavaScript API enables direct access to the social graphs of the container. Individual person objects within the graph are represented by a person class that supports more than 50 fields used with the context of user profiles on social networks. The majority of these fields are optional, meaning that the container ultimately decides which profile data they make available to their applications. Two instances of the person class are directly available in the form of the VIEWER and the OWNER. The first object here involves the current user or viewer, while the latter is the user in whose context the application is executed. This implies that the VIEWER and OWNER are the same person if a gadget is rendered in the home or canvas view. They can be two different people though in the profile view if the VIEWER views the application in the context of the OWNER's user profile.

The central characteristic of networking software is their support in the creation of targeted connections, and in viewing and traversing the own connections and those made by others within the network (Boyd & Ellison, 2007). Social applications have to access precisely these connections to be able to support the exchange of information and the interaction between users. OpenSocial enables this with the requests VIEWER_FRIENDS and OWNER_FRIENDS. These differ from one another if a person views another user's profile, but are often not disjunctive, meaning that the VIEWER can often find their own contacts within the contact list of the OWNER.

Most current networking platforms offer update feeds, which let the user know about the activities of their contacts (e.g. "What's new in my network" on XING). Users can find out here, for instance, who has changed company or been promoted, who has connected with whom and who has joined which group. Within an activity, the subject or the object(s) of this activity are linked, aimed at increasing user activity on the platform. OpenSocial gives social applications the opportunity to promote themselves in the container's update feed, hence growing organically as a result. On the one hand, an interaction between the user and the container can form an activity (e.g. the installation of a gadget or the adding of a gadget to a user's own profile page). On the other hand, an activity can also be an interaction between the user and the gadget (e.g. the upload of a file in a collaboration tool or the achieving of a new high score in a game). Containers usually implement the activity concept here in such a way that users can decide for themselves at any time whether or not they want to allow a gadget to send activities to their contact network.

In order to avoid users having a large number of the same or similar activities in their update feeds, they can be aggregated with the help of activity templates in accordance with the OpenSocial standard, in which developer define general events with placeholders for data specific to applications and users. This separation of content and presentation means that containers can display consolidated bundles of activities, thus maintaining a clearly structured update feed. The container reserves the right to determine the ultimate display and execution of each and every activity, meaning that the use of activity templates from a developer's perspective can be a mandatory requirement for a container to process activities reported by a gadget in the first place.

The sending of notifications is another method in addition to the activity concept that provides other users within the networking site with user-specific information. Social applications can feed different types of messages to the container. Once again, the container has control here over whether and how these messages are presented to the recipient (e.g. as an email or site message). To protect users' privacy, containers usually give them the freedom to choose for themselves whether a gadget may send messages to other users at all.

In order to enable data access to servers, mobile end devices and desktop computers that isn't dependent on Ajax and direct user interaction, the OpenSocial specification also includes a RESTful API (Fielding & Taylor, 2002). Applications can make use of this API analogously to the JavaScript API for accessing people, relationships, activities and messages within the context of the container. Figure 1 summarizes the data exchange between a social application and the surrounding container that is made possible by the OpenSocial standard.

STRUCTURED PARTNERSHIPS IN THE SOCIAL NETWORKING CONTEXT

In this section, it is argued that APIs such as OpenSocial enable a new form of value-creating, structured collaboration between social networks and e-ventures. For the latter, the advent of OpenSocial increases an e-venture's scope and productivity considerably, as it means that applications need only be developed once, and can then be implemented within the context of any given social network container that supports the standard. For the containers, respectively, OpenSocial APIs represent a chance to bring value-adding functionality to their community which is provided by third parties.

Theoretical Foundation

To explain why firms cooperate, the Resource-Based View (RBV) has been widely applied and accepted in strategic management literature. RBV focuses on the internal organization of firms, which is, in particular, defined by their internal resources and capabilities (Prahalad, & Hamel, 1990; Barney 1991; Wernerfeld, 1995). RBV assumes that resources are heterogeneously distributed across firms and resource differences persist over time (Amit, & Schoemaker, 1993; Wernerfeld, 1995). Hereon, researchers have theorized that when firms dispose of resources that are valuable, rare, imitable, and non-substitutable, they are able to

Figure 1. Data exchange between application and container

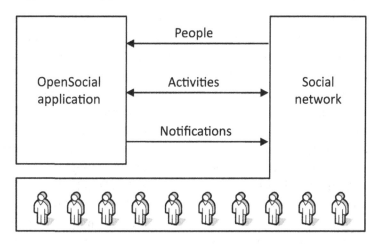

achieve competitive advantage by strategies that cannot be easily duplicated by their competitors (Barney 1991; Wernerfeld, 1995). According to RBV, cooperation results from the possibility of getting access to valuable resources and capabilities of the partner, "that cannot be efficiently obtained through market exchanges" (Das, & Teng, 2000). Similarly, hypothesizing on the concept of core competencies introduced by Prahalad and Hamel (1990), it can be argued that cooperation should be built around a set of shared competencies that provide potential access to wide markets and make a significant contribution to the perceived customer benefits. Since building competencies is often difficult and expensive, firms should concentrate on their current core competencies while outsourcing certain tasks that others can handle better.

Important to add here is that resources in the Net Economy are difficult to keep proprietary. This makes time an essential aspect of strategy and the duration of competitive advantage unpredictable (Porter 2001). Because business models and the whole market structure are often unclear, the challenge is not only achieving competitive advantage, but sustaining it (Eisenhardt, & Martin, 2000). To explain how and why firms achieve competitive advantage in such volatile industries, researchers

have extended RBV (Teece, Pisano, & Shuen, 1997). They argue that dynamic capabilities are a set of processes by which firms "integrate, reconfigure, build and release resources – to match and even create market change" (Eisenhardt, & Martin, 2000, p. 1107). In the sense of structured partnerships in the context of social networking platforms, these processes affect the external resources made accessible via the respective partners. Hence, it can be assumed that the ability to enter structured partnerships represents a dynamic capability that is a precondition to leverage partner resources to produce adaptive outcomes (Porter 2001; Eisenhardt, & Martin, 2000).

E-Ventures vs. Social Networks

Because a lack of financial means often leads to deficits in the areas of sales and market positioning, cooperation strategies play an elementary role for the growth of e-ventures (Kollmann, & Häsel, 2006; Volkmann, & Tokarski, 2006). Consequently, the possibility of gaining access to a specific national or the international user base of a large social network can be seen as the main reason for an e-venture to enter a structured partnership based on OpenSocial. Moreover, as users are not willing to maintain several high-quality profiles on the Web it is difficult for e-ventures to build and grow their own social graph. In that sense, it is not only the user base as such that is of important value for an e-venture, but rather the social graph of a given network including the user-generated content attached to it (i.e., profile and contact data). This is important as many new products on the Web are based on mass collaboration and, more specifically, the concepts of openness, peering, sharing, and acting globally (Tapscott, & Williams, 2006). As a result, structured partnerships do not only result in quantitative aspects such as an increase in profitability and a reduction of costs, but also improve the quality of customer need satisfaction which highly depends on the number of users using the product.

While e-ventures may utilize the social graph of networking sites to balance their deficits in terms of market access, operators of social networks are presented with the opportunity to expand on their own existing functionalities with additional third-party applications delivered by various e-ventures without having to relinquish control over their user data in the process. When specialized products are built and maintained by strategic partners, social networks are able to focus on what is their core competency: To build, run and maintain an infrastructure that maps a social graph and offers various core services on top of it, such as user profiles, contact management, search, messaging, and update feeds. Additional infrastructure services may include community components such as groups and forums as well as payment and billing.

While the core services offered by a social network are of horizontal nature (i.e., every member of a network is using them), the specialized products that come in via structured partnership are rather vertical, designed to meet the specific needs of a certain user segment. Consequently, structured partnerships based on OpenSocial are a perfect means to reach of what is referred to as the long tail (Andersson 2006; O'Reilly 2007), with the collective power of many vertical third-party

applications making up a social network's product portfolio. The technological implementation of each social application as well as any application-related content is delivered and maintained by the specific partner, whose core competency is focused around a specific product, but not necessarily running a social network.

Besides these core competencies in delivering horizontal vs. vertical customer needs, resources also include strategic assets such as brands (Amit, & Schoemaker, 1993). When introducing structured partnerships based on social applications, brand image and publicity of both partners may be increased when two well-established brands are featured together. At the same time, the social application brought into a social network joys a unique positioning in the community if it is carrying a well-known brand. However, while some mature Net Economy players such as eBay or Facebook have invested high amounts in building a brand or boosted their brand value due to network effects, this is not necessarily true for e-ventures. Certainly, an e-venture leverages the equity of its product when bundling with an established social network. Nevertheless, research shows that partnering even with an unknown brand is judged favourable by customers when the brands presented together are seen as providing complementary features (Samu, Krishnan, & Smith, 1999). This is true when it comes to horizontal vs. vertical features so that co-branding, even if the brand of a social application is unknown, can be assumed to be valuable for both e-ventures and social networks.

Despite its potential value for e-ventures and social networks, structured partnerships based on OpenSocial pose significant challenges. Most importantly, partners need to be equipped with the capability of keeping pace with the complexity and volatility of the OpenSocial standard and its surrounding technologies. Both e-ventures and social networks are required to build and refine expertise in the implementation of structured partnerships as well as their continuous enhancement,s both from a technical and managerial perspective.

Figure 2. Resources and capabilities brought in by e-ventures and social networks

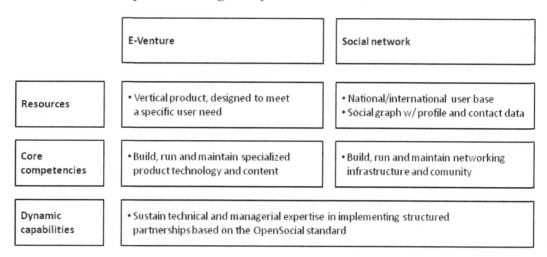

To conclude, both e-ventures and social networks need to bring in different resources and capabilities to make a partnership successful. Figure 2 summarizes the endowment of both partners in terms of resources, core competencies and capabilities.

Partnerships and Strategy

As in marketing alliances in general (Bucklin & Sengupta, 1993), the potential for serious conflict and opportunism is high when it comes to structured partnerships. Integrating very different products and business models is inherently risky. These risks can be countered if both the partner identification and the following project execution are characterized by a systematic proceeding. Especially for young businesses, however, cooperation opportunities often result from existing personal contact networks, and also the pressure of time and heavily stressed management resources may result in a rather pragmatic proceeding. In many cases, e-ventures develop ad hoc strategies, anticipating or reacting on changes in the competitive environment.

No matter whether strategy is planned or comes ad hoc, entrepreneurs and managers need to be sure whether their strategic objectives can be achieved

with the help of OpenSocial. A strategic fit is a prerequisite for a win-win situation and can only be ensured by the explicit formulation and communication of strategic objectives, as well as the pronounced engagement of both partners. "Trust and commitment are the building blocks of alliance effectiveness" (Perry, Sengupta, & Krapfel, 2004). Conversely, during the 'dot-com boom', some cooperation agreements purely aimed at increasing the partners' reputation by brand alliances. However, "The days of the [...] press releases announcing, 'I love you, you love me, we're a happy family' are over" (Ernst, Halevy, Monier, & Sarrazin, 2001, p. 92). Both social networks and e-ventures need to recognize the strategic fit, and not reduce structured partnerships to an aspect of marketing. At the same time, both partners need to prevent their businesses from arriving at a conditio sine qua non (i.e., a condition where they cannot successfully operate without the resources brought in by the partner). Methods of the portfolio theory can be applied to achieve a balanced ratio of partners and to determine whether a partner fits into the overall partnering strategy.

As partners need to perceive and treat each other as equals, Bucklin and Sengupta (1993) suggest that businesses should build relationships with partners having similar endowments in terms of resources and capabilities. Power balance is "sought by the parties as the means to ensure that neither has the incentive to exploit the other" (Bucklin, & Sengupta, 1993, p. 32). As power imbalance can be detrimental to the effectiveness of a partnership and could thus deny the potential of otherwise desirable relationships between e-ventures and social networks, partners need to mitigate the risks resulting from power imbalances by carefully drawing up a contract. To build fruitful alliances, arrangements should include termination penalties and exclusivity constraints that can be seen as pledges of commitment for the partnership (Anderson, & Weitz, 1992; Perry et al., 2004). Financial incentives in form of equity investments or direct monetary payments can be another component of the contract (Bucklin, & Sengupta, 1993). Direct payments can be unidirectional or bidirectional and may include both one-time fees and commissions on joint sales within the scope of the vertical product. Despite the complexity of a structured partnership, contractual terms effectively safeguard both partners' interests.

FUTURE RESEARCH DIRECTIONS

OpenSocial can be seen as a precursor to a paradigm shift that will ultimately see social networking sites evolve from enclosed software systems to a run time environment for social applications that provides the basic networking functionality and standardized infrastructure they need to operate. In that sense, OpenSocial is a key enabler for moving from a Web of content to a Web of loosely coupled, social applications (Raman, 2009).

Structured partnerships based on social networking APIs such as OpenSocial and the Facebook Platform can be expected to gain importance in the future. With the proliferation of the social Web as well as mobile technologies, more innovative business models that can or need to be run

in a social networking context can be expected to emerge. To understand the resulting social and economic implications, researchers need to empirically investigate the phenomenon of such structured partnerships. More specifically, vertical application partnerships within social networks need to be classified and compared according to their technical, social and economic characteristics in order to learn about the actual value they create for the involved parties.

CONCLUSION

The concepts presented in this chapter highlighted that structured partnerships in the context of social networking platforms enable the partners to create new kinds of value-creating partnerships without extending themselves beyond their own means or competencies. Based on the Resource-based view and the concept of core competencies, it has been theorized that by entering OpenSocial-enabled partnerships, e-ventures and social networks can gain sustainable competitive advantage by integrating highly complementary resources and capabilities.

The idea of being able to develop social software without having to build a new social graph from scratch opens up a wealth of different business opportunities. Internet-based enterprises can exploit this, in particular, to boost both their outreach and product quality – by positioning social applications on various networking sites. This is particularly appealing to e-ventures that have to gain a broad user base as quickly as possible with a flexible product despite the scarce resources they have available to them. For social networking sites, OpenSocial represents a secure infrastructure that enables exclusively authorized parties access to carefully specified parts of the OpenSocial APIs while the users retain control over which parties are granted access to personal data. From a strategic perspective, OpenSocial enables them to expand their core services with third-party functionality designed to meet the specific needs of vertical customer segments. Finally, both partners may benefit from structured partnerships due to brand und publicity effects. While e-ventures benefit from a unique positioning of their brand in a well-known community, social networks benefit from having a portfolio of innovative partner brands that provide complementary features. To fully exploit the potentials that go along with OpenSocial, however, entrepreneurs and managers need to approach structured partnerships in a systematic and precautious way that is backed by sound strategy and carefully drawn contractual agreements, never as an end in itself.

REFERENCES

Amit, R., & Schoemaker, P. (1993). Strategic assets and organizational rent. *Strategic Management Journal, 14*(1), 33–46. doi:10.1002/smj.4250140105

Amit, R., & Zott, C. (2001). Value creation in e-business. *Strategic Management Journal, 22*(6/7), 493520.

Anderson, C. (2006). *The Long Tail: Why the Future of Business Is Selling Less of More.* New York: Hyperion.

Anderson, E., & Weitz, B. (1992). The use of pledges to build and sustain commitment in distribution channels. *JMR, Journal of Marketing Research, 29*(1), 1834. doi:10.2307/3172490

Barney, J. B. (1991). Firm resources and sustained competitive advantage. *Journal of Management, 17*(1), 99–120. doi:10.1177/014920639101700108

Boyd, D., & Ellison, N. (2007). Social Network Sites: Definition, History, and Scholarship. *Journal of Computer-Mediated Communication, 13*(1), 210–230. doi:10.1111/j.1083-6101.2007.00393.x

Bucklin, L. P., & Sengupta, S. (1993). Organizing successful co-marketing alliances. *Journal of Marketing, 57*(4), 32–46. doi:10.2307/1252025

Das, T. K., & Teng, B.-S. (2000). A Resource-based Theory of Strategic Alliances. *Journal of Management, 26*(1), 31–61. doi:10.1016/S0149-2063(99)00037-9

Eisenhardt, K. M., & Martin, J. A. (2000). Dynamic capabilities: What are they? *Strategic Management Journal, 21*, 1105–1121. doi:10.1002/1097-0266(200010/11)21:10/11<1105::AID-SMJ133>3.0.CO;2-E

Ernst, D., Halevy, T., Monier, J.-H.J., & Sarrazin, H. (2001). A future for e-alliances. *The McKinsey Quarterly, 2001*(2), 92102.

Fielding, R. T., & Taylor, R. N. (2002). Principled design of the modern Web architecture. *ACM Transactions on Internet Technology, 2*(2), 115–150. doi:10.1145/514183.514185

Garrett, J. J. (2005). *Ajax: A New Approach to Web Applications* [white paper]. San Francisco, CA: Adaptive Path Inc.

Graham, W. (2008). *Facebook API Developers Guide.* Berkeley, CA: Apress.

Kollmann, T. (2006). What is e-entrepreneurship? – fundamentals of company founding in the Net Economy. *International Journal of Technology Management, 33*(4), 322–340. doi:10.1504/IJTM.2006.009247

Kollmann, T., & Häsel, M. (2006). *Cross-Channel Cooperation: The Bundling of Online and Offline Business Models.* Wiesbaden, Germany: Deutscher Universitäts-Verlag.

Kollmann, T., & Häsel, M. (2007). Reverse auctions in the service sector: The case of LetsWorkIt. de. *International Journal of E-Business Research, 3*(3), 57–73.

Kollmann, T., & Häsel, M. (2008). Cross-channel cooperation: A collaborative approach of integrating online and offline business models of e-entrepreneurs and traditional SMEs. *International Journal of Entrepreneurship and Small Business*, 6(2), 212–229. doi:10.1504/IJESB.2008.018629

Lumpkin, G. T., & Dess, G. G. (2004). E-business strategies and internet business models: how the internet adds value. *Organizational Dynamics*, 33(2), 161–173. doi:10.1016/j.orgdyn.2004.01.004

Matlay, H., & Westhead, P. (2005). Virtual teams and the rise of e-entrepreneurship in Europe. *International Small Business Journal*, 23(3), 279–302. doi:10.1177/0266242605052074

O'Reilly, T. (2005). *What Is Web 2.0. Design Patterns and Business Models for the Next Generation of Software*. Retrieved April 24, 2009, from http://www.oreillynet.com/pub/a/oreilly/tim/news/2005/09/30/what-is-web-20.html

OpenSocial Foundation. (2009). *OpenSocial – It's Open. It's Social. It's up to you*. Retrieved April 24, 2009, from http://www.opensocial.org

Perry, M. L., Sengupta, S., & Krapfel, R. (2004). Effectiveness of horizontal strategic alliances in technologically uncertain environments: are trust and commitment enough? *Journal of Business Research*, 57(9), 951–956. doi:10.1016/S0148-2963(02)00501-5

Porter, M. E. (2001). Strategy and the Internet. *Harvard Business Review*, 79(3), 6278.

Prahalad, C. K., & Hamel, G. (1990). The core competence of the corporation. *Harvard Business Review*, 68(3), 79–91.

Raman, T. V. (2009). Toward 2^W, Beyond Web 2.0. *Communications of the ACM*, 52(2), 52–59. doi:10.1145/1461928.1461945

Samu, S., Krishnan, S., & Smith, R. E. (1999). Using Advertising Alliances for New Product Introduction: Interactions Between Product Complementarily and Promotional Strategies. *Journal of Marketing*, 63(1), 57–74. doi:10.2307/1252001

Tapscott, D., & Williams, A. (2007). *Wikinomics: How Mass Collaboration Changes Everything*. London: Atlantic Books.

Teece, D. J., Pisano, G., & Shuen, A. (1997). Dynamic Capabilities and Strategic Management. *Strategic Management Journal*, 18(7), 509–633. doi:10.1002/(SICI)1097-0266(199708)18:7<509::AID-SMJ882>3.0.CO;2-Z

Volkmann, C., & Tokarski, K. O. (2006). Growth strategies for young e-ventures through structured collaboration. *International Journal of Services Technology and Management*, 7(1), 68–84.

Weiber, R., & Kollmann, T. (1998). Competitive advantages in virtual markets – perspectives of information-based marketing in the cyberspace. *European Journal of Marketing*, 32(7/8), 603615. doi:10.1108/03090569810224010

Wernerfeld, B. (1995). The resource-based view of the firm: ten years after. *Strategic Management Journal*, 16(3), 171–174. doi:10.1002/smj.4250160303

ADDITIONAL READING

Eisehardt, K. M., & Martin, J. A. (2002). Dynamic Capabilities: What are they? *Strategic Management Journal*, 21(21), 1105–1121.

Gamma, E., Helm, R., Johnson, R., & Vlissides, J. (1995). *Design Patterns: Elements of Reusable Object-Oriented Software*. Reading: Addison-Wesley.

Highsmith, J. A. (2002). *Agile Software Development Ecosystems*. Boston: Pearson Education.

MacCormack, A., Verganti, R., & Iansiti, M. (2001). Developing Products on Internet Time: The Anatomy of a Flexible Development Process. *Management Science, 47*(1), 133–150. doi:10.1287/mnsc.47.1.133.10663

Polanyi, M. (1967). *Tacit Dimension*. London: Routledge.

Porter, M. E. (1980). *Competitive Strategy: Techniques for Analyzing Industries and Competitors*. New York: Free Press.

Porter, M. E. (2001). Strategy and the Internet. *Harvard Business Review, 79*(3), 62–78.

Prahalad, C. K., & Hamel, G. (1990). The core competence of the corporation. *Harvard Business Review, 69*(3), 79–91.

Reich, B. H., & Benbasat, I. (2000). Factors That Influence the Social Dimension of Alignment Between Business and Information Technology Objectives. *MIS Quarterly, 24*(1), 81–113. doi:10.2307/3250980

Sveiby, K. E., & Lloyd, T. (1990). *Das Management des Know-how: Führung von Beratungs-, Kreativ- und Wissensunternehmen*. Frankfurt, Germany: Campus Verlag.

Vinekar, V., Slinkman, W., & Sridhar, N. (2006). Can agile and traditional systems development approaches coexist? An ambidextrous view. *Information Systems Management, 23*(3), 31–42. doi:10.1201/1078.10580530/46108.23.3.20060601/93705.4

Weiber, R., & Kollmann, T. (1998). Competitive advantage in virtual markets - perspectives of Information-based Marketing in cyberspace. *European Journal of Marketing, 32*(7/8), 603–615. doi:10.1108/03090569810224010

Zahra, S. A., & Bogner, W. C. (1999). Technology strategy and software new ventures' performance: Exploring the moderating effect of the competitive environment. *Journal of Business Venturing, 15*(2), 135–137. doi:10.1016/S0883-9026(98)00009-3

Chapter 17
Enabling Technologies in an Ambient Intelligence (AmI) System

Simrn Kaur Gill
National University of Ireland, Ireland

Kathryn Cormican
National University of Ireland, Ireland

ABSTRACT

This chapter introduces the concept of Ambient Intelligence (AmI) with regard to the enabling technologies and how they are combined to assist e-entrepreneurs. AmI is a new paradigm in the area of Information and Communication Technology (ICT). AmI allows for seamless interaction between the human and technology. The AmI system provides the human user with information and decision support tailored to their specific needs. To achieve seamless interaction between the human and technology requires the environment that surrounds the human to be embedded with technology in everyday objects. These technologies gather information that the AmI system uses to adapt its responses to the human user. The aim of the chapter is to provide a better understanding of the AmI process and knowledge of the AmI system and tools. To this end three of the enabling technologies are discussed: semantic web, multi-modal services, and radio frequency identification tags. These technologies are then examined within the AmI reference model. The reference model provides an understanding of how the technologies can be combined to achieve different AmI features for the human users. This toolkit can be used by a new venture in the area of e-entrepreneurship to provide AmI to service providers, new businesses and traditional industries.

INTRODUCTION

Entrepreneurship is about creating new ventures (Barba-Sánchez, del Pilar Martínez-Ruiz, & Jimé-nez-Zarco, 2007; Tetteh, 2008; Wienclaw, 2008). New ventures are young agile firms that can implement more effectively new concepts in many areas such information and communication technology (ICT). E-entrepreneurship can be defined as new ventures that apply and exploit e-technologies (Koll-

DOI: 10.4018/978-1-61520-597-4.ch017

mann, 2006). E-entrepreneurship is a knowledge intensive concept that requires up to date information on products and services which are offered (Kollmann, 2006; Matlay, 2004, 2005). There is a need to provide information and decision support to human users. This needs to be supported by an interactive man-machine interface that captures, analyses, and delivers information tailored to the human users needs. In the production setting for example, knowledge and decision support are critical to maintaining a competitive advantage in an environment where there is a rising cost base, inflation and higher wage demands. Improvements in providing knowledge and decisions-support to the stakeholders in all areas of the process setting can assist in improving flexibility, effectiveness, efficiency and adaptation to changing needs and requirements (MANUFUTURE, 2004). A new strategy needs to be adopted to assist industry to retain its competitive advantage. The new approach needs to be able to adapt seamlessly to the changing business environment and help companies become more flexible, dynamic, efficient and effective (Koska & Romano, 1988; MANUFUTURE, 2004). Ambient intelligence (AmI) is a strategy that can assist in achieving a knowledge-intensive concept like e-entrepreneurship. AmI is a young technology which holds great opportunity for new ventures in the ICT sector. The new venture can exploit AmI by implementing the concept in service providers, new businesses, and traditional industries.

AmI is a user-centered concept in the area of ICT (Giuseppe Riva, 2005). It places the user at the centre of a technology embedded environment. In essence the move is away from one computer, one user to an environment where many computers interact seamlessly with one user (Giuseppe Riva, Vatalaro, Davide, & Alcaniz, 2005). Technology in the AmI environment moves to the background by becoming embedded in everyday objects like clothes and furniture. The AmI system works on the principles of evaluating inputs and outputs from the user, as well as the process, and environment

in which the user inhabits. The technologies cater to the needs, habits, gestures, emotions, and the context awareness of the users' interaction with the environment, by tailoring its responses to the user. The responses are provided through the technologies that are embedded in the environment, being people-centered and having the ability to be intuitive and adapt to changes in the environment. The surrounding environment is sensitive and responsive to the changes in the user. It also has the ability to adapt to these changes due to its omnipresent nature (DG Information Society, 2004; Gill & Cormican, 2008a). AmI is a system composed of technologies that have the ability to adapt and learn in the physical environment that encircles the user. Different combinations of technologies are used to create different levels of human computer interaction. The use of speech recognition software (SRS) to collect user inputs to the system combined with semantic agents to assist in annotating and storing information in the most effective way to assist in retrieval of information in the future. The use of semantic agents to store information that is gathered from users, processes and the environment allow for the use of semantic searching of information that is stored. This provides for more intelligent searches of databases through improved search parameters (ISTAG, 2002).

This can be of benefit to manufacturing in the case of the shop floor operator. The AmI system can assist the shop floor operator by providing each individual with skills level task information for each task that they need to perform. The AmI system can also assist the operator in recoding machine breakdowns, material shortages, reject quantities, product traceability, and other task related issues that arise. The information that is gathered is then promptly sent to relevant personnel so that action can be taken to rectify any problems that arise on the shop floor. The value proposition for implementing AmI in a new venture can be summarized as follows:

- Reduce costs
  - Improved visibility across the system (user, process, and environment)
  - Reduction in repetition of tasks
  - Better use of resources
- Increase revenue
  - Improved efficiency
  - Improved effectiveness
- Increase expertise
  - Improved quality of captured information
- Mitigate risk
  - Better decision support through contextual information

These value propositions are examined further within the AmI System in this chapter.

The aim of the chapter is to provide a better understanding of the AmI process and knowledge of the AmI system and tools that can be exploited through e-entrepreneurship. E-entrepreneurship is a knowledge-intensive concept that involves a new venture applying and exploiting technology. To this end the chapter presents an AmI in-industry reference model that can be used to develop an AmI system that will assist the human decision maker. To accomplish this, an outline of the concept of ambient intelligence is provided. Some of technologies used in developing the AmI system are examined. These include semantic web, radio frequency identification tags (RFID) and multimodal services. The review of the concept leads to the development of an AmI in industry reference model. The reference model examines the user in the AmI system with regard to their implicit and explicit interaction with the process, environment, and the AmI system which works as both an observer and controller of the surroundings. The model outlines the generic requirements of the system in industry. The reference model contains certain AmI features that are presented. These are person-oriented features that can be achieved through combining technologies to provide the required level of interaction needed to create the

AmI system. Both the reference model and the AmI features are discussed further in the chapter. The AmI reference model will help the reader to understand the concept of AmI and help find opportunities to exploit AmI in a new venture. The concepts outlined in the chapter can be applied to other sectors. The lessons learned in this chapter can be implemented in new organizations. They will help to reduce costs, increase revenue, increase expertise, and help to mitigate risk within the new venture.

HUMAN AND TECHNOLOGY

The technology that surrounds our daily lives has evolved over time. Computers have evolved from occupying an entire room to becoming handheld devices (Giuseppe Riva, 2005; Swade, 2000). At the same time technology has adapted from being associated with only computational functions to being the facilitator of social networking between geographically dispersed individuals and groups (SIBIS, 2002). To achieve these evolutions in technology for users has required the use of user-centered design concepts. One of these concepts is the development of socio-technical systems. Socio-technical systems examine the user, process, and environment in a holistic way from the viewpoint of the user (Katsioloudes, 1996; Shani, Grant, Krishman, & Thompson, 1992; Stanton & Ashleigh, 2000). The user requirements are gathered from all users and the process and environment are examined with their active participation. The process steps are analyzed with regard to improved effectiveness and efficiency from a user perspective. The environment includes an analysis of the materials, technology, and resources as well as the building that the user occupies. User-centered development helps to create technologies that cater to the specific needs and requirements of the user. Creating a system/network of technologies that cater to the needs and requirements of the user requires the system to be omnipresent in the user environment. This is achieved by embedding sensors in the environment that surrounds the user. The sensors can collect information on the preferences of the user. This information can then be used by the system to create a profile of the user so that the responses that the system provides to the user are tailored to their specific needs and requirements. This may create certain undesirable effects for the users of the system. Some of these less desirable effects are in the area of privacy and security of user information and of boundaries between work and personal time for users of the system.

To create a system that caters to the needs and requirements of the user seamlessly gathering information regarding the users' needs, habits, gestures, emotions, and context awareness. This gathered information can have privacy and security implications if not managed correctly (see Aarts, 2004; Casal, 2004; Potter, 2005; Raisinghani et al., 2004; Wright, 2005). Equally within this type of environment the user is always contactable and accessible. This creates issues with regard to boundaries between work and personal time (see Davis, 2002; Drury & Farhoomand, 1999; Kidd, 1994).

AMBIENT INTELLIGENCE

The concept of ambient intelligence (AmI) developed from advancements in three technology areas, ubiquitous computing, ubiquitous communication, and intelligent user friendly interfaces. Ubiquitous computing involves the embedding of technology devices into everyday objects within the users environment (Alcaniz, 2005; Sørensen & Gibson, 2004; Weiser, 1993, 1999). Ubiquitous communication allows these embedded technology devices to communicate with each other (Alcaniz, 2005; Friedewald & Da Costa, 2003). Intelligent user-friendly interface provides the user with ease of interaction and access to the embedded technologies in the environment (Alcaniz, 2005; Ducatel,

Bogdanowicz, Scapolo, Leijten, & Burgelman, 2001; Friedewald & Da Costa, 2003).

In the AmI environment, technology moves into the background through the use of embedded radio frequency identification (RFID) tags and speech recognition system (SRS) which results in a more natural interaction between the user and the technology that surrounds them. The use of speech and gestures to communicate with technology creates more dynamic and flexible surroundings in manufacturing, particularly on the shop floor. Therefore AmI is an adaptive and flexible technology that caters to the needs and wants of the user by modifying its responses in line with the changing manufacturing environment. This will lead to information and decision support being provided to the users' specific requirements. This information and decision support will be explicitly presented through a man-machine interface that captures, analyses, and delivers information to the user.

Ambient intelligence is defined by numerous authors (Gill & Cormican, 2008a; Horvath, 2002; ITEA, 2003; Lindwer et al., 2003) but the most comprehensive definition is provided by ISTAG in their report 'Scenarios for Ambient Intelligence in 2010' which defines ambient intelligence as being a "seamless environment of computing, advanced network technology and specific interfaces"(Ducatel et al., 2001, p. 11). The envisioned interaction with the user is outlined as the environment is, "aware of the specific characteristics of human presence and personalities, taking care of needs and is capable of responding intelligently to spoken or gestured indications of desire, and even can engage in intelligent dialogue" (p. 11). ISTAG articulates an environment in which technology will be, "unobtrusive, often invisible; everywhere and yet in our consciousness – nowhere unless we need it". The interactions with the users "should be relaxing and enjoyable for the citizen, and not involve a steep learning curve" (Ducatel et al., 2001, p. 11).

AmI in a manufacturing scenario may present itself as a scheduling management system. Technologies have been embedded into the users surrounding environment to interact seamlessly with users of the system. All scheduling and work instruction may be managed by the AmI system and it is ready for execution. When the shop floor operator arrives in the morning they walk up the LCD monitor on the shop floor that they use to interact with the AmI system. This type of device is found at all the workstations on the shop floor. It recognizes each of the operators individually. The AmI system, through these monitors, can provide the operator with work assignments, instructions, adapt the operator to skill set and allow the operator to input problems as they arise, for example. Each of the services that are provided to the operators is unique to the individual as it caters to their specific needs and requirements in relation to skills level and experience. When a problem or irregularity is detected on the shop floor by the AmI system it will automatically inform all relevant personnel, managers, supervisors or technicians. All managers and supervisors can access and update the production progress from personal digital assistants (PDAs). This information is also tailored for example to each individual's needs and requirements. This allows for the tracking of problems and solution on the shop floor in real time.

AmI therefore would benefit new ventures by:

- Reducing costs
  - Improved visibility across the system with regard to the user, process, and environment
  - Reduction in repetition of tasks through improved visibility across the value chain
  - Better use of resources through improved decisions support
- Increasing revenue
  - Improved efficiency through greater transparency
  - Improved effectiveness through better use of resources and visibility across the user process and environment
- Increasing expertise
  - Improved quality of captured information through context awareness
- Mitigating risk
  - Better decision support through contextual information provided to users specific needs and requirements

New ICT ventures are better placed to exploit the benefits of AmI. A new venture can implement the strategic and technological components of AmI far easier than in an established firm. For these key performance indicators to be achieved by AmI there needs to be an AmI system in place. This system needs to be able to (a) gather inputs and (b) provide outputs of the information to the users of the system. This (c) data (inputs and outputs) will need to be collected from the user, process, and environment. Based on the data collected the AmI system will behave as an (d) observer or (e) controller of the AmI system to cater to the users of the system. To achieve this, the AmI system needs to have a network of technologies in the surrounding environment. These technologies will provide the means to collect, process, analyze and take action based on the data. The following section presents some of the technologies that can be combined together to create this type of AmI system.

AMBIENT INTELLIGENCE ENABLING TECHNOLOGIES

The creation of an AmI system requires the use of a combination of different technologies. The technologies that are used in combination need to cater to the user, process, and environment. In viewing the AmI system in a socio-technical manner through a holistic viewpoint the technologies need to cater to the user requirements, process steps, and the environment in which the user inhabits from a technology, materials and resources perspective. This is accomplished to ensure that the enabling technologies support the AmI system. The evolution towards the AmI system has being based on present development trends (Ducatel et al., 2001; Emiliani & Stephanidis, 2005). Services are becoming more dynamic and reconfigurable to meet the needs and requirements of users. This is achieved by the use of many devices embedded into the surrounding environment to communicate and interact with the various systems that inhabit the users environment. The interaction between the user and the system is multi-modal and interactive and is completed in a more natural way. Problem solving between the human users can occur in a more dynamic way due to increased accessibility to resources and communication which is already spreading to encompass social groups and not just person to person communication through the likes of Facebook and Bebo . (Ducatel et al., 2001; Emiliani & Stephanidis, 2005)

There are numerous enabling technologies to help create the AmI vision. Three of these technologies are discussed below. These include the semantic web, multi-modal services, and radio frequency identification tags. These three technologies were chosen as they represent the makeup of a basic AmI system when combined together. They provide for the collection of data (RFID tags), the processing, and analysis of the data (semantic web) and the action taken based on the data (multi-modal services).

Semantic Web

The present web was designed by Tim Berners-Lee. It was developed as a tool for physicists to collaborate on projects. The web has evolved into a communications enabler, which has allowed for the development of everything from Google to eBay to Blogging. The semantic web is described as the next generation of the web; in essence it will give meaning to the web's content. The semantic web is defined by Tim Berners-Lee et al (2001) as "an extension of the current" web "in which information is given well-defined meaning, better enabling computers and people to work in cooperation" (p. 29).

There are two core technologies for developing the semantic web (see Figure 1). These are eXtensible Markup Language (XML) and the Resource Description Framework (RDF). XML allows the programmer to develop their own tags. Tags are attached to differentiate the meanings of words. It is used to describe only data or content, not the meaning of the structure. The data is described using XML so that it can be processed by the computer (Berners-Lee et al., 2001; Decker et al., 2000). RDF is a markup language for describing information and resources on the semantic web. By putting information into a RDF file it allows the computer program to search, discover, pick up, collect, analyze and process information from the web (Berners-Lee et al., 2001; Decker et al., 2000).

For web pages to be read semantically, they need to have metadata with an underlining ontology (see Figure 1). Metadata is information that computers can understand that explains to them, for example, what the web resources are. It is used to provide a structured description of the characteristics of a web page in relation to the meaning and the purpose of the resource. Metadata, by providing structure, allows for more sophisticated search engines on the internet. It supports intelligent agents, helps to minimize the loss and repetition of data (Berners-Lee et al., 2001; Decker et al., 2000). Ontology is the term used to describe and explain an area of knowledge. They describe the concept, relationship and the properties of the object (Berners-Lee et al., 2001; Decker et al., 2000).

The semantic web is still in its early development stage, it has great potential to change the

Figure 1. Semantic Web

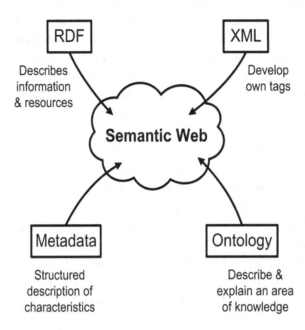

way that we use the internet. It will allow for more improved sophisticated searches of the World Wide Web. This will be done by intelligent agents having the ability to search data and information on the web in a more meaningful and intelligent way. This will allow for search results to be more relevant to the user in an ambient intelligence environment. These developments are made more user friendly through developments in the area of multi-modal services.

Multi-Modal Services

Multi-modal services provide the ability to access and interact with data on a computer through the use of multiple interfaces e.g. both text and speech. These developments allow for ease of access to the information that is gathered by the use of the semantic web. This can be accomplished through the use of a keyboard and mouse entry system as well as the voice recognition inputs and outputs. This interaction can also be accomplished through

the use of multiple input and output devices e.g. mobile telephone, PDA or computer. The implementation of multimedia applications allows for the development of the multi-modal services. To achieve this desired level of interaction the following are required:

- High processing power
- Multimedia capable file systems
- Efficient and high input/output
- Adequate storage and memory
- Network support

In the following subsection there is a focus on speech recognition software (SRS) which is one of the elements of multimodal services. SRS is chosen as it provides for more natural interaction for the user, in their interaction with technology. This provides for a more natural input of information from the user through the use of speech and vice versa.

Speech Recognition Software

Speech recognition software (SRS) has been in use for over a decade. It has advanced greatly in this time, these systems can now recognize continuous sentences compared to early systems where each word had to be spoken individually (Friedewald & Da Costa, 2003). There are two main types of SRS programs, small and large vocabulary (Rabiner & Juang, 1993; Westall, Johnston, & Lewis, 1998). The small vocabulary has the following characteristics:

- Many users
- Capable of working with variation in speech patterns
- Limited to small number of inputs, i.e. numbers and basic menu options
- Used in automated telephone answering systems

The large vocabulary has the following characteristics:

- Limited users
- Requires training to specific small user group
- Can recognize fully continuous speech, for example may have a 60,000-word vocabulary
- Used in a business environment, in some cases to replace a typist

SRS works on the principle that when we speak we create vibrations in the air. These vibrations are translated by the analog to digital converter into digital data that a computer can understand. It accomplishes this by digitizing the sound. These sounds are then filtered to remove background noise and adjusted to be at a constant volume. When this is completed the signal is separated into small segments and matched to the phonemes of the spoken language. A phoneme is the basis unit of speech that puts together makes a word i.e. "a"

or "b." The program then decides what it believes the spoken words are, or the closest match and displays them on the screen (Keller, 1994; Rabiner & Juang, 1993; Westall et al., 1998).

There are number of weakness with SRS. These are issues with background noise being collected and interfering with the spoken sounds that are collected by the system, to run the software requires a significant amount of disk space and processor speed, and the system can not differentiate between homonyms (Westall et al., 1998). Homonyms are words which are spelt different but sound the same i.e. "here" and "hear." Overcoming these drawbacks will allow for the development of natural interaction between human and computer that may, in an ambient intelligence environment, allow for the manipulation of environmental conditions through voice commands. However neither the semantic web nor multimodal services can inform the AmI environment of the movement of objects. This can be accomplished through the use of radio frequency identification which is reviewed in the following section.

Radio Frequency Identification (RFID) Tags

Radio frequency identification (RFID) is a successor to bar-coding. This technology can provide information of location and movements. It is made up of a small tag which contains an integrated circuit chip and an antenna. The chip and the antenna give the tag the ability to recognize and respond to radio waves which are transmitted from a RFID reader (Kiritsis, Bufardi, & Xirouchakis, 2003; Potter, 2005). The RFID building block is made up of three hardware components: a tag, a reader, and the data processing equipment. The tag itself contains a unique code for the item to which it is attached. The RFID reader sends and receives radio waves to read the information stored in the RFID tag. The information that is gathered is sent to the data-processing equipment. The role of the RFID tags is to carry data and have that data amended or updated as required. RFID tags are therefore programmable. They can be read-only tags, write-once read-many tags and read-write tags depending on the application and life span need from the tag.

There are two different types of tags that are in use. There are active and passive tags. The active and passive name relates to their power supply. The active tag has its own battery power supply which allows it (Kiritsis et al., 2003; Potter, 2005):

- To remain in constant contact with the RFID reader
- Longer transmission range
- Increase in the data that can be stored on the tag
- The cost is related to lifespan of the battery

The passive tag does not have an own power supply, which means that it (Kiritsis et al., 2003; Potter, 2005):

- Can only be used when the RFID reader comes into range and sends out radio wave queries
- Short transmission range
- Can be very small and are cheaper than an active tag

RFID tags can operate at different frequencies which are dictated to by the environment in which they are used. There are currently four main frequencies in use, low frequency, high frequency, ultra high frequency, and microwave. Low frequencies indicate a low rage and a slower transmission rate. The positioning of the tag is also crucial to achieving an optimal reading. For example RFID tags cannot be placed on metallic objects without a protective coating between it and the metallic object, as it interferes with transmissions to and from the RFID tag.

RFID tags have numerous benefits when integrated into an intelligent environment. An example of one of these benefits in a manufacturing setting is the reduction in the amount of manual inputs into the system, as information can be automatically scanned and this will allow for resources to be assigned to more value added activities.

To create an AmI environment the technologies described above will need to be integrated together to have the desired application experience. These technologies independently do not exhibit the characteristics of AmI. It is only when they are combined and work seamlessly together that they will achieve the AmI paradigm. At the core of the AmI paradigm is the user and the fact that the technology has to be user centered.

Summary of Key Technology Findings

AmI is a user centered concept. The AmI system is developed to surround the user, to cater to their need and requirements seamlessly. In creating a system that responds in this manner, the developer of such a system needs to consider the following areas:

- Privacy and security of information that is gathered from the AmI system is very important. Without adequate measures in place the users of the system may not feel comfortable within the technology embedded environment.
- Due to the omnipresent nature of the AmI system, the boundaries between work and personal time may become blurred. The separation between these times needs to be reinforced within an omnipresent technology environment.

These areas need to be considered with regard to the technologies used to develop the AmI system.

No single technology incorporates the characteristics of the AmI environment. Only when combined seamlessly with other enabling technologies is the concept realized. There are numerous enabling technologies to help create the AmI vision. Three of these technologies are discussed above and the key findings of each are examined below. The semantic web, multimodal services, and RFID working together in an integrated manner create an AmI solution.

- The semantic web is the next generation in the development of the web. It is designed to provide meaning to web content. By accomplishing this it allows for more intelligent searches of web content, as well as improved interaction between human and computer. In the manufacturing environment this may lead to an intelligent search of the information stored in the database by the technical staff to assist them in repairing machines on the shop floor in the most efficient manner, based on previous repairs and similar machine failures.

- Multi-modal services provide the ability to access and interact with data on a computer through the use of multiple interfaces e.g. both text and speech. This can be accomplished through the use of a keyboard and mouse entry system as well as the speech recognition system (SRS) inputs and outputs. This interaction can also be accomplished through the use of multiple input and output devices e.g. mobile telephone, personal digital assistant (PDA) or computer. In the case of a technician repairing a machine on the shop floor, they can access the previous repair history of the machine on their PDA and can, through the use of SRS input, and also receive information with regard to repairing the machine.

- Radio frequency identification (RFID) tags are considered to be the next generation of bar-coding. It can be used to track shipments around the world as well as products on the production line. Information related to products can be stored on the tag. This information can be read at different distances depending on the tag. There are two main types of tags, active and passive. Active tags as their name implies are continuously sending information to the reader. They also are more expensive then passive tags which only respond when read.

Working together they create the level of functionally required in achieving an AmI solution. The section below examines an AmI reference model which incorporates the technologies and the key findings that have been discussed to create an AmI system. The combining of technology to achieve different AmI features and solution to cater to the needs of the users of the AmI system is examined.

AMBIENT INTELLIGENCE REFERENCE MODEL

The AmI reference model is based on the findings of the previous sections. As such it takes a socio-technical view of the AmI system. The enabling technologies are combined so as to create a holistic technology environment that caters to the user. To this end the AmI reference model attempts to present a structured approach to understanding AmI in an industry setting. The AmI reference model (see Figure 2) was developed based on the findings of the AmI-4-SME project in conjunction with project partners. It has been updated and improved over time (Stokic, Kirchhoff, & Sundmaeker, 2006). The model identifies the information inputs and outputs of the system; it incorporates the user, process, and environment within the information and data retrieval, processing and output. This provides for implicit interaction between the human operator and the AmI system. The Reference model for an AmI system in industry includes the following areas:

1. Human operator input and output
2. Ambient environment input and output

Figure 2. AmI reference model adapted from Gill and Cormican (2008b)

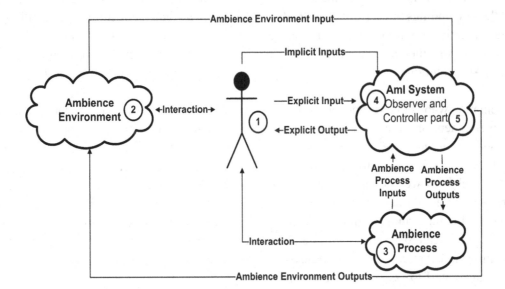

3. Ambient process input and output
4. AmI system observer part
5. AmI system controller part

This is accomplished through a network of devices that are embedded into the background and can collect information implicitly. The acquisition of information from the user, process, and environment is processed to incorporate context. To communicate the gathered information high intelligence in the system is needed. The system must provide information in context for it to be of use, to the users of the AmI system. Therefore the AmI system acts as both an observer and controller, as the information is provided to it through the network of embedded devices, and it has the ability to process the information and take action.

In the case of a machine losing calibration and slowing down production the AmI system can notify a technician of the problem immediately so that there will be less of an impact on the production schedule. The AmI system can also assist the scheduler by providing them with real-time information from the shop floor so that production can be adapted to take account of the machine that requires calibration and testing. The AmI in industry model is achieved through AmI features that are technology independent. The AmI features which are the elements of the reference model are examined in more detail below.

Ambient Intelligence Features

The AmI features are technology solutions that are independent of specific AmI technology potential needed for the human operator. The AmI features need to possess certain characteristics. It needs to be technology independent, needs to correspond to one or more characteristics and it must indicate the functional and/or non-functional requirements relevant for the human operator provided by AmI technology. A feature can therefore be defined as what an AmI system may offer, but not how it may be achieved. The AmI features are based on the reference model above. For each of the five areas of the AmI system, one or more AmI features are defined with specific AmI characteristics in that area. These AmI features were developed in conjunction with the partners of the AmI-4-SME project. The AmI features classification that serves as a reference for the identification of the AmI features and the creation of a conceptual model for the possible solution. The AmI features also provide related technologies enabling the realization of preferred features. The user, process, and environment are analyzed as well as the knowledge and context of the interaction between the three main areas that are needed to provide a level of intelligence to the system.

1. Human operator input and output
   a. Implicit inputs from human operator to the AmI system

The implicit inputs can provide an assessment of physiological data of the human operator to monitor their health and performance status. This data can be used as a reference for controlling the environmental conditions that surround the human operator. The physiological data for example can be used for automated user identification and authentication. In the shop floor environment sensors can be used by the AmI system to recognize the user as they approach a particular workstation on the shop floor.

b. Explicit inputs from human operator to the AmI system

Explicit inputs from human operator to the AmI system can be imparted through natural human input, for example: spoken language and handwriting. This can be enabled by a digital pen, handwriting recognition and speech recognition software. The information can be gathered from the human operator from mobile locations through the use of wireless handheld devices like a PDA, a mobile phone or a tablet PC. This information can be gathered on the shop floor through the use of mobile input devices. The AmI system can also be used to accept observation and experience of

the human operator so that in future this information can be used to reduce delays and improve efficiency on the shop floor. This may relate to maintenance of machines, as the technician can now input information as they are completing a task. In relation to how they repaired the machine for example so if the same error occurs the AmI system can recognize it and can provide them with the information as to how the problem was rectified the previous time. This may result in helping to improve efficiency of repairs to machines.

c. Explicit outputs of the AmI system to the human operator

Explicit outputs of the AmI system to the human operator occur by the system providing information that is personalized and context dependent to the user. This may be information that is of interest or benefit to the human operator. The information can be imparted by the use of wireless handheld devices like a PDA or Tablet PC. The output devices can also be wearable for example a handset or a head mounted display. On the shop floor this may work as a human operator approaches a workstation the PDA may provide them with all the information that they need to complete the task. The information provided may be tailored to their skills level and skill set.

2. Ambient environment input and output
   a. Ambience environment inputs to the AmI system

Ambient (environment) inputs to the AmI system include information on basic environmental conditions like temperature, humidity, and vibration. This information can be gathered by wireless networks of basic ambient sensor, like temperature, humidity and vibration sensors. Information on spatial situation and constraints in respect to the activity that is relevant to the environment for the human operator can be gathered as well as information on hazardous changes in the environment that are critical for the human operators. In the shop floor environment this may relate to the detection of health and safety issues, for example the detection of a chemical spill that will prove hazardous to the human operators in the area.

b.   AmI system outputs to the ambience environment

AmI system outputs basic changes to environmental conditions that are based on preferences and profiles of the human operators, like temperature, humidity, and light. This is accomplished by the AmI system having control over environmental conditions like air conditioning, heating systems and light. The AmI system also adapts infrastructure to the needs of the human operator and the processes that are running on the shop floor. It can also influence the environment to avoid hazardous situations. In the shop floor environment this may result in the AmI system modifying the ambient environment to suit the conditions in which the human operator is most productive. Some people may work best at 20^0C while other may work best at 15^0C. The system recognizing the user as they approach the workstation may be able to modify the ambient temperature for optimum efficiency for the human operator.

3.   Ambient process input and output
    a.   Ambience process inputs to the AmI system

Ambience process inputs to the AmI system provide information assessment of the status of process, plant, machines, products, and materials. This can be enabled through the use of wireless networks of basic ambient sensors like temperature, vibration sensors of plant systems, machines, and products. Information on location and movement of a device, products and materials can be gathered through the use of RFID tags (passive, active, smart tags) or camera systems for location and movement identification. The

information that is gathered through the use of this sensory network can be used to provide real-time information to the manager and supervisors on the shop floor.

b.   AmI system outputs to the ambience process

AmI system outputs to the ambience process involve control inputs to process plant and machines for task execution. This can contain control inputs to machines. The reconfiguration of production systems can be output in the form of the transfer of modified production programmes. Change of schedule and production plans and control information for collaboration of machines can be examples of the initiation on specific data acquisition processes. The information can be used to assist in scheduling of tasks on the shop floor to allow for better utilization of resources and improved efficiency.

4.   AmI system observer part
    a.   Knowledge about human operator

Knowledge about human operators relates to the responsiveness to user input, activity and situation awareness as well as knowledge of the current status of the human operator, knowing the social situation of users, his or her emotions, his or her identity, including models of perception and cognition. The knowledge on human operator is based on behavioral patterns. This may also include the supervision of the physiological status of the human operator to ensure the human operator's wellbeing and initiation of actions in case of abnormal situations. Elaboration of the human operator profiles interaction scenarios and behavior prediction can be used to provide supervision. Through these observations knowledge bases on the human operator's physiological state data patterns can be developed. On the shop floor the goal may be to provide information tailored to the needs and requirements of the user. This may include tasks where the information is tailored to the skills level and the previous mistakes that the operator has made, gathered by the AmI system to assist them in the improving their productivity and reducing the level of rejects generated from the process.

b.   Knowledge about ambience environment/ process and interaction

Knowledge about ambience environment/ process and interaction can be provided by the use of a location manager that can provide knowledge about current and historical status of different devices, products, materials, and users of the system. This can be achieved through the use of multi-agent technologies for the information or knowledge processing in a distributed ICT environment based upon user, ambience, and system context. The semantic connection between user interaction and process events is useful in a manufacturing environment with regard to quality control and can be enabled by semantic web technology. In relation to the maintenance of machines on the shop floor the maintenance technical may be provided with the history of the machine, which may include problems and the repairs that have been made and how they were conducted. This information should help to improve the time scale in which the machines are repaired and are again available for use in production.

c.   Knowledge on context

Knowledge on context covers numerous areas and situations. It may provide the supervision of the spatial situation of the human operator to avoid any hazardous situations. This can be realized by user movement profiles and patterns. The AmI system may identify the value-added information that supports some of the complex tasks which are completed by the human operator. This can be achieved by multi-agent technologies for the information and knowledge in a distributed ICT

environment based upon the user, ambience, and system context. To provide this environment the AmI system will need to be aware of any business rules or definition schemes, using the semantic web to filter information based upon the users' interest. This will require an extensive knowledge base as well as network interoperability and ubiquitous communication. In the shop floor example the knowledge on context may be used to maintain real-time information on the movement of parts, human operators, and equipment on the shop floor. This may assist in the calculating and improving the usage and utilization of resource (part, human operators, equipment, etc.) in the schedule.

5.   AmI system controller part
  a.   Information/Knowledge provision to human operator

The information and knowledge provision to the human operator can facilitate personalized modes of interaction between the user and the service, which is a user-oriented service creation. This may also include the offering of information that might be of interest to the human operator without being explicitly requested. This may be accomplished by the AmI system assessing the user in communicating their task to the rest of the system. The information that is provided is generated through the use of system agents that have the ability to search semantically and filter information to user's requirements. This information can be used to assist the human operators in decision making in the shop floor environment by supporting them with relevant information in the area, which has been filtered to their specific needs.

b.   Intelligent interaction with ambience environment

Intelligent interaction with the ambience environment involves the identification of activities required to change environmental conditions based on preferences and of the profiles of the human operators in the environment. As part of this it is necessary to identify the activities required to change environmental conditions for safety reasons to protect the human operator. This information can be gathered from the sensors that are found in the environment that monitor temperature, humidity, and vibration and are used to provide warnings of the development of a hazardous environment or can adapt the environment to meet the needs of the human operator.

c. Intelligent interaction with ambience process

Intelligent interaction with ambience process allows for smooth handling of errors and interruptions by dynamically adapting to the current context and situation on the shop floor. This requires an infrastructure that is tailored to the needs of the human operator and the process, by offering context-based harmonization of processes and systems operation. This can be implemented by the use of the scheduling and production planning. There also needs to be a knowledge base that can supply information related to the reconfiguration of the production systems for the shop floor.

The features which are presented are not definitive and will need to be adapted as new research in the area becomes available. The following section examines some of the future trends.

FUTURE RESEARCH DIRECTIONS

This chapter has examined the potential of new ventures in the area of e-entrepreneurship applying the AmI paradigm. New ventures by their nature are young agile firms that can implement new concepts more effectively in many areas such as ICT. AmI is a young technology which holds great opportunity for new ventures in the ICT sector. The new venture can exploit AmI by implementing the concept in service providers, new businesses,

and traditional industries. The areas of potential applications vary from product development to the management of processes. AmI provides a dynamic and flexible environment in which information and decision support is provided to the user explicitly through an interface that captures, analyses, and delivers information tailored to their specific needs and requirements.

AmI is a user-centered concept and, as such, follows a user centered development approach. The process and environment are designed around them in line with a socio-technical system:

- Improved legislation with regard to the use of electronic information that is gathered from users.
- Secure storage and management of confidential and personal information regarding the user of the system.
- Research into knowledge workers within an omnipresent technology embedded environment with regard to boundaries between work and personnel time.

AmI was developed on advancements in the technology areas of ubiquitous computing, ubiquitous communication, and intelligent user friendly interface. To achieve an AmI environment there are a number of technology requirements needed. Ducatel et al. (2001) describes these areas as being advancements in embedded technology devices, wireless connectivity, user-friendly interface, reliable and secure distributed technology network. To achieve advancements in the area highlighted by Ducatel et al. (2001) requires an amalgamation of development in the area of ICT. These developments will advance AmI systems development. These developments include (Ducatel et al., 2001; Friedewald & Da Costa, 2003; ISTAG, 2000):

- Advances in human machine interaction resulting in greater user friendliness, usability, and adaptability of technology to the needs and requirements of the human.

- Mass customizations of products through the use of wireless reconfigurable assemble lines. This can achieve greater product lifecycle monitoring, through wireless technology and greater flexibility in production processes.
- Greater visibility across the supply chain, from the raw materials to the end of life of the product.
- Improving knowledge transfer between individuals, teams and across organization by reducing the causes that obstruct knowledge generation and development.
- Advancements in collaborative working between stakeholders (suppliers, end users, and strategic partners) in the design of processes, products, and services.
- For software to gain the ability to be context aware and adapt to changes in real time. This can be supported through advancements in nanotechnology.

These developments in ICT and service trends can utilize the reference model that has been presented in the chapter to choose enabling technologies. Technologies that complement each other and that provide the key characteristics that create an AmI environment for the user.

CONCLUSION

AmI system provides a new approach in assisting e-entrepreneurs in the changing business environment. The aim of the chapter is to provide a better understanding of the AmI process and knowledge of the AmI system and tools. The toolkit that is presented in the chapter can be used by new ventures in the areas of e-entrepreneurship to exploit AmI by implementing the concept in service providers, new businesses, and traditional industries. AmI is a user-centered concept and provides seam-

less information and decision support tailored to the users' needs. AmI accomplishes this by explicitly capturing, analyzing, and delivering information to the user of the system. It can be applied in all areas; from product development to manufacturing. The AmI system is achieved by ensuring that technologies are designed and developed for industry to support flexibility and adaptability as well as improving the efficiency and effectiveness of the organization. The AmI solution accomplishes this by placing the human decision maker at the centre of the solution. Hence, optimizing the role and impact of the decision maker is a key objective of such technologies. AmI can provide greater product and service efficiency by providing improved visibility over the user, process, and environment. This visibility can be utilized to make more informed decisions by all users of the AmI system and, in turn, improves the time frame in which decisions are made, as well as providing the decision maker with the relevant information that they need to make an informed decision. This will empower the human worker to make more effective and efficient decisions. The chapter examined the concept of AmI in relation to the enabling technologies. These enabling technologies are then used with the AmI reference model in conjunction with the AmI features to create an AmI system which can also be applied to other sectors.

ACKNOWLEDGMENT

This work has been partly funded by the European Commission through IST Project AmI-4-SME: Revolution in Industrial Environment: Ambient Intelligence Technology for Systemic Innovation in Manufacturing SMEs (FP6-2004-IST-NMP-2-17120) and the National University of Ireland, Galway, College of Engineering Postgraduate Fellowship. We also wish to acknowledge our gratitude and appreciation to all the AmI-4-

SME project partners for their contribution during the development of various ideas and concepts presented in this chapter.

REFERENCES

Aarts, E. (2004). Ambient Intelligence: A Multimedia Perspective. *IEEE MultiMedia*, 12–19. doi:10.1109/MMUL.2004.1261101

Alcaniz, M. (2005). New Technologies for Ambient Intelligence. In G. Riva, F. Vatalaro, F. Davide & M. Alcaniz (Eds.), *Ambient Intelligence: the evolution of technology, communication and cognition towards the future of human-computer interaction*. Amsterdam: IOS Press.

Barba-Sánchez, V., del Pilar Martínez-Ruiz, M., & Jiménez-Zarco, A. I. (2007). Drivers, Benefits and Challenges of ICT Adoption by Small and Medium Sized Enterprises (SMEs): A Literature Review. *Problems & Perspectives in Management, 5*(1), 103–114.

Berners-Lee, T., Handler, J., & Lassila, O. (2001). The Semantic Web. *Scientific American, 284*(5), 28–37. doi:10.1038/scientificamerican0501-34

Casal, C. R. (2004). Impact of location-aware services on the privacy/security balance. *6*(2), 105-111.

Davis, G. B. (2002). Anytime/Anyplace Computing and the Future of Knowledge Work. *Communications of the ACM, 45*(12), 67–73. doi:10.1145/585597.585617

Decker, S., Melnik, S., Van Harmelen, F., Fensel, D., Klein, M., & Broekstra, J. (2000). The Semantic Web: The Roles of XML and RDF. *IEEE Internet Computing, 4*(5), 63–73. doi:10.1109/4236.877487

DG Information Society. (2004, March 11). *Ambient Intelligence*. Retrieved June 9th, 2006, from http://europa.eu.int/information_society/policy/ambienti/index_en.htm

Drury, D. H., & Farhoomand, A. (1999). Knowledge Worker Constraints in the Productive Use of Information Technology. *Computer Personnel, 19/20*(4/1), 21-42.

Ducatel, K., Bogdanowicz, M., Scapolo, F., Leijten, J., & Burgelman, J.-C. (2001). *Scenarios for Ambient Intelligence in 2010 (ISTAG 2001 Final Report)*. Seville, Spain: ISTAG (European Commission).

Emiliani, P. L., & Stephanidis, C. (2005). Universal access to ambient intelligence environment: Opportunities and challenges for people with disabilities. *IBM Systems Journal, 44*(3), 605–619.

Friedewald, M., & Da Costa, O. (2003). *Science and Technology Roadmapping: Ambient intelligence in Everyday Life (AmI@Life)*. Seville, Spain: JRC-IPTS/ESTO.

Gill, S. K., & Cormican, K. (2008a). Ambience Intelligence (AmI) Systems Development. In F. Zhao (Ed.), *Information Technology Entrepreneurship and Innovation* (pp. 1-22). Hershey, PA: Idea Group.

Gill, S. K., & Cormican, K. (2008b, 22nd – 24th October). *Implementation of an AmI system in a Manufacturing SME*. Paper presented at the eChallenges Stockholm, Sweden.

Horvath, J. (2002, December 6, 2005). Making friends with Big Brother? *Telepolis*. Retrieved from http://www.heise.de/tp/r4/artikel/12/12112/1.html

ISTAG. (2000). *Recommendations of the IST Advisory Group for Workprogramme 2001 and beyond "implementing the vision*. ISTAG (European Commission).

ISTAG. (2002). *Software technologies, embedded systems and distributed systems: A European strategy towards an Ambient Intelligent environment* ISTAG. (European Commission, ITEA. (2003). *The Ambience Project*. Retrieved September 21, 2005, from http://www.extra.research.philips.com/euprojects/ambience

Katsioloudes, M. I. (1996). Socio-Technical Analysis: A Normative Model for Participatory Planning. *Human Systems Management, 15*(4), 235–243.

Keller, E. (Ed.). (1994). *Fundamentals of speech synthesis and speech recognition: Basic concepts, state-of-the-art and future challenges* (1st ed.). Chichester, UK: John Wiley & Sons.

Kidd, A. (1994). *The Marks are on the Knowledge Worker*. Paper presented at the Conference on Human Factors in Computer Systems.

Kiritsis, D., Bufardi, A., & Xirouchakis, P. (2003). Research issues on product lifecycle management and information tracking using smart embedded systems. *Advanced Engineering Informatics, 17*(3-4), 189–202. doi:10.1016/S1474-0346(04)00018-7

Kollmann, T. (2006). What is e-entrepreneurship? – fundamentals of company founding in the net economy. *International Journal of Technology Management, 33*(4), 322–340. doi:10.1504/IJTM.2006.009247

Koska, D. K., & Romano, J. D. (1988). *Profile 21 Issues and Implications, Countdown to the Future: The Manufacturing Engineer in the 21st Century*. Dearborn, MI: Society of Manufacturing Engineers.

Lindwer, M., Marculescu, D., Basten, T., Zimmermann, R., Marculescu, R., Jung, S., et al. (2003). *Ambient Intelligence Vision and Achievement: Linking Abstract Ideas to Real-World Concepts*. Paper presented at the Design, Automation and Test in Europe Conference and Exhibition.

MANUFUTURE. (2004). *A vision for 2020: Assuring the future of manufacturing in Europe*. European Commission.

Matlay, H. (2004). E-entrepreneurship and small e-business development: towards a comparative research agenda . *Journal of Small Business and Enterprise Development, 11*(3), 408–414. doi:10.1108/14626000410551663

Matlay, H. (2005). Research entrepreneurship and education Part 1: what is entrepreneurship and does it matter? *Education and Training, 47*(8/9), 665–677. doi:10.1108/00400910510633198

Potter, B. (2005). RFID: misunderstood or untrustworthy? *Network Security*, (4): 17–18. doi:10.1016/S1353-4858(05)00184-4

Rabiner, L., & Juang, B.-H. (1993). *Fundamentals of speech recognition* (1 ed.). Upper Saddle River, NJ: Prentice Hall.

Raisinghani, M. S., Benoit, A., Ding, J., Gomez, M., Gupta, K., & Gusila, V. (2004). Ambient Intelligence: Changing Forms of Human Computer Interaction and their Social Implications. *Journal of Digital Information, 5*(4).

Riva, G. (2005). The Psychology of Ambient Intelligence: Activity, Situation and Presence. In G. Riva, F. Vatalaro, F. Davide & M. Alcaniz (Eds.), *Ambient Intelligence: the evolution of technology, communication and cognition towards the future of human-computer interaction*. Amsterdam: IOS Press.

Riva, G., Vatalaro, F., Davide, F., & Alcaniz, M. (2005). *Ambient Intelligence: the evolution of technology, communication and cognition towards the future of human-computer interaction*. Amsterdam: IOS Press.

Shani, A. B., Grant, R. M., Krishman, R., & Thompson, E. (1992). Advanced Manufacturing Systems and Organizational Choice: Sociotechnical System Approach. *California Management Review, 34*(4), 91–111.

SIBIS. (2002). *Towards the Information Society in Europe and the US: SIBIS Benchmarking Highlights 2002*. Bonn, Germany: Empirca (SIBIS project and European Communities).

Sørensen, C., & Gibson, D. (2004). Ubiquitous visions and opaque realities: professionals talking about mobile technologies . *Info, 6*(3), 188–196. doi:10.1108/14636690410549516

Stanton, N. A., & Ashleigh, M. J. (2000). A field study of team working in a new human supervisory control system. *Ergonomics, 43*(8), 1190–1209. doi:10.1080/00140130050084941

Stokic, D., Kirchhoff, U., & Sundmaeker, H. (2006). *Ambient Intelligence in Manufacturing Industry: Control System Point of View*. Paper presented at the Control and Applications 2006 Conference.

Swade, D. (2000). *The Cogwheel Brain: Charles Babbage and the Quest to Build the First Computer* (1st ed.). London: Little, Brown and Company.

Tetteh, V. A. (2008). Launching New Ventures Through Technology [Electronic Version]. *Research Starters Business*, 1-7. Retrieved February 2, 2009, from http://web.ebscohost.com/ehost/pdf?vid=7&hid=16&sid=75a1692d-8a37-460a-bb28-b8e36112cfc3%40sessionmgr2

Weiser, M. (1993). Ubiquitous computing. *IEEE Computer, 26*(10), 71–72.

Weiser, M. (1999, 9-12 May 1999). *How computers will be used differently in the next twenty years*. Paper presented at the Symposium on Security and Privacy, Oakland, CA, USA.

Westall, F. A., Johnston, R. D., & Lewis, A. V. (Eds.). (1998). *Speech technology for telecommunications* (1st ed.). London: Chapman and Hall.

Wienclaw, R. A. (2008). Technological Innovation & Entrepreneurs [Electronic Version]. *Research Starters Business*, 1-5. Retrieved February 2, 2009, from http://web.ebscohost.com/ehost/pdf?vid=7&hid=16&sid=75a1692d-8a37-460a-bb28-b8e36112cfc3%40sessionmgr2

Wright, D. (2005). The dark side of Ambient Intelligence. *Info, 7*(6), 33–51. doi:10.1108/14636690510628300

ADDITIONAL READING

Aarts, E. (2004). Ambient Intelligence: A Multimedia Perspective. *IEEE MultiMedia, 11*(1), 12–19. doi:10.1109/MMUL.2004.1261101

Aarts, E. (2005). Ambient Intelligence Drives Open Innovation. *Interaction, 12*(4), 66–68. doi:10.1145/1070960.1070996

Aarts, E., & Roovers, R. (2003). *IC Design challenges for Ambient Intelligence*. Paper presented at the Design, Automation and Test in Europe.

Austin, B. (2001). Moore's' Law: In and out of Context. *Journal of the American Society for Information Science and Technology, 52*(8), 607–609. doi:10.1002/asi.1114

Avison, D., & Fitzgerald, G. (2003). *Information Systems Development: Methodologies, Techniques and Tools* (Third ed.). Berkshire, UK: McGraw-Hill Publishing Company.

De Greene, K. B. (1981). Systems and Psychology. In J. Beishon & G. Peters (Eds.), *Systems Behaviour*. London: Harper and Row Publishers in association with The Open University Press.

den Os, E., & Boves, L. (2003, October 22). *Towards Ambient Intelligence: Multimodal Computers that Understand Our Intentions*. Paper presented at the eChallenge, Bologna, Italy.

Fitzgerald, B., Russo, N. L., & Stolterman, E. (2002). *Information Systems Development: Method in Action*. London: McGraw-Hill.

Greene, S. R., & Fiske, C. F. (1999, November 1999). Wearable Computers Open a New Era in Support Resource Management. *IEEE AES Systems Magazine*, 33-35.

Hagras, H., Callaghan, V., Colley, M., Clarke, G., Pounds-Cornish, A., & Duman, H. (2004). Creating and Ambient-Intelligence Environment Using Embedded Agents. *IEEE Intelligent Systems, 19*(6), 12–20. doi:10.1109/MIS.2004.61

Hellenschmidt, M., & Kirste, T. (2004). *A Generic Topology for Ambient Intelligence*. Paper presented at the Ambient Intelligence: Second European Symposium, EUSAI.

Hofstadter, D. R. (1980). *Gödel, Escher, Bach: An Eternal Golden Braid* (1st ed.). Harmondsworth, UK: Penguin Books Ltd.

ISTAG. (2000). *Recommendations of the IST Advisory Group for Workprogramme 2001 and beyond "implementing the vision"*. ISTAG (European Commission).

ISTAG. (2004). *ISTAG Report on Experience and Application Research "Involving Users in the Development of Ambient Intelligence"*. Luxembourg: Office for Official Publications of the European Communities, European Commission.

Jagdev, H., Vasiliu, L., Browne, J., & Zaremba, M. (2008). A semantic web service environment for B2B and B2C applications within extended and virtual enterprises. *Computers in Industry, 59*(8), 786–797. doi:10.1016/j.compind.2008.04.001

Jenkins, G. M. (1981). The Systems Approach. In J. Beishon & G. Peters (Eds.), *Systems Behaviour*. London: Harper and Row Publishers in association with The Open University Press.

Morville, P. (2005). *Ambient Findability* (First ed.). Sebastopol, CA: O'Reilly.

Mumford, E. (1983). *Designing Human Systems For New Technology: The ETHICS Method*. Manchester, UK: Manchester Business School.

Mumford, E. (2000). A Social-Technical Approach to Systems Design. *Requirements Engineering, 5*(3), 125–133. doi:10.1007/PL00010345

Porter, M. E. (1998). *Competitive Strategy: Techniques for Analyzing Industries and Competitors*. New York: The Free Press.

SIBIS. (2002). *Towards the Information Society in Europe and the US: SIBIS Benchmarking Highlights 2002*. Bonn, Germany: Empirica (SIBIS project and European Communities).

Skidmore, S., & Eva, M. (2004). *Introducing Systems Development*. New York: Palgrave MacMillan.

Wright, D. (2005). The dark side of Ambient Intelligence. *Info, 7*(6), 33–51. doi:10.1108/14636690510628300

Chapter 18
Creating Value Through Entrepreneurship:
The Case of Artificial Intelligent Agents

Andrea Bikfalvi
Universitat de Girona, Spain

Christian Serarols Tarrés
Universitat Autònoma de Barcelona, Spain

Josep Lluís de la Rosa Esteva
Universitat de Girona, Spain

ABSTRACT

The present case study describes the creation and development process of ARTIFICIAL INTELLIGENT AGENTS, S.L. (AIA), a company spun-off from the University of Girona (Spain). It describes all phases, from concept to implementation, and the problems and challenges faced by the entrepreneurial team composed of academics and professionals. AIA provides living proof of how a research group can become a company. It lays out the path from developing a technology in the field of human automation attempting to sell a user-friendly technology that would help customer intelligence and management. AIA targeted at Internet companies in general, as well as traditional businesses that used customer relationship management (CRM) extensively in their daily operations. After having developed their main product and survived financial difficulty, the company stood at crossroads and a decision regarding its strategic future had to be taken.

DOI: 10.4018/978-1-61520-597-4.ch018

INTRODUCTION

In recent years, university-based scientific inventions that translate into spin-off companies represent a potentially important and increasingly utilised option to create wealth from the commercialisation of research (Carayannis, 1998; Clarysse et al., 2005; Lockett et al., 2005; Siegel et al., 2003; Vohora et al., 2004). In this context, governments and universities all over the world have established different assistance mechanisms for aiding the creation of such companies.

Since the seminal works of Etzkowitz (1998, 2003 and 2004) that analyse the relationship and collaboration efforts between public research institutions (PRI) and the business sector and define the new role of the "entrepreneurial universities", Europe has understood the importance of the "third mission" in the university context. Traditionally, European universities centred their activities at teaching and investigating, without putting much attention on technology and knowledge transfer. With this third mission (having business creation as a main instrument), Etzkowitz illustrated the role that universities had by contributing to regional and social development through knowledge transfer via business creation (spin-off). In this sense, Etzkowitz, through the Triple Helix model, stressed the need for university-industry-government to work jointly and co-ordinately for the common purpose of stimulating knowledge-based economic development.

Recent literature (Harmon et al., 1997; Hindle, & Yencken, 2004; Ma, & Tan, 2006) states the importance of academic spin-offs for wealth creation and regional development. For example, according to Wright et al., (2004a, 2004b) university spin-offs are not only seen as contributors to a regions' economic development but also as sources of employment (Pérez, & Martínez, 2003), as mediators between basic and applied research (Autio, 1997) or as change agents of the economic landscape moving towards a knowledge-based economy.

Despite the importance of academic entrepreneurship and its assistance mechanisms to promote venture creation, we do not find in the literature empirical evidence on spin-offs' contributions to regional economic development. Furthermore, although there are plenty single case publications describing the spin-off phenomenon and/or the entrepreneurial transformation of a public research institution and its support mechanisms (Chalmers University of Technology in Jacob et al., 2003; Louis Pasteur University in Carayol, & Matt, 2004; K.U. Leuven in Debackere, & Veugelers, 2005; or Cambridge, and MIT in Acworth, 2008), this body of research has not been successful in measuring the efficiency of such companies and, for extension, of these support mechanisms. In addition, generally, the cases studied belong to what we consider elite universities, like MIT, Harvard, etc.

On the other hand, the adoption of Information and Communication Technologies is opening up a new range of possibilities and challenges in business environments. Especially, since the emergence of Internet, many companies have been trying "to digitalize" and make more efficient their operations within the value chain. There is evidence that shows that a significant percentage of academic spin-offs are ICT intensive-users or they are focusing their businesses exclusively on this new communication media. For example, we all have in mind Google, Yahoo, Sun Microsystems, etc.

Consequently, this research draws attention on academic entrepreneurship in the field of ICT. We want to study the process of creation and development of an academic spin-off specialised on intelligent agent technology development[1]. We will consider how the entrepreneurial team was formed and the problems and challenges they faced. The relevance of this case relies on the fact that it serves as a role model giving both positive and negative examples of actuations in different phases of development from creation to redefinition, as well as valuable insights and first-hand comments from the main founder. Moreover, it aims at covering an important topic that may benefit researchers, academics and practitioners involved in technology transfer from universities.

BACKGROUND

Value Creation Through ICT (Internet)

The increasing acceptance and usage of Internet and the decrease of the access' costs, provide a new broad scope of economic activities and business models. These business models are based on the production, distribution and sale information-based goods (Clemons et al., 2002; Clemons and Lang, 2003), being developed either by traditional companies or by new players identifying an opportunity in the field of ICT (internet).

The impact of the Internet at the firm level has been analysed using the value chain framework (Porter, 1985), in a number of papers including Koh and Nam (2005), Porter (2001), and Rayport and Sviokla (1995), among others. And the value creation on internet (e-business) has been studied mainly by Amit and Zott (2001). As Porter's initial value chain was found more suitable for the analysis of production and manufacturing firms than services firms (Stabell, & Fjeldstad, 1998), a virtual value chain was proposed (Rayport and Sviokla, 1995). This is based in gathering, organising, selecting, synthesising, and distributing information.

Regarding the general impacts of the Internet in the value chain, in the infrastructure activities, the Internet enhances the use of real time information for making decisions. In this sense, the Internet permits the fragmentation of business processes. This allows companies to offer only a few products and/or services, and to concentrate on some essential competences. With this, they can implement cooperation strategies with other businesses to develop secondary activities. Moreover,

the Internet allows businesses to develop new or complementary business models. These models are based on the creation of value throughout information use (Rayport, & Sviokla, 1995). Given this, businesses can create value by substituting the activities of the real value chain with activities of the virtual value chain; the latter being the most efficient and flexible of the two.

Moreover, Amit and Zott (2001) studied the value creation in e-business and identified four main drivers for it: efficiency, complementarities, lock-in, and novelty. Efficiency refers to the fact that transaction efficiency increases when the costs per transaction decrease. The greater the transaction efficiency gains to a particular e-business, the lower the costs and hence the more valuable it will be. Complementarities is related to the fact that having a bundle of goods together provides more value than the total value of having each of the goods separately. Lock-in refers to the engagement of the customers and partners with the company and prevents the migration of them to competitors. This creates value mainly by customers repeating transactions (increase of transactions volume) and partners maintaining their associations (lower opportunity costs). Novelty is related to the innovations of e-businesses in the structure of transactions.

The Internet creates new industries, reconfigures others, and has a direct impact on companies, customers, suppliers, distributors, and potential new entrants (Porter, 2001). Furthermore, it has been argued that with IT adoption, more opportunities exist for market transactions than for transactions conducted in a business hierarchy (Malone et al., 1987). IT reduces transaction costs, brings customers and producers together, and promotes electronic markets (EM) characterised by the elimination of traditional intermediaries.

Stage-Based Models

This approach implies that an additive combination of events will lead to the creation of a new

Table 1. Examples of stage-based venture creation models for university spin-offs

Author	Phases of the stage-based model
Clarysse et al. (2005)	Three stages: 1) invention; 2) transition; and 3) innovation
Clarysse and Moray (2004)	Four stages: 1) idea; 2) pre-start-up; 3) start-up; and 4) post start-up
Degroof (2002)	Six stages: 1) technology opportunity search; 2) intellectual property assessment; 3) selection of spin-off projects; 4) business plan development; 5) potential sources of funding; and 6) spin-out coaching
Hindle and Yencken (2004)	Seven stages: 1) research provider program; 2) idea/new knowledge; 3) opportunity; 4) vision; 5) technology development/proof of concept/prototype; 6) business model; 7) first customer
Lockett et al. (2005)	Five stages: 1) research; 2) opportunity; 3) pre-organisation; 4) re-orientation; and 5) sustainable
Moray and Clarysse (2005)	Five stages: 1) opportunity recognition; 2) from first market analysis to incubation; 3) incubation and business plan development; 4) transfer of intellectual property; and 5) funding process
Ndonzuau et al. (2002)	Four stages: 1) to generate business ideas from research; 2) to finalise new venture projects out of ideas; 3) to launch spin-offs; and 4) to strengthen the creation of economic value
Roberts and Malone (1996)	Four stages: 1) disclosure; 2) evaluation; 3) product development; 4) business development
Vohora et al. (2004)	Five stages: 1) research; 2) opportunity framing; 3) pre-organisation; 4) re-orientation; and 5) sustainable returns
Serarols (2008)	Four stages: 1) concept stage; 2) planning stage; 3) implementation stage; 4) redefinition-stage

Adapted from Miglorini et al. (2009)

firm. A long tradition in studying the process of new firm development stems on the assumption of a linear, unitary process, composed of a set of activities, beginning with the recognition of a business opportunity and culminating with the first sale (Kazanjian, & Drazin, 1990; Liao et al., 2005; Shane, & Venkataraman, 2000; Webster, 1976).

In general, stage-based models of spin-offs identify several phases of development and the organisational characteristics, resources, behaviours and practices exhibited within each stage. Spin-off based literature offers several models of venture creation (see Table 1). For example, Lockett et al. (2005) identified five main stages that developed iteratively: research, opportunity, pre-organization, re-orientation and sustainable. Another example is Clarysse and Moray (2004) that identified the following steps: idea, pre-start-up, start-up and post start-up or opportunity recognition.

The different stage-based models capture and map the process of spin-off creation. Spin-off literature is highly insisting on the founding team as one major importance facts in the spin-off development process (Clarysse, & Moray, 2004). The in-depth study of research-based new ventures, according to the different stages of developments and critical junctions they have to overcome, is important due to the implications these companies have at both institutional and regional levels. Even there is no an established and commonly agreed model, there are common features that make one able to find a core process. The present case study follows Serarols' (2008) most recent work due to its relevance in the field of start-ups in the Internet.

Customer Relationship Management and Intelligent Agents

At the corporate level, a CRM strategy focuses on creating and maintaining lasting relationships with customers (Ahn et al., 2003). Thus, the main goal of a CRM system is to offer the best to each client, using any available information, and arrange for supply that maximizes value in terms of rate of success, income, cost and duration (Reinartz et al., 2004). Reinartz et al. (2004) define the CRM process as "a systematic process, to manage the beginning, maintenance and conclusion of the relation with the customer through all the meeting points with the client to maximise the value of the portfolio of relations" (p.295).

At the level of contact with the customer, recommender systems and multi-agent systems (MAS) can increase the efficiency of information processing and contact effectiveness. Recommender systems integrate data about users and products to create recommendations of products that might suit customers' needs. Thus, a recommender system directly interacts with customers and helps them locate products.

According to Aciar et al. (2007, p.84) intelligent agents can be defined as "a flexible computer system situated in an environment and that is capable of flexible autonomous action in this environment in order to achieve its objectives" (Jennings, & Wooldridge, 1998; Lakshmi et al., 2005). For an agent to be considered flexible and for extension intelligent, it should have the following characteristics (Bradshaw, 1997; Jennings, & Wooldridge, 1998; Klusch, 2002): cognizant, responsive, reactive, proactive and on time to its environment, autonomous, collaborative and adaptative in its ability to learn by experience.

However, the wealth of imperfect information and the broad availability of supply to consumers makes it extremely difficult for customers to identify their own needs and preferences and a way to satisfy them. New intermediaries on the Internet, such as AIA, facilitated this interaction between supply and demand by enabling the collection, organisation and evaluation of information. The functions of a recommender system appear crucial to these activities, because the systems model customer behaviour using redundant information and thus can develop, improve and retain relations with customers while also offering them customised, value-added products. Especially on

Web sites for which consumers want advice before making a purchase, recommendations provide a powerful tool and decision aid. Figure 1 shows the general steps that a MAS follows to provide recommendations.

Briefly, for each source (S) there is a Properties' Agent (PA) responsible for valuing characteristics/properties. Each source of information is administered by an Administrator Agent (AA), which knows abstract information of the content of the source. This information is defined by the characteristics of completeness, diversity, number of relevant attributes, frequency and timeliness. The Selector Agent (SA) is in charge of selecting the sources that may provide greater information to make the recommendation. It produces an organised list of sources according to their relevance. Finally, a Recommender Agent (RA) interacts with the users. Once the sources are selected, it can make its recommendation based on the information gathered from the most relevant sources.

SETTING THE CASE

Artificial Intelligent Agents (AIA) was founded in Girona, Spain, in the summer of 2000 by a group of young researchers in the field of robotics and artificial intelligence. It was the first technology-based company spun off from University of Girona. Since then, the company has worked to develop intelligent agents that could detect and capture users' tacit preferences and thereby increase the efficiency associated with information processing and contact effectiveness.

In this sense, AIA provides living proof of how a research group could become a company. It laid out the path from developing a technology in the field of human automation to attempting to sell a user-friendly technology that would aid customer intelligence and management. The main customer targets for AIA included Internet companies in general, as well as traditional businesses that used customer relationship management (CRM)

Figure 1. Multi-agent architecture for recommendations. (Source: Aciar et al., 2007)

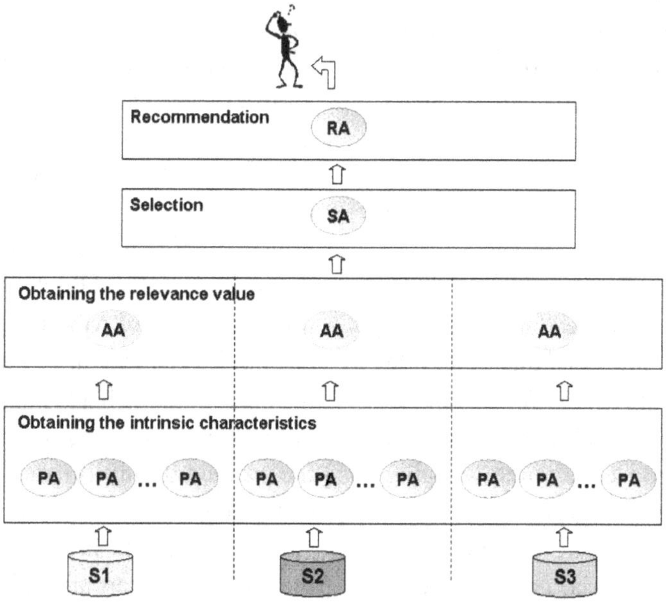

extensively in their daily operations (e.g., food, tourism, banking, insurance). Initially, AIA used recommendation agents to develop its main product, Habitat-Pro™, its recommender system for end users.

The Founding Team

Although the founding team initially was composed of seven members, only two actively worked in the business.

Core founders (working). Albert, the promoter of the business, was 33 years of age when the company was founded in August 2000. He was an associate professor at the University of Girona (UdG). Born in Mallorca, Albert came from a family without any entrepreneurial experience. He earned his M.Sc. and Ph.D. in computer engineering from the Autonomous University of Barcelona (UAB) in 1989 and 1993, respectively. Even as he pursued his doctoral degree, he retained an interest in industry. As Albert recalled, when he first explained that goal to his Ph.D. supervisor at UAB, the immediate answer was:

"Oh, ok. Take a seat in that corner, and when you finish your thesis, call me."

He found more support from a co-supervisor at Laboratoire d'Automatique et d'Analyse des Systèmes (LAAS-CNRS), who regarded Albert as

"A person that is always searching to achieve the 'theory in practice' paradigm, continuously looking for potential industrial application of his research."

Before finishing his Ph.D. in 1992, Albert accepted a lecturer position at UAB, following a conventional path before defending his dissertation.

Then after gaining his Ph.D. in 1993, he took an associate professor position at a new university, the University of Girona, which had just begun and lacked researchers within his field. He could not ignore this new challenge, which would give him great responsibilities and a free hand to manage his own research group. Of those times, Albert recalled:

"With this big responsibility I completely forgot about industry stuff until 1998, when we had a critical mass of researchers, enough to accept some industrial contracts, which were the most important private contracts for the University by that time. In the meantime, I started a new research line on intelligent agents, and we created a soccer robot based on this technology, which competed all over the world and won some prizes."

When Albert met Marc Riu, he was a 32-year-old computer engineer who had received his M.Sc. from UAB. When Albert proposed that he should join the AIA founding team, Marc was working as a chief technical officer at the Catalonia regional railway company. He had experience with big computing projects, like the European SIROCCO project to create new ticketing systems. His working experience, managerial competence in handling big computer projects and willingness to quit his former job constituted the main reasons Albert wanted to involve Marc in AIA. Convincing him to join the founding team was easy; Marc has always been an ambitious person, open to challenges and with a personal development plan that had him changing jobs every two to four years. In the previous six years, he had worked for three different companies, yet

"AIA seemed to me an opportunity, even if not the most interesting option due to the risk concerning a business that is just starting, full of university people with lots of ideas but no business experience."

Additional founders (not actively working). Since its founding, AIA maintained a large team—nine people in total—for three main reasons. First, a group of researchers and professors believed in him and his idea, and Albert needed them to gain legitimacy within the university, due to the reluctance that the third mission[2] provoked among the academic community. At that time, creating a spin-off generated controversies in academia, because it was seen as a way of to privatise public research.

Within this group, the computer engineer Dani Sala worked in the same department as Albert and shared responsibility with him for the research group and other scientific issues. His incorporation into the group was important because of his strong motivation and willingness to create a company. Familiar with the university environment, he became the specialist in searching for public and private support mechanisms, particularly funding, a competence that Albert valued greatly. Another researcher from Albert's group, Josep Coral, also joined the founding team. Albert had gotten to know him well by supervising his doctoral dissertation and considered involving Josep in the product definition area a good choice. At 37 years of age though, Josep was one of the oldest students in the department; he had already been there before Albert arrived at UdG.

Second, the group contained another set of researchers who complemented the team's existing talents and capabilities in technology development. Andreu Güell, a 25-year-old student finishing his master's degree in industrial engineering at University of Girona, had always been interested in computers and programming. When his parents bought 12-year-old Andreu his first computer, a Spectrum, he began self-teaching himself programming. When someone asked him why he had chosen industrial engineering instead of computer science, he answered that he did not need to study computer science to program applications; he could learn it by doing. Rather, to program something, he claimed he needed to understand the phenomenon, so a broad university education, like the one provided by industrial engineering, would be best. In 2004, Robert Blanc finished his Ph.D. under Albert's supervision and also joined the company, becoming its R&D director.

Third, the administrative and sales areas completed the company. This sub-group consisted of two more people: David Lopez and Jacob Negre. Albert recruited David Lopez to join the company to cover a commercial gap. He had been working as the chief technical officer for Riu Hotels, a company in the tourist sector. Albert also wanted someone with practical experience in accounting and administration, someone reliable and willing to face new challenges, and turned to Jacob Negre. Although Jacob was only 33 years of age, he had worked since he was 18 for several companies (including real estate agents, construction companies, banks); just prior to joining AIA, he had been working in one of the most well-known and prestigious accounting agencies in Girona.

Origins and Development of AIA

Gestation Stage. At the end of 1998, Albert was working as associate professor at the University of Girona, doing research in the field of intelligent agents. He already had created a research group and begun to contract research to industry. His academic path was well-defined, yet a new problem came up: For the doctoral students his research group had supervised, university positions were scarce, and the industry in Girona, and in Catalonia in general, was reluctant to hire these Ph.D.s for several reasons: (1) those with doctorates demanded higher wages than an employee with a bachelor's or master's degree; (2) most firms in the region (99.7%) were small to medium-sized enterprises with fewer than 250 workers and small R&D budgets; (3) most firms could contract research with a university or technological centre if they needed it, rather than incurring fixed R&D costs; and (4) the graduates had little industrial experience, which most companies in the region required.

As the amount of contract research within Albert's group increased, the demand for a highly qualified work force also increased. How could the group increase the contract research and industry links if it could not attract researchers because no stable jobs were available? According to Albert, the solution seemed clear:

"The only way to hire them is to create spin-offs and collaborate with industrial transfer centres. At least, these PhDs could accumulate some years

of industrial experience prior to applying for a job in the industry."

During the Christmas season of 1999, at a meeting with an officer of the Technology Transfer Office (TTO)—who later became the director of a new unit designed to support spin-off companies at UdG—the idea of creating a spin-off firm began to take form. In the following nine months, Albert held several informal meetings with friends, family and members of his research group to discuss his idea. A soccer robot the group had developed was always at the middle of these meetings: What could the group do with this robot? Of the various ideas proposed, many of them went straight to the trash, but this brainstorming process became an essential element of what later became AIA. The world seemed to offer endless opportunities, yet the group could not find a concrete business opportunity. According to Albert,

"Probably my lack of professional experience in the field of artificial intelligence or robotics, and the fact that I had never created a company before, hindered this process."

It was not until a company with an R&D contract with his research group visited that Albert seriously started thinking about creating a company. The visiting company was unsatisfied with the amount and complexity of bureaucratic, administrative and organizational procedures it confronted to gain contract research with the university, so it suggested creating a company that would ease the process and save everyone headaches and troubles. Together with the need to offer positions to his graduating students, Albert called this moment the triggering event that motivated him to create AIA.

By early 2000, public policies in Catalonia promoted the third mission of Public Research Institutions (PRIs) and funded spin-off efforts through the TTO, in the guise of units called Technological Trampolines. The regional government also provided funding and support to such companies. However, Albert faced the reality of a university environment, in which

"Except for the USA and UK, I think that the university context does not help the creation of spin-offs. There is no culture for creating wealth by transferring knowledge to the market. Internal academic structures and the whole collective of academic colleagues are hostile toward academic entrepreneurs. They still think that it is a way of making easy money from research by taking advantage of cheap university resources."

The company that had suggested the spin-off to Albert actually never became an AIA customer; it was a traditional brick-and-mortar firm looking for new opportunities during the Internet boom. However, when a traditional food company, wanting to exploit the Internet by selling and home delivering Mediterranean menus, came to visit, Albert recognized the opportunity. The food company was new in online business and eager to use the Internet as a new sales channel; it asked Albert to help create customer profiles and recommend menus that best fit those customers' expectations.

Pleased and encouraged by the request, Albert and the team did not waste much time investigating the market for this sort of services but rather decided to create their own company. Any company, in a myriad of sectors that wanted to participate in the Internet boom should also want to subscribe their services.

Planning Stage. Albert did not invest much effort initially in planning the company. Being the first technology-based company created out of University of Girona had both pros and cons. The planning phase lasted approximately nine months, from November 1999 to August 2000, and followed four main steps: definition of the business idea; competitor and market analysis; complementing the founding team; and preparation of the business plan and investment proposal.

Definition of the business opportunity. In Albert's vision, the business opportunity involved the advanced technological base, combined with the number of potential customers that wanted a presence in cyberspace. Although Albert and his team interpreted this challenge as both infinite and promising, AIA lacked a clearly defined business opportunity during this phase of development. In three years, Albert's research group had signed contract research worth 600,000€, without any commercial structure. They believed they could easily multiply this amount by ten after they had created a commercial department and developed the technology into a marketable product.

Competitors' and market analysis. Albert and his team paid little attention to AIA's potential market, in terms of potential customers and competitors. They simply lacked professional and market knowledge, and they had only a scarce understanding of the steps they needed to follow to create a spin-off company. At the moment, the TTO also lacked any specialized spin-off support unit; AIA was its first proposal, such that the spin-off support unit remained consistently one step behind AIA's development in terms of procedures, infrastructure, university involvement and information. The competitor and market analysis produced a generally positive attitude, but without any specific knowledge about writing or assessing business plans. Albert recounted visits to business fairs in which he asked participants, "Would you sell sausages through the Internet?" The answers probably reflected more what he and his team wanted to hear rather than the truth. As Albert came to realize, the entrepreneurial team had no real business model. The succession of formally and aesthetically pleasing business plans it produced had no grounding in the fundamentals. This initial lack of knowledge was accompanied by insufficient financial resources for an in-depth analysis of the market. Not until the end of 2001, with the arrival of the first seed capital, did the team seriously consider conducting a market analysis. A world-famous consultancy company charged AIA 60,000€ for market research, which indicated exactly what the entrepreneurs expected: a fabulous Internet market awaiting AIA.

Albert now confesses:

"I never realized the difficulty of applying a technology developed in a university lab to the real market. In the idea phase, you have everything clear, but you only see the complexity of it when you have to convince both your team and your potential customers."

Selecting the working team. Albert strongly believed that the founding team could ensure the project's success. All the main pillars of the business—research/technology, administration and commercial tasks, management and daily operations—and the core competences were covered by people close to Albert. He knew them before they joined the company, which generated trust and a strong belief in their future performance. Only the financial director came from outside Albert's circle of friends, family and colleagues. Those with business experience took charge of the personnel selection process after the company got its start, and Albert did not interfere with their decisions until 2002, when selecting the new president, and then again in 2004, to select the general manager. All other aspects were covered by those with some experience, which to some extent inhibited Albert's involvement, because he lacked experience in these fields.

Preparation of the business plan. In March 2000, the former vice dean of research explained to a select group of researchers performing quality research that the TTO would offer a modality: spin-off creation. Researchers were encouraged to present proposals for future companies. Albert attended this meeting and appeared among the four selected proposals. His proposal became the embryo for his first business plan. The business plan contained a considerable amount of nonsense forecasts, organised according to the requirements established by a novel and inexperienced technology transfer officer. Its selection was based on a superficial evaluation. Even though no public

initiatives easily fit the spin-off modality, the university desperately needed them.

Implementation Stage. During this phase, which lasted from August 2000 to September 2001, the group undertook a variety of definitions and redefinitions of products, services, location, team and commercial strategy.

Legal constitution. The company was officially constituted on 15 August 2000 by a public notary who registered the company's name and trademark. The initial name included the word INSIDE, which no one considered a problem. Yet in 2001, the company was forced to change its name, replacing INSIDE with INTELLIGENT, in response to a suit brought by Intel, alleging the name infringed on its INTEL INSIDE trademark.

When Albert registered the company, the vice dean offered AIA a 40-square metre office on the campus that looked rather like an accommodation block or a barrack hut. Despite the poor image it offered for a technology-based company, Albert accepted the space to resolve the cohabitation problems generated when AIA shared a laboratory with the academic researchers. The new offices

"had small and limited space, and basic services were not working properly. We often lost our supply of electrical power, Internet and e-mail services. Customers were supposed to visit us but we could not even offer them parking...."

Albert knew that one of his main detriments as a CEO was his lack of managerial experience, so soon after creating the company in October 2000, he decided to enrol in a two-year MBA offered by UdG.

The first formal business plan, focused on marketing, was produced soon after the arrival of the first seed capital. Although Albert knew he should have given more attention to the plan previously, it became decisive at this point. He subcontracted the business plan to an outsider consultancy, which appeared in retrospect to be a dismal failure. It never helped polish AIA's business opportunity, the analysis was vague and blurry and it did not indicate real customer needs. According to Albert:

"It was probably our fault. We were not able to transmit what our services and potential market were.... Anyway, we decided to go on with our first prototype."

None of the members of the founding team could foresee the threats associated with such an overly optimistic report. The general belief and the surrounding circumstances tended to imply that anything related to the Internet would succeed. Moreover, AIA had gained its first client with minimal effort; if AIA could attract its first client while working at the university, with no commercial and professional structure, it could barely predict what would happen if it were to structure its activities.

Cash problems and first round of investment. By the end of 2000, Marc, the second core founder of AIA, had joined the company as general manager, and the research-based team became a professional team, with a total of seven employees. In 2001, the team had began developing a product in response to real client requirements, Habitat-Pro™. But then,

"The bubble crashed, and the market went down in 2001. We suffered this disaster hard, since all Internet companies, our potential clients, were cutting off investments. We realized this problem very soon, since our commercial activity was not generating contracts."

In 1999, 294 Internet firms went public, raising more than $20 billion, and by 1 March 2000, Internet firms had a combined market value of $1.7 trillion, reflecting a spectacular rise in stock prices. Between January 1999 and February 2000, the Internet Stock Index (ISDEX) more than tripled in value. Perhaps even more impressive was the

subsequent fall in valuations. By the end of 2000, the ISDEX had returned to its 1 January 1999 level, then fell another 69% over the subsequent nine months, for a total decline of nearly 90%. The price drop represented a response to adverse news that triggered a significant change in investor expectations. Soon AIA was running out of cash and needed to look for money. Despite the market situation, a venture capital company chose to invest, largely on the basis of AIA's promising prototypes and excellent preliminary results.

The company also changed its location, moving away from the campus to a seventeenth-century cottage in a small village near Girona. The location was close to the university, bigger than the previous office at campus and very accessible. Yet within a year, AIA came back to campus, unable to pay the rent on its cottage.

Changes marked 2001, not just in terms of location but also employees. At the beginning of the year, AIA had three full-time employees, one remunerated shareholder and three scholarship holders. By the end of the year, after the first investment round, AIA's personnel distribution included nine full-time employees, five remunerated shareholders and from two to six scholarship holders, depending on the season.

Albert tried to reinforce the commercial activity by hiring an experienced commercial manager, but the money kept going out, and AIA was almost bankrupt. On 6 July 2001, AIA achieved a first round of investment of 540,000€; the investor cited Albert's contract research, enthusiasm, involvement and determination as reasons for investing.

The income from this first investment round covered costs, especially salaries, as well as writing the business plan, hiring the consultancy, investments and overhead. In these new and more positive circumstances, Albert believed that the general manager, together with the commercial manager, could achieve the forecasted sales. However, the investment did not help AIA gain any new customers. Some prestigious Spanish companies showed interest in AIA's products and prototypes, but none eventually became clients.

Redefinition Stage: From Products to Services. At the end of 2001, many computer companies experienced trouble commercialising licences for technological products (e.g., ISOCO) and considered providing services instead, using their technology as an alternative way to generate revenues. Habitat-Pro™ faced exactly this choice; it had never been fully commercialised, because when Albert visited Silicon Valley (California) in summer 2001 to offer it to leading Internet and ICT companies, the outcomes was not very positive. According to Albert:

"Visiting the Silicon Valley was very useful to understand how the market worked. I met 25 people, including potential customers, investors and other companies. Those people were all very open and sincere, and thus I could interact very quickly to define what would later be the new orientation of the company: service oriented instead of product oriented, because the market was already saturated with technology."

The situation was critical; the company had developed Habitat-Pro™, which cost thousands of Euros. There were 18 people working at AIA, but the product could not find a niche in the market, according to Albert's trip to Silicon Valley. A redefinition of the business model was essential, and the Silicon Valley experience forced Albert to realise that AIA had to drop the initial plan of selling licences to technological products. Rather, he decided to offer services that could fulfil customers' needs, using products that AIA previously had created.

This service, Humanation, involved an automatic software application based on MAS. It classified a company's portfolio of products and services according to customer profiles and identified specific purchasing behaviours, which the firm could use to prospect markets, generate lists of hot customers for every product and campaigns, generate customer clusters and so forth. The hot customers list generated by Habitat-Pro was 25%

more accurate than a list developed using other direct marketing techniques (e.g., RFM), and combined with the automatic message generation, it boosted accuracy up to 72% on average.

The general manager decided to fire most of the staff: From 18 people, AIA dropped to only 4 full-time and 3 part-time employees. The money raised in the first investment round ran out fast, largely because of salaries—for example, Albert's salary was close to 100,000€ per year. Cost reductions through firing, together with salary adjustments, seemed AIA's only option.

Albert also looked for a new president with solid management experience. After cutting costs everywhere, moving back to campus and convincing banks to provide more personal loans guaranteed with personal assets, Albert contacted a head-hunter and interviewed three possible candidates for the position. His choice,

"John Sodupe, 55 years old, was very skilled in all silly situations like this, and agreed to become the new president of my spin-off. He accepted to coach the two partners who were still working full-time in the company: Marc Pérez as general manager and me as chairman of the advisory board. Of course, this was not any victory; we were simply surviving after many personal, economic and professional losses. And a new project started!"

Although the headhunting operation had cost a considerable amount of money, Albert considered it a good choice, because he gained access to high-position managers from important companies. The team was looking for somebody willing to collaborate with a newly created company, give solidity to an investment project, help orient the business and coach the existing team. In general terms, it needed someone capable of helping the company.

Finally, AIA succeeded in convincing some big companies to become clients, including Telefónica, which signed a big contract in 2003. In addition, it eventually convinced Najeti Capital

Table 2. Information from the profit-and-loss account and balance sheets

	2001 (€)	2002 (€)	2003 (€)	2004 (€)	2005 (€)
Sales	0	120,000	210,000	0	236,000
Operating costs	380,000	320,000	280,000	540,000	560,000
Profit	-350,000	-100,000	-50,000	-490,000	-324,000

and HighGrowth, a French fund and a Catalan venture capitalist, respectively, to invest further in the company.

GETTING FINANCE

As Table 2 shows, AIA had significant troubles obtaining enough sales, in comparison with its operating costs, to reach a breakeven point and assure its survival. Undefined market needs, fuzzy client definition and general university and economic circumstances contributed to this incapacity to generate income.

Its success came in obtaining both public and private funds for its survival. Public money came from three major actors:

- *Concept Capital*, a seed capital fund run by the Regional Development Agency for technology-based new ventures in existence for less than two years. Its resources aim directly at promoting growth.
- *NEOTEC*, administered by Centre for the Development of Industrial Technology of the Spanish Ministry of Industry, Tourism and Trade, whose general objective is to help Spanish companies increase their technological bases. A special action line supports the generation and development of new technology-based firms.
- *ENISA loan*, from the Empresa Nacional de Innovación S.A. (ENISA), the operating arm of the Ministry for SME Policy, which expanded its actions to participatory loans.

In parallel, three venture capitalists joined the company:

- *BCNEmprèn SCR S.A.*, a venture capital company since 1999 that promoted new technological and innovative companies, using the financial instruments of investment and strategic support.
- *Najeti Capital SCR*, a French, privately owned, international investment company with subsidies in the United States and Spain. Najeti Spain, located in Madrid, provided venture capital funding and support during the growth and expansion stages to innovative biotech, telecommunications and services companies.
- *FonsINNOCAT FCR*, run by Highgrowth Partners SGECR, SA, is a financial company that follows two clearly differentiated lines of business investments in innovative companies with growth potential and offers them support, advice and guidance.

Highgrowth and Najeti both joined AIA in June 2003 and participated in the next capital extension in 2004, after it received the ENISA loan. As specialized companies in the field of detecting business opportunities, they required specific reasons to invest. At the time, AIA created a new business plan, and its first trimester sales achieved 35% of the annual forecast. Moreover, the new president and existing investors made AIA seem like a good investment opportunity, a well-oriented and well-managed start-up.

Table 3 lists the absolute and perceptual changes of shares and equity during this period.

Table 3. Distribution of shares before and after AIA's investment rounds

	Before First Investment Round, December 2001			After First Investment Round, January 2002			After Last Investment Round, June 2004	
	%	Equity - €	%	Equity - €	Surplus	%	Equity - €	Surplus
Founders	100	60.000	76	456.000	0	35	588.000	0
Venture capital	0	0	12,5	75.000	540.000	60	1.008.000	1.080.000
Others	0	0	11,5	69.000	0	5	84.000	0
Total	**100**	**60.000**	**100**	**600.000**	**540.000**	**100**	**1.680.000**	**1.080.000**

In total, AIA received approximately 2,420,000€, of which 800,000€ corresponded to public funds, aids or loans given in preferential conditions.

COMMERCIAL PATH

Initially, David Lopez was the only sales agent for AIA. He stayed in close contact with both the product developer, Josep Coral, and the research and science base, represented by Dani Sala, who tried to link AIA's research to public R&D funding. Albert's position in the company had been driven largely by personal reasons. Albert explains it:

"I knew I wanted to work with him [Dani] ... before really knowing and assessing what his position in the company would be. Somehow I felt in debt with him, because he helped me a lot in the beginning of my professional carrier in Girona. Now I see this attitude was a mistake...."

The first two customers who signed up for AIA's technological base seemed to appreciate the recommender agent and prototypes for Habitat Pro™, and despite his technical background, Dani Sala started focusing on marketing. Both the inventor and the manager thus opted for internal resources when establishing the initial sales structure.

The founders interpreted these two important early clients as indicators that the market was ready for AIA's recommender agents. The sales group set unrealistic and eventually unrealised objectives; frustrated with their actions, Albert hired an outside sales professional, who forecast more than 700,000€ in sales, even though AIA ended that year with no sales. This new sales manager, with 10 years of experience managing sales teams, seemed to offer an adequate profile, yet it was not enough. Contrary to expectations, she failed to achieve any sales, even working through concrete channels and market niches. Albert explains it:

"We did 263 presentations in less than two years. Roughly it means 11 demos per month. I remember peaks of 21 monthly presentations. This is a super-human effort for such a small team. However, it was difficult for us to capture new clients simply because we were unable to distinguish when a potential client really needed AIA's products from when they were only showing excitement, surprise and intellectual interest...."

When AIA realized that just any company operating on the Internet was not their target, the team decided to focus on more specialized marketing services. Despite clients like Telefonica and RACC, sales were barely enough for the company to survive.

In 2004, after the second investment round, AIA decided to change its marketing strategy and identify enterprises from Madrid as its main niche, instead of Catalan companies. It opened a commercial office in Madrid. The newly hired

Table 4. SWOT analysis

Strengths	Weaknesses
Good strategic approach. In line with strategic trends in technology aimed at promoting CRM, customer-oriented outlook, direct marketing, etc. **Good corporate vision.** Oriented toward people, companies or products. High degree of adaptability for multi-sector groups or mergers.	**Limited credibility.** Product and company are not well established. They have little contact with partners and are not widely known. **Limited market.** Technique is of little use to companies with a small amount of data, low-quality data or a small number of customers. **Limited market penetration.** Company's products are primarily present in banking sectors.
Opportunities	Threats
Broadening scopes in terms of sectors. By exploiting sets of values, it is possible to find a wide range of possibilities for application outside the strictly commercial field. **Take advantage of market trends.** CRM solutions or Direct marketing. **Engineer as a package.** Integrated into a product providing global solutions such as CRM or direct marketing.	**Not unique.** Alternative solutions marketed by rival companies can cover the same functionalities with satisfactory results. **Immature market.** A limited number of managers in customer companies believe in the product.

commercial manager, as his first mission, also wanted to change AIA's image. None of the demonstrations hosted out of the Madrid office led to sales. Some sales came from Catalonia, perhaps in response to previous commercial efforts. Still the company remained far from covering its accumulated expenses.

FUTURE RESEARCH DIRECTIONS

During AIA's existence, Albert had thought many times about whether his company would really be able to succeed in the long run. His enthusiasm and ingenuity, complemented by his persistence, imagination and passion, helped him overcome previous critical moments, when the company was performing so poorly. Were these personal traits still enough?

All the company's marketing activities failed, and sufficient sales had never arrived to cover AIA's expenses. This situation must have reflected some of the errors committed in the past. Assigning blame was not the point, but in these circumstances, most of the founding team gradually left the company, leaving just a minimal

operating structure by 2006, when AIA ignored its core competences and simply conducted any kinds of projects it could, just to survive.

Considering himself as the captain, last to leave the sinking ship, Albert decided to hire a consultancy company to perform a detailed analysis of AIA's services and products, as well as its technological and market potential (see Table 4 for the SWOT analysis). Everyone - shareholders, venture capitalists and the university - was curious to know where AIA failed. Was it the technology, the product, the commercial team, the company management, the founding team? Would defining the failure suggest a final solution?

CONCLUSION

Summarizing, AIA's case study follows up a newly created business venture from the first stages, crossing pitfalls and facing a variety of critical issues. Since the process has followed a learning-by-doing path translated into a try-and-error practice, the case brings valuable "do"s and "don't do"s. Thinking and interpreting those remains an individual objective of the reader. In the particular case of AIA, the ultimate outcome was a company on sale.

REFERENCES

Aciar, S.V., Serarols-Tarrés, C., & Royo-Vela, M., & de la Rosa i Esteva, J.L. (2007). Increasing effectiveness in e-commerce: recommendations applying intelligent agents. *Int. J. Business and Systems Research*, *1*(1), 81–97. doi:10.1504/IJBSR.2007.014774

Acworth, E. (2008). University–industry engagement: The formation of the Knowledge Integration Community (KIC) model at the Cambridge-MIT Institute. *Research Policy*, *37*, 1241–1254. doi:10.1016/j.respol.2008.04.022

Amit, R., & Zott, C. (2001). Value creation in E-Business. *Strategic Management Journal*, *22*, 493–520. doi:10.1002/smj.187

Autio, E. (1997). New technology-based firms in innovation networks. *Research Policy*, *26*, 263–281. doi:10.1016/S0048-7333(96)00906-7

Bradshaw, J. M. (1997). An introduction to software agents. In J.M. Bradshaw (Ed.), *Software Agents* (pp.3–46). Menlo park, CA: AAAI Press.

Brown, T. E., & Ulijn, J. M. (2004). *Innovation, Entrepreneurship and Culture. The interaction between technology, progress and economic growth*. Cheltenham, UK: Edward Elgar Publishing.

Carayannis, E. G., Rogers, E. M., Kurihara, K., & Allbritton, M. M. (1998). High technology spin-offs from government R&D laboratories and research universities. *Technovation*, *18*(1), 1–11. doi:10.1016/S0166-4972(97)00101-6

Carayol, N., & Matt, M. (2004). Does research organization influence academic production? Laboratory level evidence from a large European university. *Research Policy*, *33*, 1081–1102. doi:10.1016/j.respol.2004.03.004

Clarysse, B., & Moray, N. (2004). A process study of the entrepreneurial team formation: the case of a research-based spin-off. *Journal of Business Venturing*, *19*, 55–79. doi:10.1016/S0883-9026(02)00113-1

Clarysse, B., Wright, M., Lockett, A., Van de Velde, A., & Vohora, A. (2005). Spinning out new ventures: a typology of incubation strategies from European research institutions. *Journal of Business Venturing*, *20*, 183–216. doi:10.1016/j.jbusvent.2003.12.004

Clemons, E. K., Gu, B., & Lang, K. R. (2002). Newly Vulnerable Markets in an Age of Pure Information Products: An Analysis of Online Music and Online News. *Journal of Management Information Systems*, *19*(3), 17–41.

Clemons, E. K., & Lang, K. R. (2003). The Decoupling of Value Creation from Revenue: A Strategic Analysis of the Markets for Pure Information Goods. *Information Technology and Management*, *4*, 259–287. doi:10.1023/A:1022958530341

Degroof, J. (2002). *The phenomenon spin-off*. Unpublished doctoral dissertation, Sloan School of management, MIT.

Etzkowitz, H. (1998). The norms of entrepreneurial science: cognitive effects of the new university–industry linkages. *Research Policy*, *27*(8), 823–833. doi:10.1016/S0048-7333(98)00093-6

Etzkowitz, H. (2003). Research groups as 'quasi firms': the invention of the entrepreneurial university. *Research Policy*, *32*(1), 109–121. doi:10.1016/S0048-7333(02)00009-4

Etzkowitz, H. (2004). The evolution of the Entrepreneurial University. *International Journal of Technology and Globalization, 1*(1), 64–77.

European Union. (2009). *Creativity and innovation*. European Year 2009. Retrieved May 27, 2009, from http://create2009.europa.eu/

Harmon, B., Ardishvili, A., Cardozo, R., Elder, T., Leuthold, J., & Parshall, J. (1997). Mapping the university technology transfer process. *Journal of Business Venturing, 12*, 423–434. doi:10.1016/S0883-9026(96)00064-X

Hindle, K., & Yencken, J. (2004). Public research commercialisation, entrepreneurship and new technology based firms: an integrated model. *Technovation, 24*(10), 793–803. doi:10.1016/S0166-4972(03)00023-3

Jennings, N. R., & Wooldridge, M. (1998). *Agent Technology: Foundations, Applications, and Markets*. London: Springer.

Kazanjain, R., & Drazin, R. (1990). A stage contingent model of design and growth for technology based ventures. *Journal of Business Venturing, 5*(3), 137–150. doi:10.1016/0883-9026(90)90028-R

Klusch, M. (2002). Information agent technology for the internet: a survey. *Data & Knowledge Engineering, 36*, 337–372. doi:10.1016/S0169-023X(00)00049-5

Koh, C.E., & Nam, K.T. (2005). Business Use of the Internet: A Longitudinal Study from a Value Chain Perspective. *Industrial Management & Data Systems* (Forthcoming issue in 2005).

Kollmann, T. (2006). What is e-entrepreneurship? – fundamentals of company founding in the net economy. *International Journal of Technology Management, 33*(4), 322–340. doi:10.1504/IJTM.2006.009247

Lakshmi, I., Singh, R., & Salm, A. F. (2005). Intelligent agents to support information sharing in B2B e-marketplaces. *Information Systems Management, 22*(3), 37–49. doi:10.1201/1078/45317.22.3.20050601/88744.6

Liao, J., Welsch, H., & Tan, W. L. (2005). Venture gestation paths of nascent entrepreneurs: Exploring the temporal patterns. *The Journal of High Technology Management Research, 16*, 1–22. doi:10.1016/j.hitech.2005.06.001

Lockett, A., Siegel, D., Wright, M., & Ensley, M. (2005). The creation of spin-offs at public research institutions: Managerial and policy implications. *Research Policy, 34*, 981–993. doi:10.1016/j.respol.2005.05.010

Ma, H., & Tan, J. (2006). Key components and implications of entrepreneurship: A 4-P framework. *Journal of Business Venturing, 21*, 704–725. doi:10.1016/j.jbusvent.2005.04.009

Malone, T. W., Yates, J., & Benjamin, R. I. (1987). Electronic Markets and Electronic Hierarchies. *Communications of the ACM, 30*(6), 484–497. doi:10.1145/214762.214766

Migliorini, P., Serarols Tarrés, C., & Bikfalvi, A. (2009). *Overcoming critical junctures in spin-offs companies from non-elite universities: evidence from Catalonia*. Forthcoming in RENT Anthology 2008.

Moray, N., & Clarysse, B. (2005). Institutional change and resource endowments to science-based entrepreneurial firms. *Research Policy, 34*, 1010–1027. doi:10.1016/j.respol.2005.05.016

Ndonzuau, N. F., Pirnay, F., & Surlemont, B. (2002). A stage model of academic spin-off creation. *Technovation, 22*, 281–289. doi:10.1016/S0166-4972(01)00019-0

Pérez, M., & Martínez, A. (2003). The development of university spin-offs: early dynamics of technology transfer and networking. *Technovation*, *23*(10), 823–831. doi:10.1016/S0166-4972(02)00034-2

Pirnay, F., Surlemont, B., & Nlemvo, F. (2003). Toward a typology of university spin-offs. *Small Business Economics*, *21*(4), 355–369. doi:10.1023/A:1026167105153

Porter, M. (1985). *Competitive advantage: Creating and Sustaining Superior Performance*. New York: Free Press.

Porter, M. (2001, March). Strategy and the Internet. *Harvard Business Review*, 63–78.

Rayport, J. F., & Sviokla, J. J. (1995). Exploiting the Virtual Value Chain. *Harvard Business Review*, *73*(6), 75–85.

Reinartz, W., Krafft, M., & Hoyer, W. D. (2004). The customer relationship management process: its measurement and impact on performance. *JMR, Journal of Marketing Research*, *41*, 293–305. doi:10.1509/jmkr.41.3.293.35991

Roberts, E., & Malone, R. (1996). *Policies and structures for spinning off new companies from research and development organizations*. Retrieved July 23, 2009, from http://dspace.mit.edu/bitstream/handle/1721.1/2569/SWP-3804-32616509.pdf?sequence=1

Serarols, C. (2008). The process of business start-ups in the internet: a multiple case study. *International Journal of Technology Management*, *43*(1-3), 142–159. doi:10.1504/IJTM.2008.019412

Serarols Tarrés, C., Urbano, D., Vaillant, Y., & Bikfalvi, A. (2009). Research commercialisation via spin-off: the case of a non-elite university. *Int. J. Technology Transfer and Commercialisation*, *8*(4), 356–378. doi:10.1504/IJTTC.2009.024910

Shane, S. (2004). *Academic Entrepreneurship: University Spin-offs and Wealth Creation*. Cheltenham, UK: Edward Elgar Publishing.

Shane, S., & Venkataraman, S. (2000). The promise of entrepreneurship as a field of research. *Academy of Management Review*, *25*(1), 217–226. doi:10.2307/259271

Siegel, D. S., Waldman, D., & Link, A. (2003). Assessing the impact of organisational practices on the relative productivity of university technology transfer offices: an exploratory study. *Research Policy*, *32*, 27–48. doi:10.1016/S0048-7333(01)00196-2

Stabell, C. B., & Fjeldstad, O. D. (1998). Configuring value for competitive advantage: on chains, shops, and networks. *Strategic Management Journal*, *19*(5), 413–437. doi:10.1002/(SICI)1097-0266(199805)19:5<413::AID-SMJ946>3.0.CO;2-C

Vohora, A., Wright, M., & Lockett, A. (2004). Critical junctures in the development of university high-tech spinout companies. *Research Policy*, *33*, 147–135. doi:10.1016/S0048-7333(03)00107-0

Webster, F. (1976). A model for new venture initiation. *Academy of Management Review*, *1*(1), 26–37. doi:10.2307/257356

Wright, M., Birley, S., & Mosey, S. (2004a). Entrepreneurship and university technology transfer. *The Journal of Technology Transfer*, *29*(3/4), 235–246. doi:10.1023/B:JOTT.0000034121.02507.f3

Wright, M., Vohora, A., & Lockett, A. (2004b). The formation of high tech university spinout companies: the role of joint ventures and venture capital investors. *The Journal of Technology Transfer*, *29*(3/4), 287–310. doi:10.1023/B:JOTT.0000034124.70363.83

ENDNOTES

[1]   A flexible computer system situated in an environment that is capable of flexible autonomous action to meet its design objectives.

[2]   The third mission idea suggests that universities should be involved in technology transfer activities, in addition to their traditional roles of teaching and research. Etzkowitz provides further information about this issue

Compilation of References

Aarts, E. (2004). Ambient Intelligence: A Multimedia Perspective. *IEEE MultiMedia*, 12–19. doi:10.1109/MMUL.2004.1261101

About Lulu. *Corporate Profile*. (2009). Lulu.com. Retrieved April 30, 2009, from http://www.lulu.com/en/about/index.php

About, L. L. Bean. (2009). *Company Information*. Retrieved December 9, 2008, from http://www.llbean.com/customerService/aboutLLBean/background.html?nav=ln

Abraham, A., Windmann, S., Daum, I., & Güntürkün, O. (2005). Conceptual expansion and creative imagery as a function of psychoticism. *Consciousness and Cognition*, *14*, 520–534.

Aciar, S.V., Serarols-Tarrés, C., & Royo-Vela, M., & de la Rosa i Esteva, J.L. (2007). Increasing effectiveness in e-commerce: recommendations applying intelligent agents. *Int. J. Business and Systems Research*, *1*(1), 81–97. doi:10.1504/IJBSR.2007.014774

Acs, Z., & Audretsch, D. (1987). Innovation, Market Structure, and Firm Size. *The Review of Economics and Statistics*, *69*, 567–574. doi:10.2307/1935950

Acworth, E. (2008). University–industry engagement: The formation of the Knowledge Integration Community (KIC) model at the Cambridge-MIT Institute. *Research Policy*, *37*, 1241–1254. doi:10.1016/j.respol.2008.04.022

Alby, T. (2008). *Web 2.0 Konzepte, Anwendungen, Technologien* (3rd Ed.). München, Germany: Hanser.

Alcaniz, M. (2005). New Technologies for Ambient Intelligence. In G. Riva, F. Vatalaro, F. Davide & M.

Alcaniz (Eds.), *Ambient Intelligence: the evolution of technology, communication and cognition towards the future of human-computer interaction*. Amsterdam: IOS Press.

Aldrich, H. E., & Auster, E. R. (1986). Even Dwarfs Started Small - Liabilities of Age and Size and Their Strategic Implications. In L.L. Cummings & B.M. Staw (Eds.), *Research in Organizational Behavior* (pp. 165-189). San Francisco, CA.

Aldrich, H. E., & Fiol, C. M. (1994). Fools rush in? The institutional context of industry creation. *Academy of Management Review*, *19*(4), 645–670. doi:10.2307/258740

Aldrich, H. E., & Martinez, M. A. (2001). Many are called, but few are chosen, an evolutionary perspective for the study of entrepreneurship. *Entrepreneurship. Theory into Practice*, *25*(4), 41–56.

Alexander, J. (2000). Adaptive Strategies of Non-Profit Human Service Organizations in an Era of Devolution and New Public Management. *Nonprofit Management & Leadership*, *10*, 287–303. doi:10.1002/nml.10305

Alexy, O. (2009). *Free Revealing. How Firms Can Profit From Being Open*. Wiesbaden, Germany: Gabler.

Al-Fawaz, K., Zahran, A., & Tillal, E. (2008, May). *Critical Success Factors in ERP Implementation: a Review*. Paper presented at the European and Mediterranean Conference on Information Systems, Dubai, United Arab Emirates.

Allen, R. C. (1983). Collective Invention. *Journal of Economic Behavior & Organization*, *4*(1), 1–24. doi:10.1016/0167-2681(83)90023-9

ALTOVA. (2009). *Database mapping*. Retrieved March, 2009, from http://www.altova.com/products/mapforce/xml_to_db_database_mapping.html

Alvord, S. H., Brown, D. L., & Letts, C. W. (2004). Social Entrepreneurship and Societal Transformation: An Exploratory Study. *The Journal of Applied Behavioral Science*, *40*(3), 260–282. doi:10.1177/0021886304266847

Amabile, T. M. (1983). *The Social Psychology of Creativity*. Berlin: Springer.

Amabile, T. M. (1996). *Creativity in Context*. Boulder, CO: Westview Press.

Amazon.com. (2009). *Kindle 2: Amazon's New Wireless Reading Device (Latest Generation)*. Amazon.com, Inc. Retrieved April 30, 2009, from http://www.amazon.com/Kindle-Amazons-Wireless-Reading-Generation/dp/B00154JDAI/ref=sa_menu_kdp23_gw/188-4117823-4045537?pf_rd_m=ATVPDKIKX0DER&pf_rd_s=left-nav-1&pf_rd_r=1NS368NYM5RE5CNX6QT2&pf_rd_t=101&pf_rd_p=328655101&pf_rd_i=507846

Amit, R., & Schoemaker, P. (1993). Strategic assets and organizational rent. *Strategic Management Journal*, *14*(1), 33–46. doi:10.1002/smj.4250140105

Amit, R., & Zott, C. (2001). Value creation in e-business. *Strategic Management Journal*, *22*(6/7), 493520.

Anderseck, K. (2004). Institutional and Academic Entrepreneurship: Implications for University Governance and Management. *Higher Education in Europe*, *29*(2), 193–200. doi:10.1080/0379772042000234820

Anderson, C. (2006). *The Long Tail: Why the Future of Business Is Selling Less of More*. New York: Hyperion.

Anderson, E., & Weitz, B. (1992). The use of pledges to build and sustain commitment in distribution channels. *JMR, Journal of Marketing Research*, *29*(1), 1834. doi:10.2307/3172490

Arieti, S. (1978). From primary process to creativity. *The Journal of Creative Behavior*, *12*, 225–246.

Armstrong, J. S., & Overton, T. S. (1977). Estimating Non-Response Bias in Mail Surveys. *JMR, Journal of Marketing Research*, *14*(3), 396–402. doi:10.2307/3150783

Arranz, N., & de Arroyabe, J. (2008). The choice of partners in R&D cooperation: An empirical analysis of Spanish firms. *Technovation*, *28*, 88–100. doi:10.1016/j.technovation.2007.07.006

Ashforth, B. E., & Gibbs, B. W. (1990). The double-edge of organizational legitimation. *Organization Science*, *1*(2), 177–194. doi:10.1287/orsc.1.2.177

Ashoka. (2007). *Ashoka home page*. Retrieved August 29, 2007, from http://www.ashoka.org/ Ashoka. (n.d.). *What is a Social Entrepreneur?* Retrieved from http://ashoka.org/social_entrepreneur

Audretsch, D. (1998). Agglomeration and the location of innovative activity. *Oxford Review of Economic Activity*, *14*(2), 18–29. doi:10.1093/oxrep/14.2.18

Australian Bureau of Statistics. (1998). *1291.0 - A Guide to Major ABS Classifications*. Retrieved July, 2009, from http://www.abs.gov.au/AUSSTATS/abs@.nsf/DirClass-ManualsbyTopic/F19DB188D50D978ACA2570B30006A35D?OpenDocument

Autio, E. (1997). New technology-based firms in innovation networks. *Research Policy*, *26*, 263–281. doi:10.1016/S0048-7333(96)00906-7

Autio, E., Sapienza, H. J., & Almeida, J. G. (2000). Effects of age at entry, knowledge intensity, and imitability on international growth. *Academy of Management Journal*, *43*(5), 909–924. doi:10.2307/1556419

Awad, E., & Ghaziri, H. (2004). *Knowledge Management*. Upper Saddle River, NJ: Pearson Education.

Bagozzi, R. P. (1979). The Role of Measurement in Theory Construction and Hypothesis Testing - Toward a Holistic Model. In O.C. Ferrell, S.W. Brown & C.W. Lamb (Eds.), *Conceptual and Theoretical Developments in Marketing* (pp. 15-32). Chicago.

Bagozzi, R. P., & Dholakia, U. M. (2006). Open Source Software User Communities: A Study of participation in Linux user groups. *Management Science*, *52*(7), 1099–1115. doi:10.1287/mnsc.1060.0545

Bahra, N. (2001). *Competitive Knowledge Management.* Basingstoke, UK: Palgrave Macmillan.

Bailey, A., Johnson, G., & Daniels, K. (2000). Validation of a Multi-Dimensional Measure of Strategy Development Processes. *British Journal of Management, 11,* 151–162. doi:10.1111/1467-8551.t01-1-00157

Baldwin, C. Y., & Clark, K. B. (1997). Managing in the age of modularity. *Harvard Business Review, 75*(5), 84–93.

Baldwin, C. Y., & Clark, K. B. (2006). Clark The Architecture of Participation: Does Code Architecture Mitigate Free Riding in the Open Source Development Model? *Management Science, 52*(7), 1116–1127. doi:10.1287/mnsc.1060.0546

Baourakis, G., Kourgiantakis, M., & Migdalas, A. (2002). The impact of e-commerce on agro-food marketing: The case of agricultural co-operatives, firms and consumers in Crete. *British Food Journal, 104*(8), 580–590. doi:10.1108/00070700210425976

Barba-Sánchez, V., del Pilar Martínez-Ruiz, M., & Jiménez-Zarco, A. I. (2007). Drivers, Benefits and Challenges of ICT Adoption by Small and Medium Sized Enterprises (SMEs): A Literature Review. *Problems & Perspectives in Management, 5*(1), 103–114.

Barney, J. B. (1991). Firm resources and sustained competitive advantage. *Journal of Management, 17*(1), 99–120. doi:10.1177/014920639101700108

Baron, R. A. (2006). Opportunity recognition as pattern recognition. How entrepreneurs 'connect the dots' to identify new business opportunities. *The Academy of Management Perspectives, 20*(1), 104–119.

Basso, A., Goldberg, D., Greenspan, S., & Weimer, D. (2001). First Impressions: Emotional and Cognitive Factors Underlying Judgments of Trust in E-Commerce. In *Proceedings of the 3rd ACM Conference on Electronic Commerce,* (pp. 137-143).

Basu, A., & Muylle, S. (2002). Online Support for Commerce Processes by Web Retailers. *Decision Support Systems, 34*(4), 379–395. doi:10.1016/S0167-9236(02)00065-9

Batjargal, B. (2007). Internet entrepreneurship: social capital, human capital and performance of Internet venture in China. *Research Policy, 36,* 605–618. doi:10.1016/j.respol.2006.09.029

Baumol, W. J. (1993). *Entrepreneurship, Management and the Structure of Payoffs.* Cambridge Massachusetts, MIT.

Bausch, S., & McGiboney, M. (2009, March 9). Social Networks & Blogs now 4th most Popular Online Activity, Ahead of Personal Email. *News Report.* Retrieved http://www.nielsen-online.com/pr/pr_090309.pdf

Belch, M., Krentler, K., & Willis-Flurry, L. (2005). Teen internet mavens: influence in family decision making. *Journal of Business Research, 58,* 569–575. doi:10.1016/j.jbusres.2003.08.005

Bell, G., & McNamara, J. F. (1991). *McHigh-Tech ventures: the guide for entrepreneurial success.* New York: Perseus Books.

Benneworth, P., & Charles, D. (2005). University Spin-offs Policies and Economic Development in less Successful Regions: Learning from Two Decades of Policy Practice. *European Planning Studies, 13*(4), 537–557. doi:10.1080/09654310500107175

Bergeron, F., & Raymond, L. (1992). The Advantages of Electronic Data Interchange. *Database, 23*(4), 19–31.

Berners-Lee, T., Handler, J., & Lassila, O. (2001). The Semantic Web. *Scientific American, 284*(5), 28–37. doi:10.1038/scientificamerican0501-34

Bernoff J (2009b, March 15). Get more than an Ad, get in the conversation. *Marketing News,* 18.

Bernoff, J. (2009a, February 15). Blogs, Marketing and Trust. *Marketing news,* 17.

Berry, J. W. (1980). Acculturation as Varieties of Adaption. In A. M. Padilla (Ed.), *Theory, Models and Some Findings* (pp. 9-25). Boulder, CO: Westview Press.

Berry, J. W., Poortinga, Y. H., Segall, M. H., & Dasen, P. (1992). *Cross-Cultural Psychology: Research and Applications.* Cambridge, MA: Cambridge University Press.

Beyers, W. B., & Lindahl, D. P. (1996). Lone eagles and high fliers in rural producer services. *Rural Development Perspectives*, *11*(3), 2–10.

Bharadwaj, P. N., & Soni, R. G. (2007). E-commerce usage and perception of e-commerce issues among small firms: Results and implications from an empirical study. *Journal of Small Business Management*, *45*(4), 501521. doi:10.1111/j.1540-627X.2007.00225.x

Bhidé, A. V. (2000). *The origin and evolution of new business*. Oxford, UK: Oxford University Press.

Bieger, T., Bickhoff, N., Caspers, R., zu Knyphausen-Aufseß, D., & Reding, K. (Eds.). (2002). *Zukünftige Geschäftsmodelle: Konzept und Anwendung in der Netzökonomie*. Berlin, Germany: Springer.

Bishop, D. (2008). The small enterprise in the training market. *Training and Education*, *50*(8/9), 661–673. doi:10.1108/00400910810917046

Bitzer, J., & Schröder, P. J. H. (2005). *The Impact of Entry and Competition by Open Source Software on Innovation Activity*. Industrial Organization 0512001, EconWPA.

Bitzer, J., Schrettl, W., & Schröder, P. J. H. (2007). Intrinsic Motivation in Open Source Software Development. *Journal of Comparative Economics*, *35*, 160–169. doi:10.1016/j.jce.2006.10.001

Blomqvist, K., Hurmelinna, P., Nummela, N., & Saarenketo, S. (2008). The role of trust and contracts in the internationalization of technology-intensive Born Globals. *Journal of Engineering and Technology Management*, *25*(1-2), 123–135. doi:10.1016/j.jengtecman.2008.01.006

Bloodgood, J. M., Sapienza, H. J., & Almeida, J. G. (1996). The internationalization of new high-potential US ventures: antecedents and outcomes. *Entrepreneurship Theory & Practice*, *20*(4), 61–76.

Boag, S. (2006a). Freudian dream theory, dream bizarreness, and the disguise-censor controversy. *Neuro-psychoanalysis*, *8*(1), 5–17.

Boag, S. (2006b). Freudian dream theory, dream bizarreness, & the disguise-censor controversy: Response to Commentaries. *Neuro-psychoanalysis*, *8*(1), 60–69.

Boerner, S., & Gebert, D. (1999). The Open and the Closed Corporation as Conflicting Forms of Organization. *The Journal of Applied Behavioral Science*, *35*(3), 341–359. doi:10.1177/0021886399353006

Bok, D. (2003). *Universities in the Marketplace: The Commercialisation of Higher Education*. Princeton, NJ: Princeton University Press.

Bollen, K. A. (1989). *Structural Equations with Latent Variables*. New York: Wiley & Sons.

Bollen, K. A., & Lennox, R. (1991). Conventional Wisdom on Measurement - A Structural Equation Perspective. *Psychological Bulletin*, *110*(2), 305–314. doi:10.1037/0033-2909.110.2.305

Bollen, K. A., & Ting, K.-F. (1993). Confirmatory Tetrad Analysis. In P. Marsden (Eds.), *Sociological Methodology* (pp. 147-175). Washington, DC: Wiley-Blackwell.

Bonaccorsi, A., Giannangeli, S., & Rossi, C. (2006). Entry Strategies Under Competing Standards: Hybrid Business Models in the Open Source Software Industry. *Management Science*, *52*(7), 1085–1098. doi:10.1287/mnsc.1060.0547

Boter, H., & Homquist, C. (1996). Industry characteristics and internationalization processes in small firms. *Journal of Business Venturing*, *11*(6), 471–487. doi:10.1016/S0883-9026(96)89166-X

Boud, D., & Symes, C. (2000). Learning for real: work-based education in universities. In Symes, C., & McIntyre, J. (Eds.), *Working Knowledge: The New Vocationalism and Higher Education*. Buckingham, UK: SHRE and Oxford University Press.

Boudreau, K. (2008). Opening the platform vs. opening the complementary good? The effect on product innovation in handheld computing. *Social Science Research Network*, abstract 1251167. Retrieved August 24, 2008, from http://papers.ssrn.com/sol3/papers.cfm?abstract_id=1251167&CFID=12533725&CFTOKEN=38798633

Bourret, R. (2005). *XML and Databases*. Retrieved July, 2009, from http://www.rpbourret.com/xml/XMLAndDatabases.htm

Boutellier, R., & Rohner, N. (2006). Technologiegeschwindigkeit und Technologieplanung. In J. Gausemeier (Ed.), *Vorausschau und Technologieplanung* (pp. 291-316). Paderborn, Germany: W.V. Westfalia Druck GmbH.

Bower, G. H., & Hilgard, E. (1997). *Theories of Learning.* Upper Saddle River, NJ: Prentice-Hall.

Boyd, D., & Ellison, N. (2007). Social Network Sites: Definition, History, and Scholarship. *Journal of Computer-Mediated Communication, 13*(1), 210–230. doi:10.1111/j.1083-6101.2007.00393.x

Bradshaw, J. M. (1997). An introduction to software agents. In J.M. Bradshaw (Ed.), *Software Agents* (pp.3–46). Menlo park, CA: AAAI Press.

Braunerhjelm, P. (2007). Academic entrepreneurship: social norms, university culture and policies. *Science & Public Policy, 34*(9), 619–631. doi:10.3152/030234207X276554

Bridge, S., Hegarty, C., & Porter, S. (2008). *Rediscovering Enterprise: Exploring Entrepreneurship for Undergraduates.* Institute for Small Business and Entrepreneurship 31st Conference, Conference Proceedings. Belfast, Ireland: ISBE.

Brown, C., & Vessey, I. (2003). Managing the Next Wave of Enterprise Systems: Leveraging Lessons from ER. *MIS Quarterly Executive, 2*(1), 65–77.

Brown, J., Broderick, A., & Lee, L. (2007). Word of mouth communication within online communities: Conceptualizing the online social network. *Journal of Interactive Marketing, 21*(3), 2–20. doi:10.1002/dir.20082

Brown, S., & Eisenhardt, K. (1998). *Competing on the Edge.* Boston, MA: Harvard Business School Press.

Brown, T. E., & Ulijn, J. M. (2004). *Innovation, Entrepreneurship and Culture. The interaction between technology, progress and economic growth.* Cheltenham, UK: Edward Elgar Publishing.

Brüderl, J., & Schüssler, R. (1990). Organizational Mortality - The Liabilities of Newness and Adolescence. *Administrative Science Quarterly, 35*(3), 530–547. doi:10.2307/2393316

Bucklin, L. P., & Sengupta, S. (1993). Organizing successful co-marketing alliances. *Journal of Marketing, 57*(4), 32–46. doi:10.2307/1252025

Buhalis, D., & Main, H. (1998). Information technology in peripheral small and medium hospitality enterprises: Strategic analysis and critical factors. *International Journal of Contemporary Hospitality Management, 10*(5), 198–202. doi:10.1108/09596119810227811

Bulk, F. (2004). *Final Project: Skype* [Electronic Version]. Retrieved February 11, 2009 from http://www1.cs.columbia.edu/~salman/skype/frank.pdf

Burshtein, S., & Brodie, S. (2006, July). *Developing a modular entrepreneurship education program: The MILK Framework.* Paper presented at the Intent2006 Conference, Sao Paulo, Brazil.

Busch, P. (2008). *Tacit Knowledge in Organizational Learning.* Hershey, PA: IGI.

Busch, P., & Richards, D. (2003). Building and Utilising an IT Tacit Knowledge Inventory. In *Proceedings 14th Australasian Conference on Information Systems (ACIS2003)*, November 26-28, Perth, Australia.

Busch, P., & Richards, D. (2004). Acquisition of articulable tacit knowledge. In *Proceedings of the Pacific Knowledge Acquisition Workshop (PKAW'04), in conjunction with The 8th Pac.Rim Int.l Conf. on AI*, August 9-13, 2004, Auckland, NZ (pp. 87-101).

Busch, P., & Richards, D. (2005). An Approach to Understand, Capture and Nurture Creativity and Innovation Knowledge. In *Proc. 15th Australasian Conference on Information Systems (ACIS2005),* November 30-Dec 2nd, Sydney, Australia.

Busch, P., & Richards, D. (2006). Innovation Knowledge Acquisition: The Tacit Knowledge of Novices. In Z. Shi, K. Shimohara & D. Feng (Eds.), *Intelligent Information Processing* (IIP'2006), 20-22nd September 2006, Adelaide (pp. 259-268).

Busenitz, L. W., & Lau, C. M. (1996). A cross-cultural cognitive model of new venture creation. *Entrepreneurship Theory and Practice, 20*(4), 25–39.

Business Software. (2008). *Top 10 ERP Vendors – 2008 Profiles of the Leading Vendors*. Retrieved from http://www.BusinessSoftware.com

Butt, G., & Lance, A. (2005). Modernising the roles of support staff in primary schools: changing focus, changing function. *Educational Review, 57*(2), 131–137. doi:10.1080/0013191042000308314

Cakim, I. (2006). Online opinion leaders: a predictive guide for viral marketing campaigns. In J. Kirby & P. Marsden (Eds.) *Connected Marketing: the Viral, Buzz and Word-of-mouth Revolution* (pp. 107-118). Oxford, UK: Butterworth-Heinemann.

Carayannis, E. G., Rogers, E. M., Kurihara, K., & Allbritton, M. M. (1998). High technology spin-offs from government R&D laboratories and research universities. *Technovation, 18*(1), 1–11. doi:10.1016/S0166-4972(97)00101-6

Carayol, N., & Matt, M. (2004). Does research organization influence academic production? Laboratory level evidence from a large European university. *Research Policy, 33*, 1081–1102. doi:10.1016/j.respol.2004.03.004

Cardon, M. S., & Stvens, C. E. (2004). Managing human resources in small organizations: what do we know? *Human Resource Management Review, 14*(3), 295–323. doi:10.1016/j.hrmr.2004.06.001

Carmines, E. G., & Zeller, R. A. (1979). *Reliability and Validity Assessment.* Beverly Hills, CA: Sage.

Carson, S. H., Peterson, J. B., & Higgins, D. M. (2003a). Decreased Latent Inhibition is associated with increased creative achievement in high-functioning individuals. *Journal of Personality and Social Psychology, 85*(3), 499–506. doi:10.1037/0022-3514.85.3.499

Casal, C. R. (2004). Impact of location-aware services on the privacy/security balance. *6*(2), 105-111.

Cavusgil, S. T., Calantone, R. J., & Zhao, Y. (2003). Tacit knowledge transfer and firm innovation capacity. *Journal of Business and Industrial Marketing, 18*(1), 6–21. doi:10.1108/08858620310458615

Centre for Environment and Sustainability. (2002). Technology and Policy for Sustainable Development. *Chalmers University of Technology and the Göteborg University, 5*(February), 4.

Chakraborty, J., Hansen, L., Denenberg, D. A., & Norcio, A. F. (2008). Preliminary Investigation into the Internationalization of User Interfaces. In *Proceedings of the Applied Human Factors and Ergonomics 2nd International Conference*, Las Vegas, Nevada.

Chariton, C., & Choi, M.-H. (2002). User Interface Guidelines for Enhancing Usability of Airline Travel Agency E-Commerce Web Sites. In *Proceeding of the Conference on Human Factors in Computing Systems*, (pp. 676 – 677).

Chaston, I. (2001). *E-Marketing Strategy*. Maidenhead, UK: McGraw-Hill.

Chell, E. (2007). Social Enterprise and Entrepreneurship: Towards a Convergent Theory of the Entrepreneurial Process. *International Small Business Journal, 25*(1), 5–26. doi:10.1177/0266242607071779

Chen, M. X., Iyigun, M., & Maskus, K. E. (2007). General Public Licensing and the Intensity of Aggregate Software Development. *Economics of Innovation and New Technology, 16*(5-6), 451–466. doi:10.1080/10438590600914452

Chen, S. (2005). *Strategic Management of e-Business* (2nd ed.). Chichester, UK: John Wiley & Sons.

Chertok, M., Hamaoui, J., & Jamison, E. (2008, Spring). The funding gap. *Stanford Social Innovation Review*, 44–47.

Chesbrough, H. (2003). The Logic of Open innovation: Managing Intellectual Property. *California Management Review, 45*(3), 33–58.

Chesbrough, H. (2007). Business Model Innovation: It's Not Just About Technology Anymore. *Strategy and Leadership, 35*(6), 12–17. doi:10.1108/10878570710833714

Chesbrough, H. W., Vanhaverbeke, W., & West, J. (2008). *Open Innovation: Researching a New Paradigm*. New York: Oxford University Press.

Chesbrough, H., & Rosenbloom, R. S. (2002). The Role of the Business Model in Capturing Value from Innovation: Evidence from Xerox Corporation's Technology Spin-Off Companies. *Industrial and Corporate Change, 11*(3), 529–555. doi:10.1093/icc/11.3.529

Chetty, S., & Campbell-Hunt, C. (2003). Explosive international growth and problems of success amongst small to medium-sized firms. *International Small Business Journal, 21*(5), 5–27. doi:10.1177/0266242603021001719

Chin, W. W. (1998a). Commentary - Issues and Opinion on Structural Equation Modeling. *MIS Quarterly, 22*(1), 7–16.

Chin, W. W. (1998b). The Partial Least Squares Approach to Structural Equation Modeling. In G.A. Marcoulides (Eds.), *Modern Methods for Business Research* (pp. 295-336). Mahwah, NJ: Lawrence Erlbaum Associates.

Choi, S.-Y., Stahl, D. O., & Whinston, A. B. (1997). *The economics of electronic commerce*. Indianapolis, IN: Macmillan.

Chorev, S., & Anderson, A. R. (2006). Success in Israeli high-tech start-ups: critical factors and process. *Technovation, 26*, 162–174. doi:10.1016/j.technovation.2005.06.014

Christaller, W. (1933). *Die zentralen Orte in Süddeutschland*. Jena, Germany: Gustav Fischer.

Churchill, G. A. (1979). A Paradigm for Developing Better Measures of Marketing Constructs. *JMR, Journal of Marketing Research, 16*(1), 64–73. doi:10.2307/3150876

Churchill, N. C., & Lewis, V. L. (1983). The Five Stages of Small Business Growth. *Harvard Business Review, 61*(3), 30–50.

Clark, B. R. (1998). *Creating Entrepreneurial Universities: Organizational Pathways of Transition*. Oxford, UK: IAU Press, Elsevier.

Clark, D. (2003). *Epic survey 2003: the future of e-learning*. Retrieved February 2009 from http://www.epic.co.uk

Clarysse, B., & Moray, N. (2004). A process study of the entrepreneurial team formation: the case of a research-based spin-off. *Journal of Business Venturing, 19*, 55–79. doi:10.1016/S0883-9026(02)00113-1

Clarysse, B., Wright, M., Lockett, A., Van de Velde, A., & Vohora, A. (2005). Spinning out new ventures: a typology of incubation strategies from European research institutions. *Journal of Business Venturing, 20*, 183–216. doi:10.1016/j.jbusvent.2003.12.004

Clemons, E. K., & Lang, K. R. (2003). The Decoupling of Value Creation from Revenue: A Strategic Analysis of the Markets for Pure Information Goods. *Information Technology and Management, 4*, 259–287. doi:10.1023/A:1022958530341

Clemons, E. K., Gu, B., & Lang, K. R. (2002). Newly Vulnerable Markets in an Age of Pure Information Products: An Analysis of Online Music and Online News. *Journal of Management Information Systems, 19*(3), 17–41.

Clemson University International Center for Automotive Research. (n.d.). Retrieved from http://www.clemson.edu/autoresearch/

Clifford, A. M., & Dixon, S.A. (2005). Green-works: un modelo de negocio que combina la iniciativa emprendedora social con la mejora del medio ambiente. *Iniciativa emprendedora, 48*, 69–79.

Coetzer, A. (2006). Managers as learning facilitators in small manufacturing firms. *Journal of Small Business and Enterprise Development, 13*(3), 351–362. doi:10.1108/14626000610680244

Cohen, J. (1992). A Power Primer. *Psychological Bulletin, 112*(1), 155–160. doi:10.1037/0033-2909.112.1.155

Cohen, N. (2001). What Works: Grameen Telecom's Village Phones [Electronic Version]. *World Resources Institute Digital Dividend*, 1-15. Retrieved February 11, 2009 from http://pdf.wri.org/dd_grameen.pdf

Colombo, M. G., & Grilli, L. (2005). Founders' human capital and the growth of new technology-based firms: a competence-based view. *Research Policy, 34*, 795–816. doi:10.1016/j.respol.2005.03.010

Colombo, M. G., & Grilli, L. (2007). Technology policy for the knowledge economy: public support to young ICT service firms. *Policy, 31*, 573–591.

Cooke, P., Uranga, M. G., & Goio, E. (1997). Regional innovation systems: Institutional and organisational dimensions. *Research Policy, 26*(4), 475–491. doi:10.1016/S0048-7333(97)00025-5

Cooper, A. C. (1986). Entrepreneurship and high technology. In D. L. Sexton & R. W. Smilor (Eds.), *The Art and Science of Entrepreneurship* (pp. 153-68). Cambridge, UK: Ballinger.

Cordella, A. (2001, June). *Does Information Technology Always Lead to Lower Transaction Costs?* Paper presented at the 9th European Conference on Information Systems, Bled, Slovenia.

Cordella, A. (2006). Transaction costs and information systems: does IT add up? *Journal of Information Technology, 21*, 195–202. doi:10.1057/palgrave.jit.2000066

Cordella, A., & Simon, K. A. (1997, August). *The Impact of Information Technology on Transaction and Coordination Cost.* Paper presented at the Conference on Information Systems Research, Oslo, Norway.

Courtney, P., & Brydon, J. (2001). *Differential economic performance: Experience from two Scottish regions.* Paper presented at RICS Research Foundation Rural Research Conference, London.

Crick, D., & Spence, M. (2005). The internationalisation of high performing UK high-tech SMEs: a study of planned and unplanned strategies. *International Business Review, 14*, 167–185. doi:10.1016/j.ibusrev.2004.04.007

Cronbach, L. J. (1951). Coefficient Alpha and the Internal Structure of Tests. *Psychometrika, 16*, 297–334. doi:10.1007/BF02310555

Csikszentmihalyi, M. (1996). *Creativity: Flow and the psychology of discovery and invention.* New York: Harper Perennial.

Cutler, T. (2008). *Venturous Australia: Building Strength in Innovation. Report on the Review of the National Innovation System.* Retrieved May 5, 2009, from http:// www.industry.gov.au/innovationreview/Documents/NIS_review_Web3.pdf

Dahlander, L. (2007). Penguin in a new suit: A tale of how de novo entrants emerged to harness free and open source software communities. *Industrial and Corporate Change, 16*(5), 913–943. doi:10.1093/icc/dtm026

Dahlander, L., & Wallin, M. W. (2006). A man on the inside: Unlocking communities as complementary assets. *Research Policy, 35*, 1243–1259. doi:10.1016/j.respol.2006.09.011

Dahlander, L., Frederiksen, L., & Rullani, F. (2008). Online Communities and Open Innovation: Governance and Symbolic Value Creation. *Industry and Innovation, 15*(2), 115–123. doi:10.1080/13662710801970076

Damaskopoulos, P., & Evgeniou, T. (2003). Adoption of new economy practices by SMEs in Eastern Europe. *European Management Journal, 21*(2), 133–145. doi:10.1016/S0263-2373(03)00009-4

Daneva, M., & Wieringa, R. (2008). *Requirements Engineering for Cross-organizational ERP Implementation: Undocumented Assumptions and Potential Mismatches.* Presented at University of Twente.

Dart, R. (2004). The Legitimacy of Social Enterprise. *Nonprofit Management & Leadership, 14*(4), 411–425. doi:10.1002/nml.43

Das, T. K., & Teng, B.-S. (2000). A Resource-based Theory of Strategic Alliances. *Journal of Management, 26*(1), 31–61. doi:10.1016/S0149-2063(99)00037-9

David, P. (1997). The knowledge factor: A survey of universities. *The Economist, 4*(10), 13–17.

Davis, G. B. (2002). Anytime/Anyplace Computing and the Future of Knowledge Work. *Communications of the ACM, 45*(12), 67–73. doi:10.1145/585597.585617

Davis, K. L., Panksepp, J., & Normansell, L. (2003). The Affective Neuroscience Personality Scales: Normative data and implications. *Neuro-psychoanalysis, 5*, 57–69.

De Clercq, D., Hessels, J., & van Stel, A. (2008). Knowledge spillovers and new ventures' export orientation. *Small Business Economics, 31*, 283–303. doi:10.1007/s11187-008-9132-z

De Paoli, S., Teli, M., & d'Andrea, V. (2008). Free and Open Source Licences in Community Life: Two empirical cases. *First Monday, 13*(10). Retrieved July 24, 2009, from http://www.maurizioteli.eu/publications/DePaoliTeliDandreaInProgress.pdf

De Rond, M., & Bouchikhi, H. (2004). On the Dialectics of Strategic Alliances. *Organization Science, 15*(1), 56–69. doi:10.1287/orsc.1030.0037

Deakins, D., Galloway, L., & Mochrie, R. (2003). *The Use and Effect of ICT on Scotland's Rural Business Community.* Scotecon Report.

Decker, S., Melnik, S., Van Harmelen, F., Fensel, D., Klein, M., & Broekstra, J. (2000). The Semantic Web: The Roles of XML and RDF. *IEEE Internet Computing, 4*(5), 63–73. doi:10.1109/4236.877487

Dees, J. G. (2001). *The Meaning of Social Entrepreneurship.* Durham, NC: Duke University. Retrieved January 2009, from http://www.fuqua.duke.edu/centers/case/documents/dees_sedef.pdf

Dees, J. G., & Anderson, B. B. (2007). Framing a Theory of Social Entrepreneurship: Building on Two Schools of Practice and Thought. *Association for Research on Nonprofit Organizations and Voluntary Action (AR-NOVA) Occasional Paper Series—Research on Social Entrepreneurship:Understanding and Contributing to an Emerging Field, 1*(3), 39–66.

Dees, J. G., Emerson, J., & Economy, P. (2001). *Enterprising nonprofits: A toolkit for social entrepreneurs.* New York: John Wiley & Sons.

Defense, L. I. N. K. (2009). *US Department of Defense.* Retrieved April 30, 2009, from http://www.defenselink.mil/

Degroof, J. (2002). *The phenomenon spin-off.* Unpublished doctoral dissertation, Sloan School of management, MIT.

Dehning, B., & Stratopolous, T. (2003). Determinants of a Sustainable Competitive Advantage Due to an IT-enabled Strategy. *The Journal of Strategic Information Systems, 12*(1), 7–28. doi:10.1016/S0963-8687(02)00035-5

Del Amo, M. Q. (2007). *Critical review of scientific literature and other sources.* Retrieved May 10, 2009, from http://www.idi.ntnu.no/grupper/su/su-diploma-2007/dipl07-queroldelamo.pdf

Delany, C. (2009, February 24). Learning from Obama: Lessons for Online Communicators in 2009 and Beyond. Message posted to http://techpresident.com/blog-entry/learning-obama-lessons-online-communicators-2009-and-beyond

Delmar, F., & Shane, S. (2004). Legitimating first: Organizing activities and the survival of new ventures. *Journal of Business Venturing, 19*(3), 385–410. doi:10.1016/S0883-9026(03)00037-5

Deloitte. (2008). *In fighting shape? 2008 survey of cost-improvement trends in the Fortune 500.* Deloitte.

Dempsey, B., Weiss, D., Jones, P., & Greenberg, J. (1999). *A quantitative profile of a community of open source Linux developers.* SILS Technical Report # TR-1999-05, School of Information and Library Science, University of North Carolina, Chapel Hill, NC. Retrieved February 10, 2009, from sils.unc.edu/research/publications/reports/TR-1999-05.pdf

Deng, S., & Dart, J. (1994). Measuring Market Orientation - A Multi-Factor, Multi-Item Approach. *Journal of Marketing Management, 10*(8), 725–742.

Dennis, W. J. (2003). Raising Response Rates in Mail Surveys of Small Business Owners: Results of an Experiment. *Journal of Small Business Management, 41*(3), 278–295. doi:10.1111/1540-627X.00082

Department for Education and Skills. (2002). *Skills: Getting on in Business: Getting on in Work, White Paper.* Norwich, UK: HMSO.

Department of Defence. (2009). *Defence Materiel Organization.* Australian Government, Australia.

Deshpandé, R., Farley, J. U., & Webster, F. E. (1992). Corporate Culture, Customer Orientation and Innovativeness in Japanese Firms. In *MSI Report, Nr. 92- 100.* Cambridge, MA: Marketing Science Institute.

DG Information Society. (2004, March 11). *Ambient Intelligence.* Retrieved June 9th, 2006, from http://europa.eu.int/information_society/policy/ambienti/index_en.htm

Diamantopoulos, A., & Winklhofer, H. M. (2001). Index Construction with Formative Indicators - An Alternative to Scale Development. *JMR, Journal of Marketing Research, 38*(2), 269–277. doi:10.1509/jmkr.38.2.269.18845

DiMaggio, P. J., & Powell, W. W. (1983). The iron cage revisited: institutional isomorphism and collective rationality in organizational fields. *American Sociological Review, 48,* 147–160. doi:10.2307/2095101

Dixon, T., Thompson, B., & McAllister, P. (2002). *The Value of ICT for SMEs in the UK: A Critical Literature Review.* Report for Small Business Service Research Programme, Reading: College of Estate Management.

Domino, G., Short, J., Evans, A., & Romano, P. (2002). Creativity and ego defense mechanisms: Some exploratory empirical evidence. *Creativity Research Journal, 14,* 17–25. doi:10.1207/S15326934CRJ1401_2

Dowling, J., & Pfeffer, J. (1975). Organizational legitimacy: Social values and organizational behavior. *Pacific Sociological Review, 18*(1), 122–136.

Doyle, L., & Hughes, M. (2004). *Learning without lessons: Supporting Learning in Small Businesses.* London: LSDA.

Drucker, P. (1988). The Coming of the New Organization. *Harvard Business Review, 66*(1), 45–53.

Drucker, P. F. (1954). *The Practice of Management.* New York: Harper & Row.

Drucker, P. F., & Stone, N. (1998). *Peter Drucker on the Profession of Management.* Boston, MA: Harvard Business School Publishing.

Drury, D. H., & Farhoomand, A. (1999). Knowledge Worker Constraints in the Productive Use of Information Technology. *Computer Personnel, 19/20*(4/1), 21-42.

DTI. (2002). *Social Enterprise? A Strategy for Success.* The Department of Trade and Industry. Retrieved from http://www.dti.gov.uk

DTI. (2004). *UK National Broadband Strategy.* Retrieved July 23, 2009, from http://www.berr.gov.uk/

Duan, W., Gu, B., & Whinston, A. B. (2008). The dynamics of online word-of-mouth and product sales- An empirical investigation of the movie industry. *Journal of Interactive Marketing, 23*(2), 179–190.

Ducatel, K., Bogdanowicz, M., Scapolo, F., Leijten, J., & Burgelman, J.-C. (2001). *Scenarios for Ambient Intelligence in 2010 (ISTAG 2001 Final Report).* Seville, Spain: ISTAG (European Commission).

Duffy, T. M., & Jonassen, D. H. (Eds.). (1992). *Constructivism and the Technology of Instruction: A Conversation.* Hillsdale, NJ: Erlbaum.

Dwelly, T., Maguire, K., & Truscott, F. (2005). *Under the Radar: Tracking and supporting rural home based businesses.* Live Network Report to the Commission for Rural Communities.

Economic Research Service. (2006). *Rural development Strategies: Infrastructure.* United States Department of Agriculture. Employment Security Commission of North Carolina. (n.d.). *25 Largest Employers by County.* Retrieved November 11, 2005, from http://jobs.esc.state.nc.us/lmi/largest/largest.pdf

Economides, N., & Katsamakas, E. (2006). Two sided competition of proprietary vs. Open source technology platforms and implications for software industry. *Management Science, 52*(7), 1057–1071. doi:10.1287/mnsc.1060.0549

Edmond, N., Hillier, Y., & Price, M. (2007). Between a rock and a hard place: The role of HE and foundation degrees in workforce development. *Education and Training, 49*(3), 170–181. doi:10.1108/00400910710749305

EFER (Ed.). (2006). *20 Centers of Dynamic Entrepreneurship*. München, Germany: EFER.

Eisenhardt, K. M. (1989). Building Theories from Case Study Research. *Academy of Management Review, 14*(4), 532–550. doi:10.2307/258557

Eisenhardt, K. M., & Graebner, M. E. (2007). Theory building from cases: opportunities and challenges. *Academy of Management Journal, 50*(1), 25–32.

Eisenhardt, K. M., & Martin, J. A. (2000). Dynamic capabilities: What are they? *Strategic Management Journal, 21*, 1105–1121. doi:10.1002/1097-0266(200010/11)21:10/11<1105::AID-SMJ133>3.0.CO;2-E

Eisenmann, T. R., Parker, G., & Van Alstyne, M. (2008). *Opening platforms: How, when and why?* (Working Paper Series 09-030). Cambridge, MA: University of Cambridge, Harvard Business School.

Emiliani, P. L., & Stephanidis, C. (2005). Universal access to ambient intelligence environment: Opportunities and challenges for people with disabilities. *IBM Systems Journal, 44*(3), 605–619.

Enis, B. M. (1979). *Personal Selling: Foundations, Process, and Management*. Santa Monica, CA: Goodyear Publ.

EPS. (2009). *Secretariat of Special Assignments Minister for Electronic Government Affairs*. Retrieved April 29, 2009, from http://www.eps.gov.lv/index.php?&93

Eraut, M. (2004). Informal learning in the workplace. *Studies in Continuing Education, 26*(2), 247–273. doi:10.1080/158037042000225245

Ernst, D., Halevy, T., Monier, J.-H.J., & Sarrazin, H. (2001). A future for e-alliances. *The McKinsey Quarterly, 2001*(2), 92102.

Esteves, J., & Pastor, J. (2004). Enterprise Resource Planning Systems Research: An Annotated Bibliography. *Communications of AIS, 7*(8), 2–54.

Ethiraj, S. K., & Levinthal, D. (2004). Modularity and Innovation in Complex Systems. *Management Science, 50*, 159–174. doi:10.1287/mnsc.1030.0145

Etzkowitz, H. (1998). The norms of entrepreneurial science: cognitive effects of the new university–industry linkages. *Research Policy, 27*(8), 823–833. doi:10.1016/S0048-7333(98)00093-6

Etzkowitz, H. (2002). *MIT and the Rise of Entrepreneurial Science*. London: Routledge.

Etzkowitz, H. (2003). Research groups as 'quasi firms': the invention of the entrepreneurial university. *Research Policy, 32*(1), 109–121. doi:10.1016/S0048-7333(02)00009-4

Etzkowitz, H. (2004). The evolution of the Entrepreneurial University. *International Journal of Technology and Globalization, 1*(1), 64–77.

European Supply Chain Institute. (2007). *Euro RFID: Your Guide to RFID & GDS Solutions* [Electronic Version]. Retrieved February 11, 2009 from http://www.escinst.org/pdf/euroRFID2007.pdf

European Union. (2009). *Creativity and innovation. European Year 2009*. Retrieved May 27, 2009, from http://create2009.europa.eu/

Evans, M., Wedande, G., Ralston, L., & Van`t Hul, S. (2001). Consumer interaction in the virtual era: some qualitative insights. *Qualitative Market Research: An International Journal, 4*(3), 150–159. doi:10.1108/13522750110393053

Eysenck, H. J. (1993). Creativity and personality: Suggestions for a theory. *Psychological Inquiry, 4*, 147–178. doi:10.1207/s15327965pli0403_1

Fallgatter, M. J., & Brink, S. (2008). Zum Einfluss der Legitimation auf die Entwicklung junger Unternehmen: Eine State of the Art-Betrachtung am Beispiel von DocMorris. *Zeitschrift für Management, 3*(4), 303–319. doi:10.1007/s12354-008-0046-0

Faraj, S., & Wasko, M. (2001). The web of knowledge: An investigation of knowledge exchange in networks of practice. *MIT - Open Source Research Community*. Retrieved February 10, 2009, from http://opensource.mit.edu/papers/Farajwasko.pdf

Farrell, J., & Saloner, G. (1985). Standardisation, compatibility and innovation. *The Rand Journal of Economics*, *16*(1), 70–83. doi:10.2307/2555589

Fathian, M., Akhavan, P., & Hoorali, M. (2008). E-readiness assessment of non-profit ICT SMEs in a developing country: the case of Iran. *Technovation*, *28*, 578–590. doi:10.1016/j.technovation.2008.02.002

Feick, L. F., & Price, L. L. (1987). The Market Maven: A Diffuser of Marketplace Information. *Journal of Marketing*, *51*, 83–97. doi:10.2307/1251146

Feller, I. (1990). Universities as engines of growth: they think they can. *Research Policy*, *19*, 335–348. doi:10.1016/0048-7333(90)90017-Z

Fernández Sánchez, E. (2005). *Estrategia de innovación*. Madrid: Thomson.

Fernhaber, S. S., McDougall, P. P., & Oviatt, B. M. (2007). Exploring the role of industry structure in new venture internationalization. *Entrepreneurship Theory and Practice*, *31*, 517–542. doi:10.1111/j.1540-6520.2007.00186.x

Feser, E., Goldstein, H., Renski, H., & Renault, C. (2002). *Regional technology assets and opportunities: The geographic clustering of high-tech industry, science and innovation in Appalachia*. Prepared for the Appalachian Regional Commission. Office of Economic Development, University of North Carolina at Chapel Hill.

Feser, Edward J., Harvey A. Goldstein, & Luger, M. (1998). *At the Crossroads: North Carolina's Place in the Knowledge Economy of the Twenty-First Century*. Report for the North Carolina Alliance for Competitive Technologies and North Carolina Board of Science and Technology. Chapel Hill, NC: Univ. North Carolina at Chapel Hill.

Fielding, R. T., & Taylor, R. N. (2002). Principled design of the modern Web architecture. *ACM Transactions on Internet Technology*, *2*(2), 115–150. doi:10.1145/514183.514185

Fillis, I., & Wagner, B. (2005). E-business development – An exploratory investigation of the small firm. *International Small Business Journal*, *23*(6), 604–634. doi:10.1177/0266242605057655

Fine, G., & Deegan, J. (1996). Three principles of serendip: insight, chance and discovery in qualitative research. *Qualitative Studies in Education*, *9*(4), 434–447. doi:10.1080/0951839960090405

Finin, T., Ding, L., Zhou, L., & Joshi, A. (2005). Social networking on the semantic web. *The Learning Organization*, *12*(5), 418–435. doi:10.1108/09696470510611384

Fink, M. (2003). *The Business and Economics of Linux and Open Source*. Upper Saddle River, NJ: Prentice Hall.

Finkle, J., & Chernikoff, H. (in press). Waste Management sues SAP over software quality. *Reuters*.

Fischer, E., & Reuber, A. R. (1995). The Importance of Market Orientation for Emergent Firms. In W.D. Bygrave et al. (Eds.), *Frontiers of Entrepreneurship Research - Proceedings of the Fifteenth Annual Entrepreneurship Research Conference* (pp. 90-104).

Fitzgerald, B. (2006). The Transformation of Open Source Software. *MIS Quarterly*, *30*(3), 587–598.

Floerkemeier, C., Langheinrich, M., Fleisch, E., Mattern, F., & Sarma, S. E. (2008). *The Internet of Things: First International Conference, IOT 2008, Zurich, Switzerland, March 26-28, 2008, Proceedings*. Berlin, Germany: Springer.

Ford, J. D., & Ford, L. W. (1994). Logics of Identity, Contradiction, and Attraction in Change. *Academy of Management Review*, *19*(4), 756–785. doi:10.2307/258744

Forman, C., Goldfarb, A., & Greenstein, S. (2005). How did location affect adoption of the commercial internet? Global village vs. urban leadership. *Journal of Urban Economics*, *58*, 389–420. doi:10.1016/j.jue.2005.05.004

Fornell, C., & Larcker, D. F. (1981). Evaluating Structural Equation Models With Unobservable Variables and Measurement Error. *JMR, Journal of Marketing Research*, *18*(1), 39–50. doi:10.2307/3151312

Fosfuri, A., Giarratana, M., & Luzzi, A. (2008). The Penguin Has Entered the Building: The Commercialization of Open Source Software Products. *Organization Science*, *19*(2), 292–305. doi:10.1287/orsc.1070.0321

Foss, N. J. (1997). *Resources, Firms, and Strategies: A Reader in the Resource-Based Perspective.* Oxford, UK: Oxford University Press.

Franck, E., & Jungwirth, C. (2002). Reconciling investors and donators - The governance structure of open source, Working Papers 0008, University of Zurich, Institute for Strategy and Business Economics (ISU). Retrieved February 10, 2009, from http://econpapers.repec.org/paper/isowpaper/0008.htm

Franke, N., & Von Hippel, E. (2003). Satisfying heterogeneous user needs via toolkits: The case of the apache security software. *Research Policy, 32,* 157–178. doi:10.1016/S0048-7333(02)00006-9

Friedewald, M., & Da Costa, O. (2003). *Science and Technology Roadmapping: Ambient intelligence in Everyday Life (AmI@Life).* Seville, Spain: JRC-IPTS/ESTO.

Frischmuth, J. (2001). *Strategien und Prozesse für neue Geschäftsmodelle Praxisleitfaden für E- und mobile Business.* Berlin, Germany: Springer.

Fritsch, A., & Johannsen, K. (2004). *Ecotourism in Appalachia: Marketing the mountains.* Lexington, KY: University of Kentucky Press.

Frost, J. (2005). *Some Economic & Legal Aspects of Open Source Software.* University of Washington. Retrieved February 10, 2009, from opensource.mit.edu/papers/frost.pdf

Frumkin, P. (2002). *On Being a Non-Profit, A Conceptual and Policy Primer.* 432 H. Haugh. Cambridge, MA: Harvard University Press.

Fukuyama, F. (1999). *The Great Disruption.* London: St Edmundsbury Press.

Gabrielsson, M., Kirpalani, V. H. M., Dimitratos, P., Solberg, C. A., & Zucchella, A. (2008). Born globals: propositions to help advance the theory. *International Business Review, 17*(4), 385–401. doi:10.1016/j.ibusrev.2008.02.015

Gale, F., & McGranahan, D. (2001). Nonmetro Areas Fall Behind in the 'New Economy'. *Rural America, 16*(1), 44–52.

Gallaugher, J., & Wang, Y.-M. (2002). Understanding Network Effects in Software Markets: Evidence from Web Server Pricing. *MIS Quarterly, 26*(4), 303–327. doi:10.2307/4132311

Galloway, L. (2007). Can broadband access rescue the rural economy? *Journal of Small Business and Enterprise Development, 14*(4), 641–653. doi:10.1108/14626000710832749

Galloway, L., & Mochrie, R. (2006). Entrepreneurial Motivation, Orientation and Realisation in Rural Economies: a study of rural Scotland. *International Journal of Entrepreneurship and Innovation, 7*(3), 173–184.

Galloway, L., Mochrie, R., & Deakins, D. (2004). ICT-enabled collectivity as a positive rural business strategy. *International Journal of Entrepreneurial Behaviour and Research, 10*(4), 247–259. doi:10.1108/13552550410544213

García-Cabrera, A. M., & García-Soto, M. G. (2008). Reconocimiento de la oportunidad y emprendeduría de base tecnológica: un modelo dinámico. *Investigaciones Europeas de Dirección y Economía de la Empresa, 14*(2), 109–125.

Garrett, J. J. (2005). *Ajax: A New Approach to Web Applications* [white paper]. San Francisco, CA: Adaptive Path Inc.

Geisler, R. L. (1993). *Research and Relevant Knowledge: American Research Universities since World War II.* Oxford, UK: Oxford University Press.

George, G., & Zahra, S. A. (2002). Being Entrepreneurial and Being Market-Driven - Exploring the Interaction Effects of Entrepreneurial and Market Orientation on Firm Performance. *Frontiers of Entrepreneurship Research,* 255-266.

Geursen, G. M. (2000). The Market And Entrepreneur Led Firms: A Model For Achieving Customer Relevance. In G.E. Hills, W. Siu, & D. Malewicki (Eds.), *Research at the Marketing/Entrepreneurship Interface - Proceedings of the UIC Symposium on Marketing and Entrepreneurship* (pp. 33-56).

Geursen, G. M., & Conduit, J. L. (2002). Entrepreneurial, Market Relevant Strategies of Small and Large Firms. In G.E. Hills, D.J. Hansen, & B. Merrilees (Eds.), *Research at the Marketing/Entrepreneurship Interface - Proceedings of the UIC Symposium on Marketing and Entrepreneurship* (pp. 15-41).

Ghosh, R. A. (2004). Economic Foundations of Open Source, In J. Feller, B. Fitzgerald, S. Hissam, & K. R. Lakhani. (Ed.), *Making sense of the Bazaar: Perspectives on Open Source and Free Software*. Sebastopol, CA: O'Reilly & Associates.

Ghosh, R., & Prakash, V. V. (2000). The Orbiten Free Software Survey. *First Monday, 5*(7). Retrieved May 10, 2009, from http://firstmonday.org/issues/issue5_7/ghosh/index.html

Gibb, A. A. (1997). Small firms' training and competitiveness. Building upon small business as a learning organization. *International Small Business Journal, 15*(3), 13–29. doi:10.1177/0266242697153001

Gibbs, R. M. (1995). Going away to college and wider urban job opportunities take highly educated youth away from rural areas. *Rural Development Perspectives, 10*(3), 35–44.

Gibson, B. (2002). Methodological Individualism as the Economic Core of the Small Firm Marketing Interface. In G.E. Hills, D.J. Hansen, & B. Merrilees (Eds.), *Research at the Marketing/Entrepreneurship Interface - Proceedings of the UIC Symposium on Marketing and Entrepreneurship* (pp. 2-14).

Gill, S. K., & Cormican, K. (2008a). Ambience Intelligence (AmI) Systems Development. In F. Zhao (Ed.), *Information Technology Entrepreneurship and Innovation* (pp. 1-22). Hershey, PA: Idea Group.

Gill, S. K., & Cormican, K. (2008b, 22nd–24th October). *Implementation of an AmI system in a Manufacturing SME.* Paper presented at the eChallenges Stockholm, Sweden.

Gilmore, A., & Carson, D. (2000). SME Marketing By Networking. In G.E. Hills, W. Siu, & D. Malewicki (Eds.), *Research at the Marketing/Entrepreneurship Interface*

- Proceedings of the UIC Symposium on Marketing and Entrepreneurship (pp. 192-200).

Giunipero, L., Dawley, D., & Anthony, W. (1999). The impact of tacit knowledge on purchasing decisions. *Journal of Supply Chain Management.*

Glaeser, E. L., & Maré, D. (2001). Cities and Skills. *Journal of Labor Economics, 19*(2). doi:10.1086/319563

Glaeser, E. L., & Shleifer, A. (2001). Not-For-Profit Entrepreneurs. *Journal of Public Economics, 81*, 99–115. doi:10.1016/S0047-2727(00)00130-4

Glaser, B. G., & Strauss, A. (2008). *The discovery of grounded theory. Strategies for qualitative research* (3rd ed.). New Brunswick, NJ: Aldine.

Gleeson, D., & Keep, E. (2004). Voice without accountability: the changing relationship between employers, the State and education in England. *Oxford Review of Education, 30*(1), 37–63. doi:10.1080/0305498042000190050

Gollwitzer, P. M. (1999). Implementation intentions: Strong effects of simple plans. *The American Psychologist, 54*(7), 493–503. doi:10.1037/0003-066X.54.7.493

Gomulkiewicz, R. W. (1999). How Copyleft Uses License Rights to Succeed in the Open Source Software Revolution and the Implications for Article 2B. *Houston Law Review, 36.*

Gorard, S., & Selwyn, N. (2005). What makes a lifelong learner? *Teachers College Record, 107*(6), 1193–1216. doi:10.1111/j.1467-9620.2005.00510.x

Graham, W. (2008). *Facebook API Developers Guide.* Berkeley, CA: Apress.

Gray, P. (2003, September 30). In depth: RMIT's PeopleSoft disaster. *ZDNet Australia.*

Greene, F. J., & Saridakis, G. (2007). *Understanding the Factors Influencing Graduate Entrepreneurship* [Research Report No. 1/2007]. Birmingham, UK: National Council for Graduate Entrepreneurship.

Gregorio, D. D., Kassicieh, S. K., & De Gouvean, R. (2005). Drivers of e-business activity in developed and emerging markets. *IEEE Transactions on Engi-*

neering Management, *52*(2), 155–166. doi:10.1109/TEM.2005.844464

Grether, M. (2003). *Marktorientierung durch das Internet - Ein Wissensorientierter Ansatz für Unternehmen.* Mannheim, Germany: DUV.

Grupp, H., & Legler, H. (2000). *Hochtechnologie 2000 - Neudefinition der Hochtechnologie für die Berichterstattung zur technologischen Leistungsfähigkeit Deutschlands.* Karlsruhe/Hannover: Frauenhofer-Institut für Systemtechnik und Innovationsforschung, Niedersächsiches Institut für Wirtschaftsforschung.

Guba, E. G., & Lincoln, Y. S. (1994). Competing Paradigms in Qualitative Research. In N. K. Denzin & Y. S. Lincoln (Ed.), *Handbook of Qualitative Research* (pp. 105-117). Thousand Oaks, CA: Sage.

Gupta, V., MacMillan, I. C., & Surie, G. (2004). Entrepreneurial leadership: developing and measuring a cross-cultural construct. *Journal of Business Venturing*, *19*, 241–260. doi:10.1016/S0883-9026(03)00040-5

H&R Block – Press Center. (n.d.). *Henry W. Bloch.* Retrieved November 28, 2008, from http://www.hrblock.com/presscenter/about/hbbio.jsp

Häcki, R., & Lighton, J. (2001). The future of the networked company. *The Mckinsey Quarterly*, *3*, 26–39.

Hall, D. J., & Saias, M. A. (1980). Strategy Follows Structure! *Strategic Management Journal*, *1*(2), 149–163. doi:10.1002/smj.4250010205

Hamel, G. (2000). *Leading the Revolution.* Boston: Harvard Business School Press.

Handy, C. (2000). *La organización por dentro.* Madrid: Ed. Deusto

Hannon, P. (2007). Enterprise for all? The fragility of enterprise provision across England's HEIs. *Journal of Small Business and Enterprise Development*, *14*(2), 183–210. doi:10.1108/14626000710746646

Hannon, P., Collins, L. A., & Smith, A. J. (2005). Exploring graduate entrepreneurship: A collaborative co-learned based approach for students, entrepreneurs and educators. *Industry and Higher Education*, *19*(1), 11–24.

Hansmann, H. (1980). The role of nonprofit enterprise. *The Yale Law Journal*, *89*(5), 835–901. doi:10.2307/796089

Hanson, W. (2008). Sweden Tops 2008 E-Government Readiness Report, U.S. Drops to Fourth. *Government Technology*, Retrieved April 29, 2009, from http://www.govtech.com/gt/articles/244097.

Harhoff, D., Henkel, J., & von Hippel, E. (2003). Profiting from voluntary information spillovers: How users benefit from freely revealing their innovations. *Research Policy*, *32*, 1753–1769. doi:10.1016/S0048-7333(03)00061-1

Harmon, B., Ardishvili, A., Cardozo, R., Elder, T., Leuthold, J., & Parshall, J. (1997). Mapping the university technology transfer process. *Journal of Business Venturing*, *12*, 423–434. doi:10.1016/S0883-9026(96)00064-X

Harris, R. (2008). Developing a collaborative learning environment through technology enhanced education (TE3) support. *Education and Training*, *50*(8/9), 674–686. doi:10.1108/00400910810917055

Hars, A., & Ou, S. (2001). Working for free? - Motivations for participating in open source projects. *International Journal of Electronic Commerce*, *6*(2), 25–39.

Hawkins, R. B. (1976). Special Districts and Urban Services. In E. Ostrom (Ed.), *The Delivery of Urban Services* (pp. 171-188). Beverly Hills, CA: Sag.

Head, B. (2003). *Exchange of Pace.* Retrieved July, 2009, from http://www.theage.com.au/articles/2003/04/07/1049567609043.html

Hegarty, C., & Jones, C. (2008). Graduate Entrepreneurship: More than Child's Play. *Education and Training*, *50*(7), 626–637. doi:10.1108/00400910810909072

Helliwell, J. (2002). *Globalization and Well-Being.* Vancouver, Canada: UBC Press.

Hertel, B., Niedner, S., & Herrmann, S. (2003). Motivation of software developers in open source projects: An Internet-based survey of contributions to the Linux kernel. *Research Policy*, *32*, 1159–1177. doi:10.1016/S0048-7333(03)00047-7

Hevner, A. R., Collins, R. W., & Garfield, M. J. (2002). Product and Project Challenges in Electronic Commerce Software Development. *ACM SIGMIS Database, 33*(4), 10–22. doi:10.1145/590806.590810

Higher Education Funding Council for England (HEFCE). (2000). *Foundation Degree Prospectus*. London: HEFCE.

Hills, G. E., & LaForge, R. W. (1992). Research at the Marketing Interface to Advance Entrepreneurship Theory. *Entrepreneurship Theory and Practice, 16*(3), 33–59.

Hindle, K., & Yencken, J. (2004). Public research commercialisation, entrepreneurship and new technology based firms: an integrated model. *Technovation, 24*(10), 793–803. doi:10.1016/S0166-4972(03)00023-3

Hitt, M. A., Ireland, R. D., Camp, M., & Sexton, D. L. (2001). Guest Editors' Introduction To The Special Issue Strategic Entrepreneurship: Entrepreneurial Strategies For Wealth Creation. *Strategic Management Journal, 22*, 479–491. doi:10.1002/smj.196

Holden, R., Nabi, G., Gold, J., & Robertson, M. (2006). Building capacity in small businesses: tales from the training front. *Journal of European Industrial Training, 30*(6), 424–440. doi:10.1108/03090590610688816

Holmstrom, B. (1999). Managerial incentive problems: A dynamic perspective. *The Review of Economic Studies, 66*, 169–182. doi:10.1111/1467-937X.00083

Homburg, C., & Pflesser, C. (2000). A Multiple-Layer Model of Market-Oriented Organizational Culture: Measurement Issues and Performance Outcomes. *JMR, Journal of Marketing Research, 37*(4), 449–462. doi:10.1509/jmkr.37.4.449.18786

Hoppe, K., & Kollmer, H. (2001). *Strategie und Geschäftsmodell*. Unpublished.

Horvath, J. (2002, December 6, 2005). Making friends with Big Brother? *Telepolis*. Retrieved from http://www.heise.de/tp/r4/artikel/12/12112/1.html

Huggins, R., & Izushi, H. (2002). The digital divide and ICT learning in rural communities: Examples of good

practice service delivery. *Local Economy, 17*(2), 111–122. doi:10.1080/02690940210129870

Hunaskar, S., & Callahan, C. (1995). Creativity and Giftedness: Published Instrument Uses and Abuses. *Gifted Child Quarterly, 39*(2), 110–114. doi:10.1177/001698629503900207

Iannacci, F. (2005). Coordination processes in open source software development: The Linux case study. *Emergence: Complexity and Organization, 7*(2), 20–30.

Iansiti, M., & Richards, G. (2007). The Business of Free Software: Enterprise Incentives, Investment and Motivation in the Open Source Community (Working Paper Series 07-028). Cambridge, MA: University of Cambridge, Harvard Business School.

Income, S. A., & Estimates, P. (n.d.). U.S. Census Bureau. Retrieved from http://www.census.gov/hhes/www/saipe/county.html

Inkpen, A. C., & Tsang, E. W. K. (2005). Social capital, networks, and knowledge transfer. *Academy of Management Review, 30*(1), 146–165.

Internal Revenue Service. (2009). *Internal Revenue Service, United States Department of the Treasury*. Retrieved April 30, 2009, from http://www.irs.gov/

International Association for Impact Assessment. (1999). *Principle of Environmental Impact Assessment Best Practice, European Union*.

ISTAG. (2000). *Recommendations of the IST Advisory Group for Workprogramme 2001 and beyond "implementing the vision*. ISTAG (European Commission).

ISTAG. (2002). *Software technologies, embedded systems and distributed systems: A European strategy towards an Ambient Intelligent environment* ISTAG. (European Commission, ITEA. (2003). *The Ambience Project*. Retrieved September 21, 2005, from http://www.extra.research.philips.com/euprojects/ambience

ITU. (2009). *Measuring the Information Society: The ICT Development Index*. International Telecommunication Union, Geneva, Switzerland.

Jakob, M., Schwarz, H., Kaiser, F., & Mitschang, B. (2006). Modeling and Generating Application Logic for Data-Intensive Web Applications. In *Proceedings of the Sixth International Conference on Web Engineering* (ICWE'06) (pp. 77-84).

Jantunen, A., Nummela, N., Puumalainen, K., & Saarenketo, S. (2008). Strategic orientation of born globals - Do they really matter? *Journal of World Business, 43*, 158–170. doi:10.1016/j.jwb.2007.11.015

Jarvis, C. B., MacKenzie, S. C., & Podsakoff, P. M. (2003). A Critical Review of Construct Indicators and Measurement Model Misspecification in Marketing and Consumer Research. *The Journal of Consumer Research, 30*(2), 199–218. doi:10.1086/376806

Jaworski, B. J., & Kohli, A. K. (1993). Market Orientation - Antecedents and Consequences. *Journal of Marketing, 57*(3), 53–70. doi:10.2307/1251854

Jennings, N. R., & Wooldridge, M. (1998). *Agent Technology: Foundations, Applications, and Markets*. London: Springer.

Jennings, P., & Beaver, G. (1997). The performance and competitive advantage of small firms: a management perspective. *International Small Business Journal, 15*(2), 63–75. doi:10.1177/0266242697152004

Johnson, J. P. (2001). *Economics of open source software*. Retrieved February 4, 2009, from http://opensource.mit.edu/papers/johnsonopensource.pdf

Jutras, C. (2007). *The Total Cost of ERP Ownership in Mid Sized Companies*. Boston, MA: Aberdeen Group.

Kakati, M. (2003). Success criteria in high-tech new venture. *Technovation, 23*, 447–457. doi:10.1016/S0166-4972(02)00014-7

Kalaignanam, K., Shankar, V., & Varadarajan, R. (2007). Asymmetric New Product Development Alliances: Win-Win or Win-Lose Partnerships? *Management Science, 53*(3), 357–374. doi:10.1287/mnsc.1060.0642

Kalis, A., Mojzisch, A., Schweizer, T. S., & Kaiser, S. (2008). Weakness of will, akrasia, and the neuropsychiatry of decision making: An interdisciplinary perspective.

Cognitive, Affective & Behavioral Neuroscience, 8, 402–417. doi:10.3758/CABN.8.4.402

Karayanidis, F., Coltheart, M., Michie, P. T., & Murphy, K. (2003). Electrophysiological correlates of anticipatory and poststimulus components of task switching. *Psychophysiology, 40*, 329–348. doi:10.1111/1469-8986.00037

Karra, N., Phillips, N., & Tracey, P. (2008). Building the born global firm. Developing entrepreneurial capabilities for international new venture success. *Long Range Planning, 41*, 440–458. doi:10.1016/j.lrp.2008.05.002

Katsiouloudes, M. I. (1996). Socio-Technical Analysis: A Normative Model for Participatory Planning. *Human Systems Management, 15*(4), 235–243.

Kaufmann, G. (2002). Creativity and Problem Solving. In J. Henry (Ed.), *Creative Management* (pp. 44-63). London: Cromwell Press Ltd.

Kazanjain, R., & Drazin, R. (1990). A stage contingent model of design and growth for technology based ventures. *Journal of Business Venturing, 5*(3), 137–150. doi:10.1016/0883-9026(90)90028-R

Kazanjian, R. K. (1988). Relation of Dominant Problems to Stages of Growth in Technology-Based New Ventures. *Academy of Management Journal, 31*(2), 257–279. doi:10.2307/256548

Kazanjian, R. K., & Drazin, R. (1990). A Stage-Contingent Model of Design and Growth for Technology-Based New Ventures. *Journal of Business Venturing, 5*(3), 137–150. doi:10.1016/0883-9026(90)90028-R

Kejak, M. (2003). Stages of growth in economic development. *Journal of Economic Dynamics & Control, 27*(5), 771–800. doi:10.1016/S0165-1889(01)00071-9

Keller, E. (Ed.). (1994). *Fundamentals of speech synthesis and speech recognition: Basic concepts, state-of-the-art and future challenges* (1st ed.). Chichester, UK: John Wiley & Sons.

Kerin, R. A., Varadarajan, P. R., & Peterson, R. A. (1992). First-Mover Advantage: A Synthesis, Conceptual Framework, and Research Propositions. *JMR, Journal of Marketing Research, 56*(4), 33–53.

Khosrow-Pour, M. (2006). *Emerging Trends and Challenges in Information Technology Management.* Hershey, PA: Idea Group Inc.

Kiang, M. Y., Raghu, T. S., & Shang, K. H.-M. (2000). Marketing on the Internet — Who Can Benefit from an Online Marketing Approach? *Decision Support Systems, 27,* 383–393. doi:10.1016/S0167-9236(99)00062-7

Kidd, A. (1994). *The Marks are on the Knowledge Worker.* Paper presented at the Conference on Human Factors in Computer Systems.

Kielhofner, G. (2008). Volition. In G. Kielhofner (Ed.), *Model of Human Occupation: Theory and application* (pp. 33-509). Baltimore, MA: Lippencott Williams & Wilkins.

Kim, D. H. (1993). The Link Between Individual and Organizational Learning. *Sloan Management Review, 35*(1), 37–50.

King, D., Lee, J., Warkentin, M., & Chung, H. (2002). *Electronic commerce: a managerial perspective.* Upper Saddle River, NJ: Pearson Education International.

King, W. (2005). Ensuring ERP implementation success. *Information Systems Management, 22*(3), 83–84. doi:10.1201/1078/45317.22.3.20050601/88749.11

Kiritsis, D., Bufardi, A., & Xirouchakis, P. (2003). Research issues on product lifecycle management and information tracking using smart embedded systems. *Advanced Engineering Informatics, 17*(3-4), 189–202. doi:10.1016/S1474-0346(04)00018-7

Kirton, M. J. (2003). *Adaption-innovation: in the context of diversity and change.* London: Routledge.

Kirzner, I. (1979). *Perception, opportunity and profit.* Chicago, IL: University of Chicago Press.

Kirzner, I. M. (1973). *Competition and Entrepreneurship.* Chicago: University of Chicago Press.

Klandt, H., & Volkmann, C. (2006). Development and Prospects of Academic Entrepreneurship Education in Germany. *Higher Education in Europe, 31*(2), 195–208. doi:10.1080/03797720600940880

Klusch, M. (2002). Information agent technology for the internet: a survey. *Data & Knowledge Engineering, 36,* 337–372. doi:10.1016/S0169-023X(00)00049-5

Knight, G. A., & Cavusgil, S. T. (1996). The born global firm: a challenge to traditional internalization theory. In S.T. Cavusgil, & T. Madsen (Eds.), *Advances in International Marketing* (pp.11-26). Greenwich, CT: JAL Press.

Kogut, B., & Metiu, A. (2001). Open-source software development and distributed innovation. *Oxford Review of Economic Policy, 17*(2), 248–264. doi:10.1093/oxrep/17.2.248

Koh, C.E., & Nam, K.T. (2005). Business Use of the Internet: A Longitudinal Study from a Value Chain Perspective. *Industrial Management & Data Systems* (Forthcoming issue in 2005).

Kohli, A. K., & Jaworski, B. J. (1990). Market Orientation - The Construct, Research Propositions, and Managerial Implications. *Journal of Marketing, 54*(2), 1–18. doi:10.2307/1251866

Kohli, A. K., Jaworski, B. J., & Kumar, A. (1993). Markor - A Measure of Market Orientation. *JMR, Journal of Marketing Research, 30*(4), 467–477. doi:10.2307/3172691

Kohli, R., Devaraj, S., & Mahmood, M. A. (2004). Understanding Determinants of Online Consumer Satisfaction: A Decision Process Perspective. *Journal of Management Information Systems, 21*(1), 115–136.

Kollman, T. (2006). What is e-entrepreneurship? – Fundamentals of company founding in the net economy. *International Journal of Technology Management, 33*(4), 322–340. doi:10.1504/IJTM.2006.009247

Kollmann, T. (2001). Measuring the acceptance of electronic marketplaces. *Journal of Computer Mediated Communication, 6*(2). Retrieved July 23, 2009, from http://jcmc.indiana.edu/vol6/issue2/kollmann.html

Kollmann, T. (2005). The matching function for electronic marketplaces – determining the probability of coordinating of supply and demand. *International Journal of Electronic Business, 5*(3), 461–472. doi:10.1504/IJEB.2005.008520

Kollmann, T. (2006). What is e-entrepreneurship? – fundamentals of company founding in the Net Economy. *International Journal of Technology Management, 33*(4), 322–340. doi:10.1504/IJTM.2006.009247

Kollmann, T. (2009). E-Entrepreneurship: *Grundlagen der Unternehmensgründung in der Net Economy.* Wiesbaden, Germany: Gabler.

Kollmann, T. (2009a). *E-Entrepreneurship* (3rd Ed.). Wiesbaden, Germany: Gabler.

Kollmann, T. (2009b). *E-Business* (3rd Ed.). Wiesbaden, Germany: Gabler.

Kollmann, T., & Häsel, M. (2006). *Cross-Channel Cooperation: The Bundling of Online and Offline Business Models.* Wiesbaden, Germany: Deutscher Universitäts-Verlag.

Kollmann, T., & Häsel, M. (2007). Reverse auctions in the service sector: The case of LetsWorkIt.de. *International Journal of E-Business Research, 3*(3), 57–73.

Kollmann, T., & Häsel, M. (2007). *Web 2.0.* Wiesbaden, Germany: Gabler.

Kollmann, T., & Häsel, M. (2008). Cross-channel cooperation: A collaborative approach of integrating online and offline business models of e-entrepreneurs and traditional SMEs. *International Journal of Entrepreneurship and Small Business, 6*(2), 212–229. doi:10.1504/IJESB.2008.018629

Kollmann, T., & Kuckertz, A. (2004). Venture Capital Decision Making After the High-Tech Downturn: Considerations Based on German E-Business Investment Cases. *Journal of Private Equity, 7*(4), 48–59. doi:10.3905/jpe.2004.434766

Kollmann, T., & Kuckertz, A. (2006). Investor relations for start-ups: an analysis of venture capital investors' communicative needs. *International Journal of Technology Management, 34*(1/2), 47–62. doi:10.1504/IJTM.2006.009447

Kollmann, T., & Kuckertz, A. (in press). Evaluation uncertainty of venture capitalists' investment criteria. *Journal of Business Research.*

Koska, D. K., & Romano, J. D. (1988). *Profile 21 Issues and Implications, Countdown to the Future: The Manufacturing Engineer in the 21st Century.* Dearborn, MI: Society of Manufacturing Engineers.

Kramer, M. R. (2005). *Measuring Innovation: Evaluation in the Field of Social Entrepreneurship.* Boston: Foundation Strategy Group.

Krishnamurthy, S. (2005). An Analysis of Open Source Business Models. In J. Feller, B. Fitzgerald, S. A. Hissam, & K. R. Lakhani (Eds.), *Perspectives on Free and Open Source Software* (pp. 279-296). Cambridge, MA: MIT Press

Kuivalainen, O., Sundqvist, S., & Servais, P. (2007). Firm's degree of born-globalness, international entrepreneurial orientation and export performance. *Journal of World Business, 42*, 523–267. doi:10.1016/j.jwb.2007.04.010

Lakhani, K. R., & Von Hippel, E. (2003). How Open Source software works: "Free" User-to-User Assistance. *Research Policy, 32*, 923–943. doi:10.1016/S0048-7333(02)00095-1

Lakhani, K. R., & Wolf, R. G. (2005). Why Hackers Do What They Do: Understanding Motivation and Effort in Free/Open Source Software Projects. In J. Feller, B. Fitzgerald, S. Hissam, & K. R. Lakhani (Eds.), *Perspectives on Free and Open Source Software.* Cambridge, MA: MIT Press

Lakshmi, I., Singh, R., & Salm, A. F. (2005). Intelligent agents to support information sharing in B2B e-marketplaces. *Information Systems Management, 22*(3), 37–49. doi:10.1201/1078/45317.22.3.20050601/88744.6

Lal, K. (2004). E-business and export behavior. Evidence from Indian firms. *World Development, 32*(3), 505–517. doi:10.1016/j.worlddev.2003.10.004

Langdon, R., & Coltheart, M. (2000). The cognitive neuropsychology of delusions. *Mind & Language, 15*, 184–218. doi:10.1111/1468-0017.00129

Langlois, R. N. (2002). Modularity in technology and organization. *Journal of Economic Behavior & Organization, 49*(1), 19–37. doi:10.1016/S0167-2681(02)00056-2

Laroche, M., Pons, F., Zgolli, N., Cervellon, M. C., & Kim, C. (2003). A model of consumer response to two retail sales promotion techniques. *Journal of Business Research, 56*, 513–522. doi:10.1016/S0148-2963(01)00249-1

Laugero, G., & Globe, A. (2002). *Enterprise Content Services: Connecting Information and Profitability.* Boston, MA: Addison-Wesley Longman.

Lawson, C., & Meyenn, N. (2000). Bringing Cellular Phone Service to Rural Areas [Electronic Version]. *Public Policy for the Private Sector*, 1-4. Retrieved February 11, 2009 from http://rru.worldbank.org/documents/publicpolicyjournal/205lawson.pdf

Lawson, R., Alcock, C., Cooper, J., & Burgess, L. (2003). Factors affecting adoption of electronic commerce technologies by SMEs: An Australian study. *Journal of Small Business and Enterprise Development, 10*(3), 265–276. doi:10.1108/14626000310489727

Leatherman, J. C. (2000). Internet-based commerce: Implications for rural communities. *Reviews of Economic Development Literature and Practice, 5*. Washington, DC: US Economic Development Administration.

Lee, A. S., & Baskerville, R. L. (2003). Generalizing Generalizability in Information Systems Research. *Information Systems Research, 14*(3), 221–243. doi:10.1287/isre.14.3.221.16560

Lee, G., & Cole, R. (2003). From a Firm-Based to a Community-Based Model of Knowledge Creation: The Case of the Linux Kernel Development. *Organization Science, 14*(6), 633–649. doi:10.1287/orsc.14.6.633.24866

Lee, S.-Y. T., Kim, H.-W., & Gupta, S. (2009). Measuring open source software success. *Omega, 37*(2), 426–438. doi:10.1016/j.omega.2007.05.005

Leitch, S. (2006). *Review of Skills: Prosperity For All in the Global Economy – World Class Skills.* Norwich, UK: HMSO.

Lerner, J., & Tirole, J. (2002). Some simple economics on Open Source. *The Journal of Industrial Economics, 50*(2), 197–234.

Lerner, J., & Tirole, J. (2005). The Economics of Technology Sharing: Open Source and Beyond. *The Journal of Economic Perspectives, 19*(2), 99–120. doi:10.1257/0895330054048678

Lerner, J., Pathak, P. A., & Tirole, J. (2006). The Dynamics of Open Source Contributors. *The American Economic Review, 96*(2), 114–118. doi:10.1257/000282806777211874

Li, W.-S., Hsiung, W.-P., Po, O., Hino, K., Candan, K. S., & Agrawal, D. (2004). Challenges and Practices in Deploying Web Acceleration Solutions for Distributed Enterprise Systems. In *Proceedings of the 13th International Conference on World Wide Web* (pp. 297-308).

Liao, J., Welsch, H., & Tan, W. L. (2005). Venture gestation paths of nascent entrepreneurs: Exploring the temporal patterns. *The Journal of High Technology Management Research, 16*, 1–22. doi:10.1016/j.hitech.2005.06.001

Lichtenstein, D. R., & Burton, S. (1990). An Assessment of the Moderating Effects of Market Mavenism and Value Consciousness on Price-Quality Perception Accuracy. *Advances in Consumer Research. Association for Consumer Research (U. S.), 17*(1), 53–59.

Lichtenthaler, U. (2009). (forthcoming). Intellectual Property and Open Innovation: An Empirical Analysis. *International Journal of Technology Management.*

Light, P. C. (2007). Searching for Social Entrepreneurs: Who They Might Be, Where They Might Be Found, What They Might Do. *Association for Research on Nonprofit Organizations and Voluntary Action (ARNOVA) Occasional Paper Series—Research on Social Entrepreneurship: Understanding and Contributing to and Emerging Field, 1*(3), 13–37.

Lindwer, M., Marculescu, D., Basten, T., Zimmermann, R., Marculescu, R., Jung, S., et al. (2003). *Ambient Intelligence Vision and Achievement: Linking Abstract Ideas to Real-World Concepts.* Paper presented at the Design, Automation and Test in Europe Conference and Exhibition.

Loane, S., & Bell, J. (2006). Rapid internationalization among entrepreneurial firms in Australia, Canada, Ireland

and New Zealand. *International Marketing Review*, *23*(5), 467–485. doi:10.1108/02651330610703409

Loane, S., Bell, J., & McNaughton, R. (2007). A cross-national study on the impact of management teams on the rapid internationalization of small firms. *Journal of World Business*, *42*, 489–504. doi:10.1016/j.jwb.2007.06.009

Local Area Bearfacts. (n.d.). Bureau of Economic Analysis. U.S. Department of Commerce. Retrieved from http://www.bea.doc.gov/bea/regional/bearfacts/countybf.cfm

Lockett, A., Siegel, D., Wright, M., & Ensley, M. (2005). The creation of spin-offs at public research institutions: Managerial and policy implications. *Research Policy*, *34*, 981–993. doi:10.1016/j.respol.2005.05.010

Lodish, L., Morgan, H., & Archambeau, S. (2007). *Marketing that Works: How Entrepreneurial Marketing can Add Sustainable Value to Any Sized Company* (1st Ed.). Philadelphia, PA: Wharton School Publishing.

Lohse, G. L., & Spiller, P. (1998). Electronic Shopping. *Communications of the ACM*, *41*(7), 81–88. doi:10.1145/278476.278491

Lucas, H. C. (2001). Information Technology and Physical Space. *Communications of the ACM*, *44*(11), 89–96. doi:10.1145/384150.384167

Ludwigshafen University of Aplplied Sciences. (2004). *Enhanced Project Success Through SAP Best Practices – International Benchmarking Study*. Ludwigshafen, Germany: Ludwigshafen University.

Lumpkin, G. T. (2005). The role of organizational learning in the opportunity-recognition process. *Entrepreneurship Theory and Practice*, *29*(4), 451–472. doi:10.1111/j.1540-6520.2005.00093.x

Lumpkin, G. T., & Dess, G. G. (1996). Clarifying the entrepreneurial orientation construct and linking it to performance. *Academy of Management Review*, *21*(1), 135–172. doi:10.2307/258632

Lumpkin, G. T., & Dess, G. G. (2004). E-business strategies and internet business models: how the internet

adds value. *Organizational Dynamics*, *33*(2), 161–173. doi:10.1016/j.orgdyn.2004.01.004

Ma, H., & Tan, J. (2006). Key components and implications of entrepreneurship: A 4-P framework. *Journal of Business Venturing*, *21*, 704–725. doi:10.1016/j.jbusvent.2005.04.009

MacCallum, R. C., & Browne, M. W. (1993). The Use of Causal Indicators in Covariance Structure Models - Some Practical Issues. *Psychological Bulletin*, *114*(3), 533–541. doi:10.1037/0033-2909.114.3.533

Madsen, T. K. (1989). Successful export marketing management: some empirical evidence. *International Marketing Review*, *6*(4), 41–57. doi:10.1108/EUM0000000001518

Madsen, T. K., & Servais, P. (1997). The internationalization of born globals: an evolutionary process? *International Business Review*, *6*(6), 561–583. doi:10.1016/S0969-5931(97)00032-2

Magin, P., & Von Kortzfleisch, H. F. O. (2008, December). *Scientific Entrepreneurship engineering: Exploratory Study and Conceptual Framework for Methods and Tools to Support Entrepreneurial Activities in Universities*. Paper presented at the International Innovation Conference in Complex Social Systems, Dublin, Ireland.

Magretta, J. (1999). *Managing in the new economy*. Boston, MA: Harvard Business School.

Magretta, J. (2002). Why Business Models Matter. *Harvard Business Review*, *80*(5), 86–92.

Mair, J., & Ignasi, M. (2006). Social Entrepreneurship Research: A Source of Explanation, Prediction, and Delight. *Journal of World Business*, *41*, 36–44. doi:10.1016/j.jwb.2005.09.002

Malecki, E. J. (1997). *Technology and Economic Development: The Dynamics of Local, Regional and National Competitiveness*. Essex, UK: Addison Wesley Longman Limited.

Malecki, E. J. (2003). Digital development in rural areas: potentials and pitfalls. *Journal of Rural Studies*, *19*(2), 201–214. doi:10.1016/S0743-0167(02)00068-2

Malone, T. W., Yates, J., & Benjamin, R. I. (1987). Electronic Markets and Electronic Hierarchies. *Communications of the ACM, 30*(6), 484–497. doi:10.1145/214762.214766

MANUFUTURE. (2004). *A vision for 2020: Assuring the future of manufacturing in Europe*. European Commission.

Marfleet, J. (2008). Enterprise 2.0 _ What's your game plan?: What, if any, will be the role of the information intermediary? *Business Information Review, 25*, 152. doi:10.1177/0266382108095037

Markoff, J. (in press). Vast Spy System Loots Computers in 103 countries. *The New York Times.*

Markoff, J. (in press). Worm Infects Millions of Computers Worldwide. *The New York Times.*

Martindale, C., & Dailey, A. (1996). Creativity, primary process cognition and personality. *Personality and Individual Differences, 20*, 409–414. doi:10.1016/0191-8869(95)00202-2

Matlay, H. (2003). Small tourism firms in e-Europe: definitional, conceptual and contextual considerations. In R. Thomas (Ed.), *Small Firms in Tourism: International Perspectives* (pp. 297-312). Oxford, UK: Pergamon.

Matlay, H. (2004). E-entrepreneurship and small e-business development: towards a comparative research agenda. *Journal of Small Business and Enterprise Development, 11*, 408–414. doi:10.1108/14626000410551663

Matlay, H. (2005). Research entrepreneurship and education Part 1: what is entrepreneurship and does it matter? *Education and Training, 47*(8/9), 665–677. doi:10.1108/00400910510633198

Matlay, H., & Addis, M. (2003). Adoption of ICT and e-commerce in small businesses: an HEI-based consultancy perspective. *Journal of Small Business and Enterprise Development, 10*(3), 321–335. doi:10.1108/14626000310489790

Matlay, H., & Westhead, P. (2005). Virtual teams and the rise of e-entrepreneurship in Europe. *International Small Business Journal, 23*(3), 279–302. doi:10.1177/0266242605052074

McDougall, P. P., & Oviatt, B. M. (2000). International entrepreneurship: the intersection of two research paths. *Academy of Management Journal, 43*(5), 902–906. doi:10.2307/1556418

McDowell, G. R. (1995). Some communities are successful, others are not: toward an institutional framework for understanding the reasons why. In D.W. Sears & J.N. Reid (Eds.), *Rural Development Strategies* (pp.269-281). Chicago: Nelson-Hall.

McKay, R., Langdon, R., & Coltheart, M. (2005). Sleights of mind: Delusions, defences, and self-deception. *Cognitive Neuropsychiatry, 10*, 305–326. doi:10.1080/13546800444000074

Mckinsey. (2008 July). Building the web 2.0 enterprise. *Mckinsey Quarterly.*

Mesenbourg, T. L. (2008). *E-Stats*. US Census Bureau. Gasson, S. (2003). The Impact of E-Commerce Technology on the Air Travel Industry. In *Annals of Cases on Information Technology* (pp. 234 – 249). Hershey, PA: IGI Publishing.

Meyer, C. (2001). The second generation of speed. *Harvard Business Review, 79*(4), 24–26.

Meyer, J. W., & Rowan, B. (1977). Institutionalized organizations: Formal structure as myth and ceremony. *American Journal of Sociology, 83*(2), 340–363. doi:10.1086/226550

Meyer, P. B. (2003). Episodes of Collective Invention, Working Papers 368. *U.S. Bureau of Labor Statistics*. Retrieved February 10, 2009 from http://ssrn.com/abstract=466880

Migliorini, P., Serarols Tarrés, C., & Bikfalvi, A. (2009). *Overcoming critical junctures in spin-offs companies from non-elite universities: evidence from Catalonia*. Forthcoming in RENT Anthology 2008.

Miles, M. B., & Huberman, A. M. (1994). *Qualitative data analaysis*. Thousand Oaks, CA: Sage.

Miner, A., Eesley, D., Devaughn, M., & Rura-Polley, T. (2001). The magic beanstalk vision: commercializing university inventions and research. In C. Schoonhoven, &

E. Romanelli (Eds.), *The Entrepreneurial Dynamic* (pp. 109-146). Stanford, CA: Stanford University Press.

Mintzberg, H. (1990). Strategy formation: schools of thought. In J. W. Fredrickson (Ed.), *Perspectives on Strategic Management* (pp. 105-235). New York: Harper Business.

Mintzberg, H., Ahlstrand, B., & Lampel, J. (1998). *Strategy safari*. London: Prentice Hall Europe.

Mitchell, R. K., Agle, B. R., & Wood, D. J. (1997). Toward a Theory of Stakeholder Identification and Salience: Defining the Principle of Who and What Really Counts. *Academy of Management Review, 22*(4), 853–896. doi:10.2307/259247

Mockus, A., Fielding, R. T., & Herbsleb, J. D. (2002). Two case studies of open source software development: Apache and Mozilla. *ACM Transactions on Software Engineering and Methodology, 11*(3), 309–346. doi:10.1145/567793.567795

Monk, E., & Wagner, B. (2009). *Concepts in Enterprise Resource Planning* (3rd.ed.). Boston, MA: Course Technology Cengage Learning.

Moon, J. Y., & Sproull, L. S. (2000). Essence of Distributed Work: The Case of the Linux Kernel. *First Monday, 5*(11). Retrieved February 10, 2009, from http://www.informatik.uni-trier.de/~ley/db/journals/firstmonday/firstmonday10.html.

Moore, G. A. (1995). *Inside the Tornado: Marketing Strategies from Silicon Valley's Cutting Edge*. New York: Harper Business.

Moray, N., & Clarysse, B. (2005). Institutional change and resource endowments to science-based entrepreneurial firms. *Research Policy, 34*, 1010–1027. doi:10.1016/j.respol.2005.05.016

Morse, E. A., & Mitchell, R. K. (2006). *Case in Entrepreneurship*. London: Sage Publications, Inc.

Mort, G. S., & Weerawardena, J. (2006). Networking capability and international entrepreneurship. How networks function in Australian born global firms.

International Marketing Review, 23(5), 549–572. doi:10.1108/02651330610703445

Mowery, D., Oxley, J., & Silverman, B. (1996). Strategic Alliances and Interfirm Knowledge Transfer. *Strategic Management Journal, 17*, 77–91.

Muniagurria, M. E. (1995). Growth and research and development. *Journal of Economic Dynamics & Control, 19*(1), 207–235. doi:10.1016/0165-1889(93)00779-4

Muñiz, A. M. Jr, & O'Guinn, T. C. (2001). Brand Community. *The Journal of Consumer Research, 27*(4), 412–432. doi:10.1086/319618

Munnich, L. W., Jr., Schrock, G., & Cook, K. (2002). Rural Knowledge Clusters: The Challenge of Rural Economic Prosperity. *Reviews of Economic Development Literature and Practice,* 12. U.S. Economic Development Administration. Retrieved from http://www.eda.gov/ImageCache/EDAPublic/documents/pdfdocs/u_2eminn_2elit_2erev3_2epdf/v1/u.minn.lit.rev3.pdf

Murphy, T., & Jennex, M. (2006). Knowledge Management Systems Developed For Hurricane Katrina Response. In B. Van de Walle and M. Turoff, (Eds.), *Proceedings of the 3rd International ISCRAM Conference*, Newark, NJ, May 2006 (pp. 617-624).

Murray, F., & Stern, S. (2005). *Do Formal Intellectual Property Rights Hinder the Free Flow of Scientific Knowledge? An Empirical Test of the Anti-Commons Hypothesis.* (NBER Working Paper No. 11465). Cambridge, MA: University of Cambridge, National Bureau of Economic Research, Inc.

Mustonen, M. (2003). Copyleft – the economics of Linux and other open source software. *Information Economics and Policy, 15*(1), 99–121. doi:10.1016/S0167-6245(02)00090-2

Muzyka, D. F., & Hills, G. E. (1993). Introduction. In G.E. Hills, R.W. LaForge, & D.F. Muzyka (Eds.), *Research at the Marketing/Entrepreneurship Interface - Proceedings of the UIC Symposium on Marketing and Entrepreneurship* (pp. VII-XV).

Nabi, G., Holden, R., & Walmsley, A. (2006). Graduate Career-making and business start-up: a literature review. *Education and Training, 48*(2), 373–385. doi:10.1108/00400910610677072

Narduzzo, A., & Rossi, A. (2005). The role of modularity in free/open source software development. In S. Koch (Ed.), *Free/open source software development*. Hershey, PA: Idea Group Publishing.

Narver, J. C., & Slater, S. F. (1990). The Effect of Market Orientation on Business Profitability. *Journal of Marketing, 54*(4), 20–35. doi:10.2307/1251757

NCVO. (2002). *The U.K. Voluntary Sector Almanac 2002*. London: NCVO.

Ndonzuau, N. F., Pirnay, F., & Surlemont, B. (2002). A stage model of academic spin-off creation. *Technovation, 22*, 281–289. doi:10.1016/S0166-4972(01)00019-0

Neergaard, H. (2005). Networking activities in technology-based entrepreneurial teams. *International Small Business Journal, 23*(3), 257–278. doi:10.1177/0266242605052073

Newbert, S. L. (2005). New firm formation: a dynamic capability perspective. *Journal of Small Business Management, 43*(1), 55–77. doi:10.1111/j.1540-627X.2004.00125.x

Newslog, C. Y. B. (2009). *E-Government in Malta*. ITU-D ICT Applications and Cybersecurity Division. Retrieved April 29, 2009, from http://www.itu.int/ITU-D/cyb/newslog/EGovernment+In+Malta.aspx

Noble, C. H., Rajiv, K. S., & Kumar, A. (2002). Market Orientation and Alternative Strategic Orientations: A Longitudinal Assessment of Performance Implications. *Journal of Marketing, 66*(4), 25–39. doi:10.1509/jmkg.66.4.25.18513

North, D. C. (1990). *Institutions, Institutional Change and Economic Performance*. Cambridge, UK: Cambridge University Press.

Northwest North Carolina Advanced Materials Cluster. (n.d.). Retrieved October 26, 2006, from http://www.advancedmaterials.org/

Nunnally, J. C. (1978). *Psychometric Theory*. New York: McGraw-Hill.

Nuvolari, A. (2002). The 'Machine Breakers' and the Industrial Revolution. *The Journal of European Economic History, 31*, 393–426.

O'Donnell, A., Gilmore, A., Carson, D., & Cummins, D. (2002). Competitive advantage in small to medium-sized enterprises. *Journal of Strategic Marketing, 10*(3), 205–223. doi:10.1080/09652540210151388

O'Donnell, A., Gilmore, A., Cummins, D., & Carson, D. (2001). The network construct in entrepreneurship research: A review and critique. *Management Decision, 39*(9), 749–760. doi:10.1108/EUM0000000006220

O'Mahony, M., & Vecchi, M. (2009). R&D, Knowledge Spillovers and Company Productivity Performance. *Research Policy, 38*, 35–44. doi:10.1016/j.respol.2008.09.003

O'Mahony, S., & Ferraro, F. (2007). The emergence of Governance in an Open Source Community. *Academy of Management Journal, 50*(5), 1079–1106.

O'Reilly, T. (2005). *What Is Web 2.0. Design Patterns and Business Models for the Next Generation of Software*. Retrieved April 24, 2009, from http://www.oreillynet.com/pub/a/oreilly/tim/news/2005/09/30/what-is-web-20.html

O'Reilly, T. (2005). *What Is Web 2.0. Design patterns and business models for the next generation of software*. Retrieved March 30, 2009, from http://www.oreillynet.com/pub/a/oreilly/tim/news/2005/09/30/what-is-web-20.html

O'Shea, R., Allen, T. J., O'Gorman, C., & Roche, F. (2004). Universities and Technology Transfer: A Review of Academic Entrepreneurship Literature. *Irish Journal of Management, 25*(2), 11–29.

OECD. (2003). *The Non-profit Sector in a Changing Economy*. Paris: OECD.

Orlikowski, W. J., & Baroudi, J. J. (1991). Studying Information Technology in Organizations: Research Approaches and Assumptions. *Information Systems Research, 2*(1), 1–28. doi:10.1287/isre.2.1.1

Orlikowski, W. J., & Hofman, D. J. (1997). An Improvisational Model for Change Management: The Case of Groupware Technologies. *Sloan Management Review*, *38*(2), 11–21.

Osterloh, M., & Rota, S. (2007). Open Source development – Just another case of collective invention? *Research Policy, 36*, 157–171. doi:10.1016/j.respol.2006.10.004

Osterloh, M., B., & Frey, S. (2000). Motivation, knowledge transfer, and organizational firms. *Organization Science, 11*(5), 538–550. doi:10.1287/orsc.11.5.538.15204

Osterwalder, A., & Pigneur, Y. (2002). *Business Models and their Elements* [Electronic Version]. Retrieved February 11, 2009 from http://inforge.unil.ch/aosterwa/Documents/workshop/Osterwalder_Pigneur.pdf

Oviatt, B. M., & McDougall, P. P. (1994). Toward a theory of international new ventures. *Journal of International Business Studies, 25*(1), 45–64. doi:10.1057/palgrave.jibs.8490193

Oviatt, B. M., & McDougall, P. P. (2005). Defining international entrepreneurship and modeling the speed of internationalization. *Entrepreneurship Theory & Practice, 29*(5), 537–553. doi:10.1111/j.1540-6520.2005.00097.x

Oxenfeldt, A. R., & Moore, W. L. (1978). Customer or Competitor - Which Guideline for Marketing? *Management Review, 67*(8), 43–48.

PANGEA. (n.d.). *e-Polk – Polk County Internet Access*. Retrieved October 26, 2006, http://www.pangaea.us/

Park, J. S. (2005). Opportunity recognition and product innovation in entrepreneurial hi-tech start-ups: a new perspective and supporting case study. *Technovation, 25*, 739–752. doi:10.1016/j.technovation.2004.01.006

Patterson, H., & Henderson, D. (2003). What is really different about rural and urban firms? Some evidence from Northern Ireland. *Journal of Rural Studies, 19*(4), 477–490. doi:10.1016/S0743-0167(03)00027-5

Pavlou, P. A., & Gefen, D. (2005). Psychological contract violation in online marketplaces: Antecedents, consequences, and moderating role. *Information Systems Research, 16*(4), 372–399. doi:10.1287/isre.1050.0065

Pease, W., & Rowe, M. (2005). Use of information technology to facilitate collaboration and co-opetition between tourist operators in tourist destinations. In *Technology Enterprise Strategies: Thriving and Surviving in an Online Era Conference*, Melbourne.

Pease, W., Rowe, M., & Cooper, M. (2005). Regional tourist destinations – the role of information and communications technology in collaboration amongst tourism providers. Paper presented at *ITS Africa-Asia-Australasia Regional Conference*, Perth.

Pelham, A. M. (1997). Mediating Influences on the Relationship Between Market Orientation and Profitability in Small Industrial Firms. *Journal of Marketing Theory and Practice, 5*(3), 55–76.

Pelham, A. M. (1999). Influence of Environment, Strategy, and Market Orientation on Performance in Small Manufacturing Firms. *Journal of Business Research, 45*(1), 33–46. doi:10.1016/S0148-2963(98)00026-5

Pelham, A. M., & Wilson, D. T. (1996). A Longitudinal Study of the Impact of Market Structure, Firm Structure, Strategy and Market Orientation Culture on Dimensions of Small-Firm Performance. *Journal of the Academy of Marketing Science, 24*(1), 27–43. doi:10.1007/BF02893935

Penrose, E. T. (1959). *The Theory of the Growth of the Firm*. New York: John Wiley & Sons.

Peredo, A. M., & McLean, M. (2006). Social Entrepreneurship: A Critical Review of the Concept. *Journal of World Business, 41*, 56–65. doi:10.1016/j.jwb.2005.10.007

Perens, B. (1999). *Open Sources: Voices from the Open Source Revolution*. Sebastopol, CA: O'Reilly Media.

Pérez, M., & Martínez, A. (2003). The development of university spin-offs: early dynamics of technology transfer and networking. *Technovation, 23*(10), 823–831. doi:10.1016/S0166-4972(02)00034-2

Perrini, F. (2006). *The New Social Entrepreneurship: What Awaits Social Entrepreneurship Ventures?* Northampton, MA: Edward Elgar.

Perry, M. L., Sengupta, S., & Krapfel, R. (2004). Effectiveness of horizontal strategic alliances in technologically uncertain environments: are trust and commitment enough? *Journal of Business Research*, *57*(9), 951–956. doi:10.1016/S0148-2963(02)00501-5

Peterson, R. A., & Merino, M. C. (2003). Consumer Information Search Behavior and the Internet. *Psychology and Marketing*, *20*(2), 99–121. doi:10.1002/mar.10062

Petts, J. (1999). *Handbook of Environmental Impact Assessment*. Oxford: Blackwell.

Phau, I., & Poon, S. M. (2000). Factors Influencing the Types of Products and Services Purchased over the Internet. *Internet Research*, *10*(2), 102–113. doi:10.1108/10662240010322894

Piller, F. T., & Walcher, D. (2006). Toolkits for idea competitions: a novel method to integrate users in new product development. *R & D Management*, *36*(3), 307–318. doi:10.1111/j.1467-9310.2006.00432.x

Pinker, E. J., Seidmann, A., & Foster, R. C. (2002). Strategies for Transitioning 'Old Economy' Firms to E-Business. *Communications of the ACM*, *45*(5), 77–83. doi:10.1145/506218.506219

Pirnay, F., Surlemont, B., & Nlemvo, F. (2003). Toward a typology of university spin-offs. *Small Business Economics*, *21*(4), 355–369. doi:10.1023/A:1026167105153

Pittaway, L., & Hannon, P. (2007). Institutional strategies for developing enterprise education. *Journal of Small Business and Enterprise Development*, *15*(1), 202–226. doi:10.1108/14626000810850937

PIU – Postal Information Unit. (2000). *Counter Revolution: Modernising the Post Office Network*. London: PIU.

Platzer, M. (2001). *Cyberstates 2001: A State by State Overview of the High Technology Industry*. Paper presented at American Economic Association, Washington DC. Policy Research Initiative. (n.d.). *The Emergence of Cross-Border Regions*. Retrieved October 26, 2006, from https://recherchepolitique.gc.ca/doclib/PRI_XBorder_e.pdf

Pohle, G., & Chapman, M. (2006). IBM's global CEO report 2006: business model innovation matters. *Strategy and Leadership*, *34*(5), 34–40. doi:10.1108/10878570610701531

Polkinghorne, D. (1988). *Narrative Knowing and the Human Sciences*. New York: SUNY Press.

Popper, K. R. (1968). *The Open Society and Its Enemies: Volume 2: The High Tide of Prophecy: Hegel, Marx and the Aftermath*. London: Routledge.

Porter, M. (1985). *Competitive Advantage: Creating and Sustaining Superior Performance*. New York: Free Press.

Porter, M. (2001, March). Strategy and the Internet. *Harvard Business Review*, 63–78.

Porter, M. (2008). *On Competition*. Harvard Business School Publishing Corporation.

Porter, M. E. (1980). *Competitive Strategy: techniques for analyzing industries and competitors*. New York: The Free Press.

Porter, M. E. (1985). *Competitive Advantage*. New York: Free Press.

Porter, M. E. (1998). *Clusters and the New Economics of Competition*. Cambridge, MA: Harvard Business Review.

Porter, M. E. (2001). Strategy and the Internet. *Harvard Business Review*, *79*(3), 6278.

Porter, M. E. (2004). *Competitiveness in Rural U.S. Regions: Learning and Research Agenda*. Institute for Strategy and Competitiveness. Cambridge, MA: Harvard Business School.

Porter, M. E., & Millar, V. E. (1985). How information gives you competitive advantage. *Harvard Business Review*, *63*(4), 149–160.

Potter, B. (2005). RFID: misunderstood or untrustworthy? *Network Security*, (4): 17–18. doi:10.1016/S1353-4858(05)00184-4

Prahalad, C. K., & Hamel, G. (1990). The core competence of the corporation. *Harvard Business Review*, *68*(3), 79–91.

Pramatari, K., Doukidis, G. I., & Kourouthanassis, P. (2004). Towards Smarter Supply and Demand Chain Collaboration Practices Enabled by RFID Technology. In P. H. Vervest, E. Van Heck, K. Preiss & L.-F. Pau (Eds.), *Smart Business Networks* (pp. 187-210). Berlin, Germany: Springer.

Price, L. L., Feick, L. F., & Guskey-Federouch, A. (1988). Coupon Behaviors of the Market Maven: Profile of a Super Couponer. *Advances in Consumer Research. Association for Consumer Research (U. S.)*, *15*, 354–359.

Qu, Z. (2007). Advance Selling and Internet Intermediary: Travel Distribution Strategies in the E-Commerce Age. In *Proceedings of the Ninth International Conference on Electronic Commerce* (pp. 177-184).

Quelch, J. A., & Klein, L. R. (1996). The internet and international marketing. *Sloan Management Review*, *37*(3), 60–75.

Quigley, J. (1998). Urban Diversity and Economic Growth. *The Journal of Economic Perspectives*, *12*(2), 127–138.

Quigley, J. (2002). Rural Policy and the New Regional Economics: Implications for Rural America. UCal Berkeley.

Quinn, R. E., & Cameron, K. S. (1988). Paradox and Transformation: Toward a Theory of Change in Organization and Management. Cambridge, MA: Ballinger.

Rabiner, L., & Juang, B.-H. (1993). *Fundamentals of speech recognition* (1 ed.). Upper Saddle River, NJ: Prentice Hall.

Raciborski, N. (2004). Digital Delivery Considerations for Entertainment Media. [CIE]. *Computers in Entertainment*, *2*(4), 8. doi:10.1145/1037851.1037864

Rae, D. (2007). Connecting enterprise and graduate employability: challenges to the higher education culture and curriculum? *Education and Training*, *50*(8/9), 605–619. doi:10.1108/00400910710834049

Rae, D. (2008). Riding out the storm: graduates, enterprise and careers in turbulent economic times. *Education and Training*, *50*(8/9), 748–763. doi:10.1108/00400910810917118

Rae, D., & Carswell, M. (2000). Using a life-story approach in researching entrepreneurial learning: the development of a conceptual model and its implications in the design of learning experiences. *Education & Training*, *42*(4/5), 220–227. doi:10.1108/00400910010373660

Raisinghani, M. S., Benoit, A., Ding, J., Gomez, M., Gupta, K., & Gusila, V. (2004). Ambient Intelligence: Changing Forms of Human Computer Interaction and their Social Implications. *Journal of Digital Information*, *5*(4).

Ram, M. (1994). *Managing to Survive: Working Lives in Small Firms*. Oxford, UK: Blackwell Publishing.

Raman, T. V. (2009). Toward 2^W, Beyond Web 2.0. *Communications of the ACM*, *52*(2), 52–59. doi:10.1145/1461928.1461945

Rawls, J. (1993). *Political Liberalism (The John Dewey Lectures in Philosophy)*. New York: Columbia University Press.

Raymond, E. (2000). *The Cathedral and the Bazaar*. Sebastopol, CA: O'Reilly & Associates.

Rayport, J. F., & Sviokla, J. J. (1995). Exploiting the Virtual Value Chain. *Harvard Business Review*, *73*(6), 75–85.

Redfield, R., Linton, R., & Herskovits, M. (1936). Memorandum for the Study of Acculturation. *American Anthropologist*, *38*, 149–151. doi:10.1525/aa.1936.38.1.02a00330

Redmond developer news. (2009). Retrieved January 20, 2009, from http://www.reddevnews.com

Reinartz, W., Krafft, M., & Hoyer, W. D. (2004). The customer relationship management process: its measurement and impact on performance. *JMR, Journal of Marketing Research*, *41*, 293–305. doi:10.1509/jmkr.41.3.293.35991

Retrieved February 10, 2009, from http://www.houstonlawreview.org/1999/05/15/volume-36-number-1-symposium-1999/

Reuter, M., Panksepp, J., Schnabel, N., Kellerhoff, N., Kempel, P., & Hennig, J. (2005). Personality and biological markers of creativity. *European Journal of Personality, 19*, 83–95. doi:10.1002/per.534

Reynolds, G. W. (2010). *Information Technology for Managers*. Boston: Course Technology.

Rialp, A., Rialp, J., & Knight, G. A. (2005). The phenomenon of early internationalizing firms: what do we know after a decade (1993-2003) of scientific inquiry? *International Business Review, 14*, 147–166. doi:10.1016/j.ibusrev.2004.04.006

Richards, D., & Busch, P. (2002). Knowledge in Action: Blurring the Distinction Between Explicit and Tacit Knowledge. *Journal of Decision Systems, 11*(2), 149–164. doi:10.3166/jds.11.149-164

Richards, D., & Busch, P. (2008). Finding and Growing Innovators: Keeping ahead of the Competition. In F. Zhao (Ed.), *Handbook of Research on Information Technology Entrepreneurship and Innovation* (pp. 396-414). Hershey, PA: Idea Group Inc.

Richardson, D., Ramirez, R., & Haq, M. (2000). *Grameen Telecom's Village Phone Programme in Rural Bangladesh: a Multi-Media Case Study; Final Report* [Electronic Version]. Retrieved February 11, 2009 from http://www.telecommons.com/villagephone/finalreport.pdf

Riva, G. (2005). The Psychology of Ambient Intelligence: Activity, Situation and Presence. In G. Riva, F. Vatalaro, F. Davide & M. Alcaniz (Eds.), *Ambient Intelligence: the evolution of technology, communication and cognition towards the future of human-computer interaction*. Amsterdam: IOS Press.

Riva, G., Vatalaro, F., Davide, F., & Alcaniz, M. (2005). *Ambient Intelligence: the evolution of technology, communication and cognition towards the future of human-computer interaction*. Amsterdam: IOS Press.

Robbins, S., Bergman, R., Stagg, I., & Coulter, M. (2003). *Management* (3rd. Ed). Upper Saddle River, NJ: Prentice Hall.

Roberts, E. B. (1991). *Entrepreneurs in High-Technology - Lessons from MIT and Beyond*. New York: Oxford University Press.

Roberts, E., & Malone, R. (1996). *Policies and structures for spinning off new companies from research and development organizations*. Retrieved July 23, 2009, from http://dspace.mit.edu/bitstream/handle/1721.1/2569/SWP-3804-32616509.pdf?sequence=1

Roberts, J. A., Hann, I. H., & Slaughter, S. A. (2006). Understanding the motives, participation, and performance of open source software developers: A longitudinal study of the Apache project. *Management Science, 52*(7), 984–999. doi:10.1287/mnsc.1060.0554

Roberts, S. (2002). *Key Drivers of Economic Development and Inclusion in Rural Areas*. Initial scoping study for the socio-economic evidence base for DEFRA.

Robey, D., Wishart, N. A., & Rodriguez-Diaz, A. (1995). Merging the Metaphors for Organizational Improvement: Business Process Reengineering as a Component of Organizational Learning. *Accounting. Management & Information Technology, 5*(1), 23–39. doi:10.1016/0959-8022(95)90012-8

Rodgers, J. A., Yen, D. C., & Chou, D. C. (2002). Developing e-business: A strategic approach. *Information Management & Computer Security, 10*(4), 184–192. doi:10.1108/09685220210436985

Rogers, E. (1995). *Diffusion of Innovations* (4th Ed.). New York: Free Press.

Rosenfeld, S. (1995). *Overachievers: Business Clusters that Work: Prospects for Regional Development*. Regional Technology Strategies, Inc.

Rosenfeld, S. (2002). *Just Clusters: Economic development strategies that reach more people and places*. Regional Technology Strategies, Inc.

Rosenfeld, S. (2003). *Clusters of Creativity: Innovation and growth in Montana*. Prepared for the Montana

Governor's Office of Economic Opportunity. Regional Technology Strategies, Inc.

Rosenfeld, S. A., & Kingslow, M. (2000). *Clusters in Rural Areas: Auto Supply Chains in Tennessee and Houseboat Manufacturers in Kentucky.* Regional Technology Strategies, Inc. Retrieved from http://www.rural.org/publications/Rosenfeld00-11.pdf

Rowden, R. W. (1995). The role of human resource development in successful small to mid-sized manufacturing businesses: a comparative case study. *Human Resource Development Quarterly*, *6*(4), 355–373. doi:10.1002/hrdq.3920060405

Runco, M. A. (2004). Creativity. *Annual Review of Psychology*, *55*, 657–687. doi:10.1146/annurev.psych.55.090902.141502

Runde, S. (2007). *Memorandum der 18. Sylter Runde: Scientific Entrepreneurship: Was sollen Wissenschaftler noch alles richten?* Retrieved from http://www.sylter-runde.de

Russ, S. W. (1998). The impact of repression on creativity. *Psychological Inquiry*, *9*, 221–223. doi:10.1207/s15327965pli0903_7

Sadler-Smith, E., Hampson, Y., Chaston, I., & Badger, B. (2003). Managerial behavior, entrepreneurial style, and small firm performance. *Journal of Small Business Management*, *41*(1), 47–67. doi:10.1111/1540-627X.00066

Sakakibara, M. (2002). Formation of R&D Consortia: Industry and Company Effects. *Strategic Management Journal*, *23*(11), 1033–1050. doi:10.1002/smj.272

Saleh, K., Abdulaziz, A., & Alkattan, I. (2006). A Services – Oriented Approach to Developing Security Policies for Trustworthy Systems. In *Emerging Trends and Challenges in IT Management.* Hershey, PA: Idea Group Inc.

Sampson, R. C. (2005). Experience effects and collaborative returns in R&D alliances. *Strategic Management Journal*, *26*(11), 1009–1031. doi:10.1002/smj.483

Samu, S., Krishnan, S., & Smith, R. E. (1999). Using Advertising Alliances for New Product Introduction: Interactions Between Product Complementarily and Promotional Strategies. *Journal of Marketing*, *63*(1), 57–74. doi:10.2307/1252001

Sanchez, R., & Mahoney, J. (1996). Modularity, flexibility, and knowledge management in product and organization design. *Strategic Management Journal*, *17*, 63–76.

Sapienza, H. J., De Clercq, D., & Sandberg, W. R. (2005). Antecedents of international and domestic learning effort. *Journal of Business Venturing*, *20*, 437–457. doi:10.1016/j.jbusvent.2004.03.001

Sarasvathy, S. D. (2001). Causation and effectuation: toward a theoretical shift from economic inevitability to entrepreneurial contingency. *Academy of Management Review*, *26*(2), 243–264. doi:10.2307/259121

Sarasvathy, S. D. (2008). *Effectuation: Elements of Entrepreneurial Expertise.* Cheltenham, UK: Edward Elgar.

Sassenberg, K., & Scholl, A. (2010). Soziale Bindungen von Usern an Web 2.0-Angebote. In G. Walsh, B. H. Hass, & T. Kilian (Eds.), *Web 2.0 - Neue Perspektiven für Marketing und Medien* (2nd ed.). Heidelberg, Germany: Springer.

Schaarschmidt, M., & Von Kortzfleisch, H. F. O. (2009, December). *Divide et Impera: The Integration of External Knowledge in Firm-Driven OSS Development - An Empirical Investigation.* Paper submitted to the International Conference on Information Systems (ICIS), Phoenix, Arizona.

Schein, E. H. (1993). How can organizations learn faster? The challenge of entering the green room. *Sloan Management Review*, *34*(2), 85–92.

Schonberg, D., & Kirovski, D. (2004). Fingerprinting and Forensic Analysis of Multimedia. In *Proceedings of the 12th Annual ACM International Conference on Multimedia* (pp. 788-795).

Schumpeter, A. J. (1975). *Capitalism, Socialism and Democracy.* New York: Harper.

Schumpeter, J. A. (1931). Theorie der wirtschaftlichen Entwicklung (3rd Ed.). München, Germany: Duncker & Humblot.

Schumpeter, J. A. (1943). *Capitalism, Socialism and Democracy*. London: Allen and Unwin.

Schuster, E. W., Allen, S. J., & Brock, D. L. (2007). *Global RFID: The Value of the EPCglobal Network for Supply Chain Management*. Berlin, Germany: Springer.

Schweizer, T. S. (2006). The Psychology of Novelty Seeking, Creativity and Innovation: Neurocognitive Aspects in a Work-Psychological Perspective. *Creativity and Innovation Management*, *15*(2), 164–172. doi:10.1111/j.1467-8691.2006.00383.x

Schweizer, T. S. (2007). Neuropsychological Support to the Novelty Generation Process. In: C. Martindale & L. Dorfman (Eds.), *Innovation and Aesthetics*. Cambridge, UK: Cambridge Scholars Press.

Schweizer, T. S., Deijen, J. B., Heslenfeld, D., Nieuwenhuis, S., & Talsma, D. (2006). *Functional magnetic resonance imaging of brain activity during rigid versus creative thought processes in obsessive-compulsive patients*. Poster presented at the Cognitive Neuroscience Society Conference, San Francisco, USA.

Schweizer, T.S. (2004). An Individual Psychology of Novelty-Seeking, Creativity and Innovation. *ERIM Ph.D. Series*, 48.

Seclos, C., & Mahir, J. (2005). *La iniciativa Sekem en Varios: Mejorar la gestión de empresas*. Madrid: McGraw-Hill, IESE.

Selsky, J., Goes, J., & Oguz, B. (2007). Contrasting Perspectives of Strategy Making: Applications in 'Hyper' Environment. *Organization Studies*, *28*(1), 71–94. doi:10.1177/0170840607067681

Serarols Tarrés, C., Urbano, D., Vaillant, Y., & Bikfalvi, A. (2009). Research commercialisation via spin-off: the case of a non-elite university. *Int. J. Technology Transfer and Commercialisation*, *8*(4), 356–378. doi:10.1504/IJTTC.2009.024910

Serarols, C. (2008). The process of business start-ups in the internet: a multiple case study. *International Journal of Technology Management*, *43*(1-3), 142–159. doi:10.1504/IJTM.2008.019412

Shah, S. (2006). Motivation, Governance, and the Viability of Hybrid Forms in Open Source Development. *Management Science*, *52*(7), 1000–1014. doi:10.1287/mnsc.1060.0553

Shane, S. (2004). *Academic Entrepreneurship: University Spin-offs and Wealth Creation*. Cheltenham, UK: Edward Elgar Publishing.

Shane, S., & Stuart, T. (2002). Organizational Endowments and the Performance of University Start-ups. *Management Science*, *48*(1), 154–170. doi:10.1287/mnsc.48.1.154.14280

Shane, S., & Venkataraman, S. (2000). The promise of entrepreneurship as a field of research. *Academy of Management Review*, *25*(1), 217–226. doi:10.2307/259271

Shane, S., & Venkataraman, S. (2000). The promise of entrepreneurship as a field of research. *Academy of Management Review*, *25*(1), 218–228. doi:10.2307/259271

Shani, A. B., Grant, R. M., Krishman, R., & Thompson, E. (1992). Advanced Manufacturing Systems and Organizational Choice: Sociotechnical System Approach. *California Management Review*, *34*(4), 91–111.

Shapiro, B. P. (1988). What the Hell is "Market Oriented"? *Harvard Business Review*, *66*(6), 119–125.

Shefer, D., & Frenkel, A. (2005). R&D, firm size and innovation: an empirical analysis. *Technovation*, *25*(1), 25–32. doi:10.1016/S0166-4972(03)00152-4

SIBIS. (2002). *Towards the Information Society in Europe and the US: SIBIS Benchmarking Highlights 2002*. Bonn, Germany: Empirca (SIBIS project and European Communities).

Siegel, D. S., Waldman, D., & Link, A. (2003). Assessing the impact of organisational practices on the relative productivity of university technology transfer offices: an exploratory study. *Research Policy*, *32*, 27–48. doi:10.1016/S0048-7333(01)00196-2

Siegel, D. S., Waldman, D., Atwater, L., & Link, A. (2003). Commercial knowledge transfers from universities to firms: Improving the effectiveness of university industry collaboration. *The Journal of High Technology*

Management Research, *14*(1), 111–133. doi:10.1016/S1047-8310(03)00007-5

Simonin, B. (2004). An Empirical Investigation of the Process of Knowledge Transfer in International Strategic Alliances. *Journal of International Business Studies*, *35*(5), 407–427. doi:10.1057/palgrave.jibs.8400091

Singh, J. (2008). Distributed R&D, cross-regional knowledge integration and quality of innovative output. *Research Policy*, *37*, 77–96. doi:10.1016/j.respol.2007.09.004

Singh, J. V., Tucker, D. J., & House, R. J. (1986). Organizational legitimacy and the liability of newness. *Administrative Science Quarterly*, *31*(2), 171–193. doi:10.2307/2392787

Sinkula, J. M. (1994). Market Information Processing and Organizational Learning. *Journal of Marketing*, *58*(1), 35–45. doi:10.2307/1252249

Sisario, B. (2008, December 31). Music Sales Fell in 2008, but Climbed on the Web. *The New York Times*. Retrieved June 15, 2009, from http://www.nytimes.com

Skloot, E. (1987). Enterprise and Commerce in Non-Profit Organizations. In W. W. Powell (Ed.), *The Non-Profit Sector: A Research Handbook* (pp. 380–393). Yale University Press, New Haven.

Smallbone, D., North, D., Baldock, R., & Ekanem, I. (2002). *Encouraging and Supporting Enterprises in Rural Areas*. Report to the Small Business Service.

Smith, K. (2008). Embedding enterprise education into the curriculum at a research-led university. *Education and Training*, *50*(8/9), 713–724. doi:10.1108/00400910810917082

Smith, M. D., & Brynjolfsson, E. (2001). Consumer Decision-Making at an Internet Shopbot: Brand Still Matters. *The Journal of Industrial Economics*, *49*(4), 541–558.

Solms, M. (1997). *The neuropsychology of dreams: A clinico-anatomical study*. Mahwah, NJ: Lawrence Erlbaum Associates.

Solms, M. (2000). Dreaming and REM sleep are controlled by different brain mechanisms. *The Behavioral and Brain Sciences*, *23*, 843–850. doi:10.1017/S0140525X00003988

Sørensen, C., & Gibson, D. (2004). Ubiquitous visions and opaque realities: professionals talking about mobile technologies. *Info*, *6*(3), 188–196. doi:10.1108/14636690410549516

South Carolina Employment Security Commission. (n.d.). Top Employers by County. Retrieved November 11, 2005, from http://www.sces.org

Southwest.com. (2009). *We Weren't Just Airborne Yesterday*. Retrieved November 28, 2008, from http://www.southwest.com/about_swa/airborne.html

Spence, M., & Crick, D. (2006). A comparative investigation into the internationalisation of Canadian and UK high-tech SMEs. *International Marketing Review*, *23*(5), 524–548. doi:10.1108/02651330610703436

Spiller, P., & Lohse, Gerald L. (1997). A Classification of Internet Retail Stores. *International Journal of Electronic Commerce*, *2*(2), 29–56.

Stabell, C. B., & Fjeldstad, O. D. (1998). Configuring value for competitive advantage: on chains, shops, and networks. *Strategic Management Journal*, *19*(5), 413–437. doi:10.1002/(SICI)1097-0266(199805)19:5<413::AID-SMJ946>3.0.CO;2-C

Stabler, J. (1999). Rural America: A challenge to regional scientists. *The Annals of Regional Science*, *33*, 1–14. doi:10.1007/s001680050088

Stair, R. M., & Reynolds, G. W. (2008). *Fundamentals of Information Systems: A Managerial Approach* (4th ed.). Boston: Thomson Course Technology.

Stalk, G. Jr. (1988). Time – the next source of competitive advantage. *Harvard Business Review*, *66*(4), 28–60.

Stallman, R. (2007). *Why Open Source Misses the Point of Free Software: Open Source is a development methodology; free software is a social movement*. Retrieved February 9, 2009, from http://www.gnu.org

Stanton, N. A., & Ashleigh, M. J. (2000). A field study of team working in a new human supervisory control system. *Ergonomics, 43*(8), 1190–1209. doi:10.1080/00140130050084941

Starr, J. A., & Macmillan, I. A. (1990). Resource cooptation via social contracting: Resource acquisition strategies for new ventures. *Strategic Management Journal, 11*, 79–92. doi:10.1002/smj.4250110107

Starr, J. A., & MacMillan, I. C. (1990). Resource Cooptation and Social Contracting - Resource Acquisition Strategies for New Ventures. *Strategic Management Journal, 11*(4), 79–92.

State & County QuickFacts. (n.d.). U.S. Census Bureau. Retrieved from http://quickfacts.census.gov/qfd/

State and County Employment and Wages from the Quarterly Census of Employment and Wages. (n.d.). Bureau of Labor Statistics. U.S. Department of Labor. Retrieved from http://www.bls.gov/data/home.htm.

Stavridou, A., & Furnham, A. (1996). The relationshiop between psychoticism, trait-creativity and the attentional mechanism of cognitive inhibition. *Personality and Individual Differences, 21*, 1243–153. doi:10.1016/0191-8869(96)00030-X

Steinberg, R. (1993). Public Policy and the Performance of Non-Profit Organizations: a General Framework. *Nonprofit and Voluntary Sector Quarterly, 22*, 13–31. doi:10.1177/089976409302200103

Sternberg, R., Wagner, R., Williams, W., & Horvath, J. (1995). Testing common sense. *The American Psychologist, 50*(11), 912–927. doi:10.1037/0003-066X.50.11.912

Stewart, L., et al. (1997, May). *Connectivity Plan for North Carolina's Region A: Cherokee, Clay, Graham, Haywood, Jackson, Macon, and Swain Counties, and the Qualla Boundary.* Connect NC Project.

Stinchcombe, A. L. (1965). Social structure and organizations. In J. G. March (Ed.), *Handbook of organizations* (pp. 142-193). Chicago, IL: Rand McNally.

Stinchcombe, A. L. (1965). Social Structure and Organizations. In J.G. March (Ed.), *Handbook of Organizations* (pp. 153-193).

Stokes, D. (2000). Putting Entrepreneurship into Marketing: The Processes of Entrepreneurial Marketing. *Journal of Research in Marketing & Entrepreneurship, 2*(1), 1–16.

Stokic, D., Kirchhoff, U., & Sundmaeker, H. (2006). *Ambient Intelligence in Manufacturing Industry: Control System Point of View.* Paper presented at the Control and Applications 2006 Conference.

Stomper, A. (2006). A Theory of Banks' Industry Expertise, Market Power, and Credit Risk. *Management Science, 52*(10), 1618–1633. doi:10.1287/mnsc.1060.0559

Storey, D. (2004). Exploring the link, among small firms, between management training and firm performance: a comparison between the UK and other OECD countries. *International Journal of Human Resource Management, 15*(1), 112–130. doi:10.1080/0958519032000157375

Storey, D. J. (1994). *Understanding the Small Business Sector.* London: Routledge.

Stöttinger, B., & Schlegelmich, B. B. (1998). Explaining export development through psychic distance: enlightening or elusive? *International Business Review, 15*(5), 357–372.

Suchman, M. C. (1995). Managing Legitimacy: Strategic and Institutional Approaches. *Academy of Management Review, 20*(3), 571–610. doi:10.2307/258788

Sveiby, E. K. (2001). What is Knowledge Management? Retrieved February 2009, from www.sveiby.com/articles/KnowledgeManagement.html

Swade, D. (2000). *The Cogwheel Brain: Charles Babbage and the Quest to Build the First Computer* (1st ed.). London: Little, Brown and Company.

Swan, J., Newell, S., Scarbrough, H., & Hislop, D. (1999). Knowledge management and innovation: networks and networking. *Journal of Knowledge Management, 3*(4), 262–275. doi:10.1108/13673279910304014

Tapio, A. (2005). *Future of Telecommunication - Internet Telephony Operator Skype* [Electronic Version]. Retrieved February 11, 2009 from http://www.tml.tkk.fi/Publications/C/18/tapio.pdf

Tapscott, D., & Williams, A. (2007). *Wikinomics: How Mass Collaboration Changes Everything.* London: Atlantic Books.

Taylor, M., & Murphy, A. (2004). SMEs and e-business. *Journal of Small Business and Enterprise Development, 11*(3), 280–289. doi:10.1108/14626000410551546

Teasley, R., & Lockwood, F. (2009, March). *Unlocking Academic Entrepreneurship: The Role of Technology Maturation.* Paper presented at the workshop on Centers, Universities, and the Scientific Innovation Ecology, Arlington, Virginia.

Technorati. (n.d.). *State of the Blogsphere 2008.* Retrieved June 15, 2009, from http://technorati.com/blogging/state-of-the-blogosphere

Teece, D. J. (1986). Profiting from technological innovation: Implications for integration, collaboration, licensing and public policy. *Research Policy, 15,* 285–305. doi:10.1016/0048-7333(86)90027-2

Teece, D. J., Pisano, G., & Shuen, A. (1997). Dynamic Capabilities and Strategic Management. *Strategic Management Journal, 18*(7), 509–633. doi:10.1002/(SICI)1097-0266(199708)18:7<509::AID-SMJ882>3.0.CO;2-Z

Telford, R. (2006). *Small businesses in rural areas – how are they different?* Paper presented at the 26th ISBE Conference, Cardiff.

Tesco. (2009). *Tesco PLC.* Retrieved April 30, 2009, from http://www.tesco.com/

Tetteh, V. A. (2008). Launching New Ventures Through Technology [Electronic Version]. *Research Starters Business,* 1-7. Retrieved February 2, 2009, from http://web.ebscohost.com/ehost/pdf?vid=7&hid=16&sid=75a1692d-8a37-460a-bb28-b8e36112cfc3%40sessionmgr2

The Boston Consulting Group/ OSDN hacker survey, Release 0.73 (2002). Retrieved February 10, 2009, from flosscom.net/index.php?option=com_docman&task=doc_view&gid=45.

Thomas, B., Sparkes, A., Brooksbank, D., & Williams, R. (2002). Social aspects of the impact of information and communication technologies on agri-food SMEs in Wales. *Outlook on Agriculture, 31*(1), 35–41.

Thompson, G., Frances, J., Levavic, R., & Mitchell, J. (1991). *Markets, hierarchies and networks: the coordination of social life.* Thousand Oaks, CA: Sage.

Thompson, H. (2005). Online services and regional web portals: Exploring the social and economic impacts. In H.K. Kehal & V.P. Singh (Eds.), *Digital Economy: Impacts, Influences and Challenges.* Hershey, PA: Idea Group Publishing.

Thukral, I. S., Von Ehr, J., Walsh, S., Groen, A., Van der Sijde, P., & Adham, K. A. (2008). Entrepreneurship, emerging technologies, emerging markets. *International Small Business Journal, 26*(1), 101–116. doi:10.1177/0266242607084656

Thurstone, L. L. (1934). The vectors of the mind. *Psychological Review, 41,* 1–32. doi:10.1037/h0075959

Timmers, P. (1998). Business Models for Electronic Markets. *Electronic Markets, 8*(2), 3–8. doi:10.1080/10196789800000016

Timmons, J. A. (1994). *New Venture Creation - Entrepreneurship for the 21st Century.* Burr Ridge, IL: McGraw-Hill.

Ting, M. P., Seth, V., & Gao, J. (2004). The e-Salesman System. *Proceedings of the International Conference on Information Technology: Coding and Computing (ITCC'04)* (Vol. 2, p. 277).

Turban, A. (2008). *Information Technology for Management, Transforming Organizations in the Digital Economy.* Hoboken, NJ: John Wiley & Sons, Inc.

Turban, E., & King, D. Lee, J., & Viehland, D. (2004). *Electronic Commerce 2004: A Managerial Perspective.* Upper Saddle River, NJ: Pearson Education Inc.

Tushman, M. L., & Anderson, P. A. (1986). Technological Discontinuities and Organizational Environment. *Administrative Science Quarterly, 31*(3), 439–465. doi:10.2307/2392832

Twaalfhoven, B. W. M. (2004). *Red Paper on Entrepreneurship.* Hilversum, The Netherlands: European Foundation for Entrepreneurship Research (EFER).

Tyler, T. R., & Blader, S. L. (2000). Cooperation in Groups: Procedural Justice, Social *Identity and Behavioral Engagement*. Philadelphia, PA: Psychology Press.

Universia Knowledge Wharton. (2008). *Kiva: Cómo mejorar la vida de las personas con un pequeño préstamo*. Retrieved September 1, 2008, from http://wharton.universia.net/index.cfm?fa=viewArticle&ID=1529

Utterback, J. M., & Abernathy, W. J. (1975). A Dynamic Model of Process and Product Innovation. *Omega, 3*(6), 639–656. doi:10.1016/0305-0483(75)90068-7

Vaessen, P., & Keeble, D. (1995). Growth-oriented SMEs in Unfavourable Regional Environment. *Regional Studies, 29*, 489–505. doi:10.1080/00343409512331349133

Vakoufaris, H., Spilanis, I., & Kizos, T. (2007). Collective action in the Greek agrifood sector: evidence from the North Aegean region. *British Food Journal, 109*(10), 777–791. doi:10.1108/00070700710821322

Valloppillil, V. (1998). Open Source Software: A (New?) Development Methodology, Unpublished working paper. *Microsoft Corporation*. Retrieved February 9, 2009 from http://edge-op.org/iowa/www.iowaconsumercase.org/011607/6000/PX06501.pdf von Engelhardt, S. (2008a). The Economic Properties of Software. *Jena Economic Research Papers, 2*, Number 2008-045. Retrieved February 10, 2009, from http://zs.thulb.uni-jena.de/receive/jportal_jparticle_00101440

Van de Ven, A. H., & Poole, M. S. (1995). Explaining Development and Change in Organizations. *Academy of Management Review, 20*(3), 510–540. doi:10.2307/258786

Vanhaverbeke, W., Duysters, G., & Noorderhaven, N. (2002). External Technology Sourcing Through Alliances or Acquisitions: An Analysis of the Application-Specific Integrated Circuits Industry. *Organization Science, 13*(6), 714–733. doi:10.1287/orsc.13.6.714.496

Varadarajan, P., & Menon, A. (1988). Cause-Related Marketing: A Coalignment of Marketing Strategy and Corporate Philanthropy. *Journal of Marketing, 52*(3), 5874. doi:10.2307/1251450

Venkataraman, S. (2004). Regional Transformation through Technological Entrepreneurship. *Journal of Business Venturing, 19*(1), 153–167. doi:10.1016/j.jbusvent.2003.04.001

Venkatraman, N. (1994). IT-Enabled Business Transformation: From Automation to Business Scope Redefinition. *Sloan Management Review, 35*(2), 73–87.

Vesper, K. H., & Gartner, W. B. (1997). Measuring Progress in Entrepreneurship Education. *Journal of Business Venturing, 12*(5), 403–421. doi:10.1016/S0883-9026(97)00009-8

Victorian Auditor General. (2003). *Report of the Auditor General on RMIT's Finances*. State Government of Victoria, Australia.

Virginia Employment Commission. (n.d.). *Virginia's Top 50 Employers*. Retrieved November 11, 2005, from http://velma.virtuallmi.com/

Virkkala, S. (2006). *What is the role of peripheral areas in a knowledge economy? - A study of the innovation processes and networks of rural firms*. Conference Innovation Pressure, March 2006. Retrieved from http://www.proact2006.fi/chapter_images/302_Ref_B111_Seija_Virkkala.pdf

Vohora, A., Wright, M., & Lockett, A. (2004). Critical junctures in the development of university high-tech spinout companies. *Research Policy, 33*, 147–135. doi:10.1016/S0048-7333(03)00107-0

Volery, T. (2005). Ressourcenorientierter Ansatz von Entrepreneurship: Ressourcen sind der Kern des Wettbewerbsvorteils. *KMU Magazine, 9*, 12–14.

Volkmann, C., & Tokarski, K. O. (2006). Growth strategies for young e-ventures through structured collaboration. *International Journal of Services Technology and Management, 7*(1), 68–84.

von Engelhardt, S. (2008b). Intellectual Property Rights and Ex-Post Transaction Costs: the Case of Open and Closed Source Software, Jena Economic Research Papers 2008-047. Retrieved February 10, 2009, from http://zs.thulb.uni-jena.de/receive/jportal_jparticle_00101864.

Von Hippel, E. (1994). Sticky Information and the Locus of Problem Solving. *Management Science*, *40*, 429–439. doi:10.1287/mnsc.40.4.429

von Hippel, E. (2001). Innovation by User Communities: Learning from Open-Source Software. *MIT Sloan Management Review*, *42*(4), 82.

Von Hippel, E., & Katz, R. (2002). Shifting Innovation to Users via Toolkits. *Management Science*, *48*(7), 821–833. doi:10.1287/mnsc.48.7.821.2817

von Hippel, E., & v. Krogh, G. (2003). Open Source software and the private-collective innovation model: Issues for organization science. *Organization Science*, *14*(2), 209–223. doi:10.1287/orsc.14.2.209.14992

Von Kortzfleisch, H. F. O. (2003). *Organizational Design of Information Technology in the Context of E-Business: Methodology for Balancing Tensions between Benefits and Drawbacks.* Paper published on CD-ROM, in Proceedings of the Thirty-Sixth Annual Hawaii International Conference Systems Sciences, HICCS-36.

Von Krogh, G., & Spaeth, S. (2007). The open source software phenomenon: Characteristics that promote research. *The Journal of Strategic Information Systems*, *16*, 236–253. doi:10.1016/j.jsis.2007.06.001

Wagner, R., & Sternberg, R. (1991). *TKIM: The common sense manager: Tacit knowledge inventory for managers: Test Booklet.* San Antonio, TX: Harcourt Brace Jovanovich.

Wahlster, W., & Dengel, A. (2006). Web 3.0: Convergence of Web 2.0 and the semantic web. *Technology Feature Paper Edition*, *II*, 2–22.

Wailgum, T. (2007). *ERP: Definitions and Solutions.* Retrieved July, 2009, from http://www.ambriana.com/C298_website/ERP_CIO.pdf

Walsh, G., Gwinner, K. P., & Swanson, S. R. (2004). What Makes Mavens Tick? Exploring the Motives of Market Mavens' Initiation of Information Diffusion. *Journal of Consumer Marketing*, *21*(2), 109–122. doi:10.1108/07363760410525678

Walsh, G., Hass, B., & Kilian, T. *(2010). Web 2.0: Neue Perspektiven für Marketing und Medien (2nd Ed.). Heidelberg, Germany: Springer.*

Walsh, G., Mitchell, V. W., Wiedmann, K. P., Frenzel, T., & Duvenhorst, C. (2002). German eMavens on Internet Music Sites. In W. J. Kehoe & J. H. Lindgren (Eds.), *AMA 2002 Summer Educators' Conference 13: Proceedings: Enhancing Knowledge Development in Marketing* (pp. 435-436). Chicago: American Marketing Association.

Walton, J. (1999). *Strategic human resource development.* London: Prentice Hall.

Weaver, M., Dickson, P., & Solomon, G. (2006). Entrepreneurship and education: what is known and not known about the links between education and entrepreneurial activity? *The Small Business Economy for Data Year 2005: A Report to the President.* Washington, DC: United States Government Printing Office.

Weber, S. (2003). The Success of Open Source. Cambridge, MA: Harvard University Press.

Weber, S. (2005). *The Success of Open Source.* Boston, MA: Harvard University Press.

Webster, F. (1976). A model for new venture initiation. *Academy of Management Review*, *1*(1), 26–37. doi:10.2307/257356

Webster, F. E. (1988). Rediscovering the Marketing Concept. In *MSI Report, Nr. 88-100*. Cambridge, MA: Marketing Science Institute.

Weerawardena, J., Mort, G. S., Liesch, P. W., & Knight, G. (2007). Conceptualizing accelerated internationalization in the born global firm: a dynamic capabilities perspective. *Journal of World Business*, *42*, 294–306. doi:10.1016/j.jwb.2007.04.004

Weiber, R., & Kollmann, T. (1998). Competitive advantages in virtual markets – perspectives of information-based marketing in the cyberspace. *European Journal of Marketing*, *32*(7/8), 603615. doi:10.1108/03090569810224010

Weiber, R., & Kollmann, T. (1998). Competitive advantages in virtual markets–perspectives of Information-based

Marketing in cyberspace. *European Journal of Marketing, 32*(7/8), 603–615. doi:10.1108/03090569810224010

Weisbrod, B. A. (2004). The Pitfalls of Non-Profits. *Stanford Social Innovation Review, Winter*, 40–47.

Weiser, M. (1993). Ubiquitous computing. *IEEE Computer, 26*(10), 71–72.

Weiser, M. (1999, 9-12 May 1999). *How computers will be used differently in the next twenty years.* Paper presented at the Symposium on Security and Privacy, Oakland, CA, USA.

Wellman, B., & Gulia, M. (1999). The network basis of social support: A network is more than the sum of its ties. In B. Wellman (Ed.), *Networks in the Global Village: Life in Contemporary Communities.* Boulder, CO: Westview Press.

Wenger, A. (2008). Analysis of travel bloggers' characteristics and their communication about Austria as a tourism destination. *Journal of Vacation Marketing, 14*(2), 169–176. doi:10.1177/1356766707087525

Wernerfeld, B. (1995). The resource-based view of the firm: ten years after. *Strategic Management Journal, 16*(3), 171–174. doi:10.1002/smj.4250160303

Werthner, H., & Fodor, O. (2005). Harmonise: A Step Toward an Interoperable E-Tourism Marketplace. *International Journal of Electronic Commerce, 9*(2), 11–39.

Werthner, H., & Ricci, F. (2004). E-commerce and Tourism. *Communications of the ACM, 47*(12), 101–105. doi:10.1145/1035134.1035141

Wessner, C. (2002). The Economics of Science and Technology. *The Journal of Technology Transfer, 27,* 155–203. doi:10.1023/A:1014382532639

West, G. P. III. (2007). Collective cognition: when entrepreneurial teams, not individuals, make decisions. *Entrepreneurship Theory and Pratice, 31*(1), 77–102. doi:10.1111/j.1540-6520.2007.00164.x

West, J., & Gallagher, S. (2006). Challenges of open innovation: The paradox of firm investment in open source software. *R & D Management, 36*(3), 319–331. doi:10.1111/j.1467-9310.2006.00436.x

West, J., & Lakhani, K. (2008). Getting Clear About Communities in Open Innovation. *Industry and Innovation, 15*(2), 223–231. doi:10.1080/13662710802033734

West, J., & O'Mahony, S. (2008). The Role of Participation Architecture in Growing Sponsored Open Source Communities. *Industry and Innovation, 15*(2), 145–168. doi:10.1080/13662710801970142

Westall, F. A., Johnston, R. D., & Lewis, A. V. (Eds.). (1998). *Speech technology for telecommunications* (1st ed.). London: Chapman and Hall.

Wickham, P. (2001). *Strategic Entrepreneurship - A Decision Making Approach to New Venture Creation & Management.* Englewood Cliffs, NJ: Prentice Hall.

Wiedmann, K. P., Walsh, G., & Mitchell, V. W. (2001). The German Mannmaven: An Agent for Diffusing Market Information. *Journal of Marketing Communications, 7*(4), 1–17.

Wienclaw, R. A. (2008). Technological Innovation & Entrepreneurs [Electronic Version]. *Research Starters Business,* 1-5. Retrieved February 2, 2009, from http://web.ebscohost.com/ehost/pdf?vid=7&hid=16&sid=75a1692d-8a37-460a-bb28-b8e36112cfc3%40sessionmgr2

Wikipedia. (n.d.). *Bell's Law of Computer Classes.* Retrieved June 30, 2009, from http://en.wikipedia.org/wiki/Bell%27s_Law_of_Computer_Classes

Williams, T. G., & Slama, M. E. (1995). Market maven's purchase decision evaluative criteria: implications for brand and store promotion effort. *Journal of Consumer Marketing, 12*(3), 4–21. doi:10.1108/07363769510147218

Williamson, O. E. (1991a). Comparative Economic Organization: The Analysis of Discrete Structural Alternatives. *Administrative Science Quarterly, 36*(June), 269–296. doi:10.2307/2393356

Williamson, O. E. (1991b). Economic Institutions: Spontaneous and Intentional Governance. *Journal of Law Economics and Organization, 7*(Special Issue), 159–187.

Williamson, O. E. (1996). *The Mechanisms of Governance.* New York: Oxford University Press.

Williamson, O. E. (2000). The New Institutional Economics: Taking Stock, Looking Ahead. *Journal of Economic Literature, 38*(3), 595–613.

Williamson, O. E. (2002a). *The Lens of Contract: Private Ordering*. Berkley, CA: University of California.

Williamson, O. E. (2002b). *The Theory of the Firm as Governance Structure: from Choice to Contract*. Berkley, CA: University of California.

Williamson, O. E. (2002c). Empirical Microeconomics: Another Perspective. In M. Augier & J. March (Eds.), *The Economics of Choice, Change and Organization*. Brookfield, VT: Edward Elgar.

Wittmann, C., & Cullen, M. (2000). *B2B Internet*. First Union Securities.

Wold, H. O. (1985). Partial Least Squares. In S. Kotz & N.L. Johnson (Eds.), *Encyclopedia of Statistical Sciences* (pp. 581-591). New York: Wiley&Sons.

Wolk, A. (2007). *Social Entrepreneurship and Government*. The Small Business Economy: A Report to the President, 2007.

Wonglimpiyarat, J. (2005). The dynamic economic engine at Silicon Valley and U.S. Government programmes in financing innovations. *Technovation*.

Wood, C. M. (2004). Marketing and e-commerce as tools of development in the Asia-Pacific region: a dual path. *International Marketing Review, 21*(3), 301–320. doi:10.1108/02651330410539639

Wood, R. (1961). *1400 Governments: The Political Economy of the New York Metropolitan Region*. Cambridge, MA: Harvard University Press.

Wright, D. (2005). The dark side of Ambient Intelligence. *Info, 7*(6), 33–51. doi:10.1108/14636690510628300

Wright, M., Birley, S., & Mosey, S. (2004a). Entrepreneurship and university technology transfer. *The Journal of Technology Transfer, 29*(3/4), 235–246. doi:10.1023/B:JOTT.0000034121.02507.f3

Wright, M., Vohora, A., & Lockett, A. (2004b). The formation of high tech university spinout companies:

the role of joint ventures and venture capital investors. *The Journal of Technology Transfer, 29*(3/4), 287–310. doi:10.1023/B:JOTT.0000034124.70363.83

Wu, C.-G., Gerlach, J. H., & Young, C. E. (2007). An Empirical Analysis of Open Source Software Developers' Motivations and Continuance Intentions. *Information & Management, 44*, 253–262. doi:10.1016/j.im.2006.12.006

OpenSocial Foundation. (2009). *OpenSocial – It's Open. It's Social. It's up to you*. Retrieved April 24, 2009, from http://www.opensocial.org

Yin, R. K. (2003). *Case study research. Design and methods* (3rd ed.). Thousand Oaks, CA: Sage.

Yusuf, Y., Gunasekaran, A., & Abthprpe, M. (2004). Enterprise Information Systems Project Implementation: A Case Study of ERP in Rolls-Royce. *International Journal of Production Economics, 87*(3), 251–266. doi:10.1016/j.ijpe.2003.10.004

Zahra, S. A., Korri, J. S., & Yu, J. (2005). Cognition and international entrepreneurship: implications for research on international opportunity recognition and exploitation. *International Business Review, 14*(2), 129–146. doi:10.1016/j.ibusrev.2004.04.005

Zampetakis, L. A., & Moustakis, V. (2006). Linking creativity with entrepreneurial intentions: A structural approach. *The International Entrepreneurship and Management Journal, 2*(3), 413–428. doi:10.1007/s11365-006-0006-z

Zanes, J., Ross, S., Hatfield, R., Houtler, B., & Whitman, D. (1998). The relationship between creativity and psychosis-proneness. *Personality and Individual Differences, 24*, 879–881. doi:10.1016/S0191-8869(97)00199-2

Zeitlow, J. T. (2001). Social Entrepreneurship: Managerial, Finance and Marketing Aspects. *Journal of Nonprofit & Public Sector Marketing, 9*, 19–43. doi:10.1300/J054v09n01_03

Zhou, L. (2007). The effects of entrepreneurial proclivity and foreign market knowledge on early internationalization. *Journal of World Business, 42*, 281–293. doi:10.1016/j.jwb.2007.04.009

Zimmerman, M. A., & Zeitz, G. J. (2002). Beyond Survival: Achieving New Venture Growth by Building Legitimacy. *Academy of Management Review*, *27*(3), 414–431. doi:10.2307/4134387

Zwass, V. (2003). Electronic commerce and organizational innovation: aspects and opportunities. *International Journal of Electronic Commerce*, *7*(3), 7–37.

About the Contributors

Tobias Kollmann holds the Chair for E-Business and E-Entrepreneurship at the University of Duisburg-Essen, Campus Essen – Germany. He received his doctoral degree in 1997 from the University of Trier with a thesis on the acceptance of innovative telecommunication and multimedia systems. His main research interest is 'E-Entrepreneurship' – that is, all aspects of company founding and development in electronic business environments.

Andreas Kuckertz is an assistant professor ('akademischer Rat') teaching and researching management at the University of Duisburg-Essen, Germany, where he is a member of the e-business and e-entrepreneurship research group. The group focuses on high-technology entrepreneurship in TIMES industries. Moreover, he is an associate member of the strategy, networks, and enterprise research group at the University of Vaasa, Finland. He is Associate Editor of the International Journal of E-Entrepreneurship and Innovation (IJEEI) and serves as the Country Vice President Germany for the European Council for Small Business and Entrepreneurship (ECSB). He holds a master's degree from the University of Leipzig, Germany, and received his doctoral degree with a thesis on venture capital finance from the University of Duisburg-Essen in 2005.

Christoph Stöckmann is a post-doctoral researcher at the University of Duisburg-Essen, Germany, where he is a member of the e-business and e-entrepreneurship research group. He holds a master's degree in Business Administration and Information Science and received his doctoral degree with a thesis on exploratory and exploitative innovation and their effects on the EO-performance relationship in ICT-Ventures from the University of Duisburg-Essen, Germany.

* * *

J. A. Ariza Montes. PhD in Economic and Business Science as well as Principal Lecture of the Human Resources Area in the School of Business and Economic Science -ETEA- (Universidad de Córdoba). Researcher and professor, has published numerous articles in scientific magazines and is author of several books: Gestión integrada de personas. Una perspectiva de organización (in collaboration) (Desclée De Brouwer, 1999), El reto del equilibrio: Vida personal y profesional (Desclée De Brouwer, 2002), Dirección y Administración Integrada de Personas (in collaboration) (McGraw-Hill, 2004).

Andrea Bikfalvi is Lecturer in the Business Administration and Product Design department at the University of Girona. She has a degree in Business Administration and a PhD in the same area. She regularly cooperates with researchers at the Fraunhofer Institute for Systems and Innovation Research in Karlsruhe-Germany where she spent a one-year research stay in 2005 in the Department of Industrial and Service Innovations. Dr. Bikfalvi participated in considerable projects at regional level, conceded by the Catalan Regional Development Agency, on the topic of entrepreneurial success, industrial competitiveness, spin-off creation and regional development. Her experience also covers areas belonging to the public administration sector, participating in two competitive projects awarded by the Public Administration School of Catalonia. Her regular activities include both teaching and research having in common the topic of innovation. She coordinates networks for conducting research related to innovation in teaching among regional, national and international higher education institutions.

Ayse Bilgin is a lecturer in the Department of Statistics at Macquarie University. She teaches undergraduate and postgraduate students in various topics such as Operations Research, Data Mining and Decision Support Systems. Her research interests include statistics education and applied statistics especially in health sciences.

Roman Boutellier is since 1st October 2008 Vice President Human Resources and Infrastructure of ETH Zurich. He is professor and leads the Chair for Technology and Innovation Management at the Department of Management, Technology, and Economics (D-MTEC) at ETH Zurich since 2004. Since 1999 Prof. Dr. Boutellier is titular professor at the University of St. Gallen (HSG). In 1979 he received his PhD in mathematics and worked as postdoctoral fellow at the Imperial College in London. His works appeared in R&D Management, Harvard Business Manager, ZFO and Drug Discovery Today. Roman Boutellier has held several leading positions in the industry and he is member of the board of directors of several Swiss large-scale enterprises. The focus of his research is the management of technology driven enterprises with a specific focus on innovation.

Simon Brach (brach@uni-koblenz.de) is a Ph.D. candidate at the Institute of Management and Marketing of the University of Koblenz. He graduated in Psychology from the Friedrich-Schiller-University Jena. In his research he is interested in the intersection of psychology and marketing research.

Malte Brettel is University Professor for Business Administration and Sciences for Engineers and Scientists at RWTH Aachen University, Germany. He received his doctoral degree and his postdoctoral qualification from WHU Otto Beisheim School of Management. He has worked as a management consultant and is co-founder of JustBooks (today ABEBooks). His areas of research interest include entrepreneurial management and development, entrepreneurial marketing, entrepreneurial finance and innovation management. He has published his work in various books and journals and has presented his research at leading international conferences including the AMA Summer Marketing Educators' Conference, the AOM Annual Meeting, the FMA Annual Meeting, and the Babson Entrepreneurship Conference. He has published in prominent marketing journals such as Journal of International Marketing.

Peter Busch is a senior lecturer in the Department of Computing at Macquarie University. His areas of teaching include databases, information systems, IT project and systems management and enterprise systems integration. His research area focuses on knowledge management, organizational learning, knowledge capital and the knowledge economy. He is particularly interested in the knowledge management implications of tacit knowledge diffusion.

Kathryn Cormican lectures in the College of Engineering & Informatics at the National University of Ireland, Galway. Her research interests lie in the areas of enterprise integration and technology management. Kathryn leads a number of funded research projects in these areas. She has published widely at international conferences and in peer reviewed journals. Kathryn also works with many leading organisations helping them to design, develop and deploy new processes and systems.

David Deakins holds a Chair in enterprise Development and is Director of Dumfries Campus at the University of the West of Scotland. He is now responsible for strategic development at the Dumfries campus whilst maintaining his research interests and conferences connected with enterprise development and entrepreneurship. David's research interests include the finance of small firms, rural enterprise and ethnic minority enterprise. He co-authors a successful textbook on Entrepreneurship and Small Firms, published by McGraw-Hill and now in its 5th edition which was published in February 2009. He will take up a Chair in Small Business Management and Entrepreneurship at Massey University, NZ from 1st September 2009 and retain a Visiting Professorship at UWS.

Andreas Engelen works as a post-doc student at the chair "Business Administration and Sciences for Engineers and natural Scientist" at RWTH Aachen University., Germany. He received his master degree and his doctoral degree in business administration from RWTH Aachen University. His areas of research interest include international marketing and entrepreneurial marketing. He has presented his research at leading international marketing and entrepreneurship conferences and published in prominent marketing journals such as Journal of International Marketing.

Markus Eurich works as a scientific collaborator at the Swiss Federal Institute of Technology Zurich (ETH Zurich). He belongs to the research group of Prof. Dr. Roman Boutellier at the Department "Management, Technology, and Economics" (D-MTEC). He is a PhD candidate with a research focus on business models for information and communication technology (ICT) innovations. He received his "Dipl. Wirtsch.-Inf." (Business Informatics) from the University of Mannheim. As research associate, Markus Eurich also works in the Smart Items Research Program at SAP Research in Zurich. He joined SAP in 2001 and mainly worked in research and in the fields of Internal Business Consulting and Costumer Relationship Management in Germany and India. He is involved in the European research project SENSEI (Integrating the Physical with the Digital World of the Network of the Future) in which he is leading the task "Business Modeling - Value Creation".

Laura Galloway is a lecturer in entrepreneurship at Heriot-Watt University, Edinburgh. She recently introduced a new undergraduate degree in Management with Enterprise to the university, and leads and teaches various modules on entrepreneurship and enterprise. Her research interests include rural entrepreneurship, electronic business, entrepreneurship education and minority entrepreneurship. She publishes in a variety of peer reviewed journals and books on entrepreneurship and enterprise.

Antonia Mercedes García-Cabrera. PhD in Economic and Business Sciences and Senior Lecturer at the University of Las Palmas de Gran Canaria (Spain). She heads the doctoral program New Strategic Tendencies in Business Management and is the head of the "Strategy and International Businesses" research group. Her areas of academic interest include organizational identity, cross-cultural studies, and entrepreneurship. Her research works on issues of entrepreneurship include studies of the personal characteristics of the individual and the national cultural dimensions as factors influencing the decision to create a venture, taking into account the existence of cultural differences within a single country. Her works have been published in books (i.e., Cases on Information Technology Entrepreneurship, IGI Publishing) and national and international journals, (i.e., Entrepreneurship & Regional Development, Journal of Entrepreneurship, Revista Europea de Dirección y Economía de la Empresa, Psicología del Trabajo y de las Organizaciones, etc.).

María Gracia García-Soto. PhD in Economic and Business Sciences and University Master in Tourism Enterprise Management, she is a lecturer at the University of Las Palmas de Gran Canaria (Spain). She is a member of the "Strategy and International Businesses" research group and as such, her lines of research have been corporate governance, cross-cultural studies, and entrepreneurship. Her research in the field of entrepreneurship has centred on the study of the psychological and sociological variables that determine entrepreneurial behaviour from a dual perspective: a technological approach and a national culture view. Her works have been published in books such as Cases on Information Technology Entrepreneurship (IGI Publishing) and in national and international journals, including Entrepreneurship & Regional Development, Journal of Entrepreneurship, Corporate Ownership & Control, Revista Europea de Dirección y Economía de la Empresa, Psicología del Trabajo y de las Organizaciones, Investigaciones Europeas, etc.

Simrn Kaur Gill is a researcher working towards her PhD in the College of Engineering and Informatics at the National University of Ireland, Galway. Her research interests lie in the area of technology innovation. Simrn has contributed to EU funded R&D projects in the area of ambient intelligence for manufacturing SMEs.

Matthias Häsel is a Senior Product Manager at XING, the leading social network for business contacts in Europe. He received his Ph.D. at the E-Business and E-Entrepreneurship Research Group at the University of Duisburg-Essen, Germany, with his research focused on product development and founder competencies in Internet-based ventures. He holds a B.Sc. in Computer Science from the Osnabrück University of Applied Sciences, and a M.Sc. in Multimedia Management from the University of Kiel, Germany.

Cecilia Hegarty is a Lecturer in Entrepreneurship with the Northern Ireland Centre for Entrepreneurship at the University of Ulster and specialises in enterprise development and entrepreneurship education policy. Dr Hegarty has consulted on many EU research projects and conducted a pioneering investigation in Ireland into small and micro-scale ventures, their growth and competitiveness. She holds a PhD from Dublin and studied in Ulster and Indiana, USA. She has published peer-reviewed articles in a number of leading journals of entrepreneurship, business, education, tourism and geography and sits on editorial boards of the same.

Florian Heinemann is Assistant Professor at the Chair of Business Administration and Sciences for Engineers and Scientists at RWTH Aachen University, Germany. He received his doctoral degree from RWTH Aachen University and was Visiting Scholar at the Snider Entrepreneurial Research Center at the Wharton School. His areas of research interest include innovation management and entrepreneurial marketing. He has published his work in various journals and has presented his research at leading international conferences including the AMA Summer Marketing Educators' Conference, the AOM Annual Meeting, and the Babson Entrepreneurship Conference.

Patricia Hurschler works as research associate at the Chair of Technology and Innovation Management at the Department of Management, Technology, and Economics (D-MTEC) at ETH Zurich since 2005. She is PhD candidate in Management with focus on Business Innovation. Her research focuses on strategic procurement decisions in the triangle Switzerland, Eastern Europe and Asia based on criteria related to the procurement item, the branch, as well as the company with its business model. Patricia Hurschler gained her MSc in managerial and production sciences at ETH Zurich with emphasis on integrated product development and technology and innovation management.

Andreas Kessell is managing director of the GFIU mbH and antikoerper-online.de in Aachen, Germany. He received his master degree from the WHU Otto Beisheim School of Management and his doctoral degree from RWTH Aachen University. His research interest cover entrepreneurial marketing and organizational culture related topics.

Tobias Kollmann holds the Chair for E-Business and E-Entrepreneurship at the University of Duisburg-Essen, Campus Essen – Germany. He received his doctoral degree in 1997 from the University of Trier with a thesis on the acceptance of innovative telecommunication and multimedia systems. His main research interest is 'E-Entrepreneurship' – that is, all aspects of company founding and development in electronic business environments.

Harald F. O. von Kortzfleisch received his diploma doctoral degree in business management from the University of Cologne and currently holds the Chair for Information Management, Innovation, Entrepreneurship and Organization Design (Mi2EO) as a tenured full professor at the University of Koblenz-Landau, Campus Koblenz, in Germany. Before, he was a senior lecturer, project manager, and assistant professor at the University of Kassel, the Cologne Business School, the Euro-Business-College Bonn, as well as Kassel International Management School. He is also managing partner of VonKor GmbH in Bonn, a business and venture management consulting company, since 2006. Mr. von Kortzfleisch wrote, co-authored and edited seven books and numerous research articles. Currently, his research focus is on scientific entrepreneurship, innovation, knowledge and collaboration management as well as the organizational design relevance of information and communication systems.

Andreas Kuckertz is an assistant professor ('akademischer Rat') teaching and researching management at the University of Duisburg-Essen, Germany, where he is a member of the e-business and e-entrepreneurship research group. The group focuses on high-technology entrepreneurship in TIMES industries. Moreover, he is an associate member of the strategy, networks, and enterprise research group at the University of Vaasa, Finland. He is Associate Editor of the International Journal of E-Entrepreneurship and Innovation (IJEEI) and serves as the Country Vice President Germany for the European Council for Small Business and Entrepreneurship (ECSB). He holds a master's degree from the University of Leipzig, Germany, and received his doctoral degree with a thesis on venture capital finance from the University of Duisburg-Essen in 2005.

Carina Lomberg is a post-doctoral researcher at the École Polytechnique Fédérale de Lausanne in Switzerland. She pursued her doctoral studies at the E-Business and E-Entrepreneurship Research Group at the University of Duisburg-Essen, Germany. Her thesis deals with entrepreneurial creativity of employees. She received a master's degree in Business Administration from the University of Duisburg-Essen with an award-winning thesis on incentives schemes in entrepreneurial growth companies.

Michael Luger is Dean of the Manchester Business School (UK) and Professor of Innovation, Management and Policy. He formally was Professor of Public Policy, Business and Planning and Director of the Center for Competitive Economies at UNC-Chapel Hill. He has published widely in the areas of regional economic development, technology policy, and public finance and infrastructure. He holds a Ph.D. (Economics) and MRP from UC-Berkeley, and an AB and MPA from Princeton.

Philipp Magin finished his study of Information Management at the University of Koblenz-Landau, Campus Koblenz, Germany, in Spring 2009 with a Bachelor of Science degree with distinction. In August 2007, Mr. Magin joined the research group "Management of Information, Innovation, Entrepreneurship and Organization Design" (Mi2EO), headed by Prof. Dr. Harald F.O. von Kortzfleisch as a research assistant. In Autumn 2008, Mr. Magin already started with preliminary research for his doctoral thesis. Under the supervision of Prof. von Kortzfleisch, he became a Ph.D. student at the University of Koblenz-Landau in spring 2009 in the entrepreneurship research field. Currently, Mr. Magin works for McKinsey & Comp. as a junior fellow consultant. Since June 2005, Mr. Magin is managing partner of his own company "pm-climbing", the exclusive distributor for eXpression holds and usteto climbing in Austria, Germany and Switzerland. Furthermore, he is engaged in two other start-up companies as foundation partner.

Nick Maynard is an Associate Policy Researcher at the RAND Corporation where he focuses on information technology, S&T policy, and economic development. He is currently working at the FCC as the manager for economic analysis on the National Broadband Taskforce. Prior to RAND, Dr. Maynard was a Program Manager with Yankee Group, where he was awarded Analyst of the Year for his research on network infrastructure in developing countries. Dr. Maynard received his BA and MA from the University of Chicago in Political Science and he completed a Public Policy PhD in 2008 at University of North Carolina at Chapel Hill. His dissertation research on national ICT strategies was supported through a National Science Foundation grant.

Aaron McKethan is a research director at the Engelberg Center for Health Reform at the Brookings Institution where he focuses on payment and delivery system reforms, including health IT. He is currently assistant professorial lecturer of health policy in the Department of Health Policy at the George Washington University Medical Center, School of Public Health and Health Services. He received his PhD in Public Policy Analysis from the University of North Carolina at Chapel Hill, where he also received a Bachelor of Arts in political science.

Avi Messica is a former Hi-Tech entrepreneur and businessman who is currently with the finance department at the school of business administration of the college of management (Israel) where he also acts as the director of the entrepreneurship and innovation management center (EIM). Dr. Messica served at senior managerial positions in companies like Tower Semiconductors (TSEM) and ShellCase

(SCSEF) and co-founded and served as the CEO of several Hi-Tech companies. His research interests include entrepreneurship, innovation management in a global context, finance (with emphasis on risky projects/ventures), strategic management, R&D management and marketing, all at the focal point of high technology ventures and firms. Dr. Messica holds a PhD in nano-technology and solid-state physics from the Weizmann Institute of Science, M.Sc. in applied optics and B.Sc. in physics from the Tel-Aviv University. He spent a Post-Doctorate specializing in financing of risky ventures at the Ben-Gurion University. Dr. Messica is also a staff member of the prestigious Acton MBA program in entrepreneurship (Austin, Texas).

Vincent-Wayne Mitchell (v.mitchell@city.ac.uk) is Professor of Consumer Marketing at CASS Business School, City University London. His research focuses on consumer decision-making, complaining behavior and risk taking. He has won eight Best Paper Awards and has published over 200 academic and practitioner papers in journals such as Harvard Business Review, Journal of Business Research, British Journal of Management, Journal of Economic Psychology. He sits on the Editorial Boards of six international journals, is an Expert Adviser for the Office of Fair Trading and is Head of Marketing at CASS.

A. C. Morales Gutiérrez. Principal Lecture of Organization and Management of Business and Human Resources in the School of Business and Economic Science -ETEA- (Universidad de Córdoba). He has written several books among them: Empresas y emprendedores en Córdoba. 30 casos de éxito (2000, Diputación); Análisis y Diseño de Sistemas Organizativos (2004, Thomson-Civitas) y Dirección y Administración Integrada de Personas (in collaboration) (2004, McGraw-Hill), Análisis Económico de la Empresa Autogestionada (2004-CIRIEC). Since 1990, he lead the research group SEJ-148 Estudios Cooperativos y ENL (ETEA) subsidied by the Junta de Andalucía.

Debbie Richards is an Associate Professor in the Computing Department at Macquarie University in Sydney. Prior to joining academia in 1999 she worked for 15 years in industry in a range of IT related roles which probably accounts for her focus on finding solutions that people need and want. Many of the challenges facing organizations and society require interdisciplinary work and thinking outside the square of the discipline one has been trained in. The work in this paper crosses a number of disciplines seeking to provide some answers to the problem of identifying individuals with the potential to become entrepreneurs, which is important first step in nurturing such individuals who will play such an important role in the global knowledge economy.

Josep Lluís de la Rosa i Esteva is Associate Professor at the University of Girona (UdG) and the founding director of EASY Innova - TECNIO, and president of Strategic Attention Management S.L. He received his Ph.D. in Computer Engineering from the Autonomous University of Barcelona (UAB) in 1993, and a MBA in 2002. In 1993, he became assistant professor to the UAB, and in 1997 post-doc fellow at Laboratoire d'Architecture et d'Analyse des Systèmes (LAAS-CNRS) in Toulouse, France. His is interested in the application of intelligent agents to a variety of fields ranging from marketing and e-commerce to robotics and industrial applications. Dr. de la Rosa is a member of the Catalan Association of Artificial Intelligence ACIA (ECCAI). He is author of over one hundred scientific publications and four patents. He is now visiting Prof. Szymanski at Rensselaer Polytechnic Institute (RPI) in New York, USA, for the subject of citation auctions, an application of complementary currencies to science. He is available at peplluis@eia.udg.edu, http://eia.udg.edu/~peplluis.

John Sanders is a lecturer in strategic management in the School of Management and Languages at Heriot-Watt University. He teaches strategic management courses to both undergraduate and post-graduate students. In addition, he teaches a small business management course to final year undergraduate students. Previously he held a lecturing position at Massey University, New Zealand, and taught International Business and General Management courses. His research efforts focus on organisational alignment, small firms and innovation management. His PhD investigated strategic fit within a University setting. Beyond research and teaching, he provides academic and administrative support for Heriot-Watt University's distance-learning and International Management and Languages (IML) programmes.

Mario Schaarschmidt holds a German diploma in computer sciences from the University of Koblenz-Landau and is currently a research and teaching assistant as well as a PhD candidate at the Management, Innovation, Entrepreneurship and Organization group of Prof. von Kortzfleisch. Mr. Schaarschmidt worked as an intern for various firms in the software and telecommunication industry. He also was a visiting doctoral student at Harvard Kennedy School. Furthermore, he is involved in several research projects, partly funded by the German Federal Ministry of Education and Research. His research focus is on technology and innovation management, open innovation networks as well as the role of firms in open source software development.

Karsten Jörn Schröder is working as a business consultant in Berlin, Germany. He graduated with a diploma in business management from the University of Duisburg-Essen, Germany, after training as an industrial manager at Wilhelm Geldbach AG, Gelsenkirchen, Germany. During his studies he specialized in strategic management, controlling, and information management and wrote his diploma thesis about market positioning methods for innovative ventures. After completing his studies he worked as a business consultant at AMConsult in Bonn, Germany, focussing on purchasing and procurement strategies and developing training and coaching events.

Anthony Scime is a graduate of George Mason University with an interdisciplinary doctorate in Information Systems and Education. Currently he is an Associate Professor of Computer Science at The College at Brockport, State University of New York. Prior to joining academia, he spent over 20 years in industry and government applying information systems to solve large-scale problems. His work has been published in Expert Systems with Applications, Computer Science Education, the International Journal of Business Intelligence and Data Mining, the International Journal of Information and Communication Technology Education, and the Journal of Electronic Commerce Research and Applications. Idea Group Publishing has published his book Web Mining: Applications and Techniques. His research interests include the World Wide Web as an information system and database, information retrieval, knowledge creation and management, decision making from information, data mining in the social and behavioral sciences, and computing education.

Anthony C. Scime is a doctoral candidate in strategic management at Purdue University's Krannert School of Management. He has received an MBA from the University of Rochester, William E. Simon Graduate School of Business Administration, and a BA from Franklin & Marshall College. His work has been presented at the Academy of Management and Strategic Management Society annual conferences. His current research interests include the origin of resource advantages, particularly through strategic factor market activity, and the intersection of strategic management and information technology.

Christian Serarols Tarrés is an Associate Professor within the Business Economics Department at the Universitat Autònoma de Barcelona and director of the Research Group in "Local environment and technology-based entrepreneurship in Spain". Research interests include technology entrepreneurship and small business management, spin-off creation, technology transfer, ebusiness and electronic commerce. He has industrial engineering background, a PhD in business economics (entrepreneurship), with industrial experience in technical research, consulting and management. He has founded a high-tech enterprise in the field of content aggregation. He is also vice-president for Spain of the European Council for Small business. He has been visiting professor in several European Universities (Politecnico Milano, Montpelier, Liencheinstein, etc.) and he is a member of the editorial board of several international journals (International Journal of Entrepreneurial Venturing, International Journal of Technoentrepreneurship, etc.).

Christoph Stöckmann is a post-doctoral researcher at the University of Duisburg-Essen, Germany, where he is a member of the e-business and e-entrepreneurship research group. He holds a master's degree in Business Administration and Information Science and received his doctoral degree with a thesis on exploratory and exploitative innovation and their effects on the EO-performance relationship in ICT-Ventures from the University of Duisburg-Essen, Germany.

Doug Thomson (PhD, MBA, MIE(Aust), CPEng, MCIPS)has been with the RMIT University, Melbourne, Australia since 2002. From Sep 2005 to Sep 2007 he was the MBA Programs Manager for the Graduate School of Business and is currently a Lecturer and Course Coordinator. He has extensive global experience in the application of e-business in the private and public sectors, and worked in Vietnam for four months in 2007 at the RMIT IUV's Ha Noi campus. He has more than 20 years international experience and published extensively in ICT and e-business policy development, public and private sector e-business management, e-entrepreneurship project management, and ERP.

Gianfranco Walsh received his M.Phil. degree from UMIST (England) and Ph.D. (2001) and Habilitation (2004) degrees from Hanover (Germany). His research focuses on strategic management, service management, corporate reputation, and e-commerce. His work has been published in, amongst others, Academy of Management Journal, British Journal of Management, Journal of the Academy of Marketing Science, Journal of Business Research and International Journal of Electronic Commerce. He is a is professor for marketing and electronic retailing at the University of Koblenz-Landau and a visiting professor at the University of Strathclyde Business School in Glasgow (UK). In addition, Gianfranco Walsh teaches at GISMA Business School, Germany.

Index